Advance Praise for
# THE WOLF AT THE DOOR

"In *The Wolf at the Door,* Geoffrey Cocks has accomplished what had seemed impossible—to inhabit the inner life of the great, and highly secretive, film director Stanley Kubrick. Cocks finds in the subconscious mind behind the films meditations on war, the Holocaust, and the real and secret history of the world explored through Kubrick's iconoclastic worldview. *The Wolf at the Door* applies an astute understanding of geopolitics and psychology to the detailed facts of Kubrick's earthly existence—the results bring insight into this mysterious twentieth-century cinematic icon."

*Vincent LoBrutto, Author of* Stanley Kubrick: A Biography

# THE WOLF
AT THE DOOR

*Contemporary Film, Television, and Video*

Joanne Hershfield, General Editor

Vol. 1

PETER LANG
New York • Washington, D.C./Baltimore • Bern
Frankfurt am Main • Berlin • Brussels • Vienna • Oxford

Geoffrey Cocks

# THE WOLF AT THE DOOR

## Stanley Kubrick, History, & the Holocaust

PETER LANG
New York • Washington, D.C./Baltimore • Bern
Frankfurt am Main • Berlin • Brussels • Vienna • Oxford

Library of Congress Cataloging-in-Publication Data
Cocks, Geoffrey.
The wolf at the door: Stanley Kubrick, history, and the Holocaust /
Geoffrey Cocks.
p. cm. — (Studies in film, television, and video; vol. 1)
Includes bibliographical references and index.
1. Kubrick, Stanley—Criticism and interpretation. I. Title. II. Series.
PN1998.3.K83C63   791.4302'33'092—dc22   2003025248
ISBN 978-0-8204-7115-0
ISSN 1543-0863

Bibliographic information published by **Die Deutsche Bibliothek**.
**Die Deutsche Bibliothek** lists this publication in the "Deutsche
Nationalbibliografie"; detailed bibliographic data is available
on the Internet at http://dnb.ddb.de/.

Cover design by Lisa Barfield

The paper in this book meets the guidelines for permanence and durability
of the Committee on Production Guidelines for Book Longevity
of the Council of Library Resources.

© 2004, 2013 Peter Lang Publishing, Inc., New York
29 Broadway 18th Floor, New York, NY 10006
www.peterlang.com

All rights reserved.
Reprint or reproduction, even partially, in all forms such as microfilm,
xerography, microfiche, microcard, and offset strictly prohibited.

Printed in the United States of America

*To Sarah, Emily,
Peter, and Andrew*

*As a member of the audience, I particularly enjoy those subtle discoveries where I wonder whether the filmmaker himself was even aware that they were in the film.*
STANLEY KUBRICK

*. . . one of the things that movies can do better than any other art form . . . is to present historical subject matter.*
STANLEY KUBRICK

*Gentiles don't know how to worry.*
STANLEY KUBRICK

# CONTENTS

Acknowledgments .................................................. xi

CHAPTER 1
Toward the Blue Mercedes ........................................ 1

CHAPTER 2
A Jewish Past .................................................... 18

CHAPTER 3
The Wolf at the Door ............................................ 33

CHAPTER 4
A German Presence ............................................... 49

CHAPTER 5
Directed by Stanley Kubrick, 1953–1962 .......................... 77

CHAPTER 6
Directed by Stanley Kubrick, 1964–1999 .......................... 105

CHAPTER 7
Almost Directed by Stanley Kubrick, 1953–2001 ................... 148

| The Wolf at the Door: Stanley Kubrick, History, and the Holocaust

CHAPTER 8
    The Horror, the Horror .................................... 161

CHAPTER 9
    *The Shining* ............................................. 172

CHAPTER 10
    From Yellow Cabriolet to Eagle's Nest ...................... 196

CHAPTER 11
    The Dream of Jacob ....................................... 218

    Notes ..................................................... 257

    Filmography .............................................. 317

    Bibliography ............................................. 319

    Index .................................................... 329

# ACKNOWLEDGMENTS

Because my intellectual engagement with Stanley Kubrick began long ago in 1980 with a first viewing of *The Shining*, I am indebted to a long list of institutions and individuals for their assistance. I am grateful to Albion College for the support provided since 1994 by the Royal G. Hall and Julian S. Rammelkamp Endowed Chairs in History and to the Faculty Development Committee at Albion and the Hewlett-Mellon Foundation for timely and generous research grants. The Center for Interdisciplinary Study in History and Culture generously and efficiently sponsored a symposium on Kubrick in 1999 and the publication of a collection of essays on Kubrick, undertakings that have significantly advanced my knowledge of Kubrick, film, and film theory. The Warsaw USC Archives, Lviv Historical Archives, and Pages of Testimony from Yad Vashem in Jerusalem provided background on Kubrick's eastern European family origins, while Miriam Weiner of Routes to Roots produced a genealogy of the European Kubricks and Shelley Kellerman Pollero of Gesher Galicia was helpful on Galician Jewry in general. For information on Kubricks in North and South America, I am grateful to Pauline Chernichaw, Albert Kubrick, Linda Kubrick, Sam Kubrick, Harriet Morrison, Richard Narva, Bernard Papernik, the Bronx County Historical Society, the National Archives of Canada, and the Yivo Institute for Jewish Research in New York City. The German Federal Archive in Ludwigsburg was the source of accounts of the Nazi destruction of the Jewish community of Probużna. For information about the Harlan and Kubrick families, I am grateful to Christiane Kubrick and Jan Harlan; Jim Kelling of the National Archives and Records Administration in Suitland,

Maryland; the Gemeentearchief and Algemeen Rijksarchief in The Hague; and I. B. van Creveld and Frank Noack. Materials relevant to Kubrick's films came from the George Eastman House in Rochester, New York; the Special Collections Division of the Georgetown University Library in Washington, D.C.; the Warner Bros. Archive at the University of Southern California; the Margaret Herrick Library at the Center for Motion Picture Study in Los Angeles; the Deutsches Literaturarchiv in Marburg; the Manuscripts Department of the Cambridge University Library; the New York Historical Society; the Library of Congress; the Museum of the City of New York; and the Celeste Bartos International Film Study Center at the Museum of Modern Art in New York City. For information about the role of the Timberline Lodge in *The Shining*, I am indebted to Richard Kohnstamm and Tad Michel. I am also grateful to Hans Staats of MoMA, Wolfgang Sedat of Deutsche Grammophon Gesellschaft, and, for technical assistance, Lisa Adkins and Sharon Clayton of the Grinnell College Library, and Mitch Kyser, Ralph Houghton, and Melinda Kraft of Instructional Technology at Albion College. The following people also provided valuable assistance: Ken Adam, Jörg Baumgarter, Louis Begley, Andrew Bishop, Louis Blau, Alan Bowker, Gwendolen Buck, Noelle Carter, Tom Chambers, John Clive, Catherine Cocks, Fraser Cocks, Hanley Cocks, Sarah Cocks, Norman Cohen, Michael Coyne, Natalie Zemon Davis, David Dennis, Jim Diedrick, Sarah Eisele, Paul Elovitz, Mario Falsetto, Frank Frick, Pat Gehrke, Kim Geiger, Michelle Gerry, Robert Emma Ginna, Sara Gocke, Barbara Grabas, Andy Grossman, David Gurtler, David Gylfe, John Hall, Gay Hamilton, James B. Harris, Raul Hilberg, Matthew Jacobson, Diane Johnson, Sally Jordan, Anthony Kaes, Michael Kater, Sidney Kibrick, Jerome Kleinsasser, Manfred Klimanski, Daniel Kohn, Robert Kolker, Oxana Korol, Tim Kreider, Kristine Krueger, Vincent LoBrutto, Judy Lockyer, Peter Loewenberg, Paul Loukides, Martin Lowenberg, Jeff Melnick, Yeshaya Metal, Mark Crispin Miller, Seth Miller, Alice Wiley Moore, Harriet Morrison, Molly Mullin, Mary Munk, Adri Offenberg, Glenn Perusek, Tim Pytell, Frederic Raphael, James Rider, Jonathan Rosenbaum, Joachim Russek, Marcy Sacks, Wendy Shadwell, Elizabeth Shepard, Richard Slotkin, Gordon Stainforth, Susan Stark, Scott Taylor, Michelle G. Turner, Lloyd Ultan, Michael Van Houten, Henny van Schie, Patrick Villiers, Jenny Vogel, Andrew Wakefield, David and Launda Wheatley of the Far West Leeds Friday Film Cooperative, Bille Wickre, many students in many classes over many years at Albion College; and at Peter Lang, Lisa Dillon and Damon Zucca.

Portions of this book appeared as "Stanley Kubrick's Dream Machine: Psychoanalysis, Film, and History" in the *Annual of Psychoanalysis* 31 (2003): 35–45; and "Death by Typewriter: Stanley Kubrick, History, and the Holocaust," in *Depth of Field: Stanley Kubrick, Film, and the Uses of History*, ed. Geoffrey Cocks, James Diedrick, and Glenn Perusek (Madison: University of Wisconsin Press, 2005).

Cover photographs courtesy Auschwitz-Birkenau State Museum and Jan Harlan; photograph, page 239, courtesy Jan Harlan.

Finally, as always, I am far beyond grateful for the love and support of my wife, Sarah, and daughter, Emily, as well as for the quiet counsel of Godzilla and Fiona.

# 1

## TOWARD THE BLUE MERCEDES

Stanley Kubrick's last film, *Eyes Wide Shut* (1999), contains a scene in which actor Tom Cruise is elbowed off the sidewalk by a group of college boys. In a block packed with parked cars, the one Cruise falls against is a blue Mercedes-Benz. The choice of car against which Cruise stumbles—surely unnoticed by almost everyone who has seen the film—is anything but an idle one. As we shall see in Chapter 6, a Mercedes the color of blue is a carefully chosen reference to the Austrian novella on which *Eyes Wide Shut* is based. And, like many details small and large in Kubrick's films, it is an example of the way in which Kubrick communicates meaning. That the car is a Mercedes is, moreover, a typically tiny clue to Kubrickian passions and concerns directly related, though often indirectly expressed, to the problematic nature of human existence in general and the dangerous history of the modern world in particular.

Nineteen years earlier Kubrick had created one of the most unsettling scenes in all of cinema. A medium shot of two sets of red elevator doors flanked by vaguely *moderne* armchairs. Ominous music—Krzysztof Penderecki's *The Dream of Jacob*—on the soundtrack. One of the doors slides open, and in slow motion a thick torrent of what we know is blood pours into the corridor. The livid purple-black flow bursts into lurid red spray on the floor and walls (Figure 1, color insert). The flood languidly carries the furniture toward the camera—toward *us*—then the blood washes up the camera lens and the screen goes black.[1] A long version of this scene from Stanley Kubrick's adaptation of Stephen King's horror novel *The Shining* (1977) was first released to the public—at Christmas 1979—as the advertising trailer for the film. Such a scene appears nowhere in King's book and is thus another instance of Kubrick's inveterate shaping of the sources for his films to his own vision.[2] Upon release of the film over the Memorial Day weekend in 1980, some reviewers complained that the elevator scene was "suspended in the movie without meaning."[3] According to this line of reasoning, the image fits only as a marketing gimmick, as it certainly must have been on the part of both Kubrick and Warner Bros. But a close reading of Kubrick's life and work reveals that, in its sheer volume, the ocean of blood flowing from the elevator in *The Shining* is the blood of centuries, the blood of millions, and, in particular, the blood of war and genocide in Kubrick's own century.

It is images such as these in the cinema of Stanley Kubrick, and especially in *The Shining*, that confirm a preoccupation with the Holocaust, a concern hardly surprising for a denizen of the twentieth century. His partner in Harris-Kubrick Pictures from 1955 to 1961, James B. Harris, has confirmed Kubrick's interest in the Holocaust, but has argued that it was "no different than mine, or millions of others."[4] This is certainly the case in terms of general cultural influence, but no person's experiences or perceptions are exactly like those of another. This is particularly the case with Kubrick, who rigorously transformed his interests and concerns into art. There is copious evidence of a concern with the Holocaust in particular in Kubrick's films, especially in response to the surrounding culture's turn to almost obsessive interest in that event after 1960. Kubrick was an especially observant child of his time. He cannot be understood without knowledge of the historical specifics surrounding the experiences that informed his worldview and animated his films. For Kubrick, at varying levels of consciousness, the Holocaust was at the center of the harsh realities of the modern world entire that made up the subject matter of his films. His thirteen feature films all in one way or another address human struggles with and over power and violence. *Fear and Desire* (1953), *Paths of Glory* (1957), *Spartacus* (1960), *Dr. Strangelove* (1964), and *Full Metal Jacket* (1987) are films about war; *Killer's Kiss* (1955), *The Killing* (1956), and *A Clockwork Orange* (1971) critique society through the lens of crime; *2001: A Space Odyssey* (1968) sees alien intervention as the only solution to human folly; *Barry Lyndon* (1975) is a sorrowful meditation on ambition, social cruelty, and the birth of modern state power; *The Shining* parodies in agonizing historical fashion the horror genre; and *Lolita* (1962) and *Eyes Wide Shut* balefully examine the dangers of sexuality. But at the center of this body of work—like the Minotaur in its maze—lies *The Shining*, for in that film there slouches a deeply laid subtext that positions the Holocaust as the modern benchmark of evil. An analysis of many otherwise inexplicable visual and aural aspects of *The Shining* demonstrates that this film was an artistic and a philosophical response to the horrors of the Second World War. As such, it is modeled on German novelist Thomas Mann's similar response to the First World War in *The Magic Mountain* (1924), as well as being just as strongly influenced by Franz Kafka's unfinished novel *The Castle* (1922) and historian Raul Hilberg's *The Destruction of the European Jews* (1961). That Kubrick was able to approach the subject matter of Nazi Germany and the Holocaust only indirectly—systematically in *The Shining* and spasmodically elsewhere in his *oeuvre*—was due to the nature of the beast and the nature of the man.[5]

## Directed by Stanley Kubrick

Kubrick was a thoughtful and strong-minded filmmaker. Unlike directors chained to a collective studio enterprise geared to the marketplace, he was an *auteur* who regarded film as a way of making important creative statements about the world. Kubrick was an autodidact, a voracious reader, and a passionate observer of the world through the lens of a camera. Because of his intense interest in the human condition, especially in the modern era, Kubrick was powerfully influenced by the historical conditions of the period in which he lived. And because his own conscious and unconscious intentions strongly mediated the world he viewed through his camera, Kubrick's films cannot be understood simply as the unmediated product of various other texts, cultural discourses, and ideological formations or as merely symptomatic of a particular culture or age. It is true that Kubrick's films, like all creative works, take on a life of their own independent of their creator's intentions. They do so because their words and images draw from, and interact with, other words, images, and meanings circulating within a culture. Audiences as well therefore interact with the film to expand and enrich the meanings within and without the film, part of a process Roland Barthes labeled "intertextuality." Rather than there being just a single meaning created by the author and confirmed by the reader, in any "text" there are multiple meanings due to the fundamental distinction between words and meaning and the resultant interpretations imparted by other texts, paradigms, and readers.[6] But because Kubrick was rigorous in his conceptualization of his films—"I come up with the ideas. That is essentially the director's job"[7]—his intentions—conscious, intuitive, or unconscious—must be given primary consideration in any evaluation of his films. His reflective, interrogatory, protracted method of making films also maximized control over their meaning. This method in turn capitalized on the similarity between films and dreams in general, and Kubrick's films in particular, in their making as well as their viewing. Like music and painting, films are particularly effective at operating on more than just the conscious level. Because Kubrick was open through concentration and over time to myriad rational and irrational influences, his films were a particularly rich conduit for personal as well as supra-personal—that is, historical and cultural—concerns and issues. The openness and fullness of his films thus reduce the tension between Kubrick's insistence on his own ideas and an open narrative designed to invite audience reflection and construction.

The chief focus of this study, therefore, is on Kubrick as *auteur*. We consider the combination of his personal experience, his reaction to and consequent artistic mediation of the flow of historical events that surrounded him, and the resultant didactic aims and effects of his films. This by no means, however, excludes other meanings brought to Kubrick's cinema by the formal characteristics of film, surrounding cultural discourses, and audience reception, all richly illuminated and challenged by modern and postmodern theory. Our model is not that of *auteur* mastery over meaning but rather imperfect creative mediation of idea, context, and text. Still, meanings external to authorial intentions must be considered in the context of Kubrick's mediation to a much a greater extent than in much less reflexive and much more commercial films in various traditional genres. Readings of Kubrick's films informed by contemporary film and literary theory can reveal much that escapes even the prudent and eclectic *auteur* approach utilized in our study. But we focus principally on what was more or less under Kubrick's control in his own reading of his time and place since there is considerable evidence of such directorial mediation. Even at the level of the unconscious, Kubrick exercised some control since, contrary to the claim of Michel Foucault, the unconscious is a site of some contestation and negotiation, not a wall impervious to agency. Kubrick's response to events was also reinforced by the culture's own reaction to them. For Kubrick as well as for many European postmodern theorists, it was the Second World War and the Holocaust that placed much of modern thought and practice into serious question. In the language of psychoanalysis, rather than the unreflective "acting out" of symptoms that occurs as a result of trauma, Kubrick's films constitute a "cinematic working through" of problems raised by the trauma of modern war and mass extermination.[8]

One theoretical approach that is particularly valuable in assessing Kubrick and his films is that of psychoanalysis. This is the case because psychoanalysis has served as a rich basis for much of contemporary literary and cinematic theory. Such psychodynamic and theoretical perspectives are thus important sources for additional insight into all of Kubrick's films, including especially *The Shining*. But it is also the case because Kubrick himself was an early and messianic reader of Freud, "pressing *A General Introduction to Psychoanalysis* [1938] on friends."[9] As we shall see, Kubrick imbibed an orthodox Freudian point of view that emphasizes the phenomenon of childhood sexuality and the necessity of the child's reorientation through the Oedipus complex of sexual drive from the parent of the opposite sex to someone outside the family.

Two derivatives of Freudian theory are also relevant to Kubrick's *oeuvre* because they treat not only the psychodynamics of early childhood and the family that are reflected in his films, but also the same problems of hypermasculinity, particularly among the power elite, that are a constant Kubrickian theme. First, from the feminist perspective of Nancy Chodorow the problem with early child care in modern patriarchal society is the female monopoly on it. This leads to an asymmetry in child rearing since mothers, who have internalized their own early experiences as well as social expectations, interact differently with male infants than with female ones. In a heterosexual culture, the male's sexual object choice is thus an attempt to re-create an exclusive relationship with the original primary caregiver. Since this original relationship was bound up with threats to masculine identity and individual autonomy, sexual desire for the male becomes an expression not only of overwhelming desire but also of great fear. The result, according to Chodorow, is a defensive male "need to be superior to women."[10]

The other post-Freudian psychoanalytic theory, that propounded by Jacques Lacan, has been especially important for modern film theory. Lacan argues that from the earliest months and years of life, the human being is divided between a narcissistic sense of self ("me") and a "speaking subject" that uses language to try to achieve validation from the outside world—other people—for an authentic unity of being that is in fact fictional. This unity is imagined to be fulfilled by the original sense of infantile unity with the mother, for which there is a longing throughout life. For Lacan, there is no essential self apart from the world of symbols, as opposed to "reality," represented by language. The whole human psyche is "the construct of the Imaginary, totally consumed by illusion and compulsion,"[11] a socially constructed set of symbolic attempts through language to solicit authenticity as well as to deny the deadly chaos of the human condition in the world. Our search for an essential self at the center of our being admits the lack of such authenticity and completeness; the only reality is our *desire* for satisfaction by means of other people (or even, in a consumer society, things) of this "longing for unity."[12] A feminist reading of Lacan also especially relevant to film offers a critique of the patriarchy by way of the Lacanian insight that "identities are determined by their position in the symbolic order and by the point of view from which they see the world."[13] This critique is grounded in the concept of "the male gaze" first theorized by Laura Mulvey by which "classic Hollywood film narrative encodes a specific gendered response."[14] The patriarchal objectification of women through sight reflects Lacan's insistence on how being is a function of seeing. The male gaze is not simply a matter of the assertion of power, since we know from Chodorow and Lacan that such desire is the result of unfulfillable need and unresolved conflict. To adapt the title of Kubrick's first film, behind every desire there is fear; in Hegel's dialectical terms, "the demonstration of power starts to function as a confirmation of a fundamental impotence."[15]

However, *any one*—or even all—of these theories will not suffice to explain Kubrick in the absence of a complementary consideration of broader but also more specific historical and cultural contexts that influenced him. Postmodern theory regarding language, gender, or power is indispensable in drawing out the larger concerns that films reflect and reproduce. This may be particularly the case since Kubrick's reputation as a famously idiosyncratic *auteur* has until recently left his work undertheorized. But any theory offers only a partial view of a given historical phenomenon because any life experience is composed of a large variety of constants and variables not reducible to a single analytic approach or even several. Every theory is also culture-bound, a strength that is also a weakness. While postmodern theory argues that language shapes reality, it is also true that reality—that is, historical context—shapes language.[16] The characteristics of an age will open eyes and minds to phenomena that are then profitably theorized and have validity beyond that time and place, as with the shattering events of the Second World War that helped spawn postmodernism itself. But this specific and general validity by its dual nature cannot exclude the validity of other theories developed at different times and places. An Oedipal reading of Kubrick's work, for example, has both special merit and particular limitations because Kubrick was born into a family and an era whose structure and attitudes were similar to those on which Freud based his theory.

One must balance factors of agency and constraint. Postmodern theory privileges the explication of "signs" that point to significance more deeply expressive of—or even in disharmony with—the work's intentional use of "symbols" to convey meaning. A Lacanian interpretation of birds in Alfred Hitchcock films, for example, typically reads them as signs of "unresolved tension in intersubjective relations" arising from the desire that fills the void of the original maternal object.[17] Given the universality claimed by Lacanian theory, such dynamics can be read in—and into—Kubrick's cinema as well. But it is also the case that birds, and specifically birds of prey, play an inordinate role as intentional and intuitive symbols in Kubrick's films, a fact reflected in the names of several of his production companies: Hawk Films, Harrier Films, Hobby Films, Eagle Films, and Peregrine Productions.[18] As we shall see, the recourse to the symbolic use of birds of prey, particularly in *The Shining*, was another reaction to the world around Kubrick that indicates the specific historical conditions that shaped his cinema beyond its shared articulation of the signs of more universalized concerns.[19] The blue Mercedes in *Eyes Wide Shut*, for one, thus packs any number of meanings related to culture, commerce, or text. But this particular automobile's location in Kubrick's last film was also the result of a specific intention on the filmmaker's part and linked as well to other individual and collective concerns shared with, and communicated to, others.

## Indirected by Stanley Kubrick

Kubrick believed that film must attempt to rouse the audience to reflection instead of reconfirming comfortable assumptions in service to entertainment and commerce. In this he was a modernist, with a faith in the power of reason and art to criticize, educate, and inspire. He was also convinced of the special power of the visual space offered by film to transcend—through his mastery of "cinematic plenitude"[20] in service to, as it were, "eyedeas"—the limitations of words, which so often human beings use to hide meaning from others and from themselves. His films, particularly since *2001*, employ an "open narrative" that requires the audience to derive meaning actively rather than being passively instructed, entertained, and manipulated. This style reflects a postmodern appreciation of the volatility and ambiguity of language, the plurality of meaning, and the diversity of experience and point of view. But it was also a method by which Kubrick could bring his own musings and meanings to the screen to stimulate and interact with impressions and insights generated by the viewers—or "readers"—of his films. It was for this reason that Kubrick would never "explain" his films. As he put it early in his career: "I think for a movie or a play to say anything really truthful about life, it has to do so very obliquely, so as to avoid all pat conclusions and neatly tied-up ideas."[21] He strongly reiterated this point of view to screenwriter Frederic Raphael while working on his last film, *Eyes Wide Shut:* "You tell people what things mean, they don't mean anything anymore."[22] This position also served an overdetermined shyness Kubrick manifested toward the outside world that reinforced his valid point that what he had to say he had said best in his painstakingly produced films.[23]

Although it took many, even contradictory, forms, modernism was a revolt against nineteenth-century capitalism and materialism. The new bourgeois order had proclaimed itself the advancing edge of human development by means of rational, technical order. Life, art, and science were a matter of the discovery of external truths and their application to the progress of "mankind." Modernism argued that external truths, to the degree they existed, were not as important as internal points of view. Human subjectivity was a greater reality than scientific objectivity: Einstein established the relativity of time and space; Freud posited a mind divided and in conflict with itself; and Nietzsche argued that reality was constructed by chance, contingency, and the will of the individual. There was no single universal truth, whether scientific, philosophical, or religious, only a variety of perspectives. Postmodernism was to take this position much further, rejecting many modernists' faith in functionalism or abstraction as a universal means for enlightenment and expanding the ideal and practice of culture to include popular culture and the "voices" of non-Europeans, women, and world cultures and histories. This postmodern rejection of modernism was in part based on modernist iconoclasm magnified—sometimes into nihilism—by the pointless destruction of the First World War.[24] Modern art's interest in the blurring of the boundaries between dream and reality would find an apt pupil in Kubrick, particularly in his last film, *Eyes Wide Shut*. And Kubrick's *2001* was, as we shall see, deeply influenced by Nietzsche's *Thus Spake Zarathustra* (1892), which was a call to an entire generation to throw off the dead weight of scientific "certainty" about the world outside and create a world of becoming within each human being. Kubrick's use of open narrative extends in postmodern fashion the same ethos of the contingency of creation to the audience, while the elliptical storytelling in pursuit of this aim was also in line with modernist form. The story of *2001* in particular is, ironically given the film's genre, one of transcendence of the very human scientific culture that allowed the discovery of the means to that transcendence. And *2001*, like *Thus Spake Zarathustra*, was enthusiastically—if often shallowly—received by a new 1960s generation intent on breaking with the stultifying conformity of the modern Western social and political establishment.

This mixture of modern and postmodern lay behind Kubrick's interrogation— or deconstruction—of the various film genres he explored. This, too, was designed to encourage modernist critical reflection while also reflecting the self-conscious irony of postmodernism that debunks "truths" of form and content while embracing multiple points of view. Such interrogation took the form of making genre conventions reflexive rather than transparent—that is, apparent rather than invisible. This approach, what German playwright Bertolt Brecht called the "alienation effect," calls for the audience to recognize the artificiality of viewing a film and, rather than escaping into this artificial world that unreflectively supports the status quo, to pay attention to what the film thinks—and have the audience think—about the real world outside the theater. For example, in *The Shining* Kubrick parodies the "startle effect" by having the audience see one character sneaking up on another. Instead of the audience jumping in fright at a sudden (and dreaded) appearance, only the other character on screen is frightened. The audience is thus not afforded the convenience of simply reacting to a visual effect or identifying with the character in a superficial, sympathetic way, but is expected to *understand*, through both affect and intellect, the feelings of the characters as well as the larger historical issues *The Shining* explores. In *A Clockwork Orange*, to cite another example, the "Cat Lady," one of Alex's victims, is by conventional Hollywood standards a less than physically and personally attractive person.[25] Critics have complained that her fractious attitude, which in any case is a realistically plausible reaction to Alex's intrusion and threat, aggravates a tendency for the audience to sympathize with her killer. A conventional Hollywood film would "help" the audience sympathize with the victim by making her a personally and physically attractive woman. Apart from his view that all women, like all men, are flawed by nature and by society, Kubrick's point is that violence against women—against human beings—by men—by human beings—is wrong as violence against women—against human beings. By making his characters realistically ambiguous in the external embodiment and enactment of their human characteristics, Kubrick invites the audience to think about real violence in the world rather than the artificial violence on the movie screen. Violence against the "Cat Lady" is wrong not because she is a physically and personally attractive person, but because she is a person who is being violated. It is precisely those many movies that depict sexually attractive women as victims of male violence that represent genuine—and sexist—disdain for the audience (and humanity) in their commercial exploitation of the culture's sexual objectification of women and in their hypocritical brief for the "good" victim and against the "evil" victimizer. Kubrick's films, by contrast, display a certain, if also limited, faith in the audience to engage in a serious examination of important matters.

This, too, reflected some measured hope on Kubrick's part that art might indirectly serve to mitigate the horrors of the human condition. But Kubrick's aims and methods sourced above all from his apprehension of the disasters of a modern world spawned—and abetted—by the failed Enlightenment project of human advancement and liberation. The modern world for Kubrick was not the triumph of reason in service to good, but the triumph of will abetted by reason in service to evil. Unlike the modernist Brecht or many postmodern philosophers of gender, society, and culture, Kubrick had no ideological remedy for humanity's ills.[26] Suspicious of human nature, he distrusted enthusiasms of any sort as well as political systems designed to "solve" social problems, seeing all systems as inherently dehumanizing. Kubrick retained only a limited pragmatic faith in democracy as the least dangerous form of government.[27] There is in this again a mixture of the modern and postmodern, of hope for—and fear of—civilization in the modernist singular but also an appreciation—and fear—of the multiple manifestations of human desire. In this, too, is postmodern doubt of autonomous and rational will, but also belief in the possibility of active, coping, and humane choice between the poles of determinism and chaos. Kubrick thus embodied the hard realism of Freud, whose own critical methods and discoveries constructively undermined the very modern order of science and rationality that modernists prized and practiced.[28]

Instead of ideological prescription, therefore, Kubrick's films emphasize the thoughtful observation reflected in the first epigraph to this book: "As a member of the audience, I particularly enjoy those subtle discoveries where I wonder whether the filmmaker himself was even aware that they were in the film."[29] Kubrick's words also reveal his love of watching films, and watching them intently in order to detect the subtlest details. They also signal, as we shall see, a psychological as well as artistic investment in the powers of sight and observation. And, finally, they reflect his own craft in structuring—at various levels of individual and cultural consciousness—his films as dreams. Unlike most filmmakers about whom he wondered, Kubrick habitually invested small visual and aural details with significant meaning on the basis of the psychoanalytic insight that, especially in dreams, small things indicate large repressed forces. In this interview he had been asked about what he hoped to achieve with *A Clockwork Orange*. Kubrick refused to elaborate, arguing that any such pronouncement would reduce the issues in the film to a brief prescription that would hobble the ability of viewers to engage and expand the story's significance. This not only again demonstrates his view of the world as a multifaceted place of dangerous possibilities. It also shows that he was acutely aware of the various levels of consciousness on which the making of a film occurs, reflecting not only an appreciation of the role of the unconscious in the creative process but also the ways in which culture, history, as well as text and interpretations of text influence the meanings constructed in the process of making—and viewing—a film. Kubrick was thus intuitively aware of the variety of ways a film is received and how that reception can magnify and even diversify the meanings contained in it.[30]

For these same reasons, Kubrick's method of directing was open and inclusive, designed to bring out as much as possible the themes he was developing over the typically long course of the preparation and production of his films: "even though you have some central preoccupation with the subject, somehow when you're telling a story . . . the characters and the story develop a life of their own, and, as you go along, your central preoccupation merely serves as a kind of yardstick to measure the relevancy of what the imagination produces."[31] When it came to the cast and crew, Kubrick's refusal to explain the film's purpose was not only a way to maintain control over the ideas the film would examine, but also a means to encourage through exploration and experimentation the possibilities of meaning and expression. The many takes Kubrick demanded of his actors and himself were also a chief means by which both he and they could discover surprising and interesting elaborations on the subject matter. As his wife, Christiane, observed after his death, such an approach to filmmaking made Kubrick during shooting as much an "audience" as a "director."[32]

## Finding the World

Kubrick's thoughtful and open-minded observation was also a vital indication of both his worldview and his view of the world—that is, a philosophical point of view that arose from intense and wary observation of the world. It has been noted that Kubrick viewed the human prospect with "amused pessimism,"[33] but there has been no systematic analysis in the vast literature on Kubrick as to how and why this was the case. A careful historical analysis of his life and career provides the necessary context for fully understanding the content and form of Kubrick's films. Descended from a Jewish family that had emigrated from eastern Europe to America in 1900, Kubrick was born in 1928, fourteen years after the outbreak of the First World War in 1914 and fourteen years before the most murderous year of the Nazi Final Solution in 1942. The year 1928 was thus the exact midpoint, as it were, of "The horror! The horror!" of modern war, enslavement, torture, and extermination that Joseph Conrad had seen—and foreseen—in *Heart of Darkness* (1902). For Kubrick, as a result of his upbringing in the world, history is repetition and not progress or development. He was also "profoundly preoccupied with the dehumanizing effects of social institutions on the individual," the "iron cage" of institutions described by German sociologist Max Weber that had "disenchanted" the world into the discipline of reason, calculation, and the organization of material production and consumption.[34] Ironically, this major *change* in human history away from the irrational, the magical, and the religious only confirmed for Kubrick the lack of progress in human affairs. These fears and concerns were most manifest in his interest in modern Germany, in whose history he saw a peculiarly dangerous combination of socially conditioned aggression, technical and bureaucratic expertise, and industrial might.

Within the context of this perspective, *all* of the major political movements and trends of the modern era had created far more suffering than liberation. In particular, the era of powerful leaders in the 1930s and 1940s who often as not were evil (and whom Kubrick on an unconscious Oedipal level both feared and identified with) was decisive in his apprehension of the world. The world after Auschwitz in particular was for Kubrick proof that human beings—as the befuddled beasts they are—learn nothing, or at least not enough to overcome the malevolent forces that surround and inhabit them. The most audacious match cut in cinema history was possibly, and appropriately, inspired by the wartime film *A Canterbury Tale* (1944), in which a medieval falcon becomes a modern Spitfire. Ironically in *2001*, Kubrick's most philosophically and historically optimistic film, time leaps 4 million years when an ape enlightened to the existence of tools and weapons hurls a bone into the air. This bone, from a tapir just killed and eaten, has also just—in a retelling of the story of Cain and Abel—been used to kill another ape in a dispute over a watering hole. As the bone ascends—and then *descends*—against the sky, it turns into a weapons satellite orbiting the earth in the blackness of space in the year 2001.[35] Much less famously, in *The Shining*, Jack's repeated throwing of a tennis ball against a wall, replete with the boyish booming and whistling sound effects of modern battle, is a similar representation of the stalled and lethal trajectory of human history.[36]

Since "Kubrick saw himself more as a historian, committed to the detached perspective and the long view," his films do sacrifice the character development common to traditional film, drama, and literature.[37] The means by which human beings are controlled by other human beings and by an indifferent or hostile natural world constitute the central concern in all of Kubrick's films. His films therefore consistently display a basic taxonomy of violence, systems of control, and inherent human evil. This *idée fixe* freezes the people in his films into types rather than fully developed characters. For Kubrick, fine plots and words are trivial compared with the power of images as a means to address larger historical and cultural issues. The people in his films are caught in the web of a world of great threat and danger, evocative especially of the world of fascism, war, and mass murder that Kubrick himself first observed as a child, youth, and young adult. More than anything else, therefore, Kubrick's films represent "a dispassionate, even antiseptic study of a found world."[38] It is this "found world" of great terror and danger that is represented in *The Shining* by the Overlook Hotel, whose horrors are witnessed by Danny Torrance, a young boy with the ability to see ("shine") into the past and future. Even more than the young observers of a found world in other Kubrick films, Danny is a representation of Kubrick himself in the 1930s; even Danny's father, like Kubrick's, is named Jack. And of all the films Kubrick made from 1951 to 1999, *The Shining* is the most autobiographical: in the words of friend Alexander Walker, it is "a strange film that reveals much more about its maker than he may have intended."[39]

Even autobiography, then, was for Kubrick a means of exploring history. In touting the great historical epic about Napoleon he never made, Kubrick observed in 1972 that there had "never been a great historical film."[40] Four years later, however, in explaining why he chose to make *Barry Lyndon* after financing for "Napoleon" fell through, Kubrick argued that "one of the things that movies can do better than any other art form . . . is to present historical subject matter."[41] With respect to *Barry Lyndon*, Kubrick was making the point that film is a much better medium than literature for describing to the audience the intensely visual nature of warfare in particular. But his statement also describes "historical subject matter" in general, which betrays the central importance to Kubrick of history, and particularly that of the modern age since the year 1789 cited at the end of *Barry Lyndon*. In this age powerful states, organizations, and individuals—fueled by the anxiety and violence of patriarchal hypermasculinity—disposed of unprecedented scientific, technical, and bureaucratic resources yielded by the Enlightenment and the Industrial Revolution. And it was the first half of the twentieth century, Kubrick's century, that brought the greatest horrors of "escalating norms of violence": the senseless battlefield slaughter of the First World War, the even greater slaughter of civilians and soldiers in the Second World War—and the Holocaust, worse than senseless in its vicious rationalized irrationality.[42]

While many films about history have often failed to achieve requisite standards of accuracy or insight, they can "make cogent observations on historical events, relations, and processes."[43] When properly researched and presented, historical films can also communicate the texture and experience of human life at a particular time and place. Problems with narrative economy do arise—that is, leaving out necessary information in order to tell an effective story within the time constraints imposed by the usual length of a feature film. Filmmakers also often sacrifice complexity for driving home a particularly dramatic point or by using the past to reflect current concerns without sufficient acknowledgment of the differences in human experience as well as the similarities.[44] While Kubrick was famous—even infamous—for his insistence on correct details, most of his films are vitally concerned *with* history without being accounts *of* history. They use—and transform—various genres and fictional stories as a means to get at the human condition as Kubrick saw it through his own experience, reflection, and reading. Most of the films, *The Shining* chief among them, also display a radical indirection in detail with respect to historical events and trends designed both to encourage the audience's own active engagement with the subject matter and, especially in the case of *The Shining*, to protect Kubrick's own psychological and artistic sensibilities with respect to the most dreadful manifestations of the dark lessons he draws from history, particularly those of the century in which he lived his entire life.

Kubrick's films, regardless of genre, therefore in one way or another concern the problems of the human condition in the modern age. As we have noted, his was a realistic, resigned, and—because he was a skeptic and moralist rather than a cynic—outraged view of a found world dominated by power and victimization. As his co-writer on *The Shining*, Diane Johnson, observed: "His pessimism seems to have arisen from his idealism, an outraged yearning for a better order, a wish to impose perfection on the chaotic materials of reality."[45] For Kubrick, however, perfection in cinematic technique only could be aspired to since perfection was illusory in terms of both the realities of the world and the oppressive nature of order and perfection in and of themselves. That he was often labeled a cynic, misogynist, or misanthrope by movie reviewers was not merely a function of his pessimistic outlook, however.[46] There are plenty of serious filmmakers who have a dark view of their subject matter. But Kubrick was unique in his use of popular film genres to present his dark philosophical and historical ruminations in striking visual images within the form of big commercial films that "have strong designs upon their audience—emotional, intellectual, and commercial . . . offer[ing] insight while giving immediate pleasure."[47] This strategy often struck Kubrick's many critics as cheap exploitation of the worst instincts of the audience out of what appeared to be a disdain for humanity mirrored in what appeared to some to be caricatures rather than characters in his films.[48] This mix of "the general and cinephile" also made it appear to some that Kubrick's films were not legitimately or effectively avant-garde in either form or content.[49] But Kubrick's unique brand of filmmaking stemmed from the fact that he became a filmmaker not simply to satisfy artistic longing or commercial success, but rather as the culmination of a lifelong preoccupation with observing, analyzing, and controlling the movie-made world in which he lived and had grown up.[50]

It is true that, as with any human being, Kubrick's concentration on—and fascination with—human violence was also a function of his own aggressive and antisocial drives. His attention to detail in the preparation of his films and the composition of their images was driven by an in part aggressive desire for control and discipline over a threatening world very unlike—but also very like—the ordered world of the chessboards over which he expertly pored from his youth onward. This close supervision over all details of the production of a film drove some of his collaborators crazy and was in some significant tension with the room for expression and experimentation he allowed—or forced upon—his actors. The stakes for Kubrick, as for anyone, were personal as well as professional, for the human will to power and violence was something Kubrick felt within himself. It was manifested in the birds of prey alluded to earlier; in his lifelong interest in the military, war, and the Nazis; and in his identification with Napoleon (known as "the eagle" [*l'aigle*]). Kubrick attempted—successfully for the most part—to sublimate his own aggressive and violent desires into imperial artistic control of a world he found wanting and dangerous. This sublimation was both advanced and complicated by his Jewish background and the postwar American Jewish struggle with the threatening and laming legacy of the Holocaust.[51]

Given this preoccupation with observing the modern world, it is no surprise that Kubrick followed in the tradition of the realist school of filmmaking associated with film theorist André Bazin (1918-1958). The competing montage school, represented above all by Sergei Eisenstein (1898-1948), emphasized editing and other effects to create a unique and artistic film reality, while Kubrick utilized long takes "in the rhythm of life itself."[52] The postmodern Kubrick did not share Bazin's, Eisenstein's, or Brecht's faith in the power of the film to lead to political revolution and liberation. At the same time, however, Kubrick used popular film genres as a means of representing real world problems for the audience's exploration, utilizing, as we shall see, Expressionist forms of décor, sound, and light to take the viewer beyond and behind surface reality. The resultant intellectual and industrious filmmaking made Kubrick a fan of Vsevolod Pudovkin's *Film Technique* (1933), which argued that what distinguishes film from photography is the "artist-director's controlling vision" as manifested in writing, shooting, and editing. The purpose of such control for Kubrick was critical and satirical, not naturalistic.[53] Following Bazin, Kubrick's films usually kept the background of shots in focus, a technique called "deep focus" in film and "depth of field" in photography. But he did this not simply to exploit the reach of the camera into the real world as depicted onscreen, but to expand the space in which to present and juxtapose actors, sets, and props in terms of metaphorical meaning and ideas.[54] Kubrick was especially concerned to reveal the dark forces behind everyday normality because everyday reality in the twentieth century had in its depths proved to be devoid of natural or moral order. He thus found his literary model in the "fantastic and almost journalistic" stories of Franz Kafka that conjoin the real and the surreal for purposes of critical exploration.[55] A similar mixing of the monstrous and mundane was characteristic of two major film traditions whose legacy Kubrick absorbed: prewar German Expressionism, with its preoccupation with the irrational, and the gritty urban realism of postwar American film noir.[56] Both these genres were also reflective of—and reflective on—the disorders of the modern world that preoccupied Kubrick. So, even when Kubrick spoke of films as dreams, he did not mean disengagement from the real world.[57] As Kubrick himself knew well, in the twentieth century psychoanalysis in particular has demonstrated the powerful presence of fantasy and the unconscious in human motives and actions.

## The Jewish Perseus

But if Kubrick were so concerned about the horrors of the modern world, why did he not make a film about Nazi Germany and the Holocaust? He was on record as wanting to make such a film, telling Michael Herr in 1980 "that, probably, what he most wanted to make was a film about the Holocaust, but good luck in putting all that into a two-hour movie."[58] He subsequently wrote a screenplay, "Aryan Papers," from a novel about the Holocaust, but that film, as we shall see in Chapter 7, never got beyond pre-production. There is clearly great ambivalence about the prospect in these words and in/actions. Such ambivalence was not unique to Kubrick, but it was a powerful element of his person and his art that relates directly to the deep, rich, and curious layers of meaning and method in *The Shining*. Of course, one does not have to be Jewish to confront and struggle with the Holocaust, but that Kubrick was Jewish made him especially sensitive to the Nazi manifestation of violence and evil. This sensitivity was modulated by the events and culture of the postwar decades, becoming manifest—or manifestly latent—only as a result of changes in cultural discourse regarding Western society in general and the Holocaust in particular during the 1960s and 1970s.

Kubrick came from a secular family background and "was known to have said that he was not really a Jew, he just happened to have two Jewish parents."[59] Such a point of view was consistent with Kubrick's modern agnostic outlook, but it was also a gloss on a much more complicated relationship with the world in part determined by his Jewish past. Indeed, his remark about only having Jewish parents could have been meant jokingly as a statement about the obvious fact of his Jewish background. In any case, as a Jew in a Gentile world, Kubrick would use his position as an outsider with a deep sensitivity to social injustice to expose the dark underside of society. His deep distrust of the world stemmed at least in part from consciousness of the historically precarious position of Jews in particular within a Christian society afflicted most recently by even more radical racist notions of

Gentile superiority. As Kubrick once put it, "Gentiles don't know how to worry."[60] To be sure, this remark, too, could be passed off as a light take on cultural difference. But Herr, who worked with Kubrick on *Full Metal Jacket,* uses these words as the epigraph for a chapter on Kubrick's mania for control, rightly pointing to it as another expression of a deep fear of a hostile world born in part of being a Jew. The Holocaust in particular would also have mobilized aggressive feelings by what Conrad labeled the "fascination of the abomination" in facing great evil and horror.[61]

Frederic Raphael, who co-wrote the screenplay for *Eyes Wide Shut,* has argued that Kubrick found the extremity of the Holocaust especially threatening.[62] Raphael sees Kubrick's unwillingness to confront anti-Semitism in general and the Holocaust in particular as complementary with his choice of profession. According to Raphael, Kubrick made movies to keep the violence of the world on the other side of the camera and thus under his control. Such a judgment, if accurate, confirms the importance of being Jewish to Kubrick's outlook on affairs. But it also points to specific aspects of his worldview that rendered the Holocaust a particularly difficult topic for him to confront. First, unlike the rational systems whose *breakdown* Kubrick habitually contemplates in his films, the Nazi Final Solution was not a rational system gone wrong; it was a rational—or rationalized—*system* gone *horribly right.* Second, the Holocaust at its black core is a horrible mystery of *irrational* evil that has in new and extremely powerful ways thrown the nature and even the existence of civilization and God into question. And, third, the threat posed by the Holocaust was personal and familial. Kubrick's avoidance—or, rather, to amend Raphael, approach-avoidance—of the Holocaust indicates that its horror was too great especially for someone like Kubrick who took serious matters very seriously. Married to fear was outrage at the injustice of the world that simply could not endure a direct contemplation of the bottomless gloom of the Final Solution. Tellingly, after his death his wife recalled that the entire time he worked on the "Aryan Papers" screenplay Kubrick was horribly depressed.[63]

Kubrick's reluctance to confront the Holocaust directly in his films was also tied to ethics and aesthetics. His remark to Herr about how to get the Holocaust ("all that") into a two-hour film is evidence that his concern ranged beyond the personal. Like Theodor Adorno, who famously declared that poetry was impossible after Auschwitz, Kubrick was aware of the problem of how to do ethical and artistic justice to depiction of the horror of mass extermination. This was especially true in his case, since his chief means of critical artistic inquiry was a satire whose style reflected not only the postmodern practice of play but also the tradition of "Jewish comedy [that] mixes laughter and trembling . . . [and] pain and pleasure."[64] Kubrick himself noted that "it was only possible to be a satirist briefly nowadays, as reality soon outstripped you."[65] But Adorno also said that art in general after Auschwitz cannot ignore the Holocaust. It was, after all, despair over civilization after Auschwitz that gave decisive impetus to the postmodern critique of the Enlightenment project: "In the most general sense of progressive thought, the Enlightenment has always aimed at liberating men from fear and establishing their sovereignty. Yet the fully enlightened earth radiates disaster triumphant."[66] Many excellent films have addressed the Holocaust directly, so that when created and apprehended with proper skill and conscientiousness, art in general, as Adorno argued, is appropriate, even necessary, for an examination of the subject of mass extermination.[67] Such films have ranged from documentaries to dramas, with Claude Lanzmann's *Shoah* (1985) representing a radical critique of these traditional forms through its total reliance on contemporary filmed accounts by survivors and eyewitnesses, to the exclusion of the "impossible" re-creation of the event through historical or fictional footage. Given the especially gruesome nature of the Holocaust, another—or the only—way for art to confront it, it has also been argued, is by means of indirection, like Perseus seeing Medusa reflected in a mirror. (In terms of the Oedipal theme in Kubrick's films, it is interesting to recall that Perseus, like Oedipus, accidentally killed his own father.) As Raphael mused—reflected—in his notebook in May 1995, "S. K. proceeds by indirection . . . [his] work could be viewed, schematically, as responding, in various ways, to the unspeakable (what lies beyond spoken explanation)."[68] Here "unspeakable" means above all the Nazi evil that Kubrick could not approach directly, particularly through the medium of words he very psychoanalytically regarded as inherently inadequate and duplicitous. "He seemed not very interested in words," Raphael concludes.[69] Although, as we shall see, Kubrick often used words with great effect, he noted that "film operates on a level much closer to music and to painting than the printed word. . . . The thing a film does best is to use pictures with music" to create a dynamic living space of rich allusive potential and effect.[70]

Since Adorno, many historians and philosophers, as well as artists, have wrestled with the issue of how art can—or cannot—treat the horrors of history and the Holocaust in particular. The fundamental problem lies in "representing events that insist that they cannot be put into words even as they insist upon the need for transmission."[71] There is, first of all, the gulf between those who experienced such extremity and those who attempt only to describe or evoke it.[72] There is also the problem of finding the right balance between narrative and theory, allowing the story and the storyteller to speak from and of experience while also applying external analysis for purposes of the production of knowledge. Along with this comes the allied conundrum of attempting to find redemptive meaning in such horrors while also acknowledging the irreducible horror and meaninglessness of mass extermination.

Kubrick developed his own creative strategy for representing the Holocaust, one that expands the definition of a Holocaust film to include those reflecting a trauma-like induced discourse. Kubrick's personal hesitations and artistic sensibilities are manifested most evidently in the systematic burial of a Holocaust subtext in *The Shining*. Such indirection fit Kubrick's open-narrative style of filmmaking, the narrative economy of film, the priority he gave to images over words, and the dreamlike structure of his films. The use of a horror film might seem in particular to trivialize the Holocaust as well as satisfy indulgence of viewer and creator in the violence characteristic of the genre. Extreme indirection arguably avoids or mitigates these problems, although it risks cold abstraction, robbing the Holocaust of its specific Jewish agony, or being overlooked entirely. But such an approach can, particularly through the vehicle of a horror film, also encourage the critical contemplation of the horrors of the *real* world. An emphasis on the historical also strengthens the film's interrogation—in line with contemporaneous blurring and exploding of genre boundaries in general—of horror films' fictional and commercial conventions, while exploiting horror films' own recourse to indirection to heighten suspense and terror (e.g., Val Lewton's *Cat People* [1942], which Kubrick most likely saw in the Bronx in January 1943, and Robert Wise's *The Haunting* [1963]). These levels of discourse in *The Shining* reflect as well postmodern insights into the value of multiple narratives and points of view (e.g., Atom Egoyan's *Ararat* [2002]), which help avoid the trivialization that would come, regardless of genre, with unexamined cultural and ideological agendas and assumptions.[73] The greatest problem with Kubrick's indirect approach is that his Holocaust subtext has gone almost—*almost*—unnoticed. But this inaccessibility testifies not only to the rich subtlety of Kubrick's films in general but, in this case, to deep personal hesitations that, ironically perhaps, reveal even more about Kubrick and the times in which he lived and worked.

# 2
# A JEWISH PAST

Stanley Kubrick was born in Manhattan on July 26, 1928, at the Lying-In Hospital on Second Avenue. He was the first child of Jacob and Gertrude Kubrick. A sister, Barbara, would be born in 1934. After living in the garment district of Manhattan, in 1927 Jacob and Gertrude had moved to the West Bronx, where Jacob, a homeopathic physician, worked as a general practitioner and as a staff otolaryngologist at the newly opened Morrisania City Hospital. At the same time Dr. Kubrick adopted the more cosmopolitan name of Jacques, or Jack, likewise changing the spelling of his family name from Kubrik to Kubrick. By the 1920s, the West Bronx had become home to a large part of the growing Jewish middle class in New York City. The Bronx was even home to the First Probużna Sick Benevolent Society, through which Michael Kubrick, Stanley's great-uncle, arranged for plots at Beth Israel Cemetery in New Jersey.[1] But the Bronx also reflected the ethnic and social mix of the metropolis, with large numbers of Irish, Italian, and working-class families. From 1942 to 1944, the Kubricks lived in an elegant apartment building at 2715 Grand Concourse and 196th Street. The Grand Concourse, a six-lane boulevard built in 1909, runs north–south along the western edge of the rocky Bronx promontory, past Fordham University on the northeast and Yankee Stadium on the southwest. In its heyday it resembled the great urban boulevards of Europe.[2] From the start, therefore, Stanley Kubrick lived in and between two worlds: the New World of America and the Old World of Europe. And all of his films would look to the Old World, first from America and then from the island of Great Britain anchored, safely, off the shores of the Continent.

## The Jews of Galicia

Stanley Kubrick grew up in a middle-class and cosmopolitan environment both different from and similar to that of the family from which he was descended. His great-grandfather, Hersh Kubrik, was a tailor who emigrated from the town of Probużna in Austrian eastern Galicia in 1899. Kubrik, born in 1852 in Galicia, brought with him his second wife, Leie (Fuchs), and two of their three children, Bela and Annie. Another child, Mendel, had died in 1898, and two more children, Joseph and Michael, would be born on the Lower East Side of Manhattan in 1900 and 1904, respectively. The family had arrived in St. John, New Brunswick, on the *Lusitania* (an earlier ship, not the famous Cunard liner sunk by a German submarine in 1915) from Liverpool on April 14, 1900. Their eldest son, Elias, born in Probużna in 1877, came to New York City in 1902 from France on the *Statendam* with his wife, born Rosa Spiegelblatt in Bucharest, Romania. Like his father a tailor, following the First World War Elias Kubrik manufactured ladies' coats as an owner of Kubrik & Maslen. Two months after their arrival in the United States, Rosa Kubrik gave birth to her eldest child and only son, Jacob. Jacob married Gertrude Perveler in a Jewish ceremony on October 30, 1927. The Perveler family was also from Austria, and Stanley Kubrick's uncle, Martin Perveler, would play an important early role in his career as a filmmaker.[3]

The Kubriks and the Pervelers were part of a large wave of emigrants from Galicia between 1881 and 1910, when over a million Galicians, among them 236,000 Jews, left, most of them heading for the United States. According to Ellis Island records, thirteen of sixty Kubriks, Kobriks, Kibriks, and Kibryks who immigrated to the United States between 1893 and 1912 came from eastern Galicia. Between 1902 and 1916, moreover, four Kubricks immigrated, two from Manchester, England; one from Bohemia; and the last from Vienna. The majority came from Russia, although others came from Hungary and one, Hersch Kubrik, via Litian, China, in 1906.[4] There are Kubricks scattered throughout the United States, with major groupings in the Northeast, particularly in and around New York City, in New Jersey, and in and around Pittsburgh, with occupations mostly in small business, trades, and labor.[5] Brothers Leonard and Sidney Kibrick became child actors in Los Angeles in the 1930s, appearing in *The Little Rascals* serial and in several films. A number of Kibriks also immigrated to South America, with a large number settling in Bueno Aires.[6] The great majority had emigrated for economic reasons.[7] Poverty had become widespread throughout western Galicia, with its capital at Cracow, and eastern Galicia, centered on Lwów, and this suffering brought renewed persecution of Jews.[8]

The Kubrick homeland of Galicia had long been a place of national conflict and contention, with the Jews there regularly victimized by Austrians, Poles, Russians, and Ukrainians. Most of the region had come under the control of Austria by 1815 and was renamed Galicia. Since the eighteenth century, Jews had comprised around 10 percent of the population of Galicia, being generally concentrated in cities and towns and particularly numerous in eastern Galicia. For example, in southeastern

Galicia in 1900 Jews made up 72 percent of the residents of Brody and 57 percent in Buczacz. But overall in the southeast, they shared a distinct minority status with the Poles among the Ukrainian majority. Under Austrian administration the Jews experienced intermittent discrimination, if not outright persecution, depending on whether the Austrian government was dominated by conservatives or by liberals.[9] It was not until 1867 that an Austrian constitution granted Jews full civil rights. The autonomy granted Galicia by the constitution, however, allowed various Polish and Ukrainian oligarchies to restrict Jews, a trend that was further aggravated by the increasing severity of the region's chronic economic problems.

## The Holocaust in Eastern Galicia

Following Austrian and German defeat in the First World War, Galicia became the southern borderland of the new Polish republic. In 1939, as a result of the German and Russian invasion and partition of Poland, eastern Galicia became part of Ukraine in the western Soviet Union. By the summer of 1941, in the furious wake of the Nazi invasion of Russia, all of Galicia had been incorporated into the Nazi General Gouvernement, which included those portions of Poland not annexed outright to Germany. Sometime in 1941 Hitler decided upon the physical extermination of the Jews, and in 1942 the transport of millions of Jews from throughout Nazi-occupied Europe to the extermination camps in the General Gouvernement began.

Kubrik (or Kubryk, Kibirik, Kybryk, Kobryk, Kobrik, or Chubrik) is not a particularly common name, but it is relatively specific to eastern Galicia and Ukraine as far to the east as Kiev, Odessa, and Kharkov.[10] The name itself comes from the Ukrainian words for a small barrel (*kubryk*) and for a beggar or poor man (*kubrak*).[11] Kubriks were spread among several Jewish small towns (*shtetl*) in eastern Galicia, working in a range of typical occupations from business agent to saloonkeeper to farmer. The Holocaust Martyrs and Heroes Remembrance Authority in Israel records fifty-nine Kubriks killed in the Holocaust.[12] Three of these Kubriks were from Ataki in neighboring northern Bessarabia (Romania), just to the south and east, while several others were from Telechany, northwest of Pinsk in White Russia to the far north and east, but the bulk of them were from eastern Galicia. Seventeen were from Brody and surrounding towns and villages northeast of Lwów, including Podkamień, Michalowka, Zaloczce, and Murawica. The rest of the Kubriks in eastern Galicia had by and large lived in a long arc east of Lwów from Brody in the north to the Czortków region in the south.

Representative of the dreadful experience of Kubriks during the Holocaust is that of the branch of the family that was originally from the village of Popowce, six miles from Brody and four miles west of the border with Russia, but had settled in nearby Podkamień. Today there is no trace of the Jewish community of Podkamień and no remains of the synagogue or cemetery.[13] Yosef and Riwka (Papernik) Kubrik had nine children. Riwka died of asthma at the age of forty-four, and Yosef had a daughter with his second wife. Yosef was the business agent for a local land baron named Jablonowski. He also operated the baron's flour mills and fisheries and was the broker for the baron's lumber business. Before the First World War he built up quite a fortune and was even an appointed official of the Austrian government. But the war ruined him, and he died of prostate cancer in the 1930s. His younger brother Solomon also lived in Podkamień and had seven children. Only five members of this branch of the family survived the Holocaust, with three immigrating to the United States and two to Israel.[14] One of Yosef's daughters, Pesia, married Moshe Papernik, a cousin on her mother's side. Moshe and Pesia were forced into the Złoczów ghetto, and their daughter Yetta was sent to a labor camp. Pesia died of typhoid fever, and her husband and daughter were murdered when the ghetto was liquidated. Pesia's sister Liba escaped the liquidation with one of her granddaughters, only to be shot and killed at a relative's farm near Popowce when someone betrayed them. Pesia and Moshe's son Baruch, however, had gone into hiding in the Pieniaki forest and survived; his parents and sisters insisted that he go alone in order to have a better chance of survival. Liba's son Shopse also survived by being hidden in the home of a Christian family, stayed in Poland just after the war, and came to the United States in the 1950s. One of Solomon's children, Hersh, escaped to Russia and settled in Haifa, Israel. His brother Shimon also fled to Russia, but was killed at Babi Yar, near Kiev, where between September 1941 and August 1943 the Nazis massacred around 100,000 Jews. Shyke Kubrik, son of Pesia's brother Yitzchak, posed as a Gentile shepherd and survived. Sarah, Pesia's oldest brother's daughter, who had married distant cousin Wolfe Kubrik, was sheltered by family friends in Popowce and survived as well.[15]

We know less about the Kubriks of Probużna. There is no record of the name in the town before the 1890s, although much of the documentation in general is missing. Although it is unknown where Hersh Kubrik was born, it could have been the case that he came from around Brody, since the descendants of the Kubriks from Popowce and Podkamień have assumed a relationship with the branch of the family from which Stanley Kubrick was descended.[16] In Probużna, Hersh's sister Liba married Salman Flik and shared a house with sister Beile Kubrik and her husband, Jankel Nadler. Next door lived a Jankel Kubrik and his first wife, Zasna Zysy; Jankel and his second wife, Czarne, had a daughter, Sara Kubrik. American immigration records show that in 1904 three other Kubriks from Probużna—Chane, David, and Leie—had arrived in the United States.[17] By 1932, according to very incomplete documentation, there were no Kubriks registered as members of the Jewish community in Probużna.[18] There is only the record for this period of Salomon Kobryk, born in Probużna on April 13, 1887, and listed among the Jews deported by the Nazis from France to Auschwitz on September 23, 1942.[19]

It was Sunday, October 4, 1942, when the Nazis stormed into the small town of Probużna, population 2700, thirty miles west of Buczacz. The raiding party would have been composed of various units of the SS Security Police, the Gestapo, local gendarmes, German and Ukrainian police, as well as Reserve Police Battalion 133 based in Rawa Ruska. These operations were under the overall direction of Friedrich Katzmann, the SS and police commander for Galicia; Kurt Köllner, chief of the Security Police's Jewish Section; and Heinrich Peckmann, the Gestapo chief in Czortków.[20] October 4 was a Jewish holiday, the last day of Sukkoth, the Feast of the Tabernacles. This last day, called Simhath Torah ("rejoicing of the law"), is the end of a celebration that marked the closing of the harvest season in ancient Palestine and is observed in memory of the ancient Jews' wanderings in the wilderness. All meals are taken in a booth covered with thatch, recalling as well the Tabernacle, the portable holy place during the Jewish exile. On this day 800 Jews were driven into the market square of Probużna for deportation to the extermination camp at Bełżec and the work camp at Lemberg-Janowska.[21] Between mid-March and December 1942, 600,000 Jews would be gassed by carbon monoxide at Bełżec. In spite of overflowing mass graves at the camp, records show the arrival of trains at Bełżec in early October.[22] Probużna's Jews, who in 1921 numbered 1226, or 39 percent of the town's population, had been augmented in March when the German authorities had declared Probużna a collection point for Jews from the surrounding countryside. This could have returned Kubriks to Probużna even had there been none there since 1932. Soon after, a decree prohibited any Jew from being on the streets after 7:00 P.M. In May an SS contingent on horseback had come to Probużna, requisitioning young women for work in the tobacco factory in Jagielnica and dispatching other Jews to the work camp in Tluste. Shortly after the October operation, the 700 to 800 Jews remaining in Probużna were sent to a new ghetto in Kopyczynce, five miles to the northwest.[23] Those who were not killed on the spot, along the way, or in the ghettos or work camps, were subsequently shot into mass graves in the woods, or escaped into hiding were sent to Bełżec. By the end of October, trains were arriving there every other day.[24] After a wave of mass executions in the spring and summer of 1943, Galicia was declared *judenrein*, "cleansed" of Jews. Like millions of others, the Jews of Probużna were no more.

## Kubrick, the Bronx, and Beyond

Like Sigmund Freud, one of the Central European intellectuals who decisively influenced his view of the world (and whose father was also named Jacob), Stanley Kubrick was a descendant of the eastern European Jews (*Ostjuden*) who were the principal victims of the Nazi Final Solution. Alexander Walker observed that Kubrick had "a quality of obsession that seems . . . considerably further east, geographically speaking, than his Middle European origins in Austria suggest."[25] This was because the "Austrian" milieu from which he was descended was in fact that of the *shtetl* of southeastern Poland. Perhaps as a result, Kubrick, with his dark eye for coincidence, even pondered the cruelty imposed by the history of his time on the Hebrew word for Jews of German origin in eastern Europe: Ashkenazim. And perhaps, also like Freud, he derived a sense of mission and high self-esteem from being the first-born—and, in Kubrick's case, only—son, specially, as reported by his younger sister, indulged by his mother.[26] But even more important was the fact that Kubrick was born into a world of growing nativist anti-Semitism and ethnic prejudice. While the middle-class West Bronx where Kubrick lived was not hit hard economically by the Great Depression, that period saw an unprecedented rise in American anti-Semitism that affected all Jews in the United States.[27] More important still for Kubrick's developing outlook was the world of power, violence, and war embodied above all by events in a Europe dominated by Hitler. The deep distrust of human personality and society shared by Kubrick and Freud stemmed in great measure from consciousness of the precarious positions of Jews, particularly within a Christian culture now afflicted with even more radical racist notions of Gentile superiority. "Gentiles don't know how to worry," indeed.

The Bronx Kubrick family apparently was anything but religious. When asked by Michel Ciment in 1980 whether he had a religious upbringing, Kubrick replied, "No, not at all."[28] There is no record of synagogue attendance, and Christiane Kubrick confirms that Stanley never had a bar mitzvah.[29] Between the ages of twelve to thirteen, in any case, Stanley lived with an uncle in Pasadena, apparently because Jacques Kubrick thought that Stanley's poor performance in school might be improved through a stay in California.[30] And even though Kaddish was read at Kubrick's funeral, the ceremony was not a Jewish one.[31] After his death, in response to a question about whether Kubrick tried to deny his Jewishness, his stepdaughter, echoing a like account by her mother, observed: "He did not deny his Jewishness, not at all. But given that he wanted to make a film about the Holocaust and researched it for years, I leave it to you to decide how he felt about his religion."[32] However, although Jacob and Gertrude were married in a Jewish ceremony, Stanley's three marriages would all be civil ceremonies. Still, the Kubricks resided in a strongly Jewish section of New York City. When they lived on the Grand Concourse near 196th Street during the war, for example, the newsstand at the corner was run by local boxing legend Al Goldstein. Most of Stanley's friends were Jewish. His earliest adolescent collaborator in photography was Marvin Traub, who lived downstairs at 2715 Grand Concourse. Marvin was given a twin-lens reflex camera for his bar mitzvah and was the family photographer for at least one Passover seder. Stanley and Marvin spent hours on the streets taking pictures and developing them in Marvin's darkroom.[33] Stanley's favorite teacher at William Howard Taft High School was his English teacher Aaron Traister. Traister was born in Minsk and raised on the Lower East Side of Manhattan, his father a kosher meat inspector and a synagogue official. Aaron was forced to leave high school when he refused to be bar mitzvahed. He was to be the subject of one of the first photo essays Kubrick would photograph for *Look* magazine in 1946.[34]

Kubrick's father was by all accounts a model of the modern American assimilated Jew. As noted earlier, he went by the name Jacques (or Jack) instead of Jacob, a bid for European sophistication as well as American assimilation also undertaken by his brother-in-law Martin, who went by the name Maurice. But his identity was not simply that of an upwardly mobile American professional. His interests and convictions reflected a European sensibility that was also specific to the Jewish community of eastern Galicia. Jacques's disappointment in Stanley's failure to work up to his obvious potential in school not only was based on pragmatic considerations of future employment for his son, but also stemmed from his love of knowledge, literature, and learning. He had encouraged Stanley to read from the large library of books at home and also allowed his son to use his Graflex camera.[35] The latter encouragement was doubly ironic in the sense that Stanley's youthful preoccupation with photography, along with his constant reading, would be both a major contributor to his poor performance in school and his ultimate professional and artistic success.

Jacques's attitude paralleled—and perhaps by a convoluted familial and cultural route stemmed from—the strong tradition among the small Jewish elites of eastern Galicia of assimilation into the dominant German and Polish culture of the region.[36] Stanley Kubrick's interest in ideas paralleled—or was inspired by—this tradition. As Frederic Raphael intuited, Kubrick "had a (Jewish?) respect for scholars."[37] Assimilation and the *Haskalah* (Enlightenment) in Germany had been particularly strong among Jewish physicians.[38] Jacques's own educational and professional experience thus resembled the mix of opportunity and prejudice Jews in eastern Galicia confronted. After graduating from New York University, he studied medicine at Homeopathic Medical College and Flower Hospital, which had been founded in 1860 by a group of New York notables, including poet and publisher William Cullen Bryant. The school had a long progressive tradition, being among the first to admit women and African-Americans. The Lying-In Hospital, where Stanley was born, was a teaching hospital where many from the college took their obstetrics training. Among the fifty-three physicians listed in the hospital's annual report for 1928, there are eight who by name appear to be Jewish.[39] But Jacques still had to face the still strong remnants of anti-Semitism in American professional and medical life. Discrimination in medicine was particularly strong, which, ironically, is why so many Jews entered medicine where the autonomy of private practice protected them from the institutional anti-Semitism that also prompted the large number of Jewish hospitals. But even in medicine, especially after the Second World War, the assimilationist pattern prevailed, and Jacques Kubrick, like thousands of other Jewish doctors, prospered in the mainstream of American professional life.[40] Jacques's son would follow the path of assimilation laid down by his father and by many of the first generations of Jewish immigrants to America. One sign of his emotional debt to the values and habits of his father's generation is that Kubrick is described by those who knew him well as "a kind patriarch."[41] But Stanley Kubrick would also remain deeply influenced by the broader European and Jewish past of his family, a fact consistently and powerfully evident in his films.[42] His immediate environment, even though located in the New World, was thus heavily colored by the Old, from the Continental pretensions of the wide, tree-lined Grand Concourse and the buildings that flanked it to the cultural cornucopia in the Bronx of newly arrived Jewish, Italian, and Irish immigrants.

Direct ties to the Jewish and immigrant world of his parents and grandparents persisted even after Kubrick's childhood and youth. His first two marriages were to the daughters of recent Jewish immigrants from Europe. His first wife, Toba

Metz, was the daughter of a jeweler who left his native Latvia before the First World War and had come to the United States from Belgium in 1912. She and Stanley had met in high school and were married in 1948, Toba remaining a lifelong friend of Kubrick's mother. She was the dialogue director on Kubrick's first film, *Fear and Desire,* perhaps also appearing uncredited as an extra in one scene. She and Kubrick separated after returning to New York from filming in California and filed for divorce in late 1951.[43] Kubrick's second wife, Ruth Sobotka, whom he married in 1955, had left her native Vienna in August 1938 at the age of thirteen following Nazi Germany's annexation of Austria. Her family originally settled in Pittsburgh, where her father, an architect, had taken a position at the Carnegie Institute of Technology. A ballet dancer, Ruth appeared in Kubrick's second film, *Killer's Kiss,* and served as art director for *The Killing*. But, like Toba's, Ruth's marriage would not survive a short career in her husband's films. They separated in 1957, perhaps due in part to discontents arising from Kubrick's childhood.[44] Although his early and later life were not free of conflict and vexation, Kubrick's third marriage apparently produced a close and stable family environment.[45] Even his failure to interrupt shooting on *Full Metal Jacket* upon the death of his parents in 1985 in California might well reveal not indifference but an immersion in work as a means of coping with—or even denying—the pain of loss. Photograph and film document that he saw his parents a couple of times a year.[46]

As a boy, the bookish Stanley had stayed aloof from most of the adolescent activities around him in the West Bronx. But he had his own group, as friend Gerald Fried remembers: "When we were teenagers hanging around the Bronx, he was just another bright, neurotic, talented guy—just another guy trying to get into a game with my softball club and mess around with girls like the rest of us."[47] Aside from the fact that Kubrick was "discovered" by New York film distributor Joseph Burstyn, a Polish Jew who had emigrated to America in 1921, a large number of Jewish friends from what acquaintance Donald Silverman called "a very close knit neighborhood"[48] peopled Kubrick's early career. Alexander Singer, who was a classmate of Kubrick's at Taft High School, was a movie enthusiast who got a job at the offices of "The March of Time," a series of documentary films produced by *Life* and *Time* magazines. He and Kubrick, not lacking ambition, collaborated on a screenplay of Homer's *Iliad,* and Singer assisted on Kubrick's first documentary, *Day of the Fight* (1951) as well as on *The Killing*. He also introduced Kubrick to Fried, another boy from Kubrick's West Bronx neighborhood, who would write the music for not only *Day of the Fight* but also *Fear and Desire, Killer's Kiss, The Killing,* and *Paths of Glory*. Another friend from Taft, Howard Sackler, wrote the scripts for *Fear and Desire* and *Killer's Kiss*. Kubrick's uncle, Martin Perveler, who amassed a modest fortune in the California pharmacy business, lent Kubrick money for *Fear and Desire* and received credit as an associate producer.[49] Kubrick's habitual mode of dress, too, reflected not the usual imperial Hollywood mode of directorial attire, but rather his New York origins: "the Bronx-born director from an American Jewish family usually wore an ill-fitting, lived-in sport jacket and slacks with no tie."[50] And when he was unhappily dealing with lack of directorial control and the intimidation and arrogance of established actors and technicians, many of them Gentile, on *Spartacus*, his first and last big-budget Hollywood assignment, he found refuge in friendship with Tony Curtis, the young New York Jewish actor who was born Bernard Schwartz in 1925 at the same Flower Hospital in Manhattan that was part of the medical school at which Kubrick's father trained.[51]

Kubrick of course rebelled to some extent against his past and his parents, although this too underscored the importance of his relationship to them. His lack of interest in his schoolwork was one indication of this, although it was also a result of an innate curiosity and intellect that could not be satisfied by the routine of public schoolwork. His poor performance in school, in any case, put paid to the hopes his parents had in Kubrick becoming a doctor.[52] Perhaps his lifelong habit of a rather disheveled appearance and wearing army fatigues, "his usual uniform of casually mismatched items that might have been left over from the last war,"[53] or the "tan work pants that laborers wear"[54] was more than just a part of his association with young New York Bohemian artists in the 1950s and 1960s. They were maybe also a sign of rebellion against his father's own determined bourgeois trajectory away from his ancestors' more humble occupations. There is throughout Kubrick's films an Oedipal pattern of the struggle of youth against patriarchal authority. And his obsessive habits, while certainly not pathological, were a defense against associated feelings of rage and aggression. Whatever the specific successes or failures of characters with Oedipal lineaments (e.g., Davy Gordon in *Killer's Kiss*, Colonel Dax in *Paths of Glory*, Alex DeLarge in *A Clockwork Orange*, Redmond Barry in *Barry Lyndon*, and Danny Torrance in *The Shining*), the paternal order always reigns supreme in Kubrick's films.[55]

This Oedipal pattern is consistent with reports that he remained close to his mother. According to his third wife, Christiane, as late as 1957, when Kubrick was filming *Paths of Glory*, his mother still bought any nice clothes he would wear and was "more up on films" than Stanley's father.[56] Certainly, like any male raised principally by the mother in the common patriarchal family structure, he also had to deal with the resultant pre-Oedipal psychological difficulties of coming to terms with women as other than the original source of protection, identity, and threat. Kubrick's portrayal of women in his films has generated significant controversy, but in general it appears that he viewed them as no worse than men and also with some considerable sympathy as victims of patriarchal society. Similarly, the theme of homosexuality in his films, played in a minor but persistent key, has received some psychoanalytic attention in the literature on his films.[57]

But there is more going on in Kubrick's films than the working out of an Oedipus complex, a pre-Oedipal fixation on his mother, or the repression of homosexuality. His films reflect an ongoing confrontation with the world outside the family that in a patriarchal family structure is almost always represented in psychodynamic terms by the father. Like any son, Kubrick identified with his father and resembled him in his assimilation into the dominant culture. It was also his father who introduced him to lifelong pursuits in photography, reading, and chess.[58] But while his father was associated with the security provided by the family, he also represented an outside world that Stanley Kubrick increasingly viewed with suspicion and then horror. As he told Ciment in 1980, photography "gave me a quick education in how things happened in the world."[59] The threat to Jews in particular that became appallingly manifest before and during the Second World War was another reason to embrace the principle and practice of assimilation as a means of self-protection. But, as we shall see in Chapter 3, anti-Semitism was not just a distant European reality in the 1930s and 1940s but also a proximate American one. Stanley's interest in photography and movies from the very beginning was thus bound up with an intense desire to observe the painful realities of the world and an equally intense desire to hold them at arm's length in the pages of a book, on the squares of a chessboard, or, especially, through the lens of a camera. As he revealed to a colleague during the production of *Full Metal Jacket,* his Vietnam War film: "I feel perfectly safe in my love of war and military history because I know that I am a devout coward."[60] So while he could identify with his father through a shared interest in photography, his father embodied a façade of middle-class prosperity and security that hid a human social order with a seemingly infinite capacity for malevolence and violence. Though often exaggerated by the popular press, many of his friends and colleagues even detected hints of paranoia in Kubrick's personality. More—or other—than a possible unconscious conflict over homosexuality, any such paranoia is consistent with Kubrick's obsessive fear of the world and with his obsessive desire for control over his surroundings.[61] A bad experience piloting a plane, for example, led to a phobia—though not, of course, also rationally unfounded—about flying. Given the fears that directing films was designed to control, moreover, it is not surprising that in his one filmed address he compared film director D. W. Griffith to Icarus flying too close to the sun but also that he himself, according to Christiane, "loved to see any dumb film with a fight between airplanes."[62] Fear of flying, along with his fear of the world in general, led Kubrick to work as much as possible within the environment of his home and his family.[63] But his chief response to his fears was a perfectionist, even obsessive desire to control all aspects of life and art—indeed, to attempt to control the world by keeping it under the watchful, unblinking eye of a camera.

Kubrick's seriousness about the world was thus reflected above all in his approach, even as a youth, to photography and film. Gerald Fried recalls the movies Stanley and his friends habitually attended and how the discussions afterward "were primarily listening to Stanley kind of smirking at the tasteless sentimentality of most pictures."[64] The camera Kubrick's father gave him was to prove not a means to education into a world of preparation for academic, professional, commercial, and social success, but a method of apprehending the fundamental wrongness of the world entire. Kubrick's father in this sense for Stanley turned out to be an unreliable guide to a world revealed to be the dangerous "found world" often confronted by the young and even by children in his films. Danny Torrance in Kubrick's largely autobiographical *The Shining* is the most striking and relevant example of this fearful juxtaposition. Even the "star child" in the last shot of *2001* founding a new world—instead of finding an old one—betrays a disturbing ambiguity in its gaze, an ambiguity stripped to naked aggression in the face of young Alex DeLarge in the first shot of Kubrick's next film, *A Clockwork Orange*. The Oedipal conflict regularly played out in these films is therefore informed and reinforced by a view of human society shaped by early impressions of it in its most grotesque forms and moments. Kubrick's obsession with paternal authority in his films was therefore based on fear that was both Oedipal and historical. It involved identification with the aggressor not only as an outlet for aggression but also as a defense against destruction of the ego (the self)—a psychological as well as philosophical *wish* for protection from both internal and external violence. Kubrick's lifelong focus on the violent hypermasculine power elites that to his eye controlled the world was more artistic than neurotic, but still no less a product of early and continuing personal experience.

Perhaps revealing of neurotic as well as philosophical content was his attitude toward doctors, which also followed a pattern of avoidance often characteristic of males. Christiane Kubrick has recalled his deteriorating condition while working on *Eyes Wide Shut:* "I thought he was awfully tired, and he never slept much—ever—in his whole life. Then I thought he was really overdoing it with this last film. Sleeping less and less. He also was a doctor's son and he wouldn't see a doctor. He gave himself his own medicine if he wasn't feeling well or he would phone friends—it was the one thing he did that I thought was really stupid."[65] Was this a habit also linked to his Oedipal fear of his father? Was mistrust reinforced by Stanley's discovery and exploration of the dangerous world his father represented and by his conduct attempted to hide from his son? As we shall see, this avoidance of doctors can be regarded as consistent with a world viewed in terms of impending destruction and death. Doctors are not numerous in Kubrick's films and neither are they seemingly any better or worse than anyone else. But there is the Nazi Dr. Strangelove (not a medical doctor, to be sure), the deluded behavioral psychiatrists in *A Clockwork Orange*, the phony psychologist Dr. Zempf in *Lolita*, and a female pediatrician in *The Shining*. The only major character in a Kubrick film who is a doctor is the hapless Dr. Harford in *Eyes Wide Shut*, which may be psychologically significant in and of itself because this last film and *The Shining* were the only ones to concentrate on a single family, while *Eyes Wide Shut* was the only Kubrick film to be drawn from an Austrian source.

## Behind the Camera

But if Kubrick were so influenced by a personal past that was in a variety of ways determined by the ambiguous position of Jews in American and Western life, why then are there so few Jewish characters in his films? Characters such as Drs. Brodsky and Rubinstein in *A Clockwork Orange* and Marion and Lou Nathanson and (possibly) Victor Ziegler in *Eyes Wide Shut* are not identified as Jews beyond the possibility or certainty of their names identifying them as such. Sidney (played by the

Jewish actor and later film director Paul Mazursky) in *Fear and Desire* and Lieutenant Goldberg in *Dr. Strangelove* are only there to help compose the "all-American melting-pot" combat unit common in Second World War movies. Kubrick even wrote Jews out of the screenplays of five of the sources he filmed—Lionel White's *Clean Break* (1955), Humphrey Cobb's *Paths of Glory* (1935), Anthony Burgess's *A Clockwork Orange* (1962), William Thackeray's *The Memoirs of Barry Lyndon, Esq.* (1844), and Arthur Schnitzler's *Dream Story* (1926)—mostly (but not wholly) for reasons of narrative economy. In *Paths of Glory* Kubrick left in a character self-described as a "social undesirable," but leaves out the novel's subplot of a Jewish soldier not being selected for execution because an officer fears another political storm over anti-Semitism on the scale of the Dreyfus Affair. Cobb underscores the real existing anti-Semitism in France by having an officer justify caution because "you never know what connexions [sic] these Jews may have."[66] Cobb also exploits the irony of a Jew being spared because he is Jewish. Though Kubrick, as in all of his films, also makes rich use of irony in his *Paths of Glory*, this particular irony was not available to him in the wake of Auschwitz. As for *Eyes Wide Shut*, Kubrick had considered Woody Allen for the lead role, playing a Manhattan Jewish doctor in a dramatic, not a comedic, role.[67] But in his adaptation of the Schnitzler novella, Kubrick changed the protagonists from Jews to Gentiles, moved the location from Vienna to New York, and changed a scene of anti-Semitism to one of homophobia.

There were several reasons why Kubrick seldom portrayed Jews in his films and never as major characters. Frederic Raphael argues that Kubrick was convinced that Jewish characters do not have wide box-office appeal and so wanted his protagonist in *Eyes Wide Shut* to be "a Harrison-Fordish goy."[68] Kubrick was following the lead not only of Jewish filmmakers but also of the great Hollywood studio heads like Carl Laemmle, Louis B. Mayer, the Warner Brothers, and Adolph Zukor.[69] Although these men were Jews who had emigrated from eastern Europe and took control of much of the movie business just before and after the First World War, they made movies designed to appeal to the Christian majority in the United States. Their productions were also designed to emphasize assimilation and avoid conflict with the Gentile establishment. In other words, their movies were as much about their own *non*-Jewishness and assimilation into the dominant culture. While the Russian and Polish pogroms they had fled were sometimes reflected in their stories about the American West in particular, their movies molded the American Dream as happy escape for the individual and generic common man.[70] And these were the movies on which Kubrick grew up, another reason for him not to be concerned with the portrayal of Jews on film.[71] But there was more to Kubrick's reluctance to include Jews in his films than just pragmatic commercial considerations or identification with his father's assimilation. Kubrick persisted in avoiding Jewish characters even long after Hollywood and European films had begun featuring them during the 1960s and 1970s. A cousin of Kubrick's wife maintains that Kubrick did this because he was afraid of provoking anti-Semitism through the inclusion of Jewish characters in his films.[72] This startling observation coincides with what we have learned about Kubrick's sensitivity to the place of

Jews in a world of threat and danger. The absence of Jews in Kubrick's work is therefore anything but proof of the irrelevance of his own Jewish background. Raphael, who is also Jewish, rightly observes that it is "absurd to try to understand Stanley Kubrick without reckoning on Jewishness as a fundamental aspect of his mentality."[73]

Kubrick himself was more than reluctant to appear on film. Despite a flurry of Internet postings about a Kubrick cameo in *Eyes Wide Shut,* Kubrick never did appear in any of his (or anyone else's) films, except once by accident in *2001* when his reflection holding a handheld camera can be seen for two seconds in the visor of one of the astronauts inspecting the monolith on the moon.[74] While this choice, the norm among film directors, could also be written off as stage fright, an inability to act, or general shyness, the refusal to be the subject of the camera could be another clue to a larger pattern in his life and work. Jews are absent from Kubrick's films because the main subjects of Kubrick's films are perpetrators and not victims. For Kubrick, those with power on the scale of Hitler or Stalin are the proper subjects for an understanding of the world. Their place is before the camera because that is the place where they not only can be observed but also can be controlled by means of imprisonment within a carefully constructed fictional world. From photography through documentary films to features, the trajectory of Kubrick's film career was toward the greater control that selection, preparation, and production of fictional stories could provide. For this reason above all others, Kubrick never made a feature film from anything except a fictional source. Even in his early days as a photojournalist, Kubrick had staged some of the "candid" photos he took.[75] The obsessive control Kubrick exercised over the preparation and production of his films was part of this process of locking the world's evil into his films, where it could be observed and controlled. As Raphael has correctly noted: "Is it unduly fanciful to see fear and horror driving him to face in art the malice which he dreaded in life? The great thing about violence in films, however scandalous, is that the director at least is in control of it. He can toy with brutality, brutally, without its hurting *him.*"[76]

Along these lines, many collaborators and commentators have noticed the powerful observatory effect of Kubrick's eyes and the sense that he was always thoughtfully and intently watching everything on the set and in the world. Malcolm McDowell, who plays Alex DeLarge in *A Clockwork Orange,* once jokingly invoked an image out of the films of Fritz Lang, whose films were among those that inspired Kubrick, during an interview in New York: "Our mentor, Stanley Kubrick, is watching our every move. He just switched a button in his headquarters and a satellite picked us up."[77] John Baxter even opens "Kubrick Under the Lens," the first chapter of his biography, with the command: "Look at those eyes. *Look* at them."[78] And of course how appropriate—and purely coincidental?—in this sense that Kubrick would become a photographer for a magazine named *Look*. Kubrick's obsession with eyes and seeing is also evident in the many famous close-up images from his films in which a character peers back at the audience: the ambiguous stare of the astral fetus at the end of *2001* or the predatory gaze of Alex at the beginning of *A Clockwork Orange*, for example. These characters are in effect the film—and the filmmaker—gazing back out at the world's own predatory stare. Kubrick's—ironically last—film was even titled *Eyes Wide Shut*, a play on words about seeing and not seeing, wanting to see and not wanting to see.

This obsession was certainly fueled by elements of Kubrick's early life experience. The desire to see—scoptophilia—can be a result of castration anxiety stemming from Oedipal conflict. Although "[p]hotography is the art of the solitary, the voyeur,"[79] Kubrick was not in any clinical sense a voyeur, which is a particularly acute syndrome of scoptophilia and is a reaction to Oedipal castration fears (Sophocles's Oedipus blinded himself out of guilt over incest with his mother). Voyeurism "is based on the hunger for screen experiences, that is, for experiences sufficiently like the original to be substituted for it, but differing in the essential point and thereby giving reassurance that there is no danger."[80] Scoptophilia itself is more generally linked to the child's desire to know sexual facts, a desire that can be either stimulated or blocked by the birth of a sibling. Kubrick's sister was born in May 1934, when Stanley was about to become six, the age when the Oedipus complex is reaching a resolution. Certainly suggestive in terms of both Oedipal and visual dynamics is Kubrick's strong interest in the face of many (in the end insuperable) obstacles in making a film of Stefan Zweig's *The Burning Secret* (1914), in which a young boy keeps observation of his mother's romantic affair from his father.[81] Sadistic impulses, too, are often associated with scoptophilia, whereby seeing is destroying, seeing that something is not destroyed, or is itself even a substitute for destroying.[82] While voyeurism in the general sense of the word is probably inherent in film directors, Kubrick's famous directorial cool and calm amid the problems, conflicts, and frustrations on the set may thus in this context also be seen as a defense against unconscious feelings of rage and aggression and therefore as part of a larger sublimation of such emotions through his artistic work.[83]

But these early elements were merely fuel for more comprehensive historical, cultural, and artistic concerns on Kubrick's part. Oedipal rage sublimated into hatred and aggression against the male power-elite perpetrators of violence in his films made the films an inappropriate place for Jews psychologically as well as historically, but even more important was the fact that Kubrick's obsession with eyes and looking was overdetermined along the lines of history in particular. The two instances of close-ups of Jack's gaze in *The Shining*, for example, are unlike the looks of other characters in *The Shining* and in other Kubrick films. Jack's eyes, once while he is alive and then once in death, are directed upward and not—as, for example, Alex's in *A Clockwork Orange*—toward the audience. This lifting of the eyes is an indication of not only Jack's madness but also his willing subordination to the elevated hierarchies of power and violence in the world. Given the Holocaust subtext in the film, the direction of Jack's gaze is also expressive of the indirection of Kubrick's presentation of extreme human evil. In this horror film, otherworldly forces are not understood primarily, if at all, in terms of the supernatural but rather of the historical. And, for its part, the Holocaust is represented as beyond the pale (as it were) of direct apprehension psychologically or artistically.

Just like his obsession for control over his subject matter, therefore, Kubrick's *modus operandi* was based on a need for a sense of personal and familial security from the dangerous forces abroad in the world. Work was a refuge from a lethal world in every sense, even, as we have seen, from the death of his parents. His physical (though not intellectual or social) isolation from the world, which was inflated into legendary, infamous, and largely inaccurate status in much of the popular press, was manifested most consistently in his insistence on the long and meticulous preparation and production of his films within or near the confines of his family ("rooms in which family life and filmmaking overlap") and—after *2001* anyway—with the assistance of individual collaborators and small shooting crews.[84] Even the only film ever produced of Kubrick at work on the set, *Making The Shining* (1980), was made by his daughter Vivian. A similar venture of hers about his next film, *Full Metal Jacket,* however, was never completed, perhaps partly due to Kubrick's reticence in this regard.[85] Director Peter Bogdanovich recalls that "Kubrick's obsessions [were] film and family," the resultant process of making a film being what Diane Johnson has called "evolving and organic."[86]

Kubrick's twin obsessions were, of course, also there at the beginning. In 1955, Kubrick made his second feature film and the only one he would film in his hometown of New York City. *Killer's Kiss,* which we will study in greater detail in Chapter 5, is a crime noir film that drew a great deal of its visual style from Jules Dassin's *The Naked City* (1948). Kubrick himself had photographed the shooting of *The Naked City* for *Look* in 1947.[87] Dassin's film dramatizes the crowds and the rich ethnic background of New York, including Chinatown and two scenes on the Jewish Lower East Side. Kubrick's film, by contrast, offers only the physical landscape of the city itself, which, with the exception of scenes shot in Times Square and Penn Station, is devoid of people. But Kubrick seemingly does reflect the Irish identity of Dassin's homicide lieutenant Daniel Muldoon in his protagonist, fighter Davy Gordon. And he renders the antagonist in *Killer's Kiss* an Italian by the name of Vinny Rapallo. In his complicated way, Kubrick was commenting on the ethnic composition of the New York City of his own youth. The juxtaposition of Irish and Italian most likely is a partial reflection of the "apartment buildings filled with Jewish, Italian, and Irish families"[88] along the Grand Concourse in the Bronx—partial of course in terms of being only one possible factor among others, but also through the absence of any Jews in the film. But this absence is also in fact the presence of an absence that, in keeping with his overall detached and omniscient point of view, is addressed in many of Kubrick's films on the level of indirect historical discourse rather than in terms of discrete characters.

And, in any case, there in fact was—and is—always one Jew at the center of every Kubrick film. The one behind the camera: Stanley Kubrick.

# 3
# THE WOLF AT THE DOOR

Night. Winter. Jack Torrance is about to murder his family. He hunches at the door of the room in which his wife is trapped, the words dripping and then—as he straightens to splinter the door with an ax—lunging from his mouth:

> Little pigs, little pigs,
> Let me come in.
> Not by the hair on your chinny chin chin.
> Then I'll huff and I'll puff,
> And I'll blow your house in.[1]

In this scene from *The Shining*, the wolf is literally at the door. And he is there because Stanley Kubrick and history ordained that he be. Fairy tales play an important role in *The Shining*, and we know that Kubrick was well read (to) as a child in Grimm's fairy tales.[2] It is true that "The Three Little Pigs" is not a Grimm fairy tale: "The Story of the Three Little Pigs" was first published in England in J. Q. Halliwell's *Nursery Rhymes and Nursery Tales* in 1843. But while the story was anything but unknown in the United States, its popularity was massively boosted by the cartoon version released in movie theaters by Walt Disney on May 7, 1933.

Disney's *Three Little Pigs* became the most successful cartoon in the animator's "Silly Symphonies" series, winning an Academy Award in 1934, and the song composed for the eight-minute short by Frank Churchill, "Who's Afraid of the Big Bad Wolf?" became a national theme song in defiance of the Depression. It is anything but clear if the politically conservative Disney in fact intended the moral of the story to address the economic crisis. But the tone of the film reflects the vigorous optimism of the new Roosevelt administration in 1933 and is of course in line with the main—and very profitable—purpose of the entire Disney enterprise of "sentimental populism . . . the attempt to create a cultural space where people could experience, however briefly, freedom from fear."[3] According to Richard Schickel's iconoclastic portrait of Disney, the message in *Three Little Pigs,* however, "is more that of Hoover than of Roosevelt . . . stressing self-reliance, the old virtues of solid, conservative building and of keeping one's house in order."[4] In both constructions, in any case, the wolf retains its old European and American symbolic meaning of, originally agrarian, fear of hunger and starvation. This association had a long history. The fifteenth-century English satirical poet John Skelton wrote of keeping "the wolfe from the dore," an image given new expression by American feminist and social activist Charlotte Perkins Gilman in "The Wolf at the Door" (1897), an attack on the obscene extremes of wealth and poverty of the Gilded Age.[5] The image of the constant threat of hunger and starvation was powerfully revisited in industrial America during the Great Depression, when in 1932 the number of unemployed reached 18 million.

But, as Catherine Orenstein has pointed out in her recent study of "Little Red Riding Hood," the meanings of fairy tales change with time and place. And it was the change in the cultural meaning given to the wolf in literature and film during the 1930s that would place Kubrick's Jack Torrance at the door. For its part, "Little Red Riding Hood" originated as a seventeenth-century French warning against female promiscuity in an age of sexually predatory male court life, the wolf retaining a sexual meaning in twentieth-century American culture as well. The German Brothers Grimm, however, reflected the Victorian nineteenth century in their removal of the tale's sexual content and substitution of lethal violence and the moral of obedience. Unlike the original story by Charles Perrault, in the German version Red Riding Hood escapes being eaten when a handsome young hunter shoots the wolf.[6] The wolf underwent a change in symbolic meaning during the 1930s and 1940s due not to cultural difference but to events. The Depression went away as a result of the New Deal, the mobilization of the American economy during the Second World War, and the postwar economic boom produced by the GI Bill and the Korean and Cold Wars. Poverty, inequality, and malnutrition still existed in the United States, but general prosperity and the creation of a new large middle class all but banished the specter of starvation from public consciousness, thus rendering the original wolf at the door a quaint, if also memorably cruel, anachronism.

Overseas, the rise of fascism and militarism, and in particular Nazism, during the 1930s and the world war in the 1940s restored the image of the wolf as predator in place of his meaning as a harbinger of hunger and starvation. For centuries human populations, particularly in densely populated Europe, had to deal with the reality of wolves as a mortal danger. And as far back as Titus Maccius Plautus, the Roman comic dramatist of the third century B.C.E., who observed that "man is a wolf to men," the wolf has been a central symbol of merciless violence. In the twentieth century, the gargantuan war that spread across the entire world beginning in 1941 with the German invasion of Russia and the Japanese attack on Pearl Harbor created an international environment of massive military mobilization. And while evil was vanquished in the Second World War, its horrors remained palpable, with the Holocaust eventually emerging as a phenomenon that has permanently darkened the human prospect. To many, including Kubrick, man did indeed seem to be a wolf to men. As Kubrick put it in 1971, "man is the most remorseless killer who ever stalked the earth."[7]

This impression of the world was all the more marked for Kubrick because of the reality of anti-Semitism in America. As we saw in Chapter 2, the 1930s saw an unprecedented rise in American anti-Semitism that affected all Jews in the United States. Even after the war, according to a cousin on his wife's side of the family, Kubrick himself on at least one occasion was subjected to anti-Semitic prejudice. During location work on one of his early films out in the country, it began to rain heavily. Cast and crew repaired to a restaurant to wait out the storm. Stanley did not receive his order, and when he asked where it was, the manager replied that he did not serve Jews.[8] Kubrick remained sensitive to this issue right to the end of his life. In 1999 he remarked in a phone call to Michael Herr that the head of a motion picture studio had just bought an apartment in Manhattan and that he was the first Jew allowed to buy in that building: "Can you believe that?" Herr quotes him as saying. "What is it, 1999? And they never let a Jew in there before?"[9]

But before the war, things were much worse. One of the most disturbing effects of the Depression was the consequently greater appeal of fascism and Nazism in America. This appeal could also draw upon a long history of nativist religious, ethnic, and racial prejudice in the United States, whose "paranoid style" had been further inflamed by the large numbers of immigrants from eastern and southern Europe during the first decades of the twentieth century up until the time when the Immigration Act of 1924 put strict quotas on categories of immigrants from southern and eastern Europe. During the 1920s and 1930s, such attitudes metamorphosed into an anxious cultural discourse about "racial" threats to an idealized homogeneous Anglo-Saxon America. The domestic Nazi movements were of course the most dangerous anti-Semitic expression of this: for them, among other things, "Jewish control" of Hollywood, for example, was a major concern.[10] The accession of the Nazi party to power in Germany spawned a variety of imitators in the United States after 1933, such as the German-American Bund, the Gray Shirts, the Silver Shirts, the Black Legion, Phalanx, and the National Gentile League. These groups were supplemented by the right-wing extremism of the ilk of Father Charles Coughlin and Gerald L. K. Smith and the anti-Semitism of Henry Ford's newspaper, the *Dearborn Independent*. And New York City was a major hub of pro-Nazi activity in the 1930s, as pro-fascist meetings, rallies, marches, and demonstrations spilled out over the entire metropolitan area. Jewish businesses in the Bronx were picketed, and Nazi and "Christian Mobilizer" meetings and demonstrations in that Jewish and immigrant section of New York were common.[11] Actor Tony Curtis has recalled rabid German nationalists of the Yorkville section of Manhattan who would beat up any Jews found in their area.[12] As an organizational high point, on February 20, 1939, the German-American Bund held a rally at Madison Square Garden that attracted a crowd of 20,000. It is not known whether the Kubrick family was exposed directly or indirectly to this type of harassment, but it is unlikely that an educated family such as the Kubricks would have been oblivious to such an obvious and distressing feature of the immediate social and political landscape.

Given such dire developments inside and outside the country, it is not surprising to find that the symbolic meaning of the Big Bad Wolf in Disney cartoons began changing from hunger to aggression during the mid-1930s as Disney moved to exploit the success of *Three Little Pigs*. In 1934 *The Big Bad Wolf*, featuring "Little Red Riding Hood, The Three Little Pigs, and Grandma," was released. The Big Bad Wolf now clearly represents a more generalized threat to life and well-being in a fable about the danger of taking short cuts through a dark forest. The Practical Pig's brick house—a symbol of modern individual industriousness—is no longer enough to keep the new wolves in the world at bay. One must be armed: the Practical Pig has a corner shelf devoted to various types of "Wolf Exterminators." The hit song of 1933, "Who's Afraid of the Big Bad Wolf?" is reprised twice, the first time by the unprepared and oblivious Fife and Fiddler Pigs and the second by the entire cast (*sans* wolf) after a Wolf Exterminator has done its job. And no longer is the Big Bad Wolf run off by falling into a boiling cooking pot laced with turpentine, as in the original Disney version, which was a less violent adaptation of the English fairy tale, in which the wolf is cooked and eaten by the third little pig. This resolution indicated the wolf's status as a cultural symbol of hunger and want, while the psychological dynamics behind his demise also have to do with the satisfaction of the reader's aggressive drives as well as defensive identification with the aggressor (eat instead of being eaten). In the cartoons of the mid- to late 1930s, the implements of defense and destruction have changed to machines of war against the wolf, portrayed as foreign aggressor against peoples and nations.

This change is even more explicit in *Three Little Wolves* (1936), Disney's next attempt to capitalize on the popularity of his porcine stars. In this cartoon the wolf explicitly symbolizes an enemy that is a threat from abroad. The film opens with the Big Bad Wolf instructing his three pups in the culinary art of pork preparation, reciting with the class in a German accent, "Ist das nicht ein Sausage Meat?" and so on. On a tree near the Three Little Pigs' house, there is a sign with a horn attached that reads "Wolf Alarm," while the Practical Pig is constructing a huge mechanical contraption called a "Wolf Pacifier" (unlike "Exterminator" a bow to American isolationism or even, though early, sensitivity to the [possible] plight of Nazi victims?). To save the Fiddler and Fife Pigs (who have made the same mistake as "The Boy Who Cried 'Wolf'"), the Practical Pig disguises himself as an Italian tomato salesman and traps the Big Bad Wolf in his machine, which, after bopping him with mechanical rolling pins and kicking him with mechanized boots, uses a cannon to shoot him out of sight. The cartoon closes with the Three Little Pigs with fife, drum, and flag à la "The Spirit of '76" playing "Who's Afraid of the Big Bad Wolf?" The discourse of this cartoon clearly displays the influence of threatening events in Europe that surely aroused fear and patriotism on Disney's part reflective of trepidation—and, for most, a resultant isolationism—among the American populace as a whole.

After the attack on Pearl Harbor in December 1941, the American film industry mobilized itself to produce propaganda for the war effort. Like other characters, the wolf had new roles to play. Even those productions not—primarily or at all—inspired by patriotism reflected the change. By 1941, Universal Pictures had initiated with *The Wolf Man* what would become the most popular monster genre of the war, a clear indication of the changed status of the wolf as a cultural marker. The Wolf Man films reflected the traditional portrayal of the Old World of Europe as the locus of horror and mystery, a tradition now terribly reinforced by images of Hitler's goose-stepping legions. Even Val Lewton's *Cat People* had begun as a war story, with the people of a village in the Balkans turning into "werecats" at night to slaughter German soldiers.[13] Cartoons as well signed up for the duration. Maverick animator Tex Avery's *Blitzwolf* (1942), for example, has "the three little pigs face their old enemy the wolf, who has now taken on the persona of Adolf Hitler."[14] As a strongly patriotic American, Disney of course had his studio do its part for the war effort. *Der Fuehrer's Face* (1943), featuring Donald Duck as a flustered Nazi war worker, won Disney another Academy Award. Even before the United States entered the war, Disney had recast *Three Little Pigs* as a Canadian war bond trailer entitled *The Thrifty Pig* (1941) and dressing the wolf in Nazi armband and hat.[15] In *Home Defense* (1943) aircraft spotter Donald plays "Who's Afraid of the Big Bad Wolf?" on a bugle, which not only transforms the spirit of optimism in confronting economic disaster into a spirit of resistance to German and Japanese aggression, but is another obvious transmutation of the wolf from symbol of want to symbol of war. This association was reinforced in the daily press by the actual names of Hitler's headquarters (Wolf's Gorge, Wolf's Lair, Werewolf) echoing his nickname "Wolf," "allegedly the meaning of 'Adolf.'"[16]

In another unique, curious, and troubling way, Disney's *Three Little Pigs* reflected the impact on American culture of the events of the 1930s and 1940s in Europe in particular. There are, coincidentally enough, three versions of *Three Little Pigs* and they differ from one another in one small but significant way. In each of the versions, the original one released in 1933, a second that replaced it shortly thereafter, and a third released during the Second World War and subsequently issued on video in 1996, the wolf disguises himself as a "Fuller Brush Man" trying to work his way through college in order to trick the pigs into letting him in. The character in question is a caricature of a Jewish peddler as well as of the more recent American upward educational mobility of Jews. The only human being portrayed in *Three Little Pigs* thus gave the young Kubrick a short primer in contemporary American anti-Semitism. The wolf wears a disguise composed of a long nose; black beard; small round glasses with green lenses; a small, flat, round cap; and a long coat. On the soundtrack is eastern European fiddle music. In the original version, the wolf speaks in a "Jewish" voice and accent. The second version of the cartoon substituted a vaguely eastern and perhaps "dumb jock" voice, but kept everything else. However, in the 1940s, certainly under the impact of the Nazi persecution of the Jews, which had begun achieving a new and broadly noticed ferocity from 1938 onward, Disney made further changes in the character. He reanimated the entire scene to eliminate the nose, beard, and original glasses, leaving the coat, the same type of glasses but now perched down on the wolf's snout, a bowler hat, and the original music.[17] But Disney, who shared the polite (by and large) anti-Semitism of the day, persisted with an image of the wolf in this scene that was closer to Nazi stereotypes of the Jew than anything else. Disney's original midwestern anti-Semitism had been aggravated by difficulties with Jewish-dominated segments of the motion picture industry, something he confided to Nazi film director Leni Riefenstahl when he was one of the few in Hollywood to welcome her on a visit to Hollywood in November 1938.[18] That he changed the cartoon a second time was certainly due not only to the populist solidarity of a country at war, but probably also to the impact of growing knowledge about the unprecedented extremity of Nazi persecution of the Jews. That he did not eliminate the character entirely demonstrates the ongoing social prejudices of the day as well as Disney's own apparent reluctance to incur further criticism by admitting that anything was wrong in the first (or at least the second) place.

The "Big Bad Wolf" in *The Shining*, therefore, is the product of many years of cultural evolution and reflects in particular the transformation wrought in the symbolic meaning of the wolf during the 1930s and 1940s. It is also an indication that European and world events surrounding the threat and reality of war against the West and against the Jews were of greater moment to the solidly and securely bourgeois precocious Kubrick than poverty, unemployment, and economic catastrophe. And it is an indication of the role that the world of movies played in Kubrick's life from the very beginning, for the lines Jack quotes are those of the Disney version rather than those from "The Story of the Three Little Pigs." The wolf also satisfied to some degree Kubrick's unconscious aggression as well as serving as a defense against his fear of the dangerous world by means of an identification with the aggressor. But, however informed by personal and familial conflict, the cognitive and cultural dimensions of Kubrick's artistic investment in the figure and symbol of the wolf in *The Shining* and by general thematic extension in all of his films are even more important. As we shall see in Chapter 8, any mention of the wolf in *The Shining* is a(n) (in)direct expression of a growing preoccupation in the 1970s on Kubrick's (and the culture's) part with the subject of Nazis, the Second World War, and the Holocaust. In this respect, it is significant that Jack, like the Big Bad Wolf, does not make it through the door to get at his wife, but remains on the other side. This is in line with Kubrick's use of camera, film, and narrative and symbolic indirection as a means of distance from and control over the subject of the Holocaust in particular. Instead of his wife and son, Jack Torrance's only victim (besides himself) will be Halloran, the black cook whose arrival at the Overlook Hotel just as Jack has broken through the bathroom door saves the lives of

Wendy and Danny Torrance. By having an African-American as the victim of Jack's—and the hotel's—murderous rage, Kubrick underlines, as we shall see, a twinned theme in *The Shining* of an American and, underneath, a German past of racial persecution.

## Kubrick Seeing Pictures I

Much has rightly been made of the artistic influence on the adult Stanley Kubrick of certain—mostly European—films and filmmakers. But Kubrick was also an early fan of movies in general. Kubrick allowed as how Hollywood films of the 1930s and 1940s were very cleverly made even if their form was predictable and their content restricted to rote fantasy and happiness. He obviously included himself as a youth when he observed that they held one's attention even if they were not works of art. But because these films usually had little of real interest to say, Kubrick was not able or willing to name any American directors as favorites. When asked in 1968 whether particular European films influenced him, he responded that, first, he had not seen any until the late 1940s and, second, when he did start seeing them they impressed him in telling stories without compromises to popular tastes and commercial concern. But when further asked whether therefore he was particularly influenced by European cinema, Kubrick replied: "No. Or, rather, I am influenced by *absolutely everything I have seen*."[19]

Kubrick's declared penchant for learning from all manner of movies has been remarked upon in the literature, as has an early introduction to the cinema that in fact predated his years (1946–1949) at *Look*: "When Stanley Kubrick was a boy of 14, life was a dream prescribed by a series of images, changed semi-weekly and viewed from the velvety rococo depths of Loew's Paradise in the Bronx."[20] As they were for most Americans in the 1930s and 1940s, movies were an important part of Kubrick's daily life. What has escaped notice, however, are the specific influences on Kubrick of the subject matter of the movies he saw as a youth. While Kubrick did begin to appreciate film technique—often through its absence—in these films, just as or even more important was the conscious and subliminal effect of their contents on Kubrick. The fact that he became a filmmaker renders this influence, even if unacknowledged in specific terms by Kubrick himself, even more important. And when we consider the turn in American films during the 1930s and 1940s toward a concentration on matters of tyranny and war, we cannot help but observe that Kubrick's later career—indeed, his whole outlook on life and the world—had been decisively shaped by early viewing experiences that reflected and refracted shattering historical events. More specifically, the construction Kubrick placed on the relationship between the world and both his own life and that displayed in the cinema was one of a façade of security behind which lurked only imperfectly comprehended danger. Life as depicted on the movie screen in the 1930s and 1940s was not but a dream, but a dream hiding a nightmare, much like the happy chatter in Thomas Mann's short story of 1925, "Disorder and Early Sorrow," listened to "with a dark suspicion all the while that something is wrong somewhere."[21] This does not mean that Kubrick was traumatized by his childhood. Indeed, the real security of his early experience as well as the creative sublimation of fears and aggression that the cinema provided combined to generate nostalgia in later life. As his wife revealingly recalled after his death about Kubrick's enjoyment of cruises by ocean liner from England to the United States, it was because he "enjoyed . . . pretending to be living in 1930."[22] For the same reason, he remained all his life "a fascinated radio listener," as he had become in 1930s and 1940s when radio, broadcasting both the mirth and the mayhem of the age, was the only broadcast mass medium in the home.[23] But the nightmare behind the façade of both his life and the cinema pierced through by his restless mind and eye could be controlled as well as observed only through the lens of a camera.

Thus it seems that much, if not most, of Stanley Kubrick's early education in the world in general during the 1930s and 1940s took place not in school but in the movie houses of the West Bronx. Kubrick, as we have noted, was an indifferent student, apparently no better after his return in September 1941 from a stay with his uncle in California than before he left in June 1940. Although he played in the orchestra and swing band, worked on the school magazine, was a member of the photography club, and met Toba Metz, who would become his first wife, his years at William Howard Taft High School were relatively lost ones for him. The only scholastic enthusiasm Kubrick demonstrated at Taft was for his English teacher Aaron Traister, whose dramatic classroom renditions of Shakespeare and other poets and writers resembled performances more than lessons.[24] Alongside his early interest in photography, Kubrick, like most people in America in the 1930s, was an avid moviegoer.[25] Movies, along with radio, became the great cheap mass entertainment in America during the years of the twentieth century before television. We do not know exactly when Kubrick started going to the movies on a regular basis, but he has said that his mother took him regularly until he started going on his own.[26] So there is no doubt that as a youth he saw a large number of Hollywood films. This was not only because going to the movies was a universal habit in America in the 1930s but also because New York was where all the important movies premiered and where all the movies played in scores of neighborhood theaters—"nabes" in the parlance of the trade paper *Variety*—across the metropolitan area. As Christiane Kubrick later wrote: "You were never far away from a cinema in the Bronx and Stanley visited them all. Movies would fascinate him from an early age, and he used to say whether the picture was good, bad, or indifferent, it didn't matter, you could learn from it."[27] This behavior is also anything but surprising in light of Kubrick's contemporaneous fascination with photography and, of course, his ultimate choice of a career in film.

We may therefore assume with great confidence that if a movie played at either the RKO Fordham (R) or Loew's Paradise (L), in particular between roughly 1936 and 1946, Kubrick most likely saw it.[28] It is also the case that these movies played at other cinemas the same or other weeks, increasing the likelihood that Kubrick would see any one of them. The most distinguishing new feature of the American movie scene from the late 1930s until 1946 was of course the number of movies dealing with the Nazis and war. In this, movies in general followed a path parallel to that trod by the Big Bad Wolf in his change from economic to military threat. The Second World War itself would witness an unprecedented mobilization of media in all the combatant nations that would make this war the most filmed event in history. The film industry in America and Europe, which had reached maturity in the decades after the First World War, would play a major role in the propaganda and morale efforts of nations at war. While traditional entertainment vehicles remained important for commercial and political reasons, war films entered the genre's golden age. Even before the war, however, Hollywood had begun to take the first faltering steps toward active commentary on the ever more dangerous world situation. A battle against clear and definitive evil—West and East—was to augment the energy and effect of Hollywood's war productions after 1941.

Before the war, however, only Warner Bros., with which Kubrick would sign in the 1970s, was willing to take on the subject of the Nazi threat to America and Hitler's persecution of the Jews. Aside from wanting to continue to make pictures as profitable entertainments, Jewish studio heads did not want to fan the flames of American anti-Semitism by focusing on these issues. The studios also did not want to compromise their lucrative German and European operations by offending the new Nazi regime. Harry and Jack Warner, like Carl Laemmle of Universal, Louis B. Mayer of MGM, and Adolph Zucker of Paramount, were Polish Jews. But unlike their mogul peers, the Warner brothers, especially Harry Warner, were committed early on to making anti-fascist and anti-Nazi films. Harry himself had been born in Poland during a pogrom and was dedicated on both religious and political grounds to resisting the rise of Nazi influence in Europe and around the world. The Warner Bros. campaign began in 1933 with a Looney Tunes cartoon that lampooned Hitler's Germany. Both Jack and Harry Warner were active in support of Jewish refugees and supported the Anti-Nazi League, and in 1938 Jack Warner sponsored a dinner in honor of German novelist and anti-Nazi Thomas Mann, who had been exiled to the United States.[29] Warner Bros. had always had the reputation of making darker, edgier films than the other studios. It also regularly took on social issues, depicted the travails of the working class, and often championed the "little guy" in his struggle against "bourgeois convention."[30] The studio, finally, had a long history of producing films concerned with American foreign relations. All this stood Warner Bros. in good creative stead in its campaign to expose the Nazi menace at home and abroad.

The prewar Warner offensive against Nazi Germany was constituted by a series of major motion pictures between 1937 and 1941. The first, *Black Legion,* which premiered in New York City on January 16, 1937, was a frontal attack on one of the most violent American fascist organizations. In the early 1930s the Black Legion was behind the assassination of a Catholic autoworker who had married a Protestant. This murder, safely non-Semitic, formed the basis for the Warner Bros. film. The conservative Production Code Administration (PCA), "Hollywood's own self-censorship cum marketing arm extraordinaire,"[31] required the studio to tone down the anti-Semitism, racism, and nativism of the Black Legion—neither the word "Jew" nor "Catholic" is heard. But the screenplay and the finished product nevertheless made the xenophobia of the organization clear enough, and the film played at the RKO Fordham in the Bronx the first week of February 1937. Later in 1937 the second and third in the Warner Bros. series of anti-Nazi films were released: *The Life of Emile Zola* had its premiere in New York on August 11 and played the RKO Fordham at the end of December and then again in April 1942. It was designed as an allegory of contemporary European events that focused on past and present anti-Semitism in Europe. The PCA again insisted that overt references to Jews be removed, and Warner Bros. complied, the word "Jew" being heard only once. Fear of censorship and audience antipathy also played a role in the production of *They Won't Forget* (R, August 1937), which was a fictionalization of the murder of Leo Frank, an Atlanta businessman who defended a black employee accused of raping and killing a white woman.[32]

In 1939 Warner Bros. released *Juarez* and *Confessions of a Nazi Spy*. *Juarez*, which premiered in New York on April 25, 1939, and showed at the RKO Fordham in July, was designed as an appeal to Latin Americans to resist Nazi penetration of the Western Hemisphere. *Confessions of a Nazi Spy* opened in New York three days after *Juarez* and began a run at the RKO Fordham in early June. Like the other Warner films, it was based on actual events, in this case the breakup of a Nazi spy ring by the FBI in February 1938. Even though the film did not do well at the box office, its production and release stirred considerable national and international controversy, including a clumsy attempt by German diplomats to sabotage its production. The director, Anatole Litvak, used a semi-documentary style reminiscent of newsreels and included clips of the German-American Bund's Madison Square Garden rally and Leni Riefenstahl's Nazi propaganda film, *Triumph of the Will* (1935). Like the other Warner anti-Nazi features, however, *Confessions of a Nazi Spy* deemphasized anti-Semitism.[33] The new decade, reeling now under the outbreak of war in Europe, witnessed three more Warner Bros. attacks on the Nazis before Pearl Harbor: *Dr. Ehrlich's Magic Bullet* and *The Sea Hawk* in 1940 and *Sergeant York* in 1941. In *Dr. Ehrlich's Magic Bullet*, which played the RKO chain in Queens and Brooklyn in April, Edward G. Robinson portrays the German-Jewish scientist who developed the first cure for syphilis. This constituted a direct response to American fascists who condemned Jews as the enemies of humankind. *The Sea Hawk*, which played the RKO Fordham in September 1940 when Kubrick was in Pasadena, was another Errol Flynn swashbuckler that drew parallels between the Spanish Armada, which threatened England in 1588, and the current Nazi air assault against the British Isles. This revisited the British film *Fire over England* (1936), which equated Nazi racial totalitarianism with sixteenth-century Inquisition and Armada Spain, where "they herd souls as we herd cattle." *Sergeant York* (R, November 1941), a film about the First World War, promoted American interventionism over American isolationism.[34]

After Pearl Harbor, of course, Hollywood unleashed a barrage of war movies. The world was intruding on the movies as never before. But even before December 7, 1941, war films, including those from 1940 on from England, were a staple at the box office. The proximity of the East Coast historically and geographically to Europe certainly made films about that theater of particular interest in New York. This impact, similar to the West Coast's fear of Japanese invasion and subversion, was surely heightened after December 1941 by deadly German submarine attacks off the Atlantic coast and the subsequent blackouts. The large Jewish population in New York City also made the war against the Nazis of special moment there. So in the West Bronx as elsewhere from 1942 on, the war genre grew exponentially. At the Paradise and the Fordham alone between 1936 and 1946, Kubrick had the opportunity to see upward of 160 war films, almost three-quarters of them concerning the war against Nazi Germany. These included quite a few documentaries as well. These documentaries would provide a creative bridge toward much of Kubrick's own early work in particular because of their historical subject matter and recourse to narration. These films also formed a link back to many of the Warner Bros. anti-Nazi movies that were based on real-life events. Documentaries did not do well at the box office—even Frank Capra's Academy Award–winning *Prelude to War* (1942) did poorly in its commercial run.[35] But Kubrick, with his interest in film in general and his desire *in nuco* to document the world for purposes of enlightenment and control, no doubt watched them with great interest. The documentary tradition was also maintained in the newsreels regularly shown in movie theaters and in such special news features as "Joe Louis vs. Schmeling" (R, June 1938), which recorded the Detroit boxer's victory over Nazi Max Schmeling, who had beaten him in a previous fight. This boxing short also anticipated Kubrick's first documentary film, *Day of the Fight*, which too reflected Kubrick's view of the world largely as a place of masculine combat.

Given Kubrick's long and strong interest in the military and the organization of military operations as reflected in a number of his owns films (*Fear and Desire, The Killing, Paths of Glory, Spartacus, Dr. Strangelove, Barry Lyndon,* and *Full Metal Jacket*) as well as in several unproduced projects, it would seem that movies about the Second World War—and the war itself—were a crucial element in the evolution of his approach to his work, making Kubrick in an artistic sense a prisoner of the Second World War his entire life.[36] Even the flaws in these movies from Kubrick's perspective—the easy sentimentality, avoidance of the real pain and horror of combat, and happy endings imposed by industry and government censors as well as dictated by Hollywood's own sound commercial instincts—were motivating factors in the development of Kubrick's own filmic vision. Like his father's photography, these movies both revealed and veiled their subject matter. The real war was somewhere else, particularly when it came to the Holocaust, which was unknown territory for the movies of the time. Kubrick, while eventually deploring the intellectual and ethical as well as technical inadequacies of much of commercial cinema, would for his own reasons adopt a similar, though also only partially successful, strategy of avoidance when it came to the depiction of that horror which surpassed all others.

## Kubrick Taking Pictures

During the Second World War, Stanley Kubrick went from seeing pictures to also taking them, a process that would culminate in 1951 in his decision to go from taking pictures to making pictures. At the end of the Second World War, Kubrick entered the world of professional photojournalism. His introduction to photography had come at the beginning of the war when on his thirteenth birthday, in 1941, his father gave him his first camera.[37] He sold his first photograph to *Look* in 1942, published his first there in 1945, and joined the *Look* staff upon graduation from high school in 1946.[38] Kubrick as a result not only learned a great deal about how the professional world worked but also began seeing the ways of the real world in general. Among other things, it was photojournalism that at the end of the war brought visual confirmation to America and the world of the worst atrocity of the twentieth—or perhaps any—century. In May 1945 both *Look* and *Life* magazines published photographs taken in Nazi concentration camps. Even though public concern with the Holocaust would wane in the postwar years, the immediate effect on the public of the photographs was profound: "Images had shown themselves capable of conveying the very horror that had incapacitated words . . . [and] helped turn collective disbelief into the shock and horror of recognition."[39] These photographs were followed by newsreels of the trial of Nazi leaders at Nuremberg, which included footage of the concentration and extermination camps.[40] Kubrick was once again convinced of the power of images and of the inadequacy of words when it came to understanding and portraying a dangerous world run by dangerous men. It is no accident in this regard that the walls of the Overlook Hotel in *The Shining* are covered with black-and-white photographs of the powerful men who built and patronized it.[41]

What had Kubrick known about the Holocaust during the Second World War and how did what he might have known affect him? The Holocaust was one thing he did not learn about from the movies, for the whole subject of Nazi persecution of the Jews was treated faintly or, more often, not at all in war films of the period. Even when before the war Warner Bros. wanted to make a movie called "Concentration Camp," opposition from the Production Code Administration, other studio heads, and the Hollywood press succeeded in convincing Warner to shelve the picture.[42] (By contrast, an anti-Nazi Russian film of the same name played at the Waldorf Theatre in Manhattan in March 1939.) The studios in particular did not want American isolationists to have the additional ammunition of charging that Hollywood Jews were trying to get America involved in Europe's war. The Warner Bros. *Mr. Skeffington* (R, August–September 1944) would treat American and Nazi anti-Semitism under a formulaic veneer of romance, light comedy, and drama, but any less delicate linkage between the war and Jews, it was believed, would only aggravate persisting anti-Semitism.[43] Charlie Chaplin's *The Great Dictator* (L, April 1941) features a Jewish Hitler look-alike played by Chaplin, an alternately buffoonish and raving Hitler also played by Chaplin, and scenes in a Jewish ghetto. But the ghetto is very unlike the real ones to come, and the film focuses on lampooning Hitler and Mussolini and making a plea for common humanity. Even those films that did mention the camps did not focus on the persecution of the Jews, an exception being *The Mortal Storm* (L, August 1940), in which a Jewish professor is sent to a concentration camp. And even that movie keeps its eye firmly on the box office in its construction as a thriller and its foregrounding of non-Jewish characters.[44]

Most often the camps were mentioned in the context of political persecution and resistance. This was the case, for example, with *Casablanca* (R, March 1943, with *At the Front in North Africa*), *All Through the Night* (R, April 1942), *The Seventh Cross* (L, December 1944), and Ernst Lubitsch's *To Be or Not to Be* (L, April 1942). Movies that dealt with the Nazi leadership, such as *The Devil with Hitler* (R, December 1942), Fritz Lang's *Hangmen Also Die* (L, May 1943), *The Hitler Gang* (L, September 1944), *Nostradamus Predicts the End of Hitler* (L, February 1945), and the Warner Bros. *Hitler Lives?* (R, February 1946), also emphasize persecution and atrocity in general as well as the threat of Nazi militarism to other countries and peoples. Even *None Shall Escape* (L, April 1944), which shows Polish Jews being loaded onto cattle cars, does not depict or otherwise suggest their ultimate fate, closing with a rabbi's admonition to resist along with the other victims of the Nazis. Of course, during the war the world was only—and, for many reasons, too slowly—beginning to grasp the appalling enormity of what the Nazis were doing in Poland. The first film to depict Auschwitz was *The Last Stop* (Poland, 1948), which was shown in the United States in 1949.[45]

But there was knowledge of the Holocaust in America during the war. We do not know how closely the Kubrick family followed events in eastern Europe, but word of the extermination reached America by 1942 and most of the organized response to Nazi industrialized butchery was centered in New York City.[46] While American Jews were more sensitive to the travails of Jews in Germany and in occupied Europe than other Americans, the trend toward assimilation had lessened their sense of belonging to the Old World of Europe, which, after all, they had left in the first place. Younger Jews tended to think of themselves as American and were immersed in a culture far less dominated by the traditions of their European Jewish past. American Jewry was not only socially and religiously diverse but still, ironically perhaps given their distance from their transatlantic past, also culturally diverse: "Jews of German origin versus *Ostjuden,* and among the latter, a somewhat attenuated split between *Litvaks* and *Galitzianer.*"[47] The more recent immigrants living on the Lower East Side of Manhattan and in the Williamsburg section of Brooklyn more often tended to read the more comprehensive Yiddish press coverage of the Holocaust and to be involved in memorial activity than the descendants of earlier immigrants living in middle-class sections of the city like the Bronx.[48] And just as Jews before the war had feared stirring up the volatile pot of American anti-Semitism and isolationism, during the war they were concerned that by pressing the American government too hard on the issue of rescuing the Jews from the Nazis they would fan the flames of domestic anti-Semitism.[49] Nevertheless, especially in New York City—the commercial and media capital of the world, home to a large Jewish population, and with close links to European culture and trade—as Matthew Baigell has pointed out, "[m]ost Jewish Americans, of course, knew what was happening. I certainly knew in 1943, although I was barely ten years old."[50]

Even the Jewish-owned *New York Times* "was coy about printing Jewish-sounding bylines on its front page," but it did offer coverage of Nazi persecution of the Jews, particularly in "its massive coverage" of the Night of Broken Glass, the Nazi pogrom against German Jews in November 1938.[51] It was much more difficult to give extensive coverage to the Nazi extermination program, first of all because it was secret but also because there was a tendency to disbelieve the horrific reports that were coming out of Poland. This tendency was fed among the population in general by the memory of perceived Allied propaganda exaggerations of the First World War as well as by greater concern for the course of the military conflict and for American casualties. Jewish organizations remained fearful of arousing domestic anti-Semitism and diminishing their influence on the Roosevelt administration through too great an insistence upon action on behalf of Europe's Jews. Zionist organizations put a greater emphasis on the issue of a Jewish state in Palestine than on saving Europe's Jews, something most Jews and non-Jews agreed was impossible short of winning the war and destroying the Nazi regime.[52]

But the reports would not stop coming. The Jewish Telegraphic Agency began reporting the mass shootings of Jews in Russia during the summer of 1941. In October the *Times* ran a story entitled "Slaying of Jews in Galicia Depicted," which described the massacres of thousands of Hungarian Jews deported to Poland and also reported that "the plight of the Galician Jews is said to be so serious that they face hunger and other hardships."[53] In July 1942 the *Times* reported that the "extermination" of Jews had begun in eastern Galicia the previous summer, noted the use of gas chambers at Chelmno from November 1941 to March 1942, and quoted Szmul Zygielbojm of the Polish National Council in London on "absolutely reliable" sources, "although the story seemed too terrible and the atrocities too inhuman to be true."[54] On June 30, 1942, the *Times* for the first time used a seven-figure number to describe what was going on: "1,000,000 Jews Slain by Nazis, Report Says"; the figure of 2 million appeared in articles on September 3, November 25, and December 9. From late 1942 through the early months of 1943, large articles on New York events in response to the killings appeared in the *Times,* culminating in a front-page story on March 2, 1943, headlined "Save Doomed Jews, Huge Rally Pleads." Coverage of the story in other papers and magazines across the country was more sporadic, but on October 14, 1944, *Collier's* magazine published Jan Karski's eyewitness account of exterminations in eastern Galicia under the title "Polish Death Camp."[55]

It would be surprising to learn that the professional, literate Kubrick family was not aware of what was published in the *New York Times* or in the daily, weekly, and monthly press in general. Even if the Kubricks did not read the *Times,* they hardly could have escaped discussion of reports in the press and elsewhere of the horrible events in Europe that surely circulated through the Jewish community in the

Bronx. Even if such discussion was occasional, muted, or disbelieving, the very fact of such indirection was a sign not only of the uncertainties surrounding the information from abroad but also of the tremendous emotional impact of even the suggestion of what the Nazis might be—or probably were—doing to the Jews of Europe, particularly given Christian Europe's long history of persecution of the Jews. We do know from Stanley's sister that President Franklin Roosevelt was much admired in the Kubrick household. When FDR died in April 1945, Kubrick's mother said: "Roosevelt was a god to us."[56] Indeed, Jewish support for FDR was widespread: American Jews "believed, it was said, in three worlds: *die velt* (this world), *jene velt* (the world to come), and *Roosevelt*."[57] The Kubricks' admiration could have been created or at least buttressed by the wartime perception that the president was a champion of the Jews of Europe.[58] Although Roosevelt's actual record on the matter of saving the European Jews from the Nazis has since been the subject of considerable debate, it was Roosevelt who, more than any other leader, save for Churchill, framed the conflict with Nazi Germany as a worldwide struggle against tyranny. Hitler was Roosevelt's exact counterpart in this sense since he, too, saw the struggle as global, only against the imaginary forces of "world Jewry."[59]

Stanley's reaction to such an atmosphere can be gauged, appropriately enough, by one of his photographs. It is consistent with Kubrick's suspicious view of the world around him that the first photograph of his in *Look* was not of victory celebrations but of a downcast news dealer surrounded by headlines announcing the death of President Roosevelt. Once again, the extraordinarily alert and observant Kubrick—the *watchful* Kubrick—was confronted with the façade of proximate security and the lurking reality of deadly danger. Even a family like the Kubricks that did not regard itself as religiously Jewish certainly knew that the Nazis did not bother with such a distinction. Like most Jews in America, the Kubricks knew of paternal and maternal relatives as well as friends of their parents and grandparents consumed in the fires of Nazi fury. Christiane Kubrick has said that Stanley knew of relatives in Poland and elsewhere who had died in the Holocaust.[60] If Kubrick in later life did exhibit paranoid tendencies, he came by them honestly, in the sense that even paranoiacs—especially Jewish ones—have enemies. And if, as some authors have argued, the subjects of many of Kubrick's still photographs "expose the anguish over an imminent menace,"[61] then they too indeed reflect the world of depression, fascism, and war under whose influences Kubrick had grown up. Many of his photographs also display people surveying either the world inside the frame of the camera or the "world" outside the frame in a way that reproduces Kubrick's own concern about what is both visible and invisible in a contingent world. In either case, though, what is observed is usually invisible to the viewer, an expression of the frame as both protection and illusion.[62] Kubrick's response to the world and the people in it was not hopeless cynicism, however, for his pictures also display "his humor, his talent for observing with compassion, and his humane approach [to] . . . human fragility."[63] As Kubrick himself once said with regard to "feel-good" cinema: "You don't have to make Frank Capra movies to like people."[64]

Kubrick escaped military duty in the Second World War due to age and the Korean War due to marriage.[65] But his early career was to benefit from the cultural space created by the victory of antiracist forces both at home and abroad in 1945. Postwar films like *Crossfire* and *Gentlemen's Agreement* (both 1947) reflected new post-Holocaust tolerance, although *Home of the Brave* (1949) changed the stage play's protagonist from Jewish to African-American, substituting the stereotype of an apparently Jewish psychiatrist. Kubrick was also—ironically—free for a time to ignore the Holocaust in his work, a phenomenon that, while not absolute, was general in America and the West in the immediate postwar era. His parents, as assimilated Jews, were especially reluctant, even long after the war, to discuss the Holocaust.[66] Once again, Kubrick could live and work in security, all the while, however, searching for expression of, and control over, the darker realities beneath the social orthodoxy of calm. His turn from taking to making pictures at the end of the 1940s would in great measure be due to this desire to exert greater control over the content of his observations of the world, a desire in turn due largely to his fear of the dark forces abroad in that world. Source, script, subjects (actors), as well as structure and sequence (time) rather than the single snap of a shutter would be the means for Kubrick to pin the world's evil under the gaze of a camera's lens.

# 4

# A GERMAN PRESENCE

It is just a typewriter, but it is not just *any* typewriter. It is most probably one of Kubrick's own, an Adler, a German machine.[1] It belongs as well to Jack Torrance, the main character in *The Shining*. Jack is a self-described writer who, among other things, represents the writer and director of the film in which he appears. Kubrick himself may be seen in his daughter's own film, *Making The Shining*, typing on a small yellow Adler.[2] Kubrick opens one scene in *The Shining* with a close-up of Jack's Adler, zooming slowly back and up to show Jack at the other end of the room throwing a tennis ball against the wall.[3] The full significance of this shot will be discussed in Chapter 11, but Kubrick's focus in *The Shining* on this particular typewriter is emblematic of the treatment of the subject of Germany in his films. While Jews represent the presence of an absence in Kubrick's work, Germans were both a manifest and a latent presence in both his life and his work, always sensed if not always seen. His life and work intersect in this regard since his films reflect the style and substance of Kubrick's education in German literature and German cinema. And though there are few German characters in his films, odd, scattered references to the Germans appear throughout his *oeuvre*, a metonymic pattern that often associates Germans with machines, often and ominously machines of destruction. Neither, of course, was a difficult association to make in the first half of the twentieth century, when modern German military prowess was steeled by modern German industry and technology.

Michel Ciment is not in error, therefore, in observing in Kubrick a "fascination with things Germanic."[4] Kubrick's life and career were in fact characterized by a marked ambivalence with respect to all things German. The ambivalence had to do with what he read and thought about Germany's history in the twentieth century as well as with a certain psychological tension generated by the confluence of his Jewish background and a close family relationship with the German world. For his third wife was Christiane Harlan, a non-Jewish German he met while filming *Paths of Glory* in Germany in 1957. And even before the third of his three marriages, during his early adult life from 1945 on Kubrick's experiences brought him into regular contact with elements of German history and culture that would have a decisive effect on his life and work.

## Kubrick Seeing Pictures II

After the war and in advance of his move to Greenwich Village in May 1948 with his first wife, Kubrick was, as before and during the war in the Bronx, a regular moviegoer in Manhattan. Only this time he was seeing European and avant-garde films at Cinema 16 on Lexington Avenue, at the Guild and World Cinemas near Times Square, and at the Museum of Modern Art.[5] And while he was grateful for the chance to practice photojournalism as a staff photographer for *Look*, he later observed that his "ultimate ambition had always been to make movies," complaining that the "subject matter of my *Look* assignments was generally pretty dumb."[6] He also certainly chafed under the editorial control over his pictures.[7] In this transition, of course, Kubrick was taking a further artistic step in line with the visual culture of his times and place. But he was also responding to his own need not only for exploration of the world but also for personal, intellectual, artistic, and mechanical control over its brimming dangers. Such control was not available to him as a staff photographer, as it was in his two other postwar passions: chess and film.[8]

It was during the ten years between the end of the Second World War and his relocation to Los Angeles in late 1955 that Kubrick developed his regard for certain directors, styles, and films. He also continued to see masses of films, good, bad, and indifferent. At the Museum of Modern Art on West Fifty-third, he had the chance to see films from the earliest years up to the present, including war films such as *Confessions of a Nazi Spy*, *Casablanca*, and *The Best Years of Our Lives* (1946), which he had most likely first seen back in the Bronx. But most of the films were new to him. MoMA showed the films of Griffith, Chaplin, Lubitsch, Erich von Stroheim, Josef von Sternberg, René Clair, Friedrich Wilhelm Murnau, Carl-Theodor Dreyer, Roberto Rossellini, Akira Kurosawa, and Robert Bresson; in the summer of 1947 MoMA offered "A Survey of the Film in Germany," and a series on France included Jean Renoir's *Grand Illusion* (1937) and photographer Henri Cartier-Bresson's *Le Retour* (1945), on the return of French prisoners from German prison camps.[9]

All accounts of Kubrick's life and work as well as his films themselves reveal that, while his cinematic tastes were eclectic, he was particularly influenced by the "visual experimentation" of German Expressionist filmmaking.[10] One commentator even called Kubrick "the last expressionist."[11] Expressionism began in painting and literature early in the twentieth century as a modernist movement dedicated to expressing psychological or spiritual reality, especially the "projection of emotional states by means of imagery," in place of the naturalistic or realistic recording of external events. Expressionist filmmaking emerged in Germany following the First World War and was characterized by the use of fantasy, folktales, and legends to maximize the subjective view of both the filmmaker and the film's characters. These silent films employed highly stylized and even fantastic sets, lighting, costumes, and acting. The first was Robert Wiene's *The Cabinet of Dr. Caligari* (1919), which originated in a screenplay that condemned the merciless destruction of young lives during the First World War. The sets, with their distorted angles and decorations, reflected the inner turmoil of the human beings within them. Expressionism drew from the conservative aspects of Romanticism that focused on the individual, the internal, and the imaginary rather than seeking inspiration from contemporary radical concern with social and political conflict and justice. Expressionist films also reflected a cultural preoccupation with "Oedipal scenarios . . . incomplete families, jealousies, overpowering father figures, absent mothers . . . often . . . not remedied by an attainable or desired object choice."[12] This specifically German preoccupation arose at least in part from the fact that many modernists in Germany were reacting to the especially acute problems associated with "the political, social, and sexual repression" of the conservative, patriarchal prewar German Empire.[13] Kubrick's films share this preoccupation with the conflict between fathers and sons, while also critiquing the hypermasculinity characteristic of turn-of-the-century Prussian and German society.[14]

The harmony between this tradition in film and the cinema of Stanley Kubrick is readily apparent, particularly with respect to Kubrick's exploitation of the silent cinema's "artistic language of film based purely on the expressive qualities of the image."[15] Even in its bowdlerized form, *The Cabinet of Dr. Caligari,* which was a sensation in the 1920s in New York as well as in Europe, communicated the original antiwar message of its screenplay through visual effect.[16] Kubrick always felt that the expressive quality of images and their effect upon the subconscious imagination had been lost in cinema's transition to sound.[17] But his films are also highly intellectual as well as emotional in their preparation and impact.[18] In this concern for "eyedeas," too, Kubrick was reflecting German Expressionist film. Moreover, the film style that succeeded Expressionism in Weimar Germany, New Objectivity (*Neue Sachlichkeit*), was likewise moved by disillusionment caused by the First World War and retained the strong emotionalism of Expressionism even as it turned toward realism and social commentary. Such a fusion of fantasy and reality is evident in all of Kubrick's work. Alexander Walker has argued that this mix of Expressionism and realism in Kubrick's *oeuvre* came from the influence of postwar American film noir.[19] But in fact this stylistic convergence had already been anticipated in the cinema of the Weimar Republic between the world wars in such films as Murnau's *The Last Laugh* (1924) and the so-called street films of the New Objectivity movement like Georg Pabst's *The Joyless Street* (1925) and *Pandora's Box*

(1928), all of which played at MoMA after the war. Even though Kubrick admired many European and non-European directors, those who inspired him most were German directors such as Lang, Pabst, and Max Ophuls.[20]

During the 1930s and 1940s, moreover, many German artistic and intellectual luminaries would come to America seeking refuge from Nazism. Kubrick had direct contact in 1948 with one of these German émigrés when he photographed Georg Grosz for the June 8 issue of *Look*. Grosz was an illustrator and a member of the "verist" movement, which comprised part of the New Objectivity. Grosz attacked the narrow-mindedness, meanness, corruption, and hypocrisy of the German bourgeoisie, whom, regardless of social class or station, he labeled *Spiesser*— Philistines. Kubrick's portrait of Grosz, in suit and tie and with cigar in hand, sitting astride a chair on a sidewalk along Fifth Avenue, displays acute and ironic insight into Grosz's life and work. Many of Grosz's illustrations of *Spiesser* were set in the streets of German cities and often juxtaposed the poverty of the early 1920s in the form of ragged working-class children or disabled veterans against cruel and smug representatives of the prosperous bourgeoisie and the arrogant officer corps.[21] It is not known whether Kubrick or Grosz or both came up with the idea of posing Grosz in the street, but for Kubrick, his eyes and mind certainly wide open as always, it represented in origin or effect an understanding of Grosz's scathing indictment of modern German society. To picture the elegantly dressed Grosz on the most glamorous street of the most powerful city in the world among a few well-dressed pedestrians embraces the ambiguous, dualistic, contradictory, and even grotesque nature of society as both Kubrick and Grosz saw it. Even the—intentional, intuitive, or inadvertent—inclusion of a "No Parking" sign alongside Grosz points to his position as violator of order, a sense of violation heightened by the fact that there is a car parked alongside the sign and that all the pedestrians, as in Grosz's illustrations, are moving, all but one, a woman, away from the camera.[22] Such characteristics were particularly pointed, tragic, and horrific in the context of the most recent history of Germany as represented in Grosz's work. They also evidence the strong German influence on the formation of Kubrick's view of the world. Grosz himself at the time the picture was taken was deeply depressed by the death of his mother and "the physical destruction of the German landscape of his youth."[23] Indeed, the occasion for the Kubrick shoot would appear to have been the opening of Grosz's first postwar exhibition, at the AAA Galleries on Fifth Avenue, which featured works like those of the 1920s "deal[ing] with the themes of war, hunger, and the search for cultural values."[24]

Kubrick therefore had direct experience with the cultural fallout from Europe's recent catastrophe. And even as a youth he had a head start in his education in German film as a result of the early stages of the German catastrophe because German filmmakers had a huge influence on many Hollywood films made before and during the Second World War. It was the Germans who laid much of the basis for American film noir during the 1930s and 1940s, a dark, moody style that, as we shall see in Chapter 5, would be further invigorated in the United States after 1945 under the shattering impact of the war's events. While some European and German film talent had come to Hollywood in the 1920s, it was the rise to power of Hitler in Germany that caused a wave of German actors and directors to crash upon the shores of Hollywood in the 1930s. Actors like Conrad Veidt and Peter Lorre and directors such as Billy Wilder, Lubitsch, Ophuls, Lang, William Dieterle, and Robert Siodmak fled either for political reasons or because they were Jews. Coincidentally, Siodmak's last film in Germany, for which he was excoriated by Nazi Propaganda Minister Joseph Goebbels, was an adaptation of Stefan Zweig's *The Burning Secret*, the novella that Kubrick would attempt to adapt for the screen.[25]

These men arrived in a Hollywood that was already heavily influenced by Europeans. The wartime film *Casablanca*, for example, was directed and acted by a potpourri of European talent, quite appropriate for its theme of America rousing itself from its isolationism to mobilize its decent instincts on behalf of the world's oppressed. Even the unproduced play on which the film was based, *Everybody Comes to Rick's*, was inspired by the playwright's trip to Austria in 1938, the year that country was annexed by Nazi Germany: Murray Burnett "went to Austria as an American. He came back to America as a Jew."[26] More significant for Kubrick than European appeals for help in the struggle against Nazi Germany, however, was the subject matter and style of filmmaking brought to Hollywood by German émigré directors. Lang, Ophuls, and Stroheim, three of the most influential on Kubrick, were all Jews living in a dangerous world, and all to one extent or another had direct experience with the danger surrounding them. And although they differed from one another and reacted creatively to this threatening world in ways that were different as well as similar, they all shared the position of the endangered outsider at a time when Jews were more endangered than ever before.

Even as a youthful moviegoer, therefore, Stanley Kubrick was exposed to the German cinematic tradition. Wilder's *Five Graves to Cairo* (L, July 1943), for example, offered Kubrick an early experience of the Expressionist style. Wilder was born Samuel Wilder in Sucha, Galicia, in 1906 to a German-Jewish family. He left Germany for Paris in 1933 and arrived in Hollywood in 1934. *Five Graves to Cairo* concerns British espionage against Field Marshal Erwin Rommel's Afrika Korps, which in 1942 had just invaded Egypt. The cinematography and lighting reflect the Expressionist style, with shadows dominating the interior of the claustrophobic and menacing hotel, "much of the illumination shining obliquely through innumerable screens and grids."[27] *Five Graves to Cairo* also, however, includes scenes in which illumination comes from natural lighting within the scene. This creates the same sort of highly contrasting light and shadow characteristic of Expressionist film, but in a "realistic" fashion—that is, as a natural part of the "reality" of the scene itself. This technique reflects the evolution in mid-1920s Germany toward the more realistic filmmaking of the New Objectivity movement, which, while sharing the moody atmosphere of German Expressionism, moved away from the fantastic toward social criticism and also influenced the less political American film noir style of the succeeding decades.

A representative scene from the film has the hotel workers' quarters lighted only by a single metal-shaded light bulb hanging at about eye level from the ceiling, the same disquieting noir diegetic light arrangement Kubrick would use to great effect thirteen years later in *The Killing*.[28] That Kubrick moved away from Expressionistic lighting (though not Expressionistic themes and staging) when he moved into color film only underlines his consistent commitment to critical documentation of the world alongside his fascination with the mysterious and the fantastic. When asked by Ciment why he preferred natural lighting, Kubrick responded simply and directly: "Because it's the way we see things."[29] And that he parodied—accurately and beautifully—Expressionistic lighting in just one scene of *The Shining* confirms not only his reflexive style of filmmaking but also the primacy he placed on seeing the horrors of this world in the natural light of day—the real life of history— rather than in the standard spooky and timeless dark of horror movies.[30] Kubrick would also turn the common Expressionist juxtaposition of good and evil through light and dark, a tendency magnified in war propaganda films, into the daylight ambiguity of good and evil within all people, a theme common in film noir, where the whole world seems to be shadowed by evil without variation, exception, or escape. Typical of this central European take on human behavior is the thug Alex DeLarge in *A Clockwork Orange* who, Kubrick observed, was like Hitler in his combination of villainy and love for good music.[31]

## Stroheim

*Five Graves to Cairo* also introduced Kubrick to the acting of Erich von Stroheim, whose own directorial work Kubrick would admire after the war. Stroheim's performance in the supporting role of evil Field Marshal Rommel rivets the eye more than the British, French, and Egyptian protagonists. The character of the famous "Desert Fox" was the result of collaboration between Wilder and Stroheim and exploits one of the standard wartime German stereotypes, that of the cold, ruthless aristocratic Junker officer. This was a role Stroheim was born to play, and his physical appearance and bearing in Wilder's film resembles that of the Prussian prison camp commander von Rauffenstein he portrayed in Renoir's prewar *Grand Illusion*, which was shown at MoMA in 1949, 1951, 1952, and 1954.[32] Wilder and Stroheim also made the type of veiled reference to Nazi persecution of Jews consistent with Hollywood's careful military and commercial priorities during the war. In one scene Rommel, upset about an officer's dalliance with the French hotel maid, rages revealingly—though not too revealingly—*in German* about vulgar and degenerate behavior: "Is this the German army or a Jews' school?" Rommel also refers on another occasion to the untenable military position of his enemies by noting—in a historically ominous way—that there is no longer any Moses to part the Red Sea for the British army. And when the maid asks for his intervention on behalf of her brother in a Nazi prison camp, Rommel tells her to submit the required documents in triplicate, adding—ambiguously but once again ominously—that "we can use paper in Germany, a great deal of paper." Such a possible reference to the bureaucracy of mass murder may sound in contemporary ears rather than having been fully formed in wartime minds, but in effect at least it is just as much a metonym of murderous clerical function as Kubrick's typewriter in *The Shining*.

Whether Kubrick understood enough—or any—German as a youth to notice what Stroheim was saying about Jews—*Juden*—is uncertain. But given his family background, the community environment, and what media attention there was to the fate of Jews in Germany and Europe, it would not be surprising if he at least knew that particular German word, even though he apparently never learned German.[33] He would also admire the silent films Stroheim directed after the First World War, which showed at MoMA in 1947, 1949, 1950, 1951, and 1952—*Blind Husbands* (1919), *Foolish Wives* (1922), and *Greed* (1924)—also attending a screening of *The Merry Widow* (1925) in London in the 1960s.[34] Stroheim even parodied himself in playing the role of the autocratic director of a First World War movie in *The Lost Squadron* (1932), which MoMA presented in 1954.[35] Whether Kubrick knew it or not, there were also certain distinct similarities between himself and Stroheim. The silent film director was born Erich Oswald Stroheim in Austria, was registered as a member of the Jewish community in Vienna, but converted to Catholicism and added the "von" to his name when he immigrated to America in 1909. By 1914 he was in Hollywood as Erich Hans Carl Maria Stroheim von Nordenwall, scion of a noble Prussian military family, often playing the same role in the movies he was playing in life. During the First World War, he became "The Man You Love to Hate" by playing villainous German army officers. Like Kubrick, he was fascinated by military life but never was a soldier, and after the war he would play the same types of uniformed nobles in his own films, which savagely satirized prewar Habsburg Vienna. All of his films, like Kubrick's, deal probingly and scathingly with passion, corruption, and guilt and have rightly been praised for their unblinking realism; like Kubrick, he was a stickler for set and prop detail and required many takes during shooting.[36] During the Second World War, Stroheim played in several anti-Nazi films besides *Five Graves to Cairo*, reprising his role as the venomous German.[37]

Clearly Stroheim had a love–hate relationship with the Germans and their militarism, perhaps along the same sorts of lines of a defensive and sublimating identification with the aggressor common among human beings that was also evident in Kubrick. That such identification, at its extremes, can be the result of a variety of powerful psychodynamics such as denial, low self-esteem, and even self-hatred is exemplified in the case of Walter Rathenau. Rathenau was a Jewish businessman and government minister assassinated by right-wing terrorists in Berlin in 1922. Similar to Stroheim's preoccupation with the Austrian German elite, Rathenau "emulated the fashions, values, and ideals of the East Elbian Junkers," whose ranks, with very few exceptions, had always been closed to Jews.[38] Even these exceptions, aside from being exceedingly rare, were accompanied by conditions and suspicions, part of a social atmosphere that naturally generated psychological fears and defenses among Jews.

Kubrick's relationship with the Germans was of course not as immediate or nearly as intense and personally problematic as that of Stroheim or, especially, Rathenau. One of Kubrick's German technical collaborators, set designer Ken (Klaus) Adam, did, however, once compare Kubrick with Rommel. During the filming of *Barry Lyndon* in Ireland, Kubrick had organized Volkswagen minibuses to transport the various departments to the many shooting locations: "I had a drawing board in the back of my minibus, plus whatever files I needed. Stanley thought of us like Rommel in the desert."[39] While this comparison might say more about Rommel's fame as a commander of mobile forces or about Adam, a Berlin Jew who fled Hitler to become "the only native-born German fighter pilot to serve in the Royal Air Force"[40] in the Second World War, it is a striking comparison given Kubrick's interest in military history and the Second World War as well as his mania for directorial control. (It is also possible that Kubrick himself made the allusion.) The comparison, however, speaks to the difference between Kubrick and Stroheim. While Stroheim for personal as well as patriotic reasons played Rommel as a cold and arrogant Nazi, after the war Rommel was generally regarded with respect in the West for his "correct" observation of the rules of war and for his (however belated and conditional) opposition to Hitler.[41] In this light, the comparison between Rommel and Kubrick parallels observations of Kubrick the kind patriarch, a mixture of strictness and sensitivity reflective of a character not excessively driven or burdened by aggressive drives or compensatory identifications.

It is therefore unfair to label Kubrick a "self-hating Jew." Whatever his level of psychological conflict, the reaction to his historical environment from the 1930s on was by and large appropriate for a sensitive and creative Jew confronted by radical threats at that particular juncture of the twentieth century. *Spartacus* screenwriter Dalton Trumbo found Kubrick a mass of contradictions: Was he a Jew who hated Jews as responsible for their own afflictions or a Jew who married a German to punish the Germans?[42] Frederic Raphael has reported a variation on Kubrick's remark about the persecution of Jews alleged by the Christian Scientist Trumbo: "S. K. said to me, not long after Hitler's recent birthday, that A. H. had been 'right about almost everything.'"[43] Presumably based on this alleged remark, Raphael has been condemned for calling Kubrick a "self-hating Jew."[44] Raphael has responded that he said no such thing, and, although he expresses some animus—justified or not—against Kubrick, he contextualizes Kubrick's remark by noting his own experience with Jews mocking themselves as Jews.[45] While what Raphael says about Jews applies to human beings in general, what is likely the case is not that Kubrick was consumed by pathological self-hatred, but that he extended his realistic, mordant assessment of the human condition onto Jews as well. This view of the world reflected and supported an imperfect mastery of his psychological conflicts through defensive identification with the German aggressor and sublimation of aggression through his fascination with the history of Nazi Germany. That this fascination never resulted in a film about the Nazis or the Holocaust is another sign of the contested psychological ground on which Kubrick confronted the subjects of Germans and Jews. It would seem, therefore, that Kubrick would have said such things as he allegedly did about Jews and Nazis in sorrow over the human condition in general rather than in anger at himself as a Jew in particular. And of course the words "almost everything" clearly exclude Hitler's campaign of extermination against the Jews.

## Lang

Fritz Lang was born in 1890 in Vienna, served with the Austrian army in the First World War, and in collaboration with his wife, novelist and screenwriter Thea von Harbou, became in the 1920s a giant of the German cinema. Part-Jewish, Lang left Germany in 1933. He was otherwise quite Germanic in his bearing, even sporting from a young age in Vienna the "Prussian affectation" of a monocle.[46] He was also in the ironic position of having two of his films, *Die Nibelungen* (1924) and *Metropolis* (1927), admired by Hitler for their celebration of Germanic heritage and sheer visual power, respectively. And even though his *The Testament of Dr. Mabuse* (1932) could be seen as an anti-Nazi allegory and was banned in Nazi Germany, an admiring Goebbels showed it privately to a privileged few.[47] In *Destiny* (1921) and *Die Nibelungen,* Lang drew on German legend in contemplating the inexorability of fate and the destruction of civilizations through brutality and revenge. Such cinema resonated with Kubrick, who had been raised on Grimm's fairy tales and Greek and Roman mythology.[48] Lang's monumental settings, like Kubrick's, are shadowed cinematic spaces in which destructive, often criminal, forces seem to live and breathe, as in *Dr. Mabuse, the Gambler* (1922), *M* (1931), *The Testament of Dr. Mabuse,* and *The 1000 Eyes of Dr. Mabuse* (1960), in which a criminal mastermind uses hypnosis, psychological terror, and grotesque levels of violence in a failed bid to gain total control over society.

According to Walker, Kubrick particularly liked *M* and the *Mabuse* films, holding the almost over-the-top "expressionist thriller" *The Testament of Dr. Mabuse* in "amused esteem."[49] *The 1000 Eyes of Dr. Mabuse* was surely one source of inspiration for Kubrick's orchestration of the hotel setting in *The Shining.* Lang also made films in America that influenced Kubrick from the time he likely saw them as a youth during the Second World War. The first, *Hangmen Also Die,* dramatizes the assassination of Reinhard Heydrich, architect of the Final Solution, in Prague in 1942. The screenplay is by Bertolt Brecht and emphasizes the rigors of life in Czechoslovakia under a brutal occupation regime. Lang, more cautious than the Communist Brecht, also filmed but then left out a scene at a mass grave, "which would have constituted the first on-screen depiction of Jewish victims of the Nazi terror."[50] Once again, the young Kubrick would have been seeing the Holocaust "through a glass darkly," its real horrors in a way even more terrifying for remaining mysteriously undefined. The release of the film coincided with the American premiere of *The Testament of Dr. Mabuse,* which allowed Lang to claim in an interview in the *New York Sun* that what was explicit in *Hangmen Also Die* was implicit in his 1932 allegory of Hitler's terrorism.[51]

The second Lang film that played in Bronx theaters during the Second World War was *Ministry of Fear* (L. August 1945), "replete with ticking clocks and roaring trains, séances and spy rings, mysterious Nazis with Viennese backgrounds, and a lead character who has just been released from an insane asylum."[52] The film is appropriately dark and surreal. The sets are typical Lang, imprisoning the actors among winding staircases, mirrors, and the dark urban landscape of blacked-out London under the nightly Nazi air raids of 1940/1941 the English called the Blitz. Lang was not happy with a coda insisted on by the studio, a happy ending with the male and female leads driving along a coastline, a world away from the dark setting and mood of the rest of the film. This was just the type of movie sentimentality, as we have seen, at which Kubrick regularly scoffed as a youth. But there is one other detail from *Ministry of Fear* that seems to have struck a more positive—or at least useful—and ringing chord in Kubrick. A gateway into the insane asylum that is pictured in one of the very first shots of the film looks almost exactly like the entrance to the hedge maze in *The Shining*. The connection—on whatever level(s) of Kubrick's consciousness—seems more than likely since the maze in *The Shining* symbolizes the disordered mind of a protagonist in which his wife and son are literally and figuratively pictured as being trapped.[53] A similar quotation occurs in *Lolita* when hapless Humbert paints Lolita's toenails just like the endlessly humiliated Chris does Kitty's in Lang's *Scarlet Street* (1945).[54]

But no film by Fritz Lang arguably had a greater effect on Kubrick than *Metropolis* (MoMA, 1947, 1952), the last Expressionist film and one that Kubrick greatly admired.[55] It tells the tale of a future civilization in which workers live and labor deep underground in factories run by an elite of industrial managers in the glamorous city above. Lang's film has been widely praised for both its bold settings and cinematography and the sheer audacity of its production. It has also been criticized as nothing but a plea for benevolent despotism and for displaying a social ethic that resembles nothing so much as the Nazi ideal of a hyperindustrial "people's community." Many at the time in Germany saw the script, written by von Harbou (who in 1932 joined the Nazi party), as a betrayal of the New Objectivity through its "strange eclecticism of medieval and futuristic."[56] Critics since have analyzed such things as the film's obvious Oedipal dynamics and its objectification of the female body in service to male desire and mechanical control.[57] *Metropolis* also reflects divergent views of technology: the Expressionists' fear of it as "irrational, chaotic . . . destructive . . . dynamic, shocking, almost libidinal"; the New Objectivists' "rationalist, functionalist" faith in technology; and the Nazis' muddled fusion of the modern mechanical and the medieval mythical in service to the timeless tyrannical.[58] This ambivalence about technology forms an important part of Kubrick's worldview—fascinated by machines and their potential use in the improvement of life but also deeply fearful of them as representing an enhanced means of human aggression and disaster. In *Metropolis* the plan of scientist Rotwang to turn human beings into machines and the machinations of manager Fredersen almost lead to the destruction of the city. In the end, hope in a cooperative technological future prevails, although Lang remained ambivalent about this happy ending upon which his scenarist wife had insisted.[59]

The film Kubrick made that drew the most inspiration from *Metropolis* had no such happy ending. Indeed, as we shall see in Chapter 6, *Dr. Strangelove* has not just one, but two, absolutely catastrophic endings. Although Kubrick made the film a comedy, it is the blackest of black comedies about the blackest of topics, the destruction of—almost—all human life in the world, all rendered in the spirit of laughter "because it hurts too much to cry." The change from drama to comedy was Kubrick's idea, and it surely functioned in some part as a psychological defense against the real horror of the scenarios he envisioned.[60] And to some degree it constituted sublimation of anger and aggression. But this type of humor is also a weapon of the oppressed as well as being characteristic of a Jewish literary custom of mixing comedy with tragedy. All this gives lie to the charge that Kubrick's sense of humor was either missing in action or simply and grimly "Teutonic."[61] Indeed, the satirical nature of all of Kubrick's films, especially the Swiftian *Dr. Strangelove*, not only expressed the director's own psychological defenses and sublimations, but also represented a genial creative response to the historical environment. One can even speculate that Kubrick's appreciation for William Wellman's wartime satirical comic melodrama *Roxie Hart* was, at least in his considered retrospect, closely bound up with the overall pattern that was starting to form in him during the Second World War of recognizing that Hollywood productions hid the real horrors of the contemporary world. On the surface, the broad and even slapstick comedy of the film was perfect for a perceptive adolescent at fourteen years of age. But in retrospective construction, the fact that Roxie's story, which ends in 1928, is told in flashback in 1942 ("fourteen years ago," the storyteller declares), might have created in Kubrick an impression that the world in which *Roxie Hart* was produced was dancing on a volcano. This impression would have been reinforced by the fact that the years used in the film were significant ones for Kubrick, 1928 being the year of his birth and 1942 not only the year *Roxie Hart* played the Bronx but also the first and most lethal year of the Holocaust. It would have been further reinforced in Kubrick's memory, even if not in his adolescent consciousness, by subject matter, however lightheartedly treated, that would show up regularly in Kubrick's own films: (1) violence within families; (2) women as wronged by men but also complicit in social injustice; (3) the simultaneously casual and exuberant corruption of American urban life exploited for entertainment value; and (4) the social primacy given to appearance over substance. The last two aspects are satirically self-reflexive and reflect an overall satirical consciousness revisited in the dark cinematography of *Chicago* (2003) but otherwise missing for the sake, ironically, of entertainment in this contemporary remake of *Roxie Hart* as a musical.

The physical design of *Dr. Strangelove* also owes a heavy debt to German Expressionist film in general and to *Metropolis* in particular. As Kubrick's last black-and-white film, *Dr. Strangelove* employs the deep, malevolent *chiaroscuro* of German

Expressionism. Berlin native Ken Adam's famous design of the War Room recalls the dark cavernous sets of Lang's film, other early German science-fiction films, and even architect Albert Speer's massive erections for Hitler.[62] The War Room's semi-triangular shape, however, also reflects Kubrick's insistence on functionality and historical accuracy, in this case the structural strength necessary to withstand a nuclear strike.[63] Dr. Strangelove himself, with his "black-gloved artificial arm,"[64] while also a composite of contemporaneous American and German strategic thinkers, resembles Lang's scientist Rotwang (Dr. Strange*glove*?) as well as the mad, disabled criminal geniuses of both Lang and Murnau.[65] As we shall see in Chapter 6, Dr. Strangelove was the creation of Kubrick and actor Peter Sellers, but it was Kubrick, no doubt inspired by Lang's Rotwang, who suggested that Sellers wear one of the black gloves that Kubrick used for handling lights.[66]

The German Dr. Strangelove is also one in a Kubrick series of characters who are part human and part machine, in Strangelove's case not only the mechanical arm but also his imprisonment, like Lord Lyndon in *Barry Lyndon* and Frank Alexander in *A Clockwork Orange*, in a wheelchair. This combination is also manifest in the "character" of HAL the computer in *2001*, in the theme and very title of *A Clockwork Orange*, and in the robot boy of Kubrick's co-production of Steven Spielberg's *A.I.* (2001). This blurring of organic and mechanical reflects the Expressionist fear of technology so evident in *Metropolis:* not only Rotwang, but the evil robot Maria and the entire machine that is Lang's city of the future.[67] Its German dimensions in particular may also have been suggested to Kubrick by the German played by Stroheim in *Grand Illusion*, an officer whose body is held erect not only by traditional Prussian militaristic rigor but also, because of injuries suffered in an airplane crash, by braces of steel. Kubrick's vision of modern Germany intuited the historical reality of a volatile fusion of a militaristic and hypermasculine cultural ethos and a modern industrial society and state. This historical development was reflected in Kubrick's visual construction of the "clockwork" Prussian army in *Barry Lyndon*.[68] Finally—and reflexively—the whole enterprise of filmmaking in its union, particularly strong in the case of photographer and *auteur* Kubrick, of camera eye and human eye is also an expression of this motif.[69] And it too is represented in *Metropolis* (and *The 1000 Eyes of Dr. Mabuse* and Chaplin's *Modern Times* [1936]) by the malevolent and voyeuristic power of mechanical observation. Appropriately enough, perhaps a photograph of Kubrick on the set of *The Shining* is an apt summary of these historical, personal, and artistic dynamics: "Kubrick on the set of a film . . . peering out of a Black Forest of camera equipment, pensive, detached, and . . . black-gloved."[70]

Kubrick retained an Enlightenment respect for technology as a powerful product of reason, but he also reflected the modernist movement's ambivalence toward reason, science, and technology. While, out of pragmatism as well as fascination, he owned all sorts of high-tech devices from the dominant German and Japanese manufacturers, there would be in his films some association between Germans and machines that also reflected his personal tastes in technology. It was the Germans, after all, who led much of Western technological progress in the early twentieth century, a major historical factor conditioning the creative Kubrick association of Germans and machines. At this same time, however, Germany more than any other nation was projecting its military power in the most aggressive ways. Indeed, with the exception of Napoleon (another Kubrick object of fascination), the modern era in the West had been dominated by what can be called "the German wars" of 1740, 1756, 1864, 1866, 1870, 1914, and 1939. So, "[i]nfluenced by the West German Army's adopting the same make of truck,"[71] Kubrick owned Porsches and Mercedeses, a German computerized chess game, a German Definitiv filing system—and more than one Adler typewriter—admiring—while also fearing—the type of technical thoroughness that Germans had brought to the Final Solution as well.[72]

Kubrick was especially enthusiastic during the filming of *Paths of Glory* in Germany about Germans' technical abilities: "[They] were superb technicians, totally work-oriented," he is reported as saying.[73] On *Paths of Glory* his special effects man was Erwin Lange, who had worked on many German war films since the 1930s. The director of photography was Georg Krause, who in 1957 had won American and German awards for his work on Siodmak's *Nights, When the Devil Came* (1957) and had photographed Elia Kazan's *Man on a Tightrope* (1953). Krause had also worked on war films for the Nazis, but also on at least one film, *The Bewitched Day* (1944), banned by the Nazis for its "defeatism."[74] Set designer Ken Adam, who worked on *Barry Lyndon* as well as on *Dr. Strangelove*, coupled superb artistic sense with high German technical competence. Harry Lange, a former engineer in Wernher von Braun's Nazi rocket program, worked on *2001*, detailing spacecraft models from "molded plastic parts from Airfix kits of World War II German planes."[75] Lange's background in particular embodied Kubrick's deeper fear of—and some compensatory psychological identification with—such dangerous technology. It is the figure of Dr. Strangelove, of course, who literally incorporates technology's destructiveness. Certainly in this regard Kubrick must have been struck by the first ten minutes of *The Testament of Dr. Mabuse*, during which nothing is on the soundtrack save for the heavy drumming and rasping of machinery in the cellar of one of the hideouts of the Mabuse gang. This Kubrickian blurring of the boundaries between good and bad uses of technology reflected not only conditions in the real world (e.g., his admiration for the technical features of Second World War German gun emplacements along the French coast[76]) but also his own psychological and cultural struggles with good and evil. For Kubrick, the development of machines in the modern era represented a more pessimistic—and historically Jewish-informed—variation on Murphy's Law: not "If something can go wrong, it will" but rather "If something can go wrong, it already has." His films are filled with highly technical plans dependent on technology that go terribly wrong, although ironically, tragically, and for the mordant aspect of Kubrick's outlook logically, it was the Nazis' mechanical "solution" to the Jewish "problem" that for far too long went far too right.

## Ophuls

Max Ophuls was born Max Oppenheimer in Saarbrücken, Germany, in 1902 to a prosperous Jewish family. After beginning a career in theater and then in film, he fled Hitler in 1933. For the next seven years, he made films in France (where German Expressionism was much in vogue), the Netherlands, and Italy, but in 1940, with the Nazi invasion of France, he was once again forced to flee for his life, finally settling in Hollywood. He was unable to find work until 1947, however, directing only four films before his return to France in 1949. He went back to Germany in 1954, making his last film, *Lola Montes* (1955), at the Geiselgasteig Studios in Munich, where Kubrick found some of the dilapidated sets while filming *Paths of Glory*.[77] The dolly shots for which Kubrick would become famous owed a great deal—perhaps everything—to Ophuls, whom Kubrick placed at the top of his list of favorite directors in a 1957 interview.[78] *Paths of Glory* itself exemplifies this influence as Kubrick's camera follows the officers through their labyrinthine headquarters, its fluid, serpentine motion literally reproducing their devious, self-serving plans. And it leads the audience through the curving, claustrophobic trenches that entrap the soldiers who will pay with their lives for their officers' corruption and ruthless ambition.[79] For Kubrick, the moving camera enhanced control over the dangerous terrain of his films as well as hinting at the possibility of escape from the darker, static enclosures of German Expressionist cinema. But such movement also traced the labyrinthine nature of human personality and society at the center of Expressionist film. It resembled as well the predatory swoop of the birds of prey that expressed Kubrick's own identification with the aggressor. Significantly, this predatory association manifested itself most explicitly in the camerawork of the opening sequences of Kubrick's horror film *The Shining*.

Kubrick inherited more from Ophuls than camera technique, however. He inherited a certain sensibility also represented by Stroheim and Lang. While "Ophuls' films are almost all love stories, . . . in almost all of them love is thwarted, or impermanent, or brings disaster to one or both of the lovers."[80] Ophuls's seductive camerawork, lush settings, and sympathy for the characters, especially women in spite of their shortcomings, give his films, unlike Kubrick's, an overall mood of sweet comedic sadness. But, like Kubrick, he finds cold, powerful, and narcissistic men as the predators in human society, with women, out of their need for love and passion, as their usually complicit victims. Kubrick would also adopt the same metaphorical meaning of dance as Ophuls—that is, the flow and interweaving of desire and chance at play in a seductive but dangerous world. Viennese physician and author Arthur Schnitzler captured this coupling in his play *Der Reigen* (1903), in which a series of linked sexual encounters (i.e., "the round dance") among representatives of Vienna's social classes comments on the elusiveness of love. Ophuls begins *La Ronde* (1950), his adaptation of *Der Reigen*, with the "master of play" saying: "I am inclined to the past. It is more comforting than the present and more certain than what may come." These words reflect Ophuls's anxiety about the future, but their declaration of security in the past is meant ironically. Ophuls believed that the German and European tragedies of the first half of the twentieth century had their origins in the modern era's loss of respect for humane values of the Enlightenment and the classical era. When Ophuls visited Vienna after the war, he breathed in Schnitzler's early understanding of the dangerous human passions that would plunge the world into war and genocide. Surveying in 1950 the physical and moral ruins of one of the great cities of Europe, the city of Mozart, Beethoven, Brahms, Mahler, Freud—and Hitler—Ophuls notes how the pleasure in life of a Strauss waltz reflects "the beauty of melancholy" typical of Austrian literature and of Schnitzler in particular.[81]

Kubrick's sharing of Ophuls's unromantic view of human relationships arose from a perspective on the darkness in the human soul explored, expressed, and exercised to such shattering degrees in modern central Europe. Kubrick, too, would film a Schnitzler work. There is a sensibility in the two men's films that expresses the desire to expose and—perhaps—mitigate through art the dark underside of human society. *Le Plaisir* (1952), from three stories by Guy de Maupassant and Kubrick's very favorite, begins with a blank screen over which the narrator (Peter Ustinov) says, ambiguously, "I have always loved the night." In this, surely, Ophuls was referring to the realms of modern psychology. Virginia Woolf in 1925 predicted that the primary focus of interest for humanity in the modern era would continue to lie "very likely in the dark places of psychology."[82] All three of the stories in *Le Plaisir*, "The Mask," "The Model," and "The House of Madame Tellier," concern how in the "shadows of pleasure" desire is constant but happiness is rare. *The Earrings of Madame De . . .* (1953), another Kubrick favorite, opens with a waltz under the titles and tells a story that led *Village Voice* film critic Andrew Sarris to write perceptively upon its re-release, along with *Le Plaisir*, in 1963: "Below the glittering surfaces, the lush décor, the sensuous fabrics, there is the cruel sensibility of an artist mourning the death of this world and all other worlds to come. Inside the beautiful ladies and lovers of romance lurk the grinning skeletons of tragedy."[83] Once again, the theme is the impermanence and duplicity of human sexual relationships. As one character puts it: "The only victory in love is escape." And once again, this theme is shadowed for Ophuls by the maelstrom of the first forty-five years of the twentieth century. As in *La Ronde*, in *The Earrings of Madame De . . .* the lives of several people are linked, this time by the coincidences involving the sale and purchase of a set of earrings. Kubrick loved coincidences, in part because he believed they represented what psychologist Carl Jung defined as synchronicity, the acausality of the simultaneous occurrence of events that suggested "some other kind of order in the universe . . . parallel to the physical world."[84] Deeper down, however, Kubrick retained a darker Freudian view of the immanence of human motivation. For Freud, coincidences constitute the repression of past events in a person's life, not the portal to another world.[85] *The Earrings of Madame De . . .* shares the latter view since the sale and resale of the earrings are links in a historical chain of causality having to do with the fears and desires of the characters through whose hands they pass. As the husband says to the jeweler: "Coincidence is an extraordinary thing, because it's natural."

## Kubrick Taking Notes

Following the Second World War and his graduation from high school in June 1946, Kubrick's education in the world continued by means of night classes at City College of New York, his father's alma mater. His mediocre high-school grades did not allow him to gain acceptance into colleges now flooded with soldiers seeking an education under the GI Bill of Rights. But during the 1940s Kubrick was enthusiastically reading classic literature by Pole Joseph Conrad, Russian Fyodor Dostoyevsky, and, his favorite, the German-Jewish Franz Kafka.[86] In the early 1950s, after quitting his job at *Look,* he began auditing literature classes at Columbia University taught by Lionel Trilling, Mark Van Doren, and Moses Hadas.[87] Kubrick would be a lifelong reader and interpreter of literature in film, mostly since books fired his brooding passion for observing and illuminating the world. Van Doren, who was the film critic for the *Nation,* noted Kubrick's intense interest in extraordinary and immanent forces abroad in the world in a 1952 endorsement of Kubrick's first feature film, *Fear and Desire,* which at the preview attended by Van Doren and by James Agee was entitled "Shape of Fear" and, originally, "The Trap."[88]

While we do not know exactly which courses Kubrick attended at Columbia, we do know what the professors he named usually taught. Before the war Van Doren, a noted author, had specialized in Shakespeare, but in 1947 turned to teaching "absolute masterpieces of storytelling" such as Homer's *Iliad* and *Odyssey,* parts of the Old and New Testaments, Dante's *The Divine Comedy* (1300, 1308, 1311), Kafka's *The Castle,* and Cervantes's *Don Quixote* (1605, 1615).[89] Hadas was a classicist by training, specializing in Greek and Roman literature, but he was also a scholar of Hebrew and Latin. In *Humanism: The Greek Ideal and Its Survival* (1960), he favorably compared Greek warriors and their broad interest in the humane details of daily life with the narrow focus of Germanic knights on "pride of race and warlike prowess."[90] Hadas also translated the autobiography of Solomon Maimon, born in Poland in 1754 and a representative of the German-Jewish Enlightenment whom Hadas admired for his refusal to adhere to any community besides that of enlightened humanity.[91]

Lionel Trilling was one of America's leading literary critics and taught modern literature at Columbia from the early 1930s onward. Trilling was born the son of a German-Jewish tailor in Bialystok, Poland, who migrated to New York before the First World War. Trilling grew up in a Conservative Jewish kosher home, but he preferred the world of literature to the world of religion. His view of life was that it was "dangerous, a complicated, a bewildering thing, full of paradox: a terrible, a strong thing."[92] In 1939 he became the first Jewish member of the English faculty at Columbia. Trilling was a liberal, but he was at the same time highly critical of liberalism's reliance upon rationalism. Following flirtation and disillusionment with Marxism, Trilling became influenced by Matthew Arnold and Freud, each of whom in his own way he saw as balancing intellect and emotion in a secular Enlightenment understanding of the human condition. This position was in partial harmony with the one Kubrick would develop, in particular that of "Freud's tragic view of the human condition."[93] The greatest effect Trilling had on Kubrick, however, was his teaching the modern literature upon which Kubrick would base much of his cinema. It was certainly Trilling who, along with Van Doren, introduced Kubrick to a deeper understanding of the work of Kafka and Thomas Mann, authors who had a deep effect on Kubrick that would manifest itself most trenchantly and specifically in *The Shining* thirty years later.

Trilling believed in encouraging among his students a sense of historical context in which to place works of literature. The first term of Trilling's course began with selections from James Frazer's *The Golden Bough* (1890), a book Kubrick would still be recommending years later, since Trilling believed that modern doubt about Christianity had reopened people's minds to ancient myths of "gods dying and being reborn."[94] This surely connected with and reinforced Kubrick's childhood reading of Greek and Roman myths, but also contrasted with Kubrick's take on recent history, for Frazer—particularly as taught by Trilling—was dedicated to the triumph of reason over irrationality, including the Nazi variety. After Frazer came Nietzsche's *The Birth of Tragedy* (1872, 1886), in which the German philosopher argues that art and human experience are composed not only of rational serenity but also of irrational frenzy. Then Joseph Conrad's *Heart of Darkness* with its "strange and terrible message of ambivalence toward the life of civilization."[95] This theme of the coupling of the angelic and demonic in human society continued through Mann's *Death in Venice* (1912), Nietzsche's *The Genealogy of Morals* (1887), and Freud's *Civilization and Its Discontents* (1930). The second term of the course included Dostoyevsky's *Notes from Underground* (1864), Tolstoy's *The Death of Ivan Ilych* (1884), *The Castle*, and Mann's *The Magic Mountain*.

The German presence in Trilling's course was especially important for someone like Kubrick whose contemporaneous wrestling with the German horrors of the Second World War would manifest itself in odd and striking ways in his films. Interestingly, Kubrick's ambivalence toward Germany was similar to that of Joseph Conrad, whose most famous work, *Heart of Darkness,* Kubrick read in Trilling's class. In this short book, which explores the murderous Belgian colonial exploitation of the African Congo in the late nineteenth century, Conrad reveals his own ambivalence toward Germany and in so doing anticipates in astonishing fashion the German horrors to come in the new century. Although he was Catholic and not Jewish, Conrad, like Kubrick, had a Polish background. Conrad was attracted by German culture, but he was especially fearful of an expansionist Germany dominated by Prussian militarism. In 1913, when on the eve of the First World War he returned to Poland for the first time in many years, he found "no beacons to look for in Germany," only a central European heart of darkness.[96]

Conrad's fears of the Germans show up in *Heart of Darkness,* a curious fact because it is the atrocities carried out by Belgians and other nationalities *not* including Germans that are the subject of the novella. Kurtz, the central horrific presence in the story, is a composite of several people, including Frenchman Georges Antoine Klein, a composite designed to give the narrative a more cosmopolitan relevance.[97] Kurtz, head of a trading station in the Congo who has been systematically slaughtering Africans, adds a postscript to his report for the International Society for the Suppression of Savage Customs that reads, "Exterminate all the brutes!" and whose dying words are "The horror! The horror!" No doubt the model of the Frenchman Klein ("small" in German) played a part in Conrad naming his character Kurtz ("that means short in German—don't it?"), but it would be naïve to ignore the role played in this by Conrad's ambivalent feelings as a Pole about the Germans. This sensitivity, coupled with his recognition of the growing importance of political mobilization of the masses in Europe, gave Conrad an uncanny premonition, as it were, of worse German horrors to come: not only the extermination of the Herero people in German Southwest Africa in 1904, but also that of 6 million Jews (and 3 million Poles) between 1939 and 1945, observations, extrapolations, and/or premonitions embodied in the *Führer*-like figure of Kurtz himself that could not escape a reader like Kubrick after 1945: "A voice! A voice! . . . how that man could talk. He electrified large meetings. He had faith—don't you see?—he had the faith. He could get himself to believe anything—anything. He would have been a splendid leader of an extreme party." Conrad saw these shades in the context of his own racism and Euro-centrism, ascribing the darkness to Africa in terms of Caucasian reversion to primeval jungle barbarism. For Kubrick, however, it was the European Nazi horror of his own times that lent Conrad's words, with their own echo of the fear of Germans, their most terrible power: "a shadow insatiable of splendid appearances, of frightful realities; a shadow darker than the shadow of night, and draped nobly in the folds of a gorgeous eloquence . . . the wild crowd of obedient worshipers, the gloom of the forests, the glitter of the reach between the murky bends, the beat of the drum, regular and muffled like the beating of a heart—the heart of conquering darkness."[98]

## Kubrick Making Pictures

By the time Kubrick was taking notes at Columbia, he had embarked on the path to becoming a filmmaker. He got his start with a sixteen-minute documentary, *Day of the Fight*, which was inspired by a series of photographs Kubrick took for *Look* about a day in the life of prizefighter Walter Cartier that appeared over seven pages in the January 18, 1949, issue. Kubrick's first film was marked by his own unique style. He rented a 35mm Eyemo camera, the kind used by combat photographers in the Second World War. Although the film is narrated by CBS newsman Douglas Edwards, as filmed by this handheld camera it anticipated the gritty, unmediated and unadorned *cinema vérité* films from France and the United States of the 1950s and 1960s. *Day of the Fight* was distributed by RKO-Pathé, and in it Kubrick's pairs the Cartier brothers, identical twins and the first of many doubles in his films. When the film premiered on April 26, 1951, at the Paramount Theatre in Manhattan, Kubrick quit his post at *Look* in order to become a filmmaker.[99] Kubrick would make two more documentaries, both assignments rather than his own projects: *Flying Padre* (1951), about New Mexico parish priest Fred Stadtmueller, and *The*

*Seafarers* (1953), made for the Seafarers' International Union. He also did second unit work on *Mr. Lincoln* (1952), directed by Norman Lloyd and written by James Agee for the *Omnibus* television series.[100]

The progression from photojournalism to documentary filmmaking was a logical one, but documentaries still offered less artistic control than Kubrick would ultimately require. The first constraint was the nonfictional material itself and the second the fact that short documentaries had to be made in relatively strict accordance with the requirements of the companies willing to distribute them. All of this was even more the case when an organization or a film company hired someone to produce a film on a given subject. In these respects, making documentaries was similar to the photojournalism Kubrick had been doing. Kubrick would achieve the degree of artistic control he wanted only when he could choose and rework fictional sources and when, later in his career, he won the rare right of making films how and when he chose without interference or alteration by a studio. For Kubrick, this was vital not only for artistic reasons. This desire for control stemmed from his personal and artistic response to history and its most recent and appalling manifestations. This desire, as we have seen, was accompanied by fear that was manifested in the peculiarly constructed presence of Germans and absence of Jews in his films. As a result of Kubrick's desire to make films filled with ideas as well as the powerful historical influences on him, many details concerning German history in particular are evident in his work. Jan Harlan has argued, however, that the details in Kubrick's films—for example, the prison in *A Clockwork Orange*—are the result of meticulous research.[101] This is certainly true, but careful research was not an end for Kubrick but the means by which ideas and associations could be created.

Ironically, similar to the situation in postwar Germany, the immediate postwar years in America did not offer, even among Jews, a political environment conducive to reflecting on what would only later become known as the Holocaust. One reason for this was the marked decline in blatant American anti-Semitism as a result of the Holocaust. There was also significant anti-German feeling within the American Jewish community, leading to a tacit Jewish boycott of Volkswagen automobiles, Grundig radios, and travel to Germany.[102] As at least a titular member of the American Jewish community, Kubrick shared in the public quiescence on the subject of the Holocaust. But he also shared in his own way the uneasiness about the Germans stemming from the Second World War that would make its presence felt in the very first feature film he made and in most of the others to follow over the next almost half century.

## The House of Harlan

When Kubrick went to Munich in 1957 to film *Paths of Glory*, there was a sense in which he never returned from Germany. For in the process of hiring local talent, he met, courted, and eventually married an actress with the stage name of Susanne Christian. Susanne was in fact not a Christian, but she was a Gentile. She was also a Harlan, from a family of fairly famous—and in one case extremely infamous—members of the German artistic community during the first half of the twentieth century. Kubrick's relationship with Christiane, which would last for the rest of his life, was to entangle him suddenly and deeply with the "Aryan" side of Germanic Europe's recent history and its attendant horrors. Kubrick of course did not go to Germany with the aim of establishing intimate ties with a German family, but the effects of his attraction to Christiane Harlan were nevertheless to aggravate and stimulate, respectively, the psychological and artistic confrontation between his Jewish identity and Germany's immediate past.

Susanne Christiane Harlan was born on May 10, 1932, in Braunschweig. She was the daughter of Fritz Moritz and Ingeborg (de Freitas) Harlan, both of whom were opera singers. Christiane grew up in Karlsruhe, where she learned to dance and paint. As a girl she was a member of the Bund deutscher Mädel, the Nazi organization for girls that paralleled the Hitler Youth for boys. She liked parading about in her uniform, but has asserted—dubiously in terms of its generality—that "all this Heil Hitler thing was really tongue-in-cheek, even with the most emotionally committed Nazis."[103] She also once saw Hitler and recalls what she labels as the insanity of his voice. In late 1942 she and her younger brother Jan, along with their nanny and the nanny's family, were sent from the large city of Karlsruhe to the small village of Reihen near Heidelberg. Christiane and Jan lived on the grounds of a brick factory, went to school by train, and worked as members of the Hitler Youth in the fields alongside French prisoners of war and Ukrainian slave laborers. Christiane occupied much of her time with crafts, puppetry, and drawing. Her drawings were lent for a Russian exhibition after the war but were never returned. One of her postwar paintings, *The Brick Factory*, however, portrays aspects of life in Reihen during the war: the harvesting of grain, the firing and stacking of bricks, children's games, the crash of an American bomber, the entrance to the air-raid bunker. She later spoke of her drawings of her wartime surroundings as "a child's view of war. I was the little girl who moved in where Anne Frank was pushed out."[104] Christiane of course was right to contrast—not compare—and, as we shall see, juxtapose her war experience with that of the young Jew Anne Frank, who fled Nazi Germany with her family to Amsterdam in the Netherlands, only to be rousted out of hiding in 1944 and sent to Auschwitz.

The Harlan family would make major contributions to the production of Kubrick's films. Most important were the immediate members of his family, who created an immediate environment of love, security, artistic inspiration, and intellectual stimulation that generated a unique style of careful and richly informed filmmaking.[105] Christiane herself provided paintings for *A Clockwork Orange* and *Eyes Wide Shut* while paintings by the daughter from her first marriage, Katharina, appear in the latter film as well. Several other members of the Harlan family also became important parts of Kubrick's creative empire. Christiane's brother Jan, who did pre-production work on the ill-fated "Napoleon," served as an assistant on *A Clockwork Orange* and was executive producer for Kubrick's last four films. Jan's wife, Maria, arranged for the German version of *The Shining*, and their sons, Manuel and Dominic, have also worked for Kubrick. Manuel was video assist operator on *Full Metal Jacket* and location photographer on *Eyes Wide Shut* while Dominic played piano for Kubrick's last film.[106]

By marrying into the Harlan family, Kubrick was also once again brought into the realm of German filmmaking. Only this time it involved the controversy over Christiane's uncle Veit, an elder brother of Fritz Harlan, who had been the most prominent film director of the Nazi period. His infamy rested mostly on two films that had aggressively promoted Nazi racial and military aims: *Jew Süss* (1940) and *Kolberg* (1945). The former film, loosely based on the career of Süss Oppenheimer, a financial adviser to the prince of Württemberg in the eighteenth century, depicts its main character—and all other Jews—as members of a devious and destructive race. Oppenheimer manipulates the court to his benefit, rapes the daughter of one of the government ministers, and is hanged. *Jew Süss* was the most popular film in Germany in 1940 and was also shown around occupied Europe. Like Fritz Hippler's much less popular and even more odious "documentary" of 1940, *The Eternal Jew*, Harlan's artfully dramatic but vicious film was designed to convince "Aryans" of the necessity of dealing harshly with the fantasied social and racial parasitism of Jews. The film was even shown to concentration camp guards for this purpose.[107] After the war Harlan was brought before an Allied denazification tribunal and acquitted of crimes against humanity, but for a time was prevented from working as a filmmaker in the Federal Republic of Germany. By the early 1960s Harlan was writing his autobiography, in which he attempts to show—the public, his family, and perhaps also himself—that he was not "that strong an anti-Semite or that convinced a Nazi after all."[108]

Kubrick met Veit Harlan in 1957 and wanted to make a film about him and, in Christiane Kubrick's words, "the absolutely normal life under the protection of Joseph Goebbels."[109] Jan Harlan has recalled that Kubrick had "a very positive relationship to Germany . . . and was not prone to prejudgments."[110] This is to say, of course, that Kubrick as always was clear-eyed about the subject of human history. Surely what fascinated him most with respect to Veit Harlan was the artist's pact with the devil and the everyday insidiousness of evil as well as its blatancy. This cohabitation of the banal and horrific was the moving force behind a sixteen-hour German television serial Kubrick much admired, Edgar Reitz's study of a small town during the Third Reich, *Heimat* (1984). Indeed, when it came to the preparations for the unfilmed "Aryan Papers," Kubrick had hired Fritz Bauer, the designer and set dresser for *Heimat*, to help Jan Harlan scout locations in Hungary and Slovakia, because Kubrick wanted that look for his Holocaust film.[111] The type of traditional genre films in which Veit Harlan specialized was more effective in creating the satisfied obedience the Nazis required of the German populace than overt propaganda films were in producing active fanaticism. In this regard, films like *Jew Süss* were vitally important in advancing the regime's most horrific aims, as anodyne rather than emetic, more the narcotic discipline of Aldous Huxley's *Brave New World* (1932) than the rant and truncheon of George Orwell's *Nineteen Eighty-four* (1949). The social realities and moral challenges of life in the Third Reich were in fact as complex as they were lethal. Everyone to varying degrees, even those opposed to the regime, was morally compromised simply by functioning—as a soldier, as a professional, as an artist—within the large and complex racial, military, and industrial state forged by the Nazis. This was an extreme instance of how Kubrick viewed human society, as a moralist but also as a realist. Kubrick's films are not just about evil, but about the confrontation with evil: how people deal with the evil around them and within themselves. Some of Kubrick's characters—Colonel Dax, President Muffley, Group Captain Mandrake, Wendy and Danny Torrance, Dick Halloran, Bill Harford—confront this evil, but most don't, and many can't. The major problem for Kubrick is that evil is pervasive within the systems as well as the inhabitants of the world, all of which is a reflection of a hostile or an indifferent universe.[112] Thus attempts in Kubrick's films to counter evil fail. The pattern Kubrick saw early in life of evil lurking behind the façades of security and diversion is a deeper one, for evil is within the façades themselves. As water to fish, as air to humans, we live in it and are of it. As such, the Nazi era was exceptional for Kubrick only in the nature and degree of its evil and its violence, though exceptional to such a degree that he could not confront it directly in his films.

Kubrick's antennae thus must have been especially attuned to the critical vibrations in the Harlan family caused by sorrow and outrage over Veit Harlan's close collaboration with the Nazi cultural and political elite. Closest to him of course was Christiane, who, as Natalie Zemon Davis has observed, "must have rejected Veit Harlan's years of collaboration with Joseph Goebbels even before her lifelong companionship with Stanley."[113] Veit's children were subject to the stresses and strains of their parents' stormy marriage as well as to the legacy of their father's involvement with the Nazi regime. Although she has claimed she was forced to do it by her agent, one of Veit's daughters, actress Maria Körber (like sister Susanne and cousin Susanne), dropped the Harlan name, taking as a postwar stage name her mother's maiden name. While Körber's protestations of love for her father are no doubt sincere (she took him into her home during his final illness in 1963), it would be naïve to assume that her feelings for her father were uncomplicated.[114] She, too, would contribute to Kubrick's cinema, providing the voice of the psychiatrist in the German version of *A Clockwork Orange*.[115]

Veit's son, Thomas, had an especially complicated and confrontational relationship with his father. Thomas Christian Harlan was born in 1929, received his first model train set as a present from Goebbels, and became a leader in the Naval Hitler Youth.[116] But things change. In 1954 Thomas accompanied his father on a trip to Switzerland for a burning of the back-up print of *Jew Süss*, which critics interpreted as a publicity stunt to allow the export of his other films to Switzerland. Thomas also collaborated (as it were) with his father on the screenplay for Harlan's first postwar film, *Germany Betrayed* (1955), about a German correspondent who was a spy for the Russians in Japan during the Second World War. Since the Cold War was raging at the time, the film was censored for its pro-Soviet stance, which resulted in changes, including the abandonment of the original title, *The Case of Doctor Sorge*. This sympathy for the Russians was due to Thomas, who from his days at the University of Tübingen had embraced radical leftist politics. At the same time Thomas was preparing a stage play and film on the Warsaw Ghetto uprising of 1943, a project that was inspired by his meeting in Israel in 1953 with survivors of the revolt. While it had long been rumored that in the 1950s Thomas had set fire to theaters showing his father's films, it was only after Veit Harlan's death in 1964 that he expressed publicly his hatred for what his father had done for the Nazis.[117] In 1985 Thomas released a semi-documentary anti-Nazi film entitled *Wound Passage*. In this film a convicted mass murderer, an SS man by the name of Alfred Filbert who had been released from prison for health reasons, plays Veit Harlan, who is sadistically interrogated and condemned to death. The film is typical of the vindictive anger many in the early postwar generation in West Germany felt toward parents who had in one way or another collaborated with the Nazis. For his part, Kubrick extended some financial support to Thomas, but not as backing for *Wound Passage* or any of his other projects.[118]

Kubrick, however, had an instance of the moral challenges of the Nazi past even closer to home in the person of his father-in-law, a tale that may have had a direct or an indirect effect on a film that, unlike the unrealized project on Veit Harlan, he would make. Fritz Harlan, after beginning his singing career in Berlin in 1926, performed between 1929 and 1942 as a concert and opera singer in Lübeck, Braunschweig, and Karlsruhe before accepting a teaching post at the University of Freiburg. Before the war, around 1937 or 1938, he had taught and performed in Barcelona.[119] According to Christiane Kubrick, Harlan, like most members of the German artistic community, was closer to being a Bohemian than a German and more interested in art than in politics. Both she and her brother declare that their father never joined the Nazi party. His life, like that of most of the members of his family, seems to have been mostly that of an artist in a profession whose members were diverse and international in origin. He had served in the German army near the end of the First World War, and, in late 1942, in order to avoid being drafted again, Harlan accepted a job at the German Theater in The Hague.[120] Such enterprises were a part of overall Nazi policy in occupied Europe to strengthen German influence. The Netherlands was a showplace for this policy, and Reich Commissioner for the Netherlands, Artur Seyss-Inquart, was himself the moving force behind the establishment of the German Theater.[121] Over time, however, Harlan and his wife spent less and less time at the German Theater and more and more time entertaining troops throughout Holland. They stayed in the Netherlands until late September 1944 following the Battle of Arnhem in Belgium, which marked a failed attempt by the Allies to break the German lines in western Europe. He returned to southern Germany to be near his family, but was drafted into the army, captured by the French, and spent a year in a prison camp.[122]

In the Netherlands, Harlan and his wife had for the first time been brought face to face with Nazi racial policy. In Germany adults were usually insulated from the exercise and effects of inherent and systematic Nazi brutality. It was different with German children, Christiane Kubrick remembers, who were instructed daily in school of what it took to extend the dominion of the Master Race over all lesser human beings. It did not take long for Christiane's parents to learn the same lessons in a country under German occupation. Aside from the poor treatment of the Dutch in general by the Germans and the resultant hatred for any and all Germans, the "Aryanization" of Jewish business and property through the divestment of their owners and employees and the distribution of assets to non-Jews was well along by 1942. In the Netherlands various German looting agencies coordinated, among other things, the seizure of the premises of all Jewish music businesses and organizations as well as the confiscation of all privately owned musical instruments, books, and sheet music. The plunder was stored in Germany or distributed to German organizations in the Reich and in occupied Europe. By 1941, when the decision had been made to deport Jews from all over Europe to killing centers in the East, another material bonanza fell to Germans: the sudden massive availability of Jewish apartments and houses. Germans taking up residence in the occupied countries or "Aryans" bombed out of their homes were often provided with housing seized from Jewish owners.[123] The official and unofficial reallocation of Jewish residences to "Aryans" took the place of a systematic policy of construction and improvement of housing as well as being a means for Germans to get their hands on valuable property. An early and famous example of the latter was the elegant Jewish apartment in Cracow that German industrialist Oskar Schindler was given in 1939.[124] Germans less well connected than Schindler had to wait longer, particularly in western Europe, where the exclusion of Jews from society took longer than in the East, even though liquidation of Jewish real estate in the Netherlands had been authorized by the Germans as early as 1941.[125] The deportation of Jews from the Netherlands began in July 1942, and within fourteen months almost all of the approximately 140,000 of them had been sent east.[126]

The Nazi occupation government was therefore in the position to kindly arrange housing for the visiting members of the German Theater from Germany. Fritz and Ingeborg Harlan initially moved into lodgings on Van der Aastraat in the wealthy Benoordenhout district northeast of the city of The Hague. While in the eighteenth century most of the richer Sephardic, or Spanish, Jews had lived near the prince's court and during the eighteenth and nineteenth centuries most of the Ashkenazic Jews had lived near the town center, there had never been a Jewish district or ghetto in The Hague. In 1942 on the very short Van der Aastraat there were at least two apartments formerly owned by Jews. Erhard Bernhard Matthias and Herbert Nikolaus Waldemar Hirschland had lived at 52 Van der Aastraat, while at 51 there had resided Fanny Judith Henriëtte Oppenheim-Jospehus-Jitta. While the fate of the Hirschlands is not known, Oppenheim was deported in 1942 and died at Auschwitz. It is therefore likely that the Harlans were housed in one of these two apartments, probably that of Oppenheim since it had only two rooms and we know the Harlans found their first lodgings too small.[127] The Harlans did not live on the Van der Aastraat for long because they wanted space for their children when they visited. Jan and Christiane had been sent to Reihen to live with their nanny's family. It was the nanny's family who owned the brickworks and, unwillingly, had taken the Harlan children in. Like most of the 5 million other children who had been evacuated from cities threatened by air attacks, the Harlan children spent much of the war apart from their parents, staying in Reihen until almost the end of the war.[128] As early as Christmas 1942, however, Fritz had been allotted a larger apartment in the central Bezuidhenhout district on the Van der Bosstraat, and the children spent that holiday and several others in The Hague with their parents. This apartment, too, had been taken from its Jewish owners. Ingeborg Harlan, who had Jewish relatives, could tell from the furnishings of the apartment that its former owners were Jews. The children were also exposed to the resentment of the Dutch population against the Germans living and lording in their midst. Even the Dutch members of the German Theater had to eat in a crummy dining room while the Germans took their meals in an elegant one.[129]

Christiane has maintained that her parents were appalled and depressed by their new knowledge of the explicit evil of Nazi designs. According to a member of the Harlan family, who wishes to remain anonymous, Christiane once said that her father was indifferent to the sufferings of the Jews, had indeed taken over the apartment of a Jew or Jews who had been sent to the extermination camps in Poland, and had heartlessly thrown away many of the departed residents' possessions.[130] Kubrick herself denies that she ever said any such thing. She is, however, a member of a generation of Harlans that has, like many of the members of the postwar German generations, loudly and rightly rejected their family's Nazi associations and the preceding generation's crimes, complicities, and cowardice under the Hitler dictatorship. This was particularly the case in the decades following the war when youthful idealism and adolescent intolerance, combined with the older generation's long and culpable silence on the subject of National Socialism, produced angry condemnations on the part of many young Germans of their parents' collaboration with the Nazi regime. What is likely, therefore, is that Christiane's general criticism of her parents' crimes of omission were translated, through a mixture of error and—perhaps—animus, into the rumor of a condemnation of explicit anti-Semitism on her father's part. There is no evidence that the Harlans were involved in anything abroad (like spying) other than cultural activities. There is also a strong ring of truth in Christiane's painful memories of the encompassing sadness of her visits to The Hague, a truth—and pain—that are evident in what turns out to be a geographically literal and eloquent memory of being the child who "moved in where Anne Frank was pushed out."

The cosmopolitan artistic background Christiane inherited from her family, reinforced by the horrors of the Third Reich, in any case, caused her not only to reassert a rejection of nationalism after the war but also to develop an aversion to Germany in particular. As she has recently noted, "I am not normally a defender of Germany." Her art instructor in New York has recalled that "[s]he never talked about her German background, never."[131] Since leaving Germany with Kubrick in 1957, Christiane has avoided returning to her homeland. She, together with Stanley, only attended some family birthday celebrations there, and she, though not her husband, also went back for the funerals of her parents. Fritz Harlan, who was a cofounder of the Musik Hochschule Freiburg after the war, died in 1970. Her mother, suffering from Alzheimer's, lived briefly in England with the Kubricks and then in an institution in Germany and died in 1991.[132] That Christiane, like her cousin Susanne, married a Jew and left Germany is certainly also consistent with her uneasiness over the Nazi past of her homeland and her family. Still, she and Stanley had an apartment on the Upper East Side just two blocks south of what during the war had been "Hitler's Broadway" in German-American Yorkville.[133] Clearly, like that of Kubrick himself, Christiane's rejection of Germany was understandably colored by an ambivalence and even affection stemming from her family background.

It is certain that the echoes of these events and their discussion within the Harlan and Kubrick families found their way into Kubrick's life and work. They seem to sound geographically in a conversation with Michael Herr on the Friday before Kubrick died in 1999: "In Holland, he'd heard, there was a football team called Ajax [Amsterdam] that had once had a Jewish player, and ever since then, Dutch skinheads would go to all the team's matches and make a loud hissing noise, meant to represent the sound of gas escaping into the death chambers. 'And that's Holland, Michael. A *civilized* country.' Laughing."[134] Once again, surely, it was too sad to cry. This family referent may also be strongly represented in Kubrick's indirect Holocaust film, *The Shining*, by the empty rooms of the shuttered Overlook Hotel haunted by the ghosts of departed residents murdered in the hotel's bloody past.[135] This is likely given the common trope in Kubrick films of space and enclosure representing threat, the former communicating universal contingency and chaos and the latter representing earthbound entrapment.[136] As the characters in Kubrick's cinema move into or through these spaces, they confront a world of pervasive individual and institutional evil. It must have struck Kubrick that as Christiane's parents moved into the rooms formerly occupied by Jews who had been sent to Poland to be exterminated, the emptiness of those spaces was itself eloquent testament to the greatest of evils. Here the beauty of music through its embodiment in musicians was confronted with the pervasive evil drifting in the air of empty rooms vacated for Auschwitz, where prisoner orchestras played for Jews descending into the gas chambers. Such evil also pervaded the musicians, for music and the musicians, independent of their own goodness, were part of the system of evil through their participation in cultural projects designed to extend and bolster Nazi rule. Even Nazi fanatics, as Kubrick himself gloomily observed in discussing the marriage of Beethoven and violence in *A Clockwork Orange*, appreciated high culture: "Hitler loved good music and many top Nazis were cultured and sophisticated men, but it didn't do them, or anyone else, much good."[137]

In his films, Kubrick is not concerned primarily with whether the evil in the world is extrinsic (universal) or intrinsic (natural). He may have had a Manichean dualistic perspective on the universe as created by both good *and* evil, with the world as a battleground between these forces. He definitely did hold a modern Freudian view of the inextricable mix of good and evil in the human psyche, was eclectic in his pessimism, and with his bent for history had a strong appreciation for ambiguities of all types.[138] In *2001* he suggests the smallness of humanity's moment in the infinite sweep of time, thereby rejecting the anthropocentric bias of traditional religious belief.[139] In *A Clockwork Orange* he presents but undermines novelist Anthony Burgess's Catholic equation of morality with individual free will, a point of view that, because it does not view human beings as in part essentially evil, rejects Manichean dualism. Kubrick was also a Stoic in terms of being resigned to evil, but his films are fierce enough in their eloquence and passion to constitute the type of rebellion inconsistent with resignation, particularly in the face of horrendous mass evils like the Holocaust that make a mockery of the Stoic emphasis on *individual* acceptance of evil as part of a larger order one should humbly accept.[140] But more than divining the nature and meaning of evil in theological or philosophical terms, Kubrick is interested in how humans deal with the commingling in life of evil and good. And he is interested in this question not simply in terms of individual cases, but in the flow of time and particularly, as we have seen, over the course of the modern era. His frequent recourse to narration and voice-overs demonstrates not the conceit of godly omniscience but the fact that, as we have observed, Kubrick favored the long and detached view of the artist-as-historian. Given this historical long view, nevertheless, there does loom in his films a mythopoeic suspicion that behind all the conflicts of human existence there is "a large and inexplicable universe."[141] In the wake of the Holocaust, many Jews in particular came to the conclusion that the universe was indifferent or even hostile. The questioning or even the abandonment of a belief in a just—or any—God was replaced by a deep dread and anxiety in contemplating the realm of the divine.[142] *The Shining* presents such a trembling confrontation with the otherworldly and, even more than Kubrick's other films, conjoins realism and the fantastic in its own fearful examination of this world's problems.

The long and extensive relationship between Kubrick and the Harlan family was of course a function of his accidental attraction to Christiane as well as of the relatively small community of international filmmaking in Europe.[143] But Kubrick's marrying of his domestic and professional life also became both a cause and an effect of his intense preoccupation with things German, particularly when they had to do with the Second World War. What are we otherwise to make of the fact that when he took Christiane on a first, and rare, holiday after finishing *Lolita*, it was a five-day tour of the Normandy invasion beaches and their German bunkers?[144] Kubrick's complicated processing of his own Jewish past was now colliding directly with a German presence. Ironically, perhaps, this helped produce an enduring and satisfying marriage. Others close to Stanley and Christiane sometimes assumed a tension between them because of their different backgrounds at this particularly tragic juncture in history.[145] But if there were tensions within the Kubrick marriage and family between Jewish past and German presence, it seems certain that it was a creative tension that did little or nothing to harm either the personal or the artistic partnership. Probably a more telling indication of the dynamic status of the relationship between the German Gentile Christiane and the eastern European Jewish Stanley was a typical instance of Kubrick's ready sense of humor. Once he and Christiane were watching *Magdana's Donkey* (1955), a Soviet film co-directed by Georgians Tengiz Abuladze and Rezo Chkheidze. In one scene, 500 dark-haired bearded eastern European extras suddenly rush on camera, and Christiane remembers Kubrick exclaiming, "They all look like me!"[146]

All his adult life, Stanley Kubrick manifested a distinct and complex ambivalence toward modern Germany and the Germans. He married into a prominent German family of artists, filmmakers, and writers. He loved Black Forest cooking.[147] He admired German literature, German films, and German technology. But he feared their history. When Michel Ciment observed to him that in their use of German music (e.g., in *2001*, *A Clockwork Orange*), among other things, his films seemed "to show an attraction for Germany," Kubrick replied, "I wouldn't include German music as a relevant part of that group, nor would I say that I'm attracted but, rather, that I share the fairly widespread fascination with the Nazi period."[148] Indeed, Kubrick much more often would have recourse in his films to the music of eastern European composers, much of which had been written in response to the Nazi horror. Though often cast in shadow in his films, therefore, the Germans and their most recent Nazi past were a constant presence. For Kubrick, as for Conrad, deep within modern German history beat the most modern and savage heart of darkness.

# 5

## DIRECTED BY STANLEY KUBRICK, 1953–1962

Between 1953 and 1962, Stanley Kubrick directed six of the thirteen feature films he would make in his lifetime. These films represent a steep learning curve on Kubrick's part as well as a rate of production that would slow considerably during the rest of his career. Typical for Kubrick's films as a group, his first six films cover a range of genres, including two war films, a historical epic, a film noir, a crime thriller, and a romantic drama. In comparison with those that would come after 1962, these films are relatively conventional in subject matter and form. This was the result of Kubrick learning his craft and working within the constraints of the movie business, first in the United States and then in England. Only with *Dr. Strangelove* would he begin fully developing the unique style that would earn the adjective "Kubrickian." But his early films nevertheless contain strong traces of the basic themes, distinctive visual and narrative form, and specific symbolic means of conveying meaning (e.g., music, colors, numbers) that would be magnified in the fully Kubrickian films to come. These films also reveal a sly, if sporadic, progression of the historical preoccupation regarding the recent disasters in the world of the 1930s and 1940s we have detailed in the preceding chapters. The importance of attention to the outside world in the artistic re-creation of life had been reinforced for Kubrick by his exposure to the ideas of the Russian stage director Konstantin Stanislavsky. Just as the outside world was Kubrick's chief motive for becoming a filmmaker, observation of the outside world was a chief means for development of one's re-creation of the world on stage or screen, the only way for a director to get the actors to communicate the central idea or ideas behind the production.[1]

The richness of the visual and aural information typical of Kubrick's films is a reflection of the director's commitment to the observation and analysis of the world. Given this, careful study of his films will reveal many small and large details having directly (or indirectly) to do with his interests and concerns. It is also the case that—given the textual richness and volatility of language, the film form, and perceptions influenced by history and culture—there will be much in the films for audiences to find that was not directly, consciously, or at all intended by Kubrick. Thus Kubrick's films reflect cultural constructions around various issues, such as gender, race, and political philosophy. But, given Kubrick's painstaking construction of his films, much, if not most, of even this information will be arrayed along lines determined or at least influenced by authorial interest and intent.

## *Fear and Desire* (1953)

*Fear and Desire,* Kubrick's first feature film, was shot in the San Gabriel Mountains above Los Angeles, but it originated in the stone canyons on the island of Manhattan. Kubrick himself later disowned the film, calling it "a very inept and pretentious effort."[2] It began as a screenplay by Kubrick's friend Howard Sackler, who had written it at Kubrick's urging in 1950 under the impact of the war that had just broken out in Korea. Kubrick had originally wanted to film in upstate New York but opted for the better weather of southern California. His uncle Martin agreed to back the film, and Richard de Rochement also provided some financing. Shooting commenced in the summer of 1951 with Kubrick's friends from New York and his wife, Toba, serving as crew. Following its preview in June 1952, Kubrick succeeded in getting Joseph Burstyn, a 1921 Polish immigrant who distributed foreign films in the United States, to distribute *Fear and Desire* and it opened in New York City at the end of March 1953.

*Fear and Desire* begins with narration over a shot of dark, forested hills shrouded in clouds and fog. The words are loaded with trendy existentialism, but they also reflect Kubrick's view of a twentieth-century world beset by great wars. The narration is also reflexive in that it is saying that the film and its actors are "outside history" while fixing in mythological fashion "fear and doubt and death" as the demiurge of "our world."[3] Kubrick himself emphasized the film's open, allegorical structure, which would "mean many things to different people."[4] Kubrick at the beginning of his career is thus embracing the open narrative in a film whose setting, cinematography, and theme recall the terrifying void of truth in Akira Kurosawa's *Rashomon* (1951), the dark heart of Conrad's jungle, and—in its references to Prospero, Miranda, and humans as lonely and hostile isles—Shakespeare's *The Tempest* (1611).[5] His statement is also patently autobiographical in its evocation of a searcher in a world of danger, a self-reference underlined in the film by the strong physical resemblance of one of the actors to Kubrick as well as by the presence of a Jewish soldier, Sidney, played by Paul Mazursky.[6] And the allegorical and mythological tone of the film also evidences the distance that Kubrick would habitually place between himself and this philosophically and personally problematic historical subject matter.

But even though the story is "outside history," the landscape, uniforms, and weapons tell us that the referent—save for a couple of scenes with ferns and palm trees that betoken the primeval and the Pacific—is Europe in the Second World War. *Fear and Desire* resembles *A Walk in the Sun* (R, May 1946), a film about an American unit trapped behind Nazi lines in Italy, and its mood evokes "the Teutonic forest of Grimm."[7] This serves the theme of entrapment in an unknown and threatening environment very well, but it also underlines for us Kubrick's preoccupation with the war that in its coming, its being, and its passing had dominated the world of his childhood and youth. Kubrick's soldiers are trapped behind enemy lines when their plane crashes. Their attempt to escape involves them in a firefight at an enemy outpost, a chance meeting with three women that ends in the shooting death of one the women after an attempted rape, and an attack on an enemy headquarters that leaves two enemy and two American officers dead. A major conceit (and economy) of the film has the same actors playing both the American and the German officers. One interpretation of this is that "the basic brotherhood of mankind cannot be destroyed even by war, for the enemy is but a reflection of one's self."[8] This is an antiwar plea that will be heard again in *Paths of Glory*, *Dr. Strangelove*, and *Full Metal Jacket*. But Kubrick was not a pacifist, and he certainly would not have been one out of idealism, for his view of the world was as clear-eyed as it was bleak. His own historical environment had taught him the violent way of the world that one had to regret but could not ignore by escape from reality into simple idealism. For this reason, *Fear and Desire* has a dark mood consistent with the fact that the two Americans, Corby and Fletcher, must kill their "opposite" numbers in order to survive. Mac, the "American" sergeant, is played by Frank Silvera, a black Jamaican civil rights activist in the 1950s and 1960s.[9] The fable allows Kubrick this anachronism, since the American armed forces were not integrated until after—and as a result of—the Second World War. As such, Silvera's background is perhaps an indication of Kubrick's concern for the issue of racism—among "us" as well as "them"—which would also be alluded to, subtly but definitely, in his next three films. And the enemy officers in *Fear and Desire* are not just soldiers, after all, but Nazis.

The economy of two actors instead of four also allowed the Kubrick of Jewish past and German present to question, for personal as well as philosophical reasons, the binary opposition of "them" and "us," "good" and "evil, and "then" and "now." The referents to the European theater in the Second World War are ubiquitous. The American soldiers sport German helmets, belt buckles, and canteens, while their leader, Lieutenant Corby, wears an American bomber jacket and an Army Air Force cap that displays a wreath with a globe held by the talons of an eagle in the style of the emblem of the Nazi Luftwaffe.[10] The enemy officers wear German-style uniforms and the soldiers guarding them wear helmets that look vaguely Italian, while a large map of Europe hangs on the wall behind the "Nazi general officer."[11] The German also owns a Doberman Pinscher, another artifact of

Nazis in the world and on film, a dog tellingly named Proteus, the sea god of myth who could assume different forms. Both Kubrick and the uncle who financed *Fear and Desire* owned Dobermans, and it is likely that the dog in the film was the one that belonged to Martin Perveler.[12] In sum, that Kubrick's first directorial effort was "a drama of man deprived of material and spiritual foundations, lost in a hostile world in which he seeks to understand himself and the life around him [that] could well serve as a keynote of all of his films,"[13] only underscores the benchmark status of the Second World War, its issues, and its artifacts on Kubrick from the very beginning of his career.

## *Killer's Kiss* (1955)

For his second film, Kubrick literally returned home. *Killer's Kiss* is a film noir set—and filmed, guerrilla-style—on and in the streets and structures of New York City, with most of the locations within minutes of Kubrick's own apartment in Greenwich Village. Kubrick and Howard Sackler collaborated on the screenplay, with the final product—reflecting the theme of entrapment in a maze of violence—a Minotaur Production. Like that for *Fear and Desire*, backing for *Killer's Kiss* came from sources close to home, this time a friend of the family. The film would be distributed—on a limited basis—worldwide by United Artists.[14] *Killer's Kiss* is distinguished by its black-and-white photography, with many of its compositions resembling stills and displaying dramatic use of depth of field.[15] The film, with its location shots of New York streets, skyline, people, and objects, is almost a documentary about New York, but its theme and style are typically Expressionistic. The cinematography is a Kubrickian composite of grainy *cinema vérité* and gloomy Expressionism that reproduces the fusion of quotidian and fantastic in service to a demolition of the hypocritical norms of bourgeois society that so attracted Kubrick to the stories of Kafka.[16] The story itself lies between neo-realism, in its concentration on the everyday lives of everyday people, and a Germanic "fable of a maiden rescued by a valorous knight from the clutches of an ogre" in the confines of a nightmarish modern metropolis that resembles the realms of Hades into which the Orpheus of Greek myth descended vainly in order to save his wife, Eurydice.[17]

What *Killer's Kiss* is above all, like Kubrick's next film, *The Killing*, is a film noir. This was the name given by French critics to some Hollywood films of the 1940s and 1950s that had as their subject a bleak, criminal, corrupt world of shadows and threat. Like German Expressionist films, films noir take place mostly at night and in dark rooms and streets. Noir was an outgrowth of the Second World War in two ways. First, beginning as a self-conscious style around 1944, it was largely the product of German directors steeped in Expressionism, many of whom, like Lang, Wilder, and Siodmak, were recent émigrés from Hitler's Germany. Second, film noir not only reflected contemporary American concerns about the Cold War and the nuclear arms race in the wake of Roosevelt's death (a moment young photographer Kubrick caught), but also expressed the feeling that "the violence unleashed by the war could wreak havoc . . . [and t]he suggestion that dangerous impulses resided in the souls of American themselves."[18] The same conviction of universal evil animated the novels of Louis-Ferdinand Céline, "one of the godfathers of noir . . . in his hallucinatory novels of urban apocalypse" and a French Nazi collaborator whom Kubrick called "[m]y favorite anti-Semite."[19] Given the historical pedigree of film noir, therefore, it is hardly surprising that Kubrick turned to this genre for his second and third films or that he, as in *Fear and Desire*, invests the fable in *Killer's Kiss* with artifacts and associations drawn from the Second World War.

Kubrick's interest in boxing is at the center of *Killer's Kiss* and serves as a fitting expression of film noir's preoccupation with the dark violence of urban society. The boxing ring itself is a symbol of entrapment in a violent world. The protagonist is Davy Gordon, a boxer approaching the end of his career whom we will see fail at one last shot at a championship. He is a lonely figure, far from home with Uncle George and Aunt Grace, who live literally at the other end of the country on a ranch outside Seattle. As "wide-open spaces" music plays on the soundtrack, Davy reads a letter from his uncle while riding on the subway. Then, as his uncle urges him on the phone to come out West in the wake of his defeat in the fight with Rodriguez, Davy is alone in his dark, cramped room while in deep focus through facing windows we and Davy see the woman who will entangle him in violence outside the ring undressing in her tiny apartment.[20] Davy goes to bed and turns out the light. Following a blackout that lasts a long six seconds, he has a dream of his looming entrapment in which the camera, anticipating the Star Gate sequence in *2001*, hurtles down deserted city streets—only parked cars and one pedestrian are seen—in a negative image. The sky is black, the buildings and cars blazing ashy white or charring black. It is as if the city has been caught in the x-ray instant of a nuclear blast, an ominous augury of the ending to *Dr. Strangelove*. On the soundtrack, catcalls from the boxing crowd fade into a woman's screams, and Davy awakens to the sight of the woman across the way being assaulted by an older man.[21]

The woman, the aptly named Gloria Price, is trapped in her own ring of violence as a taxi dancer at Pleasureland (recall Ophuls's *Le Plaisir*), run by lecherous mobster Vincent Rapallo. This cinematic coupling of boxing and dancing is an initial instance of Kubrick's association of dancing in his films with patriarchal pleasure, violence, and manipulation. The Oedipal theme is more than obvious in the triangle formed by the young woman, the older man, and the younger fighter whose own parents are already dead. Gloria tells Davy her own fable-like story of Oedipal drama concerning her older sister, Iris, who grew up the beautiful image of a mother who had died giving birth to Gloria. An ailing Mr. Price favored Iris, who gave up ballet to marry an older man with money who would care for her father and sister. Upon the father's death, Gloria berated Iris, who as a result committed suicide. Seeking penance, Gloria took the job at Pleasureland and comforting herself with the thought "that at least Iris never had to dance at a place like that, a human zoo."[22] It is typically Kubrickian as well as appropriately Freudian that her job allows—or, rather, forces—her to fulfill her Oedipal fantasy through her enslavement to Rapallo. This clunky subplot of a young woman's guilt-ridden fantasy of incest with her father is told in flashback over Iris dancing alone on a foot-lit stage cloaked in darkness. This filmic construction adds to the fable-like quality that accompanies the gritty noir realism of the film as a whole. The scene, moreover, is danced by Ruth Sobotka, who was soon to become Kubrick's wife, and it is photographs of Ruth and her father, Walter Sobotka, that Davy sees on Gloria's dresser that prompts her confidence in him.[23] The references to Kubrick's own Oedipal conflict—both conscious and unconscious, involuntary and reflexive—are readily apparent, as is the Kubrick habit of investing names with meaning. Iris is the name of a part of the eye and thereby reflects Freudian Oedipal theory as well as filmmaking, while the name Price denotes both the psychological and social costs involved in human relationships.

Rapallo's self-destructive desire for Gloria also anticipates the predicament of another professor, Humbert Humbert, in *Lolita*. This desire is itself the product of Rapallo's own Oedipal longings, as his mournful glance at a portrait of his mother after hearing of Gloria's betrayal indicates.[24] The conflict between Davy and Rapallo also builds to a fight among and with mannequins, most of which are female, and ends in phallic fashion when Davy runs Rapallo through with a spiked pole as his victim lies among the mannequins. In this, as with Kubrick's problematic fascination with violence, is a patriarchal objectification of the bodies of women that reflects the times in which—and the person by which—the film was made, but again also reflects Kubrick's personal and intuitive critical awareness of the injustices of male-dominated society.[25] Rapallo in particular is the object of the film's scornful fascination in this respect, as he is the "bestial man" who manipulates people just like the mannequins he smashes with an ax. He also preys in particular upon women, a habit underlined by the camera's focus on his gaze and his body language. The standing shop-window dummies are arranged in the same way as the hostesses at Pleasureland, and it is an appropriate, whether coincidental or intentional, production detail that the same warehouse was used for Pleasureland and the mannequin storehouse.[26] Kubrick's point is made doubly dark since Rapallo is Davy's alter ego, in psychological terms, his *Doppelgänger*—a double, the "dark beast" underneath the boxer's "homogenized repressed manhood."[27] The very title of the film conveys this message since of the two people kissing Gloria, only one, Davy, is shown killing anyone. Both men are also depicted as clumsy in their duel, subverting audience identification with Davy as well as with Rapallo. At least one German audience is recorded to have laughed at the scene. In this way as well, *Killer's Kiss* recalls Kurosawa's *Rashomon,* in which one version of the duel between swordsmen portrays them as scared, clumsy, and gasping for breath.[28] Finally, what Norman Kagan calls "cookbook Freud" shows up in what would become a cinematic Kubrick habit (e.g., in *The Shining* and *Full Metal Jacket*) of close-ups of female buttocks to represent aggression as well as desire.[29] This trope is based on the psychoanalytic view of the anal stage of childhood development, when the buttocks are the seat, as it were, of struggles over rage, control, and autonomy. Here Kubrick permits himself the adolescent humor of having "The End" appear on the screen over the rear end of a female passerby in Penn Station.[30]

Kubrick's focus is not only psychological, however. In the tradition of German New Objectivity of the 1920s and American film noir of the 1940s and 1950s, he is also concerned with the dangerous and corrupt outside world. We have already mentioned the male sexual and economic exploitation of women. Kubrick highlights this visually when Rapallo hears Gloria Price's name in a telephone call telling him that she is leaving with Davy, for as he hangs up in anger and despair, he moves to reveal a poster on the wall of his office that reads "Barbara Worth."[31] Aside from its dark depiction of the urban landscape and its denizens in general, *Killer's Kiss* also deals with the problem of race in postwar America. This is appropriate for a time during which public and artistic consciousness was being raised about discrimination against African-Americans in particular. Black men and women are frequently seen on the streets in *Killer's Kiss* and in Pleasureland. But the film's subtle and indirect discourse on the subject was also informed by Kubrick's own concerns with race stemming from the horrors of the Second World War. As Rapallo moves around his office after learning of Gloria's intended desertion, his (mind's?) eye—and the camera's—falls upon a cartoon of two men grinning out a window back at him (and us). The men are dressed in hats and coats that suggest they are Irish, as is the fighter who is stealing Gloria away from him. But what is also interesting about the caricature is that the noses resemble those in racist caricatures of Jews and blacks in the late nineteenth and early twentieth centuries. Such composites were common in Caucasian presentations of the racial Other, most often in association with the dark, simian features ascribed to Africans. One film, for example, that combined such Irish and Jewish stereotypes for the enjoyment of Anglo-Saxon audiences was Edwin S. Porter's short, *Levy & Cohen: The Irish Comedians* (1902).[32]

Like the horror films of the 1930s and 1940s, *Killer's Kiss* also tends to identify the greatest evil with people and forces from Europe. Since for film noir the war in Europe between 1939 and 1945 was the source of new discomfort about American society, this places *Killer's Kiss* firmly within its own genre in this respect as well. References to the Second World War in the film are subtle but pervasive. Davy is indirectly identified as a veteran of the war, and soldiers in uniform are regularly pictured in Times Square, on Forty-second Street, and in the Pleasureland dance hall. But Kubrick also embroiders his noir with his own special German concerns. The most obvious, though in typical Kubrickian allusive/elusive fashion, is Davy's Luger pistol. It is his possession of this gun that, along with his age, identifies him as a veteran of the Second World War. The Luger is clearly a war souvenir, but one that Davy carries with him to use or—since the gun is never fired—at least to deter or to threaten. The gun appears in three separate scenes, including three one-shot close-ups.[33] Rarely (*He Walks by Night* [1948]) in film noir or on the streets of America was the Luger, because of the scarcity of ammunition and the difficulty of maintenance, the weapon of choice. But it was one of the most common symbols of Nazi brutality in American war films, having been a standard German army pistol since

1908 and exported in large numbers to America after the First World War.[34] Film noir favored American handguns like the revolvers brandished by Rapallo's gang in *Killer's Kiss* or the revolver in Jules Dassin's *The Naked City*, which was a direct inspiration for Kubrick' first noir. An instructive contrast in mid-century pulp fiction is the cover of a 1937 issue of the pulp magazine *The Feds* ("G-Men vs. Crime!"), on which appears an American naval officer carrying what looks like a Luger in a confrontation with enemy agents. This difference is clearly linked to the government's response to Nazi espionage in the late 1930s and thus unlike the domestic subject matter of most films noir. The same difference marks Dassin's film *Rififi* (1955), in which French criminals carry German Luger and Walther military pistols that are available, along with ammunition, only as a result of the long Nazi occupation of France during the Second World War. Significantly, the novel from which Dassin derived his film has its mobsters, in noir/frontier emulation of their American counterparts, packing Colt revolvers, making it possible that Dassin, like Kubrick, was making a statement about the pervasive memory of Nazi evil.[35]

The Luger also underscores Rapallo as Davy's double, an expression of Kubrick's belief in the inextricability of good and evil in the world. Rapallo pockets the Luger after a fight, and he carries it as he pursues Davy into the mannequin warehouse. In other words, the German gun is carried by both the "good" man and the "evil" one. The last we see of the pistol is when it is lying next to a box on the warehouse floor and resting, along with a loop of rope, on ads for women's dresses at "5.98" (Figure 2).[36] Rapallo's association with the weapon also revisits the "Axis alliance" in *Fear and Desire* of "German" officers and "Italian" soldiers. So his fight with Davy in the warehouse suggests as well the struggle against evil during the Second World War, in this case between the former American soldier and the "dark beast" Rapallo.[37] The war associations in the film are also heightened by music underneath the chase scenes dominated by jazzy percussion (Kubrick himself was a high-school percussionist) intended to suggest heartbeats, but that has the quality of a martial tattoo as well. This scoring closely resembles the more militarily flourished drums highlighted in Kubrick's next two films, *The Killing* and *Paths of Glory*, both of which in very different contexts examine the type of planning and execution that goes into military operations.[38] These three films, along with a Kubrick screenplay of the decade, "The German Lieutenant," thus signify a consistent underlying concern with a world dominated by the type of organized violence that the Second World War brought to unprecedented degrees of development and destructiveness. There is also a palpable sense in *Killer's Kiss*, as there was in the United States and abroad during and after the Second World War, of a young but strong America overcoming the last murderous gasps of a violent decadent Europe. Film noir also darkly questioned America's immunity from violence and decadence, a theme mirrored in Kubrick's linking of the two male antagonists in *Killer's Kiss*.

Kubrick's second film also hints at the Holocaust in a manner congruent with the "sense of silence mixed with a strong sense of the presence of the Holocaust in

*Directed by Stanley Kubrick, 1953–1962* | 85

Figure 2

the homes of those growing up in postwar Britain and America . . . in the late 1940s and 1950s."³⁹ It does so in the duel at the warehouse, in which mannequins and parts of mannequins stacked on shelves recall the heaps of bodies displayed in postwar newsreels on the liberation of the camps in 1945 (Figure 3). It is probably more than just a telling coincidence that in the concentration camps the SS imposed terms like *Figuren* (dolls or puppets), *Stücke* (pieces), or *Schmattes* (Yiddish for rags, i.e., old clothes) to dehumanize their Jewish victims by likening their corpses to dummies or mannequins.⁴⁰

This dehumanization was magnified by the industrial nature of the Nazi killing machine. Rapallo is associated visually with the torture and murder of helpless victims by means of terrible machines. This is even before he begins hacking at mannequins with an ax, a weapon that foreshadows Jack Torrance's weapon of choice in *The Shining*. On the wall of Rapallo's office at Pleasureland are what appear to be two large advertising posters for pulp fiction. The first, "Blue Jeans," shows one man about to kill another man lashed to the cutting board of a large rotary saw while a woman cowers in an upstairs office.⁴¹ The second, "The Cherry Pickers," its sexual entendre foreplay for a deliciously salacious circumlocution in *Lolita*, places a man and a woman against a wall, as a huge cannon in the absurdly tiny room appears to fire directly at them.⁴² Symbolization of the Holocaust in *Killer's Kiss* does not go nearly as far as it does in *The Shining*. It is too soon after the war, and Kubrick is only just honing his craft and shaping his historical and

86 | The Wolf at the Door: Stanley Kubrick, History, and the Holocaust

Figure 3

philosophical view of the world. We also know that the setting of a mannequin warehouse was inspired by a segment of the "The Girl Hunt" dance sequence in the MGM musical *The Bandwagon* (1953), and perhaps as well by an episode of Hans Richter's *Dreams That Money Can Buy* (1944–1947), directed by Fernand Léger, since Ruth Sobotka had appeared in another episode of Richter's series directed by Man Ray, "Ruth, Roses, and Revolvers" (1946).[43] The "unsettling visual juxtaposition" of the mannequins in a setting that is both real and surreal does, however, in all probability record the impact on Kubrick of the Nazi Final Solution.[44]

Much of *Killer's Kiss* was filmed in and around Times Square and Forty-second Street, the popular epicenter of glamour and danger in Manhattan. The number 42 was a constant presence in Kubrick's life, as it was for many residents of Manhattan, and twenty-five years later in *The Shining* Kubrick would use the number 42 as a symbol for the Holocaust. Kubrick knew the number well from the film theaters he patronized, as well as from the Academy of Chess and Checkers on Forty-second Street, which would show up in *The Killing*.[45] The area's glitz has been celebrated in such films as *42nd Street* (1933), while one sequence in "The Girl Hunt" ballet in *The Bandwagon*, which parodies the obsession with crime and violence of pulp fiction and film noir, takes place in the Times Square subway station at Forty-second Street, where a row of girders recedes into the distance, all marked with the number 42. And in one scene in *Killer's Kiss*, Gloria "wanders along the grubbiest part of 42nd Street."[46] Since Kubrick uses mirrors in this film, as in others, to comment on characters' perceptions of themselves and others, it is striking that Gloria lives on Twenty-fourth Street, for 24 is the mirror image of 42, a specific symbolic chronological juxtaposition Kubrick would in fact use in *The Shining*, just as novelist Vladimir Nabokov does for other reasons in *Lolita* (1955). In *Killer's Kiss,* 42 seems to be simply a natural artifact of the Manhattan environment, but it is also a multiple of the number 7. It is probably significant that Gloria first sees Davy through her window at ten minutes before 7 as he is leaving to fight and she is leaving to dance, since in Kubrick's *oeuvre* the number 7, starting with his next film, will be associated successively with incipient violence, war, and fate.[47] It is therefore more than reasonable to suppose that Kubrick's memory of personal associations with the number 42 made it available for use as one of the many details in his films that carry meaning and communicate ideas. This seems particularly to be the case given the number's connection in Kubrick's experience of history to the horrors of racism and war as well as his appreciative and anxious eye for coincidence.[48]

The huffing of the steam locomotive that begins and, with the wail of its whistle, ends *Killer's Kiss* is not yet a reference to the Holocaust. This train, after all, is the one on which Davy and Gloria escape the city for the wide-open spaces of the West. But what appears to be, besides *2001,* the only commercially motivated happy ending to a Kubrick film is typically Kubrickian and thus anything but a Hollywood ending. The end to *Killer's Kiss,* Michael Herr writes, is "a painful travesty of a happy ending, where the couple go off together even though we've seen them both cravenly betray and desert each other to save their own lives."[49] For Kubrick, who would in his films soon link machines with the worst that can be done, dark is already the default in the world explored by his cinema. And trains were to be a tiny but indelible presence in *The Shining* as one of the darkest possible symbols of the lethal power of machines.

## *The Killing* (1956)

In 1955 Kubrick moved to Los Angeles to shoot *The Killing* for United Artists. This film would be the first of three films produced by Harris-Kubrick Pictures, which had formed in 1955 when Kubrick's old Bronx friend Alexander Singer introduced Kubrick to James B. Harris. It would also be Kubrick's first adaptation of a novel, Lionel White's *Clean Break. The Killing,* its working titles "Day of Violence" and "Bed of Fear," represented Kubrick's big break into Hollywood studio filmmaking and the beginning of a temporary departure from the style and concerns of his first two films. This does not mean that *The Killing* was a radical departure for Kubrick in the process of adapting to Hollywood commercial standards, far from it. His basically suspicious view of the world would find excellent expression in the story of a racetrack heist that goes badly wrong. And some of the photojournalistic immediacy and Expressionistic composition of the cinematography of his first two films would be reproduced in the smoother style of California filmmaking.

More significantly, however, *The Killing,* along with *Paths of Glory, Spartacus,* and *Lolita,* would mark a departure from *Fear and Desire* and *Killer's Kiss* not only in terms of scale of production and sophistication of screenwriting, acting, and cinematography, but also in terms of subjects and themes. In those initial efforts, Kubrick's stories emerged in a process akin to psychoanalytic free association—that is, a more or less unmediated flow of personal and historical ideas and concerns that in Kubrick's case were related to early impressions of a world rent by prejudice, violence, and war. The same basic point of view and its concomitant cinematic style would remain in his next four films, but they would share space with other subject matter and with the necessity of Kubrick refining his skills in collaboration with others, as producer, screenwriter, cinematographer, and director. Since he was no longer privately financing his films, he would have to put up with the requirements of those who were providing the money. This would begin to change significantly only with *Dr. Strangelove,* a film that would mark the style and independence from outside control over content and method characteristic of the classic period of Kubrickian cinema from 1964 to 1999.[50]

To help write the screenplay, Kubrick hired Jim Thompson, a Communist, an alcoholic, and an extremely talented writer of hard-boiled fiction who was living in New York at the time. Kubrick had read Thompson's *The Killer Inside Me* (1952) and had wanted to make a film of it. But the novel's story of a deputy sheriff who is a psychopathic murderer was too raw for Hollywood at the time.[51] Even though Kubrick was learning to work with established figures in the necessarily collaborative world of feature filmmaking, he and Thompson would end up in arbitration before the Writers Guild over screenwriting credit for *The Killing.* Kubrick lost the fight, but in the process secured Thompson's help with the script for *Paths of Glory.*[52] But otherwise, as in a famous confrontation with veteran cinematographer Lucien Ballard, Kubrick demonstrated the cool, calm, complete directorial control that would mark his career.[53]

*The Killing* is a film noir set, as it were, in the suburbs. In this, it marks the beginning of Kubrick's gradual departure from the dark, Expressionist cinematography he had inherited from the German masters of the first half of the twentieth century. While certain scenes early in the film reproduce the gloomy lighting he had used in *Killer's Kiss* and inherited from German Expressionism and New Objectivity, most of the film's action takes place in bright sunlight. This was a documentary style, heightened by Kubrick's use of a narration precisely outlining times, plans, and destinations, that was becoming increasingly common in the last stages of film noir in the mid-1950s. Like Robert Aldrich's *Kiss Me Deadly* (1955), the story takes place in Los Angeles. And like John Huston's *The Asphalt Jungle* (1950), it concerns the planning and execution of an elaborate crime. These films were a reflection of the unease at modern American life that was basic to film noir, but they extended their critique to all realms of society and in doing so further reduced—or even eliminated—the social and moral distance between the criminal and the respectable. For Huston, as for Kubrick, crime was an "occupation like any other, 'a left-handed form of human endeavor.'"[54] Both Huston and Kubrick display sympathy for their crooked and doomed characters. A year after *The Killing* was released, Kubrick was quoted as saying that "I've a peculiar weakness for criminals and artists—neither takes life as it is. Any tragic story has to be in conflict with things as they are."[55] In *The Killing,* Kubrick's characters are "picturesque, lovable-type losers—a dimwitted girlfriend, a chess-playing wrestler, a puppy-loving gun dealer, even a patient, invalid wife" who are "coldly viewed" but "enormously appealing" in their unadorned humanity.[56] The subjects are of black comedy, not tragedy; they are trapped, as we all are, in a doleful Kubrickian world of sunlight—natural and just now ominously artificial as well—in which the "threat *now* seemed to be everywhere."[57] With Hitchcock's *Psycho* (1960), as we will see, the threat would enter and remain in the home itself.

Kubrick saw all human beings as equally flawed, but he balanced this critical view with an overall sympathy that was especially strong for those who were victimized by Anglo-Saxon male domination of society. This included women and Jews, of course, as we have seen, but it also included homosexuals and blacks. Homosexuals make regular supporting appearances in his films even at a time when treatment of, much less sympathy for, homosexuality was as unacceptable as homosexuality was "unnatural." In *The Killing,* Marvin Unger feels a latent "fatherly and homosexual attachment" to Johnny. Kubrick typically is not trying to raise the issue of gay rights—indeed, many have seen elements of homophobia in his films—but is concerned with all those characteristics of human beings that complicate their lives and the lives of others. Marvin, like all the characters in *The Killing,* is presented clinically but also sympathetically as another conflicted and befuddled human being with his own particular devils and angels. His feelings for Johnny—which are aggravated by the presence of Johnny's girlfriend, Fay, and the intrusion of George Peatty's sluttish wife, Sherry—lead him to drink and to endanger the robbery plan.[58] Marvin is the first in a series of homosexuals in Kubrick films whose characters serve to variegate and enrich the complex tapestry of human motive, action, and fate that Kubrick weaves on screen. In (a scene cut from the original release of) *Spartacus,* Roman patrician Crassus flirts in his bath with his body servant, the slave Antoninus. General Jack D. Ripper in *Dr. Strangelove* represses his homosexuality with a self-loathing so violent in its acting out against the outside world as to remind one of Claggart in Herman Melville's *Billy Budd* (1924). At the same time, among the few characters in *Dr. Strangelove* with whom one can have some sympathy are Group Captain Lionel Mandrake and President Merkin Muffley, both of whom project a certain femininity in stark contrast to the hypermasculine males who surround them. In *A Clockwork Orange,* in response to Alex's own homoerotic appearance, his probation officer, Deltoid, has predatory homosexual inclinations, as do some of his fellow prison inmates. For *Barry Lyndon* Kubrick invents two gentle British officers bathing in a river, as both a bridge in the narrative and a link to the Unger–Clay relationship between Barry and Captain Grogan. *The Shining* hints that Overlook Hotel manager Stuart Ullman and his assistant Bill Watson are gay, while much of Gunnery Sergeant Hartman's ranting at his recruits in *Full Metal Jacket* is homophobic. And in *Eyes Wide Shut*

Kubrick substitutes a scene of homophobia for one of anti-Semitism and also invents a scene between Bill Harford and a wildly gay hotel desk clerk that might constitute a long-delayed reaction on Kubrick's part to Catholic Legion of Decency objections to what it saw as the homosexual nature of banter between Clare Quilty and hotel clerk George Swine in *Lolita*.[59]

Kubrick's treatment of race in *The Killing* is similarly episodic, but significant in that the subject is not treated in the novel. Nikki Arane has been hired to shoot a racehorse as part of the robbery plan, and he is to do so from a parking lot overlooking the backstretch. In the novel he pretends to be a paraplegic in order to convince the parking lot attendant to let him watch the race from his car. Everything goes like clockwork: Nikki shoots the horse and drives away from the now untended lot.[60] Kubrick, however, expands the discourse and the action of this scene. It begins with Nikki faking an injury from the Battle of the Bulge in order to gain admittance to the parking lot. The other change is the casting of a black actor to play the attendant. The attendant brusquely tells Nikki to park somewhere else, but Nikki's tale of paraplegia as a result of the war, along with a bribe, changes the attendant's attitude. It is implied in the conversation that the black man also got his "bum leg" in the war, so there is also an instant solidarity between veterans that reflects both the change in racial attitudes wrought by the war and the postwar gloss over the racism still extant in American society. It is perhaps significant in this respect that the attendant is played by James Edwards, who appeared as a soldier in a number of films, including the lead in *Home of the Brave*, the first Hollywood film to take on the issue of racism in the American army during the Second World War. Nikki is anxious to unload his rifle and has to get rid of the guy. So he calls him a "nigger," and the attendant departs with a scathing "Yes, boss."[61]

At the center of *The Killing* is actor Sterling Hayden, who had appeared in *The Asphalt Jungle* and who plays Johnny Clay, just out of prison with a foolproof plan to steal $2 million from a racetrack. Just as *The Killing* carries a double meaning of delirious criminal profit and the deaths that will claim most of the conspirators, Clay's name, invented by White, mournfully suggests fallibility (feet of clay) and an easy, fragile target (a clay pigeon). Mastermind Clay has put together a team consisting of George Peatty, a track cashier who wants to use the money to win the favor of his unfaithful wife; Randy Kennan, a policeman with gambling debts; Mike O'Reilly, the track bartender who needs money for the care of an invalid wife; the shooter Nikki, who owns a shooting range; Maurice Oboukhoff, played by Kubrick's old chess buddy Kola Kwariani from the chess club on Forty-second Street, as a wrestler who will stage a fight at the track as a diversion; and Marvin Unger.[62] The film retains the book's unique structure in which the unfolding of the plan is told several times from the perspectives of each of the participants. Kubrick would later be flattered by comparisons of this structure with that of Kurosawa's *Rashomon*, but *The Killing* does not pursue, as the Japanese film does, the terrible fact of there being no truth in the world because humans are unable to see beyond their own wishes and weaknesses.[63] The structure of *The Killing* is designed to impress the viewer with the meticulousness of Clay's plan and at the same time to reinforce the impression of a smothering fate—"the workings of chance in a closed system"—that will finally doom the plan.⁶⁴ These baleful elements of chance take two forms. The first, emphasized more in the novel, are the irrational psychological conflicts and weaknesses of the foolish individuals inhabiting a supposedly foolproof rational plan. The second, emphasized more in the film, are the forces of chance and contingency in the world at large that frustrate individual plans. This frustration animates the last words of the film, as a pair of detectives, prefigured as identical paper targets in an earlier scene, close in:

> **Fay:** Johnny, you've got to run.
> **Johnny:** What's the difference?⁶⁵

More important than words is Kubrick's exploitation of visual space to underline the callous indifference of the material world in a shot just before the last scene. As Johnny and his girlfriend, Fay, walk out of the airport building, they pass the American Airlines desk. This is where supervisor Mr. Grimes (his name a foreshadowing of night manager Mr. Swine in *Lolita*?) had required Johnny to take the disastrous step of checking—and not, as planned, carrying on—the suitcase full of cash that has just burst open on the tarmac. A two-shot shows Grimes and the desk agent in front of that portion of the airline logo (and the word "American") that reads, cruelly, "RICA," the Spanish word for "rich."⁶⁶

Even though *The Killing* is one of four films that marks an interim between Kubrick's early open responses to the world in which he had grown up and his later return to greater concentration on these early issues, these larger concerns still find their way onto the screen in this film. We have noted this already in terms of patriarchal persecution of women, homosexuals, and blacks. In *The Killing* Kubrick also makes initial, though somewhat tentative or even fortuitous, use of the number 7 as a symbol of violence and the organization of violence. It is impossible to know at which stage in the long and complicated process of writing, rehearsing, shooting, and editing a film Kubrick might have introduced or noticed some detail out of which he wished to construct and communicate meaning. When it comes to the number 7, however, he could draw from a long tradition of the mystic and sacred number 7, the number of the universe and the macrocosm for starters, being arguably the most culturally loaded of all numbers: seven days in the week, seven stages of life (Shakespeare, *As You Like It* [1599]) seven graces, seven sacraments, seven virtues, seven deadly sins, seven names of God, seven arts, seven seas, seven wonders of the world, seven bodily orifices (invoked in a scene cut from *Dr. Strangelove*), and so on.⁶⁷

Kubrick's symbolic use of the number 7 is most consistent, however, with Dante's designation in the *Inferno* (1300) of the Seventh Circle of Hell as that reserved for the *violent*. Of the six films Kubrick directed between 1953 and 1962, five, including *The Killing*, have to do with the organization of violence either by states or by individuals.⁶⁸ The number is also used in its larger macrocosmic sense to symbolize a universal order or even disorder, within which human beings are buffeted and bludgeoned by forces beyond their recognition or control. Since the symbolic associations of the number 7 are so widespread, it is no surprise that White himself in his novel designates the fateful race during which the horse Black (in the film, Red) Lightning will be shot as the "Seventh race—the big race of the year."[69] Kubrick consistently places the number both aurally in the narration and visually within the action of the film to express the world's "order of chaos" as well as specific instances of violence. Instances of the latter are clustered around shooter Nikki Arane in the parking lot before and during the seventh race, with Kubrick's habitual deep focus showing a car behind Nikki's MG with a license plate that reads T177877.[70] The number 7 is also the symbolic structure within which the action of the entire film takes place. Even more than *Paths of Glory*, *The Killing* is structured around the precise timing needed for the success of a complex operation, but the number mentioned most often is that associated with fateful forces beyond human control that will in fact betray this plan. The narrator introduces us to Johnny Clay one evening at 7:00 P.M., as "perhaps the most important thread in the unfinished fabric" of a robbery will take place in seven days (two subsequent scenes are "three days later" and "four days later"). On the day of the operation, on what "might be the last day of his life," we see Johnny at "seven that morning" as he sits down on Marvin Unger's bed and wakes his friend to say goodbye. Then the narrator tells us that Johnny arrives at the airport at "exactly 7 am." This is either a mistake and/or it is done intentionally to emphasize the web-like meaning of the number. This discrepancy may also be designed to undermine the audience's faith in the narrator (as, some have argued, occurs in *Barry Lyndon*) in order to give viewers, too, the feeling of an unreliable and inexplicable universe as well as the ultimate futility of human plans. Another possible instance of this last narrative stratagem is that the seventh race, the $100,000 Lansdowne Stakes, is announced as being scheduled to start at 4:30 while the narrator tells us that Nikki "was dead at 4:24."[71] Either the race started early, a minor instance of things not going as planned, or once again we are being told not to trust the narrator as an alienation effect to underscore the chaos that undermines all human endeavors.

In addition to the nondiegetic narrator outside the action of the film, Kubrick uses diegetic sound not only to exploit the aural space created by film but also to suggest inherent chaos. As Fay is waiting for Johnny at the airport (and, foreshadowing an imminent betrayal, a Yellow Cab driver in threatening deep focus ogles her), the public-address system twice announces the arrival of American Airlines "DC-7 service." And as Johnny's bag full of cash is placed on the conveyor belt, American Airlines announces the "DC-7 service" on which Johnny and Fay are scheduled.[72] While in the novel George Peatty shoots Johnny, an act that emphasizes the psychological conflicts within and among the characters in the plot, in the film it is an impersonal fate that destroys Johnny's plans and life. A small dog runs onto the tarmac, causing the truck carrying Johnny's bag to swerve. The bag falls and bursts open, and the cash flies up and away in the prop wash of an airliner. Once again in a Kubrick film, machines—and their human inventors and operators—are agents of disruption. The role of the dog is also an example of the fact that this destructive symbiosis is shared by the contingencies of nature—organic as well as inorganic—as a whole. So it is fully appropriate that a final mechanical conveyance, along with its human operators, betrays Fay and Johnny as they attempt to escape from the airport. As Johnny stares glumly into space, Fay desperately signals three different taxis to stop. But all three Yellow Cabs speed off, at least two of which have on their doors identification codes beginning with the number 7.[73]

## *Paths of Glory* (1957)

*The Killing* marked Stanley Kubrick as a young director to watch. One of those watching was actor Kirk Douglas, to whom Kubrick sold the screenplay for a film called *Paths of Glory*.[74] Douglas got United Artists to back production of the film in Germany by his company, Bryna Productions. It would cost less to shoot the film than in France, and it was also the case that the French would not be pleased with the depiction of their officers in the film.[75] In the end, the film did not play in French theaters until 1976 and was similarly banned from American military bases.[76] Kubrick's connection to the project actually dated back to 1942 when as a fourteen-year-old he read a novel by Canadian novelist and screenwriter Humphrey Cobb. In 1934 Cobb had read an account in the *New York Times* of a trial in France in which the widows and families of men shot for mutiny in 1915 had sued the French army for damages. The case had been in the French courts for more than ten years. Before a special military tribunal, the men were acquitted and the widows received 1 franc—"7 Cents Each," the headline reads—while the families received nothing at all. But in the French case the villainy rested with the court. The motive for the low award was clearly misplaced patriotism and a desire not to harm the reputation of the army, especially at a time of renewed German threat under the new Nazi government. The men had been chosen by lot, and the 1934 tribunal ruled that the War Council would never have condemned the men if it had known how they had been chosen.[77] Cobb, himself a First World War veteran, was outraged by the decision, and the result was the novel *Paths of Glory*.

Kubrick and Harris were looking for a property to develop as a follow-up to *The Killing*. Kubrick suggested *Paths of Glory*, the script for which was written by Kubrick, Jim Thompson, and novelist Calder Willingham. Willingham would later maintain that the idea for the final scene featuring a young woman singing to the troops was his idea, not Kubrick's, while Douglas was furious with Kubrick for submitting a draft with the condemned men winning a reprieve, a happy ending Kubrick allegedly proposed for the purposes of making the film a commercial hit.[78] Kubrick's attraction to Cobb's novel almost certainly began with its title, a quotation from Thomas Gray's famous poem, "Elegy Written in a Country Churchyard" (1750): "The boast of heraldry, the pomp of pow'r, / The paths of glory lead but to the grave." The novel emphasizes the tragic juxtaposition of notions of traditional military glory and the slaughter that was trench warfare in Europe between 1914 and 1918. Cobb focuses on the lives and the deaths of the men executed for their exhausted units' refusal to advance into murderous German machine-gun fire. In the novel, the officers remain in the background, undefined and even unnamed. We see the world of war as the men in the trenches saw it. Kubrick changes the perspective to focus on the officers, while the condemned men for much of the film remain, along with their fellow soldiers, in the background.[79] Kubrick embraces the rest of the stanza in Gray's poem having to do with those whose power in life cannot save them from equality with the powerless in death. (This is also the thrust of the last line of *Barry Lyndon*.) By emphasizing the motives and actions of the officers and, behind them, the forces of the government and the press, Kubrick's view waxes more cynical than that of Gray or Cobb: the "paths of glory" are those trod by officers advancing themselves at the cost of their soldiers' lives.[80] There is no equality in death, at least in terms of who dies when and for what reason. In Kubrick's *Paths of Glory*, we see one more terrible instance of the modern state's organization of violence, the twentieth century's most deadly form of the rationalized bureaucratic system and mentality that Weber saw as replacing a world of humane values. It is no accident in this regard that Kubrick would some years later quote Matthew Arnold, about whom he learned from Trilling at Columbia, in speaking of life as "a darkling plain . . . where ignorant armies clash by night."[81]

Kubrick's film also reflects discontent with the stultifying American triumphalism of the 1950s and its attendant conformism, anti-intellectualism, and paranoid McCarthyite anti-Communism. Although Kubrick biographer John Baxter discounts the idea, there might have been intentional irony in opening *Paths of Glory* on Christmas Day in 1957.[82] At the very least, Kubrick would have seen the irony, and the effects of it are certainly not irrelevant to greater appreciation of the film's argument. Norman Kagan has pointed out that *Paths of Glory* was being developed and produced at the same time Joseph Heller was beginning to write his novel about the Second World War, *Catch-22* (1961), and that the works resemble each other in their portrait of an absurd, violent world of war.[83] The two world wars themselves were a major cause of this trend of disillusionment in experience, thought, and artistic expression, since both wars in their own unique yet shared ways brought into serious doubt the confident Western ideal of a rational universe in which knowledge and science would pave the way toward the progressive moral and material betterment of humanity. Indeed, what was so shattering about the First World War in particular was the way in which the mass production of the Industrial Revolution was, like Frankenstein's monster, turned in destructive fashion upon its human makers in the form of weapons limitless in their lethality and number.

As in Heller's novel, the war in Kubrick's film is essentially that between the officers and the men. The action in the film alternates between the grime and horror of the trenches and General Mireau's headquarters in a château behind the lines. Kubrick chose as a shooting location for the latter Schleissheim Palace outside Munich, an appropriate choice given that it was built by the Bavarian Wittelsbach dynasty in the Baroque style of controlled exuberance that celebrates the power of the state. Kubrick symbolizes this power in his usual way by naming Mireau's headquarters the "Château d'Aigle" (Eagle Castle). In contrast to the dark, claustrophobic trenches and dugouts in which the soldiers live, the château is light and airy. In this world, the sun shines only on the elite, emphasizing their distance from the dark world of everyday humanity and their resultant impersonal coldness toward those at the lower stations of humanity. The social distance between the high command composed of the old aristocracy and the common soldiery is underlined in Kubrick's symbolism by the fact that the Wittelsbachs' palace was a summer residence, just like two other Kubrick "high spaces": the Overlook Hotel in *The Shining*, open only in the summer; and the mansion in *Eyes Wide Shut* named "Somerton," which in Anglo-Saxon means "summer dwelling." On a metaphysical level, these high spaces represent the Apollonian striving for rational mastery over the world, while the labyrinths that inhabit both the high and low realms represent the Dionysian impulse toward submersion in the dynamic elemental powers of life. The Apollonian space leads to stasis and paralysis; the Dionysian labyrinth, to movement and entrapment.[84] In *Paths of Glory*, Kubrick's fluid dolly shots physically reproduce the officers' labyrinthine plots for advantage and advancement within the high rooms of Machiavellian power. The same camerawork expresses the claustrophobia of the labyrinthine trenches in which the soldiers are trapped on all sides by violent death.

The film begins with a labyrinthine conversation between General Mireau and his superior from General Headquarters, General Broulard. Broulard tempts the professionally ambitious Mireau into attacking an impregnable German position, the Anthill, by "reluctantly" mentioning a potential promotion. Mireau accepts the assignment, disavowing, of course, any selfish motives for doing so. Mireau thus lives up to his name, which rhymes with "château" and perhaps also connotes the French word for "mirror" (*miroir*) and the verbs *mirer* (to covet) and *se mirer* (to admire oneself). Broulard too earns his name, which resembles *brouillard*, or "fog." This connotes not so much the famous "fog of war" as the shadowy and devious plotting of a master Machiavellian in the sense of the German expression for stealth, *bei Nacht und Nebel* (by night and fog), also the name of a 1941 decree under which the Germans deported French prisoners to concentration camps and which Alain Resnais adopted as the title of his film about humankind's failing memory of the camps, *Nuit et Brouillard* (1955). The novel, too, plays with both French and crude Anglo-Saxon in this manner: General Assolant is Mireau, Colonel La Bouchère (butcher) is the sadistic president of the court martial, and Private Langlois (from *angois* [anguish]) is one of the condemned men.[85] Colonel Dax, a character, though a less major one, in Cobb's novel, is appalled at the plan to attack the Anthill ("the Pimple," or site of infection, in the novel), but as a good soldier accepts the order.

The attack is such a disaster that Mireau orders his own artillery to fire on French troops who have not left their trenches. Artillery commander Captain Rousseau, a Kubrick invention, asks that the order be given in writing. His request is denied, but before the shelling can begin, the attack as a whole comes to an end. Mireau, apoplectic over his men's failure to advance his career, orders a court-martial that very afternoon, rasping "If those little sweethearts won't face German bullets, they'll face French ones!" For his part, Captain Rousseau might be seen to have lived up to his name—that is, the philosopher Jean-Jacques Rousseau, who theorized that natural man uncorrupted by civilization is basically good. Kubrick undercuts this assumption by having Rousseau explain his refusal to General Mireau: "Suppose you're killed, where'll I be?"[86] His ethic is clearly that of someone looking out for himself within a hierarchy. Like everyone else, including the idealist Dax, Rousseau is trapped by the conditions of a civilization that has newly armored and organized innate human aggression through the power of modern weaponry and the ethos of bureaucratic organization.[87] The other junior officers, with the exception of course of Colonel Dax, are worse. Lieutenant Roget is a drunk, a coward, a liar, and finally a murderer. Sergeant-Major Boulanger, taken from the novel, no doubt refers to General Georges Boulanger, a French politician synonymous with extreme nationalism and militarism. It is Boulanger who efficiently and heartlessly organizes the firing squad. Major Saint-Auban, General Mireau's slick, sychophantic aide-de-camp, helps modernize his superior's old-fashioned aristocratic social prejudice into the racist Social Darwinism of the new century. Discussing the night's casualties from an artillery barrage, General Mireau criticizes the men for swarming "together like a bunch of flies" when under fire, while Saint-Auban observes: "Herd instinct, I suppose, kind of a lower animal sort of thing." Dax's response to Saint-Auban is Kubrick's: "Kind of a human sort of thing, it seems to me, or don't you make the distinction?"[88] Saint-Auban is another Kubrick name, which might connote *mettre au ban*, or "banish."

The "other" enemy of course is the German army, whose soldiers, unlike the "grotesquely helmeted figures" in the novel, are never glimpsed in the film.[89] Only the loud and lethal effects of the artillery, machine guns, and rifles fired from the teeming "Anthill" are witnessed. Aside from the West German policemen who play the soldiers in the film, the face of the German army in Kubrick's film is literally that of General Mireau, who bears a dueling scar across his right cheek peculiar to the German custom of the university duel (*Mensur*). Actor George Macready bore such a scar that was usually covered by makeup or filled by lighting. Kubrick, however, accentuates it, perhaps in part due to its coincidental German associations in the context of a war film. The duel of honor was a tradition across Europe, a practice governments largely managed to ban in the course of the nineteenth century. Only throughout Germany did university students conduct duels in which the object was not to kill for satisfaction of an insult to honor, but to wound the face and neck so as to produce the scars that would be a badge of courage and status.[90] Like Conrad's naming of Kurtz in *Heart of Darkness*, this historical misplacement "effectively internationalizes" Mireau, just as his slapping a shell-shocked soldier in the manner of Second World War American General George Patton also makes him a twentieth-century archetypal figure.[91] The scar also simply makes him look more malevolent. But one reason he looks more malevolent with a dueling scar on his face is that such a disfigurement was associated in early-twentieth-century Western culture with the evil Germans, especially Prussian Junker officers, with whom other nations often found themselves at war. Given Kubrick's immersion in the films—especially Stroheim's, among others—and the history of the period from before the Second World War, his highlighting of a German artifact was obviously, like Conrad's, personally, historically, and artistically appropriate as well.

But the Germans also serve as a means to the film's antiwar ends. The only German character in the film is the young woman who is brought into a bar to entertain the troops. Played by Susanne Christian, who would become Christiane Kubrick, the girl sings "Der Treue Husar" (1825), a folk song popular among German troops in the First World War about a "faithful soldier" who rushes to the deathbed of his beloved. This, penultimate, scene is obviously designed as a sorrowful testament to our common humanity and the tragedy of war, an effect immediately challenged by the bitter irony of the concluding scene of the film, in which Dax tells a subordinate to give the men a few more minutes before they are to be ordered to go back into the line to kill and be killed by Germans.[92] The irony and tragedy are historically magnified by the fact that a hussar was a cavalry soldier who originated in Hungary in the fifteenth century. This was exactly the type of weapon that was literally exterminated in Europe by the machinery of the First World War, a fact alluded to by a scene in the film in which a roaring motorcycle and sidecar, carrying two men, frightens a pair of horses.[93] Again Kubrick links the organic and the mechanical in historically meaningful concurrent juxtaposition, union, and conflict.

The three condemned men—Férol, Arnaud, and Paris—are victims not only of the vicious logic, or illogic, of war, but also of the cruel class system that still ruled much of European life in the early twentieth century. And Private Férol has been chosen because he is "a social undesirable," another reference to the growing trend in Europe (and America) toward eugenic thinking—that is, the necessity for societies and governments to weed out "inferior" human beings and "scientifically" promote the growth of superior human "stock."[94] Cobb places Férol in a more specifically French situation, which apparently Kubrick thought too involved for a film and its audience. In the novel Férol is a replacement for another "incorrigible," Private Meyer. Férol (among other things, a "mental defective, chronic alcoholic") is chosen in order to avoid the possible public repercussions of another Dreyfus Affair, in which a Jewish officer was falsely accused by the army of espionage and eventually exonerated as a result of public outcry.[95] Kubrick prefers to focus in this case on individual stories with which the film audience can readily identify, although he does, as we have seen, incorporate the more general modern racist eugenic thinking, if, as usual, not the specific European "problem" of Jews. Kubrick does not let other classes off the hook, however, for unlike the actual event reflected in the novel the film has only one of the men, Private Arnaud, chosen by lot. Corporal Paris is chosen by the bourgeois Lieutenant Roget in order to eliminate the only witness to his accidental killing of Private Lejeune (from *jeune* [young]), a name that revisits in a particularly murderous fashion the fundamental conflict in *The Cabinet of Dr. Caligari* of old men condemning young men to death.

The chief antagonists, Mireau and Broulard, represent the declining but still powerful old order of aristocratic privilege, while the lawyer Dax is one of those Kubrick intermediate figures who attempt in vain (or don't attempt) to intercede with the masters on behalf of victims.[96] On the night before the execution, officers and ladies are shown dancing in the château. (The condemned men are being kept in a horse barn.) The couples are dancing to Johann Strauss's "The Artist's Life Waltz" (1872), a typically reflexive Kubrick choice that not only joins the world of art and beauty to the world of power and violence, but also offers an oblique comment on the artist Kubrick's own fascination with the men who preside over the world of power and violence. But what is most striking about this particular dance sequence are the figures of General Mireau and his partner. In contrast to the other couples who turn waltzing circles around the floor, Mireau unsmilingly moves his partner back and forth ("in-and-out," as it were) in a stiff and lifeless parody of a dance designed to express the emotional as well as, in the words of Mireau soul mate General Ripper in *Dr. Strangelove*, "the physical act of love."[97] The general shoves his partner in the way he fatally pushes his men into battle for the sake of his own vanity and ambition. In the scene that follows, Kubrick toys with the audience's possible expectation of a reprieve for the men as Dax reports to Broulard that Mireau ordered Rousseau to fire on his own men. Broulard *is* concerned, but not for the men. It is only after the execution that we learn that, instead of saving face by saving the men, Broulard has decided to make Mireau the scapegoat for the failed attack in order to convince the government and the press that the army is doing its job. Broulard even offers an outraged Dax Mireau's job, assuming that is what Dax wanted all along.[98]

Kubrick's damning portrayal of human beings at war with one another is advanced by even greater symbolic recourse to the number 7. This strategy is of course rendered easy by the organizational and decorative practices of military life. Kubrick changes the unit numbers used in the novel to ones dominated by 7 and displays them prominently in several close-ups: Dax's regiment is the 701st, the court-martial officers are from the 727th, and the 710th supplies the firing squad, while Mireau promises support from the attack, which is to commence at 7:00 A.M., from the 72nd Division.[99] Kubrick's message is subtle yet clear. The macrocosm is webbed darkly with fate, as signaled by that number most associated with both the divine and the malevolent. As a result, Kubrick's *Paths of Glory* is an antiwar film but not a pacifist one. Kubrick offers no solutions except, possibly, efforts at mitigation, which, however, are likely to fail. The game is rigged in favor of the amoral and immoral powerful. In this, Kubrick was partly a pragmatist. As he pointed out in an interview in 1968, he was not sure what pacifism meant since the Second World War, the most destructive war in history, was also a just war against Hitler. But "there have been tragically senseless wars such as World War One and the current mess in Vietnam and the plethora of religious wars that pockmark history."[100] His pragmatism was not instrumental, however, but a result of bitter realism and pessimism. For Kubrick, the historical record, particularly and painfully in the modern era, is one of regular triumphs of aggression and violence. In *Paths of*

*Glory*, therefore, the theme is not resistance but victimization. The men realize they have no chance. They are trapped. As are we all.

## *Spartacus* (1960)

In 1959 Kirk Douglas's Bryna Productions was making *Spartacus* for Universal International when Douglas called Kubrick to replace Anthony Mann as director. Due to lack of directorial control, *Spartacus* is a bastard child that Kubrick disowned. An early and apparently easy decision Kubrick did make was to fire German actress Sabine Bethmann as the female lead; she was replaced by English actress Jean Simmons. He had a much harder time dealing with big-name actors Laurence Olivier, Charles Laughton, Peter Ustinov, and Douglas himself. Kubrick was not pushed around to the degree that one might think he would have been, but he was compelled to compromise his vision for the film given all the Hollywood firepower assembled in front of and behind the camera. The most important effect of *Spartacus* on Kubrick, therefore, was "to strengthen his resolve to safeguard his artistic independence in making future films."[101]

Kubrick's biggest complaint was his lack of control over the script, which he thought contained a weak story. In this criticism, he was reflecting the fact that even though he had not planned on making a film about the Roman slave revolt led by Spartacus from 73 to 71 B.C.E., he had read at least one book on the subject.[102] And in that book, Arthur Koestler's *The Gladiators* (1939), the theme is not the idealistic portrayal of a struggle for liberation that animated the script that Dalton Trumbo had written for *Spartacus*, but the story of "why revolutions go wrong."[103]

Koestler for seven years had been a German Communist who, disillusioned by Stalin's ruthless dictatorship in the Soviet Union, had quit the Communist Party in 1938. Trumbo, who had gone to jail in the late 1940s for refusing to name names in the House Un-American Affairs Committee investigation of alleged Communist influence in Hollywood, had been blacklisted and reduced to writing (very successful) scripts at a discount and under pseudonym from exile in Mexico. Douglas hired Trumbo to write, as "Sam Jackson," the script for a film that would romanticize the timeless struggle for human freedom. In this, the film reflected not only—or even not so much—Trumbo's Depression-era sympathy for social classes trod down by a system of wealth and corruption but also—or perhaps rather—the common American and Hollywood heroic image of everyman's struggle for individual freedom most recently threatened by McCarthyism. This approach was behind the original casting idea that the slaves be played by American actors, with their pedestrian accents, and the Romans by English actors, with their patrician ones. Another trace of the American context for the film was the casting of African-American actor Woody Strode as the gladiator Draba. Draba, who lectures Spartacus on the wisdom of gladiators not making friends with one another since they all live in a kill-or-be-killed environment, spares Spartacus's life in their duel out of outrage at the patrician spectators. He rushes the tribune where they sit and is killed. His body is then strung up in the gladiators' quarters as an example. This episode seems a clear reference to the civil rights struggle just beginning in the United States. The display of his body resembles a southern lynching, while his saving of the life of a white man is a way to generate respect for him in a white audience while also reassuring that audience they have nothing to fear from blacks. Howard Fast, who had written the novel on which the screenplay was based and who had been jailed for his politics, was more radical in his Marxist views than Trumbo. Fast had written the original draft of the screenplay and hated Trumbo's script for what he saw as truckling to comfortable American bourgeois opinion. For his part, Trumbo felt that his script had been sabotaged by Kubrick, a view held by other commentators in noting the clichéd montage sequences that approach parody in the second half of the film. It also seems, however, that the film had progressively become much more Douglas's than Trumbo's or Kubrick's.[104] Since *Spartacus,* as written, was a mishmash of sentimental Marxism and American liberalism, it did not accord with Kubrick's less sanguine view of humanity. He was much more sympathetic to Koestler's disillusionment with the present "century of abortive revolutions" and the concomitant growth in state power for which Koestler found expression in the brutal actions of a slave army twenty-one centuries ago.[105]

Kubrick later said that his chief objection to the Trumbo script was that it was not historically accurate. This was true, though the reasons were various. For example, in Fast's novel, the last slave crucified by the victorious Romans, David (mentioned once and only by name in the film), is a Jew. Whether this is historically accurate or not, Fast's story reflects the fact that many Jews were among the slaves of the Roman Republic, something that presumably for reasons of narrative and box-office economy was written out of the film. One of Kirk Douglas's original motives for wanting to film Fast's novel was that the Jewish Douglas identified with the slaves. For Douglas, it was the general principle of affirming human dignity. For Fast and Trumbo, it was the more specific issue of their own political persecution. For both these reasons, the film does accurately portray Rome as a decadent slave state.[106] But Trumbo's insistence on a victory for Spartacus in the eventual decline of the Roman Republic under Crassus is inaccurate and reflects Trumbo's desire to bury American McCarthyism once and for all. He even has incipient dictator Crassus declare that "lists of the disloyal have been compiled."[107] Trumbo disliked the changes Douglas and Kubrick made that softened this impression of long-term political victory for the revolt. As usual, Kubrick was better at portraying the perpetrators and the effects upon their victims than at exalting the oppressed, however much he sympathized with them. He focused on problems rather than solutions. In *Spartacus,* as in his "own" films, Kubrick portrays the oppressed as being crushed by the superior force of the machine-like legions of Roman soldiers massing onto the battlefield. Even Trumbo was impressed with the battlefield sequence and its sad, bloody outcome. In this, he was seeing the antiwar Kubrick of *Paths of Glory, Dr. Strangelove,* and *Full Metal Jacket* who could offer little hope but a great deal of sobering, and perhaps instructive, reality.[108]

Instead of Trumbo's political triumph, Kubrick and Douglas came up with a concluding scene of tragic personal justification in which Varinia holds up their son to Spartacus as he dies on a cross along the Appian Way, on which Varinia and Spartacus's son are riding to freedom. Natalie Zemon Davis has pointed out that such an ending corresponds with a practice among slaves to establish marriages and families in spite of Roman prohibition. As such, she argues, the film highlights a form of slave resistance relatively unexplored by historians up until that time. (It was also good box office, since it allowed the foregrounding of the love story between Varinia and Spartacus.) Davis has speculated that Kubrick was moved to this type of ending in part because of the birth of his daughter Anya in 1959.[109] As it turns out, Trumbo had his own idea about using marriage as a sign of resistance to oppression: a mass-marriage scene of slaves just before the last battle with the Roman legions. According to Trumbo, Kubrick rejected this scene by saying that it reminded him of the marriage of Hitler and Eva Braun. Trumbo and Kubrick simply had a different generational and personal experience of history: "Kubrick's view of human behavior and its dangers was more somber than that of the 'progressive' older man. Trumbo's youth had been marked by his anger at the bosses, his hopes as a union member, and his dreams as a socialist; Kubrick's youth by the horrors of World War II, the Nazi assault on the Jews, and the atomic bomb."[110]

## *Lolita* (1962)

In 1955 Vladimir Nabokov's novel *Lolita* was becoming a best-seller and *cause célèbre* against censorship. Backed by United Artists, Harris-Kubrick Pictures purchased an option on the book. Because of the controversy over the book's subject matter of adult sexual interest in a child between the ages of nine and fourteen, for which in the book Nabokov created the neologism "nymphet," Harris-Kubrick had trouble getting a studio interested in actually bankrolling a film. Kubrick invited Nabokov to come to Los Angeles in order to write a new screenplay. Harris and Kubrick had decided that the only way to film the story was to make Lolita a somewhat wily and even predatory teenager of around fourteen and thus an obvious — if still young — sex object rather than a child. This in fact coincided with one of the original characteristics of the Nabokovian nymphet: her ability to manipulate on the basis of an almost demoniac quality. Nabokov wrote a very long screenplay, which Kubrick and Harris pared down radically. Predictably, Kubrick was not willing to accede to studio control and set about looking for a backer not under the constraints of American censorship. He found it in England, where Associated Artists, as Seven Arts UK, benefited from a British cinema industry program to promote productions in England; the casting of English actors James Mason and Peter Sellers satisfied one of the requirements for British financial support. In the end, script alterations managed to avoid censorship not only in England but also in the United States. The film was produced by

Harris-Kubrick through a Swiss corporation, Anya Productions, named after Stanley and Christiane's first daughter, and was distributed by MGM. In 1961 Kubrick bought himself out of his association with Bryna Productions, and a year later he and Harris agreed to dissolve their partnership. Both Harris and Kubrick had decided that they wanted to strike off on their own.[111]

Nabokov's *Lolita* appealed to Kubrick in many ways: its rich, symbolic, playful, sexual language (Camp Q for Girls on Lake Climax, Mona Farlow, Ramsdale [New Hampshire], the Frigid Queen malt shop, Beardsley College); its exploration of "the red sun of desire and decision (the two things that create a live world)," which create in Humbert Humbert "a cesspool of rotting monsters"; and its stripping examination of Humbert's "masked lust" for that which is abhorred (because desired) by respectable society.[112] Even with the movie censorship of the time, Kubrick was able to add to the sort of sexual wordplay just cited (all of which made it into the film), as, for example, when during the game of Ping-Pong Quilty says, "I'll take the service again, if you don't mind. I sort of like to have it up this end."[113] Kubrick was also intrigued by Nabokov's use of a *Doppelgänger* for Humbert in the figure of the smutty and—invisible or disguised—omnipresent Quilty ("guilt," "quill" [writer], "quilt" [patchwork]). Kubrick was equally impressed with Sellers, whose improvisational ability to assume the masks of other people intensified the uncanny effect of Quilty's role as the embodiment of all of Humbert's fears and desires, such as when Quilty with typical uncanny effect poses as a policeman during a State Police Convention at the Enchanted Hunters Hotel:

**Humbert:** I thought perhaps you had someone with you.
**Quilty:** I'm not really with someone. I'm with you.[114]

Nabokov, for his part, later had both positive and negative things to say about Kubrick's "munificent" film.[115] Although the focus of the film is on Humbert's sexual obsessiveness, homosexual panic, and paranoia, Nabokov, unlike Kubrick, thought Freud to be "crude" and "medieval" with drab excuses for sin and crime.[116] While Kubrick embraced Freud's appreciation for the gray shades that compose the psychological and moral life of humanity, in *Lolita* he too parodies the profession in sexual and political terms in the figure of Peter Sellers's Germanic Dr. Zempf (*Senf* [mustard], as in the sexual "cut the mustard"), who also refers to an associate named Dr. Cutler ("cuddler"; "cut" or "geld").

The novel and the film share the patriarchal perspective on women, homosexuals, and African-Americans that reflects the culture of the times, while the film reflects Kubrick's thoroughgoing critique of a male-dominated society. The film, even if only obliquely, also links a Nabokov mention of German domestic help to the larger issue of American racism through Charlotte's reference to "a colored girl" as a domestic; black help is also seen at the Enchanted Hunters Hotel and at a hospital.[117] Such casual—or is it?—inclusion of blacks as part of the social landscape of menial work might only be a thoughtless artifact of early 1960s American filmmaking. Or, given Kubrick's previous and subsequent condemnation of the dominant Western social order, it might be critically intentioned. Finally, Kubrick, like Nabokov, does not spare women critique. Just as Nabokov's Lolita is the sexually predatory nymphet, her equally predatory mother in one scene in the film wears a leopard-print belt and in three others a leopard-print dress.[118]

There are also small details that were to become symbolic elements in Kubrick's brooding on the Holocaust. Even though these details existed for other reasons in *Lolita,* the coincidence of their appearance and context registered in Kubrick's observant eye and omnivorous mind enough that they were available for historical use later. For example, there is the association between death at the hands of the state and the color yellow, which would achieve significant symbolic expression in *The Shining:* Quilty, just shot by Humbert, who is stalking him up a staircase, oddly mentions that electric chairs are painted yellow.[119] A similar association with Nazi mechanics of murder that would show up in *The Shining* possibly also had its genesis or reinforcement in Kubrick's mind when in the novel Humbert considers the possibility of murdering Charlotte in words that would be transported almost wholly into the film:

> I sat down beside my wife so noiselessly that she started.
> "Shall we go in?" she asked.
> "We shall in a minute. Let me follow a train of thought."
> I thought. More than a minute passed.
> "All right. Come on."
> "Was I on that train?"
> "You certainly were."[120]

A more significant coincidence-cum-inspiration in terms of Kubrick's symbolic legacy is Nabokov's use of the number 42 as an instance of the workings of what Humbert darkly labels "McFate." The room number at the Enchanted Hunters, where Humbert has taken Lolita to consummate their relationship, is 342; the Haze home in Ramsdale is at 342 Lawn Street; Humbert later notes that he has stayed at 342 hotels, motels, and tourist homes during his travels with Lolita; and it is in 1952, when he is forty-two years old, that he dies after writing the account of his affair with Lolita.[121] In the screenplay Nabokov further emphasizes the fateful reappearance of the number: a scene at 42, rue Baudelaire in Paris, Humbert's hometown; rooms 242, 342, and 442 at the hotel; a highway 42; and room 342 at Beardsley College.[122] As Kubrick would in *The Shining,* Nabokov in connection with 42 also uses mirrors as well as multiples of 7: Humbert's second encounter with a "nymphet" occurs (in 1947) twenty-four years after his first; 24 Pritchard Road; Sunday, the 24th ("*Brute Force* and *Possessed* were coming to both theaters"); 14 Thayer Street; and in the screenplay and film the very American Haze phone number, Ramsdale 1776.[123] Only room 242 at the Enchanted Hunters Hotel appears in the film, though Kubrick invokes the number 7 by having Charlotte's husband dead for seven years.[124]

While Nabokov apparently makes nothing of any symbolic historical import of the number 42, there are in the novel scattered Humbert references to anti-Semitism and one to the Holocaust about "the brown wigs of tragic old women who had just been gassed."[125] These survive in the film only in an oblique conversation between Humbert and Charlotte regarding his belief in God and in one more of Quilty's *avant-mort* ravings ("You are either Australian, or a German refugee. This is a Gentile's house—you better run along."), leaving out, though, Quilty's reference to "an old Stern-Luger."[126] However, the film does invoke Nazis, as in Lolita's "Sieg Heil!" to her mother and in the disquieting figure of Dr. Zempf.[127]

While Kubrick in *Lolita* makes nothing at all of the symbolic association of the number 42 with the Holocaust that he would make in *The Shining*, the origins of that later association lie at least partly in this earlier film. That the one instance of the uncanny reappearance of the number from Nabokov's novel that he does include is associated with a hotel is particularly important in this respect. For the Overlook Hotel in *The Shining* is the physical and historical location for the manifestation of the Holocaust also symbolized by the number 42. Kubrick rightly sees the degree to which Nabokov emphasizes the appearance of the number with respect to places of lodging other than one's home. (For Nabokov himself, a 1940 émigré from St. Nazaire just ahead of *les Nazis*, they were homes since all his adult life he lived in hotels around the world.[128]) And these places in Nabokov's novel are ones of imprisonment, threat, and danger: Humbert/Lolita's room 342 is near that sign of greatest institutionalized danger, the fire escape.[129] Kubrick's *Lolita* also opens with a shot anticipating the opening sequence of *The Shining*: Humbert's station wagon driving into the mist toward Quilty's mansion, which seems less a home than an elegant hotel for a jumbled disarray of old European (like Humbert himself) cultural artifacts. In this opening traveling shot, the camera follows the station wagon just as Humbert and Lolita are stalked by Quilty while on their car trip, and just as Jack Torrance's car is literally pursued by an airborne camera up a serpentine mountain road leading to the Overlook Hotel. That these large residences are places of potential and actual terror and murder are emphasized in both films by regular reference to the fear and horror embedded in fables and fairy tales. Alexander Walker has noted that the opening shot of *Lolita* "emerges out of a ground mist that might have drifted over from German legend."[130] This is certainly no accident, for Nabokov writes that Quilty's "ancestral home" is located on Grimm Road.[131] Kubrick himself shot this second-unit footage in America, coincidentally "at Gettysburg in the fog [as] we drove through the battlefield with all these statues and monuments."[132]

The year 1962 marks the end of the early phase of Kubrick's filmmaking. *Lolita* was both the first and the last Kubrick film based on an in/famous novel. From now on, Kubrick would, as before, choose little-known works for ideas "crystallizing out of his more general concerns."[133] This would free him from popular and critical expectations and, in allowing him to present his own vision all the way from the source to the screen, give him the control he so desired for personal and artistic reasons.

# 6
# DIRECTED BY STANLEY KUBRICK, 1964–1999

During the 1960s Stanley Kubrick, like almost everyone else, was affected by the political and cultural changes that were overtaking the Western world. In Kubrick's own world of film, the Hollywood studios were beginning to feel the first stirrings early in the decade of challenge to their style of, and monopoly over, modern commercial film. The old moguls were gone, to some extent replaced by new moguls but also accompanied by individuals and institutions that found new ways to make lots of art as well as lots of money. Many of the new filmmakers, including Kubrick, wanted their films to matter in terms of addressing and dramatizing old and new struggles against injustice, oppression, and authority. For Kubrick, this meant returning to original concerns about the second Great War of the twentieth century that had left certain strong traces in his earliest films. This would strengthen Kubrick's recourse in the later films to the communication of ideas, particularly through the selective use of objects, colors, numbers, and music. This strategy reached its most systematic and historically informed expression in *The Shining*, a film we study in subsequent chapters. Usually these selections would, in their provenance and association, demonstrate Kubrick's preoccupation with the increasingly looming presence in his films of the powers wielded by elites and, in particular, by the state. While his early films often concentrate in this respect on the results of the organization of violence by the state in the form of war, Kubrick's later films more thoroughly and consistently consider the institutional power behind the organization of war and the influence of the power of the state and its minions in and on society generally. For example, while Kubrick's introduction of the police into *Lolita*, the romantic drama (of sorts) that closed the first phase of his filmmaking career, is an example of concern with the disciplining—the taming—powers of the earth, it is still more a representation of Humbert's paranoia generally and as embodied in Quilty than it is a reference to the state or the powers behind the state. Contrast this with the murderous power brokers represented by Victor (*Victor!*) Ziegler in *Eyes Wide Shut*, the romantic drama (of sorts) that closed the second, final phase of Kubrick's career. This representation of malevolent earthly powers was added by Kubrick to the original source in order to emphasize in a much more systematic and direct way his concern with the organization and exercise of violence and control from the top down that dominated the twentieth century.

One small Kubrick gesture in the early 1960s is emblematic of the metaphorical as well as literal sea change in his artistic environment. When young filmmaker Kevin Brownlow was looking for help in making a counterfactual drama about the Nazi occupation of Britain during the Second World War, he had the good fortune to run into Kubrick at a showing of Stroheim's *The Merry Widow* at the National Film Theatre in London. Kubrick told Brownlow that when he was starting out the main problem was raw film stock and asked how he was set for 35mm film. When Brownlow replied that he did not have much, Kubrick arranged for him to "have the short ends from *Dr. Strangelove* [which the neophyte] used on the big surrender scene, the climax of . . . years of location shooting."[1] Kubrick's return to his original sources of historical concern was hastened by developments in the 1960s that gave witness to a growing realization of the significance of what would come to be generally known as the Holocaust. The Israeli capture and trial of one of the major architects of the Nazi Final Solution, Adolf Eichmann, at the opening of the decade was accompanied by the first major history of the Nazi extermination campaign by Raul Hilberg. Both of these events, as we shall see in Chapter 8, helped launch testimony, study, and expression surrounding the Holocaust that would grow exponentially during the 1970s.

Kubrick was now transforming his cinema into a distinctive and unavoidable part of the world's changing cultural landscape. He was becoming one of the most talked-about and admired filmmakers of his generation.[2] His decision to stay in England after completing *Lolita* was largely based upon his desire to be independent of the commercial craziness of Hollywood. It was also the case that he and his family felt safer in England than in New York City. But his proximity to Europe also geographically confirmed and intensified his long-standing commitment to a European style of filmmaking that preferred artistic expression and the exploration of ideas to the escapism of Hollywood entertainments. He would thus enjoy the creative control he craved: on *Dr. Strangelove*, writer Terry Southern noted that Kubrick "scarcely let as much as a trouser pleat go unsupervised."[3] Kubrick was also a part of the increasing momentum toward transatlantic cultural exchange that became associated with the 1960s. As an American, Kubrick was a product of that extension of European civilization to the so-called New World beginning in the fifteenth century. Ironically, he was returning to the Old World at a time when it, and in particular England, was in the vanguard of the New World of youth culture that also represented the leading edge of the Americanization of Western society and culture. The Old World was also the New World for Kubrick in terms of his rediscovery of it for himself at the end of his family's long trajectory from Poland to the United States. At the same time, though, Europe remained for him the Old World of recent remembered horrors as well as part of the entire earth now threatened by the possibility of nuclear destruction papered over by the complacent American liberal consensus of economic prosperity, scientific progress, and national security.[4]

## Dr. Strangelove (1964)

Kubrick's second film in England ended up a black comedy about the end of the world. A Hawk Film produced by Kubrick and released by Columbia Pictures, *Dr. Strangelove, or: How I Learned to Stop Worrying and Love the Bomb*, started out as a serious dramatic thriller about a nuclear catastrophe based on the book *Red Alert* (1958) by former Royal Air Force pilot Peter George and published the same year in Britain under the pseudonym Peter Bryant and the title *Two Hours to Doom*. In August 1961 the East German regime began building the Berlin Wall, and only a year later the world seemed on the brink of this war as the United States confronted Russia over Soviet missiles in Cuba. It was this crisis and the accompanying public fatalism about nuclear war that moved Kubrick to make a film on the subject.[5] *Dr. Strangelove* would be Kubrick's last black-and-white film, reflecting Kubrick's documentary concern with current events and recent history, his investment in photography since the 1930s, and the Expressionistic use of light and shadow typical of High German Cinema in the 1920s to highlight the grim and threatening confluence of human irrationality with dark, indeed elemental, forces of nature.[6]

Peter George's novel proposes a foolproof system of nuclear deterrence whereby once, in the words of Soviet ambassador Zorubin, "both sides have missiles which will automatically retaliate, war becomes profitless."[7] The Americans and Russians agree on such a system after a crisis triggered by an American wing commander's attempt to launch a nuclear attack on the Soviet Union in order to correct what he sees as an inherent disadvantage to the United States in the current nuclear standoff with Russia. Unlike Kubrick's General Jack D. Ripper, Brigadier General Quinten is not clearly insane. He is approaching a breakdown and is about to be relieved, but his motive for launching a preemptive strike against the Russians is based on a flawed though rational analysis of the strategic situation. George's book is filled with technical concepts and jargon, and Kubrick was certainly fascinated with such technological arcana, but the effect of discussing the book with Harris finally just struck Kubrick as so incongruous as to make what he called "a nightmare comedy" the best way of getting at the terrible truth of the nuclear arms race. To this end, Kubrick added hot and provocative 1960s satirical novelist Terry Southern to the writing staff.[8] Kubrick was again exploiting his Jewish heritage in using laughter as a historically safe means of criticizing authority, leavening his own pessimism, and embracing a 1960s ethos of seizing the day before the earth is overwhelmed by disaster.[9]

In contrast to George's book, at the nucleus of Kubrick's film is his usual conviction that systems of control, no matter how—or especially when—technically sophisticated, are always ultimately subject to the disorder in the universe, principally that manifested in the form of human folly. And for Kubrick there is no greater reservoir of human folly than men drunk with power. General Ripper is convinced there is an international Communist conspiracy "to sap and impurify all of our precious bodily fluids" by means of fluoridation of public drinking water.[10] (There was in fact a campaign against fluoridation of water by the radically anti-Communist John Birch Society after the Second World War.) In order to defeat this conspiracy, Ripper exploits a loophole in "Wing Attack Plan R" to order his bombers to attack the Soviet Union, hoping this will commit the United States to full-scale nuclear assault and total victory. President Merkin Muffley is determined to have the bombers stopped, while General Buck Turgidson, head of the Strategic Air Command, accepts the grim logic of Ripper's plan and urges an all-out offensive, with American civilian losses of "no more than ten-to-twenty million, tops, depending on the breaks."[11] In the course of discussions with Soviet premier Dmitri Kissoff, the Americans learn through Ambassador Alexander de Sadesky that the Russians have rendered operational a "Doomsday Machine" designed to cover the entire earth with radiation in the case of a nuclear attack. This was to be the ultimate deterrent, but unfortunately the announcement of the existence of the weapon had been put off until the next week for the opening of the Party Congress. If just one of the American bombers drops its bombs, the Doomsday Machine will activate. There is no way to switch off the Doomsday Machine; this is the genius of its value as a deterrent. It is thus precisely the logic of the solution in George's book that in Kubrick's film becomes the guarantor of the destruction of all life on earth. And when one of the American planes does in fact drop its bombs, the Doomsday Machine is set off. It is at this juncture that the president's National Security Adviser, the wheelchair-bound Dr. Strangelove, proposes an alternative to civilization's imminent demise. The solution is for a group of a few highly qualified men and a large number of extremely nubile women to descend into abandoned mine shafts, in which their descendants would wait for about a century for the "Doomsday shroud" to dissipate. All the men in the War Room are convinced this is a good idea, although Buck Turgidson fears the Russians might stash a "big bomb" in their mine shafts so "they could take over" when the survivors come out. The film ends with Dr. Strangelove rising from his wheelchair followed by footage of exploding nuclear bombs.

*Dr. Strangelove* is Kubrick's most explicit and savage satire in the tradition of Jonathan Swift's *A Modest Proposal for Preventing the Children of Poor People from Being a Burden on Their Parents or the Country* (1749), which proposed—modestly in the spirit of enlightened cannibalism—that the problem of starving children in Ireland could be solved by feeding them to the rich. Swift is even referenced directly in *Dr. Strangelove* in the name of one of the Russian targets for American bombers, "the ICBM complex at Laputa."[12] In Swift's *Gulliver's Travels* (1726), the island of Laputa is a kingdom of quack scientists who employ people to hit them on the head to bring them to consciousness of the external world. But *Dr. Strangelove* is more particularly Kubrick's harshest and most outrageous condemnation of the hypermasculinity that has dominated all or most of human history. In Kubrick's view, this hypermasculinity has found its most horrendous and dangerous manifestation in the modern world of high-tech weaponry. This was not simply a matter of augmented destructive power, but a further anxious articulation à la Weber of the dehumanization that comes with the exaltation of science and rational order at the expense of broader humane interests. In *Dr. Strangelove* Kubrick is not only reaching back to Lang's fusion of man and machine in *Metropolis* and the *Mabuse* films, but also anticipating the perceptive paranoia of countercultural writers like Thomas Pynchon, who in *Gravity's Rainbow* (1973) wrote of the inventor of the Nazis' V-2 rocket as "somebody with a name and penis . . . [who] wanted to chuck a ton of Amatol 300 miles and blow up a block full of civilians."[13] These are men who reject in others and themselves "a human and loving sexuality." Kubrick's eponym—"strange love," indeed—is their embodiment: "Dr. Strangelove's half-machine, half-Nazi character provides the crowning symbol for all these characters' inhuman and lifeless sexual perversions."[14]

Kubrick no doubt also drew some inspiration from Swift's Master Bates in *Gulliver's Travels*, for all of the male characters in *Dr. Strangelove* have names suggestive of sex, violence, or defecation. Ripper's superior, General Turgidson, bears a last name whose first syllable means "swollen" or "engorged" and a first name, Buck, that refers of course to the male deer, or stag. Kubrick had originally named him Buck Schmuck, using the obscene Yiddish word for "penis." B-52 pilot Major T. J. "King" Kong, who dies astride a long, thick bomb that blooms in ultimate orgasm as it hits the earth, is another—and cinematic—symbol of the sexualized male animal. The names of Dr. Strangelove, Premier Kissoff, Ambassador de Sadesky, Colonel "Bat" Guano (bat shit), Admiral Pooper, General Faceman, and Mr. Staines are all along the same corporeal lines of sex, aggression, sadism, and anality. It is thus singularly—and comically—appropriate that Ripper shoots himself in his bathroom and that when General Turgidson learns of General Ripper's actions he is on the toilet in the middle of the night while "secretary" Miss Scott takes the call from her position on his bed and says the two are "catching up on some of the General's paperwork."[15] With Burpelson Air Force Base, eructation is the referent, appropriate in light of the film's emphasis on eating, which suggests not only another animal function but also the cannibalism at the heart—or, rather, the belly—of Swift's *A Modest Proposal*.[16] Even the abbreviation ICBM is an adolescent and alimentary play on words. This constant invocation of the crude language of the body points toward the animal instincts and appetites newly empowered, encouraged, dehumanized, and embodied by modern erectile weaponry.

The opening credits initiate literally this Kubrickian coupling of the human and the mechanical. Under scenes of copulative in-flight refueling of a B-52, the soundtrack plays an instrumental arrangement of "Try a Little Tenderness" (1932). The detonation of the Doomsday bombs at the end of the film, with Dr. Strangelove now standing erect, represents the orgasmic outcome of this copulation in a union of men's neurotic joining of sex and aggression. Under that final scene, we hear Vera Lynn singing "We'll Meet Again" (1939), which became a British anthem of longing during the Second World War both on the concert stage and in the film *We'll Meet Again* (1942). Aside from the black irony of the lyrics "We'll meet again, don't know where, don't know when" accompanying the destruction of the world, the song's invocation of the last war underscores both psychologically and historically what Freud called "repetition compulsion"—that is, what happens when neuroses are acted out over and over because they have not been confronted or resolved.[17] For the first time, Kubrick drew extra-diegetic music from history rather than commissioning a soundtrack for the film. This emphasized not only Kubrick's own historical reference points but also the active construction of meaning on the part of both filmmaker and audience rather than the unreflective evocation of a scene's mood. This would be a device Kubrick would use to great effect in the rest of his films, including in the most subtle but also specific way with reference to the Holocaust in *The Shining*. The content and the context of musical pieces that Kubrick used from now on would matter as much in terms of their historical relevance in the broadest sense as in fitting the mood of a scene. And, starting with *2001*, Kubrick would be able to extend the same function to the use of color.[18]

*Dr. Strangelove*'s heavily armored hypermasculinity has as its main target women. The opening lines of "Try a Little Tenderness" are pregnant with meaning in just this sense: "She may be weary, women do get weary." The single woman in *Dr. Strangelove* in particular embodies the sexual objectification of women imposed by patriarchal society. The bikinied Miss Scott, who also appears as a *Playboy* centerfold with a copy of *Foreign Affairs* over her derriere, embodies—literally— all those male desires and fears that stem from maternal domination of early child care and from the Oedipus complex, as does Vera Lynn, "the voice of the one woman we once upon a time all knew."[19] The fact that the in-flight refueling at the beginning of the film can also be seen as a mother breastfeeding an infant is a representation of the former nexus of conflict. The Oedipal crisis is suggested in the location of the targeted "ICBM complex," Laputa, which means "whore" (*la puta*) in Spanish. A civil defense poster at Burpelson that reads "Gee, Dad! Thanks for thinking of us" expresses Oedipally tinged iconoclasm in the irony of the inadequacy of bomb shelters erected by fathers in protecting against "techno-phallic" bombs launched by other men out of their own self-destructive needs and desires.[20] There is even a presumably unintended but still pregnant joke in Miss Scott's bikini, for Bikini Atoll in the west central Pacific was the main site of American atomic-bomb testing from 1946 to 1958. Moreover, the first atomic bomb dropped there was named "Gilda" and carried on it a picture of Hollywood "bombshell" Rita Hayworth, whose pinup also graced the bomb (code-named "Little Boy") dropped on Hiroshima by a B-29 named *Enola Gay* in honor of the pilot's mother.[21]

Wing Commander General Jack D. Ripper is ground zero for the film's fascinated study of male desire for, fear of, and consequent violence toward women. That Kubrick, true to the patriarchal male form he inherited from his social milieu, is fascinated by the perpetrators of violence is problematic in intent and effect, but it also represents an honest and effective critique of feelings that Kubrick as a male knew especially well. There are few characters in literature or film that rival Ripper as an instructive caricature of the technologically enhanced hypermasculinity that has been one feature of the modern age. Ripper claims to have discovered the secret of the Communist fluoridation conspiracy to weaken men during the act of sex when, after ejaculation, he felt a "profound sense of fatigue, a feeling of emptiness." Since that time, he has resolved to share the power of "the life essence" he claims women seek from him but also to deny them his "essence." This of course means not ejaculating and thus not losing his erection, a symbol of his power that also signals male fear and desire.[22] Ripper's phallic preoccupation, and that of men in general, are represented visually in the film by Ripper's long cigar, his .45 automatic, the machine gun he wields in defense of his air base, as well as the planes and bombs he sends against the Russians. It can be argued that Kubrick's depiction of the attitudes and behaviors of the men who run the military establishments of America and Russia are inaccurate or at least incomplete. After all, the Cold War of deterrence and diplomacy did not turn into a Hot War of nuclear detonation and fallout. However, there is historical evidence to suggest that in linking hypermasculinity to nuclear strategy Kubrick was on to something. A culture of air war took wing in the twentieth century composed of cold, calculating bureaucratic mentality and fantasies of freedom, fear, and power surrounding the airplane. A mix of "technological fanaticism" and "apocalyptic fantasy" among American strategic thinkers during and after the Second World War was augmented by "militarized masculinity and decontextualized rationality" among postwar "defense intellectuals."[23]

The two usual Kubrickian intermediate figures who try—and fail—to control a militarized universe spinning into self-destruction are President Merkin Muffley and Group Captain Lionel Mandrake. Like Colonel Dax, they represent Kubrick's own position as someone who tries to warn and mitigate. Kubrick observed that the cynicism in *Dr. Strangelove* was above all a way to engage constructively the threat of nuclear destruction.[24] Both Muffley and Mandrake are serious and sober, in contrast to the cartoon characters that surround them, although each, in typical Kubrick unblinking fashion, has his faults as well. And both of these men, in opposing the mad adventurism of Ripper and Turgidson, are portrayed as somewhat feminine in appearance, attitude, and activity. President Muffley, whose bald head suggests President Eisenhower, was modeled on Eisenhower's failed challenger in 1952 and 1956: Adlai Stevenson. In contrast to the Second World War military hero Eisenhower, Stevenson was often denigrated as an "egghead" of less than manly presidential stature.[25] Muffley speaks in a high, even hysterical voice, and his name is composed of words, "merkin" and "muff," descriptive of the female genitalia. In the novel the unnamed president is a hardheaded realist. He reveals to the military leaders the existence of the Doomsday device and observes that the Russian leader, as a dictator, would act just like Hitler and bring the world down in flames when facing defeat. By revealing contrast, Muffley's invocation of Hitler comes in response to General Turgidson's recommendation for an all-out attack and suggests, in typical Kubrickian and 1960s fashion, not only the president's humane—and "feminine"—instincts but the potential Hitler in everyone: "I will not go down in history as the greatest mass murderer since Adolf Hitler!"[26] For his part, Mandrake, Ripper's British adjutant under the "Officer Exchange Program," like his brothers in arms, bears a name of male sexual power: the lion (which is also a symbol of Britain) in Lionel and Mandrake, which includes "man" and "drake," a male duck. The mandrake itself is an herb with a root shaped like a human and is a narcotic member of the nightshade family traditionally regarded as a source of sexual potency. Mandrake, while bearing the uniform and name of a member of the "real men's" club, is horrified by what Ripper has done and works to undo his commander's madness. For his efforts and for a voice that, in American ears, has a prissy and lisping British quality, he is labeled a "prevert [sic]" by Colonel Guano.[27]

The concern Dr. Strangelove expresses about the prospect of nuclear war was one of the first manifestations of the more general political and cultural unrest that characterized the 1960s in the West. Among other manifestations of this unrest was the "Ban the Bomb" movement, which originated in Britain.[28] While Dr. Strangelove expressed Kubrick's liberal, rationalist hope of prevention (and not "preversion") through reason, a virtue represented in the figures of President Muffley and Group Captain Mandrake, the film's paranoia fit an age in which conspiracy at the top of the political and social order would grow to become a prevailing concern among members of the counterculture.[29] Kubrick himself, as usual, was concerned with larger and longer continuities in human history and the modern age in particular. So Dr. Strangelove is filled with references to the Second World War. Mandrake is a former RAF Spitfire pilot and prisoner of the Japanese, while the narrator tells us that each B-52 carries more explosive power than all the munitions used in the Second World War. In a more elaborate reference, General Ripper, in a parody of General George Patton, carries a pearl-handled automatic. Patton sometimes wore ivory-handled pistols, which he hated to have characterized as pearl because only "St. Louis pimps wear pearl-tipped guns."[30] More generally, the Cold War, nuclear weapons, and the American Strategic Air Command (SAC) were all creations of that war. Both Ripper and Turgidson are caricatures of General Curtis LeMay, who created SAC in 1948. Ripper is the cigar-chomping LeMay who directed the B-29 firebombing raids that obliterated Japan's cities in 1944 and 1945. Turgidson is the tough and bombastic LeMay who, representing the Air Force, was a member of the Joint Chiefs of Staff (another innovation of the Second World War) that advised Presidents Eisenhower and Kennedy during the hottest years of the Cold War.[31]

The walls of Ripper's office are covered with aerial photography of Second World War bombing raids, reflecting LeMay's own experience of flying and commanding

B-17s and B-24s in the air campaign against Nazi Germany. That B-52 bombers ever since the Cold War hold at "fail-safe" points in the air until given an order to *attack* is a legacy of both the 1930s American strategic idea of using B-17 bombers to *defend* the United States at a distance out over the Atlantic and Pacific Oceans and the American determination to avoid another surprise attack like Pearl Harbor. In two back-projection shots, Kubrick even has a B-52 throw the shadow of a *B-17*, which demonstrates the technological, institutional, and attitudinal continuities between the Second World War and the Cold War.[32] This typically reflexive Kubrick detail arose from the convenient fact that Kubrick was using a surplus B-17 for second-unit filming under director of photography Gilbert Taylor. Taylor had flown missions over Germany as a combat photographer, filmed the horrors of Belsen and Buchenwald in 1945, and shot low-level aerial footage for the British Second World War drama, *The Dam Busters* (1955).[33] And that Kubrick changed the name of the B-52 from the book's *Alabama Angel* to *Leper Colony* not only foreshadows impending doom but forges another blackly ironic link with the history and cinema of the Second World War, for *Leper Colony* is the name of the B-17 in Henry King's *Twelve O'Clock High* (1949) to which "the losers and slackers of Gregory Peck's squadron are relegated."[34] Finally, in constructing the crew of the plane, Kubrick once again employed the common Second World War film trope of the "ethnic sample crew" (e.g., *Air Force*, R, May 1943) that includes African-American bombardier Lothar Zogg, Jewish radio operator B. Goldberg, and a comic cowboy John Wayne commander played by Texas actor Slim Pickens.[35] The music for the scenes in the *Leper Colony* en route to the target is the Civil War ballad "When Johnny Comes Marching Home" (1863), of course blackly ironic in the context of nuclear war (*When Johnny Comes Marching Home*, R, March 1943).

Once again, however, it is the German side of the Second World War that in *Dr. Strangelove* takes pride of place. This, too, was a function of Kubrick's own particular obsessions and the historical legacy of the conflict, but it was also an artifact of the critical cultural reaction during the 1960s to the prospect of nuclear war. Concern over nuclear war, coupled with the growing unease about the conspiracies of men in high places, drew energy from an emerging new discourse on what very soon would become known as the Holocaust. In the late 1950s and early 1960s, the usual term for the destruction of the earth by thermonuclear weapons (the hydrogen bomb) was the appropriately biblical "Armageddon." Around the same time, the word "Holocaust" came into widespread use to describe the Nazi extermination of the Jews in the Second World War. The first public use of the word in America came as the translation of the Hebrew word *shoah* in a television documentary on the Eichmann trial, *Verdict for Tomorrow*, which aired in the autumn of 1961. In the 1970s and 1980s, "holocaust" replaced "Armageddon" in discourse about nuclear war and became a common, and debatable, noun for a variety of problems and tragedies.[36] But long before then, "[t]he issues raised in any understanding of Nazi Germany's 'Final Solution'—from basic human morality and individual willingness to participate in the extermination of human beings to the definition of criminal state authority and the meaning of obedience to such authority—found a new currency and applicability in America's new age of thermonuclear peril."[37] No longer was Auschwitz a symbol of a horror past in contrast to Hiroshima as a horror present; now both were viewed as the twin pillars of a new age of mass extermination.[38] There was a new cultural atmosphere of foreboding. Stanley Kramer's film *Judgment at Nuremburg* (1961) was an immediate response to the Eichmann trial in Israel. The same year, Kurt Vonnegut published *Mother Night*, a black comedy about an American who becomes a propagandist for the Nazis but who is also an American spy. This novel, too, was a response to the Eichmann trial and its revelations about the surprisingly murky and ambiguous nature of evil. Like Kubrick's films, works such as these in the 1960s targeted easy wartime and postwar dichotomies about good (us) and evil (them). A late example of the collapsing of Nazi and American exercise of power came in Francis Ford Coppola's *Apocalypse Now* (1979), which transports Conrad's *Heart of Darkness* to Vietnam and in one combat scene plays Wagner's "Ride of the Valkyries."

Dr. Strangelove himself, whom Kubrick lumped together with *Lolita*'s Dr. Zempf, as "parodies of movie clichés about Nazis,"[39] is the mechanical chimera of modern horror. Sociologist Lewis Mumford in 1964 anointed him as the "central symbol of the scientifically organized nightmare of mass extermination."[40] Dr. Strangelove is another Kubrickian half-machine "sitting man" who is also criminally crippled inside and who thereby fearfully threatens the world with destruction. Strangelove, as a Germanic Kubrickian villain, also recalls the hybrid wanderers between two worlds embodied in the Jewish legend of the *dybbuk* (ghost) and the *golem* (automaton).[41] Strangelove is chillingly and expressionistically portrayed in just this way by the cut to him sitting in stark shadow following the words "valley of fear" in Turgidson's prayer of thanksgiving for deliverance from the "wings of the angel of death" when it appears that all the American bombers have been recalled. The shot is one looking up at Strangelove's grim-faced visage as Turgidson in all pompous error and black irony concludes: "You have seen fit to deliver us from the forces of evil."[42] Turgidson is indeed doubly wrong, for not only has the final crisis not been averted but Dr. Strangelove himself emerges, literally as well as figuratively, as a diabolical *Satanas ex machina* who in terms of the influence of his technical expertise indicates "the extent to which Germany *won* the last world war."[43]

Strangelove is also a composite of historical personages who to a great extent determined nuclear policy in a postwar America whose military system had been reforged during the Second World War. Kubrick never named anyone in particular, saying only that he had in mind "an American college professor who rises to sex and politics by becoming a nuclear wise man."[44] Whatever Kubrick's intentions or associations, the character of Dr. Strangelove surely reflected his wide reading on what he labeled at the time "the nuclear nightmare."[45] This included Henry Kissinger's *Nuclear Weapons and Foreign Policy* (1957) and *The Necessity for Choice* (1961). Kissinger—a Harvard professor, an adviser to President Kennedy, and a Jewish émigré with a thick German accent—argued for the virtues of nuclear deterrence. Herman Kahn, the author of *Thermonuclear War* (1960) and *Thinking About the Unthinkable* (1962), proposed—but ultimately rejected—automatic nuclear response systems while also arguing that nuclear wars were survivable. Kahn, whose 1960 book Kubrick had read, was a strategist for the RAND Corporation, the famous "think tank" and the model for Strangelove's affiliation with the "Bland Corporation."[46] Another prominent nuclear strategist of the day was Albert Wohlstetter, also an analyst for RAND, the title of whose seminal article of 1959 in *Foreign Affairs,* "The Delicate Balance of Terror," became the working title of the original comic screenplay, replacing the working title, "Edge of Doom," for the dramatic treatment.[47] Finally, there was Edward Teller, a Hungarian émigré from Hitler's Europe, who developed the fusion, or thermonuclear, device known as the hydrogen bomb and who was a fierce proponent of the expansion of America's nuclear arsenal.[48]

In another relevant historical category is Wernher von Braun, who had invented the V-2 rocket that Hitler fired against London and other cities. Von Braun had become the leader of America's space program in the 1950s. By late in the decade, von Braun not only was lionized as a hero in the competition in rocketry and space with the Russians, but also was an object of criticism concerning the alliance of old Nazis with new Cold Warriors. Comedian Mort Sahl, for one, invented an acid subtitle for a movie about von Braun's life, *I Aim at the Stars* (1959): "But sometimes I hit London."[49] The film about von Braun was itself part of a new—and, for some, troubling—relationship between Americans and Germans since it was an American–West German co-production. Kubrick's own ruminations with regard to the legacy of Nazi Germany are evident in the fact that Dr. Strangelove (*né* Merkwürdigliebe) is, like von Braun, a former Nazi now working for the Americans.[50] The original screenplay tells us: "He was a recluse and perhaps had been made so by the effects of the British bombing of Peenemünde, where he was working on the German V-2 rocket. His black-gloved right hand was a memento of this."[51] In the film this direct link to the Nazi regime is manifested in Strangelove's difficulty in keeping his mechanical right arm from rising in a Nazi salute and in refraining from calling President Muffley "mein Führer."[52] And when Muffley expresses doubt about the ability of people to survive in mine shafts for a hundred years, Strangelove, eerily hinting at future denial of the Holocaust, responds: "the conditions would be far superior to those of the *so-called* concentration camps, where there is ample evidence most of the wretched creatures clung desperately to life."[53]

The second sense in which Dr. Strangelove is a creature of the Second World War is even more malevolent and has been only imperfectly recognized. Thomas Allen Nelson has characterized the predicament at the end of the film as "a world caught between a Doomsday Auschwitz and Mine Shaft Dachau" and Strangelove as "the New Man who will lead the chosen people into darkness."[54] This refers to Strangelove's plan to select people to survive deep underground until the radiation spread across the world by the Doomsday Machine has dissipated. But there are in fact *two* endings to *Dr. Strangelove*. The first, and clearly recognized, is the destruction of the earth in "Doomsday Auschwitz." The second is the construction of not so much, if at all, a "Mine Shaft Dachau" but a "Mine Shaft Berchtesgaden."

Dr. Strangelove does not mention "Aryans" or "Jews," only the categories—and racist code words?—of "youth, health, sexual fertility, intelligence, and the cross section of necessary skills." We can be anything but reassured in this regard given Strangelove's enduring corporeal loyalty to Hitler and the three words redolent of Nazism to which he gives inordinate vocal emphasis in his various speeches: "will," "fear," and "slaughtered." Everyone in the world is going to die except for a nucleus of desirable types, "top government and military men," and a ratio of ten women "selected for their sexual characteristics . . . of a highly stimulating nature." This recommendation for the perpetuation of the human race recalls the "mass marriage" that Dalton Trumbo proposed for *Spartacus* that reminded Kubrick of the marriage of Adolf Hitler and Eva Braun.[55] Let us be quite clear about how *Dr. Strangelove really* ends—with the suggestion of a "Final Solution" to the "problem" of "inferior" human beings and the creation of a new Nazi "Master Race" to emerge in a hundred years to rule the earth. Kubrick thus joins the burning of a nuclear Armageddon to the burning of the Jewish Holocaust. In this context, the song that ends the film, "We'll Meet Again," not only satirizes human nature and gender constellations but also communicates the blackest, most unbearable historical irony just like the film's last spoken words, the now suddenly toddling Strangelove's "Mein Führer, I can walk!"

### *2001: A Space Odyssey* (1968)

In 1953 Arthur C. Clarke wrote one of the great postwar science-fiction novels, *Childhood's End,* in which the human race evolves into a higher species through the intervention of a superior alien entity called the Overmind. At the end of the novel, the human race is "consumed by a holocaust from which New Man will emerge."[56] Kubrick had read both *Childhood's End* and Clarke's short story "The Sentinel" (1948). Reflecting his recent reading on the history of the atomic bomb, Kubrick named the subsequent exploratory work by his New York City production team "The Manhattan Project." The film would be shot in Cinerama, the new Hollywood rage of the day in the battle with television for the eyes and dollars of the public. What became "Journey Beyond the Stars" and then *2001: A Space Odyssey* would be produced and directed by Kubrick for MGM.[57] Ironically, the most futuristic of Kubrick's films is also the most similar to the old silent cinema he admired his entire life. There are only about forty-six minutes of dialogue in a film that runs just twenty-one minutes short of three hours. In recalling the experimentation of the early sound era (and the 1960s) in cinema, the rest of the soundtrack is taken up by music, silence, and, in two extended scenes, the sound only of (Kubrick's own) respiration. *2001* was both traditional and revolutionary in its fusion of popular genre movie and avant-garde cinema. It is also an example of Kubrick's penchant for open narrative, in this case allowing the emotive force of music to break the boundaries often set to meaning by words.[58]

A protest against the political, military, and scientific authorities descended from the experience of the Second World War, *Dr. Strangelove* addressed the critical fears of the late 1950s and early 1960s. As its wildly cultic response among members of the younger generation of the time attests, *2001* indulged the 1960s search for meaning beyond the dull and dangerous conformities of established society. This search had many routes and destinations—sexual, musical, herbal, pharmaceutical, political, and spiritual. At the center of *2001*, Kubrick said on many occasions, is "the God concept."[59] While some have commented on the seeming ambiguity of the ending to *2001*, Kubrick always maintained that the ending was optimistic. Since *2001*, like *Dr. Strangelove*, arose as well out of Kubrick's own concerns, it must be seen as a response to the hopelessness of the dual conclusion to *Dr. Strangelove*. For Kubrick, the key to a possible happy future for humankind rested on a combination of luck and strength to surmount the cold darkness of an indifferent universe. This was partially a Nietzschean vision of the human prospect: humanity must overcome its crippling reliance on the myth of God and assert its own heroic morality. While Dr. Strangelove's ravings reflect the Nazi racist ideal of a "superman," a perversion of Nietzsche's "overman" (*Übermensch*), *2001* offers a hymn of praise for Nietzsche's original concept. It is no accident in this regard that Kubrick exploited Richard Strauss's Nietzschean *Thus Spake Zarathustra* (1896) as the opening and closing music for *2001* and, in speaking about the film, drew from Matthew Arnold the observation that in the modern era "'the sea of faith' recedes around the world with a 'melancholy, long, withdrawing roar.'"[60] Kubrick's desire, however, to embrace cosmic evolution as a way out of the literal dead end of the machinations of Nazis like Strangelove ignores, as does Strauss's music, Nietzsche's doctrine of eternal recurrence, by which the overman does not evolve onto a higher plane of existence but simply asserts himself against the constant repetition of history, a view Kubrick otherwise shares.[61]

*2001* begins with "The Dawn of Man," when 4 million years ago a mysterious monolith appears among a group of apes. These apes are herbivores living in a desert environment—no verdant biblical Garden of Eden this—in which they are subject to attacks by carnivorous cats and to fights with other apes over a water hole—"man-apes on the long, pathetic road to racial extinction."[62] The monolith punctuates the apes' evolutionary equilibrium by enabling them to discover the concept of tools and weaponry: a bone that can be used to kill game and wrest control of the water hole back from their enemies. The accompaniment of Strauss's *Thus Spake Zarathustra* to this moment of enlightenment constitutes a reprise of Kubrick's sober view of human history exemplified in the weapon-happy bellicosity of most of the characters in *Dr. Strangelove*. Ensuing is the famous match-cut between weapons 4 million years apart.[63] Satellites and earth rotate to the strains of Johann Strauss's "Blue Danube Waltz," music originally and ironically written as a choral piece to assuage Austrian feelings in the wake of crushing military defeat by Prussia in 1867.[64] Kubrick himself described this music as appropriate both for communicating the beauty of movement in space and for liberating the viewer from the science-fiction convention of space as eerie and strange.[65]

As in *Dr. Strangelove,* the music Kubrick uses in *2001* was written to carry ideas, address human concerns, and not just dress a movie.[66] And the reasons Kubrick chose particular compositions, and in the end not using a film score written by Alex North, overlapped with the reasons the works were written. This is clear at the end of the film when the music under the credits continues for several minutes after the credits have run. The audience—which ironically is almost certainly no longer there—sees only a black screen and hears only the "Blue Danube." This juxtaposition, while also typical play-out music, communicates both the human perception of and presence in space, but also intimates something of the cold indifference of the universe. At the same time, the music is boldly and joyously beautiful, thus expressing the hope embodied by the overman. The subject in the end, as in the beginning, therefore, is not the exploration of space but the exploration of self. The odyssey is that of the aptly named Homer: Odysseus, after all, was on his way *home,* just as the Star-Child, the successor to humanity, at the end of *2001* returns to earth.[67]

Kubrick's choice of music was also determined by his own interests and background, especially his long-standing interest in German folktales and in the music of central and eastern Europe. While there are competing claims over the sources and timing of his selection of music for *2001,* there is no doubt that the final determination of what to use was Kubrick's alone. As early as the writing of the script, Kubrick and Clarke listened to German composer Carl Orff's *Carmina Burana* (1937) and even considered commissioning Orff, who had composed an opera entitled *The Moon* (1939) based on the Grimm fairy tale of the same name, to write a score for their film. Kubrick also thought of using Gustav Mahler's Third Symphony (1902), which was based on German folktales and includes a theme on Nietzsche's *Zarathustra,* and Felix Mendelssohn's *A Midsummer Night's Dream* (1826). When he chose Strauss instead, he selected a rendition by the Berlin Philharmonic conducted by Herbert von Karajan.[68]

Kubrick's other musical selections, by Hungarian György Ligeti and Armenian Aram Khachaturian (1903–1978), bear traces of the Second World War. In *2001* Kubrick uses Ligeti's *Atmosphères* (1961), *Requiem* (1963–1965; winner of the Bonn Beethoven Prize, 1967), *Aventures* (1962), and *Lux aeterna* (1966). Ligeti, a Hungarian Jew who lost his family and endured forced labor during the war, fled Communism in 1956 and emerged as a leader in "new music" during the 1960s with work that was often a combination of wit, satire, and dark comedy. Such an approach to his art was not surprising in light of his experience with the persecution that comes with being regarded as dangerously different.[69] Ligeti's artistic response was to write music as part of a worldview that condemned any form of racism, nationalism, or intolerance. Moreover, the choral atonality of Ligeti's compositions arose, in a striking parallel to Kubrick's enduring response to the world, from, in his own words, "the fantasy of a child excluded from his parents' secrets."[70] The result is music that emphasizes the inextricability of wonder and unease at the world and the universe that moves within *2001.* The adagio from Khachaturian's *Gayaneh Ballet* (1942), which accompanies *Discovery*'s transit to Jupiter, similarly expresses the indifference of the universe and the hopelessness of a mission that will end in extinction for the crew. In the course of five scenes over seven minutes, the adagio introduces us to HAL and the crew and captures the cold loneliness of space travel. But the music was written, as part of the Soviet war effort, to convey the anxiety of a collective farm on the eve of the Nazi invasion.[71] Khachaturian's piece is a prime example of how Kubrick's choice of music—as opposed to commissioning another composer's treatment of the film—could be a matter of both knowledge of the specific origins and intents of the composition and/or a response to the historically conditioned mood of the music in line with his own concerns about modern history in particular.

With its positive outlook, *2001* does not concern itself with the Nazi past, but it does also introduce a brief but significant "von Karajan effect" that would play a role in three of the four films that Kubrick made from 1968 to 1980. In two of these films, Kubrick makes prominent use of orchestral works conducted by Herbert von Karajan, and in all four films the recording produced by Deutsche Grammophon Gesellschaft features the Berlin Philharmonic. Deutsche Grammophon is the leading classical record company in the world, while von Karajan (1908–1989) is widely regarded as the finest conductor ever to wield a baton. Kubrick said that the DG recording of the Strauss waltz used in *2001* was chosen not so much for the composition as for the particular performance by the Berlin Philharmonic under the direction of von Karajan.[72] The choice of von Karajan, a choice Kubrick would revisit with greater historical specificity and artistic consequence in *The Shining,* reflects his abiding concern with the curious and disturbing occlusion of beauty and horror in human life that reached its nadir in Nazi Germany. Herbert von Karajan first rose to musical prominence in Nazi Germany and is an example of the bright young people who used—and were used by—the regime to further their careers. Karajan joined the Nazi party in his native Austria in 1933 and supported Hitler by "conducting orchestras for party functions, playing in occupied Paris, [and] performing for Hitler's birthday."[73] Kubrick probably knew something about this, if for no other reason than in the 1950s Jewish groups in America had loudly protested engagements by former Nazi party members such as von Karajan and soprano Elisabeth Schwarzkopf.[74]

For his part, *Zarathustra* composer Strauss (1864–1949) was compromised by a more ambiguous association with the Nazis. As Germany's greatest living composer, in 1933 he was chosen to head the new Reich Music Chamber. The same year Strauss stood in for conductor Bruno Walter, who, as a Jew, was no longer welcome to conduct in Germany. Strauss never joined the Nazi party since he had Jewish associates and relatives and a cosmopolitan outlook, and politically was an old guard conservative.[75] Even his *Zarathustra* failed to embrace the radical Romantic implications of Nietzsche's philosophy.[76] Orff (1895–1982) was an idiosyncratic modernist whose interest in German folk songs gave him as well a place in the new Nazi order celebrating ancient Germanic virtues. Both *Carmina Burana* and *The Moon* were successes in the Third Reich since they spanned the divide between earlier artistic traditions and new political and racial enthusiasms. *Carmina Burana* has even been labeled "fascist trash" and "a Christmas greeting from Nazi Germany."[77] *The Moon* is a case in point for the dangers in the real world that come with a fascination—a fascination problematically shared by Kubrick—with the dark and the mysterious in art and life. Its Brothers Grimm plot involves foolish boys who steal the moon, are killed, and then share the underworld with the moon, including as staged "dead people and dark underworld scenes—untimely reminders of lethal bombings and terrifying anti-air-raid blackouts."[78] Orff even wrote incidental music for a 1939 production of Shakespeare's *A Midsummer Night's Dream* (1600) to replace the original music written for the play by Felix Mendelssohn, a Jew.[79]

The waltzing of spacecraft in *2001* suggests Kubrick's old theme of the union of humans and machines, expressed in *2001* in terms of the degree to which human beings are becoming cold and increasingly impotent machines themselves. There are regular reminders in the second part of *2001* of bodily functions—food, a zero-gravity toilet—but, with the exception of Poole's jogging and shadow-boxing, the only athleticism appears on televisions or in the vector and whirl of machines.[80] Indeed, the whole point of the first segment of the film is that human beings not only have become enslaved by their machines, but are almost clones of them within soul-deadening bureaucracies of experts and functionaries. Far from progress, therefore, the history of humanity is a tale of repetition, for man also remains a violent animal, the only difference being the polite, flaccid hypocrisies of modern civilization. Just as the apes fight noisily over a water hole, American Heywood Floyd and his Russian counterpart Andrezj Smyslov—watched by three female scientists—joust diplomatically around a table of drinks.[81] Dr. Floyd flies in the ships *Orion* and *Aries,* named after the mythological figures and zodiacal constellations. Orion, a giant and hunter, boasted that he would rid the earth of wild beasts while Aries was the ram whose Golden Fleece was the object of the voyage of Jason and the Argonauts. Even the name of one of the astronauts, Frank Poole, recalls the earlier prehistoric confrontation, while the name of his pea-in-the-pod *Doppelgänger,* Dave Bowman, signifies in an obviously phallic way the human as the eternal carrier of weapons. Recalling Poole's shadowboxing, even the space pods the astronauts use to leave the mother ship have mechanical arms held in the position of raised fists. Finally, there is the old Kubrick symbol of state power, a gold eagle against a black background on the astronauts' shoulder patches.[82]

The discovery of a second monolith buried on the moon leads to the long middle of the film—bisected punningly by an intermission—concerning an international space mission to Jupiter. The spaceship *Discovery* is run by a supercomputer named HAL, an acronym for "*H*euristically Programmed *Al*gorithmic Computer." HAL, who is built to serve but who appears to wish to dominate by virtue of his intelligence, is an almost Kafkaesque symbol of cold, complex reason. As he is lobotomized by Bowman after trying to take over the ship, he sings the song he was taught by his programmer, "Daisy Bell (A Bicycle Built for Two)" (1892), a song of sweet emotion in which a machine of conveyance is a means and symbol of human love and companionship, unlike HAL's interplanetary conveyance *Discovery,* which is a means and symbol of cold and lonely high intellect. HAL has made an error and, given his inability to admit a mistake, has descended into murderous paranoia. Because HAL was created by human beings, he is not the infallible entity he believes himself to be. It is therefore highly ironic that when confronted with a different analysis of the problem by a computer back on earth, HAL blames human error for the *other* computer's "mistake."[83]

Kubrick uses color as well as music in *2001* as a vehicle for ideas. Against the blackness of space, Kubrick films most of the interiors in a blinding and shadowless "high key against white" that expresses the sterile rationalism of scientific enterprise. Allied with this is a frigid blue, which will appear with both similar and different meanings in *Barry Lyndon* and *The Shining* in particular and which symbolizes "the cool man-made apparatus [that] has lulled its passengers into a necessary unawareness of the infinite, keeping them equilibrated, calm, their heads and stomachs filled, in order to ensure that they stay poised to keep the apparatus, and themselves, on the usual blind belligerent course."[84] This is another of Kubrick's "high spaces" (as it were) in which cold and banal intellect—Floyd's obsequious underling is named *Hal*vorsen—serves the crippling system of human and technological power. Even—or especially—sex in this world is furtive and cooled, perhaps as in a "blue movie": "'A blue, woman's cashmere sweater has been found in the restroom,' a robotic female voice announces, twice, over the space station's PA system just after Doctor Floyd's arrival" (and just so we know who is still in charge, the woman concludes by saying that the sweater may be claimed "at the manager's desk").[85]

Aside from blue, red and yellow are associated with the body and with danger, and with ineluctable passion and violence. We first see red in the Olivier Morgue furniture in the space station, their stabbing sanguinary hue reminding us of their maker's coincidentally mordant name. The Lunar Transfer Vehicle *Aries* descends into the red womblike docking bay of the Clavius moon base, with a cut to a cool blue conference room containing eleven men and two women. HAL's panoptic eye is a hellish furnace of red and yellow aurally stoked by the roaring of *Discovery*'s machinery. According to Georg Seesslen, HAL's name is midway between the words "hell" and "hail" (as in "Heil Hitler!") and is thereby a "fascist machine" that kills out of cold reason.[86] HAL also recalls Hel in *Metropolis,* in Norse mythology the goddess of the underworld, half dead and half alive, and in Lang's film the woman Rotwang lost to a rival and whom he has re-created in the robot ("All it is missing is a soul!") that assumes the identity of Maria to lead the workers and the city to destruction. When Dave shuts HAL down, he floats in an enclosure suffused with red light that symbolizes the death of a humanoid machine. Bowman and Poole alternate wearing red and yellow spacesuits, and when Bowman takes on—and takes out—HAL, his spacesuit is red and his helmet is green. While this clash is a function of the plot, green (the color between yellow and blue) carries verdant associations with vitality and youth and with sickness and envy as well as meaning "go" in traffic parlance. Dave could be all these things: his brain vital while HAL's dies, his mind an immature anticipation of that of the Star-Child, his body deteriorating at the end of his journey, and even his mind filled with intellectual jealousy of HAL.[87]

The conclusion to *2001* represents the transition of Dave Bowman and thus of all humanity into a higher life form. The journey through the Star Gate is clearly a scene of copulation and fertilization, which, coupled with other scenes of phallic and vaginal mechanism and the almost completely marginal role of women in the film, represents a patriarchal and sexist tradition in science fiction concerning technology as a masculine means to usurp female reproductive powers.[88] But Kubrick the male is also as usual consciously as well as intuitively pursuing an artistic and philosophical agenda shaped by other conditions and considerations. Kubrick's setting for the conclusion of *2001* is a windowless and doorless room decorated in what most commentators agree is Louis XVI style and with a lighted floor that suggests a birth canal to the outside world.[89] What seem like alien voices on the soundtrack (mixed in from Ligeti's *Aventures*) suggest that Bowman is being observed. From the *Discovery* pod in which he passed through the Star Gate, he sees himself standing in the room in his spacesuit. Then from the spacesuit, he sees himself as a much older man eating a meal from a wheeled cart. In the silence of the room, the sound of utensils is sharp, suggesting the dry sloughing off of skin or chrysalis in the process of transformation as well as perhaps the parched and cracked ground associated with the husks of the "hollow men" at the end of the world in T. S. Eliot's *The Waste Land* (1922). Old seated Bowman knocks a wineglass to the floor and it shatters, which suggests the breaking of the goblet in the *Odyssey* that represents Odysseus's "triumphant reclamation of his home."[90] It has also been observed—dubiously, though Kubrick himself observed that the ending of the film constituted the coming of a new Messiah—that this action also reflects the breaking of a glass in the Jewish wedding ceremony, symbolizing the destruction of the temple in Jerusalem in 70 C.E. and the change from one way of life to a new one.[91] The eighteenth-century setting of the room makes historical sense in just this respect, since Louis XVI was the last Bourbon king of France from 1774 to 1792 and was beheaded in 1793 during the French Revolution. This signaled the start of the modern age, which in Kubrick's *2001* is coming to an end. The 1700s were also the age of rationalism, a human capacity frozen during the modern era into the hard, functional shell Kubrick coldly traces in *2001*. The Palladian arches over the paintings in the Star Gate room remind us of Pallas Athene, since Palladian refers both to the architectural style of Andrea Palladio (1518–1580), much copied in eighteenth-century England, and to the Greek goddess of wisdom, industry, and war.[92]

The final scene of the film brings us in an ironic and even disturbing way back to the conclusion of *Dr. Strangelove*. Clarke's novel ends (on a page without a page number) with the Star-Child destroying the nuclear weapons orbiting the earth.[93] Since Clarke retains great faith in the power of reason and the ultimate improvement of humankind, this is an ending of progress. But *2001* reminds us of the extinction of the human race at the conclusion of *Childhood's End*, which carries with it alarming tremors of rational and inhumane Enlightenment projects for human "improvement." Kubrick, while admiring reason and technology, also *feared* the consequences of thought, in particular the entire modern ethos of reason and technology in the hands of men with flaws made even worse by the pursuit and maintenance of power. But to end the film with the blooming of nuclear explosions would not only repeat the ending of *Dr. Strangelove* and thereby distract the audience from the optimism of *2001*'s conclusion, but also suggest the vital—and volatile—questions raised by Clarke's ending: What has happened—or will happen—to the human beings on earth? Have they all been transformed along with Bowman? Are they to be governed by the Star-Child? Or are they to die out "naturally" in evolutionary competition with the new species? *Or?*

Kubrick could not face this final "or." Not only because he wanted to avoid the detonating end-of-the-world pessimism of his last film revisited in the equation of human knowledge with weapons use in *2001*, but because the whole point of *2001* is the salvation of humanity by means of the creation of, as it were, a new Master Race. This very flirting with the concept of a new race may be the chief source of the ambiguity many have felt in the gaze of the Star-Child, and it of course reflects an ambiguity inherent in the plotting and surely felt by Kubrick himself.[94] After all, the twentieth-century precedents for designs to "improve" humanity were not, to say the least, encouraging. What is more, *2001*'s ending, particularly with the possible allusion through the breaking of the glass to the Jewish marriage ceremony, again recalls the mass-marriage proposal by Dalton Trumbo for *Spartacus* that Kubrick dismissed as Nazi claptrap. There is indeed, therefore, hope for the new in *2001*, but also fear of the old, what Kubrick spoke of as "the ultimate genocide" that lay in the possibility of nuclear war. Left unspoken, however, is the ultimate genocide that is not just possibility but historical reality and to which President Muffley irately compares the argument for a first-strike against the Soviet Union in *Dr. Strangelove*.[95] In his very next film—indeed, in his very next shot—Kubrick would show the face of a human future far more in accord with his dark view of the human past.

## *A Clockwork Orange* (1971)

Just as in the last shot of *2001* a face stares at us from the screen, so it is in the first shot of *A Clockwork Orange*. Only this time the face is not that of the Star-Child, who represents the evolution of humanity away from its dull and destructive ways, but of "the Star-Child of the Id."[96] This time the face is that of young thug Alexander DeLarge sometime in an indefinite future that also reflects the definite present of British and Western society. Like Orwell's *Nineteen Eighty-four*, the title of which literally mirrors the time of its writing, Kubrick's film elides present and past instead of bifurcating them, as he so radically does in *2001*, between an "old" present and a "new" future. To emphasize this "imminent future," Kubrick carries over Burgess's reference to Orwell in the name of the prison to which Alex is remanded, Staja 84F, shorthand for one "State Jail" among many that also recalls the nomenclature of the Soviet Gulag and the German *Stalags* of the Second World War.[97] The film also opens its examination of the death of civil society past, present, and future with an electronic rendering of Henry Purcell's "Music for the

Funeral of Queen Mary" (1694); the teenage language is a mixture of medieval and modern English combined with Russian; the police wear traditional uniforms, but the clothing and the architecture in general are extensions of contemporaneous trends; even a prominently displayed license plate on a futuristic "Durango 95" ends in "Q," a rare letter designation that appears on "cars of indeterminate age."[98]

Kubrick had read Anthony Burgess's novel *A Clockwork Orange* on the recommendation of Terry Southern while working on *Dr. Strangelove*. It is a story told by fourteen-year-old Alex Burgess, who goes by the name of Alex DeLarge and who with his gang terrorizes the society of Britain in the indeterminate future. Burgess based the sexual violence in the book on the experience of his wife, who, while he was in the army at Gibraltar in 1944, was beaten and robbed in London by four American deserters. Alex is finally imprisoned and subjected to the Ludovico Technique, a chemical aversion therapy that causes him to become nauseated whenever he feels aggression or lust. The government is exploiting this scientific behavioral regime because it wants to reduce crime and clear out the prisons for the incarceration of political opponents.[99] Alex, who narrates the story, is victimized upon his release from prison by those he victimized. He also becomes a pawn in the struggle of the liberal left against the proto-fascist government, ending up finally as a *cause célèbre* in the government's campaign to destroy the opposition. A last chapter of Part Three, Chapter 7, has Alex at the age of twenty-one looking back on his life from the mature perspective of marriage and the family. The point of the book is that moral choice had to be a result of free will and not imposed by conditioning or authority. Burgess was a Pelagian Catholic who rejected the idea of original sin and embraced "the notion of moral progress."[100] Without choice, Burgess argues, a human being is nothing more than "a clockwork orange," with only the appearance of a living thing covering a mechanical interior. The American edition (1963) of the novel on which Kubrick based his screenplay, however, omitted the last chapter, and so the film ends on a grimmer note that also reflects a postmodern view of society bound by domination. The film's union of Alex, overcoming the effects of the Ludovico treatment, and the proto-fascist government represented by the Minister of the Interior, with "his stern blue" eyes, resounds with Kubrick's mordant sense of the dangerous found world that remained the basic subject in all of his films.[101] A Hawk Film for Warner Bros., *Orange* was released at Christmas in 1971 to some acclaim but also furious controversy and condemnation. Like Nabokov with *Lolita*, Burgess was of two minds about it, regretting the omission of the final chapter but admiring many of its provocative formal and thematic features.[102]

Kubrick was also attracted to thug Alex's love for great German music: Bach, Handel, Mozart, and especially Beethoven's Ninth Symphony (1824)—in Alex's own teenage (nadsat) slang: "Music always sort of sharpened me up, O my brothers, and made me feel like Bog himself, ready to make with the old donner and blitzen and have vecks and ptitsas creeching away in my ha ha ha power."[103] Burgess was intent on exploring the connection between violence and German music in particular, a theme that engaged not only Kubrick's ambivalence about Germany but also his conviction about the inextricability of good and evil within all human beings: art critic Robert Hughes wrote that the film challenges the idea that fine art "provide[s] moral uplift."[104] By contrast, the soundtrack also features a silly tune that characterizes his bland, tamed parents' taste.[105] For reasons of narrative economy, Kubrick imports only Beethoven from the book, but foregrounds it aurally and visually to spectacularly disturbing effect. He satirically underscores Alex's artful, dancing "ultra-violence" by using Giaocchino Rossini's overture from *The Thieving Magpie* (1817) in two scenes (including one in an abandoned theater) of Alex-led criminality, while Alex himself sings the bouncy, joyful "Singin' in the Rain" (1952) while beating a husband and raping his wife.[106] And in Alex's enjoyment of material possession as well as of sex and violence, Kubrick accurately portrays the youth culture as basically materialistic and consumerist. As usual with Kubrick, no one escapes blame—all of us are all too human. From Kubrick's ironic point of view, there is no solution to any problem that does not bring with it further problems and leaves it up to the audience to consider such dilemmas.[107]

Unlike *2001*, the film is shot through with Nazi imagery. Burgess himself had visited Nazi Germany, witnessed the Nazi obsession with classical "Aryan" art, and experienced the visceral appeal of the ancient symbol of the swastika, which everywhere fluttered "its arrogance on the Berlin skyline."[108] The close association between Wagner's myth-laden Teutonic music and Hitler rendered Beethoven, with his dedication to human liberation, a much better choice for Burgess and for Kubrick (who eschewed Wagner in his films anyway), particularly the selection of the fourth movement of the Ninth Symphony based on Friedrich Schiller's poem "Ode to Joy" (1785). Kubrick, like Burgess, amplifies this terrible juxtaposition, no more so than when Alex's last Ludovico session accompanies scenes from Leni Riefenstahl's Nazi propaganda masterpiece *Triumph of the Will* and German war newsreels with an electronic version of the fourth movement that thereby links the first half of the nineteenth century with both halves of the twentieth and whose buzzy jauntiness mocks deadly Nazi grimness and its commercial representations. Burgess uses the Fifth Symphony for the Ludovico treatment, while Kubrick, for reasons of narrative economy as well as to concentrate the juxtaposition between odish joy and Nazi horror, scores Beethoven's Ninth for both the Ludovico sessions and Frank Alexander's subsequent "treatment" of Alex. In the book it is the "violent" Third Symphony of the fictional Otto Skadelig ("harmful" in Danish) that Alexander plays and not Beethoven's hopeful Ninth. A huge concrete eagle and swastika from *Triumph of the Will* flashes on the screen as Alex's words goose-step over the music on the soundtrack: "It was Ludwig van. Ninth Symphony. Fourth Movement." Kubrick's recourse once again to the eagle as a symbol of state power and violence is underlined when Alex, while reading the Bible in prison, imagines himself as a Roman soldier, his helmet sporting an eagle, scourging Christ.[109]

The Nazi presence in the film is thus as pervasive as in the novel, although attenuated in one vital respect in comparison with Burgess's treatment. In the film a British street gang wears Nazi regalia; another white-clad "droog" in the Korova Milkbar wears a black Nazi SS helmet; and one low-angle shot taken from the point of view of a congregation of prisoners consists of trusty Alex in black uniform and red armband à la SS, a guard with somewhat of a Hitler mustache and certainly Hitler mien and posture, and the chaplain with his arm in the position of Nazi salute (Figure 4, color insert).[110]

In the novel Alex is forced to watch bloody and gruesome atrocity films from the Second World War involving both the Japanese and the Germans. Kubrick, partly again for reasons of narrative economy, shows only German footage that, except for the Riefenstahl clips, consists of wartime newsreel footage featuring airplanes, tanks, and soldiers. Machines of death take the place of the bloody, mangled corpses in Burgess's text. The only blood we see is the manifestly fake blood in the clips from bad movies of sex and violence. While most of the German newsreel scenes seem to be from the campaign in Russia (a tank barrel precedes the camera through a seemingly endless field of sunflowers; a famous shot shows ruined buildings in Stalingrad), Kubrick attenuates the novel's references to the ghettos and the camps: "And there it was again all clear before my glazzies, these Germans prodding like beseeching and weeping Jews—vecks and cheenas and malchicks and devotchkas—into mestos where they would all snuff it with poison gas."[111] In the film Alex describes how he became conditioned against Beethoven's Ninth: "while they were showing me a particularly bad film of like a concentration camp, the background music was playing Beethoven."[112] But all we have seen on the screen during Beethoven's Ninth are scenes of combat and of Hitler and Himmler at Nuremberg commemorating German dead of the First World War. That Kubrick consigns "concentration camp" to words rather than to pictures reverses his usual preference for visual over spoken information, showing that he has significant artistic and personal reasons in line with the thesis of this book for doing so. Kubrick's reluctance—or refusal—to show the mortal consequences of war and persecution stemmed, as noted, from artistic considerations regarding the depiction of atrocity. But they also stemmed from an individual unwillingness to confront the horrors of the Holocaust in particular. While Kubrick's juxtaposition of a comic electronic rendition of Beethoven's Ninth with Nazi films is an instance of his finely honed sense of satirical humor, it also indicates a desire to use satire not only as a sword but also as a shield.

True to this form as well is Kubrick's (again also economic) decision to omit the character of "Big Jew," one of Alex's cell mates, although he retains Burgess's references to Alex identifying with Old Testament "Hebrew vino" and "yahoodies tolchocking each other." Also true to form, moreover, is Kubrick's indirect insinuation of the issue of Jews and anti-Semitism in two scenes. Before the attack on Miss Weathers, the "Cat Lady," at Woodmere Health Farm, gang member Georgie justifies robbing her because her house "is full up with like gold, and silver, and like jewels."[113] That this might be an echo of a common stereotype of Jews is suggested by the fact that the woman is played by Miriam Karlin. Karlin is a British actress active in Jewish causes and a prominent member in the 1970s of the Anti-Nazi League, which was one of the responses to the stirrings of neo-fascism in Britain at the time. Her mother came to England from Holland, and had lost her entire family at

Auschwitz.[114] An equally sly, even unconscious, vignette in this respect comes from the government's demonstration of the effectiveness of the Ludovico Technique on Alex. Before an audience of experts and dignitaries, Alex is insulted, struck, and pushed to the floor by an "actor." He is incapacitated by nausea brought on by his anger and, flat on his back, is forced to lick the sole of the man's shoe. What is very odd about the scene (in an *Annie Hall* [1977] sort of way) is that the actor's enunciation of the line "You see that shoe?" sounds like "You see that, Jew?" John Clive, who played the part, recalls no discussion of the line, its enunciation, or any subtext. He even thinks he ad-libbed the line, a practice Kubrick, as we saw especially with Peter Sellers, encouraged. Clive also remembers that he was called back alone to do this particular (and common Kubrickian) shot, from Alex's point of view looking upward past the shoe into the actor's face: "Stanley decided that he wanted to shoot that himself. . . . So he took the camera and laid down on the floor at my feet. Something I never expected. . . . And I had to put my foot in front of his face and tell him to lick it. Like I said, right out of left field."[115] It all went quite quickly, according to Clive, perhaps in a single take. Given Kubrick's insistence on getting something he wanted no matter how many takes it took, he was obviously satisfied. It is hardly farfetched to argue that at one level of consciousness or another Kubrick, flat on his back with a camera in his hands and a foot in his face, found (at the time and/or during editing) personal and artistic meaning in the sound of the words in terms, as we shall see in Chapter 8, of a recently heightened conscious and unconscious preoccupation with modern power, Jews, and the Holocaust. As one reviewer observed, this scene, reprising Big Brother's "boot stamping on a human face—forever" in *Nineteen Eighty-four*, "shows Kubrick's genius for fixing an aspect of the human condition in a single image, here Subjugation itself."[116]

Appropriately enough given its title, *A Clockwork Orange* is awash in the bright colors of contemporary and future pop art. Alex and his "droogs," by doubled literal and metaphorical contrast, are clothed (like the Teutonic knights in Eisenstein's *Alexander Nevsky* [1938]?) in white overalls and black hats. Red is prominent, of course, as the color of blood in the fact and fantasy of Alex and his gang. Once again, for Kubrick red is the color of the passions of body and of mind. Pale blue, as in *2001*, represents the cold, detached realms of authority, here especially scientific authority, as when Alex is "spotlighted in a dehumanized blue color to demonstrate before an audience the curative wonders of the Ludovico Technique."[117] In identical shots at "HOME," Frank Alexander types on a red IBM Selectric and later on a light blue one.[118] When Alexander and his political gang are driving Alex to suicide with Beethoven's Ninth, the speakers lie on a snooker table along with brightly colored balls, most of which are red.[119] Numbers, on the contrary, do not seem to play much of a role in the film, even though Burgess makes much of the number 21 in his novel, which has twenty-one chapters, as the symbol of the measure of maturity that Alex achieves. But since Kubrick ended his film with Burgess's penultimate chapter, perhaps it comes as no surprise that he does not make a creative departure from Burgess's penchant for arithmology except in the conditioning Serum 114, a pun on the CRM 114 code device in *Dr. Strangelove*.[120]

At the end of the film, the Nazi referent is amplified in Kubrick's own uniquely indirect way through his emphasis on the intervention of the state. Burgess, as we have noted, ends the novel from the perspective of family, while Kubrick concludes his film with the alliance between Alex and the Minister of the Interior that ends the American edition of the novel. For Kubrick, the "state has become the thug."[121] As he once told writer Joseph Laitin, "I've always been terrified by cops."[122] All the authority figures in the film are at least partly malevolent. Writer Frank Alexander, who opposes the government and seeks to use Alex for political purposes (the blue typewriter) and out of personal revenge for the rape and subsequent death of his wife (the red typewriter), is by name Alex's *Doppelgänger* in both their similarities and their differences. He is another manipulative but impotent man who, as a result of the beating by Alex and his gang, is, very much à la Kubrick, confined to a wheelchair that mirrors his earlier imprisonment behind his typewriter.[123] Kubrick's film ends with the alliance between Alex, who is recovering in a hospital from injuries suffered while trying to escape the illness brought on by Alexander's blasting him with Beethoven's Ninth, and the Minister of the Interior, a title that has a much more sinister, Germanic ring to it than the actual British title of Home Secretary. That the first name of the minister, who is unnamed in the novel, is Frederick (he and Alex are going to be great friends) also strikes the ear with a Teutonic clang. The name is perhaps traceable to Kubrick's work at the time on his film about Napoleon, before, during, and after whose era Prussian kings were all named Frederick. In any case, the minister has imprisoned Frank Alexander and his cohorts and has cashiered Dr. Brodsky and the Ludovico Technique. It appears as if the government is going to rely on the police and prosperity rather than on science to tame the population. In the final shot, the sexually ambiguous Alex has wet dream sex with a young woman while ladies and gentlemen in formal Ascot fashion applaud. The id is now in service to power, with Alex growling in delight, "I was cured all right."[124]

## *Barry Lyndon* (1975)

*Barry Lyndon* was not the next film Kubrick wanted to make. He wanted to make a film about Napoleon, but Hollywood studios were at the time reluctant to fund big-budget spectaculars. So Kubrick elected to make a film of a novel about the eighteenth century that would allow him to stage some of the kind of battlefield scenes he was planning for his Napoleon film.[125] *The Memoirs of Barry Lyndon, Esq.* by William Makepeace Thackeray (1811–1863) is a picaresque tale of the rise and fall in English society of a boastful young Irish rogue named Redmond Barry. An eighteenth-century setting also gave Kubrick the chance to return to the Age of Enlightenment, an era whose faith in reason had always fascinated, inspired, but also disappointed him. *Barry Lyndon* succeeds as a historical film on two levels: first, as a meticulous re-creation of the pace and appearance of the aristocratic life in the last years before the French Revolution, and, second, as a metahistorical contemplation of the end of one era and the beginning of another. The ensuing modern era would produce horrors beyond any scale imagined beforehand, culminating in the Holocaust: "The dream which Western man conceived in the eighteenth century, whose dawn he thought he saw in 1789, and which, until August 2, 1914, had grown stronger with the progress of enlightenment and the discoveries of science—this dream vanished finally ... before ... trainloads of little children."[126]

Produced for Warner Bros. as a Peregrine Film from Hawk Films, *Barry Lyndon* is a satirical and yet sympathetic Kubrick tale of an outsider who is defeated by the calcifying social order of the Old Regime on the brink of disaster. Unlike the novel, however, Kubrick puts much greater emphasis on the "pastness" of the historical and cultural context, a choice underlined by the fact that the film ends in the revolutionary year of 1789 instead of 1811, the year of Thackeray's birth during the long reign of George III (1760-1820). Partly again for reasons of economy, Kubrick in the end replaces the first-person narration of the novel with an omniscient narrator who ironically reflects society's point of view rather than just that of Barry himself.[127] While Kubrick exercises his usual satirical disdain for social snobbery and oppression that alienate humans from their vitality, *Barry Lyndon* also mourns the passing of a simpler and less destructive age of order. But its tone is "elegiac rather than nostalgic,"[128] reminding one of the sorrowful accounting of timeless human failings in the eighteenth-century poem referenced in the title of *Paths of Glory*. The elegy is not just for an age—it is for all ages. In particular, Kubrick mourns the woeful trajectory of history toward ever more stifling control and escalating atrocity in the modern era.[129]

The temporal connection between premodern and modern present is made clear through references to *A Clockwork Orange*. Kubrick is not just being reflexive in form, for he seeks to emphasize that the society that began its final death throes in 1789 was giving way to—while also anticipating—not just the nineteenth century but the twentieth and beyond. The first words spoken by a character in the film are those of Barry's cousin Nora Brady, whom he is paralytically wooing over a game of cards. She wins a hand and says, "Now, what shall it be?" which almost duplicates the opening words of Burgess's *A Clockwork Orange:* "What's it going to be then, eh?"[130] These are the words of the prison chaplain, the character who represents the author's point of view that human beings are not human if they lack the ability to make moral choice. Nora is mirroring the choice that love-struck Barry cannot make while also foreshadowing the eventual defeat of all his social ambitions in words that recall a larger human issue as well as the whole question of what the future of history holds. Later Barry admires the use of blues in a painting by the fictional "Ludovico Corday, a disciple of Alexandro Allori," a significant reference to *A Clockwork Orange* that takes on dark coloring.[131] Even the final title card of the film, which comments on the era's cruel and silly squabbles for rank by noting that the protagonists "are all equal now," is an ironic and tragic comment on the fate of the equality promised by the French Revolution.

*Barry Lyndon* reflects Kubrick's abiding Freudian concern with human desire and fear, particularly Oedipal conflict between sons and fathers and male struggles over isolation versus intimacy.[132] But the chief aim of the film is to explore history in terms of the social and national conflict that lays bare, according to Kubrick, the violence behind the façades of individuals and institutions. Kubrick shared with Thackeray a great distrust of power and a belief in "the unworthiness of the mighty."[133] When Redmond Barry becomes the titled Barry Lyndon, his new name expresses the social, cultural, and historical conflict and prejudice that makes his climb up the social pyramid unsuccessful in the end.[134] Kubrick himself was reminded of the legacy of bitterness between the Irish and the English. While filming *Barry Lyndon* in Ireland in the winter of 1973/1974, Kubrick received a death threat from someone claiming affiliation with the Irish Republican Army. Kubrick decided to do all further filming in England, confirming an old preference to remain close to home, directing his attention outward to the dangerous surrounding world from the much safer family environment.[135]

Kubrick, with traditional economy, significantly pared down the number of characters and incidents, characteristically leaving out a series of episodes involving Jewish diamond merchants and moneylenders. Perhaps along the same lines, Kubrick changed the name of Barry's army mentor and friend from Fagan to Grogan, fearing a distracting association in viewers' minds with the old Jewish crook Fagin in Dickens's *Oliver Twist* (1838).[136] There are two parts to the film. The first part charts Barry's "rise." He is forced to flee Ireland after a duel with the British Captain Quin over Nora. Kubrick's visual sense of humor is much in evidence in the conflict between Barry and Quin. Immediately following the scene in which Nora teases Barry by hiding a ribbon in her décolletage, Kubrick cuts to Captain Quin's regiment on parade to the skirl and rap of "British Grenadiers." While the camera performs the "stately pullback" that is one of the visual hallmarks of *Barry Lyndon,* behind the oncoming troops appears a cairned peak in the Comeragh Mountains the shape of a woman's breast and nipple while the narrator intones, "About this time the United Kingdom was in a state of great excitement."[137] Robbed by highwaymen, Barry joins the British army and goes off to Germany to fight in the Seven Years War (1756–1763), in which the French, Austrians, Russians, and Swedes are fighting the Prussians and the British. After a picaresque series of events, Barry meets, woos, and wins widow Lady Harriet Lyndon. The second part of the film begins with the marriage, whereby Redmond Barry becomes Barry Lyndon. At the end of a disastrous series of events, Barry leaves England to escape debtors' prison.

Kubrick's changes make Barry a more passive and melancholy figure than the ingenious and boisterous rogue of Thackeray's novel, for Kubrick's subject is the dreadful course of history and not just the picaresque adventures of an ambitious young Irishman.[138] This mournful tone is communicated by much of the period music used in the film, a peculiarly strong instance of Kubrick's attention to the historical specificity of musical selection also evident in music chosen for other films, including *The Shining*. This is especially the case with the title theme, a slow, sad sarabande by Georg Friedrich Handel (1685–1759), whose mournful minor key communicates Barry's loneliness as well as his sad end while also serving as an elegiac hymn for the entire age.[139] The sarabande is heard for a total of thirty-two minutes and underscores the most crucial events in Barry's life: the duel with Captain Quin, the injury and death of his son Bryan, and Barry's rapid fall after his duel with his stepson.[140] Similarly dolorous is the adagio from a cello concerto by Antonio Vivaldi (1678–1741) that accompanies Bryan's birth and Barry's reflection on his imminent decline.[141] Music from *Idomeneo* (1781) by Wolfgang Amadeus Mozart (1756–1791) ushers Barry into European high society after his military service, an appropriate accompaniment because the core of Mozart's opera is an Oedipal drama that characterizes Barry's youthful challenge to the patriarchs of the Old Regime aristocracy.[142] Kubrick's reliance on music specific to the period is also evident in the satirical use of the "Hohenfriedberger March" (1745?), written in honor of a famous Prussian victory over the Austrians, which plays over scenes of Barry's service with the Prussians.[143] The cavatina from *The Barber of Seville* (1782) by Giovanni Paisiello (1740–1816) accompanies two scenes of Barry and the Chevalier gambling, which reflects the opera's portrayal of the challenge to the decadent *ancien regime* posed by the rise of dynamic new classes.[144] The only music selections not from the eighteenth century are by Franz Schubert (1797–1828), in particular the andante from the Trio in E Flat (1828) for the romance between Barry and Lady Lyndon. Kubrick felt that there were no "tragic love-themes in eighteenth-century music" and used the alternating minor and major keys of the andante to dramatize the ebb and flow of emotion within the scenes.[145]

The symbolic use of color in *Barry Lyndon* is, like words, subordinated to the use of the medium of painting in the cinematography to represent the static and confining nature of eighteenth-century aristocratic society as well as the importance that society put on surface appearances of order and beauty.[146] Kubrick's cold blue is in evidence, but more apparent are the period candlelit scenes made possible by lightning-fast Zeiss lenses. Color is otherwise monopolized by the demands of historical accuracy, although the color of the Prussian uniforms has perhaps a deeper and darker meaning for Kubrick, as we shall discuss in Chapter 11. One clear instance of the symbolic use of color is the boat with the bright red sail that passes behind the skiff carrying Barry and Lady Lyndon just after the scene in which they first kiss. The waters are calm, but the boat with the red sail moves quickly and as the shot ends is turning toward the two lovers, a clear representation of dangers to come.[147] Numbers quite naturally take on historical significance rather than carry symbolic value, although the Seven Years War is consistent with Kubrick's use of that number as a symbol for military organization and violence. Its presence in Thackeray's novel was probably coincidence, but it could have served as part of the attraction of the story to Kubrick in constructing symbolic patterns.

More than anything else, *Barry Lyndon* concerns a world in which "power appears to be everything."[148] In Kubrick's eye, this is particularly true of military power, because he foregrounds Thackeray's antiwar sentiment through the use of an omniscient narrator who is much more given to sweeping philosophical statements than is Thackeray's Barry, who narrates his own story and sorrowfully emphasizes his own struggles. So Kubrick takes care to paraphrase Thackeray's only explicit condemnation of war and the military. Over a scene of British troops plundering a farmhouse, the narrator sadly intones: "Gentleman may talk of the age of chivalry, but remember the plowmen, poachers, and pickpockets whom they lead. It is with these shocking instruments that your great warriors and kings have been doing their murderous work in the world."[149] Kubrick also invents a humorous vignette concerning two homosexual British officers bathing in a stream not only, as he had said, as a bridge in the action but once again as a commentary on the cold, loveless world of hypermasculine warfare. While their exchange is a parody of the genuine human sentiment that is so lacking in *Barry Lyndon*, these two men—along with Grogan and Barry in the scene immediately preceding—are the only ones in the film who express tender affection. The scene is also in line with the British literary response to the First World War in which naked soldiers bathing was a commonplace in almost every English war memoir and symbolized the erotic, the pastoral, and the awful vulnerability of flesh to the swift, hard metal of modern industrial warfare.[150] Similarly, the juxtaposition of the breast-like hill and the British military parade expresses the gulf—and tie—between love and war.

Kubrick focuses in particular in this regard on the Prussian army, renowned for its efficiency, effectiveness, and brutal discipline. One of its critics called it a "'clockwork' army . . . of ferociously drilled but poorly motivated soldiers."[151] Thackeray, too, strongly condemned Prussian militarism under Frederick the Great, a criticism made in the context of his exceptional interest in, and some considerable sympathy for, German lands and people.[152] These complementary characteristics were aggravated by the attrition during the Seven Years War that compelled the Prussians to forcibly enroll prisoners of war and subjects of occupied countries into their army. Kubrick includes a scene of such impressments along with commentary from the novel, and Barry himself becomes one of them when Prussian captain Potzdorf discovers that he is a deserter from the English army.[153] The most fearsome images of this "clockwork" army are as, in a zoom/telephoto shot, the "Prussian army marches toward us, completely fills the screen, we see no breath [*Hauch*] of nature or sky . . . a foreboding of . . . mechanized war."[154] In their Kubrickian dualism of the mechanical and the organic, these shots recall the menacing unseen German soldiers of the Anthill in *Paths of Glory*. The satirical use of the "Hohenfriedberger March," a triumphal piece that Mark Crispin Miller has observed would not be out of place in *A Clockwork Orange*, introduces an allied dualism in *Barry Lyndon* having to do with the Prussian monarch, Frederick II. Frederick the Great (1712–1786) was the model of the enlightened monarch, a man of great learning and a composer whose works may have included the "Hohenfriedberger March," but who was also a brilliant and ruthless military leader. Frederick the Great, like Napoleon, thus embodied the inextricable union of creativity and violence that Kubrick saw as one great root of eternal human suffering.[155]

However, as in *Paths of Glory*, Kubrick juxtaposes a symbol of female German innocence, "a young German girl in peasant dress [who] materializes like a spirit in fairy tale" in contrast to "the loveless uprightness of the Prussians."[156] In the novel this woman, Lischen, whose husband is off in the war, is involved in some larceny, but the film only shows her and Barry sharing a tender romantic interlude that underlines Barry's failed search for genuine love and security. A certainly sad, perhaps sexist, but also ultimately cynical note, however, is provided by Thackeray's and Kubrick's narrator: "A lady who sets her heart upon a lad in uniform must prepare to change lovers pretty quickly, or her life will be but a sad one. This heart of Lischen's was like many a neighboring town that had been stormed and occupied many times before Barry came to invest it."[157] Kubrick once again displays his ambivalence toward things German in a way that was reflective of his family life. *Barry Lyndon* was also one of a trilogy of Kubrick films between *2001* and *Full Metal Jacket* that in one way or another addressed issues of the family—and the human race—in general. This was part of a Western cultural discourse in film and literature in the 1970s reflecting social and sexual challenges to the patriarchal family and to traditional gender roles. *A Clockwork Orange, Barry Lyndon,* and *The Shining* addressed, intentionally and unintentionally, terrors in and around the modern family. *The Shining,* as we have seen and will see, in 1980 would address the Holocaust as the darkest horror in the history of the human family.

## *Full Metal Jacket* (1987)

Like many other directors, Kubrick was seeking a property on the American war in Vietnam, which had come to such an ignominious close in 1975. In his usual way, he was reading everything he could on the subject and had been very impressed by Michael Herr's *Dispatches* (1977), a collection of eloquent reports from the battlefields of Southeast Asia as a frontline "soldier" of the critical "New Journalism." Coincidentally, the first film Herr saw upon his return from Vietnam was *2001*, and, just out of what American soldiers called "the world of shit," he was moved to tears by the film's optimistic ending. Kubrick told Herr that *Dispatches* would not make a film because it did not have a story, but in 1982 he came across Gustav Hasford's *The Short-Timers* (1979), a novel that in its terseness and economy seemed perfect. Kubrick hired Herr to help write a screenplay that, in contrast to the Expressionism of Coppola's *Apocalypse Now* or the formal conventionality and redemptive ending of Oliver Stone's *Platoon* (1986), would provide the basis for Kubrick's usual poetic realism.[158]

Since he wished to focus on the experience of the frontline troops and not on the officers or civilian leaders, Vietnam veteran Hasford chose as his title the term used by infantrymen ("grunts") to describe the 385 days of a normal Marine rotation in Vietnam. The term, an expression of human mortality in general, was also used to describe the last couple of weeks of a tour of duty, when the possibility of being killed or horribly wounded took on cruel irony and even greater tragedy.[159] Kubrick's title, which he found in a gun catalogue, not only describes the organic beings that are being turned into clockwork killing machines but also expresses the baleful ironies of good and evil. As he put it, "[a] 'full metal jacket' refers to a bullet design used by police and military the world over in which a lead bullet is encased in a copper jacket. It helps it feed into the gun better. It also keeps the lead from expanding inside the wound: which the Geneva Convention on Warfare makes a point of—I guess . . . it's meant to be more humane."[160]

Such irony tells us that Kubrick's antiwar views were another reason he was attracted to *The Short-Timers,* a novel that consciously follows in the absurdist tradition of *Catch-22*—for example, an officer named General Motors—characteristic of much of countercultural criticism of the American and Western postwar establishment. Kubrick surely was also struck by the fact that *The Short-Timers* was dedicated to a combat photographer killed in action in Vietnam and that in the novel the gentle combat photographer Rafter Man is run over by an American tank. Hasford's protagonist is James T. Davis, who is given the name Joker by his drill instructor for his sarcastic imitation of John Wayne. He is assigned out of training at Parris Island as a correspondent for *Stars and Stripes,* not a surprise since Hasford himself was a military correspondent in Vietnam. Joker's name thus assumes metaphorical significance in the sense of military journalism being to journalism what military music is to music. Kubrick's creative scoptophilic tendencies were thus fully engaged, particularly since the subject was the human activity known as war, which had so concerned him since youth. As Herr wrote of his experience in Vietnam: "You know how it is, you want to look and you don't want to look. I can remember the strange feelings I had when I was a kid looking at war photographs in *Life;* the ones that showed dead people or a lot of dead people lying close together in a field or a street, often touching, seeming to hold each other. . . . I was there to watch."[161]

It is thus appropriate that Kubrick in three scenes reflexively shows film coverage of the war, including one scene in which a Marine refers to "Vietnam, the Movie." But Joker and Rafter Man—as well as Hasford and Herr—also represent for the photographer and filmmaker Kubrick the possibility of mitigation of the horrors of the world through observation and education. Kubrick noted the American military's attempt to sell the war to the American people through advertising techniques, but also observed that media coverage of the war made another mass-mobilization war much less likely due to the gruesome images brought into American homes by the television networks.[162] While Kubrick as usual offers the audience no easy pieties or satisfying sentimentalism, there is a *soupçon* of hope in the film that does not exist in the novel. This is why Jung's "duality of man"—also engaging Kubrick's cinematic use of "the double"—rather than Freud's more despairing view of the inextricability of good and bad seems to prevail in *Full Metal Jacket.* And whereas in the book Joker becomes one of the hard men of the Marine Corps, in the film he undertakes a journey that preserves in him a fear of death that saves him "from the greater fear of losing his humanity."[163] But what Kubrick giveth, Kubrick taketh away, for, as in the novel, Rafter Man is horrifically brutalized by combat. There is some authorial guilt in having the *photographer* (who in the film survives) and not the journalist succumbing to the ethos of destruction, since Kubrick has noted that war films have a visceral appeal, something he himself no doubt felt keenly during a lifetime of careful, concerned, but also fascinated observation of a dangerous found and filmed world. This is reflexively represented in the double-entendre of the words spoken into the camera directly above repeatedly—in English—by the sniper mortally wounded by Rafter Man: "Shoot me." Kubrick underscores this identification by including his daughter Vivian (who was also making a documentary on *Full Metal Jacket* and, as Abigail Mead, composed music for the film) photographing a mass grave.[164] Kubrick's storyline therefore actually parallels Hasford's since in both novel and film it is the character most closely identified with the artist—that is, filmmaker and correspondent, respectively—who is brutalized.

Kubrick divides *Full Metal Jacket*, like *Barry Lyndon*, into two distinct parts. The first covers the training of Marine Corps Platoon 3092 at Parris Island, South Carolina, detailing the strictly mapped construction of the killing machines the corps requires.[165] The construction of hypermasculinity in Marine Corps training transforms "boys into men through the suppression of the feminine within and through the identification of sex with violence."[166] Women, including sisters and mothers, are degraded into nothing but sexual objects subordinated to phallic desire and power. Homosexuality, ironically fostered by the all-male military environment, must for that and other reasons be vigorously defended against. The men also relate to one another in scatological terms, partly because military regimentation requires the socialization of that most private part of the body and because anality is developmentally linked from infancy on with aggression. Kubrick visualizes this anal culture dramatically in the barracks head, a narrow white klieglightish bright corridor with a long row of toilets on each wall facing each other. The nickname given to a soft-bodied and fatally dysfunctional Marine, Gomer Pyle, itself incorporates both these sexual and scatological dynamics. The name is a reference to the homosexual actor who played Gomer Pyle on television, while the last name is a collective term for excrement and also recalls an old term, "piles" (from the Middle English *pyle*), for hemorrhoids.[167]

The second part of the film follows Joker into the dreadfully contingent and psychosexually ambiguous world of Da Nang, Phu Bai, and, finally, the city of Hué during the Communist Tet Offensive in February 1968. During the fighting in Hué, a sniper kills several members of the squad that Joker and Rafter Man have joined. Kubrick's purpose in the second part of *Full Metal Jacket* is to demonstrate the failure of militarized hypermasculinity to protect against the mechanized threats to a human body that, however hardened by training, remains soft, vulnerable flesh much—or, rather, exactly—like a woman's. The fear of passivity in the face of overwhelming weaponry, which is one motive for macho Marine posturing, dates back at least to the First World War, as dramatized in Pat Barker's novel *Regeneration* (1991). That the men of the Lusthog Squad in Hué are penetrated in slow bloody motion by the bullets of a sniper who turns out to be a young woman not only evidences the fact that modern weapons discount male physical superiority, but also signifies the failure of hypermasculine denial of common human vulnerability. Kubrick, in departing from the novel, makes this episode the final one in the film to emphasize just this point. Indeed, the second part of the film ends much as it begins, with a woman exercising her power over Marines: the film fades directly from Pyle's suicide on a toilet at Parris Island to a street in Da Nang. A prostitute enters the frame from behind the camera, which slowly follows her advance on Joker and Rafter Man. They bargain over sex until a young man grabs Rafter Man's camera and escapes with a confederate on a motorbike. The music over and under the scene is Nancy Sinatra singing "These Boots Are Made for Walkin'" (1966), which carries meanings of aggression and abandonment associated with both Marine boot camp and the dangerous world of sex and crime in Vietnam. The prostitute is probably working with the thieves, while Joker observes that half the whores are Viet Cong and—as the woman at his hip coughs—the other half have tuberculosis.[168] At the end of the film, it is Joker who kills the dreadfully mangled sniper rather than letting her rot, as Lusthog Squad mate Animal Mother recommends. We then hear a soldier off screen speak in a double-entendre linking pornography and the corps ("body" of men): "Hard core, man, fucking hard core."[169]

Perhaps surprisingly, Kubrick's film is much less brutal in its depiction of war and atrocity than Hasford's book. We are spared scenes of the mutilation of bodies, including that of the young sniper, who has her feet, ring finger, and head cut off. In a way, though, this makes Kubrick's film even darker than the novel, since we do not have the luxury of putting all the blame on sadists who inhabit Hasford's Marine Corps. We have "normal" guys like Joker, who can show mercy only through killing and whose kind mentorship only helps Leonard Lawrence ("Gomer Pyle") to become a killer. And there is Rafter Man, who exults lustily in his killing of the sniper. Kubrick concentrates outright sadism in the character of Animal Mother and in a scene taken from Herr's *Dispatches*—that is, from real-life reportage—in which a helicopter machine-gunner takes crazy delight in slaughtering men, women, children, and animals. The last shots of the film show the squad marching at night against the backdrop of the burning city and, as members of the first television generation fighting the first television war, singing the "Mickey Mouse Club Song." The 1985 screenplay ends with Joker's funeral after his death in Vietnam and—in flashback—as eight-year-old Jimmy Davis playing war, but in the film Joker's words from Vietnam in narration, taken from the middle of Hasford's book, are the last we hear: "I'm in a world of shit, yes, but I am alive. And I am not afraid."[170] The many pop songs in the film similarly do not allow us to slip into the comfort of moral fables or generate nostalgia for a period we have—physically at least—survived. These songs are not the obvious antiwar or countercultural anthems of the era, and all of them predate 1968, which means they are songs from the soldiers' peaceful early civilian lives. As with "These Boots Are Made for Walkin'," they are tied to specific scenes to suggest and reinforce ideas connected with the rupture in the lives of soldiers represented by the war in Vietnam.[171]

Kubrick moves Hasford's novel into the realm of his own concerns by removing the action from the typical jungle environment of Vietnam represented in American literature and film. Familiar symbols in the form of numbers and colors also appear that replace or accentuate aspects of the novel in accord with the director's vision. For example, while instances of 7 in *The Short-Timers* probably just reflect the significant presence in our culture of the number 7, in *Full Metal Jacket* 7 is the usual Kubrick sign of the military order since it appears in the first shot of the film narrative, a white 7 against a red field on the wall behind Sergeant Hartman as he "welcomes" his new recruits to boot camp. In two instances, Kubrick changes or invents numbers in order to increase the subtle, and therefore disquieting, presence of 7 in his story. He changes a unit called simply One-Five to Hotel Two-Five, recalling in the conjunction of military oral alphabetization and numbering two potent symbols of inhumanity in *The Shining*.[172] Kubrick also changes the Military Occupation Specialty (MOS) Number that Joker is given for his assignment to "Basic Military Journalism" from 4312 (Print Journalist) to the wholly invented 4212, a number that reflects multiples of the number 7 (42 as well as the mirror of 21 in 12) in a manner again used extensively in *The Shining*. Joker's "rotation date" out of Vietnam, moreover, written on his helmet is "7-12-68."[173]

The usual Kubrick colors appear, though they are subordinated to the colors of nature and battle. As the attack on Hué opens, Kubrick shows the wreckage of red and yellow cars as a warning of deadly danger.[174] A Kubrick cold blue suffuses the night scenes in which Pyle is beaten by his squad mates and in which he kills Hartman and himself. The beating, which, according to the novel and the screenplay, occurs on the first day of the seventh week of training, is to punish Pyle for the failings for which Hartman punishes the entire squad. It takes place "in a disconcertingly beautiful cerulean light" that represents the cool internalization of violent authority by the recruits. Pyle is pinned to his bunk and beaten with bars of soap wrapped in towels, which recalls the gauntlet of blue-jacketed soldiers whipping a malefactor shown in *Barry Lyndon* as a graphic example of brutal Prussian army discipline, while the celesta on the soundtrack revisits a major musical motif of *The Shining* tied directly to fascism in the 1930s.[175]

In line with antiestablishment literature of the 1960s and 1970s, Hasford makes regular reference to the recent Nazi past as the benchmark of modern evil. The opening of *The Short-Timers* describes Parris Island as "a suburban death camp" and the transfer to advanced infantry training at Camp Geiger in North Carolina on "cattle-car buses," while there are also references to Hitler, Goebbels, and Göring, as well as to the cruel words above the gate to Auschwitz: "Arbeit Macht Frei."[176] Kubrick, as a means of economy and artistry, substitutes image for word. Though it is used in only one scene, the image Kubrick chooses—the swastika—has unrivaled recognition, power, and relevance. The Nazi use of the swastika has imprinted it, a symbol originally of "well-being," with evil and revulsion, along with whatever appeal it might still—or, terribly, also therefore—possess. The swastika was a widely used symbol in Asian cultures as in the West before Hitler. It often appears in ornamental and architectural designs, representing renewal and metamorphosis in the linking, replicating, and reversing of its arms throughout a pattern. But the labyrinthine quality of the ornamental swastika also recalls Kubrick's habitual use of the maze as a symbol of violent entrapment. It is just such a pattern based on the swastika that dominates the ornamental grilles in the ruined, flaming concrete room in which the Marines confront and kill the sniper (Figures 5 and 6, color inserts).[177]

For Kubrick, of course, as for all late-twentieth-century moderns, the swastika symbolizes the absolute extreme of racial hatred and violence. It is also the most extreme and ironic expression of the labyrinthine inextricability of good and evil—the worst with the best (or "best")—that for Kubrick characterizes human life. So not only do mazed, mirrored, swelling, and swirling swastikas loom in the final killing scene of *Full Metal Jacket,* but they set themselves in opposition to or harmony with other subjects in the film. The swastika contrasts with the peace button Joker wears, a symbol of opposition to the Vietnam War itself. The peace symbol itself was drawn in 1958 as part of a British movement for nuclear disarmament, a Strangelovian subject also referenced by "I Am Become Death" written on Animal Mother's helmet, words from the *Bhagavad-Gita* that scientist J. Robert Oppenheimer remembered upon witnessing the detonation of the first atomic bomb in 1945.[178] The swastika also punctuates the racism that surfaces throughout the film. To the grunts, all Vietnamese are "gooks" or "zipperheads." Animal Mother takes a whore away from black Eightball with an easy racist jibe fleshed out by sexual innuendo and chilling historical reference: "all fucking niggers must fucking hang."[179] With his usual avoidance of Jewish characters, Kubrick omits the novel's fragging of a Jewish officer, substituting a Polish Catholic (Walter J. Schinoski) killed by enemy fire, and leaves a Jew out of the traditional Second World War all-American platoon. Hartman does once refer to "kikes," but only as part of a list that embraces "niggers, wops, and greasers."[180]

Apart from the ornamental swastikas, the Holocaust itself probably does not come into even indirect discourse in *Full Metal Jacket* unless one wishes to view the piles of hair of new recruits on the floor under the opening credits as also a reference to the concentration camps, or a tall column of flaming and smoking concrete in one scene during the battle for Hué as the chimney of a crematorium.[181] The importance of the latter shot, however, is that it is part of the blasted noir-like cityscape of Hué that calls up "images of World War II, New York dereliction, and *1984*" or "a concrete nightmare in broad daylight, a firebombed Dresden on the day after, that oddly resembles the blank, vacant New York urban corridors from the last part of *Killer's Kiss.*"[182] Kubrick, by choosing to film his battle sequence in the abandoned Beckton Gasworks (1868–1969) in London's East End, emphasizes that war is both literally and figuratively manmade. In so doing, he avoids the dangerous implication in accounts from *Heart of Darkness* onward that the depredations of civilized Western man are best expressed through the metaphor of dark, primitive peoples and places. In the case of Vietnam, Hollywood (and film noir) has tended to conflate Asia with dangerous sexuality, treacherous women, and male homoeroticism, a tendency *Full Metal Jacket* may not fully escape. But whatever the cultural streams that fed into Kubrick's own creative Mekong Delta, he was also following his own line of vision, one that had been sharpened to keenness on the horrors of the Western world since the 1930s in particular. The 1930s concrete architecture at the Beckton Gasworks that had survived the Second World War resembled that of French-built Hué, so Kubrick was figuratively as well as literally on familiar European ground. Moreover, Kubrick's habit of self-reference arguably appears in the 1985 screenplay in the form of *The Shining*'s Holocaust skein of yellow, seven, paper, and gas:

> The master sergeant is writing on a piece of yellow paper on a clipboard. He doesn't look up, but jerks his thumb over his shoulder.
> "Two-five. Gasworks . . . a click north."
> "Gasworks. Outstanding. Thanks, top."
> The master sergeant walks away, writing on the yellow paper.[183]

Like the novel, the film concentrates on the infantrymen, but the threat and reality of power—*temporal* power—from above is omnipresent and militarized. It is thus as threatening as it is appalling that the drill instructor praises the marksmanship of former Marines Charles Whitman, who gunned down civilians at the University of Texas, and Lee Harvey Oswald, who shot President Kennedy in Dallas.[184] Once again, to a degree, this power wears a German face. Hasford gives his drill instructor a German name, Gunnery Sergeant Gerheim, which Kubrick changes to Hartman, stressing the construction of "hard" (German *hart*, echoed in Hartman's mantra "it is the hard heart that kills"[185]) men, "the storm troopers of America."[186] Hartman's observation that they will become "ministers of death, praying for war," thus conveys, like the title Minister of the Interior in *A Clockwork Orange*, fascistic as well as religious associations. In spite or because of such intentions, *Full Metal Jacket*, like *A Clockwork Orange*, has become for some viewers a male fetish object. This is a danger given the subject matter and approach, but such nefarious effects can be outweighed by Kubrick's humane instincts. The frequently reflexive humor he brings to his treatment makes it easier—or too easy—to indulge oneself in the evil perpetrated by his characters: Hartman announcing Christmas services by "Chaplain Charlie" or a soldier's reference to Oswald shooting from "that book suppository building."[187] But the effect on the thoughtful and empathic viewer should be Kafkaesque. For Kubrick, as for Conrad, darkness is the lesson drawn from the heart of hardness.

## *Eyes Wide Shut* (1999)

What would be his last film constituted a double odyssey for Kubrick. For the first time since *Killer's Kiss*, Kubrick places a film in his hometown of New York City. And the film he places there is based on a story written about Vienna, the capital of the empire under whose double-eagle symbol his ancestors had lived before emigrating to New York in 1899. Kubrick had purchased the rights to Arthur Schnitzler's novella *Dream Story* in the late 1960s. That he waited for thirty years to film his adaptation of Schnitzler's novella testifies not only to the many other projects he had in mind, but also to the fact that the subject matter required a more mature and wiser perspective on the lifelong struggles that constitute human sexuality and emotional life.[188] This film, which immediately before his death he described as "my best movie ever," was one he obviously wished to make.[189] But that he was also ambivalent about it is clear from the long period of creative gestation and avoidance. The subject of men and women is a consistent theme in Kubrick's films, and four of his last five films (*A Clockwork Orange, Barry Lyndon, The Shining,* and *Eyes Wide Shut*) in one way or another focus on the family unit. As in *2001, A Clockwork Orange,* and *Full Metal Jacket,* a Kubrick daughter, this time Katharina Kubrick Hobbs, appears, as the mother of a patient, while paintings by Hobbs and Christiane Kubrick adorn the film. These paintings, most of them in a family's apartment, show fields, flowers, or germinating seeds. In another, palatial home, a large painting of a naked pregnant woman hangs in a bathroom above a chair in which a naked, overdosed prostitute sprawls. This juxtaposition dramatizes the film's concern with the procreative and nurturing value of family and the home, whatever the difficulties humans bring to their every interaction within as well as without it.[190] Growing introspection as well as the prospect of death therefore may have been behind Kubrick's desire to make a final statement on love, marriage, and family as the primitive and enduring basis for humankind.[191]

Kubrick again links the events of everyday life with the history of the human race in general but also with that of central Europe. The most substantial link between *Eyes Wide Shut* and *Dream Story* is psychoanalysis. Arthur Schnitzler (1862–1931) was a physician and writer whose fiction explored the psyche in a way that paralleled the work of Freud. Freud in fact regarded Schnitzler as his *Doppelgänger.* But Schnitzler was not concerned simply with the intrapsychic; he was also interested in the problems of the family and of society. It is in these respects that he made the central theme of his works the world of Vienna around 1900. Schnitzler, like Freud, saw that behind the stiff conventions of society raged the tumults of love and death within and among people.[192]

Schnitzler's *Dream Story* concerns Fridolin, a physician embodying Schnitzler's sensitivity to Jews' social vulnerability, and his wife, Albertine. At a masked ball, both flirt with others and then each subsequently confesses to the other previous temptations and fantasies at a seaside resort in Denmark, she with an officer and he with a young girl on the beach. Fridolin feels betrayed since he makes no distinction between dream and behavior. He fantasizes about taking revenge by having affairs and then confessing them to her. Beneath the apparently smooth surface of this marriage lie the turbulent seas of desire and aggression. Fridolin then embarks on a series of bizarre, unconsummated encounters over a period of two days, first with a patient's daughter who confesses her love for him, then with a young prostitute dying of tuberculosis, and finally at a masked orgy at which he is saved from humiliation and maybe worse by an anonymous woman whose corpse he later discovers in a morgue. He had been directed to the orgy by his *Doppelgänger,* a friend who had left medical school and since has made a living as a pianist. The story ends with the laughter of Fridolin and Albertine's daughter over a spring day and with her parents recognizing both the fragility and the strength of their family bonds.

Both Schnitzler's story and Kubrick's film demarcate the boundaries between dream and reality in order to make the point that in two senses human beings live with their eyes wide shut. On the one hand, we live oblivious to the workings of our unconscious minds; that is, our wide-open eyes do not see the unconscious drives behind our feelings and actions. On the other hand, shutting our eyes allows us to dream and thereby have insight into our unconscious lives.[193] In *Eyes Wide Shut* this insight is available to the audience but not to the characters through form and content structured, as in the novella, like a dream. Tiny visual and aural clues and coincidences hint at unconscious emotional conflicts. Dream structure and imagery accompany the masking and misleading dialogue, the film substituting such imagery for the first-person voice-overs originally in the screenplay.[194] Specific dream forms are reproduced: one variety of anxiety dream is one in which the dreamer arrives late into a situation, has no control over it, no understanding of its context, and thus risks being unmasked and humiliated. Kubrick's Bill Harford, Schnitzler's Fridolin, has several such experiences: he arrives upstairs at the party that opens the film to find a naked prostitute with a drug overdose; twice at a costume shop he confronts two Japanese men and a half-naked girl; he arrives late at the masked orgy and is literally unmasked; he goes to Nick's hotel, only to learn that Nick has been taken away; a return to the first prostitute's apartment reveals that she is HIV positive (Bill passes the Lotto Store on both occasions[195]); he discovers a "lost" mask on his pillow next to his sleeping wife; and his search at a hospital for the prostitute who saved him at the orgy ends with the news that she has already died. A dream of progression through a series of rooms, according to Freud, can be a brothel dream, which Kubrick represents directly in Bill's tour of the mansion in which the (anti)climactic orgy takes place.[196] The entrance to the mansion is carpeted in red and leads "through heavy velvet drapes into a vast hall . . . carved in white marble," vagina imagery also reflected in the previous scene in which the half-naked daughter of the Slavic Milich at the costume shop whispers in Bill's ear that he "should have a cloak lined in ermine."[197]

In *Eyes Wide Shut* "virtually every scene has to do with sexual desire and the creation of obstacles to its realization."[198] As Bill seeks revenge on his wife for her fantasized infidelity, he experiences paranoia, doubt, delay, and frustration during a literal odyssey of desire.[199] His response to his wife's confession is preempted by a call concerning the death of a patient; his flirtation at the party is interrupted by another medical emergency; he starts to have sex with a prostitute, but then answers his cell phone to talk to his wife; a conversation with another prostitute is broken off by the discovery of his illicit presence at the orgy; and the same prostitute intervenes in Bill's subsequent interrogation. Other interruptions mirror this dynamic: Bill's conversation with his old friend by the host's secretary and the dead man's daughter's confession of love by the arrival of her fiancé.[200] Such interruptions, more frequent in the film than in the novella, are common in dreams and usually signal continuing repression of conflict and/or fantasies surrounding desire and death. The interruptions in *Eyes Wide Shut* therefore represent not only Bill's desire and his conflicts, including guilt and punishment, over desire (including homosexuality, pedophilia, and necrophilia), but also fantasies of maternal salvation. Kubrick's old theme of hostile and needy male images of females reflects here Schnitzler's treatment of the Freudian split between "the mother and the whore" made more complicated (and thus more realistic) by making Bill's wife, Alice, like Albertine, the cruel woman who reveals her own aggression in dreams of Bill's humiliation and punishment, while the prostitute is the maternal rescuer. At the same time, his wife (and, through her, his mother) is clearly the one he has been searching for all along, as the doubling of women (Domino, which is a type of mask, and her roommate Sally; the overdosed hooker at Ziegler's and Mandy at the orgy) indicates. And it is Bill's wife as well who has possibly saved his life by calling him before he had sex with an HIV-positive woman. Given the centrality of the woman in this odyssey, one can apply to the scenario the Chodorovian and Lacanian analysis of the power of the mother as the object of primal symbiotic desire as well as the *Ur*-reminder of limit and mortality.[201]

*Eyes Wide Shut* also differs from *Dream Story*, but the differences only underscore important psychological and artistic linkages between the world of central Europe at the outset of the twentieth century and the world of America at century's end. The principal difference between the film and the novella is that what was originally set in Vienna at the end of the nineteenth century is now set in New York at the end of the twentieth. From the beginning, apparently, Kubrick wished to establish something essential about human desires, fears, and relationships that transcend the boundaries of time and place. In a revealing exchange with screenwriter Frederic Raphael, Kubrick made this intention quite clear:

> F. R.: Things have changed a lot between men and women since Schnitzler's time.
> S. K.: Have they? I don't think they have.[202]

Kubrick in fact had nothing less in mind than to compare the decadence of the declining Austro-Hungarian Empire at the beginning of the twentieth century with the decadence of the declining American empire at the century's end. Kubrick's camera glides in, out, and around the rooms of New York City in a way strongly reminiscent not only of a dreamer's progress through a dream but of the flowing camera of Ophuls that recorded the lives within the sumptuous and decadent mansions of old Europe. In Kubrick's film, America is exposed as the place where everything, including people, is for sale. Women in particular are commodities. Bill, using the typically banal words that hide psychological truths from others and from himself, has as his first words in the film, "Honey, have you seen my wallet?" which associate him with money and power. Alice's first and equally banal words when we see her are "How do I look?" Alice and all the women in the film are concerned with their physical appearance, in or out of clothes. For its part, Bill's obsession with sex inevitably calls up associations, whether intended or not, with President Bill Clinton as a sign of American *fin-de-siècle* decadence.[203]

Like the quotations of Strauss in *2001* and *A.I.*, fusion of the Austrian past and the American present emphasizes the degree to which Kubrick's own past was a constant psychological and creative reference point for his life and work. The music that opens the film, Dmitri Shostakovich's "Waltz 2" from *Jazz Suite No. 2* (1938) represents a union of distinctively Viennese and American musical forms, waltz and jazz, to underscore the continuity Kubrick sees between the Austrian then and the American now. This musical junction of past and present is dramatized cinematically by transforming the Shostakovitch piece from nondiegetic to diegetic music. Under the music we follow Bill and Alice through their preparations to attend a party. As the couple leaves their bedroom, Bill switches off the radio and the music on the soundtrack ends. The other main musical theme in *Eyes Wide Shut* is also of central European origin, György Ligeti's *Musica Ricercata* (1953), along with contemporary pieces by Jocelyn Pook. Kubrick further links the Old World and the New by means of eleven American romantic instrumentals from 1924 to 1974 that fill much of the film's score, all "dance music that might have descended collaterally from [the waltzes of] Strauss."[204] Kubrick reinforces the Viennese origins of the story by quoting from Mozart's C Minor Mass, *Requiem* (1783), and from the morose and modernist "Grey Clouds" (1881) by Franz Liszt (1811–1886). He draws from Beethoven's only opera, *Fidelio* (1805), the original subtitle to which was *Die eheliche Liebe* (*Conjugal Love*), by substituting as the password to the orgy "Fidelio" for Schnitzler's "Denmark." The word is ironic since in Italian it means "he who is faithful," the central moral issue in the story. (It also reinforces the confusion of sexual identity in *Eyes Wide Shut* since in the opera Fidelio is in fact Leonora, who has disguised herself as a prison guard in an attempt to free her husband.) Fragmented and dreamlike Italian associations include the Roman erotic poet Ovid, the Verona Restaurant, the Venetian carnival masks and Catholic-*manqué* ceremony at the orgy, and a scene on television that Alice watches from Paul Mazursky's *Blume in Love* (1975)—a film about marital infidelity that takes place in Venice, California, and Venice, Italy—in which a café orchestra plays Rudolf Sieczynski's "Vienna, You City of My Dreams" (1913). Indeed, *Eyes Wide Shut* itself is constructed like a sonata (from the Italian *sonàta*), a tripartite structure of "opposing themes and key relationships" resolved into a whole, a form that was predominant in Austro-German music in the late eighteenth and early nineteenth centuries and that in the film (with its Sonata Café advertising "Sonata jazz") expresses the real conflicts but also the possible harmony between and among people.[205] These Italian references are what break through the repression barrier in Bill's (and Alice's) mind and indicate the underlying conflict inhabiting their dreams and days, the struggle for and with fidelity against the drives of desire.

Kubrick has also changed the protagonists from Jews into Gentiles. Kubrick told Raphael that he did not want either Bill Harford or friend Nick Nightingale to be Jewish.[206] Ironically, part of the appeal of *Dream Story* to Kubrick was most likely the outsider status of its Jewish characters, in particular Nachtigal (nightingale), a Polish Jew from Galicia whose origins are reflected in dreamlike fashion in the locale for the orgy: the fancy western suburb of Vienna called Galitzinberg.[207] There are in all this surely considerations of narrative economy as well as an eye— an eye wide open—for the box office. Traces of Schnitzler's concern with the marginal status of Jews in central Europe before the First World War nevertheless persist in *Eyes Wide Shut*. Bill's patients have Jewish names and the only clearly Jewish character in *Eyes Wide Shut,* Lou Nathanson, is a corpse taking the place of the dead Austrian government councilor in the novella whose death calls Fridolin out from the exchange with Albertine of tales of sexual temptation. Raphael adopted the name from someone he knew, but the filmic constructions around Nathanson in *Eyes Wide Shut* show that it is more than likely that the name struck a conscious and creative chord within Kubrick.[208] First, Nathan is the son of the biblical Jacob referenced in a musical composition used in *The Shining* and the prophet who attacked King David for his infidelity with the wife of Uriah. Second, in the play *Nathan der Weise* (1779) by Gotthold Lessing (1729–1781), it is the Jewish patriarch Nathan who makes an Enlightenment plea for religious tolerance. That Nathanson's corpse represents the dead eighteenth century is indicated in a dreamlike manner by the French royal *fleur-de-lis* pattern on the light blue walls and drapes of the bedroom that has become a death chamber.[209] For Nathan's sons, as it were, the anti-Semitism of the succeeding modern age that is highlighted in Schnitzler's novella leaves this ecumenical eighteenth-century ideal as cold and dead as Nathanson's corpse.

A similarly indirect but surely intentional retention of the theme of anti-Semitism occurs in a confrontation on the street between Bill and a group of college students. In the novella, the students are members of an anti-Semitic fraternity, but Kubrick changes the scene to one of gay bashing. This sharpens the film's focus on matters of sexual fear and desire. But this connection between the subjects of anti-Semitism and homosexuality suggests Schnitzler's own concomitant concern with external threats to Jews in particular. Anti-Semitic caricatures have often represented Jews as weak or effeminate and therefore a threat, ironically as well as illogically, to the dominant religious, social, or racial order. This conception of order was increasingly characterized in the late nineteenth and early twentieth centuries by an emphasis, especially on the radical right, on hypermasculine identities coincident with the power and symbols of an authoritarian state and a racially homogeneous society. That this particular historical phenomenon might have informed Kubrick's choices for indirect citation in *Eyes Wide Shut* is suggested by Kubrick's substitution in his *A Clockwork Orange* of a pair of generic prison homosexuals for Burgess's lisping "Big Jew, a very fat sweaty veck lying flat on his bunk, like dead."[210] There is also a possible reference along these lines to *Scarlet Street,* the postwar Lang film that Kubrick referenced in *Lolita,* in the red sign reading "Jewelry" seen behind Bill just before he rounds the corner and comes upon the college boys. Tom Conley has read a Greenwich Village jewelry sign in *Scarlet Street* as a rebus—that is, a written hieroglyph within the film image containing other words and meanings, in this case the word "Jewry," which reflects the synchronous liberation of the concentration camps and the problematic American confrontation with their reality. That Kubrick juxtaposes this sign with the one explicit reference to Schnitzler's portrayal of anti-Semitism strongly suggests that it is a representation of Lang's image, particularly since the street scenes were filmed on exactingly constructed sets that are, typically for Kubrick, realistic but not naturalistic.[211]

Another aspect of Kubrick's preservation of the subtext of anti-Semitism in this particular scene involves his habitual use of color to carry ideas. The homophobes who harass Bill on the street wear Yale shirts and jackets that refer to the blue caps worn by the anti-Semitic Alemannia fraternity boys who wordlessly elbow Fridolin aside in the novella. The reference is all the more historically powerful since Yale, like other Ivy League universities until after the Second World War, limited the enrollment and employment of Jews in favor of Gentiles like Bill. And Kubrick, employing a classic example of a dream's capacity to signify the large in the small, has Bill shoved by a *blond* boy against a blue Mercedes-Benz: a Kubrickian reference to cold authority, Schnitzler's subject of anti-Semitism, and Bill's sexual paranoia (a blue Mercedes in *The Man in the Glass Booth* [1975] represents the paranoia of a Holocaust survivor in Manhattan who pretends to be a concentration camp commander). These details are not fortuitous, according to *Eyes Wide Shut* cinematographer Larry Smith: "Stanley had a phenomenal eye for small details. If we didn't like the color of the walls or something else in the scene, he'd have them changed."[212] Save for the Yellow Cabs in fourteen scenes (7M96, which Bill hails at least four times at night in scenes 8, 16, 27, and 31, recalls the conclusion to *The Killing*), yellow is infrequent. But such exclusivity may signify the earlier and subsequent plight of Jews in Europe, since the most apparent use of the color is the warm yellow of the entrance and hallways of the ornate Nathanson apartment. For yellow is not only a color often associated with disease, infection, and decay that coincides literally as well as metaphorically with Nathanson's illness and death, but also a color associated with cowardice and betrayal and thus often historically and tragically in the Christian world with Jews.

Since the film is concerned primarily and powerfully with sexuality and fidelity, colors are more often used as vehicles (so to speak) for these more universal human dynamics. Kubrick utilizes a wide range of bold and also subtle colors to capture a particular mood or emotional setting. For example, various hues of blue, from icy to deep cerulean, are omnipresent and associated with "the cold presence of fear of emotional exposure."[213] While the deeper shade of blue is not inconsistent with its employment in other Kubrick films, it is much more in evidence in *Eyes Wide Shut*. By contrast, as we shall see, blue in *The Shining* quantitatively and qualitatively took on more of its habitual Kubrickian representation of chilling authority as well as the color's traditional associations with transcendence, ghosts, and death. Here the deeper blue might also seem to promise some degree of emotional warmth, while also—as in Bill's "blue movie" daydreams of his wife's infidelity that spell "whore"—anticipating the more sexual and violent reds and purples (red + blue) that dominate the second half of the film. Throughout the film, red is an omnipresent color. In nearly *every* scene of the film there are the reds of the Christmas season, of sexual passion, of the darker couplings of passion and power in the high houses of the mighty. We have already mentioned the sexual symbolism of the red trappings of the Long Island mansion. Equally striking and significant is the bright red baize on the pool table around which Ziegler lets Bill know of the dangerous game (that is no game) in which he has involved himself. Even the Harfords' babysitter and the Nathansons' maid are named Roz and Rosa, respectively.[214]

The other major difference between *Dream Story* and *Eyes Wide Shut* is Kubrick's addition of the character of Victor Ziegler, who hosts the party at the beginning of the film, attends the orgy on Long Island, and, in a concluding scene, instructs Bill in the ways of the world. Ziegler represents the economic and political power elite ("all the best people" of *Barry Lyndon* and *The Shining*) that ignores "ordinary people" and manipulates Kubrickian intermediaries like Bill who serve—or, recklessly, question—them.[215] Raphael invented this name too, but it may have struck an unconscious chord in Kubrick since in German it means "brick maker," perhaps recalling Christiane's wartime exile at the brickworks in Reihen. Ziegler, another fearsome Kubrick father, is also Bill's *Doppelgänger,* for he embodies in maximal form the evil that, according to Kubrick, is within all human beings and thus reminds us that even in Schnitzler's story there was a sense that for Jews in particular a "couple's cocoon will not protect them from the madness that's already taking hold of Europe."[216] Ziegler lives in a palatial Manhattan apartment with an upstairs bathroom tricked out like a den, which suggests the mixture of cold reason and twisted passion typical of Kubrick villains. The orgy, likewise a "ritual devoted not to pleasure but to authority and fear," takes place at an even larger mansion named Somerton.[217] Somerton resembles the Overlook Hotel in *The Shining,* which is open only in the summer and is a playground for the rich and infamous, as well as the summer palace Schleissheim in *Paths of Glory* and Summering in *The Burning Secret.* Its architectonic assertion of obscene and mighty power stands in contrast the "modest, single-story Empire-style villa" in *Dream Story.*[218]

Given this habitual Kubrickian theme of dangerous temporal power, it is no surprise that the music in *Eyes Wide Shut* carries subtle but significant associations with Nazism and totalitarianism. Russian composer Shostakovich finished the waltz in his *Jazz Suite No. 2* in the autumn of 1938 surely under the impact of the annexation of Austria by Nazi Germany, which had occurred that March. It is probably for this reason that the music can accurately be characterized, in the words of Michael Herr, as a "rose with a canker in it."[219] For its part, Ligeti's piercingly repeated striking of a single piano key in *Musica Ricercata* captures how deeply Bill in particular has been affected by his odyssey. Ligeti had written this music as "a knife in Stalin's heart" and dedicated it to the memory of Hungarian composer Béla Bartók, who had written some similar music in the 1930s to protest fascism.[220] Beethoven's *Fidelio* carries a second meaning in just this respect, since the opera concerns a man freed by his wife from imprisonment for having attempted to expose political corruption.

In the end, recapitulating the family environment in which Kubrick always lived, Bill seeks the company, counsel, and comfort of women as well as his own "latent female sensitivity."[221] While anything but a social revolutionary, Bill at the end of the film no longer regards his masters as he did at the beginning. His patient at Ziegler's party, the overdosed hooker Mandy, is allegedly dead. In this, Bill is like Colonel Dax in *Paths of Glory,* still trapped in a violent world of power and passion but no longer (as) naïve about its realities. Perhaps like Florestan in *Fidelio,* he is being freed from the prison of a corrupt political and social hierarchy by his own Leonora(s). There is thus some optimism in the use of Beethoven's music in *Eyes Wide Shut* in a way that was not the case in the cynical invocation of the Ninth Symphony in *A Clockwork Orange*. For its part, Alice's dream does not have the elements of sadism that mark Albertine's, even though her word to Bill, "Fuck," that concludes the film contains elements of psychological aggression as well as physical passion that also mark a significant cinematic predecessor: Nicholas Roeg's *Bad Timing: A Sensual Obsession* (1980).[222] At the end, Bill, Alice, and Helena are in FAO Schwarz (originally of Vienna), with all its false and commercial gaiety ringing out over rows and rows of stuffed toy animals. But the family is together, Christmas (like *2001*) marks a male birth, and Helena wants an old-fashioned baby carriage for her doll Sabrina or perhaps for the child her parents will, in "fucking," conceive. Sabrina is also the modern Cinderella of three films (two directed by Billy Wilder and Sydney Pollack, respectively) who does not confine herself to dependence on a Prince Charming.[223] This reference, too, might indicate some hope for families that can nurture men different from Victor Ziegler, different from Gunnery Sergeant Hartman, different from Redmond Barry, different from Alex DeLarge, different from Dr. Floyd, different from General Ripper, different from Dr. Strangelove.

# 7
# ALMOST DIRECTED BY STANLEY KUBRICK, 1953–2001

From his earliest years as a filmmaker to the end of his filmmaking career, Kubrick considered and developed many other film projects than the ones he brought to the screen. Some never went beyond the acquisition of rights or the initial planning stages, while some others in the end produced scripts. In 1953 the Production Code Administration rejected "Along Came a Spider" for the script's treatment of rape, violence, illicit sex, and absence of "compensating moral values." It also rejected "The Snatchers" (1955), from an unpublished novel by Lionel White, which fell afoul of the PCA's "kidnapping clause." The latter, however, was later released as *The Night of the Following Day* (1968), starring Marlon Brando. "Lunatic at Large" (1955) was the draft of a screenplay by Jim Thompson "about an American soldier and a psychopathic female with homicidal tendencies," and Harris-Kubrick also took an option on Martin Russ's *The Last Parallel: A Marine's War Journal* (1957) about the Korean War. "I Stole 16 Million Dollars" (also known as "The Theft") was another script by Lionel White and based on the life of safecracker Herbert Emerson Wilson. Kubrick also considered a television series based on the Second World War comedy *Operation Mad Ball* (1957), while "The 7th Virginia Cavalry Raider" (1958) was a partially completed Kubrick script on the Civil War adventures of Confederate officer John Singleton Mosby. Finally, "The Passion Flower Hotel" featured young women at an all-girls school who sell sexual services to a nearby all-boys school.[1]

Harris-Kubrick was also interested in directing a film based on Felix Jackson's novel *So Help Me God* (1955), which attacks the anti-Communist witch-hunts that damaged or destroyed many Hollywood careers, including those of writers like Trumbo and directors like Dassin, both of whose work Kubrick knew well. The novel also makes clear the accusatory equation between Communists and Jews so common in the Cold War years of the 1950s, even drawing a parallel between the persecution at that time in the United States and Germany just after Hitler's rise to power.[2] The PCA would not approve the novel as a basis for a screenplay, however, since it violated the principle that "prominent institutions be not misrepresented."[3] This project was part of a pattern of interest that, on the prominent basis of *Paths of Glory* and *Spartacus*, earned Kubrick an inaccurate or at least simplistic reputation as a liberal or even a socialist in the late 1950s and early 1960s. Kubrick's pessimism precluded Marxist sympathies, and he was equally skeptical about the possibility of solving social problems through traditional liberal nostrums.[4] But he still had too much heart to be a reactionary or even a conservative.

Nevertheless, a dark view of society was surely what prompted Kubrick to consider an option on Calder Willingham's novel *Natural Child* (1952), which also was deemed unacceptable by the PCA because it deals with abortion and illicit sex.[5] The setting is Manhattan, and there is another reminder for Kubrick of postwar anti-Semitism through disparaging references to Galitzianers as "white" Jews and Litvaks as "black."[6]

The picture at this time that Kubrick came closest to making was Marlon Brando's *One-Eyed Jacks* (1961). Brando, who had been impressed by *The Killing* and *Paths of Glory*, hired Kubrick to direct the film of a novel by Charles Neider about Billy the Kid, *The Authentic Death of Hendry Jones* (1956). The title of the film is a southern card-playing expression, which in Neider's novel symbolizes the hidden sides of people and which, in the form of the Jack of Spades, Kubrick himself had used in one scene in *Killer's Kiss* to dramatize Gloria's apparent betrayal of Davy.[7] But the project had always remained Brando's, and Kubrick was fired after telling Brando, "Marlon, I don't know what this picture's about."[8] Brando had indeed changed the story from the death of a killer to the survival of a hero. *One-Eyed Jacks* has the look and feel of the new genre of anti-Westerns filled with the tragic lives of antiheroes that, like film noir, challenged the complacency and conformity of the Eisenhower years in America, but, as Neider himself concluded, "the film sentimentalizes the novel [through] a romantic, perhaps adolescent bitter-sweetness that distinguishes it from other westerns."[9] A Kubrick telling of the tale would have been very different, of course, certainly realizing the "melancholy nihilism" of Neider's book in its depiction of life as a rigged game of chance, all expressed in the Conradian atmosphere of the novel's setting at the Punta del Diablo (Devil's Point) on the California coast: "There was a smell of seaweed in the air and the breakers looked like burning oil. Everything turned gloomy and blue and the trees stuck out black against the ocean light."[10]

The projects Kubrick considered from the mid-1960s on have been subject to far greater misinformation than those documented for the early phase of his career before he became a star, a celebrity, and, for some, a *bête noire*. During the production of *Dr. Strangelove* writer Terry Southern, who also proposed sequels to *Dr.*

*Strangelove* to Kubrick, encouraged him to think about making a film about a studio director making a big-budget Hollywood pornographic movie. Southern wrote a screenplay entitled "Blue Movie" about a director resembling Kubrick, but Kubrick decided in the end that such a film was impossible. Southern published the script as the novel *Blue Movie* (1970), dedicating it to Kubrick, and the idea ended up as part of the film *S.O.B.* (1981).[11] Kubrick also briefly considered filming Diane Johnson's novel *The Shadow Knows* (1974), about a divorced woman's growing fear for her life, but instead hired Johnson to help write the screenplay for *The Shining*.[12]

Kubrick also worked on or considered a number of projects involving German subjects.[13] When it came to direct confrontation with artistic treatment of the Nazi era, however, his approach-avoidance syndrome kicked in. After giving up on the idea of a film about Veit Harlan, Kubrick entertained the idea of filming Thomas Keneally's *Schindler's Ark* (1982), which ended up as Steven Spielberg's *Schindler's List* (1993). Earlier he had turned down the idea of making a film of the memoirs of Hitler's architect Albert Speer, *Inside the Third Reich* (1970).[14] When presented with a screenplay for the Speer film, Kubrick expressed great interest but said that because it was in effect a love story between Hitler and Speer he could not do it: "It's fascinating stuff. But, you know, the thing is—how can I do it when I'm Jewish? I would love to make it, but how can I as a Jew?"[15] There were also reports that Kubrick considered making a film of Patrick Süskind's deconstructionist Hitler allegory *Perfume: The Story of a Murderer* (1985). But even though that book is a historically metaphoric treatment of the Holocaust and, like *Barry Lyndon*, takes place at the time of the Enlightenment and the Seven Years War, Jan Harlan has said that Kubrick never contemplated making a film of it and had not even read the book when the first reports of such plans appeared.[16]

In addition to these flirtations, there were five projects over Kubrick's career that developed into more serious, if also unconsummated, relationships. While even screenplays, especially for Kubrick films, tell relatively little about the finished product, the history of their development and analysis of their contents offer further instructive context for an understanding of Kubrick's interests and influences.

## *The Burning Secret*

When in 1956 MGM turned down the Harris-Kubrick idea for a film of Humphrey Cobb's *Paths of Glory*, the studio told the two young producers to look through the MGM Story Department for another source for a film. They came across Stefan Zweig's novella *The Burning Secret*, with which, according to Harris, Kubrick was already familiar and about which he was most enthusiastic. Zweig had been born in Vienna in 1881 and became part of that city's great turn-of-the-century cultural efflorescence and was a friend of Freud and Schnitzler. His stories and biographies made it to Hollywood, where Ophuls made *Letter from an Unknown Woman* (1948) from a book by Zweig. The Jewish Zweig was forced to flee the Nazis in 1938. He went to Brazil, where in February 1942 he and his mistress, devastated by the destruction of the culture and peoples of Europe, committed suicide in Petrópolis, a suburb of Rio de Janeiro. His last work, *Chess Novella* (1942), had used chess as an analogy for the psychological deterioration of a Jew being interrogated by the Gestapo. *The Burning Secret,* published the year the First World War broke out, is a Freudian tale that concerns a young baron who, while at Summering, a spa in the mountains, seeks to seduce a beautiful Jewish woman. As a means to this end, the baron befriends the woman's twelve-year-old son. The boy becomes increasingly anxious and resentful as he senses what the baron is after. He flees to his grandmother's house, to which his father has come from Vienna to find out what is going on. Just as the boy is about to tell him, he sees his mother put her finger to her lips and he lies in order to save her reputation. Terribly excited by the story, Kubrick once again hired Calder Willingham to write the screenplay, but studio and Production Code problems doomed the project.[17]

Surely one of the appeals of the story to Kubrick, and one that at the same time made the PCA so skittish, was its strong Oedipal content. The issue of childhood sexual curiosity, discovery, and challenge is a Kubrick trope, animating in particular *Lolita, Barry Lyndon, The Shining,* and *Eyes Wide Shut.*[18] But in *The Burning Secret* the dynamics of secrecy and duplicity in sexual matters are especially marked, and in this respect the story also resonates with the pattern established early in Kubrick's life to suspect—and inspect—dangerous forces behind the façade of the world's civility. This connection of the psychological-sexual and historical-political is represented by Summering, another of Kubrick's high summer rooms like Somerton in *Eyes Wide Shut* and the Overlook in *The Shining,* where the intersection of power, sex, and violence serves as an expression of fundamental human dilemmas and outrages. The title of Zweig's novella by coincidence communicates more to a latter-day reader such as Kubrick in this respect than was ever intended, for, aside from his own growing sexual awareness, the greatest "burning secret" of Kubrick's fourteenth year, the year of Zweig's suicide, was the Holocaust. Nine years before, in 1933, Zweig himself was certainly conscious of the words of the nineteenth-century German-Jewish poet Heinrich Heine: "Wherever they first burn books, they end by burning people." Neither Zweig nor Heine, of course, had any idea of how many people were to be burned by the Nazis in 1942 and in the other interminable years of the Holocaust. But in 1933, by another coincidence, Zweig found *The Burning Secret* at the center of a Nazi storm that would by 1942 turn from wind and rain, as it were, to gas and fire. Ironically, the controversy involved the first film version of *The Burning Secret,* the consequences from which, Zweig believed, he was saved by his association with "Aryan" composer Richard Strauss.[19]

## "The German Lieutenant"

In 1958 Kubrick was strongly interested in making another war film to follow *Paths of Glory*. Richard Adams, a former paratrooper in Korea, had written a screenplay based partly on his own experiences, but Kubrick apparently wanted to do for the Second World War what his last film had done for the First. The story was to be as gritty as *Paths of Glory*, only this time told from the German side. The studios were cool to the idea since Marlon Brando was just then playing a German officer in the film of Irwin Shaw's novel *The Young Lions* (1958).[20] But once again, Kubrick was planning a film directly concerned with war and the futility of operational planning. And clearly the Second World War in particular continued to be on and in his mind, just as under other influences in succeeding decades Kubrick would—reluctantly and fitfully—turn his artistic attention to the operational planning and execution of the most boundless atrocity of the Second World War. Adams and Kubrick therefore co-authored a revised screenplay entitled "The German Lieutenant" for Harris-Kubrick Pictures.

As the film opens, it is 1945, in the last weeks of the war, and the roads are filled with retreating German troops and civilian refugees. Along the roadsides dangle the bodies of deserters hanged by the SS. The first scene shows a dozen German paratroop officers watching newsreels on events leading up to the outbreak of the war and the German Blitzkrieg victories in Poland and France. These films are to be followed by *Romance on the Danube* (1936)—in Kubrickian fashion linking prewar Vienna to the Third Reich—and as Lieutenant Oskar Kraus leaves, the music of Strauss's "Blue Danube Waltz" fills the soundtrack. Kraus and Lieutenant Paul Dietrich are going to Karlstadt to tell the wife of a comrade of her husband's death. They first go to a bar where men and women are seeking a few last desperate moments of pleasure in the escalating chaos of the Nazi defeat. Kraus leads a toast to those who "have survived twelve years of madness, each in their own way."[21] As he leaves the bar, Dietrich is arrested by the Gestapo for defeatism, but he kills the agent and escapes. He then visits Anna Koenig and tells her that her husband, Klaus, died honorably. Anna wants Paul, as many others apparently have, to make love to her. He refuses in disgust, but she shouts: "You don't have the right to be so smug. I have brought much more happiness to the world than all you little tin soldier boys playing at being heroes."[22]

The next day Colonel von Sperling announces that the unit is to be dropped behind enemy lines in order to blow up a railway bridge over the Main River. Dietrich is enlivened by the order, but other officers object to the mission as suicidal. One even refuses the order and is ordered shot. Dietrich is given command of the operation and asks in vain that the condemned man be spared. Kraus decides to desert, but because Dietrich will not desert with him he goes along. The Gestapo shows up, inquiring about the agent's death. Dietrich admits responsibility to von Sperling, but the colonel protects him by blaming the man who has been shot for refusing to follow orders. The original plan for the mission had called for a night drop and a march to the target, but rain delays the operation. Begun "at 0700" in broad daylight, the drop results in the killing and wounding of many of the men. It also turns out that they have been dropped in the wrong place. From hiding, they watch endless columns of American tanks and troops advancing through the German countryside. A skirmish results in the capture of an American soldier. As in *Fear and*

*Desire,* though in a more naturalistic style, much is made of the similarities between American and German soldiers. Dietrich agrees to let Corporal Scott go in exchange for American medical care of his wounded, but Kraus foolishly reveals the object of the mission and Dietrich is thereby forced to have the American shot.

A long combat scene ensues on the approaches to the bridge. Kraus proves to be a coward, but he argues that the war is lost and what matters is their children's future.[23] Dietrich draws his pistol but does not wish to kill his old friend. He tells Kraus to stay with the wounded and surrender to the Americans. But Kraus swears that he will tell the Americans of the German plan. Dietrich then pummels Kraus until he agrees to continue the mission. Dietrich and another man wire the bridge while Kraus organizes a defensive perimeter. But when the Americans show up, Kraus wants to surrender to them. The Germans are taken prisoner and forced to wait for transportation into captivity in the middle of the bridge, since the American commander rightly believes the bridge has been wired high up on the span. Dietrich urges the men to remain on the bridge so as not to betray the mission. They are all frightened but do not appear so from a distance to the Americans, who do not want to risk their engineers' lives unless absolutely necessary. Dietrich encourages his men: "You will tell your grandchildren about it, and they will tell theirs. At this moment we are living like few men have ever lived." The men's faces "begin to glow with a weird kind of enthusiasm and emotion, seldom seen."[24] Captain Jones then decides that the Germans might lose their composure once they are off the bridge. At his order, the Germans leave the bridge, singing, and the bridge blows up behind them. The final scene of the screenplay shows Dietrich ten years later as a postal clerk, lost in the monotony of his job.

This screenplay is a scant guide to Kubrick's intentions, particularly since he later told Jan Harlan that he could no longer remember why he was ever interested in this script.[25] But "The German Lieutenant," while sketchy and even implausible in parts, does resemble other Kubrick films in its depiction of human beings at the mercy of a senseless environment and their own fears and desires. It also, typically for Kubrick, denies the viewer any sort of easy identification with a "good" character as opposed to a "bad" one. In fact, the two German lieutenants are each other's *Doppelgänger.* Kraus appears to be a coward, but he is right about not only the fruitlessness of death for a lost cause but also, by (the audience's?) extension, the unjustness of the German cause in the Second World War. It might be intentionally ironic that the gung-ho officer, Paul Dietrich, has the same first name as the hero of Erich Maria Remarque's German pacifist classic of the First World War, *All Quiet on the Western Front* (1928), particularly in light of his ruthless, though militarily necessary, decision to have the captured American soldier killed. But an evaluation of his character, too, is complicated by the Gestapo charge of defeatism, his desire to spare Kraus, and his attempt to save the life of the officer who refused von Sperling's order. The ending of the film, with the "hero" Dietrich imprisoned in a job he obviously finds anonymous and meaningless, also has a definite Kubrickian cast to it. Obviously, Dietrich's grandchildren, if he has any, could care less about his wartime heroism. At the same time, Dietrich's prediction of postwar pointlessness in contrast to the moment of bravery on the bridge ("the war is over and what the hell are we going to do with ourselves anyway?") suggests that men (and especially Germans?) not at war are fish out of water.[26] The script, typical for films of the era about the Second World War, does not address Nazi racism or the Holocaust, confining itself to the Gestapo's pursuit of "good" Germans who have displayed doubts about whether the war is good for Germany, a question raised by Germans much more often when Germany was losing than when Germany was winning, which may also have been part of Kubrick's point.

## "Napoleon"

The film that Kubrick most wanted to make that he never made was about the French general and emperor Napoleon Bonaparte (1769–1821), the only man in the modern era besides Hitler to conquer nearly all of Europe. The film was never made due to inadequate financial backing.[27] Kubrick, consciously at least, did not so much admire Napoleon's conquest as he identified with Napoleon's great capacity to amass, store, and analyze large amounts of information. Kubrick was also fascinated with the man of genius and action brought down as much by fatal flaws as by fate and the historical contingencies of the outside world.[28] Kubrick once provided a virtual Baedeker guide of his own interests and concerns reflected in Napoleon's life: a "sex life worthy of . . . Schnitzler"; an "obsessional passion" for his wife, Josephine; and a career that shaped "our own world" as well as embodying the great issues of the abuse of power, the course of revolution, and "the relationship of the individual to the state."[29] Kubrick marshaled experts such as Napoleon scholar Felix Markham of Oxford University and produced reams of research about all aspects of Napoleon's life and times. The script highlights Napoleon's meticulously rational preparations for battle, the failures that nevertheless accompanied his successes, and the cruel and capricious infidelities of both Napoleon and Josephine. Not surprisingly, Kubrick also used Napoleon as a vehicle for the director's own view that society is corrupt because human beings are corrupt and that "authority's main job is to keep man from being at his worst."[30]

For Kubrick, the French emperor was an embodiment of Lord Acton's dictum, "Power corrupts, and absolute power corrupts absolutely." Napoleon has remained a controversial figure among historians, but Kubrick's historical adviser, Felix Markham, was unwilling to compare Napoleon with the subsequent conqueror of Europe: Hitler.[31] Subsequent historical research has confirmed the fact, however, that Napoleon was the individual catalyst for the undermining of the old world order and the establishment of the modern age of unprecedented state power. As such, Kubrick's "Napoleon" bears some of the lineaments of Anthony Burgess's *Napoleon Symphony* (1974), in which Burgess suggests parallels as well as causal relationships between Napoleon's increasingly tyrannical rule over Europe and Hitler's. Burgess portrays the Napoleonic age as one that not only helped generate the nationalism in the German lands that would contribute to the rise of Hitler but, even more portentous, also presaged the more vicious tyrannies of the twentieth century. Burgess thought of Napoleon in Kubrickian terms "as a great demonic force, and essentially as a very modern man, really a very contemporary man, because he's . . . half animal and half computer."[32] Early in his career, Napoleon was a creature of the Enlightenment, for which Kubrick had such admiration and trepidation, as well as an idealist who believed in the liberating power of reason and republicanism. But Napoleon increasingly became a captive of his own egocentrism and thus an agent of evil. Unlike the older Markham but like the younger Kubrick, Burgess had come to intellectual and artistic maturity in a world lit by the fires of Auschwitz. Burgess, no doubt influenced by the 1970s preoccupation with Nazi Germany and the Holocaust, has his Napoleon voice the following method of dealing with the inhabitants of a captured enemy city: "Consider, for instance, the efficient annihilation of a whole disaffected city. The unventilated room crammed with subjects—we must not think of victims, prisoners, the terms being emotive—and the introduction, by a simple pumping device, of some venomous inhalant."[33] While Kubrick's screenplay makes no such obvious, or even indirect, references to the Holocaust, shards of the worst of the modern dictatorial state lie within it: Napoleon's reputation, like Hitler's, as a reckless gambler; Napoleon's view of the Russians as barbarians; and the Russians' view (with their secret police) of the French army as one composed of criminals.[34] And perhaps Kubrick's decision to focus on the Russian campaign of 1812/1813 rather than on Napoleon's final defeat at Waterloo in Belgium in 1815 was meant to reflect the time and place of the most ruthless total war of the twentieth century, fought over much of the burning ground of the Nazi Final Solution.

These differing generational views of the Second World War and the Holocaust are also exemplified in Dutch historian Pieter Geyl's book, *Napoleon, For and Against* (1946). The book was written in 1944 during the darkest days of the Nazi occupation of the Netherlands. Geyl had begun studying Napoleon early in 1940 when western Europe was threatened with German invasion. After the invasion that came that spring, Geyl, at one time a political prisoner in Buchenwald, found that the audiences to whom he lectured saw obvious parallels between Napoleon and Hitler. In a preface written on October 14, 1944, for the original postwar Dutch edition of the book, Geyl recalls hearing British prime minister Winston Churchill on the BBC say that he always hated to compare Hitler with Napoleon but then did so anyway, noting only that Napoleon's conquests carried civilization along with them while Hitler's regime lacked "any civilization at all." [35] For his part, Geyl saw another parallel between Napoleon's rule and Hitler's: the joining of power to conviction through the means of the state.[36]

The chief difference of course was the German treatment of the Jews. That Geyl twice labels this treatment "persecution" rather than "extermination" is an artifact of the years from 1944 to 1963, in which he was writing and publishing the three editions of *Napoleon, For and Against*.[37] For Kubrick, the surrounding culture adopted the more accurate term "extermination," the word (*Ausrottung*) the Nazis used. Twenty years after the end of the Second World War, therefore, the difference between Hitler and Napoleon was seen as greater than it had been during and just after the war. But, and this was certainly the case with Kubrick, this more piercing view of the Holocaust also put into serious question the entire trajectory of the modern age, which was born of the French Revolution at the end of the eighteenth century and raised by the Napoleonic Wars and Industrial Revolution of the nineteenth century. From this perspective, a relatively humane age had given way to an industriously inhumane one, certainly at least part of the reason Kubrick could consider a film on Napoleon but not one on Hitler.

### "Aryan Papers"

The outright Holocaust film Kubrick came closest to making—and in the event not all that close—was to be based on Louis Begley's novel *Wartime Lies* but became only a screenplay entitled "Aryan Papers." The novel concerns a young Polish Jew—another child confronting a dark "found world"—who under the Nazi occupation is hidden as a Catholic. "Aryan papers" was the term used to describe living under a false identity with the protection of phony documents proving one was not Jewish.[38] Begley himself had lived in Poland during the war and so had autobiographical knowledge of the time, the place, and the events, a fact underlined by the first-person narration by the young boy Maciek as well as the novel's personal and contemplative tone. Kubrick and his associates poured a great deal of work into the project, including the scouting of the Czech town of Brno to serve as wartime Warsaw.[39] The novel obviously had personal appeal for Kubrick on a number of grounds. Begley, first of all, draws extensively on Freud to describe the heavily charged Oedipal scenario of a young boy living alone and being protected by his audacious and courageous aunt Tania, who had always been his surrogate mother, replacing the real mother who had died giving him birth. There is also the repeated motif, familiar to Kubrick at American remove, of the boy Maciek's identification with the aggressor. This takes the form of admiring the hard, efficient, and apparently invincible German Wehrmacht and SS as well as relying on the "heart-freezing Teutonic efficiency" of his aunt-protector: "I could be a hunter and an aggressor, like SS units destroying partisans in the forest or, very soon, rebellious Jews in the ghetto of Warsaw."[40] Even the German soldier Reinhard, who falsely promises to protect Tania and "Janek," must have struck a responsive and ironic chord in Kubrick due to the fact that he wears a Strangelovian glove on the end of a mechanical arm.[41]

Begley's novel also represents an indirect approach to the subject matter of the Holocaust since it is the first-person fictional account of a Jew in hiding from the Nazis rather than a factual account of the Nazi extermination of the Jews. And the theme contained in its very title offered a reprise of Kubrick's own much more benign experience of the façade of Hollywood films and general wartime disinclination to fully comprehend reports of the extermination. In addition to a mention of "talk of a camp in Bełżec, near Lublin," Kubrick's approach-avoidance syndrome must also have been engaged by Maciek's words that open the novel: "I was born a few months after the burning of the Reichstag in T., a town of about forty thousand in a part of Poland that before the Great War had belonged to the Austrian-Hungarian Empire. My father was T.'s leading physician. . . . My mother's older sister was . . . [of] the close world of wealthy Galician Jews."[42] T. by its population has to be Tarnopol, the only town of that size in Galicia beginning with that letter. It was thus close to Buczacz and Probużna, while Kubrick's father too, as we know, was a physician. Begley's book, due to its detailed geographic proximity to the history of Kubrick's own family, was both attractive and threatening to Kubrick and one of the reasons why, as we learned in Chapter 1, he was dreadfully depressed the entire time he was writing the screenplay for "Aryan Papers." The personal nature of the project was also reflected in his decision to write the screenplay alone, but that only compounded the emotional burden; he never even spoke directly with Begley.[43] He was therefore even more distracted by two other projects, one that became the posthumous production *A.I.* and the other *Eyes Wide Shut*. And, finally, perhaps in this regard *The Shining* had satisfied—and/or repelled—him at some subliminal level. *That* perhaps was as close as he felt he could come to the subject.

Kubrick also apparently felt that Spielberg's *Schindler's List* had beaten him to the punch.[44] This rationale, while commercially logical, seems somewhat lame in light of Kubrick's deserved reputation as a courageous risk taker. It is also artistically questionable since Kubrick, like others, later went on record that Spielberg's film was not about the Holocaust. As he told Frederic Raphael: "The Holocaust is about six million people who get killed. *Schindler's List* was about six hundred who don't."[45] Interestingly, Kubrick uses the present tense for the event and the past tense for the film, indicating the proximity the Holocaust itself had to Kubrick as well as dismissal of the film by consigning it to history. He was moved once again (see Chapter 8) to contact Holocaust historian Raul Hilberg, saying that Spielberg had not made the right film. He even invited Hilberg to St. Albans, but Hilberg did not have the time. Kubrick suggested that Hilberg read the novels of John Dos Passos to see how characters could disappear in the middle of a film and be replaced by other characters, but Hilberg thought this would be too "panoramic" and reminiscent of the flawed American television miniseries *Holocaust* (1978). Subsequently, Hilberg thought that a film simply titled *Auschwitz* and chronicling the construction of mass destruction would be compelling. He almost called Kubrick "to remind him we were mortal," but did not since Kubrick by then was already working on what would become his last film, *Eyes Wide Shut*.[46]

Kubrick's dismissal of Spielberg's *Schindler's List* is problematic in terms of the projected "Aryan Papers," revealing once again his personal and artistic hesitations in directly addressing the subject. Begley's novel—unless Kubrick was going to change the ending—involves physical if not complete psychological survival for Maciek. Jan Harlan has suggested that Kubrick took his cue in dropping the project from the response of Isaac Bashevis Singer (see Chapter 8) to his earlier request to write a screenplay on the Holocaust. Singer had said that he was honored, but the problem was he did not know anything about the Holocaust. Kubrick, who had never even been (and would never be) in eastern Europe, could well have taken this as an artistic admonition to say nothing about a subject that was not just unsettling to him but inexplicable to everyone. Indeed, to approach Singer, whose work concentrates on the intimate world of pre-Holocaust Jewry in eastern Europe, was perhaps itself an indication of reluctance to confront the subject.[47] Kubrick's hesitations about the subject had been manifest as early as 1962 when he turned down an offer to direct the film (Sidney Lumet, 1965) of Edward Wallant's novel *The Pawnbroker* (1961).[48] Kubrick's personal and artistic hesitations were also reflected in, and reinforced by, the general culture, a culture, as we shall see, that in the 1970s was about to change. Among other things, this change would play a great role in ushering Kubrick toward a devilishly unique treatment of the horror genre in *The Shining*.

### A.I. Artificial Intelligence

As early as 1980, Kubrick was interested in adapting a story by Brian Aldiss, "Supertoys Last All Summer Long" (1969), for the screen. But by the 1980s he was convinced that the story was one that he should not direct, and so he began thinking about producing the film with Steven Spielberg as the director. This was in fact the arrangement under which *A.I.* finally appeared in 2001, two years after Kubrick's death. Spielberg took Kubrick's ninety-page treatment along with myriad storyboards and created a film that reflects, inevitably but also somewhat uneasily, both a pessimistic Kubrickian and an optimistic Spielbergian point of view. As Tim Kreider has observed, the Spielbergian "story for children is the one the narrator tells, but the story for adults, presented visually" is a Kubrickian one.[49]

Kubrick had long since moved away from the original Aldiss story of the robot boy who had to confront the fact that he is a machine. At first, he wanted to incorporate the Italian children's story *Pinocchio: The Adventures of a Marionette* (1880), in which a puppet wishes to be a real boy, but learns that in order to do so he must overcome laziness, selfishness, and cruelty. After surmounting a series of dangerous adventures involving the puppeteer Stromboli and the worldly Lampwick, among others, Pinocchio is reunited with his maker, Gepetto, in the belly of a shark and transformed into a real boy by the Blue Fairy. The original story was clearly a fable for the moral edification of children. *A.I.*, however, ends up closer to the Walt Disney feature cartoon *Pinocchio* (1940), in which the emphasis is not on moral development but on the boy David's desire to be reunited with his mother, an Oedipal scenario consistent with long-standing Kubrick concerns. *A.I.* also reflects the original story's dark view, as in the words of Gepetto to Pinocchio that could be a mantra for Kubrick's world of dangerous contingency: "My dear boy, no one ever knows what may happen in this world, so always be prepared for the worst."[50] And Kubrick's traditional preoccupation with the relationship between men and machines is also present, resembling *2001* in the prediction that the "evolution" of humanity into a higher species, this time through the triumph of artificial intelligence,—that is, robots—will result in "a more environmentally adaptable form of human being."[51] But this time the vision is darker, since "evolution" has been replaced by extinction as highly evolved robots take over in the wake of humanity's demise as a result of global climate change due to human disruption of the environment.

*A.I.* thus re-creates the mommy-odyssey that has characterized many Spielberg films.[52] But it also reminds us of its Kubrickian origins, including his similar as well as dissimilar search for the maternal. Many shots and scenes in the film recall Kubrickian settings and themes and constitute a Spielberg homage to several Kubrick films.[53] Also included in the film at Kubrick's specific insistence is a sentimental waltz from the Richard Strauss opera *Der Rosenkavalier* (1911) as David and Joe drive into Rouge City through bridge arches and abutments that in their design as women's mouths recall the vaginal and mammalian furnishings of the Korova Milkbar in *A Clockwork Orange*. While Kubrick apparently did not specify where in the film this music should go, music director John Williams has said that it was obviously important to Kubrick.[54] That in its sweet, nostalgic strains there is a sense of returning to ancestral and artistic roots in the world of old Vienna, this choice of music certainly makes sense in terms of what we have learned were matters of central importance and inspiration to Kubrick.

More significant, though, are the traces of larger Kubrick concerns that Spielberg allows to overwhelm in the viewer's memory the artificially happy ending he reflexively pins onto the picture. Besides the Oedipal dynamics, there is the preoccupation with the fluid boundary between men and machines. Humans in *A.I.* are revealed to be as programmed in their desires as robots are, and choice as the definition of what is human, as preached in *A Clockwork Orange,* is gone. This Freudian determinism is evident in David's imprinted narcissistic obsession with finding his mother in lieu of any other moral or practical consideration. Love is coldly artificial in a world where robots are produced to provide the love that humans themselves cannot give to one another. Even David himself is abandoned by everyone, including what he in his first memory thought was the image of God, which in fact is only the statue of a woman with her arms outstretched like wings that is the Cybertronics corporate logo. This is what Professor Hobby (another bird of prey) describes to David, who has just smashed his double (among countless others), as "the great human flaw, to wish for things that don't exist."[55] In the angry clash between orgas and mechas, there is Kubrick's preoccupation with violent prejudice and racism. The Flesh Fair, in which old robots are torn, as it were, limb from limb, is as dark an indictment of frenzied hatred and murder as can be found in Kubrick's cinema. According to Aldiss, Kubrick originally considered having David consigned to a place called Tin City, a concentration camp where unwanted robots are worked to death. The remains of this conception appear in a scene in *A.I.* in which "David, lost in the woods, comes across a truck dumping a load of dismembered mecha bodies . . . as synechdochic of suffering as the heaps of stolen watches, jewelry, and gold fillings in *Schindler's List*."[56] But, as with the camps shown to Alex in *A Clockwork Orange* but not to us, creative instinct and psychological reservation prevailed once again, and Kubrick finally told Aldiss: "Brian, this concentration camp stuff is all shit."[57]

# 8

## THE HORROR, THE HORROR

In 1975 Kubrick had his executive producer Jan Harlan read Raul Hilberg's *The Destruction of the European Jews*. He also sent him that year to ask Isaac Bashevis Singer, the most famous Yiddish writer on the Jewish communities of prewar Poland, to help write a screenplay for a Holocaust film.[1] In 1980 Kubrick sent a copy of the Hilberg tome to Michael Herr, who correctly notes that it is "a complete log of the Final Solution."[2] Kubrick, in speaking of his desire to make a film about the Holocaust, told Herr that the book was *"monumental."*[3] Kubrick then wrote Hilberg himself in the early 1980s to ask for a recommendation of a book on which to base a Holocaust film. Hilberg, whose family had left northeastern Austria-Hungary a few years after Kubrick's, suggested the diary of Warsaw ghetto leader Adam Czerniakow, which had been published in 1979, but Kubrick rejected the idea, saying such a film would be anti-Semitic.[4] This rejection was presumably founded on Czerniakow's role in carrying out Nazi deportation orders, a practice Czerniakow, who finally committed suicide upon being ordered to deport ghetto orphans, had hoped might prevent the complete liquidation of the ghetto. Hilberg's own critical stance toward Jewish elders' passivity in the face of Nazi predation reflected another dismaying aspect of the Holocaust that surely aggravated Kubrick's personal and artistic reservations about the entire subject. Kubrick was now pondering with obvious ambivalence the film about the Holocaust he had told Herr he "probably . . . most wanted" to make.

Kubrick's turn toward a film project on the Holocaust was not, however, occasioned only by his own intentions. While he would never make a film about the Holocaust per se, two developments in Western culture during the 1970s in particular would decisively influence Kubrick's cinematic shaping of Stephen King's Gothic horror novel *The Shining* into an indirect meditation on the Nazi Final Solution. Without understanding these influences, there is no understanding the many subtly laid visual and aural historical referents in Kubrick's *The Shining*. The first and most important of the contemporaneous cultural developments was the relatively sudden and massive growth in the 1960s and 1970s in cultural consciousness of, knowledge about, and discourse on the nature and history of the Holocaust. The second development was that during the 1970s horror films in America began to reflect a crisis within the patriarchal family. This cinematic commentary was an outgrowth of social criticism of Western patriarchal culture exploding out of the counterculture of the 1960s. Kubrick, on various levels of consciousness, was alive to these developments because he was an inveterate watcher of the world and because this cultural wave caused massive displacements within cultural discourse that no one at all creatively or politically engaged in contemporary society could ignore. But since these developments also took place in the two realms of his greatest interest, film and history, Kubrick in particular could not have helped noticing and reflecting powerfully on them. That the change in horror films was generated to a great extent in the United States was also no bar to its effect on Kubrick, since by this time American movies had begun their commercial dominance of the popular culture of the entire Western world. Kubrick was of course in any case plugged into developments worldwide in cinema and literature, while also maintaining a lifelong interest in events in general in his native America.[5]

As we have observed, confrontation with the darkest heart of the Nazi darkness was attenuated in the late 1940s and the 1950s. This did not mean that the Holocaust was not a strong, if silent, presence—or at least a presence of an absence—in postwar Britain and America. Holocaust themes inevitably found their way into cultural discourse and artistic texts as, for example, in Fritz Lang's *Rancho Notorious* (1952), which has recently been read as a generic and allegorical response to the Holocaust.[6] Similar degrees of more or less conscious intention arising from past as well as present concerns certainly played a role in Kubrick's reworking of King's novel in the 1970s. This certainly was more the case with Kubrick than with Lang, who was of a generation of German directors who had less distance in time and space from the Nazi regime and thus less ability to confront it directly. Lang's persistent concern with crime and violence in his films made his receptivity to some degree of inscription of Nazism and the Holocaust greater than that of some of his contemporaries, however. *Rancho Notorious* dealt with the war and the camps "in even more direct ways"[7] than Lang's own earlier *Scarlet Street* and, as we will see, an even later Lang film would take on the chief perpetrators, if not the chief victims, of the Nazis. Kubrick, even with his familial and artistic hesitations about confronting the Holocaust, was a child of the 1930s and 1940s and, as a result of his orientations and experiences, had a even greater generational compulsion to attempt to work in—and through—the Holocaust in his films.

Explicit creative and public attention was certainly paid to the Holocaust even during the late 1940s and 1950s, but such treatments tended to shy away from a full accounting of the event. American television productions of the 1950s that dealt with the Nazi persecution of the Jews most often attempted to derive affirmation of life and of virtue by portraying the Holocaust as a lesson by which humanity could redeem the millions of lives lost through a commitment to a better civilization in the future. This was certainly the case with *The Diary of Anne Frank,* a telecast in 1952, a stage play in 1955, and a film by 1959. Television programs in the United States were further compromised by the conditions of a commercial medium. Not only was Abby Mann's teleplay *Judgment at Nuremburg* (1959) as usual interrupted by commercials, but the American Gas Association even succeeded in forcing CBS to blank out the word "gas" whenever the term "gas chambers" was used![8] Then television, along with literature and film, was thrown into a new realm of confrontation with the Holocaust by worldwide broadcast of the trial of Adolf Eichmann in Israel in 1961. Eichmann, who had been in charge of the deportation of Jews to the extermination camps, was captured by Israeli agents in Argentina in 1960 to stand trial for crimes against humanity. The trial reinforced the already prodigious effect of the publication of 1930s Berlin correspondent William Shirer's *The Rise and Fall of the Third Reich* (1960) and Hilberg's *The Destruction of the European Jews,* the translation into English of the Holocaust memoir *Night* (1960) by Elie Wiesel, the release of Stanley Kramer's film version of *Judgment at Nuremburg,* and the appearance of Richard Rubenstein's *After Auschwitz: History, Theology, and Contemporary Judaism* (1966).

For the first time, the focus in accounts of the Holocaust was now exclusively on Jews, and so both Gentiles and Jews were confronted with issues that had largely been submerged by earlier coy and generic accounts of "man's inhumanity to man." Even Resnais's classic short documentary film on the concentration camps, *Night and Fog,* had depicted Jews only as among the other victims of the Nazis.[9] The Eichmann trial, by contrast, presented the Holocaust "as an entity in its own right, distinct from Nazi barbarism in general."[10] Jews were now beginning to be understood as the only group targeted by the Nazis for complete extermination. Other issues crowded in as well. Philosopher Hannah Arendt, who attended the Eichmann trial, described in *Eichmann in Jerusalem: A Report on the Banality of Evil* (1963) what she saw as the ordinariness of a dull, efficient bureaucrat of mass death. This clashed with most people's view of Nazis as demonic monsters. Arendt made no secret of her loathing for Eichmann, but her book suggested that evil in the modern world was as much a function of normal, rational routine as of irrational passion or persuasion. Meanwhile, Yale psychologist Stanley Milgram, seeking to understand the behavior of the functionaries of the Nazi Final Solution, had conducted experiments that seemed to bear out Arendt's thesis that a totalitarian environment can determine behavior. Milgram concluded that most people, when confronted by any type of authority, follow orders.

The most controversial issue, however, was the contemporary analysis of the behavior of the Jewish victims of the Holocaust. Arendt had observed that totalitarianism had made any Jewish resistance as weak and ineffectual as it was rare. Psychologist Bruno Bettelheim even criticized the family of Anne Frank for not having killed the police who came to arrest them in their hiding place, arguing that such failure to resist was typical among the Jews and had only helped the Nazis do their murderous work. Arendt disputed Bettelheim by saying that the totalitarian conditions under which Jews lived at the time made significant resistance futile. Like Hilberg, Arendt focused her criticism on the Jewish leaders who believed that cooperation with the Nazis would reduce the number of Jewish victims.[11] This was a fatal miscalculation based on earlier murderous outbreaks of anti-Semitism, which were spasmodic and relatively limited in duration.

Israel's stunning military victory in the May 1967 war seemed, along with the apparent sympathy of a world now increasingly knowledgeable about Jewish suffering under the Nazis, to diminish significantly the threat of another Holocaust. The Israeli victory was all the more comforting because it came in a war that originally seemed to threaten the existence of Israel. These fears were revisited in the Yom Kippur War of 1973, when Israel once again appeared to be on the brink of destruction. In contrast to the 1967 war, this war was accompanied by renewed fears of a rise in worldwide anti-Semitism and thus of another Holocaust. Even in West Germany there had been a resurgence of anti-Semitism in the late 1950s, while the Communist East German regime had consistently followed the Soviet line of associating Jews with capitalism and Israel with Western imperialism. By coincidence, it was in 1967 that a plaque was unveiled at the extermination center of Auschwitz-Birkenau that, in line with Polish Communist policy, made no mention of the Jewishness of the vast majority of the people killed there.[12] Jews in the West, like other ethnic groups in the roiling political years of the 1960s, responded with an increased sense of collective identity and solidarity in terms of shared historical victimization. The growing public discourse on the Holocaust increased the sense of solidarity among Jews, especially in America, who previously had only a marginal Jewish identity.[13]

## The Hitler Wave and *Holocaust*

As a result of the sea change in consciousness of the Holocaust, in 1968 the Library of Congress had created a new subject entry, "Holocaust—Jewish, 1939–1945," and in 1971 the *Reader's Guide to Periodical Literature* likewise introduced the cross-listing "Holocaust."[14] American writer and critic Alfred Kazin reflected this surging contemporary cultural discourse when he observed in the 1970s that the Holocaust was "the nightmare that will haunt me to my last breath."[15]

Greater public consciousness of the Holocaust was accompanied in the 1970s by greater interest in Hitler and the Nazis. While interest in the history of the Second World War in general had always been strong, especially among "war buffs," only in the 1970s did there emerge what quickly came to be known as the "Hitler Wave." This was a series of books and films on Hitler and on the Third Reich that captured worldwide attention and also created widespread controversy. As usual, the effect of pictures in the visual culture of the twentieth century was even more widespread than that of books. Apart from sexploitation trash like *Ilsa, She-Wolf of the SS* (1975), feature films such as *Stavisky* (1974), *The Serpent's Egg* (1977), *Salo: The 120 Days of Sodom* (1975), *Lacombe, Lucien* (1974), *Seven Beauties* (1975), *The Night Porter* (1974), *Hitler—A Film from Germany* (1978), *Swastika* (1974), *The Damned* (1969), *The Sorrow and the Pity* (1970), and *The Man in the Glass Booth* engaged the subject of Nazi Germany with widely varying degrees of effectiveness and sensitivity.[16]

For more than a few, this increased interest in fascism and Nazism represented a dangerous cultural trend. Susan Sontag was among those who decried this trend in film, literature, and the media in general, most famously in an essay of 1974 entitled "Fascinating Fascism." Sontag argued that much of 1970s culture, including Kubrick's *2001*, was erected on the basis of "fascist aesthetics" concerned with the pure and the impure, the dominant and the submissive, and the mass and the leader, a "choreography [that] alternates between ceaseless motion and a congealed static 'virile' posing [that] glorifies surrender, exalts mindlessness, [and] glamorizes death."[17] She saw this as nostalgia for simpler styles of artistic expression in place of "the demanding complexities of modernist art" and condemned in particular the "eroticizing" of fascism in films such as *The Damned* and *The Night Porter*, not to mention the repellent and arty *Salon Kitty* (1975).[18]

This association of a trend in artistic expression in the 1970s with fascism was an outgrowth of more general social and political criticism of "the Establishment" on the part of 1960s radicalism. The struggle for racial equality in America, the disillusionment with American public authority that came with the Watergate scandal, and the ever growing opposition to the war in Vietnam produced a tendency for some to equate those in power in the West with fascists and Nazis. Typical of this rhetoric was the common radical characterization of the police as "fascist pigs" and, especially in Europe, the Nazi-Germanic label of "Amerika" applied to the United States—the name, ironically enough, of Hitler's headquarters train during the Second World War.[19] Reflecting this conflation, Coppola's Vietnam film, *Apocalypse Now*, as we have seen, used Nazi-inflected music from Wagner's *Die Walküre* (1870) as the music the Strangelovian Colonel Kilgore plays as his helicopters with great exuberance strafe and bomb a village. Wagner was Hitler's favorite composer, and so the reference is quite clear: in Vietnam, we are the Nazis. *Apocalypse Now*, based on Conrad's *Heart of Darkness*, also invokes the historical horrors of the Second World War more generally in the now American Kurtz's written admonition, "Drop the Bomb. Exterminate them all." This was another tradition in the cinema of the 1970s, that of increasing questioning of the American status quo, as in Roman Polanski's film noir, *Chinatown* (1974), in which a 1930s Los Angeles detective played by Jack Nicholson, Kubrick's Jack Torrance in *The Shining*, discovers that "the myth of individualistic justice collides with the power of evil and chance in the world."[20] *Chinatown* is more than anything else typical of the cultural criticism in and of the West that was peculiarly strong in the 1970s, as represented in the black humor of Pynchon's "psychedelirious" *Gravity's Rainbow*, a work that exemplifies the postmodern crisis in the novel brought about by the disorienting horrors of the Second World War.[21]

Kubrick's films certainly fit into this tradition in terms of both their embrace of social criticism and their seeming flirtation with fascist frenzy. Sontag's criticism of *2001* was based on what she saw as the fascist aesthetic of its cold, technological suppression of the human and the humane. But in Kubrick's films, as in the modern and postmodern literature of the absurd, there is also the "comedy of language" and the "combination of humorous burlesque and high seriousness" that support the active, sympathetic engagement of the audience in confronting the world's threats to humanity and humaneness.[22] An even more specific charge of Kubrick flirting with fascism came as part of the stormy public and critical response to *A Clockwork Orange*, a film that spawned copycat beatings and rapes as well as death threats against Kubrick and his family that prompted him to withdraw the film from circulation in Great Britain.[23] In America, a Kubrick nemesis, film critic Pauline Kael, found the film "Teutonic in its humor" and "sucking up to the thugs in the audience."[24] Because of the nudity and sex in the film, it was given an "X" rating, which banned those under the age of seventeen or eighteen from seeing the film and prompted some newspapers in the United States not to accept advertising for it. Kubrick, reflecting the discourse of the decade, responded in one case with an angry letter to the editor of the *Detroit News* quoting "Adolph [sic] Hitler" on "approved" and "degenerate" art.[25] *A Clockwork Orange* was also attacked in the United States along 1970s Sontagian lines as "psychedelic fascism" and "deeply anti-liberal totalitarian nihilism."[26] Kubrick replied that to be a pessimist is not to be a tyrant and that to consider him a fascist is the same thing as accusing the Jonathan Swift of *A Modest Proposal* of being a cannibal. Kubrick marshaled Arthur Koestler in support of his pessimistic view of humanity and also criticized Rousseau's idea of the "noble savage" by citing the work of Robert Ardrey, anthropologist and author of *African Genesis* (1962) and *The Social Contract* (1970). Kubrick, in following Ardrey, argued that a recognition of humanity's flawed condition ("a risen ape . . . rather than a fallen angel") is actually a more optimistic point of view than Rousseau's since it regards civilization at least in part as a process of education and achievement, however blighted in particular by the "dizzying and frightening vistas of the intellectual future" opened up by the Enlightenment.[27]

Near the end of the decade, the debate over art and fascism was recast by an American television event. In 1978 NBC broadcast a television miniseries by Gerald Green entitled *Holocaust*. Among other things, *Holocaust* was Hollywood's response to the widely publicized march of American Nazis through a Jewish neighborhood in Skokie, Illinois, the previous year and to the more general rise in neo-fascism and neo-Nazism in Europe and America during the 1970s. *Holocaust* invented two families, one of assimilated German Jews and the other of an SS officer, to survey all the major landmarks of the Nazi attempt to exterminate the Jews of Europe. The broadcast over four days was preceded by a media and organizational blitz to publicize the program and provide background for its viewing. The miniseries generated significant discussion after its showing, which concluded during the week before Passover and on the thirty-fifth anniversary of the Warsaw ghetto uprising. Millions of people were prompted to discuss an event that to them had hitherto been relatively insignificant. But many regarded the miniseries as a trivialization of a great tragedy and as proof that commercial television was the wrong medium in which to present such material. Aside from the censorship of violence and nudity that softened—and trivialized—the actual horror of the historical events, commercials for products such as Gas-X and a household disinfectant struck a bizarrely inappropriate note amid scenes of mass chemical extermination. And yet, the broadcast of *Holocaust* did mark a decisive turning point in awareness of the Holocaust that brought forth a number of initiatives to memorialize the victims and underscore the lessons, including President Carter's support for an American Holocaust memorial museum. In 1979 the miniseries was broadcast in Britain, West Germany, Israel, and France. The effect in West Germany was galvanizing. It was as if—*as if*—the Germans had never before heard of the Nazi persecution of the Jews. The glossy, highly competent melodrama at which Hollywood excels had a tremendous impact in the homes of German viewers. Literally for the first time, the Holocaust was brought home to many Germans in a form that encouraged identification and sympathy for victims that were no longer faceless millions of the long dead. For the first time, the Holocaust became the subject of public discussion in Germany, while in America, five television miniseries having to do with the Holocaust ensued over the following decade.[28] Perhaps Kubrick's co-writer on *The Shining*, Diane Johnson, had intuitively anticipated what now seems like the inevitable union of television and the Holocaust in her 1974 novel, *The Shadow Knows*, her protagonist noting darkly one evening "the pale blue lights of television sets and . . . the baying of the German shepherds on their chains."[29]

It is therefore no surprise that in the 1970s Kubrick began actively pursuing the possibility of his own Holocaust film. Even before the steps he took in this direction in 1975, the early years of the decade would leave latent traces of Kubrick's very specific artistic concern with the Holocaust in *A Clockwork Orange* and *Barry Lyndon*. Such wisplike traces were to be manifested almost as subtly but also much more numerously and powerfully in *The Shining*. It was in the genre of horror that Kubrick found the medium for an indirect treatment of the subject that satisfied, at least partially, his personal and artistic concerns about the subject of the Holocaust. This discovery, too, was a reflection of the immediate cultural environment, for it was the horror genre that more than any other dominated popular cinema in the 1970s.

## The Other Horror

The boom in horror films that occurred beginning in the 1970s was no exception to the unparalleled capacity of film to shape and reflect popular attitudes.[30] The spate of horror films that lurched and lunged across the movie screens of America in that decade continued a tradition peculiar to the whole genre of "horror art, [which] seems to grow best in the soil of communal insecurity."[31] This had arguably been the case ever since the emergence of the literary genre in Europe between 1780 and 1820. The so-called Gothic novel or Gothic romance (German, *Schauerroman* [shudder novel]) usually concerned young women who go to live in gloomy mansions of familial mystery and supernatural danger. Horace Walpole's *The Castle of Otranto, a Gothic Story* (1764) is generally acknowledged as the first example of the genre. Gothic in general is the artistic expression of the hidden, the unconscious, and the fearful represented, among others, by Henry Fuseli's painting *The Nightmare* (1781). As we will see in our discussion of *The Shining*, the modern concept of the uncanny is also central to this type of expression. The uncanny (in German, *unheimlich*, literally, "unhomelike") includes those things that seem foreign and inexplicable but are actually intimate to human experience and thus in fact explicable. The fantastic, also a signal element of Gothic and horror art, is in the realm of the marvelous and therefore truly inexplicable. This literature in the nineteenth century was a reaction against the burgeoning dominance of the rational and the material in the dawning modern age. Even the modern itself—in the work of Darwin, Freud, and Nietzsche, among others—undermined reason by positing the existence of *irrational* forces at best only imperfectly understood or controlled by human reason. As Francisco Goya painted it in 1798, *The Sleep of Reason Breeds Monsters*. In the twentieth century, psychoanalysis would have a great deal to say about the appeal of horror, and of the mass-market horror film in particular, to repressed drives, especially among adolescents dealing with the strong, awakening fears and desires of sexuality and sexual identity.[32]

Horror also embraces the grotesque, that combination of human and animal forms that highlights "the excesses of the body" in contrast to, but also in dreadful connection with, the elevated realms of thought, spirit, and ideals.[33] The grotesque tradition, in contrast to the Gothic, moreover, assumes no essential natural or moral order in the universe, a view in line with a powerful tradition of modern thought both before and after the Second World War in particular. This perspective can preempt critical analysis of the real struggles and conflicts within individuals and societies in the world. But even the critical social realism of artists like William Hogarth in the eighteenth century and George Grosz in the twentieth took on grotesque form through the depiction of distorted "images of the normal [and] human perversion and transformation."[34] This grotesquerie actually added power to their social criticism rather than detracting—or distracting—from it. Even Dickens used the grotesque—for example, the spontaneous combustion of Krook in *Bleak House* (1853)—with an eye toward improvement through the shaking of personal and social complacency. The same was true of Kubrick. Whatever his own tendency toward an obsession with disorder, mystery, and disaster, he retained a humane spirit that can be detected in the tone of disappointment, not cynicism, that suffuses his films. And to whatever extent his characters are caricatures, this too is in service to the artistic communication of ideas that Kubrick believed essential for any chance at contributing to the overcoming—or, rather, limiting—of disorder and disaster in the world.[35]

It was the two world wars that provided a decided impetus to the creation of the modern horror film. *The Cabinet of Dr. Caligari,* while not the first horror film, was the first blockbuster of the genre and had an effect on cinematic expectations that David Skal has likened to that of *2001* forty-nine years later.[36] *Caligari,* as we have seen, was a direct response to the horrors of the First World War. It was an uncompromising attack on military psychiatry and the authoritarian society that allowed old men to send young men to war to kill, die, or be driven mad. To press home their point, scriptwriters Carl Mayer and Hans Janowitz constructed a horror story about a doctor who directs a somnambulist to kill on command, and the film uses highly Expressionistic sets to represent the psychological terrors that lurk beneath the surface and in the shadows of contemporary society. The First World War also influenced the growth of the horror film genre through the impact of the thousands of disfigured soldiers who returned from the war. Lon Chaney's facially disfigured characters in *The Hunchback of Notre Dame* (1923) and *The Phantom of the Opera* (1925) grotesquely mirror the "smashed features, missing noses, and mouths full of broken teeth" of the disabled veterans who "haunted Europe and America" and who as members of the Union des Gueules Cassées (Union of Smashed Faces) in France often led the Armistice Day parades. Members of this organization were also mobilized to appear in Abel Gance's *J'Accuse* (1937), in which they appear among the legions of soldiers of the First World War called forth from the dead to march in protest against the prospect of another war.[37] The Second World War had a similar, though lesser, impact upon art in general—for example in the paintings of Francis Bacon that present grotesque "humanimal" shapes that produce an "artistic correlative for moral shock at bodies torn apart by bombs, men and women reduced to primal greed in concentration camps, Hitler in his bunker, Mussolini's body dangling from a meat hook in the center of Milan."[38] Horror films in the Cold War environment of the 1950s metamorphosed worldwide into science-fiction films in response to the development during the Second World War of atomic energy and ballistic missiles.[39]

Traditional horror films began making a comeback in the 1960s, but there was now a crucial difference in their construction. Whereas before horror films had reflected the tradition of Gothic literature that emphasized the supernatural in the gloomy settings of fading aristocratic Europe, now horror, chief among other characteristics, was located in domestic American settings of contemporary family and society. The seminal film in this regard was Alfred Hitchcock's *Psycho,* in which a clean, bright motel bathroom in the semirural American West becomes a place of sudden, savage murder. The world is unpredictable and no place is safe from the depredations not of nature, aliens, or monsters but of other human beings, depredations often, as we shall see in Chapter 9, carried out in and therefore in the name of realms of the public and the commercial rather than the old private aristocratic venues of nineteenth-century horror. Bathrooms also engage what might be regarded as the three essential strategies of the horror genre: mystery, confinement, and the sense of doom that comes with consciousness of the mortal physicality of the body. Kubrick, too, would subsequently use the bathroom as premonition, threat, place, and memory of death, respectively, in *Eyes Wide Shut, The Shining, Dr. Strangelove,* and *A Clockwork Orange*.[40]

In the 1970s, with the commercial explosion of the horror genre, this domestic orientation became more highly and horrifically articulated. As was the case with horror films in the past, these new versions revealed fault lines in the American psyche and society and worked, however obliviously, "to show exactly what would melt down the nuclear family."[41] During this "Golden Age of the American horror film," American culture was a landscape of massive repressions coming into conflict, and thus consciousness, with forces of social challenge and disruption. Among the repressions of American bourgeois ideology were sexuality, bisexuality, female sexuality, and a variety of anxious conceptions of the Other: women, the lower classes, foreigners, ethnic groups, alternative ideologies, and children. The last category became the chief mode of critical horror expression in the 1970s, not only because of the Oedipal dynamics habitually addressed in the genre but also because of the contemporaneous challenges of the young generation of the 1960s to the social, political, and sexual norms of the established culture in America and the West. Since horror films had a history of disrepute within the culture and since they are preoccupied with monsters, the abnormal, and the ambiguities, ambivalences, and terrors of the realms of dream and nightmare, they were the perfect vehicles for the treatment of all these subjects.[42]

American horror films of the 1970s, which of course circulated and inspired similar films worldwide, focused on the nuclear family of the reigning bourgeois patriarchal culture. It was the child within this family who, beginning around 1968, was the most critical character. Vivian Sobchack has argued that it was two films of 1968, Kubrick's *2001* and Roman Polanski's *Rosemary's Baby*, that introduced the child in its youngest form as "a visible site of ambiguity, ambivalence, and contradiction" and as herald of exterminatory change.[43] This reflected the effect of the young generation that was then challenging "the Establishment." The child was no longer the darling of the family, but rather it—*it*—was now an alien force of change and danger. A spate of films in the 1970s represented children this way. But among these films there were differences. Earlier films highlighted the demonic powers of the child, while later films tended toward the victimization of the child by a "weak" father possessed to destroy his family. In general, what is questioned in these horror films—and in others, such as *Kramer vs. Kramer* (1979)—is patriarchal power, although the representation of homicidal fathers also constitutes an acting out of the rage of established society over its besieged and flagging powers.[44] In this context, Kubrick's *A Clockwork Orange* at the beginning of the decade represents a similar, though philosophically more complex, meditation on the corrosive agency of the brutally socialized child within and against the nuclear family. And all three Kubrick films of the decade deal in one way or another with the challenge of the young against the old: the victory of thugs by collaboration with the state in

*A Clockwork Orange,* failed social ambition in *Barry Lyndon,* and personal triumph but historical disaster in *The Shining*.

*The Shining* has been seen as a culmination of the horror films of the 1970s. But it was also a culmination of Kubrick's lifelong approach-avoidance syndrome with regard to the Nazis and the Holocaust. In terms of his own personal and artistic struggle with historical evil, Kubrick in *The Shining* was also realizing one of the cardinal elements of the horror film that emerged beginning in the late 1960s, a lack of resolution and closure. This was pioneered by Roman Polanski's *The Fearless Vampire Killers* (1967), which represents a deep foreboding about the world, a foreboding reflected as well in Holocaust survivor Polanski's *The Tenant* (1976).[45] *The Shining* displays an even more specific historical subtext exemplifying the deep ties between the fictional and factual worlds of horror in our time. There may in fact often be a link through the minds of viewers and performers between screen terror in particular and the horrors of the real world. The actors playing the two antagonists of *Caligari,* the primal father of the horror film genre, went opposite ways after 1919, Conrad Veidt leaving Germany to play Nazi villains in Hollywood and Werner Kraus staying in Germany to play Jewish ones for Hitler.[46]

# 9

## THE SHINING

Stanley Kubrick wanted to make a film about the Holocaust. Stanley Kubrick never made a film about the Holocaust. Until he did. It was not the film he said he would make. But it is the one he made.

In 1977 horror-fiction writer Stephen King published *The Shining*, a tale of terror about a family trapped by a mountain winter in a haunted hotel. Coincidentally, ironically, and perhaps also portentously, King had been inspired to write this novel as a result of a stay at the Stanley Hotel in Estes Park, Colorado, in 1974. When King made a television miniseries of *The Shining* in 1997, he filmed it at the Stanley.[1] There might have been some conscious or unconscious satisfaction in this for King, since he had long been on record as disliking Stanley Kubrick's adaptation of his novel. King thought that Kubrick made a horror film that was not scary. This was true, since it was Kubrick's purpose to interrogate the horror genre for purposes of an investigation of human character and human history. King also believed that Kubrick gave the film a happy ending with a final shot showing Jack in an old photograph of a hotel party. This is flat wrong, since Kubrick's point, as we shall see (again), is history as repetition rather than progress, what Freud called "the return of the repressed"—that is, the neurotic repetition of the symptoms of psychological conflict in place of personal insight and improvement. King was in no position to appreciate this point of view, since he went on record as saying, again wrongly even in his own case, that no one, including Kubrick, had a Freudian perspective anymore.[2] By filming at the Stanley, in any case King could, psychologically at least, punctuate his response to Kubrick's film with a symbolic reminder of the other SK's alleged betrayal and failure in the translation of the novel to the screen.

## From King to Kubrick

According to Kubrick himself, he came across Stephen King's *The Shining* quite by accident when John Calley, an executive at Warner Bros., sent him advance proofs of the novel. King had emerged during the 1970s as a master storyteller of horror, and Kubrick was convinced that *The Shining* would make an excellent film. He had not read any of King's other books and had not seriously considered making a horror film until he read *The Shining*. But his choice was certainly determined to a significant extent by his own reactions to the events of the decade we outlined in Chapter 8 and reinforced by the filmic and literary precedents we will discuss in this chapter. King's story itself displayed characteristics appealing to Kubrick, such as its strong Oedipal theme and, especially, the ability of horror stories "to show us the archetypes of the unconscious: we can see the dark side without having to confront it directly."[3] Kubrick was also impressed with the combination of natural and supernatural in the story, a characteristic he had always admired on a much higher literary level in the works of Kafka in particular. In the case of *The Shining*, Kubrick saw an opportunity to explore the interface between the sensible and the insensible world, even suggesting that the possibility of the existence of ghosts perhaps constituted a promise of life after death.[4] But this speculation did not make the ending to the film a happy one, for like all Kubrick films *The Shining* remains grounded in the terrestrial and the historical rather than in the supernatural. Kubrick was especially attracted to the character of Jack Torrance for the same reason, because the idea of a father threatening a child seemed the best way of getting at the rage and fear within human families, rage and fear that of course also scar human history writ large and long.[5] Finally, Kubrick was no doubt attracted by the autobiographical aspects of a novel about a man isolating himself to write. This mold fit Kubrick as much as King, for the circumstances of his life reinforced personal reference in this film in particular. It was during preproduction on *The Shining* that Kubrick moved away from London to familial isolation at St. Albans in rural Hertfordshire.[6]

King's novel tells the story of the Torrance family—Jack, Wendy, and five-year-old son Danny—who spend the winter in the Overlook Hotel high in the Colorado Rockies. Jack has taken the job of winter caretaker. An ex-teacher, he is working on a play and thinks that the isolation is just what he needs in order to finish it. But the hotel is haunted by ghosts of its guests as well as by a former caretaker named Grady, who murdered his wife and two daughters. Jack himself has a history of alcoholism and violence, one incident involving a former student and the other his son. Since hurting his son, he has vowed to reform, but the hotel environment literally as well as figuratively brings out his inner demons. The Overlook itself is a symbol of corrupt American power, and, as Jack peruses a scrapbook detailing the hotel's history, he is compelled—or enslaved—by the spirits in the hotel to write about it. Both Danny and the hotel's chef, Dick Halloran, have telepathic powers ("shining") that allow them to see into the past and the future. Danny's "insights" into the true nature of the place prompt the hotel's ghostly masters to instruct Jack to kill both his son and his wife. Halloran, who has been "contacted" by Danny, returns to save Wendy and Danny. Since Jack has not attended to the hotel's boilers, they explode and the Overlook and Jack go up in flames.

Kubrick and his co-writer, novelist Diane Johnson, left out the supernatural phenomena in the novel: a topiary garden of fierce animals (including a lion that reminds one in the shining Danny of the biblical Daniel, who can read the handwriting on the wall[7]) that come alive to defend the hotel, a wasp's nest that mysteriously generates wasps after being emptied, and a fire hose that unreels itself and attacks like a snake. Drawing, as we shall see in Chapter 10, on Freud's essay on the uncanny and on Bruno Bettelheim's psychoanalytic study of fairy tales, Kubrick and Johnson concentrated on the psychological dynamics of their characters, in particular Jack. Appropriately, given this emphasis on the psychological, Kubrick late in the writing substituted for the topiary animals a hedge maze with walls thirteen feet high that represents the labyrinthine passageways of the human psyche. And instead of having, like King, the possessed Jack perform such stock monstrosities as dance "an eerie, shuffling polka," Kubrick has him limp like an injured human being (though also like "horror film cripples and hunchbacks of the 1930s"), just like Oedipus, whose name means "swollen foot."[8] Finally, in place of the supernatural "great hollow boom" of the mallet Jack carries in the book, Kubrick substitutes the booming of a ball thrown against a wall in forming a symbolic historical tableau centered on Jack's quite natural typewriter.[9]

Kubrick also ostensibly changes the character of Wendy from an attractive and self-confident woman to that of a nervous, even hysterical one. Kubrick remorselessly criticized actress Shelley Duvall during the filming in order to put her on edge and thus heighten her hysteria onscreen. He took this approach because he felt that the confident blonde bombshell in King's novel was not the sort of woman who would put up so long with a self-indulgent and violent loser like Jack. The result onscreen is an unnerving—and, for some, distracting—combination in Wendy of stunned immobility and frenetic panic. Actress Shelley Duvall's strikingly idiosyncratic physical appearance also lends her character a vulnerable individuality in contrast to the stock horror story sexuality of King's Wendy. Her cluelessness, or at least Jack's addled perception of it, is underlined early in the film when he notes that she is "a confirmed ghost story and horror film addict."[10] This reflexive remark recalls King's Wendy, who reads Gothic novels, though in the film we see her halfway through J. D. Salinger's *The Catcher in the Rye* (1951). This (along with her smoking Virginia Slims, the first cigarette marketed to "independent women") indicates, in contrast to traditional ghost stories and horror films, at least some exposure to a more modern and critical view of the arrested male development behind the authoritarianism that Jack displays. As Salinger's protagonist himself, Holden Caulfield, puts it, "You can't stop a teacher when they want to do something. They just *do* it."[11] Kubrick's Wendy, however, is anything but helpless. It is Wendy who, in contrast to the novel, checks the hotel's boiler pressure, thus preventing the conflagration that destroys the hotel in the book. And, like her literary counterpart, in the end she fights back successfully against her husband in order to save herself and her child. The arguable cost in this approach is a loss of the well-rounded character that Diane Johnson wrote, but once again Kubrick was sacrificing traditional characterization for the sake of emotional extremity in service to the ideas behind the film.[12]

An early treatment by Kubrick of the novel had the black chef Hallorann become possessed and kill Wendy and Danny. This idea, inspired by the novel's depiction of a failed attempt by the hotel to sway Hallorann to murder, survived in a subsequent treatment in which Wendy stabs Jack to death and Hallorann arrives as the "monstrous and threatening figure that Danny has seen in his dreams." Hallorann chases Danny with an ax, but the "maddened, demonical figure" of Wendy comes "howling out of a doorway, stabbing in a frenzy, with her long boning knife, so that the old lady in 'Psycho' will look like a pushover in comparison. There will be no question about how she is able to kill a homicidal maniac. She will temporarily have become one herself."[13] Subsequently, it was Johnson who argued strongly for having Danny die in order to underline the horror in the story, but in the end Kubrick and Johnson decided that Hallorann should be the one to die. This would emphasize the racial dimension to the history Kubrick's film treats, a dimension whose Western Caucasian thrust would have been undercut by having Halloran become possessed. Having Hallorann and Wendy become murderers also would have appealed to Kubrick's own personal and creative tendency toward defensive and offensive identification with the aggressor. It would also have underlined his bleak view of humanity in general. But, according to Johnson, Kubrick "had a soft spot for Wendy and Danny," and so they would in the end survive.[14] But so, too, would the hotel.

Kubrick, finally, changed the ending of the story. He had filmed a coda similar to that in the book in which Wendy and Danny safely recuperate far from the Overlook Hotel. The coda included hotel manager Stuart Ullman, from whom Danny learns that his "shining" had indeed revealed the secrets of the Overlook's past and future. This ending corresponded with an earlier version of the script Kubrick and Johnson had written in which the entire family is seen as ghosts at the Overlook. King, too, changed the ending when he filmed *The Shining* for television. Danny graduates from college and, as he is being congratulated by Wendy and Hallorann, sees the image of his father smiling his congratulations as well. This ending is consistent with that of the novel, since instead of killing his son, Jack, in a moment of lucidity and love, tells Danny to run away from him before the demons within him again prevail and the hotel explodes and burns.[15] After negative test audience reactions to his coda, Kubrick concluded the film with a still photograph on a hotel wall of Jack from July 4, 1921. This ending more directly and economically (though also more enigmatically) emphasizes the historical content and continuity that links King's America to Kubrick's Europe. It also both differs from and resembles the conclusion to *The Magic Mountain*. While Hans Castorp escapes freezing to death in the snow, he dies as part of the history of the First World War. Jack Torrance is frozen to death in the maze, but he is also frozen into the history of the Overlook Hotel instead of being consumed with it by fire.[16]

As early as the treatment just cited, Kubrick had removed a postwar American referent in King's novel for an interwar European one. In the novel a post-Nagasaki party takes place on August 29, 1945, with the hotel lit by "glowing Japanese lanterns," as Jack learns when he reads an invitation on behalf of the founder of the Overlook stuck into a scrapbook he found in the hotel basement.[17] The party is modeled on Poe's "Masque of the Red Death" (1842) that collapses the entire time period from 1914 to 1945 as a means to critique crisis-ridden 1970s America.[18] Kubrick's treatment mentions 1930s dress, 1930s music of a "dance band," and a "silk banner" reading "Happy 1919," which, like the British accents of Grady and his daughters and of a party ghost who greets Wendy, take on British and Continental associations in the film. This interwar chronological blur is abetted in the film by a concluding invocation of a 1921 party that links years across the century by means of multiples of the number 7. The music permissions sought as late as April 1980 ranged over more than forty songs from as early as 1920 to as late as 1937, but all four of the songs chosen for the film are from the 1930s and recorded by British musicians, creating geographical and historical blur as well.[19] Kubrick's film and its ending, therefore, underscore more than King's the historical continuity of human evil, since the hotel and its accumulated historical horrors survive. Unlike America in 1945, in the film the war is not almost over. For interwar Europe, it is only just beginning and, in a sense, never ending. Ironically, while in the film the Overlook Hotel does not burn to ground, the hotel set was itself destroyed by fire just before the film wrapped in the spring of 1979 after almost eleven months of shooting. The fire was caused by the 700,000 watts of light used to reproduce winter's glare pouring into one of the most elaborate sets ever built. But Kubrick got the ending he wanted in this as well. He had the entire set rebuilt on another soundstage.[20]

King's conclusion offers the comfort of the basically conservative Gothic belief in universal order, while Kubrick's, revealing and exploiting the horror genre's own inner contradictions, leaves us with the grotesque's intimation of disorder and dread. The novel represents in typical Gothic style the intrusion of the supernatural *into* the natural world. King wrote in the naturalist tradition of Frank Norris, while Kubrick rejected Norris and embraced the realistic tradition that, in the tradition of Kafka, depicts the fantastic and grotesque aspects *of* the real world: "The hotel's labyrinthine layout and huge rooms, I believed, would alone provide an eerie enough atmosphere. This realistic approach was also followed in the lighting, and in every aspect of the décor. It seemed to me that the perfect guide could be found in Kafka's writing style. His stories are fantastic and allegorical, but his writing is simple and straightforward, almost journalistic."[21] King's novel, besides referencing "The Masque of the Red Death," recalls Shirley Jackson's *The Haunting of Hill House* (1959) and Don Siegel's film *The Invasion of the Body Snatchers* (1956).

Kubrick's film, while reflecting and parodying Gothic form, follows, in addition to Kafka and others, Conrad's *Heart of Darkness*.[22] The Gothic conventions of Poe and King do not engage history; rather they exploit formulas for evoking timeless horror in the reader. While Kubrick too is interested in the continuity of human motivation and behavior regardless of time period, he is also vitally concerned with the modern historical specifics of their effects. Unlike Poe, *Heart of Darkness* is interested in the horror that "originates not from within the mind but from without."[23] The drama is in the mind's attempt to deal with the experience of horror, and its depiction demands indirection due to "an opacity or silence at the heart of historical catastrophe."[24] In Kubrick's *The Shining*, the most radical historical evil requires the most radical indirection. The breadth and depth of its concerns thus offer "the spectator an almost endless array of interpretive possibilities."[25] At the center of this maze of meanings are the recent horrors of the world and their difficult apprehension. Kubrick's Jack, overdetermined as Kubrick and as Kubrick's father, is also the perpetrator, is both Conrad's Marlow and Conrad's Kurtz, the voyager into darkness who, unlike Marlow and Kubrick's Danny, does not remain its stunned observer but becomes its oblivious agent.

## From Blue Hotel to Berghof

The Overlook Hotel in a very real sense is the central character of both the novel and the film of *The Shining*. In both novel and film, it stands as a symbol of great human evil, whose masters and agents seek to extend their control over all those who dare to reside within its walls. Kubrick in particular, through the sheer visual audacity of his set and his cinematography, imbues the Overlook with a paradoxical combination of both boundless and claustrophobic vulnerability characteristic of much of his work since his earliest days as a photographer.[26] King's hotel, modeled on the Stanley, has about it much of the darkness of the old haunted houses of traditional horror and also some of the frontier architecture and furnishing of the American West. The common areas of Kubrick's Overlook have towering white walls bathed in light, which, while reflecting the physical grandiosity of German Expressionistic set design and even Albert Speer's cruel Nazi monumentalism, emphasizes not the formulaic gloom of fictional horror, but the daylight in which the real horrors of the world take place. And there is no doubt in the selection of architecture that the horrors that preoccupy Kubrick the most are those connected with Europe and the world in the first half of the twentieth century. The style, taken primarily from the Ahwahnee ("deep, grassy valley") Hotel, built in 1927 in California's Yosemite Valley, is mostly Art Deco—the sleek, cold interwar successor to Art Nouveau. The exterior of the Overlook is modeled on that of the Timberline Lodge on Oregon's Mount Hood, a location that is a clever reference, like Danny's Big Wheel, to the luminaries the Overlook serves. The location refers as well to the fate of the hotel in King's novel, since, as Kubrick himself pointed out, Mount Hood is a dormant volcano whose neighbor, Mount St. Helens, in fact erupted the same month as the release of *The Shining*. The Timberline, too, is an interwar phenomenon, completed under the Work Projects Administration in 1937 and restored as a National Historic Landmark in the 1970s. Kubrick even used the pictures on the Timberline manager's office wall in the film.[27] Kubrick's choice of styles for the hotel also reflected the trend in the 1970s toward interest in the interwar period, the most dramatic and often troubling manifestation of which was, as Sontag complained, nostalgia for the brutal simplicities of fascism. Among the simplicities Sontag listed was Art Deco, "the fascist style at its best, with its sharp lines and blunt massing of material, its petrified eroticism."[28] Kubrick was again tapping into the times and, to follow Sontag's critique of Art Deco, indulging his own aggression and defensive identification with the aggressor. But he was also critically confronting humanity's worst crimes.

Thus the Overlook Hotel adds another level of meaning onto *The Shining* that distinguishes it from other horror films of the 1970s in particular also concerned with the crisis of the patriarchal family as well as from films such as *The Godfather* (1972) and *Slaughterhouse-Five* (1972) that portrayed America as a corrupt and violent society. Kubrick's hotel, even more than King's, is informed by a rich literary and cinematic tradition in the depiction of and discourse about hotels. This was of course a function of Kubrick's exhaustive reading and viewing that certainly continued through the 1960s and 1970s. The representation of the hotel in literature and film increasingly reflected its changing commercial and political position within modern society. During the first half of the twentieth century, the hotel became a location and symbol of public danger and state power. Hotels could still offer to their guest "secrecy and anonymity for the person attempting to maintain control."[29] But, especially in Kubrick's films, the hotel is also another place for individuals (e.g., Johnny in *The Killing* and Humbert in *Lolita*) to lose to the forces of worldly power and universal indifference. This metaphorical use of the hotel, combined with the especially volatile history of the twentieth century, was, as we shall shortly see, intensified in the decade before Kubrick filmed *The Shining*. The Overlook Hotel therefore not only represented Kubrick's own personal and artistic concerns, but also embodied an evolving cultural discourse that in the previous decade had taken on even more specific expressions of social disquiet. This disquiet was informed by powerful and pervasive confrontations with the Second World War and the Holocaust that would further transform the literary and cinematic representation of hotels. We must remind ourselves at this juncture that the fact that Kubrick himself never commented in specific terms about these meanings and associations is not in and of itself an argument against the existence and importance of such meanings and associations. This is the case not just because the percolation of cultural and textual forms and contents is not a function alone, or even at all, of authorial intentions. It is also the case, as the highly intent and intentional Kubrick himself had declared, that for a filmmaker to explain the meaning of a work is to rob of it of much or all of its meaning.

An immediate inspiration for Kubrick's Overlook was Stephen Crane's story "The Blue Hotel" (1898), which had been turned into a film script in 1949 by James Agee and became an episode in the *Omnibus* television series in 1956. Kubrick had done second-unit work on Agee's five-part *Mr. Lincoln* for *Omnibus* and Agee, as we have seen, had also previewed Kubrick's first film, *Fear and Desire*.[30] "The Blue Hotel" concerns a Swedish immigrant who arrives in Fort Romper, Nebraska, one cold, bleak winter in the 1880s. Inflamed, as many Europeans were, about the violent, lawless American Western frontier, he is disposed to distrust everyone in the Palace Hotel.[31] Indeed, it is apparent from his remarks that he thinks someone is going to murder him. This prophecy begins to fulfill itself when he accuses the son of the hotel owner of cheating at cards. He beats up the young man and leaves the hotel and goes to a saloon. When a gambler there refuses to drink with him, the belligerent Swede attacks him and is stabbed to death. It turns out, however, that young Johnnie Scully *was* cheating, and so the Swede's death cannot be ascribed simply to groundless paranoia. This depiction of the world as a place of danger and evil seemed particularly relevant in the film noir wake of the Second World War. The world for Crane, as for his friend Joseph Conrad, was one of contingency and chance against which human will rather than human reason is the only—and still inadequate—defense. Human beings are estranged not only from the universe, but also from one another. As in *Rashomon,* the universe serves people not as window but as mirror. What one sees *in* the world and *as* the world are only reflections of a needy sense of self.[32]

Agee's 1949 script follows Crane's narrative, capturing the cold, chaotic, and indifferent "blizzard of the universe" that surrounds the characters in the story with a pessimistic determinism.[33] The pervasive sense in the face of the horrors of the world war (and the one that preceded it) that there was something dreadfully amiss in the universe could not but provoke a creative response to Crane's grim take on the universe. The film's opening dramatizes this atmosphere through the juxtaposition of a mechanical device rasping the music of Emile Waldteufel ("forest devil," 1837–1915) with a surrealistic and grotesque picturing of the Swede.[34] The script cannot help but elaborate on Crane's exposition in terms of the postwar environment in which it was written: Agee introduces international relations into Crane's portrayal of the Easterner, who desperately tries to make causal sense of the killing and to assign collective responsibility for it: "That's right, shrug it off; it's a small matter. It's why wars are fought; why a great nation can fall apart like rotten meat."[35] These words would easily have been heard in the audience as a reference to the Axis powers in the recently concluded war. When coupled with Agee's paraphrase of the further words of Crane's Easterner, this reference to the Second World War would have been magnified by the staining of the word "collaboration" as a result of the long Nazi occupation of Europe: "Every sin is a collaboration. Everybody is responsible for everything."[36] Indeed, whether fully intended or not, the addressing of the recent war in the script gave the Easterner's words a moral and intellectual weight that they arguably do not possess in the original story. Instead of the Easterner as merely—or is it for Crane only mostly?—an example of a hapless holder of "a dream of order in a reality ruled by the forces of chaos," the lesson of the teleplay could be taken as the necessity of good people banding together to defeat or prevent evil.[37]

A similar ethos seems to inform Czech director Jan Kadar's teleplay "The Blue Hotel" (1977). In the 1960s Kadar had made the anti-Nazi film *Death Is Called Engelchen* (1963) and a classic film on the Holocaust, *The Shop on Main Street* (1965). Kadar (1918–1979), whose parents and sister had died in Auschwitz, immigrated to the United States in 1968 after the Soviet suppression of reform in Czechoslovakia. He had begun his career as a filmmaker with a short documentary, "Life Is Rising from the Ruins" (1945), and in the 1970s made two films, *The Angel Levine* (1970) and *Lies My Father Told Me* (1975), which concern Jewish life.[38] Kadar had apparently been introduced to "The Blue Hotel" by Alfred Kazin, and the film ends with a note of special appreciation to him. Kazin, an authority on American literature, notes that Crane, who was born in New Jersey in 1871 and died in Germany in 1900, was skeptical of American power after the Civil War, was convinced that the universe was indifferent to human aims and desires, and consequently advocated stoicism as the only recourse against what Kazin calls "the Wagnerian music of blood lust, imperialism and war" into which the nineteenth century was expiring at his death.[39] For Crane, therefore, according to a Kazin haunted by the Holocaust, life is nothing less than a state of war. Writing in 1977, Kazin sees the Swede in "The Blue Hotel" as a crazy brute force no less volatile than Hitler who "is done in by the group as a whole," a denouement that renders the "'blue' hotel in a snowstorm . . . a bad dream about ourselves."[40]

Kadar himself, who, like the Swede, had grown up with the European image of the violent American West, was attracted to what he saw as Crane's anticipation of the existentialism that was one philosophical response to the world wars. He was also particularly intrigued by the "silent conspiracy" of indifference to the Swede's self-destruction, which Kadar felt was the characteristic attitude toward "condemned people" he had witnessed in his own country. In order to emphasize this conspiracy and the inevitability of its fatal outcome, Kadar eliminates the scene in the saloon and instead has the Swede killed by "The Stranger," a dark-haired, sharp-featured man who checks into the hotel just as the Swede is about to check out. His appearance, in both senses of the word, has about it a visual and formal quality of a *Satanas ex machina* that indicates a post-Holocaust emphasis on the deadly determinism in Crane's story. It would seem, therefore, that the literary and cinematic environment of the 1970s, combined with Kadar's and Kazin's ongoing individual confrontation with the Nazi extermination of the Jews, had an effect on this version of "The Blue Hotel" as well.[41]

Kubrick of course had his own reasons for being attracted to features of the story, some of which would be incorporated into *The Shining*, such as the "psychological misdirection" that also marks King's novel. Just as the reader of King's novel is initially misled into thinking that the supernatural events at the Overlook Hotel are all projections of Jack's disordered mind, the reader of "The Blue Hotel"

**Figure 1.** The Shining

**Figure 4.** A Clockwork Orange

**Figure 5.** Full Metal Jacket

**Figure 6.** Full Metal Jacket

**Figure 7.** The Shining

**Figure 8.** The Shining

**Figure 9.** The Shining

**Figure 11.** Barry Lyndon

initially sees the Swede as paranoid, only to discover that his suspicions of the world around him are justified.[42] But a close examination of Crane's story reveals details of form and content that explain even more fully the place of "The Blue Hotel" in Kubrick's construction of *The Shining*. The opening sentences of the story instantly remind one of the setting of the Overlook, absent only the mountains.[43] Right away we are reminded of Kubrick's "high rooms." The hotel is "isolated mysterious, highly symbolic"—in Kubrick's films the places, usually suffused with the cold blue light that, for instance, pours through the windows of the Overlook Hotel, where the human high and mighty hold court and where mysterious forces of and over which humans have little or no cognizance or control hold sway. Crane's blue is the expression of human irrationality and of a cold, indifferent universe.[44] Against the Palace Hotel, Crane sets the saloon, a naturalistic, amoral, and contingent world of human passion bathed in shades of red and yellow that are revisited in the living quarters and the bar of the Overlook. Of course, the Palace Hotel is its own sort of hell, so red and yellow show up there as well.[45]

Kubrick would also have been struck by the account of the arrival of the Swede in which the commercial efficiency of hotel proprietor Pat Scully is couched in jovial but shadowed irony made much darker by any idea of what was to come. Readers after 1945 of course had even more of such an impression in the description of the lugubrious arrival of the train, "with its long string of freight cars," and Scully's "catching" of his "prisoners" for escort to the hotel, a "temple for an enormous stove . . . humming with godlike violence", its "iron . . . yellow from the heat."[46] This digestion of people from train into hotel, with its sly inkling of the unexpected and the unwanted, was certainly reinforced in Kubrick's artistic consciousness by the similar opening to Zweig's *The Burning Secret:* "The train, with a shrill whistle, pulled into Summering. For a moment the black coaches stood still in the silvery light of the uplands to eject a few vivid human figures and to swallow up others. Exacerbated voices called back and forth; then, with a puffing and a chugging and another shrill shriek, the dark train clattered into the opening of the tunnel, and once more the landscape stretched before the view unbroken in all its wide expanse, the background swept clean by the moist wind." And it would be the same train, freighted of course with obvious sexual symbolism, that would take the young boy Edgar farther into the enticing but also perilous adult world: "He drew a great sigh of relief when at last the first whistle sounded in the distance, and the rumbling came closer and closer, and the train that was to carry him out into the great world puffed and snorted into the station."[47] Agee, like Zweig, made more atmospheric and symbolic use of trains than did Crane. The film as written, like Kadar's, begins and ends with their sound: from "the humming, then hammering of rails" to "a train's whistle. In the silence after it, the cold stars sharpen; and very slowly, like a prodigious wheel, the whole sky begins to turn."[48] These sounds and images of the film reinforce the sense of doom in the original story, as the whole universe turns away (and onward toward murder?) like the iron wheels of a train. This fusion of human violence and mechanical power *à la Kubrickienne* also marks an Agee image of the Swede after his fight with young Scully standing "like an idling locomotive."[49]

There is another difference between Crane and Agee that too reflects the different times in which the story and the film were created. Crane's emphasis is on the *will* of the Swede in acting as he does against his environment. For Crane, this is all one can do, a matter of defeat rather than triumph of the will, in Crane's terms "the eagle ... giving way to the crows."[50] The twentieth century, however, brought confrontation with a scale of violence that rendered the late-nineteenth-century concern with individual action somewhat quaint and outmoded. Increasingly, people and artists began thinking more often in terms of perpetrators and victims, particularly in the terms of collaboration with murderous Nazi persecution. In this frame of reference, the Swede after 1945 can be viewed as the outsider, the foreigner, who confronts a society that, in the words of the production company for Kadar's 1984 teleplay, "punishes outsiders for being different." In this context, Crane's own use of the word "holocaust" takes on an expanded significance: "Suddenly a holocaust of warlike desire caught the cowboy, and he bolted forward with the speed of a broncho [*sic*]. 'Go it, Johnnie! go it! Kill him! Kill him!'"[51] For Crane, of course, the word had none of the modern historical meaning it would later assume. It would also probably not have been read this way in 1946, although Kazin has noted that he began hearing the word applied to "the destruction of the Jews" as soon as the first years after the war.[52] But as Kubrick recalled or even re-read the story later in his preparations for *The Shining*, the word would have had this added meaning within the story's overall concern with murder in a cold, indifferent universe. Trains too were for Kubrick another example of the general modern problem of men and machinery, a problem gruesomely magnified in Hilberg's account of trains skirling and drumming all over iron Europe toward the extermination camps.[53] In *The Shining* Kubrick would almost vanishingly re-create the sight and sound of trains that subtly and intermittently inhabit Crane's story and Agee's film. And these invisible trains would serve a discourse most dreadfully informed not by holocaust but by the Holocaust.

Unlike "The Blue Hotel," King's *The Shining* employs the specific Gothic horror tradition of "the terrible house" that was also the basis of *The Haunting*, a film Kubrick admired. But King's book was also part of a turn in the literature and cinema of horror toward replacing the old aristocratic haunted house with the modern hotel. This turn reflected the *fin-de-siècle* change in American hotels from a domestic environment to a dedicated commercial one, from strangers gathered in a communal environment to commercially individualized strangers.[54] Whatever else they may be — a place of romance, adventure, wealth, or intrigue — the literary or cinematic hotel — and, ever since *Psycho,* motel — is a home that is not home, a place of privacy but also of vulnerability, of collectivity but also of isolation. The horrors of *The Shining* and *Psycho* in particular are Kafkaesque since they take place not in the gloomy shadows of an old private home, but in the often bright, though also often deserted, public rooms of modern life and activity.[55] With respect to its public loneliness, Kubrick's Overlook reminded one viewer of Ingmar Bergman's *The Silence* (1963).[56] As early as the 1920s, German sociologist Siegfried Kracauer had identified the hotel lobby in particular as "a space that does not refer beyond itself . . . [a] space of unrelatedness [in which] the change of environments does not leave purposive activity behind, but brackets it for the sake of a freedom that can refer only to itself and therefore sinks into relaxation and indifference."[57] Beyond the lobby, moreover, are the corridors of rooms, the realm not only of further isolation but also of mystery and danger. Just as a room is a purchase of a temporary home, one's "own" space inhabited by some of one's personal possessions, one is also closely surrounded by—and yet also isolated from—others whose presence is that of the strange and potentially dangerous. The corridors therefore are also places of danger—a door (or doors!), after all, could open any second extruding or inviting peril. Kubrick himself read of this in the Oedipal terms of Zweig's *The Burning Secret* when a young boy, as in *The Silence,* spies on his mother and the baron: "From window to window he went peeping, always outside the hotel for fear if he went inside he might run up against them in one of the corridors."[58]

Appropriately enough, a coincidence also linked *The Shining* to an early important film in the hotel "genre," *Grand Hotel* (1932). Diane Johnson, Kubrick's co-writer on *The Shining,* had only ever once before written a screenplay, for director Mike Nichols for a remake of *Grand Hotel* that was in fact was never made.[59] The original film, starring Greta Garbo, had begun the tradition of linking the intrigue, mystery, and danger of large urban hotels to contemporary political events of the greatest gravity that would by the 1940s include the Third Reich and, in the 1970s, the Holocaust. *Grand Hotel* was the product of a screenplay written by German novelist Vicki Baum of her novel *Menschen im Hotel* (1929). Baum (1888–1960) was a Jewish native of Vienna who was afflicted with many illnesses as a child and had spent a lot of time in hospitals. During the First World War, she served as a nurse and again spent time as a patient in hospitals after the war. These early experiences drew her to the hotel as a human pageant, a place not only (or so much) of residence as of arrival and departure in which, as in a hospital, one's bed is left for another to occupy: "A hospital is a great experience, every room, every bed a history."[60] From 1926 to 1931, Baum worked for purposes of research as a chambermaid at the Hotel Bristol in Berlin. The Hollywood film was a great success and inspired three separate musical productions. Baum became an American citizen in 1938, the same year her books were burned in Austria by the Nazis. During the Second World War, she wrote a sequel to her most famous novel, *Hotel Berlin '43,* which was serialized in *Collier's* in 1943/1944. In this story the hotel serves as a much more dangerous and even delirious microcosm of the surrounding society. In both novels, the hotel used a model was the Art Deco Hotel Adlon in Berlin, which during the Third Reich became, as Baum writes in *Hotel Berlin '43,* "less a hotel for passing guests than a half-official branch of the Government, a comfortable island set apart from the rest of the country" filled with "Hitler's elite . . . officials . . . industrialists bombed out of their towers . . . privileged people . . . Quislings and collaborationists . . . big, important foreign bankers and magnates, and . . . small, shady foreign agents,"[61] to paraphrase—or, rather, not to paraphrase—Kubrick, all the *worst* people. And all around the hotel are hospital trains filled with wounded soldiers pouring into a Nazi capital increasingly reduced to chaos by massive air raids. The escalating chaos even begins to creep into the hotel, where Gestapo agents in search of defeatists have already spread the paralyzing fear of suspicion, arrest, torture, and death. Ordinary people, members of the resistance, and even Jews in hiding take up residence in the hotel. Not surprisingly, this book too was made into a film, *Hotel Berlin,* focusing on a member of the underground and an actress involved with a general, which played at the RKO Fordham in the Bronx, May 3–10, 1945, the week that Nazi Germany surrendered.

In general, the hotel mode has been roomy enough to encompass gritty noir films such as the French *Hotel du Nord* (1938), a Hungarian wartime comedy called *The Blue Star Hotel* (1941), the war film *Five Graves to Cairo,* stock dramas such as *Hotel* (1967), thrillers like *The Towering Inferno* (1974), as well as psychological studies such as *The Silence.* Between 1898 and 2001, there were made in the world no fewer than 289 films just on hotels per se, as well as 42 television films and 38 television series. After the Second World War there emerged a trend to use hotel allusions when referring to the Nazi concentration camps or to use concentration camp imagery when addressing issues of institutional residence and regimentation. An example of the first practice is Resnais's *Night and Fog,* in which the narrator observes that camps were "built, like a stadium or a Grand Hotel."[62]

The most bizarre instance of the latter approach is Roy Rowland's frankly unsettling *The 5000 Fingers of Dr. T* (1953), based on an idea and a screenplay by Theodore Geisel, aka Dr. Seuss. This musical is a live-action cartoon nightmare about a fascistic piano teacher who imprisons young boys in a fortress-like piano camp. Seuss, who during the war created U.S. government cartoons under the direction of Frank Capra, uses Nazi architecture, imagery, and policies to emphasize the importance of enlightened child rearing with an emphasis on free play, inquiry, and imagination. Dr. Terwilliker, played by Hans Conreid, is a Hitlerian figure who wants to eliminate all musicians except pianists as a means to world domination. Conreid, who in physical appearance resembles Seuss caricatures of Hitler, had done German voices for anti-Nazi films, and his conductor's uniform is "a combination of circus band drum major, Carmen Miranda, and Hermann Göring." Most of Dr. T's henchmen have German names, and his soldiers goosestep around in blue helmets carrying huge "Happy Fingers" logos as if in a scene from *Triumph of the Will.* Ironically, the composer of the score had studied under Richard Strauss, worked with Max Reinhardt in Berlin, and directed the music for Josef von Sternberg's *The Blue Angel* (1930). The concentration camp references, badly trivialized by the Technicolor musical setting, are blatant. The boys arrive in accurately but also conveniently ominous *yellow* school buses. They are escorted through a large gate in the "poison ivy walls" with electrified barbed wire and stripped of their possessions. Growing gaunt in their striped prison garb, they live in dark underground cells just above a dungeon outfitted with, a hooded elevator operator sings, "gas chambers." The young boy Bart, who has this nightmare, lost his father in the Second World War, but he and his mother are befriended by plumber August Zabladowski. Zabladowski, who wears an Eisenhower jacket and drives a Jeep, is described in the original script as being a Slav from eastern Europe, which augments associations with Nazi mass persecution and murder. Although the substitution of a Pole for a Jew follows 1950s generic Holocaust victimology, Dr. T wants Zabladowski, who has been hired to fix the sinks in the institute, "disintegrated" after he has made the place "sanitary."[63]

It was two later films, both released in 1960, that, given Kubrick's interests and concerns, undoubtedly had a direct influence on *The Shining:* Lang's *The 1000 Eyes of Dr. Mabuse* and Hitchcock's *Psycho*. Shelley Duvall noted that "Kubrick was crazy about Hitchcock."[64] And reviewers of *The Shining* have detected quotations—with alterations—from *Psycho:* two scenes that recall a staircase murder sequence, and the scene in the bathroom of room 237 in which Danny and Jack discover a nude woman in the tub that recalls the shower murder in *Psycho*. Besides being unflattering portraits of America, both films, it has been argued, present a feminized male dealing with Oedipal issues. In *Psycho,* investigator Arbogast ascends a staircase—a common Freudian dream symbol for sexual intercourse—only to be knifed at the top by Norman Bates, who is dressed as his own mother. Jack backs Wendy, who is armed with a baseball bat, up the stairs until struck by the bat and then falls backward, arms flailing, just like Arbogast. In the other scene, Wendy runs up stairways wielding the same kind of knife as the cross-dressed Bates. The bathroom sequence involves a reflexive reversal in that the woman at the Overlook Hotel emerges from the tub to tempt—and then horrify—Jack by changing from a sexually alluring naked young woman into a rotting old hag. Kubrick's reversal, however, also represents the original in that the woman in the tub, who had attacked Danny, is the ghost of a woman murdered in the tub at some time in the hotel's past. The woman's transformation also embodies a condemnation of America as a place of materialistic promise and boundless violence.[65]

The other bathroom scene in *The Shining,* in which Jack attempts to hack through the door with an ax to get at Wendy, forges an even more important link to *Psycho*. This is because it, more than the others, addresses the issue of the changing venue of horror in modern American and Western life. As we have noted, *Psycho* marked a turning point in horror cinema by bringing horror in from its origins far away and long ago into the contemporary domestic scene. *Psycho* also extended the modern commercial "terrible house" of the hotel to the motel, that previously snug island of safety from the terrors—and extension of the freedom—represented by the American road. The advertised appeal of a "home away from home" here takes on, along with the horror of invasion of the home, the literal awfulness of the adjective "away." Unlike the rooms of an old haunted house, the bathroom in the Bates Motel in which the murder of Marion Crane takes place is brightly lit. While the traditional haunted house, as represented in *Psycho* by the Bates house, presents a dark, foreboding exterior, the motel presents a clean, modest façade of comfort and security.[66] Even the interior of the old and movie-creepy Bates house somewhat belies its exterior, since its acts of murder and attempted murder occur as well in the light. The motel bathroom in particular is transformed from a place of privacy (recall "your ass belongs to the Corps" in *Full Metal Jacket*), security, and comfort into a location of naked vulnerability. Aside from any patriarchal voyeurism, the naked woman being stabbed to death in the shower in *Psycho* is a representation not merely of psychological evil in society, the Freudian association (reproduced by Kubrick) between anality and aggression, or later feminist constructions around the bathtub in particular as a place of both female security and vulnerability. The greatest horrors of the twentieth century, as increasingly reflected in horror films, take place within the public institutions of modern society, not in haunted houses of purely private home life.

Hitchcock, like Wilder, worked on a concentration camp documentary, but it would be too much to say that *Psycho* references the Holocaust insofar as the murder is that of a naked person and in a shower, the euphemism for the gas chamber the Nazis used in the extermination camps to deceive their victims. Overall, the horror in *Psycho* "is not particularly of death or symbolic evil; the fear is instead of living in crazy world, a world in which one can be mutilated physically in close-up."[67] But an anecdote from the filming of *The Shining* suggests the volatile symbolic and historical ground on which any film about horror and murder treads amid the ashes of the Final Solution. Diane Johnson recalls commenting on the tiling in the set of the Torrances' bathroom in which Wendy hides as Jack comes to murder her (and not just with a knife, as in *Psycho,* but with a fireman's ax). At the time, the tiles ran all the way up to the ceiling, which, Johnson said to Kubrick, made it look "like a gas-chamber. Bathroom tiles mostly stop at the height of the shower door."[68] Kubrick had the tiles torn out, and in the film the wall of tiles, marked by a single horizontal black strip, ends about halfway up the white walls. In *Psycho,* while the white tiles end just above the level of the showerhead, in the shots in the shower the victim is shown against nothing but tiles. Johnson's intuitive association has merit at the very least in terms of the institutional quality of a cold, white, tiled enclosure that excludes the individualized domestic warmth of detail in favor of a hard, uniform surface easy to clean. Such institutional standards are also historically synonymous with what the Nazis saw as the cleansing operation made necessary by the noxious existence of Jews. Hence, along with a memory of the shower scene in *Psycho*, which is part of American cultural consciousness, Johnson's impression of a gas chamber effect in the original set of the bathroom for *The Shining* is in harmony with the historical discourse of some horror films of the era as well as that which Kubrick would develop in his own.

Lang's *The 1000 Eyes of Dr. Mabuse* brings this filmic discourse closer to 1970s constructions around hotels, Nazis, and the Holocaust. Lang had returned to Germany to direct this film, constructing a continuity between the explorations of mystery and terror of pre-Hitler German Expressionism in order to examine the Nazi era in a way similar to that of Peter Lorre's *The Lost One* (1951). As early as 1952, as we saw in Chapter 8, the communal setting of Lang's *Rancho Notorious* was imbued with Holocaust associations. *The 1000 Eyes of Dr. Mabuse*, an updating of Lang's *The Testament of Dr. Mabuse,* also reaches back to his *Ministry of Fear,* in which a murder attempt takes place in a hotel. And the film recalls the two Baum novels by making the Hotel Adlon the basis for Lang's Hotel Luxor. The Nazis apparently planned to bug the Adlon, as they had the SS brothel Salon Kitty, in preparation for the foreign businessmen and diplomats Berlin would attract as the capital of Nazi Europe. This plan represented an expansion as well as a technological advance over the German Abwehr's "Hotel Organization," which employed hotel staff to watch enemy agents and help recruit foreigners for counterespionage work abroad.[69] According to one of the characters in the film, the Nazis began building the Luxor in May 1944 for exactly this purpose. Lang's story thus constitutes an elaboration on the historical fact built upon by Baum that the Adlon was a hotel frequented by foreigners and diplomats and penetrated by government security. More generally, Lang's film exploits the hotel as a place of residence peculiarly suited for surveillance as well as the realization of the inherent threat, represented by such institutions, of the violation of individual privacy and security. Every room in the Luxor is surveyed by a television camera, 1000 eyes controlled by an unnamed successor to Dr. Mabuse from a basement room hidden inside a fake boiler. Just as with *The 5000 Fingers of Dr. T,* a number in the thousands suggests masses of victims as well as oppressors. The plot involves Mabuse's plan to acquire the nuclear power holdings of a young American staying in room 1414 of the hotel. The false Mabuse is clearly a Hitler figure, the ultimate realization of Lang's vision of the "inexorable inhumanity" that issues from "the battle of the individual against circumstance."[70]

As with *The Shining*'s symbolic use of the typewriter, Lang emphasizes the bureaucracy of "faceless functionaries" who run modern systems of domination.[71] Also like *The Shining, The 1000 Eyes of Dr. Mabuse* incorporates a Mephistopheles figure serving the devil. In Kubrick's film, it is Lloyd the bartender, who plies Jack with liquor on behalf of the lords of the Overlook. Lloyd appears as Jack, sitting at the empty hotel bar for the first time, says: "I'd give my goddam soul for just a glass of beer."[72] Mabuse's avatar has a clubfoot, just like Hitler's propaganda minister Joseph Goebbels. This allusiveness makes the impact of the film's concern with history all the greater, especially since the genre each film employs, mystery and horror, respectively, is otherwise inadequate to the task of representing the Nazi legacy in a serious manner.[73] Since we know that Kubrick admired Lang and that Kubrick himself was a master of architectural space on film, it is no accident that this analysis of *The 1000 Eyes of Dr. Mabuse* could easily—or even necessarily—be applied to *The Shining*. Even had Kubrick no knowledge of Lang's film, the similarities between the settings of the two films and the subject of their concerns would suggest a strong draft from the same trench of cultural and historical representation. Kubrick, moreover, had the even more daunting artistic and personal task of addressing the Holocaust and not just the Nazi regime, which is why *The Shining* has an allusiveness—and elusiveness—all its own when it comes to its treatment of history, and German history in particular.

Luis Buñuel's *The Exterminating Angel* appeared two years later. Like Kubrick (one thinks in this temporal and thematic regard of the Enchanted Hunters Hotel in *Lolita*), Buñuel was dedicated to the Kafkaesque—that is, the evocation of the incongruous and the fantastic within realistic settings. This 1962 film concerns a group of upper-class Mexicans gathering after the opera in a fancy urban mansion.

The servants, sensing something amiss, leave and the guests discover that some mysterious force has imprisoned them in the salon. The situation brings out the worst in the smug and striving bourgeoisie that Buñuel habitually made the target of his art. The angel, a painting of which adorns the door to the claustrophobic cupboard used as a lavatory, symbolizes the entrapping social roles of bourgeois conformism that mask and pervert desire. As with *The Shining*, Freud's concept of the "uncanny" strongly informs *The Exterminating Angel:* Buñuel, like Freud, sees human fears and desires as a result of the repression of early experiences and conflicts that are then projected onto the outside world to create the monsters that we thus find both strange and familiar. The ornate house in *The Exterminating Angel* resembles, in its appointments and darknesses, the "terrible house" of Gothic literature but, like the hotel in *The Shining*, also assumes metaphorical and historical meaning. Like the modern hotel in film, it is a place where people find themselves housed with others, but, like *The Shining*, the film concentrates on the internal and external forces that rip civility, society, and family apart and bring out "a wolf of a man."[74] The police place a yellow flag of quarantine on the house, but when the imprisoning spell is broken, "the plague," as Buñuel calls it, spreads to a church, also adorned with a yellow (papal) flag that likewise turns into a prison for the priests and parishioners.[75] Buñuel and Kubrick—along with Hitchcock—also shared a wariness of—and (therefore) an attraction to—birds, particularly birds of prey like eagles and hawks. They admired each other's work, and so it is likely that Buñuel's films influenced Kubrick and that *The Exterminating Angel* informed *The Shining*.[76]

One can even speculate that the shared Kafkaesque perspective of these two filmmakers is reflected in a possible curious coincidence of cinematic reference. Buñuel's attraction to the surreal made him a fan of the Gothic horror film *The Beast with Five Fingers* (1946), in which the severed hand of a pianist (*à la* Dr. T?) takes on a life of its own in the mind of an underling played by Peter Lorre. In homage to this surreal vision, a severed hand is seen crawling across the floor of the mansion in *The Exterminating Angel*.[77] The human hand as monster (as in *The Clutching Hand* [1915] and *The Hands of Orlac* [1924]) is consistent with one of the themes in *The Shining*—the human functionaries of modern systems of domination and oppression. The mechanical embodiment, as it were, of this theme in Kubrick's film is the typewriter, the primary weapon of the SS bureaucrats of the Final Solution who have rightly been designated "desk murderers" (*Schreibtischmörder*). There is no better example of Kubrick's emphasis on the natural sources of evil in contrast to King's stress on the supernatural: "Kubrick puts the typewriter on a long, empty table in the Overlook's long, empty, sterile lobby, in perfect, cold symmetry with the hotel's space. Jack's compulsive peckings, which echo down the corridors in a stark equation of sound and space, index his gradual breakdown. The relentlessly mechanical sound, issuing *from* the activity of character rather than trying to drown it out, replaces King's howling wind as the hotel's menacing voice."[78] But, given Kubrick's metaphysical and historical intentions, the symbolism here is not only psychological, even though the motif of the severed hand has been closely aligned in horror film with the concept of the double so important to *The Shining*. In conceiving of the human being as the monster, Kubrick has sundered the image of the severed hand from the timeless evil of the Gothic and reconnected it in service to the historical. It is chilling in this connection to note that during the Second World War one of the rehabilitation centers for wounded SS soldiers worked at turning out one-armed typists. Such men would be available to help process the reams of paper that Stroheim's Rommel in *Five Graves to Cairo*—itself set in the desert Hotel Imperial—had so ominously said Germany would require. A German newspaper of the time headlined this rehabilitation as "Five Fingers Will Do"—the beast with five fingers, indeed.[79]

By the late 1960s and the 1970s, film and literature were ever more frequently addressing both the Nazi perpetrators (Luchino Visconti's *The Damned*) and the Jewish victims (D. M. Thomas, *The White Hotel* [1981]) of the Holocaust. The 1970s witnessed the first great wave of films dealing with the subject. Many of these films were controversial, since aesthetic and commercial forms are problematic in dealing with this subject matter. Typical in this regard is Liliana Cavani's *The Night Porter*. Unlike *The Damned,* which sees Nazism as the ugly fruit of political and economic collaboration between racists and capitalists, *The Night Porter* focuses on fascism as a form of cruel psychological and sexual conflict.[80] In *The Night Porter* a hotel in Vienna becomes the re-creation of a concentration camp for a former guard and one of his prisoners. For many, as a result, the film was nothing but, in the words of Pauline Kael, an exercise in "porno-gothic . . . [in] "an s-m Grand Hotel."[81] Cavani herself declared that the intent of the film was to collapse the absolute dichotomy of victim and murderer and explore the mutual unconscious complicities of the victim–executioner dynamic in all relationships, a perspective Holocaust survivor Primo Levi found objectionable in the most fundamental way: "I was a guiltless victim and I was not a murderer." However, Levi himself also wrote of "the gray zone" into which the Nazis cast their victims that forced their participation in the extermination of others, thus dehumanizing them in a mad and usually hopeless struggle for survival.[82] Almost all of the film's action takes place within the walls of the Hotel zur Oper, which literally becomes a time machine into the labyrinths of the repressed psychological and historical past of the night porter, Max, and a hotel guest, Lucia. In particular, the "hotel lobby, Max's own territory, becomes the visible site of erotic and dark fantasies."[83] Like Kubrick, Cavani prefers the statement of image to the statement of language: mirrors, gates, bars, and walls become metaphors of past and present imprisonment.

It is 1957, just after the departure of Soviet occupation troops in compliance with Austria's new neutral status, and Lucia Atherton, a concentration camp survivor and wife of an orchestra conductor on tour, checks into the Hotel zur Oper. The night porter, Max Aldorfer, was the concentration camp officer who filmed prisoners arriving at the camp. Lucia, a fourteen-year-old imprisoned as a "Viennese socialist," becomes Max's sexual partner in a sado-masochistic relationship. *The Night Porter* is built around flashbacks to this concentration camp relationship as Lucia takes up again with Max (her husband has left Vienna on his tour) and eventually moves into his apartment (see also Polanski's *The Tenant*). The hotel is thus the gateway to a timeless concentration camp of the unconscious in which Max and Lucia are again imprisoned by their unresolved conflicts and morbid sexual passions. Even the abstract pattern of the blue wallpaper in Max's apartment resembles fencing composed of broken swastikas. Cavani, like Hitchcock and Kubrick, also exploits the space of the bathroom as a place of violated privacy and naked, mirrored, vulnerability. But also like *The Shining*, Cavani's film is not restricted to the psychological. Max is a member of an underground SS organization that wants him to eliminate Lucia, since she is a potential witness against them. She is, in the terms of a Nazi bureaucratic euphemism, to be "filed away." Max refuses, barricading himself and Lucia in his apartment until—starving—both are shot down in the street. *The Night Porter* is an important artifact of the 1970s since it adopted the point of view that fascism in general was not only still an underground presence in Europe but also a generalized potential of contemporary civilization.[84]

Cavani portrays the Nazis as beset by the same sort of hypermasculine panic over—and unconscious indulgence in—ambiguous sexuality that Kubrick depicts among American Marines in *Full Metal Jacket*. Max is the same sort of feminized male who occupies *The Shining* and many of the films of the decade. At the same time, Cavani attempts to universalize her message by Lucia not being Jewish. This runs the risk of missing the central element of the Holocaust, the same risk Kubrick runs by rendering his discourse on the Holocaust so indirect. Kubrick never said anything publicly about *The Night Porter*, but if he saw it, he would have noticed the cohabitation of beauty and evil that so transfixed him when it came to Hitler's Germany.[85] In one scene, a nearly nude man dances for the SS to the music of *Der Rosenkavalier*, the comedy of lost and found love by Strauss and Hofmannstahl quoted as well at Kubrick's insistence in *A.I.* In another scene, both Max and Lucia exchange glances during a performance of Mozart's *The Magic Flute* (1791) conducted by her husband, while scenes of a concentration camp rape are intercut with lyrics about the sanctity of the bonds between man and wife. Like the Beethoven opera *Fidelio* referenced in *Eyes Wide Shut*, *The Magic Flute* has intents blackly ironic in the context of Cavani's film: the celebration of the victory of humanitarianism and "the bourgeois ideology of marriage."[86]

The ever more explicit association of a hotel setting with the Holocaust only gathered momentum during and after Kubrick's production of *The Shining* from 1978 to 1980. Especially relevant as well as representative are Aharon Appelfeld's *Badenheim 1939* (1980) and Joel and Ethan Coen's *Barton Fink* (1991). Appelfeld escaped from the Transnistria concentration camp in Romania, served with the Red Army, and immigrated to Palestine in 1946. In his novel of "nervous detail," Appelfeld imagines a resort town for Jews located in the Sudetenland region of Czechoslovakia ceded to the Germans in September 1938.[87] It is now the spring of 1939, and the resort has come alive for the new season: "The hotel was a hive of activity. The spring light and the laughter of the people filled the streets, and in the hotel gardens the porters once more carried the brightly colored baggage." But: "The days slipped by. A cold light broke out of the north and spread through the long corridor. It seemed not like light but needles cutting the carpet into squares. The people hugged the walls like shadows."[88] At first there are only small portents, like the story of the fish in the hotel aquarium slaughtered the year before by some new blue Cambium fish. The hotel owner disposed of the perpetrators and has brought in new fish, but now worries that the two new varieties ought to be separated. One day it is discovered that the more retiring green fish have disappeared without a trace.[89] At the same time, the naiveté of the newly arrived residents is demonstrated by their inability to comprehend the true meaning of the edicts that gradually begin to circulate in the town. The Sanitation Department has directed that all guest must register in the Golden Book while posters appear that tout the virtues of living in Poland, a destination that for the Jews in the book calls up family origins but for the reader portends the abyss. Particularly ominous and yet unnoticed are the references to the fresher air in the East that for any reader are, in spite of their elliptical nature, clear and cruelly ironic references to gas chambers and extermination.[90] The color yellow, in its associations with warning, disease, and ages-old discrimination against Jews, also becomes a grim harbinger. Thus it is that "[t]he last days of Badenheim were illuminated by a dull, yellow light."[91]

*Barton Fink* constitutes a fitting conclusion to our discussion of the role of hotel film and literature in the construction of Kubrick's *The Shining*. This is because *Barton Fink* is to some extent an homage to *The Shining*. The film concerns a Jewish playwright from New York with writer's block living in the dark, claustrophobic 1930s Art Deco Hotel Earle (motto: "A Day or a Lifetime") in Los Angeles in late 1941. The cinematographic influence of Kubrick can be seen not only in the décor of the hotel but also in the many dolly shots, in particular down the hotel corridors, while the entire situation of the film also reminds one of Kafka and the black humor of central European Jews that was central to Kubrick's *oeuvre*.[92] The historical content of *The Shining* as well finds dramatic and more direct expression in *Barton Fink*. In particular, Holocaust referents and imagery confirm the significant degree of inspiration and intuition based on *The Shining* as well as the power of the cultural discourse on the Holocaust that would reach one of its most famous and controversial cinematic moments with *Schindler's List* just two years later.

Barton Fink has been hired to write a B-movie about wrestling for Wallace Beery, an actor who, coincidentally or not, had appeared in *Grand Hotel*. The plot line takes on mordant gravity when it becomes apparent that this movie script is like the wall*paper* peeling with the mounting heat in the Hotel Earle: it failingly masks the real and escalating violence in the world. Like Kubrick, Fink is confronted with a world of horror that renders his writing task ludicrous, for the hotel itself contains secrets of the most murderous kind. Sitting over his typewriter, Fink hears faint sounds through the wall behind the typewriter coming from the next room, which is occupied by folksy insurance salesman Charlie Meadows. A gender analysis à la Chodorow and Lacan demonstrates that *Barton Fink* engages issues of male desire for the original female caretaker (a rear view of a young woman sitting on a beach looking out to sea; a journey into the hotel's plumbing during Barton's coupling with Audrey Taylor). But, as in *The Shining*, it is history that assumes the greatest metaphorical and actual presence. Barton's first hint of the real violence of the world beyond his typewriter comes in the form of a novel given to him by screenwriter Bill Mayhew (a character modeled on William Faulkner) entitled *Nebuchadnezzar*. Nebuchadnezzar, the greatest king of the warrior kingdom of Assyria, has the Jewish prophet Daniel interpret one of his dreams. The dream is of a giant with feet of clay, symbolizing the strengths and weaknesses of worldly realms that will one day be succeeded by the kingdom of God. Nebuchanezzar misunderstands the dream as an invitation to establish his own eternal kingdom, which is symbolized by a giant golden image. When three Jewish governors refuse to bow down to the image, the king has them placed in a fiery furnace heated "seven times more than it was wont to be heated" (Daniel 3:19). The three are saved from burning by the Son of God. The film uses this story ironically, since Barton is brought face to face with evil and not salvation, although he, like Danny in *The Shining*, escapes the hotel even though it is burning.[93]

The horror begins the morning after his tryst with Mayhew's companion, Audrey. A mosquito that has been plaguing Barton bites Audrey's naked hip. Barton watches the small spot of blood give way to a tide of blood—recalling the Overlook elevator as well as invoking the male desire for and terror before the female body—soaking the mattress. He turns Audrey over and finds her butchered. Charlie disposes of the body for him. But then Barton learns from detectives Mastrionotti and Deutsch that Charlie is mass murderer Karl Mundt. The detectives, whose names in oneiric fashion reflect the contemporaneous Axis alliance of Italy and Germany, accuse Barton of being Mundt's accomplice in the murder of the woman. As they are grilling Fink in his sixth-floor room, the hotel, as it has throughout the film, is growing hotter and hotter. The detectives hear the sound of the elevator and go into the hall to see if it is Mundt. The elevator doors open, and smoke wafts out. Flames flicker along an elevator threshold that reads "Meyersberg Bros." Mundt (German *Mund* [mouth] and *Mond* [moon]; Italian *mondo* [world]) steps from the elevator carrying a large policy case. Just as the Overlook's elevator disgorges oceans of blood, the Earle's vomits waves of fire. Flames multiply along the walls, recalling—for us at least—the "gas jets" lighting the corridors of the hotel in Zweig's *The Burning Secret,* as Mundt takes a shotgun from the case and kills one of the detectives.[94] He pursues the other detective down an endless corridor sprouting flames. Over the fire's roar, Mundt shouts "Look upon me" and then, over and over, "I'll show you the life of the mind." As he places the shotgun's barrel to the fallen man's forehead before pulling the trigger, Mundt says calmly, "Heil Hitler." Barton the writer has called himself a soldier of the mind, but Mundt's claim about the nature of the mind in December 1941 carries greater historical weight. This is the real world, not the Hollywood world of wrestling movies with titles like *The Devil on Canvas* that the studio has Barton watch for inspiration. No less than the Overlook Hotel, the Hotel Earle is therefore a symbol of the violent real world of twentieth-century mass murder. Unlike Jack, though, Barton, regardless of what the Axis police project onto the Jew, does not become an accomplice to horror. He remains only its observer, sitting at the end of the film on the beach behind the bathing beauty looking out over the ocean with the square head-shaped box Mundt gave him resting in the sand at his side. Richard Jameson has called these allusions to Hitler and the Holocaust in *Barton Fink* "some supremely silly historical allegory," but offers no argument as to why the allegory is silly.[95] These allusions to history in fact offer further evidence of a cultural discourse on the century's—or history's—greatest atrocity, an atrocity that had received supremely eloquent—and almost completely unnoticed—artistic cinematic expression eleven years before in *The Shining*. At some level of artistic intuition, the Coen brothers had noticed.

For almost a century, therefore, from "The Blue Hotel" to *Barton Fink*, the hotel has served as a vital, evolving cultural and artistic site for contemplation of the human condition, even latterly taking on the heavy historical weight of the Holocaust. Kubrick's *The Shining*, unbeknownst to almost everyone, was a signal instance of this artistic turn. His film, however, also derived significant inspiration from Thomas Mann's novel *The Magic Mountain*, the great twentieth-century metaphorical treatment of an exclusive and luxurious mountaintop institutional residence in Davos, Switzerland, for the social, economic, cultural, and political elite of Europe, the International Sanatorium Berghof.

## *The Magic Mountain*

In its remoteness and in its attendant symbols, Kubrick's Overlook Hotel more than anything else resembles the Sanatorium Berghof in Mann's 1924 novel. Kubrick was certainly familiar with the novel from his study at Columbia University. Unless one relies exclusively on the view that texts derive meaning only from other texts and not from their creators, there are too many parallels between Mann's novel and Kubrick's *The Shining* not to assume conscious as well as unconscious and cultural construction from Kubrick's first reading of *The Shining* onward. It is consistent with Kubrick's avoidance of the unreflective established interpretations that accompany famous works of literature that he never revealed this source of inspiration even to Diane Johnson or to his family.[96] Although Stephen King has also never said anything about it, it is possible that King too was aware of the parallel of location in his novel and Mann's. It may be just a logical coincidence that both books have chapters entitled "Snow," although of course Mann's chapter is much longer in length and infinitely deeper in thought than King's. It is probably also just a coincidence that King's brief "Snow" is Chapter 24, but less of a coincidence in just this respect that Kubrick in his film includes a television news report about a twenty-four-year-old woman who "disappeared while on a hunting trip with her husband."[97] Kubrick's love for coincidence surely made him aware of the coincidence of the name of the sanitarium in Mann's novel and Hitler's Berghof (mountain manor) at Berchtesgaden. He was probably also aware that Franz Kafka, his favorite writer, had, like Conrad, died in 1924 and of tuberculosis, the very disease Mann's sanitarium is dedicated to treating.[98] He was probably unaware of the dark irony that during the Third Reich, the Waldsanatorium in Davos, Switzerland, where in 1912 Mann's wife had gone for a cure, came under the direction of the leader of the Swiss Nazi party and during war was filled with tubercular German soldiers.[99]

Mann wrote *The Magic Mountain* as an artistic and philosophical response to what he saw as the decline of European civilization to and through the First World War.[100] Mann had grave doubts about the modern world. His protagonist in *The Magic Mountain*, Hans Castorp, whose name in syllable, sound, and cadence resembles that of Jack Torrance and who unlike Jack escapes death from freezing in the snow, dies in the war that breaks out in 1914: "Hans willingly, even enthusiastically, becomes the cannon fodder of the historical moment. It is difficult to take seriously the idea that Hans Castorp's post-mountain self mirrors the image of a social and political ideal. The First World War was a famously spurious answer to the era's ennui, and so also to Hans Castorp's emptiness, his yearning for a sense of life's purpose and meaning. Rather the war gave full vent to Europe's most deep-seated, destructive impulses."[101] But Mann, who was not Jewish and had not yet witnessed the world during and after Auschwitz, retained at least some faith in human reason to overcome the decline of civilization and the 10 million dead of the war of 1914 to 1918. Kubrick, as we know, was an artistic child of the world during and after Auschwitz. *The Magic Mountain* remains a *Bildungsroman*, a novel of education and self-discovery, as well as a study of an era of decline and futility. *The Shining*, in doubly ironic fashion since Jack is a schoolteacher, is a rueful contemplation of how history shows that human beings learn nothing, or at least not enough to overcome the malevolent forces that surround and inhabit them.[102] Just as Mann's novel was a meditation on Europe's descent toward and through the First World War, so is Kubrick's film a meditation on the modern world's collapse into the horrors of the Second World War. And just as Kubrick's view, as a Jew in the wake of Auschwitz, could not be as sanguine as Mann's, his personal and artistic struggle with filming the Holocaust parallels Mann's own problematic struggle to come to terms with the Third Reich and the Second World War in *Doctor Faustus* (1947).

The philosophical struggle in *The Magic Mountain* between the rationalist, materialist, and anticlerical idealist Lodovico Settembrini and the nihilistic, anarchical Jewish Jesuit Leo Naphta would have appealed to Kubrick's sense of the world as a place of conflict between faith and reason, between spirit and matter, particularly since Mann demonstrates the insufficiency of both positions and the failure of the "moral authority of ideas" in general.[103] When Settembrini and Naphta duel, the former (like Barry Lyndon) purposely misses, whereupon Naphta (unlike Lord Bullingdon) shoots himself. Mynheer Peeperkorn, from The Hague, is the advocate of unrestrained power, but he too commits suicide. Kubrick might have been struck by the fact that Naphta is from Galicia and his father, Elie, as a result of "the unexplained death of two gentile boys, a popular uprising, a panic of rage . . . had died horribly, nailed crucifix-wise on the door of his burning home."[104] Like Kubrick, Mann created few Jewish characters and infrequently treated anti-Semitism, but their very infrequency only makes them stand out. Mann's wife, Katia, was in fact Jewish, but Mann had grown up under the influence of standard upper-class German anti-Semitism, regarded the Pringsheim family not as Jewish but as well-off and cultivated, and would overcome his own anti-Semitism only during his exile from Hitler's Germany.[105] Apart from the many large conceptual details of Mann's novel that find a place in Kubrick's *The Shining*—in particular, the shared symbolic use of the number 7, the color yellow, and doubles—other, smaller details of the novel might have been resorted to in Kubrick's construction of *The Shining,* such as its hedge garden and its white walls. And the Berghof, like the Overlook in King's novel, sits in bright winter blue and white near the very top of a high mountain, at the end of "a steep and steady climb that seems never to come to an end."[106]

Given Kubrick's interests and concerns, especially in connection with the history of Nazi Germany and the Holocaust, it is hard even to imagine that the trends described in this chapter and in the one preceding would not have had an influence on *The Shining*. Indeed, such trends help provide a ready entrée into, and explanation of, many otherwise unnoticed and inexplicable visual, aural, and thematic patterns in the film. In turn, a study of the deep Holocaust subtext in *The Shining* adds new material for understanding a cultural, historical, and artistic discourse that had dominated the previous two decades.

# 10

# FROM YELLOW CABRIOLET TO EAGLE'S NEST

A black screen becomes mountains and sky over water as a small, treed island glides toward us. The camera—for it is we who are moving through the air—banks past the island and over the dark lake toward a mountain wall. The island, shaped like a battleship with the trees as superstructure, disappears to our left. We are on our own, every man an island. The tiny tip of our waking mind is now behind us, and we are suspended over the deeply submerged topography of our unconscious fears and desires. The mountains and sky loom both over and under us, doubled in the black mirror of the lake's surface like the other, darker side of the human personality.

On the soundtrack is a modern electronic rendering of the medieval "Dies Irae," whose opening words are "The day of wrath, that day / which will reduce the world to ashes." The musical setting of the dirge Kubrick chose was Hector Berlioz's *Symphonie fantastique* (1830), in which an artist dreams he has killed the woman he loves, is executed by guillotine, and at whose funeral witches and monsters dance. It is this final scene of a witches' Sabbath in which the "Dies Irae" is heard. The story of this program music, which in the 1970s "was the subject of four important publications,"[1] parallels that of *The Shining*. The death by guillotine in Berlioz's piece even engages the psychoanalytic insight that decapitation is linked in males to scoptophilia and fear of castration.[2] But there is also a historical level to this music related to Kubrick's concerns. For the Frenchman Berlioz, the guillotine called forth the horrors of the Terror during the French Revolution.[3] (Like the full metal jacket cartridge in *Full Metal Jacket* to which Kubrick pointed as an ironic and oxymoronic example of "humane warfare," the guillotine was originally invented as a technologically humane option to execution by ax.) Both Berlioz and Kubrick, therefore, link personal violence within human families to political violence within the human family in general. As with another electronic setting by Wendy Carlos and Rachel Elkind of seventeenth-century funeral music in the opening of *A Clockwork Orange,* Kubrick at the beginning of *The Shining* links the human past and the human present through an equally funereal fusion of ancient and modern music.[4] And here the "Dies Irae" expresses more despair over modern evil ascendant than medieval punishment of evildoers on the Day of Judgment.

Now we are directly overhead a serpentine road snaking its way through tall evergreens. We hear reptilian hissing and rattling on the soundtrack and subsequently learn that this is the twenty-five-mile slither of road to the Overlook Hotel from the town of Sidewinder.[5] There is a tiny car alone on the road, and, with a cut to an open vista overlooking mountains and water, the flying camera approaches a yellow Volkswagen Beetle from behind. It is autumn, and Jack Torrance is driving to his job interview at the Overlook. Another cut and the VW is moving along a road cut above water. The camera swoops in on the car like a post-Ophuls bird of prey as the first line of credits, "A Stanley Kubrick Film," rolls up the screen. As the camera passes close by the car and crosses the double yellow line, "Jack Nicholson" appears, followed by "Shelley Duvall" as we fly off the edge of the road out toward the black lake. "Danny Lloyd" then ascends the screen as the Volkswagen approaches a tunnel on a high mountain road. A white station wagon, looking like an ambulance, is parked on the right side of the road. After the Volkswagen emerges from the tunnel, a black car with a white top, looking like a police car, appears on the left. Along with the yellow color of warning of the Volkswagen, we see in the colors of these other vehicles that we are being alerted to danger ahead.

*The Shining* is the only film in which Kubrick uses scrolling credits, with the very small exception of the disclaimer added at the insistence of the U.S. Air Force to *Dr. Strangelove.* Since the color Kubrick uses for the lettering is light blue, we are aware that his choice of scrolling is not an accident, for the color of the lettering signals the symbolic importance that blue assumes in *The Shining.* Just as the scrolling of the credits upward follows the course of the Volkswagen higher and higher up into the mountains, the light blue ascending into the bluish-white sky reminds of the association of blue with regions beyond the sensible. Kubrick had read in Eisenstein's 1942 essay, "Color and Meaning," that in the Japanese theater blue "is the color of villains . . . supernatural creatures . . . ghosts and fiends."[6] The German poet Johann Wolfgang von Goethe (1749–1832) noted that blue—in water, sky, and smoke—is "a stimulating negation" that draws the eye and mind into cold, clear distance and darkness.[7] Blue is at once the color of mood and melancholy, of transcendence (like the Blue Fairy in *A.I.*), and thus also of death.[8] Mann uses blue (and yellow) in *The Magic Mountain* to signify not only the pallor of those dying of tuberculosis but also the lack of oxygen at high altitude. It is this that Hans Castorp, like Jack Torrance and his family, detects in his initial ascent to the Berghof on "being carried upward into regions where he had never before drawn breath...water roared in the abysses... among rocks, dark fir-trees aspired toward a stone-grey sky... through pitch-black tunnels... wide chasms... narrow defiles, with traces of snow in chinks and crannies... above the zone of shade trees... a sense of impoverishment of life... the more distant ranges showed a cold, slaty blue."[9] This ascent into the ether in *The Shining* is also underscored by the music: over the dark, tramping notes of "Dies Irae" high keening voices soar into breathless evanescence.

Ironically, Jack's arrival at the Overlook—and later that of him and his family—brings him—and them—back down to earth. The hotel, along with the unctuous and patronizing representatives of its management Jack meets, make it clear that he and his family are common folk. Unlike marine engineer Castorp, who arrives at the International Sanitarium Berghof in an elegant carriage, a "yellow cabriolet," Jack arrives in a Volkswagen that is, in King's words, "shopworn," "battered," and "farting blue smoke," an old, cheap car—Hitler's "people's car"—common in America in the 1970s that shows in no uncertain terms the Torrances' modest station in life. Jack's yellow VW (which in the novel and in King's film is red) is seen in three aerial shots against the peak of the mountain, the first time along with five other VWs among the cars parked in the lot and then all alone. And in all three shots it is dwarfed by the "impersonal and Kafkaesque corporate state" that is the Overlook.[10] As with Kafka's K. in *The Castle*, this is Jack's big chance, even bigger—and more fateful—than he imagines, since, in Kafka's words, "anyone who was taken into the Castle service could do a great deal for his family."[11] K. was summoned to the Castle (*das Schloss*, from the verb "to close, shut, lock") to be appointed a land surveyor, although he ends up only as a school janitor, a striking parallel to Jack the caretaker, a schoolteacher who wants to be a writer. Torrance lacks the sense of quest for answers to essential questions that characterizes Kafka's protagonist, but he is similarly frustrated in his attempt to improve his lot and that of his family. Indeed, his fate is worse than that projected by Kafka for K. Jack, unlike K., becomes an agent of the Overlook's murderous designs, whereas K. is simply prevented from penetrating the grounds and secrets of the almost invisible Castle above. Like both Agee's and Kadar's "The Blue Hotel," therefore, Kubrick's post-Auschwitz film emphasizes evil and collaboration with evil rather than, as in *The Castle*, the imperviousness to surveillance and examination of a celestial and worldly authority itself unsure of its power.

The word "overlook" itself carries several meanings germane to the symbolic role of the hotel in *The Shining*. Most literally, it means to look over the top of something in order to see what is beyond. This definition encompasses not only the physical act of viewing, however. In the context of King's story, it also refers to the ability of both Danny and Hallorann to "shine," to see beyond the present into the past and future. Furthermore, this meaning is linked with another much less ordinary meaning in line with the subject matter of horror stories in general: to bewitch or to look upon with the evil eye. To overlook also means not to see something, to pass over without notice, to disregard—meanings that are particularly apropos for the Freudian perspective of a film in which, as in dreams, large hidden forces are indicated only by the smallest of details and thus are easily and willfully overlooked. To overlook in both these senses also suggests the paranoia that Kubrick himself rightly entertained in the hidden face of the horrors of the world his father and society were covering up. To overlook is also to look down upon, to command a view, and to survey from above—an accurate description of the physical location of the Overlook Hotel that also embraces an allied meaning: to watch over officially, keep an eye on, look after, superintend, oversee. Connected with this definition of function is one of social or intellectual position and attitude: to look down upon, to slight, treat with contempt, to despise.[12] Some of these meanings apply as well to *The Castle*—as with the failure of K.'s quest to become a surveyor—and—as with Krokowski's psychoanalysis and interest in occult phenomena—to *The Magic Mountain*. But most of all, Kubrick's Overlook is the Art Deco locus of a level of historical power and violence—from ashes to axes—inherited by Kubrick from the 1930s, 1940s, and, as revisited, 1970s. This world was no longer that of the mysteries and forebodings of Kafka and Mann. The Overlook, in its blueness, is a Kubrick "high room" of cold authority—indeed, one of the "killing machines" represented in the grand and malovelent spaces of many Kubrick films. The Overlook is an aerie around which the eyes of eagles soar and swoop on pinions to survey and mark the trepid ascent of those from below.[13]

## "Well, It's Very Homey"

In dispensing with most of the supernatural features of the novel, Kubrick and Diane Johnson reworked *The Shining* to focus on scenes of domestic life. As Janet Maslin put it in her review of the film: "The Overlook is something far more fearsome than a haunted house—it's a home."[14] Johnson brought to the task of helping to write the screenplay not only her knowledge of Gothic literature and her experience as a writer, but also Kubrick's attraction to her last novel, *The Shadow Knows*, about the blue-hotelish paranoia induced in women by the history of "husbands killing wives."[15] *The Shining*, the last in the 1970s Kubrick trilogy of films about the family—past (*Barry Lyndon*), present (*The Shining*), and future (*A Clockwork Orange*)—is, as we observed in Chapter 9, the only one of Kubrick's films that is thoroughly autobiographical. Like *Eyes Wide Shut*, the story focuses on a single-family triad of husband, wife, and child without the usual Kubrick mediation of a distancing narrator. Much more than the novel, the film focuses on a father who is trying to be a writer: as we have noted, even the typewriter in the film is one of Kubrick's own. Jack Torrance also has the same first name as Kubrick's father, Jacob, who went by Jack or Jacques, while a large part of the soundtrack is given over to Krzysztof Penderecki's Old Testament composition, *The Dream of Jacob*. That Kubrick has observed that the use of this composition "in the scene when Jack wakes up from his nightmare [is] a strange coincidence" is—consciously and/or unconsciously—an extremely misleading statement, as we shall see in particular in Chapter 11.[16]

All this does not reduce the film to a simple expression of Kubrick's own unconscious hostilities, even as it engages the common legacies of early childhood conflict and growth.[17] Indeed, as we have seen, Kubrick's own family life was apparently quite stable, rewarding, and a chief component of his creative process. In making *The Shining,* Kubrick stuck to his habit of shooting his films close to home and involving family members in ongoing discussions about myriad aspects of the film, while at the same time keeping the central conceptions of the film to himself.[18] Members of his family were, even more than usual, a constant presence during the long production schedule of *The Shining.* Kubrick allowed his daughter Vivian, who also appears in one scene in *The Shining,* to make the only formal record of him at work, although he reserved the right of final cut on that film as well.[19] *Making The Shining* even shows Kubrick's parents, both of whom would die in 1985, making an on-set visit to their son. Whether in degree causal or coincidental, the presence of family further joined the personal with the historical in the finished product. This participatory process also, as usual, extended to the actors, as when Jack Nicholson suggested from his own life the scene in which Jack Torrance cruelly and profanely excoriates Wendy for interrupting his work.[20] Kubrick kept to himself, however, signal elements of his artistic intention and thus the final decision regarding all matters of form and content. This combination of constant feedback and constant control had always maintained his films' "consistency and deeply mediated effect."[21] While also a sign of Kubrick's anxious conviction of the insufficiency of a single, comprehensive artistic grasp of human reality in the fullness of past and present, this process both advanced and mirrored the open narrative style of the finished film. This is because it allowed a large amount of unconscious and conscious material to inhabit the work. This of course happens in the production and consumption of any creative project.[22] But it happened especially with *The Shining,* given the personal and historical place of its subject in Kubrick's mind.

At the time Kubrick told an interviewer that, while a film about historical subject matter required a great deal of research, he had done comparatively little reading in the preparation of *The Shining.*[23] This relative lack of research had in part to do with the horror genre, which, unlike a historical film like *Barry Lyndon* or the projected "Napoleon," does not require nearly the same level of reading to ensure accuracy of detail and theme. It also means, however, that the history in the film is that history of the modern world in which Kubrick had schooled himself all his life. And it reflects the very personal nature of the family subject matter and its treatment that Kubrick links with the historical in *The Shining.* This again demonstrates the change from the emphasis in King's novel on the supernatural to the emphasis in the film on reality and history, even though for reasons of narrative economy Kubrick cut most of the novel's specifics of the family's proximate and immediate past.[24] The internal and unconscious dynamics of the characters in the film, particularly Jack, are what drive everyday "reality," further emphasized, as in *Eyes Wide Shut,* by the rare absence of a narrator. And while Kubrick himself, as we have seen, noted that *The Shining* suggests that ghosts do exist, the symbols and signs in the film refer not to the realm beyond nature but to the historical past. Kubrick admired King's book in part because it fools the reader into thinking that Jack is simply insane but then reveals the supernatural forces at work in the Overlook Hotel. But the ghosts in the Overlook in both novel and film are the ghosts of the past, and it is the historical referents rather than the novel's supernatural effects that Kubrick addresses.

Kubrick demonstrates this in *The Shining* by twenty-seven slow lap dissolves, beginning with the first scenes of the film, in which usually a person or persons gradually become as transparent as horror movie ghosts as a new group or individual emerges. This links past and present as well as represents the timelessness of the unconscious. One example of such a ghostly dissolve comes just after Wendy remarks about how the Overlook in winter must be like "a ghost ship"; she and her three companions in the shot then disappear into a close-up of Hallorann's face and head.[25] Furthermore, Kubrick observed on more than one occasion that people who had seen ghosts described them not as ethereal but "as being as solid and real as someone actually standing in the room."[26] This is how the ghosts appear in *The Shining*, which only further concretizes the film's emphasis on the ties between the real past and the real present while making the dissolves and their reference to traditionally portrayed ghosts doubly reflexive. It is for "historical" reasons as well that the Grady girls, who play only a small role in the novel, assume, as we shall see in Chapter 11, central importance in the film. This reflects not only Kubrick's own immediate familial environment but also the proximate and distant historical forces that threaten all of us. Ultimately, *The Shining* is not about ghosts, but is about death—that is, how people become the ghosts we imagine. More specifically, it is about murder—indeed, about mass murder—including the genocide of the Jews that Kubrick could not directly represent, in great measure because the threat was not only ruthless but also personal and familial.

In reworking the novel into a screenplay, Kubrick and Johnson drew upon two sources that emphasize both the psychological tensions within families and the influence of the past upon the present: Sigmund Freud's essay "The 'Uncanny'" (1919) and Bruno Bettelheim's psychoanalytic book on fairy tales, *The Uses of Enchantment* (1976).[27] Freud defines the strange yet somehow familiar experiences we call the uncanny as that "class of the frightening which leads back to what is known of old and long familiar . . . in the mind and which has become alienated from it only through the process of repression."[28] Freud makes much of the fact the German word for "comfortable," "homelike," "cozy," or "familiar" (*heimlich*) also means "secret" or "concealed" and in certain contexts comes to mean its opposite— that is, "uncomfortable," "sinister," or "uncanny" (*unheimlich*). In English, this same ambiguity of meaning about what is familiar and agreeable and what is hidden and disagreeable is carried within the English word "canny," which can mean "cosy" but also "occult" or "uncanny" and which also includes among its definitions "supernatural" and "(of a house) haunted." Clearly the Torrance family and the Overlook Hotel are locations for the dangerous human dynamics contained in these words and serve as another exercise in Kubrick's conviction that good and evil are conjoined and bedded deeply and tightly together within human individuals and institutions. The purpose of Kubrick's horror film, therefore, is not horror and certainly not terror, but communication of the deep unease that accompanies contemplation of the human condition to the present day. Kubrick's reliance on Freud's study of the etymology of the word "uncanny" is apparent early on in *The Shining* with Jack's reactions during his and Wendy's tour of their living quarters in the oldest part of the hotel: on Danny's bedroom: "Perfect for a child"; their bedroom: "Cozy"; and the bathroom in which he will attempt to murder his wife: "Well, it's very homey."[29]

Freud cites E. T. A. Hoffman's story "The Sandman" (1814) as an example of the uncanny in literature. Hoffmann (1776–1822) was a German Romantic writer who was also a legal councilor in the Prussian civil service. The Sandman is he who, according to the mother and the nursemaid in the story, tears out the eyes of children who do not go to bed on time. Freud highlights Oedipal content by noting that the young boy, Nathaniel, is haunted not only by memories of the Sandman but also by the mysterious death of his father. According to Freud, Hoffman's story is an example of how a child's fear of blindness or of damaging his eyes substitutes for the dread of castration by the father as punishment for the sexual desire he feels for his mother. The feeling of the uncanny aroused by the story is therefore based on the combination of our childhood familiarity with such fears and desires and our adult repression of them.

Freud also analyzes the use of doubles—mirrors, shadows, spirits—in the literature of the fantastic as another manifestation of childhood conflicts. The double is originally the child's assurance of immortality that arises from the original and exclusive love of the self, what Freud called "primary narcissism." Beyond childhood, however, the double becomes "the uncanny harbinger of death," which explains the frequency of its appearance in horror literature and film.[30] It is no accident in this regard that in both "The Sandman" and in Kubrick's film the story begins at the end of October, when in Celtic and Western tradition dark spirits roam the earth.[31] Kubrick, as we have seen, also embraced Carl Jung's concept of the double as a portal to the collective unconscious, as in his remarks about the possibility of the existence of ghosts as well as in the explicit reference to Jung in his very next film, *Full Metal Jacket*. But *The Shining* is beholden to a Freudian view of the world both inside and outside the family circle. Freud argues in "The 'Uncanny'" that the repetition of behavior we perceive as uncanny and thus safely inexplicable is the chief signal of unconscious neurotic conflict inherited from childhood.[32] For Kubrick, this is the story of human history entire, a story he inscribes into the objects, colors, and sounds of the Overlook in *The Shining*. As a reflection of this dark underside of the human psyche, Jack and his deed—"REDRUM" as scrawled by Danny in his mother's lipstick on the bathroom door—are on several occasions reflected in mirrors.[33]

The Oedipal trajectory of Freud's thought and of Kubrick's film enriches the character of Danny in terms of Kubrick's long-standing trope of a child learning, indirectly and painfully, of the dark secrets of humankind, from sexuality to war and atrocity. So it is that mother Monica's wail to robot son David as she abandons him in the woods in *A.I.*, "I'm sorry I didn't tell you about the world," thus represents a final, tragic expression of Kubrick's long education in the history of the late modern era.[34] Danny's own education began with abuse by his father, and in the film he is between five and six years of age, a period when the Oedipal crisis is beginning to reach its resolution. Three years before their arrival at the Overlook, Jack in a drunken rage had dislocated Danny's shoulder. Danny's response to this "castratory gesture" was to invent an imaginary friend, Tony, who lives in his mouth and is the vehicle for Danny's ability to see into the past and the future.[35] This imaginary friend, of course, is a "double" that represents the boy's attempt to deal with the fears and desires that are part and parcel of human sexuality and mortality. These Oedipal dynamics are communicated not only by the film's dialogue, but also in the form of symbols that, in the form of dreamwork as described by Freud, appear as small visual details. Such odd, obscure—though in the context of each scene also naturalistic—details are the products of the conscious mind's repression of unconscious emotions. For example, when the bartender ghost Lloyd serves Jack the liquor he had given up as a result of his injuring Danny, it is Jack Daniel's, a bottle of whiskey on whose label appears the name of both father and son. And to demonstrate the constant pressure of the unconscious on the conscious mind that results in such symbols in dreams, the bottle not only is foregrounded in the scenes between Jack and Lloyd in the Overlook's bar, but also appears in the background of two scenes in which Halloran is calling Colorado from Miami after receiving Danny's telepathic calls for help.[36] While Kubrick said that the first names of the actors and the characters, Jack and Danny (Lloyd), were a coincidence, there can be little doubt that the choice of liquor bottle was intentional.[37] There is even a photograph of Kubrick carefully arranging cans and bottles on the set of the storeroom in which Wendy imprisons Jack.[38] While such attention to detail on Kubrick's part was certainly in part a matter of visual composition, we have seen that he was also powerfully concerned in his films with the communication of "eyedeas" through colors, music, and objects.[39] This visual exploitation of objects has been especially effective in the oblique and poetic discourse common to the literature of the grotesque, which makes it thus doubly appropriate for Kubrick to translate into the open narrative style of his cinema.[40]

In the end, Jack does die while Danny escapes in Oedipal triumph with his mother, symbolized by Danny's brandishing a long knife over a sleeping Wendy and his evasion of Jack in the hedge maze. In the latter, Kubrick invokes another Greek myth: Danny is Theseus slaying the Minotaur, the half-man, half-beast to whom annually seven maidens and seven youths were fed. This reference is as intentional as those to Freud, since King Minos lived in the "Palace of the Ax" and it is an ax that Jack carries into the maze, a setting that—coincidentally?—appears seven times in *The Shining*.[41] (We also recall that *Killer's Kiss*, Kubrick's first professionally produced film, was a Minotaur Production.) That Theseus was led out of the maze by Ariadne, the king's daughter whom he married and then abandoned, also links it directly with the Oedipus complex. The maze itself is typical of the labyrinths one regularly finds in Kubrick's films and has traditionally been associated with both entrapment and escape. Mazes have also been seen as representative of postmodern discourse in which the emphasis falls on the process and ambiguity of language and meaning in place of the modern linear pursuit of certain knowledge.[42] But, even more important, Kubrick's maze is also charged in terms of sexual and gender dynamics related to every child's task in establishing his or her sexual and individual identity independent of the woman who, in modern times at least, dominates infancy. This is a vital theme in Robert Wise's *The Haunting*, which, as we have noted, was a signal influence on Kubrick's horror film.[43] In *The Shining* the maze represents male desire and fear in particular with regard to the female body. The labyrinth can be thus seen to represent the womb as a place of both protection and entrapment, a dynamic woven into the spermatozoically labyrinthine patterns of the 1970s Deco carpeting inside and outside room 237.[44] The same masculine preoccupation with the eerie feminine space of human origin is represented in Danny's vision of the deep and narrow corridor in which the Grady girls lie butchered and of the hemorrhaging elevator that represents "an image of menstruation—blood pouring from one of the two shafts into a long narrow hall."[45] Danny's androgynous appearance therefore reflects not only the sexual conflicts within him but also his struggle for a male identity in breaking away from the care-giving woman who dominated his infancy. And the wish Jack expresses to Danny to stay at the Overlook "forever, and ever, and ever" represents the kind of endless gratification associated with the return to the womb as well as Lacan's idea of "the primordial void," the desire for which is an end in itself. But all this is a threat to masculine identity and autonomy in particular.[46] This paradox is the reason why, according to Freud in his 1919 essay, neurotic men undergoing psychoanalysis often say that they perceive female genital organs as being mysterious and uncanny. Freud analyzes this in terms of the female genitals being the entrance to the womb, the original home (*Heim*) of all human beings, "the place where each one of us lived once upon a time and in the beginning."[47]

Much psychoanalytic thought since Freud, as we have seen, incorporates a gender perspective that sees in such feelings and fantasies a male denial of dependence on, and desire for, the original caretaker. Much of the need for males to prove their superiority in the competitive environment of work as well as male violence toward women, it has been argued, stems from this angry denial of dependence as well as from resentment of the genuine creativity of women in conceiving, carrying, and giving life. In *The Shining*, this conception of the caretaker is underlined by the fact that it is Wendy who takes care of the hotel while it is Jack, "the caretaker," who (unlike in the novel) does nothing but sit—as it turns out, destructively rather than constructively—at his typewriter. Indeed, it is the "Others" in *The Shining* who do productive work: besides Wendy, the female pediatrician who examines Danny, the "shiners" Hallorann and Danny, and Hallorann's African-American garage owner friend, Larry Durkin.[48] And it is Jack who rages at Wendy that she is the one, through her concern with getting Danny away from the suddenly violent Overlook, who is going to "fuck up" his chance finally to get into his work and make something of himself.[49] Kubrick's habitual employment of what Richard Jameson has called a "central vacancy principle," in which a bright light from the back of a scene occupies the center of a shot, is closely related to this construction.[50] Rather than, or in addition to, being a reference to realms beyond human experience, this light can represent a denial of the darkness of the womb, darkness that calls up male fear in particular of extinction and the loss of the self, as well as dependence on, and love for, the original caretaker. In *2001*, we recall, the penultimate scene takes place in an astral room with a lighted floor that can be seen as the light at the end of the birth canal through which the Star-Child will pass. But the "womb" itself too is brightly lit, at once a denial of dread and death as well as an affirmation of desire for eternal union with the source of life. It is this context that explains the deeper meaning of the rolling of the name "Shelley Duvall" in the opening credits as the camera flies off toward the water. In this psychological and artistic construction, the woman is the water surrounding the obliviously lonely male island, armed—as it were—for battle, at its center.[51]

Bathrooms, too, are part of this construction since water is often unconsciously associated with return to the womb. In strictly traditional Freudian terms, however, the bathroom is also connected with the anal-sadistic stage of infancy during which the child's struggle against unconscious drives and for autonomy assumes the form of passive and active aggression against the parents. Three of the white men in the film associated with Overlook, Stuart Ullman, Bill Watson, and Jack, are identified early in the film as anal types when Hallorann, leaving the food locker with Wendy and Danny, says, laughing, in reference to prunes: "You know, Mrs. Torrance, you gotta keep regular if you gonna be happy." As he closes the door while saying this, in the background we see Stu, Jack, and Bill as they march, all business and unsmiling, down the hall toward the trio of others in the foreground. The two red alarms bells on a column camera left give lie to the cordiality of the thin smiles they put on as they arrive. As we then watch the backs of the others walking away down the corridor, Danny and Hallorann discuss chocolate ice cream, a reference to both Hallorann's color and the color associated with anality.[52] All the white males in *The Shining* (Jack, Ullman, Watson, Lloyd, and Delbert Grady) serve the Overlook Hotel, a painful blend of banal *bonhomie* and barely repressed rage filling the words and conversations among them. Grady, the obsequious but murderously racist interwar waiter who is the double of 1970 caretaker Charles Grady, is the one, in a bathroom, who urges Jack to "correct" his wife and child, as he did, as well as later assisting him in pursuit of this homicidal task. Delbert, too, is a classic case of the repressed anal type who stresses order and cleanliness, as when he fussily—like a Delbert—insists on cleaning up Jack after spilling a drink on him.[53]

It is no accident, therefore, that Kubrick places several scenes concerning violence and murder in bathrooms. Danny has his first vision of the bloody elevator in the pink bathroom of the Torrance's Boulder apartment. Jack and Wendy's tour of the Overlook ends with their standing in the tiny white bathroom of their quarters. A dead woman attempts to strangle (Freud: castrate) Danny in room 237; in the same bathroom, Jack confronts a nude young woman who turns into a decaying old hag after slowly running her hands seductively but also ominously around his neck. Grady's proposal to Jack takes place in a blood-red "gentleman's room" next to the bar in the palatial Gold Room. And Jack, voicing the toilet double-entendre television greeting "Here's *Johnny!*" attempts murder by trying to break into the Torrances' bathroom, in which Wendy has locked herself. Other scenes of the discussion of murder take place in the kitchen and the food locker, both of which settings symbolize the oral stage of infancy in which the child is dependent, usually, on a woman for nourishment and in which, as with the anal stage, sadism and even fantasies of cannibalism play a role. It is such dynamics that complicate the already complicated emotional and sexual relationships between men and women. A final scene of the actual threat of murder occurs as Jack mounts a staircase, a common dream symbol of sexual arousal, in pursuit of his wife, though the narrative itself tells us that there is of course much more going on than direct sexual desire.[54]

Along the same psychodynamic lines, *The Shining* juxtaposes play as the arena of the relatively unrepressed nurturing and creative spirit against the world of work in which a cold passion for order is a symptom of repressed aggressive and sadistic impulses. The world of modern work is often peopled with obsessive-compulsive personalities who are, in Freudian terms, "generally and obviously concerned about conflicts between aggressiveness and submissiveness, cruelty and gentleness, dirtiness and cleanliness, disorder and order."[55] Such individuals, who emphasize control, rationality, and accountability, often make excellent bureaucrats since their regression to the anal-sadistic stage of infancy calls up mighty defensive energies to control oneself and one's environment in harmony with social demands. At the same time, however, these very same aggressive wishes can find an outlet in controlling and even persecuting others through the power conferred by functional—and, appropriately enough, seated as on a toilet—obedience to a powerful authority. Jack is another of those sad sitting Kubrick functionaries who, very much in the Freudian language and logic of anal aggression, do the "dirty work" of their masters. Kubrick expresses Jack's own resultantly lamed sense of the sadness of his existence—"feminized" as putative "caretaker" and "castrated" through clerical enslavement to the hotel's masters—by the pleading tone that accompanies the anger of his final tirades against Wendy.[56] This contrast between Jack's repressed and regressive world of work and the much less repressive and regressive world of play that Danny and Wendy inhabit is made clear by three successive sequences of shots all linked by an excerpt from a Bartók composition. Two of the sequences are also joined together by dissolves, again that filmic technique rare in Kubrick's films that expresses a particularly close thematic connection between and among scenes and characters by having one scene gradually fade in as the preceding scene slowly fades out.

In the first scene Jack, instead of sitting at his typewriter, is shown throwing a yellow tennis ball against one of the walls of the Colorado Lounge. The ball is being thrown very hard and makes a huge booming sound as it strikes a large Native American wall painting over a massive fireplace. The aggressive and joyless nature of Jack's "play" is stressed by the whistling noise he makes on one throw, a typically boyish imitation of the sounds of shells or bombs flying through the air. Jack's hurling figure dissolves to Danny and Wendy outside the hotel in a race toward the hedge maze, as Wendy playfully calls out, in a variation on an environmental slogan of the day, "The loser has to keep America clean, how's that?" The juxtaposition of "loser" and "clean" signifies social and historical victims, Jack as functionary, and the psychodynamics of anality and aggression. Anality is visually punctuated by a stack of sewer pipes in the background of the outdoor dolly shot and by Danny twice repeating Wendy's words about the loser having to keep America clean. Wendy and Danny are then shown walking through the maze until another slow dissolve brings a scowling Jack into view wandering through the hotel lobby. He slams the tennis ball down hard against the floor and then flings it down a corridor where, its bounces reverberating loudly, it disappears. Then Jack goes over to a large table model of the hedge maze and gazes down upon it. A shot of the maze from Jack's point of view above pictures the tiny figures of Wendy and Danny in the maze's center. The camera zooms in slowly on the pair until an abrupt cut shows Wendy and Danny walking toward us. A jump cut timed to the abrupt end of the music brings a black title board to the screen bearing the word "Tuesday" (the day of Mars). This final cut is a parody of the startle effect, which also works to startle because the audience, sensing the end of the music, has been set up to expect something (i.e., the Minotaur) to jump out at Wendy and Danny in the middle of the maze. That the Minotaur is Jack up in the hotel looking down on the model of a maze that is the symbol of his own labyrinthine psyche of course only confirms the film's concentration on the historically immanent rather than on the supernaturally transcendent.[57]

The psychological juxtaposition of work and play culminates in one of the most horrific scenes in the film when Wendy discovers that Jack's hours, days, weeks, and months of work typing at his writing table in the Colorado Lounge are nothing but a typology, as it were, of madness. Armed with a baseball bat, Wendy is looking for Jack, her own mobilized anal aggression signaled, as in *Killer's Kiss* and *Full Metal Jacket*, with a close-up of her rear end as she moves past the camera to get the bat and start her search. Not finding Jack, she examines the sheet of paper in the typewriter and is shocked to see that it contains only repetitions, replete with typographical errors, of the same statement: "All work and no play makes Jack a dull boy." Her horror grows as she looks through the ream of paper in a box to one side of the typewriter. Every page is filled top to bottom with the same sentence, words that in form as well as content signal grim pathological obsession and compulsion.[58] As with K. in *The Castle* replacing a picture on the wall with the letter of appointment from the castle, there is no "work" here in terms of creativity or fulfillment. There are only the dead lines of bureaucratic repetition, barely suppressing anger and conflict and serving a cruel authority that exercises control and violence through paper, contracts, and deeds. Jack represents Kafka's fear, as expressed in "Metamorphosis" (1912), of the deadening effect of modern office work. For Gregor Samsa, to wake up one morning as a bug (*Ungeziefer* [vermin or noxious insect]) is, in the grotesque logic and atmosphere of Kafka's story, to be more of an individual in harmony with nature than those around him who become little more than automatons of routine and uniformity. That Jack drives a Volkswagen, called a "beetle" or a "bug" (*Käfer*), forges another link between Kafka's story and Kubrick's film.[59]

Danny's victory at the end of the film is of course illusory, since the Overlook Hotel, with Jack now and forever one of its ghostly inhabitants, remains standing as a symbol of the eternal return of the repressed in the form of endless familial and historical conflict and violence. Kubrick even responds to *2001*'s evolutionary perspective by having Jack almost literally *devolve* into a howling ape at the end of *The Shining*.[60] Danny, therefore, is, along with Jack, the most obvious autobiographical character in Kubrick's *oeuvre* in the sense that he is the ultimate expression of the child confronting a found world of great mystery and danger, beginning with desire for the body of the mother, fear of the violence of the father, and horror at the even greater horrors of the world at large.[61] Danny is also the most empowered of Kubrick youth, his ability to "shine" seemingly a psychological analogue to Kubrick's own impressive ability to observe and create a vision of the world. Arguably, all of Kubrick's films from 1962 on may be seen to center on youth in confrontation with the established world of patriarchal power. *Lolita* is the "child in the woman" that Humbert seeks for his sexual and psychological satisfaction. *Dr. Strangelove* has no children in it, but at its end we are left with the prospect of Strangelove's Nazi progeny emerging, as if out of hell, from deep within the earth. In *2001*, Kubrick's most—or only—optimistic film, a Star-Child, the interstellar evolutionary savior, gazes down upon the violent, dying world of old humanity. *A Clockwork Orange* is the despairing answer to *2001*'s question about the future of humankind with a teenager gone very bad and made even worse through opportunistic exploitation by adults with political power. *Barry Lyndon* traces the rise and fall of a young man seduced and abandoned by the greedy and arrogant social standards of his day. *Full Metal Jacket* sees young men stripped of their humanity and sent off to kill and be killed. In *Eyes Wide Shut*, as in *Barry Lyndon*, one notices the Harfords' youth in contrast to the corrupt powerbrokers they serve, along with the ambiguous future faced by their daughter, Helena. And the posthumous *A.I.* tragically engages a young boy's confrontation with a cruel world of humans on its way to the evolutionary scrap heap.

## "I'll Have to Leave a Trail of Breadcrumbs"

*The Shining* is filled with references to fairy tales. This is hardly surprising, since traditional fairy tales are closely related to the literature of horror and terror. And since fairy tales have been an integral part of child rearing in the modern West, it makes sense that in *The Shining* they help transmit Danny's perspective on the world.[62] But fairy tales in *The Shining* are more than simply an accurate detail of a child's world. Bruno Bettelheim's argument in *The Uses of Enchantment* is that fairy tales help a child deal with the effects of the unconscious conflicts within by making intuitively clear that such "bad" thoughts and feelings are normal and can be overcome in some significant and satisfying degree of harmony with social demands and expectations. Kubrick and Johnson dispensed with this idea of the therapeutic value of fairy tales. But one could argue that Kubrick's overall didactic intent constitutes an attempt to assist the audience in recognizing the difference Bettelheim sees between fairy tales that help teach life lessons and modern cartoons, which only entertain, merchandise, and corrupt.

Kubrick emphasizes the horrific content of fairy tales as part of his argument about the violence and hatred repeated over and over in history. He chooses to reference only two of the fairy tales that Bettelheim analyzes in his book. The most evident is, as we have seen, when Jack invokes the Big Bad Wolf's demand that the Three Little Pigs open their doors. According to Bettelheim, who survived Dachau and Buchenwald, the wolf "stands for all asocial, unconscious, devouring powers," which must be overcome by the child's ego.[63] Jack is thereby identified directly as the wolf in wolf's clothing, as he also is through the picture of a wolf and pups by the bathroom in which he will wolfishly regard a naked woman. The other reference occurs as Hallorann conducts Wendy and Danny on a tour of the Overlook's cavernous kitchen. After passing through a huge sliding black metal door with large white letters reading "Fire Exit Must Be Kept Clear," Wendy comments that the kitchen is so big that she will "have to leave a trail of breadcrumbs every time I come in it." This of course is a reference to "Hansel and Gretel," in which, according to Bettelheim, infantile "cannibalistic inclinations are given body in the figure of the witch."[64] Bettelheim takes his analysis in the direction of the necessity of the child growing away from selfish oral gratification and dependence on the mother, mastering fears of forces both within and without, and maturing into productive relationships with parents and society. Kubrick, as elsewhere in *The Shining*, constructs this kitchen scene around both the spoken and the shown words in order to communicate danger. The realistic, though also disquietingly large, fire exit (followed by an equally realistic "No Smoking" sign in red) refers to the witch's oven, in which the children are to be cooked, as well as to the revenge the children will have upon the witch when they shove her into the oven. Kubrick's message here is the suppression of aggression represented in the witch's destruction as well as the threat of destruction and death itself as documented by history.

Kubrick also addresses cannibalism as another representation of violence within the human family. He gives us a tight shot of the Torrances packed claustrophobically in their tiny car on the drive up to the Overlook. The subject of conversation is cannibalism. Wendy, more ominously than she can possibly know, asks if the Rocky Mountains are where the Donner Party (1846–1847) was stranded. Jack, ever the teacher, replies that it was farther West, in the Sierra Nevada ("snow-covered mountain range" in Spanish). Danny asks what the Donner (German for "thunder") Party was, and Jack answers that they were a group of settlers stranded by storms who resorted to cannibalism. Overriding a mousy demurral from Wendy, Jack expands with a wolfish grin on how eating one another was necessary for survival. Danny, reflecting his own unconscious emotions, reassures his mother by saying that he knows "all about cannibalism" since he "saw it on TV."[65] Jack then interjects with a sarcastic appraisal of the value of television that is a reflexive criticism of all visual-entertainment media.

Jack's sarcasm is an example of Kubrick's parody of the horror genre in order to comment on its ahistorical and melodramatic excesses. Kubrick, in deliberately subverting the genre, is even willing to parody himself, as with the poster that reads "Camera Walk" at the beginning of the almost ostentatiously impressive Steadicam sequence of Danny riding his Big Wheel (itself a joke on the Overlook's patrons and a burlesque of a famous scene in the child-possession film *The Omen* [1976]) around the Overlook's Colorado Lounge.[66] Kubrick also "reverses the conventional meanings of light and darkness" as a means to the Kafkaesque union of the real and the fantastic.[67] And at a crucial juncture in the film, just as Wendy has discovered to her horror and sorrow the truth about Jack's writing project, Kubrick forgoes scaring the audience in favor of directing our attention to Wendy's fright. He does this by showing Jack coming up behind her and not, as convention would have it, sneaking up on the audience as well.[68] Instead of our jumping in fright, only Wendy does. The film in this way works to have the audience understand, through both affect and intellect, the feelings of the characters as well as the larger historical issues it explores. The properly attentive audience will also think about how horror films, their makers, and their customers exploit the subject of human violence, fear, and suffering for purposes of commerce and diversion. *The Shining* therefore links enjoyment of fictional horror to the repression of factual horror, a dynamic also represented in the deep burial—like Poe's purloined letter, in plain sight—of visual references to historical horrors, including the Holocaust. The result is not the "good scare" of a conventional movie of terror, but a lingering and informed sadness at the horrors of life as well as deep unease at the human condition that is—or should be—*really* scary.

Jack's response to Danny is also an affirmation of another of Bettelheim's arguments. Bettelheim contends that modern-day cartoon versions of fairy tales are nothing more than "empty-headed entertainment" robbed "of all deeper significance."[69] Modern cartoons lack the open narrative style of fairy tales that allows children intuitively to work through the hard lessons of psychological maturation for themselves, a meaningful internalization that cannot be achieved by explicit instruction through the voice of an adult. This contrast is evident in *The Shining* in the visual and aural wallpaper of cartoons that decorates modern daily life blaring out from televisions and adorning Danny's clothes and the walls of his room.[70] For Kubrick, however, even the vacuous cartoons in *The Shining* are also dreamlike expressions of violent human impulses in general as well as specific manifestations of them in history. The Roadrunner cartoons that Danny watches on television are the major cartoon motif in *The Shining*. We never see these cartoons, but in two important scenes, one early and one late in the film, their sound plays obtrusively over the action. In all its affectless activity, this particular cartoon series employs the motif of an indigenous American bird constantly pursued by a coyote utilizing the self-destructive technology of a modern industrial society. Like Kubrick, the cartoon's creator, Chuck Jones, loved silent movies and in particular the slapstick chase scenes of the Keystone Kops variety. The Roadrunner ("Accerleratii incredibilus") and his nemesis, Wile E. Coyote ("Eternali famishus"), debuted in 1949 and appeared together in forty-two cartoons over the next forty-five years. The sympathy of the audience is with the hapless coyote, who never catches the Roadrunner and endures all sorts of self-inflicted injuries from the Acme devices he buys. In Southwest Native American myth, in fact, the coyote is the admirable trickster, the "witty agent" for negotiating the ironies and outrages of the world, as well as "a figure for the always problematic, always potent tie of meaning and bodies."[71] But of course Jack the Big Bad Wolf is also reflected in the figure of the coyote, or prairie wolf, whose sympathetic position reminds us of Jack as fallible human being, not inhuman monster.

Danny is nicknamed "Doc" by his parents (the doctor Stanley did not become?), a reference to Bugs Bunny's salutation, "What's up, Doc?" once echoed to him by Hallorann. Danny wears a shirt with Bugs Bunny on it in three scenes at the beginning of the film, including one in which he is seen by a doctor.[72] The only prominent visual use of a cartoon character, however, occurs in the one scene in the film in which Danny and his father appear alone together. Jack, unshaven and unable to sleep, is sitting on the bed when Danny enters the apartment to get his fire engine. His father tells Danny he wants to talk to him, and Danny comes and sits on his lap. The scene, a protracted two-shot, is photographed in cold blue winter light pouring through the window, a sharp, flat illumination accentuated but not much warmed by Jack's blue bathrobe and pajamas or Danny's blue sweater. The sad, slow conversation addresses Jack's exhaustion, his need to work instead of sleep, and how much he loves living at the Overlook. Danny is not enthusiastic about the hotel. Then he asks his father if he would ever hurt him or his mother. Jack wants to know if his mother ever said that to him. The scene ends with Jack assuring Danny that he loves him and would never do anything to hurt him. But the light blue front of Danny's sweater bears a scene from *Touchdown Mickey* (1932) showing a black-and-white Mickey Mouse kicking a football. The first Mickey Mouse cartoon appeared in 1928, and over the next seven years Disney produced thirty-four black-and-white cartoons starring his popular—and controversial—new creation. Mickey Mouse was controversial because for the first years of his existence he was a naughty creature, which prompted many complaints from parents. Building upon the fundamentally uncanny quality that accompanies the mixing of human and animal characteristics, Disney had produced a character that, in psychoanalytic terms, represents the unbridled pleasure principle of freedom from physical, moral, and instinctual constraint.[73] For Kubrick's purposes, Mickey expresses the anarchic forces that simmer beneath the surface in every family, while football suggests a peculiarly American expression of physical violence in the form of play ("Come and play with us, Danny"). And this black-and-white cartoon character debuting the year of Kubrick's birth draws the narrative back into the era that is the chief historical touchstone for *The Shining*.

## "Is There Something Bad Here?"

In both King's novel and Kubrick's film, the Overlook Hotel is manifestly a symbol of America. A small American flag rests on the manager's desk. A large American flag and that of the 1876 "Centennial State," Colorado, hang in the grand room where Jack works. Manager Stuart Ullman (whose initials transposed are "U.S.") initially wears a red tie, a white shirt with red stripes, and a blue suit.[74] The United States also chose as one of its symbols an indigenous American bird much different from the Roadrunner, the bald eagle. The eagle has been a common symbol of imperial power in Western history, and it is therefore no surprise that a dark eagle rests on the windowsill in Ullman's office and that Jack in one scene wears a "Stovington Eagles" T-shirt emblazoned with an eagle.[75] *The Shining* itself is a Peregrine Film made by Hawk Films; the production company for Vivian Kubrick's *Making The Shining* was Eagle Films.

American history suffuses the place in the form of oppressors and victims. Danny learns this about the Overlook from one of America's victims, the black cook Hallorann, in response to his question "Is there something bad here?"[76] The hotel, in Ullman's words, catered to a turn-of-the century "jet set" of "all the best people," their decadence recalling "all the best people" of the eighteenth century in *Barry Lyndon* and anticipating Kubrick's equation of modern Austrian and American decadence in *Eyes Wide Shut*.[77] According to Ullman, the hotel was built on a Native American burial ground and several attacks had to be repelled during the initial phases of construction. (This detail was added by Kubrick to *The Shining*, and, although King uses the idea in other stories, in Kubrick's telling it is not the ghosts of "Indians" who haunt the Overlook but those of the European perpetrators.) All that is left of Native Americans are the artifacts littered throughout the hotel in the form of the decorations in the Colorado (Spanish for "red") Lounge, the "Indian chief" logo on the cans of Calumet (meaning "peace pipe") baking powder conspicuously displayed in the kitchen storeroom, the line of three separate profiles of Hallorann's face, and the electronically synthesized voices to the music in the opening credits and later in the film. Moreover, in one scene Wendy wears a yellow jacket with Indian designs on it, in the ghost party scene the women wear headbands adorned with a single feather, and Danny is Indian-clever in the maze to elude the tramping violence of his father.[78] These past victims of white male American society thus have their modern counterparts: an African-American, a child, and a woman.[79] The special extreme victimization of African-Americans through slavery and racism is highlighted by the fact that Hallorann is the only person Jack kills, axed to death in front of the cashiers' cages of the hotel. In addition, a television news report speaks of a "1968 shooting," not only reflexively referring to the release in 1968 of Kubrick's "shooting" of *2001*, but in more historically relevant fashion to the assassinations that year of Martin Luther King Jr. and Robert Kennedy and perhaps as well the American massacre of civilians at My Lai in Vietnam. And when Danny is choked by the woman in room 237, he is wearing a sweater with a cartoon representation of a

United States Apollo Program moon rocket. It is this same woman who turns from alluring young sexual temptress to decaying hag in Jack's arms.[80] While Apollo was the "two-faced" god of antiquity—that is, another "double" in *The Shining*—on the level of more recent history it is the glory of the American space program and the beauty of the American way that are thereby shown to have another, darker side that is (castratingly) destructive and hateful.

Kubrick also utilizes numbers to tie together past and present. As in the book, we learn from Ullman that construction on the Overlook began in 1907 and that in the winter of 1970 a previous caretaker, Charles Grady, killed his family with an ax before committing suicide.[81] While the party Jack visits in the novel is a chronological composite of the 1920s and 1940s, at the end of the film Kubrick freezes Jack in a party photograph from the seventh month of 1921, on July 4. This bridge of time is built with multiples of 7, a number traditionally associated with duration.[82] Not surprisingly, the number 7 also has a long history in the cinema. For example, the morgue in *Niagara* (1953) is room 7a, while the murder of passion occurs, as the elevator dial shows, on floor 7 of the bell tower. And in one of Kubrick's favorite films, *Wild Strawberries* (1957), director Ingmar Bergman, in oneiric Kubrickian fashion, constructs a psychological unity out of the protagonist's life by means of the number: Dr. Isak Borg was born in 1879; he is seventy-eight years old in the film (the same age as the actor, director Viktor Sjöström, who plays him); his wife was unfaithful to him on May 1, 1917, and died in 1927; and the film itself is set and was released in 1957.[83] In *The Shining*, Kubrick, like King, exploits the number for its spooky qualities, but he also systematically mines it as a multiple and a mirror (7 × 10; 07/70) for historically didactic purposes. Specifically, he wants to link past with present in order to demonstrate the historical continuity of human violence in the modern era in particular. The Overlook is thus very much the "Hotel Two-Five," which is an echo of *The Shining* in *Full Metal Jacket*.[84]

Kubrick was, however, also following the lead of Mann, who observed in *The Magic Mountain* that "seven is a good handy figure in its way, picturesque, with a savor of the mythical; one might even say that it is more filling to the spirit than a dull academic half-dozen."[85] This intention was widely noted among readers and writers at the time Kubrick would have been reading Mann in his coursework at Columbia. Norman Mailer in his novel about the Second World War, *The Naked and the Dead* (1948), noted: "The number seven has deep significance to Mann. Hans Castorp spends seven years on the mountain, and if you will remember the first seven days are given great emphasis. Most of the major characters have seven letters in their name, Castorp, Clavidia, Joachim, even Settembrini fulfills it in that the Latin root of his name stands for seven."[86] Kubrick must have been struck by the coincidence, if that is what it was, in King's novel of the construction of the Overlook beginning in 1907, the same year Hans Castorp began what Mann later called "the seven fairy-tale years of his enchanted stay" at the Berghof that ended with his departure for war in 1914.[87] Mann's pervasive pattern of permutations of the number 7 in *The Magic Mountain* has been read primarily as a symbol of his faith in the rational self-overcoming of the human fascination with evil and destruction. The seven sections of Mann's long novel bulge with the number in various forms: Castorp, whom Mann identifies with the medieval Christian "Seven Sleepers" martyrs, intends his stay to last twenty-one days and not seven years; new experiences at the Berghof occur at seven-day, seven-week, or seven-month intervals; note is made of the fact that summer begins on June 21; Joachim returns to room 28 (4 × 7) one July and dies one evening in November at 7:00 P.M.; Castorp's room number is 34 (3 + 4) and that of Mme. Chauchat is 7, among many other instances.[88] *The Shining* is likewise filled with the number 7: Jack's liquor of choice is Jack Daniel's Black Label No. 7; Jack drives to the Overlook from Boulder in 3½ hours, a round trip of 7 hours; Sidewinder is 25 (2 + 5) miles from the hotel; cases of 7-Up are stacked in the kitchen corridors; a circular figure with seven spokes adorns the back of Jack's writing chair; and Jack knocks seven times on the door to the bathroom in which Wendy is hiding.[89] This subtle yet pervasive appearance of the number 7 enhances its unsettling effect, just as details of a dream are small but persistent indications of the pressure of larger forces hidden beneath and within.

Considering the location of the Overlook Hotel and its embodiment of the European conquest of Native Americans, Kubrick's discourse also reflects the history of the nineteenth-century American West in particular. The Colorado Lounge, where Jack sits typing, resembles nothing less than the grand office of an imperial outpost on the American frontier.[90] It is no surprise, therefore, that Jack is identified with the American cowboy and with the popular American movie genre of Westerns. Kubrick accomplishes this identification in two extremely subtle ways. First, as Wendy speaks with Jack on the phone about the job offer he has just accepted at the Overlook, a scene from a Western plays on a television behind her in the Boulder apartment. Two men in cowboy hats are talking, and one man takes a piece of paper out of his pocket. Since the scene is not from any Western of note or in particular, it serves as a generic representation of the business Jack and the men at the Overlook have just transacted. But since the movie from which the scene is taken is a Western, it also represents the modern historical continuity of Caucasian male domination of other peoples. That a piece of paper is involved connects the scene not only to the contract Jack has just signed but also to the paper—a great deal of paper—that will pass through his typewriter.[91] Second, Jack is identified with the Western male masters of the frontier through his preference for Marlboro cigarettes, a hard pack of which rests next to the typewriter. In 1972 Marlboro cigarettes became the largest-selling cigarette in the world and in 1975 overtook Winston as the best-selling cigarette in America. This was due largely to a massive advertising campaign begun in 1963 that featured rugged, young, handsome cowboys under the slogan "The Marlboro Man." Kubrick, as did Polanski in *The Tenant*, responded to this commercial and cultural trend by using Marlboro as a symbol of masculinity and male sexuality, both asserted and doubted, in his last three films: *The Shining, Full Metal Jacket,* and *Eyes Wide Shut*.[92]

But, true to its maker's origins and concerns, *The Shining* does not restrict itself to American historical referents. It hardly can in any case, since the establishment of the United States of America represents historically the expansion of European civilization and conquest in the modern era. Kubrick's reliance on Mann, Freud, and Kafka—and Hilberg—further expands the narrative from the specifically American one of King's novel to the broader European subject matter of the film. Finally, the modern industrial civilization of which America became a part was the culmination of centuries of social, political, and economic development in Europe. One major visual key to understanding these broader European referents in *The Shining* is Jack's typewriter. This typewriter is not merely a sign and means of Jack's pathetic attempt to become a writer. It is a symbol of his role as a functionary of the Overlook Hotel, just as another mechanical device, the elevator, is also a symbol of the "work" of the Overlook. For what Jack is typing is based upon his discovery of a scrapbook detailing the hotel's history. We see this scrapbook in several scenes in the film, recalling Kafka's description of one of the offices of the mysterious Castle: "On the desk there are great books lying open."[93] As a function of filmic economy and open narrative, it is one of only several props in the scenes. This also adds to the uncanny quality and dreamlike structure of the film that is accentuated by an apparent continuity error: in the middle of one scene, the scrapbook goes from being open to being closed.[94] The same type of discontinuity occurs in another scene, when a chair and table behind Jack disappear from one shot to another, an error (?) similarly consistent with the spooky intents of the horror genre as well as with reflexive directorial commentary on them.[95] However, unlike the extensive descriptions of the scrapbook in King's novel that fully detail the specifically American history of the Overlook, the marginalization of it in the film serves Kubrick's aim to generalize history to Europe and the West as a whole; similarly, when Jack and Danny confront the ghosts of Delbert Grady and his daughters, they speak in English accents, which in effect even if not in intent link the violence of the Old World to that of the New.[96]

Jack is also a latter-day Faust, representing the modern Western urge for discovery and mastery that Kubrick always admired but also found so problematic and destructive. But Jack is unlike the protagonist of Goethe's *Faust* (1808, 1832), who makes a deal with the devil's lieutenant Mephistopheles to satisfy his desire for the inexhaustible search after new knowledge and experience. Jack is a Faust *manqué* who, as we have observed, sells his soul for a drink to the Mephistophelian Overlook bartender Lloyd.[97] Condemned to (and by) a Western capitalist ethic of competition, his damnation—and ours—is to serve as an office boy for the powerful ghostly masters of the Overlook, who in the end order him to kill his own family, the human family.[98] Long before he destroys himself in this attempt, he continually responds to Wendy's and Danny's invitations to abandon his "work" for the "play" of human relationship with increasingly mordant assertions of duty. Wendy's request that he take her for a walk on a beautiful fall day before he has really gotten started on his writing elicits: "I suppose I ought to try to do some writing first." Once he has discovered the Overlook's history, any patience and humanity begin to slip away. His response to a subsequent interruption by Wendy, "I just wanna finish my work," is the quickly burning fuse to a conversation that will end in cool and cruel profanity. When Danny asks his father why he doesn't sleep if he's so tired, Jack mumbles, "I can't. I have too much to do." And then when Wendy suggests that they ought to leave the Overlook in order to protect Danny, Jack explodes at her for trying to hold him back at the very moment when "I'm really into my work." Finally, once Wendy has seen the results of his "work," Jack rages wildly at her about his "responsibilities to my employer" in a childishly pedantic but also absolutely terrifying prelude to a grinning promise of murder.[99]

Perhaps the most trenchant of the resemblances between Kubrick's film and Kafka's last, unfinished, novel is the use of the eagle as a symbol of temporal and universal power. Kubrick directly ties the American eagle visually referenced in the film to the mechanical means of Jack's "work," his typewriter. The scene described earlier in which Jack wears a T-shirt with an eagle on it gradually dissolves to a close-up of Jack's Adler typewriter, a German machine bearing an eagle (in German, *Adler*). In *The Castle,* the eagle is a symbol of the mysterious and possibly malevolent power of the Castle. K. has received a letter from Klamm, Chief of Department X, who is associated with eagles and who, as with Kubrick's own self-identification with birds of prey, also represents Kafka's insight into aspects of his own personality. Kafka's description of Klamm (German for "close, compact, narrow, stiff [with cold], numb") recalls the swooping camerawork of the opening sequences of *The Shining:* "Once the landlady had compared Klamm to an eagle, and that had seemed absurd in K.'s eyes, but it did not seem absurd now; he thought of Klamm's remoteness, of his impregnable dwelling, of his silence, broken perhaps only by cries such as K. had never yet heard, of his downward-pressing gaze, which could never be proved or disproved, of his wheelings which could never be disturbed by anything that K. did down below, which far above he followed at the behest of incomprehensible laws and which only for instants were visible—all these things Klamm and the eagle had in common."[100] Like *The Shining,* moreover, the structure of *The Castle* is labyrinthine in spite of its action in a high space open to the sky. Both works, like *The Magic Mountain* and *Heart of Darkness,* compress not only space but also time. *The Castle* covers a period of just seven days that parallels the seven years of Mann's novel. *The Shining* compresses time, as registered by title boards, from months to days to hours to emphasize claustrophobic entrapment as well as the everyday history of human lives.[101] Both emphasize a journey inward to states of mind. Both the Castle and the Overlook sit high in the mountains and are places of mystery that transcend time. The Overlook's exterior even has as its entrance a fortress-like stone stairway.[102] Both works emphasize the difficulty and failure of communication. In *The Shining* the hotel is isolated by a blizzard that cuts off the road to Sidewinder and downs the phone lines; Jack completes the isolation by sabotaging the two-way radio to the Forest Service.[103] Kubrick, like Kafka, employs the device of doubles. There are Charles and Delbert Grady (*both* equally evil) and the Grady sisters, while Ullman's assistant Bill Watson mirrors Jack in appearance, camera position, and subordination to the Overlook manager.[104] Both novel and film reflect sexual disorientation, in *The Shining* that of Jack in particular, and both works explore the failures of systems of control.[105]

But there is a major difference between *The Castle* and *The Shining*. Kafka describes a juncture in the history of central Europe at which "the larger culture embodied a state ready to collapse from its own dead weight . . . [while] the state and its institutions were sealing themselves off, hoping that by isolating themselves from the new they could control their destiny . . . as a powerless power that must disguise itself as though it were an empire, impregnable and unassailable."[106] Such a perspective allows room even for slapstick comedy, something that would be badly out of place in Kubrick's film.[107] The state power Kubrick confronts is more certain and more malevolent. In the world after 1945, Kubrick reminds us, not only does the eagle have wings, it has talons.

# 11

## THE DREAM OF JACOB

It is the Holocaust that lies at the dark heart of *The Shining,* and it is therefore the Nazi devil that dwells deepest in the details of the film. Given Kubrick's life course, the persistent themes and concerns of his films, and his 1975 preoccupation with Hilberg's book on the Final Solution, such a historical subtext should be anything but surprising. This chapter will demonstrate that patterns of meaning contained principally in numbers, colors, and music (and, in terms of the strength of historical specificity, especially in numbers and music) confirm the powerful presence of an indirect discourse on the Holocaust in Stanley Kubrick's horror film. There are also hosts of smaller and more naturalistic details in *The Shining* that can be seen to fit into this discourse. With the exception of Jack's typewriter, these details by themselves probably would not constitute components of a discourse on the Holocaust. But they are in their aggregate and in the context of certain numbers, colors, and music arguably part of a pattern of symbols of the Holocaust. That such details *can* carry meaning, whatever the meaning or meanings might be, is without question. As we have seen, Kubrick was convinced of the artistic necessity of the Kafkaesque juxtaposition of the realistic and the fantastic for purposes of commentary and critique. The presence of meaningful details is, as we have also seen, typical as well of Kubrick's rigorous exploitation of the visual depth of field offered by film for the simultaneous presentation of "multiple objects, signs, codes, connections, and relations."[1] Such details are also scattered and indirect due to the various artistic and personal reasons we have discussed. If one wishes to argue that these patterns are merely coincidental, there are enough of them to beg not only the question of when the frequency of coincidence stops being coincidental but also the question of the point at which Kubrick's love of coincidences prompted him to notice, create, or exploit them. Probably more than ever with *The Shining*, given its deep personal and familial associations, Kubrick was open over the lengthy and intense process of planning, shooting, and editing to the full, rich range of his subconscious, intuitive, and conscious faculties in the construction of historical meaning in and among the everyday objects in the film. And even if one or another, or several, of the symbols or signs were not intentional at any level of Kubrick's consciousness, the overall pattern of concerns and connections demonstrates a more general guiding intention in line with long-standing authorial concerns. These concerns were in turn reinforced by a burgeoning cultural discourse on the Holocaust as well as by the presence in both the novel and the film of *The Shining* of more apparent historical references to similar events in the American past. These American referents Kubrick crystallizes most significantly into an elliptical comparison of Nazi genocide with the cultural genocide of Native Americans, whose numbers under the assault of European imperialism declined over around 400 years by various means, including mass murder, from around 10 million to 1 million.[2]

References to the Holocaust in such details could even purely be the traces of the more general cultural discourse regarding the Holocaust in the postwar era and especially, as we have seen, in the 1970s. There is s a strong body of recent theory and practice that suggests that such a reading of *The Shining*, when based upon the detection of patterns of visual, aural, and structural evidence, can in and of itself have validity as an expression of cultural discourse and meaning even in the complete or partial absence of authorial intention. For example, we do not know how many viewers of the film, when confronted with the repeated shots of the Grady sisters, might have thought of the infamous "medical research" on twin children by Dr. Josef Mengele at Auschwitz. Knowledge of Mengele's misdeeds has long been part of the general association of Nazis with the extremities of cruelty and evil.[3] The context of Kubrick's horror film, in particular the sisters' juxtaposition with the elevator spewing blood, could have mobilized this connection in viewers' minds. This is particularly the case given the multiple meanings that inhabit a horror genre further opened to interpretation by Kubrick's intentional and intuitive interrogation. The possible accuracy of this speculation is also strengthened by the fact that on several occasions when audiences have been presented with evidence of a Holocaust subtext to *The Shining*, some have responded with an unprompted question about the Grady girls being a representation of the Mengele twins. Even though the girls are not twins, their appearance, as we shall discuss, is such that they are often mistaken as such. And even though there is no evidence of Kubrick himself making such an association, the fact of the widespread knowledge of Mengele and his twins might mean that Kubrick, too, was familiar with this gruesomely bizarre aspect of the history of Auschwitz. In his book on the Final Solution, Raul Hilberg mentions Mengele's murderous experiments on human beings as well as his protected exile in South America, which prompted Israeli extradition requests in 1959 and 1960.[4] And, as we have noted, in the 1970s there was a popular novel and film, *The Boys from Brazil* (1978), that imagines a postwar campaign by Mengele to clone Hitler.

But whatever the cultural environment, the cinematic construction of *The Shining* was also the result of Kubrick's own personal and artistic struggle concerning his century's most awful atrocity. That his most direct, though deeply indirect, creative confrontation with the Holocaust would come in a film that is his most autobiographical, the only one that deals with writing, and treats *writer's block* ("lots of ideas, no good ones," Jack says ominously) is testimony to the complications as well as the depths of Kubrick's feeling and thought on the subject.[5] As a result of all this, Kubrick's habitual use of objects, numbers, colors, and music to convey ideas reaches—inside a single huge set of a hotel—its highest stage of development in *The Shining*.[6] In this film Kubrick, for reasons we have discussed in the preceding chapters, is finally taking on in a most comprehensive fashion the horrors of human existence in general and of recent human history in particular. Once again, Kubrick is linking the personal with the political, in this case equating *a* human family with *the* human family, another joining of a modern interest in the history of big events and a postmodern concentration on the small events of people's lives.[7] But since he could not confront it directly in his work, his solution to the artistic and personal problem of representing the Holocaust, the acme of organized evil, was to bury references to it deep within the pattern of cinematic meaning conveyed by objects in *The Shining*. Such burial usefully represents the way in which the horrors of history have been repressed, particularly in reflexive contrast to—and here in the formal context of—commercial exploitation of terror and violence in horror films. This didactic exploitation of genre also utilizes the façade/reality syndrome Kubrick inherited from his early movie going. *The Shining*'s resultant abstraction of indirection avoids Jewish stereotyping of the type found in *Mr. Skeffington* (see Chapter 3), a film that may have served as one subliminal prototype for Kubrick's indirect treatment of the Holocaust. Finally, his approach serves not only the demands of filmic economy but also Kubrick's aim to have his film audiences work to derive meaning, their own as well as his.

In the language of literature, an object as symbol constitutes a metonym, whereby an attribute of a thing stands for it. In the language of psychoanalysis, and that of the cinema of Stanley Kubrick, such objects and forms constitute the topography of a dream, in which the smallest details, particularly when they are repeated and linked with other symbols, represent the most dreaded—and consequently most repressed—subjects. According to the Freud that Kubrick read, dreams basically consist of two levels of content. The manifest level is the narrative of the dream, but this story is only a cover for the latent content of the dream, whereby details and patterns convey unconscious conflicts that have been distorted through repression by the ego and the superego. The contents of the unconscious are unacceptable to the conscious mind either because they threaten the fragile sense of cohesion held together by the ego, or self, or because they represent desires unacceptable to the superego, or conscience. It is also the case that in dreams, words and objects are "overdetermined"; that is, they constitute "'nodal points' upon which a great number of dream-thoughts [converge and thus have] several meanings in connection with the interpretation of the dream."[8] This, too, is the work of repression, but in *The Shining* such multiple meanings again allow Kubrick to address issues in a cinematically economic and didactic fashion.

As we have already seen, there is a historically meaningful juxtaposition of the eagle and the typewriter in *The Shining*. In tandem, the eagle and the typewriter most generally symbolize the oversight of the bureaucratic state that preoccupied Kubrick's favorite writer, Kafka. In the pattern of symbols in *The Shining*, however, Jack's (and Stanley's) Adler typewriter also represents more specifically the bureaucracy of the Nazi Final Solution. Like Dr. Strangelove in his wheelchair, Jack is (part of) a machine, in Kubrick films always a sign of deadly danger. In *The Shining* the German typewriter, together with its mechanical cousin in crime, the elevator gushing blood, is a representation of the most extreme danger posed by the heartless rational systems of the modern European and North American era. These systems had been analyzed with great trepidation by Max Weber in *Science as a Vocation* (1919) and in *The Protestant Ethic and the Spirit of Capitalism* (1920) as "mechanized ossification" of "specialists without mind, pleasure seekers without heart."[9] It is also precisely the Nazi machinery of extermination directed against the Jews that is the subject of the book by Hilberg that would serve as Kubrick's historical guide to the Holocaust. Hilberg notes in the preface to *The Destruction of the European Jews* that his aim is to "describe the vast organization of the Nazi machinery of destruction and the men who performed important functions in this machine . . . [and to] reveal the correspondence, memoranda, and conference minutes which were passed from desk to desk as the German bureaucracy made its weighty and drastic decisions to destroy, utterly and completely, the Jews of Europe."[10]

The typewriter in *The Shining* is as central to Kubrick's film as typewriters are to Spielberg's *Schindler's List*. Spielberg's film, however, resolves the typing of thousands of lists of Jewish victims into a thematic focus on the typing of one list of Jews who will be saved. By contrast, given his outlook and cinematic strategy, it was all but inevitable that with the symbols in *The Shining* Kubrick would follow Hilberg's concentration on the German perpetrators rather than on the Jewish victims. It is also the case that there are no Jewish characters in King's novel, which relieved Kubrick of the necessity of again writing them out, although he tolerated the coincidence—or is it more than that?—of the prominent display of a large can labeled "Kosher Dill Slices" in one shot of the film. The typewriter in *The Shining* thus appropriately represents in metonymic fashion the very many murderers of the Final Solution rather than, as in *Schindler's List*, the very few saviors in the history of the Holocaust. When Kubrick's camera dissolves from Jack in his eagle T-shirt and then pulls up, and—frightened?—away from the close-up of the typewriter (Figure 7, color insert), we hear only a deep hollow boom repeated again and again.[11] As already noted, Kubrick had taken the booming horror effect in King's novel and transformed it into a representation of history. And, as we saw in Chapter 10, Kubrick's film of *The Shining* in various ways expands King's references to the blood splashed across American history into a more general pattern of reference to the modern history of Europe and the West as a whole. In *The Shining*, Kubrick once again places a particularly strong emphasis on the subject of race by forging a thematic and symbolic link between the white male European decimation of Native Americans that culminated during the nineteenth century and the white male Nazi extermination of the Jews that bloodied the middle years of the twentieth. In the pan upward from the Adler typewriter, the booming sound comes from Jack throwing a ball violently against a wall decorated with Native American figures. The temporal direction of this shot is into the past: from Jack in the present to the booming German death machine and back—with Jack's repeated throws symbolizing history as repetition—to the European decimation of Native Americans in centuries past.

The association of Nazis with eagles could well have been reinforced in Kubrick's mind by the coincidence of the names of the sanitarium in *The Magic Mountain* and Hitler's own Berghof at Berchtesgaden. This was because during the 1930s and 1940s the symbol of the eagle, like that of the wolf, had become closely linked in general cultural consciousness with Hitler and the Nazis. Hitler's "Eagle's Nest," a small tea house built in 1938 on the rocky Kehlstein spur above the Berghof, became the name abroad for the entire Nazi compound.[12] The small, close, and ultimately murderous world of mid-twentieth-century central Europe is also contained in a stunning, and grim, irony involving the buildings on the Obersalzberg. The same cottage in which in July 1929 Freud had written the first draft of his gloomy *Civilization and Its Discontents* (1930) became the house owned and occupied by Hitler's second-in-command, Hermann Göring, a cousin of whose, in a further cruel twist of irony, directed an institute for psychotherapy that strove to practice a properly "non-Jewish" form of psychoanalysis in service to the Nazi regime. And yet more irony—or tragedy: another house in the compound was the one in which Freud had begun work on *The Interpretation of Dreams* (1900) thirty years before.[13]

There is in *The Shining* a similar symbolic association between a machine and an animal represented in Jack's Volkswagen, the popular postwar car originally promised to the Germans by Hitler. Jack's Volkswagen is also linked, in film as in life, with an animal that has symbolic historical meaning in *The Shining*, the wolf. Volkswagens were and are manufactured in Wolfsburg, Germany. This factory town, which was completed in 1939, did not receive its name until after the war, but Nazi officials long before 1945 had it in mind to name the city Wolfsburg in honor of Hitler's code- and nickname.[14] In June 1945, Nazi sympathizers among local officials formally decided on the name Wolfsburg, or Wolf's Castle, and the Volkswagen company created a stylized wolf and castle arch design for the hub of the steering wheel.[15] Hitler's hypermasculine *nom du guerre* picked up by American popular culture in the 1930s was revived during the "Hitler Wave" in the 1970s. In a novel written at the end of the decade about the capture and trial of Adolf Hitler in South America, George Steiner summarizes Hitler's grisly achievement in just this way: "He took garbage and made it into wolves."[16] Kubrick underscores the link between Jack's Volkswagen and his role as the Big Bad Wolf in a way that also forges a connection with the memory of the Second World War in Europe. Late in the film Halloran is driving to the Overlook Hotel in response to a "shine" of help from Danny. Just before his car passes a red Volkswagen crushed under a jackknifed (!) semi-trailer, the car radio—tuned to KHOW, a stereotypical reference to Native Americans—announces that the mountain passes of Wolf Creek and Red Mountain have been closed and that the chain law is in effect at the Eisenhower Tunnel. Both Wolf Creek and the Eisenhower Tunnel are real locations in the Colorado Rockies, but in the context of *The Shining*'s historical concerns they together call up associations with the war against Hitler, particularly when we recall that Kubrick had on two occasions in the early 1950s photographed former Supreme Allied Commander Dwight Eisenhower when he was president of Columbia University.[17]

Kubrick also introduces two other mechanical contrivances early in the film that he connects with human violence in general and, through a pattern of oneiric images, the Holocaust in particular. The most apparent of these is the repeated slow-motion shot of the elevator spewing blood. As usual, Kubrick would not comment on the meaning of this shot. When asked by Michel Ciment about departing from King's rather more elaborate dramatic use of the Overlook's elevator, Kubrick would say only that his decision to use just his own single shot of it was a matter of the narrative economy imposed by film. And yet, admittedly like everything else in this as in every Kubrick film, a great deal of time was taken in the shooting of this scene.[18] One suspects that Kubrick's desire to get this shot right was based on more than his usual obsessive insistence on cinematographic craftsmanship and artistry. And the effect of this shot in particular would have been reduced or even eliminated by a comment from Kubrick on what he had in mind. While it may be taken as a parody of stock horror-effect shots, it also connects logically and viscerally with other themes in the film, including, as we shall see, the horrors of history gruesomely crowned by the Holocaust. Indeed, because of its nature and its repeated appearance throughout the film, the scene can well be considered *the* symbol of the irreducible and inexplicable horrors of human existence in general and the Holocaust in particular.[19]

The other machine, the train, that Kubrick brings into the discourse of *The Shining* on history and the Holocaust is the mostly deeply buried. It is referenced in only two scenes, which might be an indication of how closely in reality and in representation (e.g., in Lanzmann's *Shoah*) trains and cattle cars are associated with the machinations of the Final Solution. Their seemingly incidental appearance in *The Shining* does recall their brief but powerful presence in Agee's and Kadar's film treatments of Crane's *The Blue Hotel*. Like the other historically symbolic objects (ash, smoke, fire, gas, and ovens) we discuss in this particular early sequence of scenes, the train in *The Shining* is of course also overdetermined, carrying other associations and meanings dependent on or even independent of authorial intent. But it is nonetheless linked in a pattern of visual meaning that reinforces its associations with modern mechanical means of horror that, in the broader context of other symbols in *The Shining*, emphasize the special place of the Holocaust in the film's discourse. As with other historically meaningful machines in *The Shining*, the train is introduced early in the film. As Jack is just sitting down with Ullman up at the Overlook Hotel, we dissolve to the exterior of the Torrances' Boulder apartment house. A dog is barking over the sounds of children playing as the camera zooms in on the building. A shot follows of Wendy and Danny eating lunch. Danny has a sandwich and is watching a Roadrunner cartoon on a television off screen. Wendy reads while smoke from her cigarette columns up from an ashtray in the center of the table. As they discuss the possibility of spending the winter at the hotel, the roar of an oncoming train and the wail of its whistle come from the television.[20] Over cartoon music, Wendy reassures a reluctant Danny about the good time they will have at the Overlook. The one-shot of Wendy slowly dissolves back into Jack's conversation with Ullman and Watson, followed by a dissolve to his telephone call about getting the job and a cut to Danny's first vision of the hemorrhagic elevator that ends the sequence.

Over a black screen we hear a woman's voice. Danny has fainted from his vision and is told by the doctor to stay in bed for the afternoon. As the doctor and Wendy enter the living room to talk, they pass quickly by a dark painting on the white wall. The painting is *Horse and Train* (1954) by Alex Colville, which shows a dark horse in the foreground galloping down a railroad track at twilight toward an oncoming steam locomotive. The painting was inspired by two lines in a poem by Roy Campbell, "Dedication to Mary Campbell" (1949): "Against a regiment I oppose a brain / And a dark horse against an armored train."[21] Campbell's autobiography is titled *Light on a Dark Horse* (1951), and the poem that inspired Colville was a complaint against war ("I scorn the goose-step of their massed attack / And fight with my guitar slung on my back"). More generally, both Campbell and Colville were moved to oppose art (the horse) and death (the train). But Colville, too, had direct experience with mechanized warfare, since he served as a war artist with the Canadian army in Europe during the Second World War. His war paintings focus on the huge armored vehicles that dwarf and dominate the men around and within them. His postwar art, by contrast, turned away from machines toward the affirmation of life and value to be found in landscapes and animals. Kubrick was certainly receptive to such an opposition of the organic and the mechanical, as is shown again by his placing of another Colville painting in the Torrances' apartment, *Woman and Terrier* (1963). This portrait was painted after the death of Colville's mother and symbolizes the innocence of human life and the freeing of the soul from the body.[22] Kubrick, however, juxtaposes *Woman and Terrier* ominously with the two cowboys transacting "business" (read Jack and Ullman), with all the order, control, and rage that implies, on a television directly below the painting. This painting's appearance also immediately precedes Danny's first elevator vision.[23] Kubrick was of course just as responsive to Colville's representation of the artist observing and criticizing a violent world. As far back as the title to *Paths of Glory* he had quoted poetry in criticism of war and in one scene in that film had even shown horses being spooked by a motorcycle. Whether *Horse and Train* had inspired or influenced Kubrick in 1957 is unknown, but its use in *The Shining* is appropriately menacing and most likely directly related to the specific historical concerns of the film as well. With his predilection for the symbolic use of mirrors and numbers, Kubrick might even have noticed that the year of the painting is the partial mirror of 1945.

The bracketing of the sound of a train with the painting of a train around Danny's vision only emphasizes a communication of symbolic meaning articulated further by other signs and symbols that follow immediately upon them. The progression, as it were, from the train sounds of silly cartoon violence (featuring a prairie wolf) to the artistic expression of the train as symbol of death in Colville's painting is the immediate prelude to revelations of family violence and visual symbols of even larger inhumanities. The doctor learns from Wendy that Jack had "accidentally" separated Danny's shoulder after returning home drunk one evening. Danny had apparently committed the most grievous crime possible against a teacher—or, rather, against a *bureaucrat*—as Jack later rages to Lloyd, "the little fucker had thrown all my papers all over the room." According to Wendy, however, some good came from it because Jack had pledged never to drink again and had in fact been sober for five months. Even this "best face on it" scenario, however, is subject to some doubt since Jack whines to Lloyd that the injury occurred "three goddamn years ago." If this is true, it means there was quite some time before Jack's regret kicked in enough to give up booze.[24] But, as usual in a Kubrick scene, there is much more information being conveyed by pictures than by elliptical and duplicitous words. As Wendy talks with the pediatrician, she nervously lights and smokes a long Virginia Slims cigarette. There are six separate one-shots of Wendy holding the cigarette straight up in the air next to her head. And since the shots are close-ups, we are painfully aware of the ash on the cigarette getting longer and longer as this conversation about Jack's drunkenness and violence goes on. Clearly, the ash—and the audience's parodied horror film suspense about whether it will fall off—is a symbol of the tension and destructiveness within the Torrance family. But it also forms a chain of historical association with the heard and seen trains as well as with the (unheard) text on ashes in the opening "Dies Irae." Behind Wendy, moreover, in three two-shots is a gas oven, which her head, like Ullman's hiding the eagle on his office windowsill, conceals in close-up. Kubrick heightens the dreamlike quality of the objects by cuts that alternately hide and reveal them, capturing both the dynamic of repression in dreams as well as the constant pressure exerted by the unconscious and by memory on the conscious mind. Even Danny's ability to see into the past and the future, as when he stands before his bathroom mirror and Tony shows him the hotel elevator, is communicated in this scene by the sight three times of a thick book on an end table between Wendy and the doctor whose title appears to be *The Wise Child*.[25]

The gas oven in the Torrances' tiny kitchen mirrors the gas oven visible in the huge Overlook kitchen behind Danny as he and Hallorann discuss the "not all good" things in the hotel's past. King naturalistically makes much of the huge size of the oven in Wendy's mind as Hallorann shows it off and notes, as most professional chefs would, "I love gas."[26] Both ovens in the film are out of focus in their scenes' one-shots but in focus in the two-shots, another instance of the "now you see it, now you don't" construction of dreams. These details of smoke, ash, and gas ovens, along with their attendant historical associations, may be purely incidental, but they do resound with the at least one clearly intentional and historically rich reference to trains that immediately precede them as well as with the more explicit meanings carried by the numbers, colors, and music we highlight in this chapter. Wendy's cigarette ash also links with her smoking ashtray in a previous scene, a smoking ashtray in the close-up of Jack's typewriter in a subsequent one, and the "thin thread of smoke" drifting up the Overlook's chimney that in one exterior shot is "a token of the vulnerable lives inside."[27] And the fact that Hallorann characterizes the traces of evil in the hotel as being the smell of burned toast not only is a natural thing for a chef to say, but also is linked to murder in the hotel's past.[28] Even the racks of meat in the kitchen freezer that Hallorann proudly shows Wendy and Danny recall the image of the concentration-camp-like shelves of mannequin parts in *Killer's Kiss*.[29] Along the same lines, the Overlook's maze and the model of it in the hotel lobby come to resemble nothing so much as the layout of a concentration camp. The exterior walls of the labyrinth are ringed with towers reminiscent of the asylum gate in Lang's wartime *Ministry of Fear*. And, in a visual construction subsequently made whole and explicit in a labyrinthine and amplifying manner in the concrete room of fire, war, and death at the end of *Full Metal Jacket*, some of the maze's interior walls take on the form of partial or broken swastikas.[30] Finally, fires and fireplaces, again quite naturalistic features of the setting, play a suggestive role in terms of race and destruction. In two of the three scenes in which we hear and see Jack typing, a huge fire roars in the fireplace of the Colorado Lounge; during the tour, Ullman, recalling "all the best people," leads the Torrances past another massive and blackened stone fireplace that overwhelms a shallow sitting area that has a portrait of a Native American chief on the opposite wall; and in one scene, forming a triad of emergency vehicles with the "ambulance" and "police car" alongside the road on Jack's drive to the Overlook, Danny, once again symbolically in anticipation of trouble in the family, insists on going to his room to get his fire engine.[31]

It was of course human beings, and not machines, who conceived and ran the Nazi machinery of death, a particularly horrendous instance of the combination of "mecha" and "orga" treated in Kubrick's cinema. In particular, a cast of mind that is comfortable only with the certainties and securities of rote order is another major theme of Hilberg's book on the Final Solution. Hilberg explains that formal order was not the only desideratum of the process. Order was also a function of deep-seated psychological conflict, one of which was denial. In the Nazi hierarchy, euphemisms like "migration," "evacuation," and "resettlement" were used to keep the reality of mass extermination from the outside world.[32] But these terms also masked the reality of mass murder from the perpetrators themselves. In *The Shining*, similar circumlocutions are heard in the bathroom conversation between Grady and Jack concerning the need for Jack to "correct" his wife and child in the name of "duty," by which Grady means murder on behalf of the management of the Overlook. But euphemism is not just a matter of denying gruesome reality. It is also an expression of the psychological conflict underlying racism. For here is the only time in the film we hear a racial epithet, as twice Grady refers to Hallorann as a "nigger," a slur echoed once by Jack. Women and children, too, are thrown into the conversation as impediments to masculine work and duty. Surrounded by the blindingly blood-red walls and white urinals, sinks, and toilets in the brightly lit, painfully clean, and extensively mirrored "gentleman's room," Grady recalls how he "corrected" his daughters after one of them tried to burn down the Overlook Hotel. He also "corrected" his wife when she tried to stop him. Such dark and inferior beings have no place in the bright, clean world of men, so they must be sent, through the plumbing, as it were, into the soil as human waste. The venue of a bathroom thus revisits the anal sadism and racial hysteria of Nazism as well as the orderly, repressed regimen of the bureaucracy of murder. Hilberg, too, describes the Nazi obsession with racial purity and the threat to it posed by Jews along such lines.[33] For the Nazis, Jews and other "darker races" represented fears of weakness, sexuality, and intimacy to be contained and channeled by repression into service to the hard duty of racial warfare. This line of lunacy was reinforced by long-standing convictions among many Europeans and Germans that nation, state, and war were all manifestations of masculine power and virtue. By this illusory standard, Jews and other "inferior" races were also like women, who lacked the physical and mental capacities of men and masculine peoples ordained to lead and prosper: "White man's burden, Lloyd, my man, white man's burden," Jack says to Lloyd about his trouble with Wendy ("the old sperm bank"), quoting Rudyard Kipling's poem "White Man's Burden" (1889, the year of Hitler's birth), on the duty of the British Empire to protect and advance the lesser peoples ("Half-devil and half-child") it ruled.[34]

This imposition of ordered male violence upon the weak is reflected in the sign beside the door from the Gold Room: "Toilets and Powder Room," in which the latter term connotes not only a defensive euphemism for female "difference" but also powder magazine, a compartment for the storage of ammunition and explosives.[35] The word "correct" also takes on a significant double meaning in this murderous context, referring with grim irony both to Jack's role as a teacher and to Grady's veneer of polite obedience and restrained expression. Grady also notes that he and Jack have "always been here," which underscores Kubrick's theme of the continuities of human behavior over time. Grady, who "patiently nudges Jack towards a final solution to the problem of his unruly family,"[36] is not only an avatar of early-twentieth-century American racism. He is a European reminding an American of the history of his country's own violent racism, as also evident in Ullman's patronizing attitude toward Dick Hallorann. Jack's recognition of Grady from old newspaper clippings about the Overlook is another confirmation of Grady's embodiment of historical identity.[37]

Kubrick's reading of Hilberg, his knowledge and application of Freud, and the growing discourse in the 1970s on the Holocaust and the psychology and sociology of fascism informed at least an intuitive grasp on Kubrick's part of the type of people involved in the Final Solution. Both the anal and oral forms of repressed and expressed aggression are represented as well in "Hansel and Gretel" and "The Three Little Pigs," the fairy tales referenced in *The Shining*, and also contained within the film's allusions to cannibalism. In one scene, Jack noisily eats the breakfast Wendy has brought to him in bed, using the bacon to spoon egg yolk with great gusto into his mouth. This anticipates his later role as the predatory male who will seek to kill his family, just as the Big Bad Wolf sought to devour the little pigs.[38] But it is also this image of Jack that fades in a dissolve to the close-up of his booming typewriter, which visually and aurally reinforces the connection among fairy tales, oral and anal rage, and his clerical job in service to the murderous hotel. The violent psychic disorder within Jack that lurks behind a façade of order and control is also represented visually in *The Shining* in the contrast between his work and home environment. Unlike Jack's irregular pecking in the novel, his typing—and its product, "All work and no play makes Jack a dull boy"—is steady and anally *regular*, as orderly and repressed as it is relentless and ruthless.[39] His writing desk at the Overlook is a model of bureaucratic, Germanic tidiness: typing paper snug in its box and any pencils and pens not in their proper holder lined up carefully on the table. In the Boulder and Overlook apartments, by contrast, magazines and papers are scattered everywhere while books tilt or lie drunkenly on shelves, tables, and a window ledge. Since Jack is the teacher and writer of the family, it is clear that the books, the papers, and the disorder are his.

Jack's transition from the violent master of an emotionally disordered home to a dutiful servant of an orderly, if no less emotionally disordered and violent, hotel is marked by the fate of a single piece of furniture, a couch that appears but then disappears from the Colorado Lounge. During the tour, it is backed against what will become Jack's writing table, in bureaucratic language, his "office." In the first shot of Jack's "office," however, the couch has been moved away from the table and now faces it over a coffee table. And on it and on the coffee table in the shot that begins with the close-up of Jack's typewriter are scattered in great disorder various newspapers and magazines, a mess that reproduces the disorder in the Torrances' Boulder apartment. But in subsequent shots of the Colorado Lounge, the sofa has vanished altogether as Jack's internal disorder has been mastered for the sake of service to a larger organization with an ultimately murderous purpose to which it can apply both Jack's obedience and rage. There are issues of realism, continuity, and the uncanny in these differences. Jack could have moved the sofa away from his writing table (realism), but probably would not have removed it from the room entirely (continuity, uncanny). But of course the question of the sofa is not so much, if at all, what *Jack* did with it but what *Kubrick* did.[40]

Another typically tiny, hidden expression in *The Shining* of the psychodynamic underpinnings of order, rage, and cleanliness that reached its historical nadir at Auschwitz, a place some there called the *anus mundi*, are the many signs in the bright, spotless, and cavernous kitchen of the Overlook. Just like several reading "No Smoking," these signs are quite naturalistic for the setting. But the fact that there are so many of them and that they appear only in passing and in the background of scenes emphasizes both the dynamics of repression and the nature of dreams to signal latent content from the unconscious in small, indirect ways. All of them, some with Briticisms, are admonitions having to do with order and cleanliness, which connect with the basic psychological and historical preoccupations of *The Shining* and therefore with its indirect discourse on the Holocaust: "No Eating or Drinking"; "Keep This Area Clean" (thrice); "Have You Got Your Requisition for Tomorrow"; "Please Shut Down After Use"; "Have You Washed Your Hands"; "Notice to All Employees: The Area Below Should Be Kept Clean and Tidy"; "Put Cups and Other Garbage in the Bins Provided" (twice); and, above the Torrances' eating table in the kitchen, "No Eating or Drinking in the Kitchen."[41] The great majority of these signs appear early in the film—that is, before Jack's violence actually breaks out. Thus the signs represent the strict but permeable apparatus of repression. Like the blood in the elevator, rage and aggression are being contained only temporarily and with difficulty behind the hotel walls on which the signs, which appear to be paper and not metal or plastic, are pasted.

Whatever the other meanings of each of these and other details in *The Shining*, one thing in any case is certain. For Kubrick, it is not the supernatural that haunts us. What haunts us is history.

### "Which Room Was It?"

As we know, Kubrick had a penchant for using the number 7 as a symbol for violence and warfare in his films. In this, of course, he was drawing from a deep wellspring in Western culture from the medieval to the modern. As we noted in Chapter 5, it is the Seventh Circle of Dante's Hell that is reserved for the violent. The number's traditional associations with mystery and dread also make it a common trope in the horror genre, while in psychoanalytic theory it has been associated with obsessional neurosis. And it has also been frequently used in connection with the Holocaust. For example, the architecture of the new Jewish Museum in Berlin, in following kabbalistic numerology, includes seven "voids" that represent the exclusion of Jews from German life. Holocaust survivor Elie Wiesel biblically labels his life "seven times cursed and seven times sealed" from the time of his first night in Auschwitz.[42] We have also seen how Kubrick, following Mann's *The Magic Mountain*, employs multiples and mirrors of 7 in *The Shining* to link years, events, and characters.[43] In *The Shining* Kubrick uses the number 7 to reference a specific time period as well as specific years in the first half of the twentieth century. These multiples of 7 connoting years from 1907 to 1970 again of course include the year of Kubrick's birth, 1928, as well as the American referents in the national (1776) and state (1876) flags displayed in the Overlook Hotel. Jack's question in response to Wendy's news of Danny's injury in one of the hotel rooms, "Which room was it?" thus carries with it authorial, cultural, numerical, and historical specificity insofar as it stems at least in part from Kubrick's acute sense of the world of his own past we have observed and analyzed.[44]

Considering this, it is not surprising that the film uses a multiple of 7 to represent the year in which, according to Hilberg, more Jews were murdered—2.7 million, including most of the 1500 Jews from the village of Probużna—than in all the other years of the Third Reich combined. As historian Christopher Browning has chillingly put it, in "mid-March of 1942, some 75 to 80 percent of all victims of the Holocaust were still alive . . . [while] a mere eleven months later, 75 to 80 percent of all Holocaust victims were already dead."[45] The major reason for this was that it was only on January 20, 1942, in the middle of winter, that the Nazis began officially organizing what they called the Final Solution to the "Jewish problem" in Europe. While mass shootings of Jews had been going on for seven months and gassing of Jews had begun in early December 1941 at Chelmno in Poland, the so-called Wannsee Conference on January 20, 1942, brought together in a palatial Berlin mansion key Nazi bureaucrats whose authority, competence, and expertise was necessary for the full implementation of the policy to exterminate the 11 million Jews of Europe by shipping them to extermination camps in Poland. Seven of the men at the meeting had doctoral degrees. The meeting took less than ninety minutes, and by its end SS Security Chief Reinhard Heydrich, who had chaired the meeting as Himmler's deputy, had the agreement he needed for the implementation of Hitler's order to kill all the Jews in German hands. This agreement was fleshed out in subsequent meetings of many of the principals in March and October 1942.

While it is not certain that the number 42 has taken on an association with the Holocaust within Western culture in general, it has on occasion in works devoted to the Holocaust. Resnais's *Night and Fog* devotes a single shot and beat of music to the narrator's "1942." In Jan Nemec's short film, *A Bite to Eat* (1960), the counting of 56 (8 × 7) seconds between sentries is the key to an attempted theft of a loaf of bread from a railcar. It is near the end of the war, and concentration camp prisoners are being transported to other camps inside Germany. As one of the prisoners passes along a line of cattle cars, a 42, much larger than the other numbers on the cars, appears behind him just after a prisoner in the background says "Damned Jews!"[46] In 1980 Vasily Grossman, a Russian Jew and Soviet war correspondent, published *Life and Fate,* a novel about the Second World War modeled on Leo Tolstoy's *War and Peace* (1872). Grossman devotes a single page to Chapter 42 of Part 1 to describe the flood tide of Nazi fortunes during the year 1942 and concludes the page with the words, "Adolf Hitler and the Party leadership had decided upon the final destruction of the Jewish nation."[47] Such literary tendencies reflect not only a modern tradition of the purposive construction of ideas, but also the postmodern virtue of play that is both a method and a theme of *The Shining* (Jack's problem is "all work and no play") as well as one characteristic of Kubrick's cinema overall.

It is also hard to say what specific role Kubrick's own psyche played in the odd and persistent appearance (and disappearance) of this particular number in *The Shining*. But there are some curious and compelling considerations along these lines having to do with two closely related numbers, 6 and 7, that when multiplied produce 42. Symbolic and scientific relationships between these two particular numbers come from the realm of culture, literature, and psychoanalysis and might well have had emotional and intellectual resonance in Kubrick's consciousness. As we have seen, *The Magic Mountain* mentions the number 6 as a rather mundane counterpoint to the number 7. The term "at sixes and sevens" means "the hazard of one's whole fortune, or carelessness as to the consequences of one's actions, and in later use the creation or existence of, or neglect to remove, confusion, disorder, or disagreement." While the origins of this expression apparently lie in games of chance involving dice, psychoanalytic theory says that the resolution, often accompanied by particularly intense conflict, of the Oedipus complex usually occurs around the age of six. Such conflict can be aggravated by the birth of a younger sibling, who in the traditional patriarchal family in particular represents a rival for the attentions of the mother. Kubrick's own sister, Barbara, was born when Stanley was just going on six. Mann's novel, too, implies an Oedipal dynamic in its frequent juxtaposition of the two numbers. His account of his protagonist's childhood, for example, embodies repression, denial, and resolution of the crisis: "Hans Castorp retained only pale memories of his parental home. His father and mother he had barely known; they had both dropped away in the brief period between his fifth and seventh birthday."[48] What is more, Mann seems to associate six with a place of observation, an age when childhood conflict is in the process of being surmounted and the child is beginning to emerge onto a view—an overlook, if you will—of the world of compromise and ambition beyond childhood and the family.[49] For Mann and Freud, of course, the end of childhood conflict was not the entrée to an adult paradise. This was at least just as much the case with Kubrick, for whom the world beyond childhood, spatially as well as chronologically, had always been a place of danger acutely sensed by a preternaturally observant mind and eye. In this connection, Kubrick might have recalled from his reading of Hilberg that the Nazis constructed six extermination camps in 1941 and 1942: Bełżec Maidanek, Sobibor, Kulmhof (Chelmno), Treblinka, and Auschwitz.[50]

What is certain is that in *The Shining* the number 42 repeatedly appears and therefore demands explanation. It takes on a general meaning, as in *Lolita*, of malevolent fate as well as the specific extreme evil of the Holocaust. It is in fact the key Holocaust referent in *The Shining* since it fits into the chronological symbolic structure descended from *The Magic Mountain*. All the other possible, probable, and definite symbols of the Holocaust in the film depend to one degree or another upon it for their allied meaning. Although we hardly—if at all—notice it, we are introduced to 42 very early on in *The Shining*. We likely do not notice it because, as usual, Kubrick includes it only in the most natural but also most unobtrusive manner possible, as the number on Danny's Bugs Bunny jersey ("What's up, *Doc*?" a link to his father?). It is equally unlikely that the number is accidental, since it is another multiple of 7 that fits logically into the several specific years, 1907, 1921, and 1970, to which the film alludes. It is also the double of 21, the year of the July 4 party at which Jack is pictured at the end of the film. To emphasize the minatory quality of the number 7, this photograph is one of twenty-one pictures on a wall in three rows of seven that seals and documents Jack's permanent employment at the Overlook as a symbol that people and society remain the same, that is, ready to do a cruel master's bidding.[51] Our first glimpse of the number 42 is, appropriately for the oneiric structure of the film, a partial one: on the left sleeve of Danny's jersey as he eats with his mother in the Boulder apartment. The second ends a dolly shot past a Disney cartoon of Dopey from *Snow White and the Seven Dwarfs* (1937; R, July 1944), showing most of the 42 on the right sleeve as Danny has his first vision of the overflowing elevator (Figure 8, color insert). It is this scene, with the number foregrounded—again hidden in plain sight—that establishes without any doubt the importance of the number in the historical disquisition that is *The Shining*. This shot is the first of several of the elevator's disgorgement of an ocean of blood, and its repetition reinforces its seminal symbolic importance as a Holocaust referent. This historical reference is further underscored, as we shall presently see, by the music that accompanies it as well as by its association with the number 42.

The very next scene also foregrounds 42 by having it appear and disappear over the span of eight successive crosscut one-shots of Danny as he is being questioned by the doctor. In the first four close-ups, only the edge of the 2 on Danny's right sleeve can be seen. Then in the fifth shot, almost the entire 42 appears, subsequently disappearing in the sixth shot (as Danny, referring to Tony, says, "Because he hides") and reappearing in shots seven and eight. One might view this effect as a continuity error, since the successive shots of Danny lying on his bed alternately hide and reveal the number without Danny otherwise changing position. It is likely that Kubrick was again emphasizing, over a number of takes, the overall dramatic quality of the scene. But, particularly in the editing of the film that as usual took Kubrick a very long time, he was certainly visually aware of the entire scene, including the close-ups of Danny in which 42 flashes on and off. This visual alternation draws attention to the number and, once again, adds to the dreamlike quality of the scene in the distortion and repression characteristic of dreamwork. And that the subject of the conversation is Danny's imaginary friend Tony and what Tony shows him only confirms the historical content of the scene signaled by 42, especially since Danny ends the conversation by refusing to say anything about the horrible scene that caused him to black out.[52]

And the number will not leave us alone. A television news report, fading under the electronic scream on the soundtrack of Danny's shining, mentions a $42 million spending bill.[53] More significantly, Wendy, with a blizzard howling outside, watches the movie *Summer of '42* (1971) on a television in the hotel lobby. The movie is the story of three high-school friends on vacation at the coast. The chief attraction for the boys, in a tale of sweet (and sexist) adolescent Oedipal nostalgia, is a young married woman whose husband is off in the war. In the scene Wendy is watching, one of the boys, who at the end of the film will have his first sexual experience with the suddenly widowed and grieving young wife, has just helped the woman bring in her groceries. The discussion centers on his eagerness to leave high school and become a paratrooper like his brother. She tells him not to be in such a hurry. Once again, Kubrick has slipped in an overdetermined dream fragment consisting of sexual desire and conflict, the Second World War, and even, in the symbolic form of the year in the title of the film that links with earlier dis/appearances of the number 42, the Holocaust.[54] With January at Wannsee and *Summer of '42,* Kubrick juxtaposes winter and summer as doubles of the evil that inhabits humankind year round. As with other grand Kubrick summerhouses of cold power, this doubling of cold reason and hot irrationality appears in other small details in *The Shining,* such as the Denver television weatherman named Sonny who announces a blizzard and the Miami weatherman, Walter Croneis (German *Kroneis* [ice crown]), on a local heat wave as well as the blizzard ("railroad tracks are frozen").[55]

The same overdetermination occurs with respect to room 237, which is the room (with double doors) in which Danny is attacked by a ghost who subsequently attracts and repels Jack. While also representing the mysteries of sex and gender, room 237 serves as a central symbol and symptom of the hotel's evil and bloody past. As Danny is about to pass through the mysteriously opened door to the room (with a white "237" on a red key tag hanging from the lock), he calls out, "Mom, are you in there?" This can be explained in terms of logic and the social dynamic of the family, since Danny by now knows very well that it is his mother who does all the work around the hotel and that his father can be found only "at work" in his "office." But the tableau is clearly Oedipal as well, along with its allied representation of the visceral male attraction to, and fear of, the female womb. The scene in fact opens with Danny playing on the floor in front of a set of red elevator doors and on a carpet composed of geometrically stylized insertions and enclosures with red centers.[56] It is also the case that the product of the three digits of 237 is 42 and that Kubrick changed the number from room 217 in King's novel. The ostensible reason for this was that the management of the Timberline Lodge, whose exterior doubles for the Overlook Hotel, did not want guests to be afraid of staying in their room 217. The Timberline also has a room 227, so Kubrick, if he wanted to maintain a certain harmony with the original source and also to include another 7, would logically therefore have chosen 237.[57] But there is evidence that there was more to the choice than this—that is, that Kubrick's decision for 237 was overdetermined. *The Shining*'s assistant editor, Gordon Stainforth, recalls discussing with Kubrick Fibonacci numbers, a series (2, 3, 5, 8, 13, 21 . . .) in which each number is the sum of the two preceding numbers.[58] And on Kubrick's copy of the screenplay for *The Shining* shown in Jan Harlan's film about his career, Kubrick has written "Their address 217 N. Elm," Feb. 17," and "2.17." This would seem to indicate that Kubrick was fiddling with the number 7 in a way strongly reminiscent of Nabokov in *Lolita,* who scattered repetitions, including hotel room numbers, of the number 42 throughout his novel as an expression of Humbert's fear of the constant workings of dark destiny he called "McFate" (see Chapter 5). The memory of Nabokov's 42 in particular might well have moved Kubrick to choose 237 as another means of revealing—and hiding—a number that in *The Shining* bears the full weight of the century's most terrible year.[59]

A final possible reinforcement for Kubrick's use of the 237 as a hiding place for the number 42 is a coincidence involving "The 'Uncanny'" in which Freud cites the example of a man who keeps coming across the number 62 (Freud had turned sixty-two the year before): "a cloakroom ticket . . . cabin on a ship . . . addresses, hotel rooms, compartments in railway trains."[60] Freud argues that such "involuntary repetition which surrounds what would otherwise be innocent enough with an uncanny atmosphere . . . forces upon us the idea of something fateful and inescapable, when otherwise we should have spoken only of 'chance.'"[61] And coincidentally, Freud's discussion of the uncanny recurrence of the number 62 begins on page 237 of volume 17 of *The Standard Edition* of Freud's works published in London in 1955. Did Kubrick use *The Standard Edition*? Diane Johnson is not sure, but recalls using a Modern Library one-volume collection of Freud's main writings.[62] But that widely published work, edited by American A. A. Brill, does not contain Freud's essay on the uncanny. At the very least, however, we know that Kubrick read of the recurrence of the number 62 in "The 'Uncanny,'" repetition mirrored in the appearances of the number 42 in *The Shining*. Both Nabokov, who disdained psychoanalysis, and Kubrick, who did not, exploited the very juxtaposition posited by Freud of chance and fate in the uncanny. For Kubrick, moreover, the subject is not just the individual, as it was for Nabokov, but history. Freud locates the source of the uncanny effect of recurrences in the infantile and instinctual compulsion to repeat, behavior both he and Kubrick found to be a characteristic of human history in general. Bound by the past, according to Freud and Kubrick, we are condemned to repeat it no matter how much we may seek to learn from it.[63]

The most indirect visual reference to 42 in *The Shining* serves to place it in its immediate historical context. After Wendy has slugged Jack with a baseball bat and shut him in the food locker, Grady intervenes to free Jack so he can murder his family. But Grady wants to be sure that Jack is up to the task, that he has, in his British expression, "the belly for it." As Jack and Grady converse at some length through the locker door, behind Jack are shelves of jars, bottles, and cans that surround him with American material plenty. Large cans of Calumet baking powder, with its Indian head logo, fill one shelf while *above* that is a shelf full of large cans of Tang, the drink of American astronauts (also an oneiric reference to Danny's *Apollo 11* sweater). The center of the shot is composed of Jack and a stack of boxes against the wall immediately to his left. One box in particular stands out since it not only shares the center of the frame with Jack but is chest-high with large numbers that stand out from smaller surrounding numbers and letters. The box itself contains cans of "Yellow Cling Sliced Peaches." The obtrusiveness of this particular object is evidenced by one particularly careful critique of the film that pairs the sliced peaches with a big container of Heinz tomato ketchup behind Jack as signs of "the father's desire to cannibalize one family to insure the 'survival' of another."[64] The prominent numbers on the box, 01439, serve to raise the symbolic discourse in the scene to the level of history. In line with the chief symbolic pattern of chronological numbers in the film, the number 01439 denotes the years of the outbreak of the two world wars, 1914 and 1939, that also bracket Kubrick's interwar setting. Directly above on the box is the number 39000, which appears on other boxes in the food locker and symbolizes the special minatory artistic status of the Second World War and its horrors, particularly those of the Holocaust represented by 42, the metonym for the year 1942.[65] Delbert Grady, the European, speaking through the door to Jack, thus represents the "Big Leagues" of the mass murder that is war in the twentieth century. That Kubrick during *The Shining* was, as ever, mindful of the Second World War has been recalled by the manager of the Timberline Lodge at the time, Tad Michel, who went to England as "Hotel Consultant" and had occasion to learn that Kubrick "was very well-versed in the history of World War II."[66] On the historical level of discourse in *The Shining*, therefore, Jack in this scene emerges, thanks to Grady, from his American house of plenty to a twentieth-century scale of murder in a hellish return of the repressed.

## "It Tends to Stain"

Three colors—red, blue, and yellow—are of significance in *The Shining*. The presence and cumulative effect of specific symbolic references to the Holocaust in the film increases the probability of similar specific associations among these colors in line with their more general meanings. In general, the palette in the film moves from thin, cold blue to intense, suffocating red and yellow. This reproduces the thematic color progression of Crane's *The Blue Hotel* from the cold ethereal environment of the Palace Hotel to the passionate red contingencies of earthly life and death in the Fort Romper saloon. This transition is evident in Jack's clothing, which passes from warm brown and green toward murky red and blue. Wendy and Danny, by contrast, start out in bright red and blue and move toward earthy brown and green representative both of the natural and nurturing soil of the family and of their potential fate at Jack's hands as corpses in the ground. The change in the film's palette occurs around the time Danny first comes upon room 237 and when Jack discovers that the Gold Room suddenly has a ghostly well-stocked bar.[67] The thematic continuity in this color transformation is demonstrated by the lettering on the sign outside the Gold Room that at first glance makes it appear to read "Cold Room" (featuring the musical stylings of "The Unwinding Hours").[68] For as Jack moves toward the murderous passion signified by red, he is doing so on behalf of the historical masters of the Overlook Hotel who live in the bluish Kubrickian high rooms of cold, transcendent—and, in *The Shining*, ghostly—authority. This use of color recalls the reverse but analogous change in the color of Frank Alexander's typewriter in *A Clockwork Orange* from red in an early domestic and conjugal scene (his wife, soon to be raped and to die, is dressed in red) to light blue in a second scene shot in exactly the same fashion and in which Alexander, now consigned to a wheelchair, has become a vengeful manipulator of politics. The same mix of bureaucratic calculation and murderous passion animates Jack to an even greater extent, since he represents *both* the murderous passion of his own—and human society's—devils and the cold, rational bureaucratic means by which modern mass murder is effected.

Red also assumes its usual symbolic meaning of danger in *The Shining*. Red fire alarms and bells appear repeatedly, particularly in scenes leading up to the transition in color just noted from violence in the offing to violence beginning to be played out.[69] Hallorann's telephone in Miami is red, as is his rental car inside and out; red Avis (French *avis* [warning], from the Latin *visere* [to contemplate]) Rent-a-Car brochures sit on the hotel desk as Jack phones Wendy about getting the job; the hotel's Sno-Cat is red; Danny is wearing a red jacket when he comes upon the Grady sisters in the hallway; and the cover of the paperback copy of *The Catcher in the Rye* that Wendy reads displays gold letters on a dark red cover almost exactly the color of the burgundy jacket Jack wears in the second, violent half of the film.[70] Then of course there is the blood flowing from the elevator, with its greater gravity since it is recall, warning, and prediction. While red has long been associated with warmth, seriousness, dignity, grace, and charm, it is of course the color of blood, of life *and* death, as well as of danger. In *The Shining*, the elevator's bloody discharge explodes into a lurid red spray from a thick flow of blackish purple that is the extreme union of blue-red that Goethe called "dark, turbulent, unbearable."[71]

Blue in *The Shining* carries, as we have seen, its traditional Kubrickian meaning of natural, emotional, and hierarchical cold. It is also linked closely to its traditional association with the transcendent and therefore with death and ghosts. Given the genre and the historical subtext to *The Shining*, the subject of death is particularly important in the color scheme of the film. We have already seen how the light blue credits at the beginning of the film scroll upward into the heavens. Among the entities with which Goethe identified the color blue along these lines were sky — and smoke, a juxtaposition also made by Holocaust survivor Wiesel in his poem "Never Shall I Forget."[72] Kubrick himself had forged a creative connection among the color blue, sky, and mass murder as early as the conclusion to *Dr. Strangelove* when Second World War chanteuse Vera Lynn sings of "blue skies" that "drive the dark clouds away," words that are satanically ironic in light of the mushroom clouds ending the world over which the song plays. In his own way as well, Kubrick in *The Shining* links the color blue to murder. Following King, the the film makes visual reference to the legend of Bluebeard as also dramatized in the fairy tale by Charles Perrault (1697) and the Bartók opera *Bluebeard's Castle* (1911). Bluebeard's young wife is given the keys to the castle but told never to open one specific room. She does, of course, and finds the bodies of Bluebeard's former wives.[73] By the 1970s, the story of Bluebeard had also become one metaphor for the descent of civilization into the machined mass slaughter of modern warfare and "liquidation." In March 1971, for example, linguist George Steiner gave a lecture entitled "In Bluebeard's Castle" at the University of Kent in Canterbury. The lecture focused on the growth of organized violence since 1789 and 1815 that culminated most significantly in the end of the European order in 1915 [*sic*] and in the Holocaust during the Second World War.[74] Finally, when Jack, asleep at his desk, has his dream of murdering his family, his Adler typewriter, once gray and black, has turned a rich solid blue as a symbol of deadly service to the cold hierarchy of the hotel.[75]

*The Dream of Jacob* | 237

More significantly, the Grady sisters, murdered by their father in 1970, also wear this blue mark of death. They appear to Danny dressed in identical blue dresses (Figure 9, color insert) and are, along with the woman in room 237, the chief representation in the film of murder behind closed doors. The girls first appear on the screen for just one second in the midst of Danny's Boulder vision of the elevator. This fleeting shot is repeated as Danny later tries the locked double door of room 237, a juxtaposition that also establishes their association with the legend of Bluebeard. In between these visitations, the girls appear while Danny is in the hotel game room during his parents' tour of the Overlook. He then confronts them coming around a corner on his Big Wheel in the old section of the hotel. They stand at the end of the hall dressed in blue and holding hands just as in his previous visions of them. Only this time they speak to him, asking him to come and play and stay with them "forever, and ever, and ever." What they mean is clear as Danny shines to their butchered bodies in the past lying in the same hallway in which he now sits in horror on his Big Wheel. The walls then, as now, are dressed in white or pale yellow wallpaper with a pattern of blue flowers (forget-me-nots?). The woodwork is a dull yellow, and a deep blue runner covers the center of the dark wood floors. Camera left hangs a red fire alarm and bell, while camera right a fire hose coils under glass.[76]

The prominence accorded the Grady sisters in the film, as contrasted to a single mention of them in the novel, is once again evidence of Kubrick's emphasis on human beings trapped in grotesque reality rather than a reliance on the staple supernatural conventions of the horror genre. The Grady sisters also represent another pair of doubles in *The Shining*, a common feature of Kubrick's films and the literature and cinema of the fantastic. Kubrick even doubles these doubles in the form of two young women of strikingly similar appearance who on closing day say goodbye to Ullman (and whose behinds Jack ogles) in a bright blue hallway outside the Torrance quarters. Ullman's breezy "Goodbye, girls" resonates with his recent recapitulation to Jack (and to us) of the Grady girls' murder, while Jack's ogling also accents in the manner of overdetermination characteristic of dreams the darkness underneath the polite conventions of male–female relationships.[77] The appearance, in both senses of the word, of the Grady girls in the film is also a function of Kubrick's own past as well as of the observed and feared world of that past. It has been widely noticed that the Grady sisters are reminiscent of a famous photograph by Diane Arbus, *Identical Twins* (1967). There can be little doubt of the influence of Arbus on Kubrick, since he worked with her. The Arbus photograph, too, has an uncanny quality, since the girls pictured are not twins but sisters who, like the girls who play the Grady sisters, look remarkably alike. Kubrick himself had two daughters of his own with Christiane, and there is somewhat of a facial resemblance between the Grady and Kubrick sisters, especially Anya, as well as with Kubrick himself as a boy.[78]

There is also an equally striking resemblance between the composition of this Grady girls scene in *The Shining* and another photograph Kubrick himself had taken many years before. And this similarity even suggests both a conscious and an unconscious construction in Kubrick's mind related to the Holocaust. In 1948 Kubrick was assigned by *Look* to photograph employees of the Electric Light and Power Companies. One of the photographs that appeared in the May 25 issue is of two girls saved from carbon-monoxide poisoning (Figure 10). As Kubrick biographer Vincent LoBrutto observes about these double images: "The Grady girls stay with the viewer long after *The Shining* has unspooled. The image of the two murdered girls standing side by side smiling into the camera as they court and taunt Danny Torrance resonates with a photographic history that goes beyond the imagination of Stephen King."[79] It is possible that there is an even broader historical continuity of form and content between Phyllis and Barbara (the name of Kubrick's sister and only sibling) and the representation of the Grady girls in *The Shining*. By the 1970s, as we have learned, artistic and public preoccupation with the Holocaust had reached unprecedented extent and intensity, and Kubrick on various levels of consciousness had been deeply affected by this spreading discourse. There are reasons to speculate that the intersection of Kubrick's lifelong concerns about the world with his experience and memory of his 1948 photograph decisively informed some of the personal and creative associations he was forming in the decade before he made *The Shining*, a film that, as we have seen, is the most personal and autobiographical of all his films.

The first connection along these lines that Kubrick, perhaps only subconsciously, might have made in terms of the 1948 photograph was that carbon monoxide was the gas the Nazis used at Bełżec to kill, among hundreds of thousands of others, the Jews of the Kubrick ancestral home of Probużna. While the *New York Times* carried reports beginning as early as 1942 of gassing at Bełżec and other locations, Kubrick knew about carbon monoxide being used at Bełżec from reading about it in Hilberg's book in the 1960s or 1970s. And the color of the dresses the Grady sisters wear might also have been partially determined by something else he learned from reading Hilberg, that in "the carbon monoxide camps the agony was prolonged.... Not only was the gassing operation longer in the carbon monoxide chambers it also left a bigger mess. When the gas chamber doors were opened, 'the bodies were thrown out blue, wet with sweat and urine, the legs covered with excrement and menstrual blood.'"[80]

There is yet another possible connection involving the color blue that Kubrick may have made along the same lines. Hilberg describes in great detail the Nazi switch from carbon monoxide to Zyklon B, a hydrogen cyanide gas the Nazis found killed much more quickly than carbon monoxide. At Auschwitz, the mass production of death by means of Zyklon B occurred in "huge underground gas chamber[s] ... complete with an electric elevator for hauling up the bodies" to the ovens in the crematoria directly above.[81] Zyklon B was a brand of pesticide that issued from the discovery of hydrocyanic acid in Germany in the 1780s. This acid was a derivative of the first modern synthetic dye developed in Berlin, the capital of Prussia, in 1704 and so became known as "prussic acid." In 1691 the Prussian army had adopted uniforms of both dark and light blue, and as a result the dark blue pigment itself had been named "Prussian blue." As early as 1813 a Berlin pharmacist had even

**SAVED TWO LITTLE GIRLS** Phyllis, 5 years old, and Barbara, 8, were overcome by carbon monoxide. Henry F. and Edward B., trained in life saving methods, rushed over in time to save two precious lives.

Figure 10

suggested affixing rags soaked with the acid to the bayonets of the Prussian infantry as an early form of chemical warfare.[82] It is therefore precisely this blue, as we observed in Chapter 6, that fills and "suffocates" the screen in *Barry Lyndon* with the head-on telephoto shots of the Prussian army marching in the Seven Years War (Figure 11, color insert). The other Kubrick film of the 1970s, the icily brilliant *A Clockwork Orange* with its Nazi regalia, also perhaps contains an instance of this (unconscious?) ongoing construction of color in the form of the Volkswagen run off the road that shows up light blue in the headlights of Alex's car.[83] And in the preparation of *The Shining* itself, as we have seen, Diane Johnson reminded Kubrick of the architecture of gas chambers and herself had juxtaposed the color blue and German shepherds as part of a novel about fear of pervasive murder that prompted Kubrick to hire her to help write his horror film. Thus even the cold blue light and air that fills the Overlook like a gas is in deep historical accord with the chambering claustrophobia effected through the progressive compression of time and space in the labyrinthine hotel.[84] The same association between closed space and lack of air is made, as we saw in Chapter 10, in the tight shot of the Torrances in their Volkswagen on the way up to the Overlook that also recalls the thin, strangulating blue air of altitude that is a symbol in *The Magic Mountain* of the passage from life to death.

Also as in *The Magic Mountain*, it is, however, yellow that is the most dominant color in *The Shining*. One indication of its importance is that Kubrick set the Saul Bass illustration for the original-release poster into a background of deep yellow, a design that also served as the cover of the new paperback edition of King's novel republished upon release of the film.[85] Like any color, yellow covers a wide range of associations, from happiness and warmth as the color closest to light to, as in *The Magic Mountain*, illness and death.[86] But in the early sections of *The Shining* yellow is a symbol of danger, as with Jack's yellow Volkswagen and the yellow tennis ball that rolls up to Danny and leads him to the opened door of room 237. According to Shelley Duvall, it is the Grady sisters who have rolled the ball to Danny as an extension of their invitation to "Come and play with us."[87] Yellow also appears early on in the film as a natural part of the realistic settings in *The Shining*, but these objects too take on—in formulaic anticipation, considered retrospect, or subsequent viewing—a minatory quality that adds to the other unsettling features of the film: a yellow laundry basket and wastebasket (both objects having to do with the disposal of dirt) in the kitchen of the Boulder apartment; a yellow duck peeking from behind the shower curtain in the bathroom; a record jacket in Danny's room with the word "TIGER" on a green and yellow background; and Wendy pouring bright yellow fruit cocktail into a brownish-yellow bowl as she listens in the Overlook kitchen to the television report of a woman's disappearance on a hunting trip.[88] The color yellow becomes "even more symbolically assertive" as the Overlook and Jack converge in violence and murder:

> The Grady murder corridor is decorated in yellow wallpaper; a lamp next to Jack's typewriter gives the paper a yellow texture; his face and eyes turn yellow like the

bourbon in his glass during his talk with Lloyd; the hallway into the Torrance apartment is decorated with yellow-flowered wallpaper; as Jack stands outside the bathroom with the ax, his face and the walls take on a yellowish glow from another lamp . . . and when he moves on his murderous course to intercept Hallorann, the hotel's interior lighting transforms the walls from daytime white into evening yellow. In addition, the gold corridor and the Gold Room convert the warmth and beauty of yellow (as in the aspens behind the credits) into into something akin to the unnatural and discordant.[89]

Yellow, even more so than red, is the color associated with the murders planned and perpetrated in the second half of the film. The scattering of Danny's toy trucks and cars around the hotel in the first half of the film is ominously reproduced in a windup tank with a yellow key on the bedside table in the Torrances' bedroom before and during Jack's attempt to reprise Grady's ax murder of his wife and children. In the old hall where the Grady girls were murdered, what was originally a different color—the white, *pace* Nelson, of the hallway wallpaper—is stained a pale yellow by the light to match the woodwork. In the Torrance bedroom, the light yellow woodwork is similarly deepened. This use of light indicates a murderous transformation of character, relationship, and event. In using yellow light in this way, Kubrick is once again commenting on the inextricability of good and evil, since it is ironic as well as tragic that the color of life's light and warmth becomes the messenger of death's dark and cold. The pink walls of the apartment suggest the pink walls of the original home, the womb, while their washing and framing with yellow, accompanied by the actual yellow flowered wallpaper in the entryway, prompts one to think of an early condemnation of the domestic suffocation of a woman's body, mind, and spirit, Charlotte Perkins Gilman's "The Yellow Wall-Paper" (1892), in which a woman locks herself in a room papered in yellow. This theme was expanded and modernized in Diane Johnson's *The Shadow Knows* from the fate of imprisonment to a woman's conviction that "we are going to be murdered."[90] Although Johnson was not influenced by Gilman's story and does not remember discussing it with Kubrick, the parallels with the film, including a parody of the haunted houses of Gothic romances, are striking. Not only is there the yellow wallpaper, but in the story there is also an anticipation of Jack's means of getting at Wendy: "Why there's John at the door! It is no use, young man, you can't open it! How he does call and pound? Now he's crying for an ax!"[91]

More so than with red or blue, it is the cultural and the historical meanings applied to the color yellow that take on greatest significance in *The Shining*. This is because the overall symbolic structure of the film constructed around history and the Holocaust—the span of years 1907–1921–1942–1970 represented by numbers and the similarities in symbol, structure, and purpose to *The Magic Mountain*—makes manifest specific cultural and historical associations with yellow. As in Appelfeld's *Badenheim 1939,* yellow has had a distinct symbolic as well as literal association in literature with the Holocaust. Kubrick himself had received early instruction in both the general and the specific historical and cultural constructions around the color yellow in particular. In the essay of his that Kubrick knew very well, "Color and Meaning," Sergei Eisenstein had taken yellow as his example of the use of color in film discourse. Inspired no doubt by George Gershwin's composition *Rhapsody in Blue* (1924), Eisenstein in his wartime essay proposes a "rhapsody in yellow" as part of an exaltation of reason applied to art in contrast to the "freedom from reason attainable among our fascist neighbors."[92] Yellow's associations with its immediate neighbor on the color spectrum, green, are negative in that green is linked directly with life and young life in particular, while greenish-yellow calls up images of decay and death. Eisenstein selects American poet Walt Whitman (1819–1892) as an example of artistic use of yellow as an evocation of life from the natural warmth of the sun but one that also recognizes the "minor key" of yellow's (and blue's) sign of death and decay.[93] In this context, the bright autumn yellow at the beginning of *The Shining* not only stands in contrast to the dark story to come, but is symbolically as well as naturally the harbinger of winter and death. Eisenstein then charts the ways in which Western culture in particular began to lend the color a sinister aspect antipodal to its positive natural associations. In ancient sacred languages, yellow was the color of both union of the soul with God and its opposite, infidelity. Christianity, according to psychologist Havelock Ellis, rejected the Classical love of red and yellow as symbols of joy and pride. As a result, in the Christian view yellow "became the color of jealousy, of envy, of treachery. Judas was painted in yellow garments and in some countries Jews were compelled to be so dressed. In France in the sixteenth century the doors of traitors and felons were daubed with yellow. In Spain heretics who recanted were enjoined to wear a yellow cross as a penance and the Inquisition required them to appear at public *autos de fe* in penitential garments and carrying a yellow candle."[94] A related American colloquial usage unmentioned by Eisenstein associates yellow with cowardice, an example of which is found in a single sequence from Agee's screenplay of Crane's "The Blue Hotel" that also refers to cheating and the "thirty pieces of silver" for which Judas betrayed Jesus.[95]

Eisenstein makes clear that the meanings ascribed to yellow are not inherent but are the sign of increasing social and cultural construction over time. Eisenstein chooses Goethe as an example, quoting the German poet's discussion of both concrete associations having to do with textures and a more psychological and social approach having to do with emotions and values: "771. When a yellow color is communicated to dull and coarse surfaces, such as common cloth, felt, or the like, on which it does not appear with full energy, the disagreeable effect alluded to is apparent. By a slight and scarcely perceptible change, the beautiful impression of fire and gold is transformed into one not undeserving the epithet foul; and the color of honor and joy reversed to that of ignominy and aversion. To this impression the yellow hats of bankrupts and the yellow circles on the mantles of Jews, may have owed their origin. Cuckold yellow is really nothing but a dirty yellow."[96] Then in acute reference to the Nazi war and atrocity engulfing his country and the world, Eisenstein notes parenthetically that the "yellow path" (as in Oz?) that he and his reader have been following "seems to have landed us among Nazi revivals of medieval darkness!"[97] At the very time these words were published, the Jewish community in the Netherlands, for one, was suffering under the Nazi edict that required Jews to wear a yellow Star of David that was "a sickly, jaundiced yellow suggestive of envy and misery . . . humiliation . . . and . . . ostracism."[98]

The fact that Kubrick, according to friend Alexander Walker, was a "keen student" of Eisenstein is thus crucial with respect to the use of the color yellow in *The Shining*.[99] It is further evidence that specific historical and cultural associations of this color are likely to have been in Kubrick's mind when he was conceiving and arranging the other symbols having to do with history in this film. The Eisenstein whom Kubrick knew was also keen on history. A major example of the use of color he cites in "Color and Meaning" is, remarkably enough since it was a black-and-white film, his own *Alexander Nevsky*. In this film, in much the same way that Kubrick interrogates genres by reversing conventions, Eisenstein switched the traditional associations of black and white: black (or dark) was associated with the heroism and patriotism of the Russians, while "the white robes of the Teuton *Ritter* [knights] were associated with the themes of cruelty, oppression and death."[100] In 1946 Kubrick's early friend Alexander Singer had begun introducing him to foreign films, including *Alexander Nevsky*, whose use of the classical music of Sergei Prokofiev (1891–1953), particularly in the famous battle on the ice sequence, Kubrick found captivating.[101] But there was even more to *Alexander Nevsky* than music and color. Eisenstein had created the film as a clear analogy to the threat of invasion by Nazi Germany (and Imperial Japan) in the 1930s. The German invaders in the film, the thirteenth-century Teutonic Knights, wear white robes with large black crosses, the standards they carry display eagles *sans* swastika but otherwise identical to those of the Third Reich, and the German soldiers wear helmets and ride armored horses that clearly invoke the infantry and panzer divisions that by the time "Color and Meaning" appeared in print had crashed across most of western and eastern Europe. All of this must have worked an influence on Kubrick, especially since Moses Hadas at Columbia had condemned the racist warrior ethos of the Teutonic Knights in particular. All this offers another important reason that the historical meanings attached to the color yellow must be taken into serious account when analyzing its use as a marker of very specific epochs and events in history in *The Shining*. Whatever the external influences of form or content upon his work, Kubrick was, as we know, a meticulous researcher and builder of his films. He certainly would have agreed with Eisenstein's own conclusion about the symbolic and affective use of color (and music, as we will see) when he read it: *"we do not obey some 'all-pervading law' of absolute 'meanings' and correspondences between colors and sounds—and absolute relations between these and specific emotions, but it does mean that we ourselves decide which colors and sounds will best serve the given assignments or emotion as we need them."*[102]

Kubrick was also familiar from his reading of Hilberg with the long tradition of marking Jews with yellow. In 1215, for example, the Fourth Lateran Council decreed that Christians should wear blue belts and Jews yellow belts.[103] He and his family were certainly aware of reports in the American press on the even more nefarious

Nazi practice of so marking Jews in occupied Europe from 1939 on. In late 1941 the *New York Times* ran a story cabled from Berlin that observed: "The compulsory wearing of the Star of David, imposed on the Jews in September, again called the plight of the Jew to the attention of the public, which had been permitted more or less to forget it."[104] And Kubrick later learned from Hilberg's systematic reconstruction of the Nazi bureaucracy of persecution of the three means by which Jews in Germany were identified: first by paper, through the issuing of documents identifying people as Jews; second by name, requiring in 1938 that Jews take the middle name Israel or Sara; and, third, in a decree of September 1, 1941, ordaining that all Jews over six years of age must wear a black Star of David on a yellow background with the word *Jude* in black at the center of the star. Hilberg details the devastating effect this had on Jews, in terms of both the paralyzing fear it produced and the advantage it gave to the authorities in identifying Jews for deportation and destruction.[105] Hilberg's concomitant emphasis on the helplessness of the European Jews, which has been challenged and qualified by subsequent research, would also have fit with Kubrick's dark view of a world of oppressors and victims.

Yellow was not only a means for the Nazis to identify Jews, but also a color that communicated the Nazi association of Jews with vermin and disease and thus the "biological necessity" of their extermination by means of a pesticide that first came into widespread use against the lice that carried the typhus endemic in eastern Europe and spread through immigration into Germany. As an expert on Napoleon, Kubrick certainly knew it was typhus that had devastated the Grand Army in Russia in 1812.[106] It is no accident historically as well as psychologically, therefore, that the yellow with which the Nazis marked the Jews was also the traditional color of the quarantine signs they erected around Jewish ghettos in eastern Europe warning of the danger of typhus and other diseases. (We recall the yellow flag of quarantine in Buñuel's *The Exterminating Angel*.) In Poland, typhus itself had for a long time been regarded as a disease particularly common among Jews, a perception the Germans fully racialized during the Second World War by labeling typhus "Jew fever" (*Judenfieber*).[107] It was in the dark wake of such beliefs and the resultant atrocities of the Second World War that German sociologist Theodor Adorno reinterpreted Kafka's "Metamorphosis" as an anticipation of Nazi treatment of the Jews as lice and of the extermination camps' "grotesque deception of a delousing installation . . . supported by signs 'to the baths' and 'to disinfection,' by false shower heads, dummy pieces of soap, the issuing of towels, 'changing rooms' with numbered hooks."[108] The war Nazi Germany unleashed with the invasion of Poland in September 1939 thus was not just the means of acquiring "living space" (*Lebensraum*) for the Master Race, but also designed to get at the greatest source of Jewish "contamination" as symbolized by the traditional association of the color yellow with diseases as well as with Jews. In *The Shining* this association between war and the persecution of the Jews is arguably represented in typical dreamlike fashion (like "Kosher Dill Slices" seen earlier?) by the legend "Yellow Cling Sliced Peaches" on the box with the numbers 01439 and 39000 which, as we have argued, symbolize the two world wars and in particular the Second World War and the

Holocaust. This resonates historically, if debatably, in *The Shining* with referents to European persecution of Native Americans, a theme Diane Johnson has confirmed intrigued Kubrick as a historical basis for the violent curse of the Overlook Hotel.[109]

There is, finally, one other instance of the symbolic use of the color yellow in *The Shining* that may also carry associations with the Holocaust. As Jack moves away from the Gold Room bar during the interwar ghost party, he bumps into a waiter—it is Delbert Grady—who is carrying a tray of drinks that spill all over Jack. Grady dismisses Jack's assurances of no harm done with the remark, "I'm afraid it's Advocaat, sir. It tends to stain."[110] Advocaat is an egg liqueur of Dutch origin. When the Dutch drove the Portuguese from Java, they inherited a drink known as *abacate*, made from a combination of brandy and the pulp of a Brazilian tropical fruit, the avocado, which the Portuguese had introduced to Indonesia. In the Netherlands the Dutch substituted egg yolks for the *abacate*, which made the drink even more yellow in color than its original greenish-yellow. Over time, the drink became known by the similar-sounding Dutch word for lawyer, *Advocaat*. How did Kubrick come to choose Advocaat for this scene? Considering its color and the importance of yellow in particular in scenes such as this one late in the film, we are entitled, even obliged, to search for symbols and meaning. There is in this, first of all, arguably another allusion to the history of European colonialism elsewhere referenced in *The Shining*: northern Europeans in North America; Kipling and the British in Africa and India; and the Portuguese and the Dutch in South America and Southeast Asia. Given the symbolic significance of yellow, it is likely that Kubrick started with color as the desideratum rather than with the name of the liqueur.[111] But Advocaat also links up with the Hoffmann story "The Sandman," discussed in Freud's essay on the uncanny, which suggests an intention to tie this scene in with the theme of the uncanny, the grotesque, and the Gothic. This is likely the case since the connection goes through the *bête noire* of "The Sandman," the lawyer (German *Advokat*) Coppelius. Kubrick's habitual working mode of contemplation and consultation over a long period of time would certainly have occasioned discussions with Christiane, Jan, and others about this subject. Such discussions could easily have touched upon one of the German words for lawyer even had Kubrick not already been familiar with it.

But where is a link to the Holocaust in this beyond the color yellow in and of itself? First, we should note that Coppelius is described in Hoffmann's story as "a horrible and unearthly monster who wreaked grief, misery, and destruction—temporal and eternal—wherever he appeared" and whose appearance was marked by "an ochre-yellow face, bushy grey eyebrows from beneath which a pair of greenish cat's eyes sparkled piercingly, and with a large nose that curved over the upper lip."[112] If Kubrick knew the story itself and not just Freud's analysis of it, he certainly would have recognized this description as identical with the Nazi caricature of Jews. Such loathsome caricatures were used to depict Jews and against Jewish doctors, bankers, and lawyers in particular. Such associations could also have marshaled creative reinforcement from knowledge of Harlan childhood memories of the yellow stars seen on occasion in both Germany and the Netherlands. In any case, both green and yellow show up in the Advocaat since there is a hint of green in the yellow from the Advocaat that marks Jack's dark red jacket and blue jeans. More significant is the construction around the action of the incident, which displays the usual Freudian and Kubrickian mechanisms common in dreams. Grady spills the yellow liqueur Advocaat on Jack just as the Nazi "law" marked Jews with the stain of prejudice, ostracism, and persecution. In line with the displacement and condensation of latent meaning in dreams, the perpetrator Jack (who, like Grady, will take the fall for his masters) is stained, like his yellow VW, with the sign of the victim just as Grady is marked since Jack, symbolizing his upcoming collaboration with him and finding an outlet for the anger he had not expressed for Grady's clumsiness, pats him on the back with a stained hand.[113] There is, finally, a similarity in all this to Kafka's "The Penal Colony" (1919), in which laws are literally and fatally inscribed by machine onto the flesh of offenders.

That this activity occurs in the Gold Room, moreover, reinforces allusions to the riches of Colorado exploited by the descendants of the new white European masters of America. It also invokes, in line with the yellow badge of condemnation, the religious and racist stereotype of greedy Jews amassing gold, as represented, for example, by one of the dissolves in Veit Harlan's *Jew Süss*. Some of the literature of cultural critique in the 1960s and 1970s regarded such accusations as projections of Western civilization's own anal obsessions with order and the accumulation of wealth as a means to deny the common mortality that is signaled by excrement. Eisenstein wrote along similar lines in "Color and Meaning" with respect to antipodal meanings within words: "gold, a symbol of *highest value*, also serves as a popular metaphor signifying—filth . . . the Russian language . . . contains the term 'zolotar' ('zoloto,' the root—gold), having the specific meaning of 'cess-pool cleaner.'"[114] In this sense, therefore, Kubrick's film recalls *The Gold Rush* (1925), re-released and shown in the Bronx at the RKO Fordham during the first week of August 1942. *The Shining* revisits Chaplin's film in terms of not only being an elaboration on that film's comic theme of "cabin fever" but also satirically depicting greed ("filthy rich"), murder, and cannibalism.[115]

## "The Most Horrible Dream I Ever Had"

The music in *The Shining* also bears the heavy historical weight of the Holocaust. With just a very few exceptions we shall presently discuss, the film's music comes from eastern Europe during the era of that region's greatest suffering and tragedy. It is somewhat ironic in this regard that *The Shining* follows the lead of *The Magic Mountain* in its use of music. Mann had adopted Richard Wagner's concept of a *leitmotif*, a unifying theme that preserves "the inward unity and abiding presentness of the whole at each moment."[116] Mann, however, rejected Wagner's surrender "to the irrational power of nature" in music, fearing the abandonment of reason in "the catastrophic music of Dionysian frenzy."[117] Kubrick, too, listened to Wagner.[118] But he never used a Wagner composition in any of his films, since he, like Mann, must have distrusted Wagner for his elevation of feeling over reason. Kubrick of course also had a sad advantage in this respect over Mann, for he had had occasion to observe the worst possible consequences of the loosing of "feeling with the blood" in the fact that Wagner scored much of the soundtrack for the Third Reich. This close identification with Hitler and Nazism made Wagner for Kubrick an inappropriate choice of film music, even—or especially—for *The Shining*. Wagnerian motifs also would have made it distractingly easy for a post-1970s audience to create associations with Nazism. For Kubrick as artist and individual, Wagner was too close to the beast to be as good an example of the cohabitation of good and evil as, say, Beethoven in *A Clockwork Orange*. And finally, although *The Shining*, like other Kubrick films, focuses on the perpetrators of evil—in this case, Jack—the music in the film is predominantly that associated with the eastern European victims. Because of his personal and artistic reservations about the cinematic depiction of the Holocaust, the more intuitive, indirect means of music too allowed him to confront and express this particular historical agony.

In general, as we have already seen, Kubrick always chose music appropriate for the mood of a given scene, seeking to exploit the quality of great music in deeply touching the emotions as well as the intellect. While Kubrick's facility with numbers, his abilities as a chess player, his penchant for organization, and his eye for detail marked him as left-brained and thus sensitive to the modern communication—by music as by other means—of ideas, he was also right-brained in his ability to intuit the meanings and effects of music congruent with a postmodern artistic indulgence in play.[119] But this combination of cognitive and intuitive artistic ability was also nourished by his great knowledge of, and interest in, history. And this meant that the music he chose appealed to him not only in terms of mood or of universal message but also on the basis of its reflection of—and his own reflection on—the historical and cultural conditions that influenced its aims and effect. Ever since *2001*, moreover, Kubrick's musical interests for the most part gravitated to the past, most often toward that music composed in nineteenth- and twentieth-century central and eastern Europe.[120] As we saw in Chapter 10, the popular dance music he uses diegetically in *The Shining* was drawn exclusively from the 1930s. These four tunes play during the interwar party Jack discovers in the Gold Room after storming out on Wendy at her suggestion that they leave the hotel. Another example of Kubrickian objects communicating ideas, all the songs have titles directly suggestive of the social and historical concerns of the film: "Masquerade" (1932), "Midnight with the Stars and You" (1932), "It's All Forgotten Now" (1932), and "Home (When Shadows Fall)" (1931). With the exception of two Carlos/Elkind electronic treatments ("Dies Irae" and "Rocky Mountains") and the unnerving atmospheric use of Ligeti's *Lontano* (1967) that accompanies Danny's first visit by the Grady sisters at the Overlook, the extra-diegetic music used in *The Shining*, more than in any other Kubrick film, reflects by theme and/or by time period the horrors—observed, anticipated, or recalled—of Nazism and the Second World

War. Two compositions, one by Hungarian Béla Bartók (1881–1945) and the other by Pole Krzysztof Penderecki, predominate, expressing "the disarray of contemporary humanity in the face of his maladjustment to the world, the failure of his beliefs . . . terrified by past cataclysms and agonized by the apocalypse to come."[121]

Musicologists have argued that the value and meaning of such music is formal, written for reasons intrinsic to the artistic form rather than to comment, consciously or unconsciously, on the outside world. But there is evidence that both Bártók and Penderecki were very much influenced by the historical events that intruded upon their lives and that imprints of such intrusion are left in the music to affect and inform the listener about the world in which the music was written. Even in the unlikely event of Kubrick having no knowledge of the lives and concerns of these composers, he would have intuited them through their expression in the music. This was especially the case since their historical concerns overlapped with his, for both Bartók and Penderecki were directly affected by the disasters of fascism, Nazism, and war. The former, a vehement anti-Nazi, immigrated to the United States in 1940, while the latter lived his youth in the Poland of German jackboots and extermination camps. Bartók refused to play in Germany after the Nazis came to power; his last performance there came seven days before Hitler became chancellor at the end of January 1933. In 1937 Bartók even forbade broadcasts of his music in Fascist Italy and Nazi Germany. His *Music for Strings, Percussion, and Celesta* (1936) was created as a "solemn" work for the tenth anniversary of a chamber orchestra in Basel, Switzerland: "it soars from the initial fugue, through a turbulent dance fantasy and a nocturnal monologue, to the hymnic dithyramb, thereby symbolizing in itself the Inferno of the age and its progress toward Paradise."[122] Just as Bartók's *The Miraculous Mandarin* (1923) had reflected the chaos in Hungary after 1921, his 1936 composition marked a direct and concerted attempt in part to confront and musically overcome the massing darkness of fascism in the 1930s.

But while Bartók, in spite of all his own troubles and those of the world, would maintain the overall optimistic structure of the 1936 composition in his music until his death in 1945, Kubrick characteristically as well as appropriately uses the one section of *Music for Strings, Percussion, and Celesta*, the "night music" of the third movement, an apprehensive adagio that reflects the black shadow of prewar Nazism. Kubrick plays over nine minutes of the adagio (which itself is only a little over eight minutes in length) in the course of three scenes early in the film. Kubrick places this music, by intuition and/or by calculation, in a manner congruent with its original historical context as well as with the mood of a film of horror. The nocturne plays exclusively beneath scenes early in the film that, like central Europe in the 1930s, quiver with dread at anticipated horrors to come. We first hear a sad creepy passage from the adagio after the dissolve from our initial sight of Jack and his typewriter to Wendy and Danny as they enter the hedge maze for the first time. Then, under strings, Bartók's signature single urgent celesta note rings as Jack approaches the model of the maze in the hotel lobby, the repeating and accelerating tempo of the note suggesting the germination in his mind of the single, piercing thought of murder. This music ends abruptly and loudly in Kubrick's parody of the startle effect with the title card "Tuesday." The same musical passage resumes in the middle of the next sequence as Danny rides his Big Wheel into the more modern wing of the hotel and passes the double, locked doors of room 237. The music continues unbroken to Jack typing, ending abruptly once again as he, interrupted by the arrival of Wendy, pulls a sheet of paper from the typewriter. The final segment of the Bartók is heard four scenes later. This time, following directly upon the *Summer of '42* scene, Kubrick quotes the opening measures of the piece, which begin with the deep, bulging notes of tympani followed by the single high celesta key struck sharply and ever more rapidly. The celesta creates a disquieting urgency that inspired the Ligeti theme written against Stalin that Kubrick would use in *Eyes Wide Shut*. The passage continues under the only conversation between Jack and Danny in the entire film, during which Danny first begins to intuit the danger to himself and his mother that his father represents. The soundtrack carries this apprehension into the next scene with a seamless segue into Penderecki's *The Dream of Jacob,* the film's "elevator music," as Danny plays in front of the elevator before venturing into the suddenly unlocked room 237.[123]

There is an additional, and ironic, aspect to the use in *The Shining* of *Music for Strings, Percussion, and Celesta*. Kubrick's historical blade is twisted by the music credits for the piece that appear at the end of the film. The performance Kubrick chose is from 1966 by the Berlin Philharmonic under the direction of Herbert von Karajan and recorded on Deutsche Grammophon. The Bartók credit appears first among the music credits, and it is the only one that includes the name of the composition, the conductor, the orchestra, and the recording company. There is a prosaic reason for this: permissions for Deutsche Grammophon recordings by von Karajan normally stipulated listing his name and that of the company.[124] This may be seen to be the case with *2001, A Clockwork Orange,* and *Barry Lyndon* as well as with *The Shining*. However, considering Kubrick's historical interests and his maniacal eye for detail, it seems likely that he was aware of the irony of having the music of the anti-Nazi Bartók played by a German orchestra under a German conductor. Of course, the Berlin Philharmonic in the 1960s and 1970s was not the same orchestra as it was under the Nazis. But, as we saw in Chapter 6, von Karajan had first risen to musical prominence during the Third Reich. This diegetic-cum-nondiegetic fusion of anti-Nazi composer and Nazi conductor appears to be another dreamlike construction built from Kubrick's Freudian conviction that good and evil, beauty and horror, are inextricably woven together deep in human character and history.

Given the close relationship of the extended Harlan family to the Nazi cultural empire under Joseph Goebbels and Kubrick's great interest in that particular realm of the Third Reich, it would not be surprising if he had long been aware of von Karajan's career as a conductor during the Third Reich, particularly since, as we also have noted, von Karajan was the object of American Jewish boycotts in the 1950s. Whether he knew of Bartók's anti-fascism is perhaps more open to question, but once again we should not be surprised if Kubrick's interest in the period and his wide reading gave him knowledge of that as well. His appreciation for irony would also have made him alert to the juxtaposition of anti-Nazi composer and former-Nazi conductor. And if he did not know before, the typically long gestation of Kubrick's films would have given him ample opportunity to learn of it, particularly since music is one of the last things added to a film. It is possible that the original inspiration for using Bartók was a line in King's novel about Wendy: "Today even Bartók would have made her sleepy, and it wasn't Bartók on the little phonograph, it was Bach."[125] But the key is not the state of articulation of Kubrick's inspiration at the start of work on a film, but the state and articulation of expression in the finished product. And even in the unlikely event that Kubrick had no inkling of historical irony in the prominent placement of these music credits, the irony is there and contributes to the effect on the audience of those symbols and representations relating to Nazi Germany and the Holocaust in *The Shining* for which there is considerable evidence of authorial intent as well as cultural influence.

In contrast to the Bartók composition, which presages the renewed outbreak of violence at the Overlook Hotel, the music of Penderecki accompanies the actual horrors of the Overlook past and present. This is significant, for Penderecki's father was a lawyer during the Second World War when the Nazis killed a large percentage of the lawyers in Poland.[126] Born in 1933, Penderecki watched Jews being taken away by the Germans and has devoted his subsequent postwar musical career to the exploration of the themes of tolerance and intolerance. His compositions therefore convey a universal human message about the presence and challenge of evil that is also intensely personal and emotional. His *Threnody for the Victims of Hiroshima* (1961), with its coruscating, burning electronic screams, is perhaps the most famous example of this preoccupation with suffering in history. A Second World War companion piece, the *Dies Irae* (1967), composed for a commemoration at Auschwitz, had grown out of personal experience: "the problem of the great Apocalypse (Auschwitz), that great war crime, has undoubtedly been in my subconscious mind since the war, when, as a child, I saw the destruction of the ghetto in my small native town of Debiça."[127]

Penderecki has most often conveyed his message in works based on Christian Scripture and liturgy, two of which Kubrick uses in *The Shining* to link Christianity, Judaism, and Poland into a cinematically reproduced locus for contemplation of the Holocaust. In keeping with the oneiric structure of the film as well as with his own personal and artistic commitment to indirect discourse on the subject of the Holocaust, Kubrick provides one extremely subtle visual clue to this geographic and historical construction. In so doing, Kubrick dramatizes the partial breaks in our repression of past horrors that allow only distorted fragments of the underlying events to be expressed in dreams. And since the Holocaust was the greatest horror of our or perhaps any time, it is buried the deepest and thus traces of it are especially rare, odd, and difficult to detect. This was particularly the case with Kubrick, as we have seen, for at whatever level of consciousness he chose to symbolize the geography of the Holocaust in this manner, his reluctance to confront the subject directly in his art shines through the fact that this particular detail requires special attention to detect. If one looks closely, one can see that the baseball bat with which Wendy slugs Jack bears the signature of Carl Yastrzemski. We know this because Wendy holds the side of the bat with Yastrzemski's signature facing the camera in fourteen extended one-shots in the scene that leads up to her at-bat. Most of the sequence is composed of Steadicam shot/reverse shots between a retreating Wendy and an advancing Jack so the name on the bat flashes on and off at us just like the 42 on Danny's jersey during his conversation with the doctor.[128] This underscores the dreamlike nature of the name's appearance as well as its significance as a sign of greater underlying meaning and association. Because the unconscious exerts constant pressure on the conscious mind, such symbols not only are overdetermined but also occur singly and without apparent relevance to the immediate context. Is the name on the bat important? Or was its choice arbitrary? Given the number of takes on which Kubrick usually insisted and the fact that the name is exposed to the camera in every one of fourteen separate shots over two scenes, intention seems evident. Moreover, there is no bat in the novel, only one incidental mention of a cap that Danny wears backward like Boston catcher Carlton Fisk. Narrative economy led Kubrick to create a bat from a hat and substitute it for the novel's roque mallet. And since the Torrances are from Vermont, it makes sense that Danny would have Red Sox paraphernalia. Kubrick's own commitment to realism would thus have prompted him to get a bat with a famous Boston player's name on it. But since there are consistent and dynamic levels of historical symbolism in the film, it is also likely that Yastrzemski was chosen since he was the only baseball star in the 1970s of *Polish* extraction. This connects his repeatedly displayed name with the musical references to Poland as the geographical location of the Nazi Final Solution.[129]

This same indirection applies to the use of Penderecki's music. Kubrick excerpts six Penderecki pieces in *The Shining: Polymorphia* (1961), *Kanon* (1962), *De Natura Sonoris No. 1* (1966), *Utrenja* (1969–1970), *De Natura Sonoris No. 2* (1971), and *The Dream of Jacob* (1974). Kubrick did not use Penderecki's *Dies Irae*, also known as the *Auschwitz Oratorio*. But the similarity of sections of the *Auschwitz Oratorio* and parts of *Utrenja* and *Polymorphia* led one reviewer of *The Shining* to hear Penderecki's *Dies Irae* in the film while another just as wrongly concluded that the Carlos/Elkind/Berlioz "Dies Irae" under the opening credits was that of Penderecki.[130] If Kubrick knew the *Auschwitz Oratorio*, he probably found it too direct by subject and by title for his indirect discourse on the Holocaust. And he may have found the musical qualities of the pieces he did pick more suitable for the manifest universal message of *The Shining* than the more idiosyncratic sonic ruptures of voice and instrument characteristic of the *Oratorio*. In any case, while the other Penderecki pieces lend only their eerie and dramatic quality to the mood of their respective scenes, *Utrenja* and *The Dream of Jacob* (also called *The Awakening of Jacob*) are closely related to the Holocaust subtext of the film. *Utrenja*, Ukrainian for "Morning Prayer," is a choral piece based on the Eastern Orthodox liturgy for Christ's Entombment and Resurrection. Kubrick, with savage irony, uses excerpts ("The dead shall rise again!") from this composition to underscore the emergence of the Overlook Hotel's murderous horrors near and at the end of the film: as Wendy defends herself with the baseball bat; when she sees Danny's scrawl of "Murder" in the bedroom mirror; when Jack axes through the bathroom door and chases Danny through the maze; and as Wendy discovers Hallorann's corpse, witnesses the Overlook's ghosts coming to life, and sees blood flowing from the elevator.[131] We are reminded of the deep and dark irony of the marriage of this music to these scenes since Easter represents the good tidings of the redemption of the world through Christ as well as the human victory over death. These are of course not the messages the hotel or the film sends. There is only the bloody history of the Overlook as a representation of the deadly horrors of the world.

It is *The Dream of Jacob* that assumes the greatest importance in the film's Holocaust subtext, for it is the music heard before, during, and after Danny's first, extended vision of the blood flowing from the hotel elevator. The opening ninety seconds of the piece play immediately after Jack's (reflexive) remark about Wendy being "a confirmed ghost story and horror film addict" that concludes the Overlook interview scene. It also accompanies Danny's vision of Jack's exploration of room 237, and it underscores Jack's own dream ("the most horrible dream I ever had") of killing his family.[132] Kubrick once commented on *The Dream of Jacob* when asked about the type of music he used in *The Shining*. After listing Bartók, Carlos and Elkind, and Ligeti, Kubrick said most of the music was by Penderecki. Then he brought up several coincidences, including the "strange coincidence" of *Jack's* dream being accompanied by *The Dream of Jacob*.[133] One can imagine that Kubrick initially chose the music and only later noticed the similarity of the names. But given what we know about Kubrick's meticulous preparation and investment of objects, colors, and music with meaning, we should assume some levels of intention with regard to the composition's name at one or more junctures in the construction of historical significance in *The Shining*. There is in any case a whiff of "doth protest too much" in this ostensibly offhand statement, as if Kubrick wanted to suggest something to us—and to himself—by seeming not to suggest it, that is, to dismiss the possibility of significance out of hand. Since he shared Freud's view of coincidence as personal and historical, he was most likely aware that instances of his father's name were anything but merely accidental. Dismissed intention would also be consistent with Kubrick's desire for the audience to construct meaning actively in response to the symbols and ideas he places in his films. The other remarkable "coincidence" in Jacob being his physician father's name is that Danny's first vision of the elevator occurs as he stares into the mirror of a *medicine* cabinet. We must also remember Kubrick's flirtation with Jung's concept of coincidence as a sign of larger forces at work in the world and as a basis for hope in higher, beneficent powers. This provided some psychological compensation for his basic Freudian pessimism about a cold, indifferent universe, a universe that most recently and horribly had permitted the Holocaust.

Jacob, moreover, is he in the Old Testament who is renamed Israel and whose sons are the ancestors of the twelve tribes of the Jewish people. The text is Genesis 28:16: "And Jacob awaked out of his sleep, and he said, 'Surely the Lord is in this place; and I knew *it* not'" (emphasis in original). Jacob is experiencing a torment of the soul in the presence of the divine. The context of a horror film itself reminds us of a psychic "slippery slope between gods and monsters."[134] In *The Idea of the Holy* (1917), Rudolf Otto describes the monstrous as a suitable expression of the holy. He points out that the Hebrew word for "dreadful," which Jacob uses to describe the place of the Lord, might be rendered as *unheimlich*, or "uncanny," in the sense of the Old English meaning of the word "awe-ful." Our awe at the mystery of the universe is shaded by fear and of a feeling of the uncanny, that which is familiar and strange, comforting and disquieting, all at the same time. This is the fearful realm of the ultimate questions of evil, suffering, and the possibility of redemption in the face of death. Richard Rubenstein, in *After Auschwitz*, has also suggested that the pact between God and man represented, among other things, by God's promise to Jacob that his posterity would inherit the land of Canaan has been a means by which human beings have disenchanted the world by making a transcendent God the repository of all value. Contained within this construction is the temptation to murder God so that all things may be permitted on an earth now freed from natural limits. This temptation is a manifestation of hubris, "man's rebellion against his limits," as acted out symbolically in the crucifixion of Christ. According to Rubinstein, Christians have often projected this wish to usurp God's moral authority onto the Jews, a myth the Nazis used in their campaign toward genocide.[135] The Nazi genocide itself drew much of its organizational strength from the Judeo-Christian disenchantment of the world that was a result of placing all moral authority in God. Instead of the ancient natural world of magic and divinity that human beings had to appease, now they only had to believe in and obey God. The Protestant belief in salvation through faith alone was the culmination of this trend. The world was now free to be organized by rational, secular authority and it is no accident, again according to Rubenstein, that it was in the land of the Protestant Reformation, Germany, that the modern bureaucratic order was first perfected. It was this system that Weber described as heartless and dehumanized and whose deadly efficiency under the Nazis Hilberg detailed in *The Destruction of the European Jews*.[136]

In *The Shining*, therefore, *The Dream of Jacob* is testament to violent repetition in history, for this music accompanies Jack's dream of the future (the murder of his family) as well as Danny's visions of the past (the Grady sisters) and the present (Jack in room 237). As with the shared stain of Advocaat, the overdetermination of dreamwork that also serves narrative economy comes into play since music associated with the victims of the Holocaust here underscores the dream of perpetrator Jack. Kubrick reinforces the explicit links among these dreams and visions by subtle but powerful visual clues in one darkly eloquent sequence that once again, by means of a Kafkaesque grotesquerie of the fantastic in the everyday, underscores in particular the modern mechanical means of mass murder. As Wendy checks the heating and electrical systems in the basement, we hear the deep, slow, opening chords of *The Dream of Jacob*. All around her in the dark boiler room filled with ominous machinery are reminders and prophecies of death. Right next to one of the boilers (real and not fake, as in *The 1000 Eyes of Dr. Mabuse*) and on top of a white refrigerator sits an antique picture of two little girls, the juxtaposed machines themselves a menacing symbol of the cold of human organization and the heat of murderous human passion. As the camera follows Wendy in a panning shot to the left, we see in one corner of a bulletin board over a desk a large Red Cross logo and in the other corner a sign on what to do in the event of choking. This anticipates the Torrances' discovery in the very next scene of Danny having apparently been grabbed around the neck by the naked corpse of the woman in room 237. The bulletin board itself is surrounded, realistically but also symbolically and presciently in terms of what Jack will discover in the bathroom of room 237, by pin-ups of nude women. The camera concludes its pan with the red "Danger High Voltage" warning sign on the hotel's large electrical box. Camera left in the resultant stationary shot is the dark gray flank of a large engine with a single yellow pipe elbowed off toward the edge of the screen. It is at this moment that Wendy hears Jack's cries and screams from his nightmare and rushes upstairs as the music builds in intensity behind her. As she leaves the boiler room, she passes a large red fuel tank, a red fire extinguisher, a red fire alarm with bell, a large red circular casing on the wall, another set of Red Cross and choking posters over a row of green washing machines, and, finally, several tall yellow institutional gas dryers. Cuts to Jack during this Steadicam exit sequence show him slumped forward in his chair with his head on the desk next to the red-and-white "crush-proof" pack of Marlboros and the now solid blue Adler typewriter.[137] *The Dream of Jacob* continues as Wendy lamely reassures Jack that everything is all right and as Danny arrives bruised and mute from his experience in room 237. The music then segues into *De Natura Sonoris No. 2* as Wendy accuses her husband of abusing Danny, and Jack, confused and then enraged, finds his way to the Gold Room for an appointment with Lloyd and Jack Daniel.[138]

For Kubrick, like Hilberg a Jewish child of the twentieth century, the most vital questions of history are those manifested most horribly in the Holocaust. The coincidence of the fearsome and the divine as expressed especially in *The Dream of Jacob* represents another of Kubrick's abiding concerns, the inextricability of good and evil, and precisely here in its highest cosmic sense and its worst terrestrial one. For Kubrick, the cosmic is the inscription of the mundane. As Kafka also held, the realm of the monstrous, the grotesque, and the uncanny is not that of demons beyond our world, but our own history: "the realm of primitive fears, of what has been forgotten and left behind, yet returns on occasion to plague us; it is the sense of alienation, of things we have made turning against us, of historical and social forces that we are helping to shape and that yet escape our control and even our knowledge; and it may be also be a sense of the 'wholly other' invading our lives, of a *deus absconditus* choosing, suddenly, to reveal himself."[139] Even this God is of our own making. In the modern era we have killed God while failing to assert a new morality in God's place. We are adrift, paradoxically, in an iron cage of institutions out of which fall, like hammers, the hard edicts of the heartless. The implications of *The Dream of Jacob* as composed and as placed within the dreamlike symbolic structure of *The Shining* are rendered brutally clear. The world has often been an abattoir and never more so than during the Holocaust. As, in Danny's inner eye, the mountain of blood cascades from the elevator (a mechanical Jacob's ladder), we are instructed in the single most terrible lesson of modern history: in twentieth-century Christian and Nazi Poland the descendants of Jacob—Israel's father and Stanley's—would awaken not, like the biblical Jacob, to salvation, but to slaughter.

## Fade to Black

*The Shining* can be appreciated and criticized on many levels. As a horror film, it has been read as subversive of the social order, as supportive of it, and as expressive or even exploitative of its worst violence.[140] As a map of the male psyche, it can be read as an Oedipal fantasy of paternal violence; as actual patriarchal violence within family, society, and culture; as misogyny; or as male fear and desire of return to the womb of the original caretaker. And, like most of Kubrick's films, *The Shining* engages both modern and postmodern modes of discourse and interrogation. But *The Shining* can most trenchantly be seen as the creative and conflicted result of a complex set of historical influences on Kubrick's life and work. His Jewish past had made a slow dissolve into a boyhood of pictures, both moving and still, in the deepening Nazi gloom of the 1930s and 1940s. A German presence composed of contemporary history and the tradition of Expressionist cinema crosscut to a Cold War montage of Hollywood and Harlans. And just when the world was belatedly discovering the Holocaust during the 1960s and 1970s, Kubrick was framing his *oeuvre* in new and even darker dimensions. *The Shining* thus became the chief personal and artistic expression of Kubrick's ongoing struggle with the ghosts of the Holocaust. That Kubrick's response was genuine, deep, and creative cannot be doubted, although its indirect articulation in his films has made it less than accessible. But once this indirection has been deciphered, the integrity and richness of Kubrick's approach shines through and, especially in *The Shining*, can be seen to connect with larger and widely recognized themes and forms in his *oeuvre* and within Western culture.

Whatever the virtues or limitations of his creative aims and means with respect to the Holocaust in *The Shining*, Kubrick follows his approach to the very end of the film, concluding the soundtrack near the close of white credits on a black screen—when everyone will have left the theater—with the crackle of applause and the drone of conversation following a British dance number recorded in 1932: "Midnight with the Stars and You."[141] The title of this song is a perfect expression of Kubrick's view of the world: not the romantic rendezvous under the stars, but alone—dangerously—with another human being in the dark deep of night beneath the cold, silent emptiness of space. Dance too, as we have seen, is a symbol in Kubrick's cinema of the dangerous coupling or opposition of fear and desire. But the Holocaust is too black a subject for such a sedate symbol. In *The Shining* we view dancing just once, and barely, far in the background of two extended shots of Jack, to the tune of "Midnight with the Stars and You," at the postwar/interwar/prewar party.[142] At the very end of the film, the dance is over. The message is clear and, ironically and appropriately, unheard. We are that oblivious and complicit audience of applauding dancers on the cusp of Nazi power, in our century, the century of genocide.

# NOTES

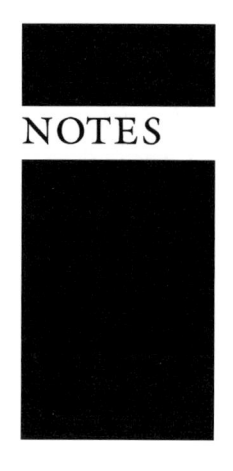

## Chapter 1

1. *The Shining,* DVD, scene 4, 11.40–12:08.
2. William Wilson, "Riding the Crest of the Horror Craze," 63.
3. David Denby, "Death Warmed Over," 61; Pauline Kael, "Devolution," 135.
4. James. B. Harris, personal communication, September 9, 1998.
5. Natalie Zemon Davis, "Trumbo and Kubrick Argue History," 186.
6. Peter Brunette, "Post-Structuralism and Deconstruction," in *Film Studies: Critical Approaches,* ed. John Hill and Pamela Church Gibson (Oxford: Oxford University Press, 2000), 89–93.
7. Philip Strick and Penelope Houston, "Modern Times: An Interview with Stanley Kubrick" (1972), in Gene D. Phillips, ed., *Stanley Kubrick: Interviews,* 136; cf. Frederic Raphael, "The Pumpkinification of Stanley Kubrick."
8. Walter Metz, "A Very Notorious Ranch, Indeed: Fritz Lang, Allegory, and the Holocaust," 74; Morris Dickstein, "Literary Theory and Historical Understanding," *Chronicle Review,* May 23, 2003, B8, 9; Thomas Windschuttle, *The Killing of History: How Literary Critics and Social Theorists Are Murdering Our Past* (New York: Free Press, 1997), 124.
9. John Baxter, *Stanley Kubrick,* 60; Hans Feldmann, "Kubrick and His Discontents," 192. On Baxter's quotation without attribution of interviews with Kubrick, see also Gene D. Phillips, "Meeting Mr. Kubrick," *Sight and Sound* 10:6 (June 2000): 64.
10. Nancy Chodorow, *The Reproduction of Mothering: Psychoanalysis and the Sociology of Gender* (Berkeley: University of California Press, 1978), 181, 198, 214.

11. Dominick LaCapra, *Representing the Holocaust: History, Theory, Trauma* (Ithaca: Cornell University Press, 1994), 207; Slavoj Žižek, *Looking Awry: An Introduction to Jacques Lacan through Popular Culture* (Cambridge, Mass.: MIT Press, 1991).
12. Dana Dragunoiu, "Psychoanalysis, Film Theory, and the Case of *Being John Malkovich*," *Film Criticism* 16:2 (Winter 2001/2002): 12.
13. Dragunoiu, "Psychoanalysis," 6–7.
14. Dragunoiu, "Psychoanalysis," 7; Laura Mulvey, "Visual Pleasure and Narrative Cinema" (1975), in *Feminist Film Theory: A Reader*, ed. Sue Thornham (New York: New York University Press, 1999), 58–69
15. Slavoj Žižek, *The Sublime Object of Ideology* (London: Verso, 1989), 157.
16. Luis Mainar, *Narrative and Stylistic Patterns in the Films of Stanley Kubrick*, 241, 244; Victoria E. Bonnell and Lynn Hunt, eds., *Beyond the Cultural Turn: New Directions in the Study of Society and Culture* (Berkeley: University of California Press, 1999), 13.
17. Žižek, *Looking Awry*, 99.
18. Baxter, *Stanley Kubrick*, 174.
19. Pat J. Gehrke and Gina Ercolini, "Subjected Wills"; Pat J. Gehrke, "Deviant Subjects in Foucault and *A Clockwork Orange*"; Metz, "Notorious Ranch," 78.
20. Mark Crispin Miller, "Kubrick's Anti-Reading of *The Luck of Barry Lyndon*," 240.
21. Stanley Kubrick, "Words and Movies," 14.
22. Quoted in Frederic Raphael, *Eyes Wide Open*, 75.
23. Christiane Kubrick, quoted in Urs Jenny and Martin Wolf, "Er war einfach schüchtern," 196; Peter Bogdanovich, "What They Say About Stanley Kubrick," 25, 44.
24. Robert Wohl, "Heart of Darkness: Modernism and Its Historians," *Journal of Modern History* 74 (2002): 573–621; Ilan Avisar, *Screening the Holocaust: Cinema's Images of the Unimaginable* (Bloomington: Indiana University Press, 1988), 181.
25. *A Clockwork Orange*, DVD, scene 14, 36.37–42.43; Robert P. Kolker, "*A Clockwork Orange* . . . Ticking," 35; Krin Gabbard and Shailja Sharma, "Stanley Kubrick and the Art Cinema," 85, 96, 98.
26. Robert Kolker, *A Cinema of Loneliness*, 162, 167–68.
27. Michel Ciment, *Kubrick*, 163; Eric Nordern, "*Playboy* Interview: Stanley Kubrick" (1968), in Phillips, ed., *Interviews*, 70–71; Baxter, *Stanley Kubrick*, 174, 199; Kolker, *A Cinema of Loneliness*, 162, 167–68.
28. Peter J. Loewenberg, "Freud as a Cultural Subversive," *Annual of Psychoanalysis* 24 (2001): 129; Gehrke and Ercolini, "Subjected Wills."
29. Quoted in Alexander Walker, *Stanley Kubrick*, 38.
30. Noel King, "Hermeneutics, Reception Aesthetics, and Film Interpretation," in Hill and Gibson, eds., *Film Studies*, 210–19; Jostein Gripsrud, "Film Audiences," in Hill and Gibson, eds., *Film Studies*, 200–209.
31. Quoted in Walker, *Stanley Kubrick*, 37–38.
32. Jan Harlan, *Stanley Kubrick: A Life in Pictures*, DVD, scene 12, 42.28–35.
33. Frederic Raphael, quoted in Ciment, *Kubrick*, 269.
34. Tony Pipolo, "The Modernist and the Misanthrope," 10; Richard L. Rubenstein, *The Cunning of History: Mass Death and the American Future* (New York: Harper & Row, 1975), 92; Max Weber, *The Protestant Ethic and the "Spirit" of Capitalism*, ed. and trans. Peter Baehr (New York: Penguin, 2002), 120–21, 124.
35. *2001: A Space Odyssey*, DVD, scene 3, 19.43–53; Mark Crispin Miller, "*2001*: A Cold Descent"; Mainar, *Narrative and Stylistic Patterns*, 30; Geoffrey Cocks, James Diedrick,

and Glenn Perusek, "Deep Focus: An Introduction," in Cocks, Diedrick, and Perusek, eds., *Depth of Field;* David Hughes, *The Complete Kubrick,* 148.
36. *The Shining,* DVD, scene 11, 37.30–38.00.
37. Baxter, *Stanley Kubrick,* 333.
38. Dana S. Pollan, "Materiality and Sociality," 97.
39. Walker, *Stanley Kubrick,* 271.
40. Phillips, ed., *Interviews,* 138.
41. Quoted in Ciment, *Kubrick,* 167.
42. Mark Mazower, "Violence and the State in the Twentieth Century," *American Historical Review* 107 (2002): 1169; Rubenstein, *Cunning of History,* 86; Avisar, *Screening the Holocaust,* 179–80.
43. Natalie Zemon Davis, "Film as Historical Narrative," in Davis, *Slaves on Screen,* 5.
44. Natalie Zemon Davis, *The Return of Martin Guerre* (Cambridge, Mass.: Harvard University Press, 1983); Marc Ferro, *Cinema and History,* trans. Naomi Greene (Detroit: Wayne State University Press, 1988).
45. Diane Johnson, "Stanley Kubrick," 28; see also Baxter, *Stanley Kubrick,* 60
46. For example, Pauline Kael, "Kubrick's Golden Age," *New Yorker,* December 27, 1975, 68.
47. Kolker, *Cinema of Loneliness,* 98, 99.
48. See, for example, Pauline Kael, "*A Clockwork Orange:* Stanley Strangelove"; Michael Harrington, "Painful Weight of Pretension," *Spectator,* July 24, 1999, 36; and Lee Russell, "Stanley Kubrick," *New Left Review* 26 (Summer 1964): 73.
49. Thirty-fourth International Film Festival La Biennale di Venezia, "Tribute to Stanley Kubrick," www.aiwass.freeserve.co.uk/memories/page 14.htm., July 29, 1999; Stanley Kauffmann, "The Dulling," *New Republic,* June 14, 1980, 26–27; Stanley Kauffmann, "Blank Cartridge," *New Republic,* July 27, 1987, 28.
50. Patricia Moraz, "Il Faut Courir le Risque," 20.
51. Anthony Lane, "The Last Emperor," *New Yorker,* March 22, 1999, 120–23; Matthew Baigell, *Jewish-American Artists and the Holocaust* (New Brunswick: Rutgers University Press, 1997), 18–19, 41–42; Anna Freud, *The Ego and the Mechanisms of Defense,* rev. ed. (New York: International Universities Press, 1966), 109–21, 134n; Anna Freud and Dorothy Burlingham, *War and Children* (New York: Medical War Books, 1943), 20–24, 67–70; Baxter, *Stanley Kubrick,* 254.
52. Andrey Tarkovsky, *Time Within Time: The Diaries, 1970–1986,* trans. Kitty Hunter-Blair (Calcutta: Seagull, 1991), 56; Katharina Kubrick Hobbs FAQ, 7.
53. Thomas Allen Nelson, *Kubrick,* 8; Walker, *Stanley Kubrick,* 13; Tim Cahill, "The *Rolling Stone* Interview: Stanley Kubrick" (1987), in Phillips, ed., *Interviews,* 199; Rainer Rother, "Das Kunstwerk als Konstruktionsaufgabe," 393; Penelope Gilliat, "Heavy Metal," 22.
54. Mainar, *Narrative and Stylistic Patterns,* 16, 41; Robert B. Kolker, "Film Text and Film Form," in Hill and Gibson, eds., *Film Studies,* 14; Nelson, *Kubrick,* 14; cf. Judy Lee Kinney, "Mastering the Maze," *Quarterly Review of Film Studies* 9 (Spring 1984): 138–42.
55. Stanley Kubrick, quoted in Vincent LoBrutto, *Stanley Kubrick,* 418; Mainar, *Narrative and Stylistic Patterns,* 5; Judy Lee Kinney, "Text and Pretext: Stanley Kubrick's Adaptations," 4, 22–23, 184.
56. Walker, *Stanley Kubrick,* 208; Cédric Anger, "Le Dernier Expressioniste," 28.

57. Penelope Houston, "Kubrick Country" (1971), in Phillips, ed., *Interviews*, 110; Michael Herr, *Kubrick*, 84.
58. Herr, *Kubrick*, 7–8.
59. Raphael, *Eyes Wide Open*, 108.
60. Quoted in Herr, *Kubrick*, 53.
61. Joseph Conrad, *Heart of Darkness* (New York: Dover, 1990), 4.
62. Raphael, *Eyes Wide Open*, 151.
63. Harlan, *A Life in Pictures*, DVD, scene 22, 1:56.31–1:57; see also 1:56.11–17; Christiane Kubrick, personal communication, November 20, 2002.
64. Lester D. Friedman, "'Canyons of Nightmare': The Jewish Horror Film," in *Planks of Reason: Essays on the Horror Film*, ed. Barry Keith Grant (Metuchen, N.J.: Scarecrow, 1984), 142, 147; cf. Walker, *Stanley Kubrick*, 30. For example, Kubrick admired Jiri Menzel's *Closely Watched Trains* (1966), a film about Hungary in the Second World War in this vein (Hobbs FAQ, 7).
65. Quoted in Christiane Kubrick, *Stanley Kubrick*, 101.
66. Theodor Adorno and Max Horkheimer, *Dialectic of Enlightenment*, trans. John Cumming (New York: Herder and Herder, 1972), 179; Jean-François Lyotard, *The Postmodern Condition: A Report on Knowledge*, trans. Geoff Bennington and Brian Massumi (Minneapolis: University of Minnesota Press, 1984), 6.
67. Annette Insdorf, *Indelible Shadows: Film and the Holocaust*, 2nd ed. (New York: Random House, 1990); Judith E. Doneson, *The Holocaust in American Film* (Syracuse: Syracuse University Press, 2002).
68. Raphael, *Eyes Wide Open*, 153.
69. Raphael, *Eyes Wide Open*, 120; cf. Vincent LoBrutto, "The Written Word and the Very Visual Stanley Kubrick."
70. Joseph Gelmis, "The Film Director as Superstar: Stanley Kubrick" (1970), in Phillips, ed., *Interviews*, 90; Phillips, ed., *Interviews*, 133.
71. Lea Wernick Fridman, *Words and Witness: Narrative and Aesthetic Strategies in the Representation of the Holocaust* (Albany: State University of New York Press, 2000), 6.
72. Saul Friedlander, "Trauma, Transference, and 'Working Through,'" *History and Memory* 4 (1992): 51.
73. Steven Alan Carr, "The Holocaust in the Text: Victor Hugo's *Les Misérables* and the Allegorical Film Adaptation," *Film Criticism* 27:1 (2002): 51–2, 64; Omer Bartov, *Murder in Our Midst: The Holocaust, Industrial Killing, and Representation* (New York: Oxford University Press, 1996), 171–72, 223n55; Avisar, *Screening the Holocaust*, 87; Insdorf, *Indelible Shadows*, 126; David Dresser, "The Return of the Repressed: The Jew on Film," *Quarterly Review of Film Studies* 9:2 (1984): 131.

## Chapter 2

1. Cemetary [sic] Release, n.d., First Probuzna [sic] Sick Benevolent Society, RG 1017, Yivo Institute for Jewish Research, New York; Francis J. Loperfido, *A Medical Chronicle of the Bronx* (New York: Bronx County Medical Society, 1964), 19, 21, 23, 25, 27, 28.
2. Baxter, *Stanley Kubrick*, 17; LoBrutto, *Stanley Kubrick*, 7–11; Beth S. Wenger, *New York Jews and the Great Depression: Uncertain Promise* (New Haven: Yale University Press, 1996), 83.

3. LoBrutto, *Stanley Kubrick*, 5–7; Ship Arrivals, Reel T-504, National Archives of Canada, Ottawa; Hersh Kubrik, Petition for Naturalization, August 7, 1912; Elias Kubrik, Petition for Naturalization, July 12, 1910, New York City Hall of Records.
4. Passenger Records, www.ellisisland.org, September 16, 2002.
5. John Bodnar et al., *Lives of Their Own: Blacks, Italians, and Poles in Pittsburgh, 1900–1960* (Urbana: University of Illinois Press, 1982), 24–25, 27, 175–76; Linda Kubrick, personal communication, February 2, 2001.
6. Richard Narva, personal communication, January 29, 2002.
7. Piotr Wróbel, "The Jews of Galicia under Austrian-Polish Rule, 1867–1918: Part II," *Galitzianer* 8:4 (August 2001): 14.
8. Suzan Wynne, "Demographic Records of Galicia, 1772–1919," *Galitzianer* 1:1 (Fall 1993): 16.
9. Piotr Wróbel, "The Jews of Galicia under Austrian-Polish Rule, 1867–1918: Part I," *Galitzianer* 8:2, 3 (May 2001): 17.
10. Daniel Kohn, personal communication, January 13, 2001.
11. Alexander Beider, *A Dictionary of Jewish Surnames from the Russian Empire* (Teaneck, N.J.: Avotaynu, 1993), 347.
12. Pages of Testimony, Hall of Names, Yad Vashem, Jerusalem.
13. *Galitzianer* 2:2 (Winter, 1994/1995): 15.
14. Bernard Papernik, personal communication, February 18, 2001.
15. Bernard Papernik, personal communication, June 19, 2001; Pauline Chernichaw, personal communication, March 15, 2001.
16. Bernard Papernik, personal communication, February 18, 2001; Linda Kubrick, personal communication, February 2, 2001.
17. Passenger Records, www.ellisisland.org, September 16, 2002.
18. Probezhna Jewish Community, Births, Warsaw USC Archives, Warsaw, Poland.
19. French Deportation Lists, Yad Vashem Archives, Jerusalem; Serge Klarsfeld, *Memorial to the Jews Deported from France* (New York: B. Klarsfeld Foundation, 1983), 303.
20. Thomas Sandkühler, "Judenpolitik und Judenmord in Distrikt Galizien, 1941–1942," in Ulrich Herbert ed. *Nationalsozialistische Vernichtungspolitik, 1939–1945*, (Frankfurt a.M.: Fischer, 1998), 142; Thomas Sandkühler, *"Endlösung" in Galizien* (Bonn: Dietz, 1996), 250; Roza Rut Dobrocka, Beglaubigte Übersetzung, February 4, 1965, 208 AR-Z 239/59, Volume 2, 718, Bundesarchiv, Aussenstelle Ludwigsburg, Germany; Dieter Pohl, *Nationalsozialistische Judenverfolgung in Ostgalizien, 1941–1944* (Munich: Oldenbourg, 1996), 240; Christopher Browning, *Ordinary Men: Reserve Police Battalion 101 and The Final Solution in Poland*, rev. ed. (New York: HarperCollins, 1992), 132; Georg Tessin, "Die Stäbe und Truppeneinheiten der Ordnungspolizei," in *Zur Geschichte der Ordnungspolizei 1936–1945* (Coblenz, 1957), 2:98; Raul Hilberg, *The Destruction of the European Jews*, 148, 312–17, 329–30.
21. Benio Bazar, Verhandlungsniederschrift, October 31, 1966, 208 AR-Z 239/59, Volume 9, 3345. Today Probużna is Probezhna in Ukraine; see Miriam Weiner, *Jewish Roots in Ukraine and Moldova* (New York: YIVO Institute, 1999), 204–5, 498–99, 576.
22. Rudolf Reder, *Bełżec* (Cracow: Fundacja Judaica, 1999), 90
23. Bazar, Verhandlungsniederschrift, 3345; Martin Gilbert, *Atlas of the Holocaust* (New York: Morrow, 1993), 128; Sandkühler, *"Endlösung,"* 253, 254; Pohl, *Judenrverfolgung*, 243; Werner Präg and Wolfgang Jacobmeyer, eds., *Das Diensttagebuch des deutschen Generalgouverneurs in Polen, 1939–1945*, (Stuttgart: Deutsche Verlags-

Anstalt, 1975), 509, 521; *Pinkas Hakehillot Encyclopedia of Jewish Communities: Poland,* vol. 2, *Eastern Galicia* (Jerusalem: Yad Vashem, 1980), 422; Weiner, *Jewish Roots in Ukraine,* 204.

24. Pohl, *Judenverfolgung,* 240.
25. Alexander Walker, "Inexactly Expressed Sentiments about the Most Private Person I Know," 301.
26. Peter Gay, *Freud: A Life for Our Time* (New York: Norton, 1988), 506; Harlan, *A Life in Pictures,* DVD, scene 2, 5.32–53.
27. Wenger, *New York Jews,* 91–92, 197–201.
28. Stanley Kubrick, quoted in Ciment, *Kubrick,* 196.
29. Christiane Kubrick, personal communication, November 20, 2002; Herr, *Kubrick,* 19, 21, 22.
30. LoBrutto, *Stanley Kubrick,* 9; Bronx County Historical Society, personal communication, October 4, 2002.
31. Walker, *Stanley Kubrick,* 373.
32. Hobbs FAQ, 4; Christiane Kubrick, quoted in Nick James, "At Home with the Kubricks," 15.
33. LoBrutto, *Stanley Kubrick,* 10–13.
34. LoBrutto, *Stanley Kubrick,* 20–22.
35. LoBrutto, *Stanley Kubrick,* 10; Ron Magid, "Quest for Perfection," 41.
36. Wróbel, "Jews of Galicia, Part I," 22; Ben Solomowitz, "Brody," *Galitzianer* 7:4 and 8:1 (February 2001): 12.
37. Raphael, *Eyes Wide Open,* 74.
38. John M. Efron, *Medicine and the German Jews: A History* (New Haven: Yale University Press, 2001), 41–44, 64–65, 82–86, 89–91.
39. The Society of the Lying-In Hospital of the City of New York, *Annual Report 1928,* 9–10, New York Weill Cornell Medical Center Archives, New York.
40. Paul Starr, *The Social Transformation of American Medicine* (New York: Basic Books, 1982), 175–76.
41. Ken Adam, quoted in Bogdanovich, "Stanley Kubrick," 25; Anya Kubrick, quoted in James, "At Home with the Kubricks," 13.
42. Baxter, *Stanley Kubrick,* 13.
43. LoBrutto, *Stanley Kubrick,* 31, 39; Baxter, *Stanley Kubrick,* 346.
44. LoBrutto, *Stanley Kubrick,* 92–93, 101; Baxter, *Stanley Kubrick,* 84, 91; Walter and Gisela Sobotka, "The Story of Ruth Sobotka" (1968), www.users.sisna.com/ruth sobotka/storyruth.htm, September 10, 2002; see also Kirk Douglas, *The Ragman's Son: An Autobiography* (New York: Simon and Schuster, 1988), 186; Michelle G. Turner, "Ruth Sobotka (1925–1967)," unpub. ms.
45. Christiane Kubrick, *Stanley Kubrick,* 19–29.
46. Craig McGregor, "Nice Boy from the Bronx?" 13; Christiane Kubrick, *Stanley Kubrick,* 82; Harlan, *A Life in Pictures,* DVD, scenes 2, 3.22–26; 8, 23.38–42; Baxter, *Stanley Kubrick,* 346; LoBrutto, *Stanley Kubrick,* 478.
47. Quoted in Bogdanovich, "Stanley Kubrick," 21.
48. Quoted in LoBrutto, *Stanley Kubrick,* 13.
49. LoBrutto, *Stanley Kubrick,* 13, 26–28, 58–70, 77, 78–79, 80–82, 86, 87–88, 95, 96, 98, 104, 114, 118–20, 123–24, 148–50; Baxter, *Stanley Kubrick,* 25, 34–35, 37–39, 45–46, 49, 50, 55, 63, 94, 105; Renaud Walter, "Entretien avec Stanley Kubrick," 30.

50. LoBrutto, *Stanley Kubrick*, 257.
51. Christiane Kubrick, *Stanley Kubrick*, 75; Christiane Kubrick, quoted in Bogdanovich, "Stanley Kubrick," 22; Tony Curtis and Barry Paris, *Tony Curtis: The Autobiography* (New York: Morrow, 1993), 26, 181, 185, 256.
52. Ginna, "The Odyssey Begins," 17.
53. Walker, "Inexactly Expressed Sentiments," 302; Baxter, *Stanley Kubrick*, 303.
54. Marie Windsor and Colleen Gray, quoted in Bogdanovich, "Stanley Kubrick," 21; Baxter, *Stanley Kubrick*, 60, 73, 74; Paul Mazursky, quoted in Harlan, *A Life in Pictures*, DVD, scene 5, 11.25–33.
55. Ciment, *Kubrick*, 146–47; Baxter, *Stanley Kubrick*, 300.
56. Christiane Kubrick, quoted in Bogdanovich, "Stanley Kubrick," 22; Christiane Kubrick, *Stanley Kubrick*, 28, 53, 62, 64, 87, 106; Christiane Kubrick, quoted in Jack Kroll, "Kubrick's Brilliant Vision," 30; Baxter, *Stanley Kubrick*, 60, 67, 73, 74; LoBrutto, *Stanley Kubrick*, 41, 80, 93, 98.
57. Peter Loewenberg, "Freud, Schnitzler, and *Eyes Wide Shut*."
58. Baxter, *Stanley Kubrick*, 18, 20; LoBrutto, *Stanley Kubrick*, 10; *Chess Fever* (Vsevolod Pudovkin, 1925), a film set in a Polish revolt against Russia in 1776, MoMA, May 1945, November 1947, April 1950, Exhibitions 32, 35, 41, Box 2.
59. Quoted in Ciment, *Kubrick*, 196.
60. Quoted by John Milius in Bogdanovich, "Stanley Kubrick," 23; Christiane and Anya Kubrick, quoted in James, "At Home with the Kubricks," 18; Raphael, *Eyes Wide Open*, 108.
61. Fried, Milius, and Arliss Howard, quoted in Bogdanovich, "Stanley Kubrick," 22, 23, 25, 40; see also Baxter, *Stanley Kubrick*, 167; and Magid, "Quest for Perfection," 4; Christiane Kubrick, quoted in James, "At Home with the Kubricks," 18; Walker, "Inexactly Expressed Sentiments," 294. There is a widespread story about Kubrick never allowing a car in which he was riding to travel over 30 mph, but this appears to be a generalization from a specific instance (Christiane Kubrick, quoted in James, 14; Herr, *Kubrick*, 30).
62. Quoted in James, "At Home with the Kubricks," 18; James Harris, quoted in Bogdanovich, "Stanley Kubrick," 22; Magid, "Quest for Perfection," 42; Kubrick on Griffith and His Wings of Fortune, www.dga.org/news/mag_archives/v22-2/kubrick.htm, October 22, 2002; Baxter, *Stanley Kubrick*, 167–68.
63. Matthew Modine, quoted in Bogdanovich, "Stanley Kubrick," 40; Johnson, "Writing *The Shining*"; Anya Kubrick, quoted in James, "At Home with the Kubricks," 13.
64. Quoted in Bogdanovich, "Stanley Kubrick," 21; see also Phillips, ed., *Interviews*, 198.
65. Quoted in Bogdanovich, "Stanley Kubrick," 48; quoted in James, "At Home with the Kubricks," 18; LoBrutto, *Stanley Kubrick*, 328; Christiane Kubrick, *Stanley Kubrick*, 110.
66. Humphrey Cobb, *Paths of Glory*, 178; Bier, "Cobb and Kubrick," 457, 463–64, 468–69, 470.
67. Jenny and Wolf, "Er war einfach schüchtern," 198; Rolf Thissen, *Stanley Kubrick*, 222.
68. Raphael, *Eyes Wide Open*, 59; see also 70–71, 89–90.
69. Michael E. Birdwell, *Celluloid Soldiers: The Warner Bros. Campaign against Nazism* (New York: New York University Press, 1999), 16.
70. Neal Gabler, *An Empire of Their Own: How the Jews Invented Hollywood* (New York: Crown, 1988); *Hollywood: An Empire of Their Own* (New York: New Video Group, 1998).

71. R. M. Friedman, "Exorcising the Past: Jewish Figures in Contemporary Film," *Journal of Contemporary History* 19 (1984): 512; Steven Carr, *Hollywood and Anti-Semitism: A Cultural History Up to World War II* (Cambridge: Cambridge University Press, 2001).
72. Marc Hairapetian and Claudia Tour-Sarkissian, "Ohne ihn ist die Welt viel kälter geworden," 2.
73. Raphael, *Eyes Wide Open,* 107-8.
74. *2001: A Space Odyssey,* DVD, scene 11, 52.55-57; Rod Munday, The New "alt.movies.kubrick" faq, www.visual-memory.co.uk/faq/, 49, August 18, 2000. Keir Dullea and Christiane Kubrick, quoted in Bogdanovich, "Stanley Kubrick," 24, 25; Herr, *Kubrick,* 15.
75. Baxter, *Stanley Kubrick,* 29-30.
76. Raphael, *Eyes Wide Open,* 108 (emphasis in original); see also LoBrutto, *Stanley Kubrick,* 9, 117, 120, 127, 193, 490.
77. Malcolm McDowell, quoted in Baxter, *Stanley Kubrick,* 266; see also Shelley Winters, quoted in Bogdanovich, "Stanley Kubrick," 22.
78. Baxter, *Stanley Kubrick,* 9 (emphasis in original).
79. Baxter, *Stanley Kubrick,* 21.
80. Otto Fenichel, *The Psychoanalytic Theory of Neurosis* (New York: Norton, 1945), 346.
81. Baxter, *Stanley Kubrick,* 86-89; LoBrutto, *Stanley Kubrick,* 131.
82. Fenichel, *Psychoanalytic Theory of Neurosis,* 71, 72, 92-93, 227.
83. Bogdanovich, "Stanley Kubrick," 23; Herr, *Kubrick,* 80.
84. Phillips, ed., *Interviews,* 127; LoBrutto, *Stanley Kubrick,* 1-2, 117, 120, 127, 193, 490; Baxter, *Stanley Kubrick,* 13-14, 19, 43-44, 167, 295-96, 298, 300, 328, 359, 364.
85. Christiane Kubrick, *Stanley Kubrick,* 153, 156, 161.
86. Bogdanovich, "Stanley Kubrick," 20; Johnson, "Writing *The Shining*"; see also Christiane Kubrick, *Stanley Kubrick,* 127-29, 145, 153.
87. Christiane Kubrick, *Stanley Kubrick,* 35, 38, 46-55; Baxter, *Stanley Kubrick,* 22.
88. LoBrutto, *Stanley Kubrick,* 10.

## Chapter 3

1. *The Shining,* DVD, scene 33, 2:03.10-33.
2. Baxter, *Stanley Kubrick,* 18.
3. Jackson Lears, "The Mouse that Roared," *New Republic,* June 15, 1998, 29; Steven Watts, *The Magic Kingdom: Walt Disney and the American Way of Life* (Boston: Houghton Mifflin, 1997), 77-82, 85, 237.
4. Richard Schickel, *The Disney Version: The Life, Times, Art and Commerce of Walt Disney* (New York: Simon and Schuster, 1968), 154; Watts, *Magic Kingdom,* 449-51.
5. "Charlotte Perkins Gilman: A Daring Humorist of Reform" (1897), in *Critical Essays on Charlotte Perkins Gilman,* ed. Joanne B. Karpinski (New York: Hall, 1992), 46; Catherine Orenstein, *Little Red Riding Hood Uncloaked: Sex, Morality, and the Evolution of a Fairy Tale* (New York: Basic Books, 2002), 94.
6. Orenstein, *Little Red Riding Hood Uncloaked,* 36, 46, 52-55, 60-61.
7. Quoted in Kroll, "Kubrick's Brilliant Vision," 29.
8. Hairapetian and Tour-Sarkissian, "Ohne ihn ist die Welt," 1.
9. Quoted in Herr, *Kubrick,* 69.

10. Carr, *Hollywood and Anti-Semitism*, 12–16.
11. John Roy Carlson, *Under Cover: My Four Years in the Nazi Underworld of America* (New York: Dutton, 1943), 27–28, 59, 66–67, 75–77, 78, 87–88, 97, 101, 105.
12. Curtis, *Autobiography*, 15.
13. David J. Skal, *The Monster Show: A Cultural History of Horror* (New York: Penguin, 1993), 213–20.
14. Orenstein, *Little Red Riding Hood Uncloaked*, 116.
15. Richard Shale, *Donald Duck Joins Up: The Walt Disney Studio During World War II* (Ann Arbor: UMI Research Press, 1982), 17 and Plate 5.
16. Ian Kershaw, *Hitler, 1936–1945: Nemesis* (New York: Norton, 2000), 395–98, 527.
17. Schickel, *The Disney Version*, 95, 155, 270.
18. Leni Riefenstahl, *A Memoir* (New York: St. Martin's Press, 1993), 239–40; Birdwell, *Celluloid Soldiers*, 29.
19. Walter, "Entretien avec Stanley Kubrick," 25–26 (emphasis added). In this French interview, Kubrick did mention one European favorite, *Carnival in Flanders* (Jacques Feyder, 1936), which showed at MoMA in 1947 (Exhibition 35); see also Robert Emma Ginna, "The Odyssey Begins," 17, 22; Elaine Dundy, "Stanley Kubrick and *Dr. Strangelove*" (1963), in Phillips, ed., *Interviews*, 14–15; LoBrutto, *Stanley Kubrick*, 93; Kroll, "Kubrick's Brilliant Vision," 31; and lists of Kubrick's favorite films and directors in Ciment, *Kubrick*, 34, and Herr, *Kubrick*, 27.
20. Joanne Stang, "Film Fan to Film Maker," 35.
21. Thomas Mann, *Stories of Three Decades*, trans. H. T. Lowe-Porter (New York: Knopf, 1936), 503; Robert Brustein, "Out of This World," 137.
22. Quoted in James, "At Home with the Kubricks," 14.
23. Alexander Walker, "Random Thoughts on the Englishness (or Otherwise) of English Film Actors," in Walker, *"It's Only a Movie, Ingrid,"* 207.
24. LoBrutto, *Stanley Kubrick*, 15–18; Baxter, *Stanley Kubrick*, 23–25; "Teacher Puts 'Ham' in *Hamlet*," *Look*, April 2, 1946.
25. Baxter, *Stanley Kubrick*, 20; LoBrutto, *Stanley Kubrick*, 14, 15.
26. Kroll, "Kubrick's Brilliant Vision," 31.
27. Christiane Kubrick, *Stanley Kubrick*, 33.
28. Play dates are from advertisements in the *New York Times*.
29. Birdwell, *Celluloid Soldiers*, 1, 3, 5, 10, 16, 17, 19, 25, 27.
30. Birdwell, *Celluloid Soldiers*, 11.
31. Carr, *Hollywood and Anti-Semitism*, 6.
32. Birdwell, *Celluloid Soldiers*, 61–63.
33. Birdwell, *Celluloid Soldiers*, 66–78.
34. Birdwell, *Celluloid Soldiers*, 81–82, 87–153; Ferro, *Cinema and History*, 111–17.
35. Clayton R. Koppes and Gregory D. Black, *Hollywood Goes to War* (New York: Free Press, 1987), 125.
36. Glenn Perusek, "Kubrick's Armies."
37. Jeremy Bernstein, "Profile: Stanley Kubrick" (1966), in Phillips, ed., *Interviews*, 23.
38. Kroll, "Kubrick's Brilliant Vision," 31; Look Collection, Library of Congress, Washington, D.C.; Museum of the City of New York.
39. Barbie Zelizer, *Remembering to Forget: Holocaust Memory Through the Camera's Eye* (Chicago: University of Chicago Press, 1998), 138, 139; Peter Novick, *The Holocaust in American Life*, 66.
40. Roger Manvell, *Films and the Second World War* (New York: Dell, 1976), 241, 361–62.

41. Walker, *Stanley Kubrick*, 290. It is typical, in effect at least, of Kubrick's sardonic, self-reflexive style that the photographs are of Warner Bros. executives and functionaries.
42. Birdwell, *Celluloid Soldiers*, 60.
43. Baigell, *Jewish-American Artists and the Holocaust*, 11.
44. Manvell, *Films and the Second World War*, 33–34.
45. Bernard F. Dick, *The Star-Spangled Screen: The American World War II Film* (Lexington: University Press of Kentucky, 1985), 207–8; Insdorf, *Indelible Shadows*, 129–33; see also Novick, *Holocaust in American Life*, 303n21.
46. David S. Wyman, *The Abandonment of the Jews: America and the Holocaust, 1941–1945* (New York: Pantheon, 1984), 79–91.
47. Novick, *Holocaust in American Life*, 31.
48. Novick, *Holocaust in American Life*, 35; Haskel Lookstein, "American Jewry's Public Response to the Holocaust 1938–1944" (Ph.D. diss., Yeshiva University, 1979); Alfred Kazin, *A Walker in the City* (New York: Grove Press, 1951), 34–39. Litvaks were Jews mostly from along the Baltic coast within the Jewish Pale of Settlement in Russia.
49. Novick, *Holocaust in American Life*, 40.
50. Baigell, *Jewish-American Artists*, 17–18.
51. Novick, *Holocaust in American Life*, 41.
52. Novick, *Holocaust in American Life*, 42–59.
53. *New York Times*, October 26, 1941, 6.
54. "Allies Are Urged to Execute Nazis," *New York Times*, July 2, 1942, 6.
55. Wyman, *Abandonment of the Jews*, 20–49, 61–63, 73.
56. Harlan, *Stanley Kubrick*, DVD, scene 3, 7.54–8:32.
57. Novick, *Holocaust in American Life*, 42.
58. "President Renews Pledges to Jews," *New York Times*, December 9, 1942, 20; *New York Times*, August 22 and October 8, 1942, 1; Novick, *Holocaust in American Life*, 42.
59. David Reynolds, "The Origins of the Two 'World Wars': Historical Discourse and International Politics," *Journal of Contemporary History* 38:1 (2003): 38–41.
60. Christiane Kubrick, personal communication, November 20, 2002.
61. Hubertus von Amelunxen, "Points de Vue Imaginaries et Réels," 201.
62. Georg Seesslen and Fernand Jung, *Stanley Kubrick und seine Filme*, 11.
63. Rainer Crone and Petrus Graf Schaesberg, *Stanley Kubrick: Still Moving Pictures*, 27; see also *Look at America: New York City*, rev. ed. (Boston: Houghton Mifflin, 1956), 344; and "Kubrick's Photojournalism," *Sight and Sound* 11:2 (February 1, 2001): 64–65.
64. Quoted in Gene Siskel, "Candidly Kubrick" (1987), in Phillips, ed., *Interviews*, 187.
65. Siskel, "Candidly Kubrick," 186.
66. Christiane Kubrick, personal communication, November 20, 2002.

# Chapter 4

1. Alan Bowker, Stanley's Room, January 1984, www.Bowkera.com/stanleys_room.htm, January 3, 2001, p. 1; Jenny and Wolf, "Er war einfach schüchtern," 198.
2. Vivian Kubrick, *Making The Shining*, *The Shining*, DVD, 10.50–11.29.
3. *The Shining*, DVD, scene 11, 37.31–53.
4. Pipolo, "Modernist and the Misanthrope," 7.

5. Phillips, ed., *Interviews*, 104; Walker, *Stanley Kubrick*, 13; LoBrutto, *Stanley Kubrick*, 57; Baxter, *Stanley Kubrick*, 31–32, 45.
6. Quoted in Ciment, *Kubrick*, 196.
7. Enrico Ghezzi, "T(eye)me Blink," in *Stanley Kubrick Ladro di Sguardi*, 4.
8. Ciment, *Kubrick*, 32–33, 67, 88, 196; Walker, *Stanley Kubrick*, 11; Baxter, *Stanley Kubrick*, 32–33, 40–42, 166, 187; LoBrutto, *Stanley Kubrick*, 10, 19, 62, 93, 105–6, 120, 282, 347, 374–75, 423, 432–33, 435; Phillips, ed., *Interviews*, 22, 32–33, 44–46, 81, 175, 196–97; Christiane Kubrick, *Stanley Kubrick*, 96–97, 100.
9. Department of Film Exhibitions, Boxes 2 and 3 (1944–1955), Celeste Bartos International Film Study Center, Museum of Modern Art, New York.
10. Ciment, *Kubrick*, 114.
11. Anger, "Le Dernier Expressioniste," 28.
12. Thomas Elsaesser, "Germany: The Weimar Years," in *The Oxford History of World Cinema*, ed. Geoffrey Nowell-Smith (Oxford: Oxford University Press, 1996), 143.
13. Wohl, "Modernism and Its Historians," 584.
14. David Blackbourn, *The Long Nineteenth Century: A History of Germany, 1780–1918* (New York: Oxford University Press, 1998), 367, 377, 379, 402, 407, 410, 427, 433, 467.
15. Geoffrey Nowell-Smith, "The Heyday of the Silents," in Nowell-Smith, ed., *Oxford History of World Cinema*, 201.
16. Neil Donahue, "Unjustly Framed: Politics and Art in Das Cabinet des Dr. Caligari," *German Politics and Society* 32 (1994): 76–88; Anton Kaes, *Der Expressionismus in Amerika: Rezeption und Innovation* (Tübingen: Max Niemeyer Verlag, 1975), 64–67.
17. Phillips, ed., *Interviews*, 7–8, 47–48, 77–79, 89–92, 106, 153, 159, 160, 163–64, 165, 190.
18. Cf. Baxter, *Stanley Kubrick*, 11.
19. Walker, *Stanley Kubrick*, 110; Ciment, *Kubrick*, 110.
20. A History of the Motion Picture, 1895–1946, September 16–December 27, 1948, Exhibition 35, Box 2; New Loans and Acquisitions, January 5–July 4, 1948, Exhibition 37, Box 2; The Film Till Now, December 26, 1949–July 15, 1951, Exhibition 41, Box 2; The Art of the Film, July 16, 1951–August 31, 1952, Exhibition 42, and September 1, 1952–September 6, 1953, Exhibition 44, Box 2; Raymond Haine, "Bonjour Monsieur Kubrick," 17–18.
21. George Grosz, *Der Spiesser-Spiegel: 60 Zeichnungen mit einer Selbstdarstellung*, 9th ed. (Dresden: Carl Reissner Verlag, 1932).
22. Crone and Schaesberg, *Still Moving Pictures*, 24–25; LoBrutto, *Stanley Kubrick*, 45–46; Herr, *Kubrick*, 25.
23. M. Kay Flavell, *George Grosz: A Biography* (New Haven: Yale University Press, 1988), 254.
24. Flavell, *George Grosz*, 260.
25. Klaus Kreimeier, *The Ufa Story: A History of Germany's Greatest Film Company, 1918–1945*, trans. Robert and Rita Kimber (New York: Hill and Wang, 1996), 212, 214, 324.
26. Aljean Harmetz, *Round Up the Usual Suspects: The Making of Casablanca—Bogart, Bergman, and World War II* (New York: Hyperion, 1992), 53.
27. Ed Sikov, *On Sunset Boulevard: The Life and Times of Billy Wilder* (New York: Hyperion, 1998), 187; Cameron Crowe, *Conversations with Wilder* (New York: Knopf, 2001), 23–24, 214, 293, 337; Gene D. Phillips and Rodney Hill, eds., *The Encyclopedia of Stanley Kubrick*, xv.
28. *The Killing*, DVD, scenes 9, 11; Mainar, *Narrative and Stylistic Patterns*, 54.

29. Ciment, *Kubrick*, 176.
30. *The Shining*, DVD, scene 21, 1:15.55–1:16.09.
31. Quoted in Ciment, *Kubrick*, 163, 265–66; Pipolo, "Modernist and Misanthrope," 7.
32. MoMA Exhibitions 39, 41, 42, 46, Box 2.
33. Kubrick quoted in Raphael, *Eyes Wide Open*, 142; Phillips, ed., *Interviews*, 65.
34. Baxter, *Stanley Kubrick*, 32; MoMA Exhibitions 35, 41, 42, 43, 44, Box 2; Kevin Brownlow, *How It Happened Here: The Making of a Film* (Garden City, N.Y.: Doubleday, 1968), 147; Walker, *Stanley Kubrick*, 351.
35. MoMA Exhibition 51, Box 3.
36. Ciment, *Kubrick*, 42, 75; Nelson, *Kubrick*, 12.
37. Patrick Montgomery, *The Man You Love to Hate* (Film Profiles, Inc., 1979).
38. Peter Loewenberg, "The Murder and Mythification of Walther Rathenau," in Loewenberg, *Fantasy and Reality in History* (New York: Oxford University Press, 1995), 112–13.
39. Quoted in LoBrutto, *Stanley Kubrick*, 383; see also Phillips, ed., *Interviews*, 11; Baxter, *Stanley Kubrick*, 235; Jerome Agel, ed., *The Making of Kubrick's 2001*, 300; Thissen, *Stanley Kubrick*, 213–214, 230; and Pauline Kael, "Trash, Art, and the Movies," *Harper's*, February 1969, 81, on Kubrick as "Field Marshal," "General," and even "*Führer*."
40. Phillips and Hill, eds., *Encyclopedia*, 1; "Ken Adam," *Film Dope* 39 (1983): 3; James Delson, "Ken Adam Interviewed," *Film Comment* 18:1 (January–February 1983): 36; Vincent LoBrutto, "Ken Adam," in LoBrutto, *By Design: Interviews with Film Production Designers* (Westport, Conn.: Praeger, 1992), 37; Hughes, *Complete Kubrick*, 127–28; Nigel Andrews, "Designer of the Kubrick Era," *Financial Times*, March 14, 1999, 7.
41. Desmond Young, *Rommel: The Desert Fox* (New York: Harper & Brothers, 1950), which served as the basis for the film *The Desert Fox* (1951), in which James Mason, who would star in Kubrick's *Lolita*, plays a sympathetically drawn Rommel; Stuart Y. McDougal, "'What's it going to be then, eh?': Questioning Kubrick's *Clockwork*," 18n3.
42. Quoted in Davis, "Trumbo and Kubrick Argue History," 180; Dalton Trumbo Papers, State Historical Society of Wisconsin, Madison.
43. Raphael, *Eyes Wide Open*, 152.
44. Herr, *Kubrick*, 74.
45. Raphael, *Eyes Wide Open*, 152; Raphael, "The Pumpkinification of Stanley Kubrick."
46. Patrick McGilligan, *Fritz Lang: The Nature of the Beast* (New York: St. Martin's Press, 1997), 42.
47. McGilligan, *Fritz Lang*, 102, 169–85.
48. Walker, *Stanley Kubrick*, 13; MoMA Exhibitions 35, 39, 41, Box 2.
49. Walker, *Stanley Kubrick*, 14, 367.
50. McGilligan, *Fritz Lang*, 296.
51. "Picture Plays and Players: Fritz Lang Discusses Two of His Films," *New York Sun*, March 20, 1943, quoted in McGilligan, *Fritz Lang*, 288.
52. McGilligan, *Fritz Lang*, 305.
53. *The Shining*, DVD, scene 11, 38.16, 39.35–40.27.
54. Tom Gunning, *The Films of Fritz Lang: Allegories of Vision and Modernity* (London: British Film Institute, 2000), 329.
55. Hobbs FAQ, p. 7; MoMA Exhibitions 35, 44, Box 2.
56. Holger Bachmann, "The Production and Contemporary Reception of *Metropolis*," in *Fritz Lang's Metropolis: Cinematic Visions of Technology and Fear*, ed. Michael Minden and Holger Bachmann (Rochester, N.Y.: Camden House, 2000), 28.

57. Patricia Mellenkamp, "Oedipus and the Robot in *Metropolis*," *Enclitic* 5:1 (Spring 1982): 20–42; Andreas Huyssen, "The Vamp and the Machine: Fritz Lang's *Metropolis*," in Minden and Bachmann, eds., *Fritz Lang's Metropolis*, 198–215; Siegfried Kracauer, *From Caligari to Hitler: A Psychological History of the German Film* (Princeton: Princeton University Press, 1947), 149–50, 162–64.
58. R. L. Ruttsky, "The Mediation of Technology and Gender: *Metropolis*, Nazism, Modernism," in Minden and Bachmann, eds., *Fritz Lang's Metropolis*, 217–45.
59. McGilligan, *Fritz Lang*, 126–28.
60. Walter, "Entretien avec Stanley Kubrick," 37.
61. Kael, "*A Clockwork Orange:* Stanley Strangelove," 134.
62. LoBrutto, "Ken Adam," 38; Walker, *Stanley Kubrick*, 107, 363; Roger Hudson, "Three Designers," *Sight and Sound* 34:1 (Winter 1964/1965): 26.
63. Walker, *Stanley Kubrick*, 129; Walker, "Inexactly Expressed Sentiments," 298; Baxter, *Stanley Kubrick*, 176; Ciment, *Kubrick*, 208.
64. Walker, *Stanley Kubrick*, 149; Baxter, *Stanley Kubrick*, 87; Gunning, *Films of Fritz Lang*, 53.
65. *Inside the Making of Dr. Strangelove*, 19.40–20.05, *Dr. Strangelove*, DVD.
66. James Howard, *Stanley Kubrick Companion*, 93; Hughes, *Complete Kubrick*, 122; Walker, quoted in *Inside the Making of Dr. Strangelove*, 19.25–36; Walker, "Inexactly Expressed Sentiments," 297; Alexander Walker, *Peter Sellers: The Authorized Biography* (New York: Macmillan, 1981), 137–38, 155; Ed Sikov, *Mr. Strangelove: A Biography of Peter Sellers* (New York: Hyperion, 2002), 195; Siegbert Prawer, *Caligari's Children: The Film as Tale of Terror* (Oxford: Oxford University Press, 1980), 64.
67. On *2001* as homage to *Metropolis*, set in the year 2000, see Gene Phillips, "Stop the World: Stanley Kubrick" (1973), in Phillips, ed., *Interviews*, 153.
68. The term "clockwork" was Prussian military reformer Hermann von Boyen's term for the "ferociously disciplined but poorly motivated" regular army (Blackbourn, *Long Nineteenth Century*, 61).
69. Geoffrey Cocks, "Stanley Kubrick's Dream Machine."
70. Walker, "Inexactly Expressed Sentiments," 297.
71. Walker, "Inexactly Expressed Sentiments," 292.
72. Baxter, *Stanley Kubrick*, 7, 167, 169, 225, 299; LoBrutto, *Stanley Kubrick*, 357; Herr, *Kubrick*, 30; Paul Joyce, *The Last Movie* (Channel 4, 1999); Walker, *Stanley Kubrick*, 9, 369; Phillips, ed., *Interviews*, 178, 200; Thissen, *Stanley Kubrick*, 218, 220.
73. Quoted in Walker, *Stanley Kubrick*, 20.
74. Frank Noack, personal communication, August 31, 1999; LoBrutto, *Stanley Kubrick*, 140.
75. Baxter, *Stanley Kubrick*, 216–17; Piers Bizony, *2001: Filming the Future*, 98, 111.
76. Walker, *Stanley Kubrick*, 9.
77. Walker, *Stanley Kubrick*, 14; see also Phillips, ed., *Interviews*, 80, 104.
78. Haine, "Bonjour Monsieur Kubrick," 16; Walker, *Stanley Kubrick*, 72n.
79. Walker, *Stanley Kubrick*, 72.
80. Geoffrey Nowell-Smith, "Max Ophuls (1902–1957)," in Nowell-Smith, ed., *Oxford History of World Cinema*, 252.
81. Quoted in Helmut G. Asper, *Max Ophüls: Eine Biographie* (Berlin: Bertz, 1998), 549–50.
82. Virginia Woolf, "Modern Fiction" (1925), in Woolf, *The Common Reader* (London: Hogarth Press, 1929), 192.

83. Andrew Sarris, "*The Elusive Corporal*" (1963), in Sarris, *Confessions of a Cultist: On the Cinema, 1955–1969* (New York: Simon and Schuster, 1970), 74; Haine, "Bonjour Monsieur Kubrick," 16–17; Walter, "Entretien avec Stanley Kubrick," 32.
84. Robert L. Van de Castle, *Our Dreaming Mind* (New York: Ballantine, 1994), 171; LoBrutto, *Stanley Kubrick*, 481.
85. Sigmund Freud, *The Psychopathology of Everyday Life*, trans. Alan Tyson (New York: Norton, 1965), 262–65.
86. LoBrutto, *Stanley Kubrick*, 21, 32, 33, 34, 55, 56, 525; Herr, *Kubrick*, 12–13; McGregor, "Nice Boy from the Bronx?" 13; Walker, *Stanley Kubrick*, 17.
87. Walker, *Stanley Kubrick*, 12; Ciment, *Kubrick*, 33; Martha Duffy and Richard Schickel, "Kubrick's Grandest Gamble: *Barry Lyndon*" (1975), in Phillips, ed., *Interviews*, 165, see also 186–87.
88. Baxter, *Stanley Kubrick*, 53; LoBrutto, *Stanley Kubrick*, 86.
89. Mark Van Doren, *The Autobiography of Mark Van Doren* (New York: Harcourt, Brace, 1958), 283; Walker, *Stanley Kubrick*, 17; E. M. Forster, *Aspects of the Novel* (New York: Harcourt, Brace, 1956); Haine, "Bonjour Monsieur Kubrick," 13.
90. Moses Hades, *Humanism: The Greek Ideal and Its Survival* (New York: Harper & Brothers, 1960), 29.
91. Solomon Maimon, *An Autobiography*, ed. Moses Hadas (New York: Schocken, 1967), xi–xiii, 3–4; Robin W. Winks, *Cloak and Gown: Scholars in the Secret War, 1939–1961* (New York: Morrow, 1987), 213–14.
92. Quoted in Stephen L. Tanner, *Lionel Trilling* (Boston: Hall, 1988), 8.
93. Edward Joseph Shoben, Jr., *Lionel Trilling* (New York: Ungar, 1981), 63; Avisar, *Screening the Holocaust*, 179–80.
94. Lionel Trilling, *Beyond Culture: Essays on Literature and Learning* (New York: Viking, 1965), 14; see also Walker, *Stanley Kubrick*, 13; Boyd, "Mode and Meaning in *2001*," 213; Shoben, *Lionel Trilling*, 66, 70, 78–79, 180; and Herr, *Kubrick*, 9–10, 13.
95. Trilling, *Beyond Culture*, 19.
96. Frederick R. Karl, *Joseph Conrad: The Three Lives* (New York: Farrar, Straus and Giroux, 1979), 758.
97. Adam Hochschild, *King Leopold's Ghost: A Story of Greed, Terror, and Heroism in Colonial Africa* (Boston: Houghton Mifflin, 1998), 144–45; *Joseph Conrad's Letters to R. B. Cunninghame Graham* (Cambridge: Cambridge University Press, 1969), 41.
98. Conrad, *Heart of Darkness*, 46, 54, 55, 64, 67, 68; David Denby, "Jungle Fever," *New Yorker*, November 6, 1995, 119–29. See also Feldmann, "Kubrick and His Discontents," 199; and Bartov, *Murders in Our Midst*, 160. Andrew Birkin allegedly sent Kubrick Nazi materials from Namibia (formerly German Southwest Africa) (Baxter, *Stanley Kubrick*, 276; Bizony, 2001, 132).
99. Baxter, *Stanley Kubrick*, 35–39; LoBrutto, *Stanley Kubrick*, 58–70.
100. LoBrutto, *Stanley Kubrick*, 71–75, 82–85; Phillips and Hill, eds., *Encyclopedia*, 257–58. Baxter claims that Kubrick made one other documentary for the World Assembly of Youth in 1952, of which there is no known print (*Stanley Kubrick*, 51).
101. Jan Harlan, personal communication, December 9, 2002.
102. Novick, *Holocaust in American Life*, 91, 109, 113.
103. Ann Morrow, "Christiane Kubrick: Flowers and Violent Images," *The Times*, February 5, 1973, 10.
104. Quoted in LoBrutto, *Stanley Kubrick*, 147; see also Marina Vaizey, "Christiane Kubrick," in Christiane Kubrick, *Paintings*, 7, 11; and Claus Larass, *Der Zug der*

Kinder: KLV—Die Evakuierung 5 Millionen deutscher Kinder im 2. Weltkrieg (Munich: Meyster, 1983).
105. Harlan, *Stanley Kubrick*, DVD, scene 24.
106. Kubrick and Raphael, *Eyes Wide Shut*, 167, 168, 169; LoBrutto, *Stanley Kubrick*, 148, 352, 447, 469, 499; Baxter, *Stanley Kubrick*, 149, 254, 285, 299; Frank Noack, *Veit Harlan*, 35–36; Phillips and Hill, eds., *Encyclopedia*, 144; Thissen, *Stanley Kubrick*, 178, 211–13.
107. Eric Rentschler, *The Ministry of Illusion: Nazi Cinema and Its Afterlife* (Cambridge, Mass.: Harvard University Press, 1996), 154.
108. Davis, "Trumbo and Kubrick Argue History," 189; Noack, *Veit Harlan*, 305. Veit and Fritz were allegedly envious of each other's success (Frank Noack, personal communication, December 8, 2000).
109. Jenny and Wolf, "Er war einfach schüchtern," 198; Marc Hairapetian, "Stanley hätte applaudiert!"; Raphael, *Eyes Wide Open*, 60.
110. Hairapetian, "Stanley hätte applaudiert."
111. Thissen, *Stanley Kubrick*, 217; Jan Harlan, personal communication, December 9, 2002.
112. Baxter, *Stanley Kubrick*, 11.
113. Davis, "Trumbo and Kubrick Argue History," 179.
114. Noack, *Veit Harlan*, 305, 397; "Maria Körber feierte ihren 70sten mit Schauspielern," *Die Welt*, October 30, 2000.
115. Hummel et al., *Stanley Kubrick*, 294.
116. Frank Noack, "Nazizögling wider Willen: Ein alternativer Blubo-Roman von Thomas Harlan," *Die Welt*, October 30, 2000; Noack, *Veit Harlan*, 60, 69.
117. Noack, *Veit Harlan*, 345–47, 349, 352, 393, 397.
118. Noack, *Veit Harlan*, 397; Anton Kaes, *From Hitler to Heimat: The Return of History as Film* (Cambridge, Mass.: Harvard University Press, 1989), 141; Frank Noack, personal communication, July 25, 1998; Jan Harlan, personal communication, November 22, 2002.
119. Noack, *Veit Harlan*, 35; Christiane Kubrick, personal communication, November 20, 2002.
120. Erich Traumann, "Hilversum: Pflegestätte europäischer Musik," *Maanblad der Nederlandsch-Duitsche Kultuurgemeenschap*, May 1943, 22; "Kammersänger Fritz Harlan," January 1944, 20, Haags Gemeentearchief, The Hague; *Documentatie: Status en Werkzaamheid van organisaties en instellingen uit de tijd der Duitse bezetting van Nederland* ([Amsterdam]: Uitgave, [1941]), 260–65; Christiane Kubrick, personal communication, November 20, 2002; cf. Ortsgruppenkartei, National Archives, Suitland, Maryland.
121. Michael Meyer, *The Politics of Music in the Third Reich* (New York: Peter Lang, 1991), 183; Christiane Kubrick, personal communication, November 20, 2002.
122. Christiane Kubrick, personal communication, November 20, 2002.
123. "Nazis Seek to Rid Europe of All Jews," *New York Times*, October 28, 1941, 24.
124. Thomas Keneally, *Schindler's List* (New York: Simon and Schuster, 1982), 51; Gerhard Botz, *Wohnungspolitik und Judendeportationen in Wien 1938 bis 1945: Zur Funktion des Antisemitismus als Ersatz nationalsozialistischer Sozialpolitik* (Vienna: Geyer, 1975), 59–65, 120–21.
125. J. Presser, *The Destruction of the Dutch Jews*, trans. Arnold Pomerans (New York: Dutton, 1969), 73.
126. Louis de Jong, *The Netherlands and Nazi Germany* (Cambridge, Mass.: Harvard University Press, 1990), 3–25.

272 | The Wolf at the Door: Stanley Kubrick, History, and the Holocaust

127. I. B. van Creveld, personal communication, November 10, 2000; NB 90834, 90835, 90837, Algemeen Rijksarchief, The Hague; Christiane Kubrick, personal communication, November 20, 2002.
128. Earl R. Beck, *Under the Bombs: The German Home Front, 1942–1945* (Lexington: University Press of Kentucky, 1986), 74.
129. Christiane Kubrick, personal communication, November 20, 2002.
130. Frank Noack, personal communication, July 25, 1998.
131. Harry Sternberg, quoted in LoBrutto, *Stanley Kubrick*, 225, see also 224, 372; Christiane Kubrick, personal communication, November 20, 2002; Walker, *Stanley Kubrick*, 361; Baxter, *Stanley Kubrick*, 165, 196; Barry Miles, *Paul McCartney: Many Years From Now* (New York: Holt, 1997), 508–9, 515.
132. Morrow, "Flowers and Violent Images," 10; James, "At Home with the Kubricks," 13; Harlan, *A Life in Pictures*, DVD, scene 25, 2:15.40–42; Frank Noack, personal communication, July 4, 2000; Veit Harlan, *Im Schatten meiner Filme: Selbstbiographie*, ed. H. C. Opfermann (Gütersloh: Mohn, 1966), 17. Kubrick did sign Fritz Harlan's death certificate (Manfred Klimanski, personal communication, September 10, 2003).
133. John Dunning, *Two O'Clock Eastern Wartime* (New York: Scribner, 2001), 29.
134. Quoted in Herr, *Kubrick*, 69.
135. I am grateful to Frank Noack for suggesting this association. Susanne, who acted in her father's postwar films under the name Susanne Körber, converted to Judaism and, after considering Israel, moved to New York, where as Susanna Jacoby she practiced veterinary medicine. She committed suicide in 1989. See Noack, *Veit Harlan*, 310, 397.
136. Nelson, *Kubrick*, 34–35, 144, 175–76, 205–7, 212, 214, 229–30.
137. Quoted in Ciment, *Kubrick*, 163.
138. Baxter, *Stanley Kubrick*, 11, 47; Ciment, *Kubrick*, 241.
139. Phillips, ed., *Interviews*, 49–50, 74.
140. Marilyn McCord Adams and Robert Merrihew Adams, eds., *The Problem of Evil* (Oxford: Oxford University Press, 1990), 1, 10, 12, 20–21.
141. Nelson, *Kubrick*, 84.
142. Richard L. Rubenstein, *After Auschwitz: History, Theology, and Contemporary Judaism*, 2nd ed. (Baltimore: Johns Hopkins University Press, 1992).
143. Noack, *Veit Harlan*, 347.
144. Baxter, *Stanley Kubrick*, 162; Walker, *Stanley Kubrick*, 368; Walker, "Inexactly Expressed Sentiments," 294.
145. LoBrutto, *Stanley Kubrick*, 225; Baxter, *Stanley Kubrick*, 95.
146. Christiane Kubrick, personal communication, November 20, 2002; cf. Walker, *Stanley Kubrick*, 369; LoBrutto, *Stanley Kubrick*, 342.
147. Christiane Kubrick, personal communication, November 20, 2002; Walker, *Stanley Kubrick*, 361; Walker, "Inexactly Expressed Sentiments," 286.
148. Quoted in Ciment, *Kubrick*, 156; see also 92.

## Chapter 5

1. Nikolai M. Gorchakov, *Stanislavsky Directs*, trans. Miriam Goldina (New York: Funk & Wagnalls, 1954), 16, 394; Ciment, *Kubrick*, 202; Walker, *Stanley Kubrick*, 21; Nelson, *Kubrick*, 61, 251; Vsevolod Pudovkin, *Film Technique*, 84, 109; Kinney, "Text and Pretext," 91.

2. Quoted in Norman Kagan, *Cinema of Stanley Kubrick,* 17.
3. Quoted in Kagan, *Cinema of Stanley Kubrick,* 9; see also LoBrutto, *Stanley Kubrick,* 88; and Phillips, *Stanley Kubrick,* 17.
4. Kubrick to Joseph Burstyn, November 16, 1952, quoted in Kagan, *Cinema of Stanley Kubrick,* 9; see also LoBrutto, *Stanley Kubrick,* 89–90.
5. Kagan, *Cinema of Stanley Kubrick,* 10, 17; Phillips, *Stanley Kubrick,* 17; LoBrutto, *Stanley Kubrick,* 89.
6. LoBrutto, *Stanley Kubrick,* 89; Phillips, *Stanley Kubrick,* 16.
7. Baxter, *Stanley Kubrick,* 46–47.
8. Phillips, *Stanley Kubrick,* 17.
9. Paul Mazursky, *Show Me the Magic* (New York: Simon and Schuster, 1999), 20–21; Phillips and Hill, eds., *Encyclopedia,* 332; Garland Lee Thompson, "Who Was Frank Silvera?" www.fsww.org/whois.html, January 15, 2003.
10. Kagan, *Cinema of Stanley Kubrick,* 13; Ciment, *Kubrick,* 48; Harlan, *A Life in Pictures,* DVD, scene 5, 10.52–54.
11. Nelson, *Kubrick,* 21.
12. Baxter, *Stanley Kubrick,* 31, 49; Mazursky, *Show Me the Magic,* 19, 21, 23; for an interesting coincidence of New York City, a Doberman Pinscher, and a ballet dancer that reproduces elements of Kubrick's first two marriages, see also J. D. Salinger, *The Catcher in the Rye* (New York: New American Library, 1953), 31.
13. Phillips and Hill, eds., *Encyclopedia,* 113.
14. Baxter, *Stanley Kubrick,* 61–63, 69; LoBrutto, *Stanley Kubrick,* 95, 102.
15. Walker, *Stanley Kubrick,* 45, 50–51; Susanna Ott, "Reshaping Life," 202–18.
16. Walker, *Stanley Kubrick,* 50; Phillips, *Stanley Kubrick,* 22; LoBrutto, *Stanley Kubrick,* 103; Seesslen and Jung, *Stanley Kubrick,* 87; Chris Chase, "Present at the Creation with Kubrick," *Los Angeles Times,* March 14, 1999.
17. Walker, *Stanley Kubrick,* 46; Seesslen and Jung, *Stanley Kubrick,* 87, 92; on the identical similarity between Kubrick and French novelist Gustave Flaubert, see Kay Kirschmann, *Stanley Kubrick,* 167–69; see also Ciment, *Kubrick,* 232.
18. John Bodnar, "*Saving Private Ryan* and Postwar Memory in America," *American Historical Review* 106 (2001): 812; Gene Philips, *Stanley Kubrick,* 18; see also Alain Silver and Elizabeth Ward, eds., *Film Noir,* 3rd ed. (Woodstock, N.Y.: Overlook Press, 1992), 154–56; and Phillips and Hill, eds., *Encyclopedia,* 113–15, 181–83.
19. Quoted in Herr, *Kubrick,* 12; Nicholas Christopher, *Somewhere in the Night: Film Noir and the American City* (New York: Free Press, 1997), 42.
20. *Killer's Kiss,* DVD, scenes 4, 7.
21. *Killer's Kiss,* DVD, scenes 7, 20.14–20; 8, 20.21–40; Kagan, *Cinema of Stanley Kubrick,* 23; Phillips, *Stanley Kubrick,* 20; Kolker, *Cinema of Loneliness,* 100.
22. Quoted in Phillips, *Stanley Kubrick,* 21.
23. www.users.sisna.com/ruthsobotka/filmappearancesindex.html, July 24, 2002.
24. *Killer's Kiss,* DVD, scene 11, 35.10–19; Nelson, *Kubrick,* 26–27; MoMA Exhibitions 37, 41.
25. Pollan, "Materiality and Sociality," 88–89, 94; Hummel et al., *Stanley Kubrick,* 28.
26. Mainar, *Narrative and Stylistic Patterns,* 7, 17, 50; Nelson, *Kubrick,* 28.
27. Nelson, *Kubrick,* 24, 198. In a close-up of Rapallo in the mannequin warehouse, there can be seen an eagle drawn on the door he is facing, an association in Kubrick's cinema that identifies those with power (*Killer's Kiss,* DVD, scene 18, 1:04.25–31). A medium shot of Davy at the same door reduces the eagle almost too invisibility, an indication of a lesser manifestation of male aggression. A huge eagle sits behind the desk of the

director in Matthew Chapman's *Stranger's Kiss* (Kill Productions, 1983), a fictional account of the making of *Killer's Kiss* (Baxter, *Stanley Kubrick,* 331). And what is probably a continuity error ends up playing to Kubrick's theme of the inextricability of good and evil. When Davy escapes from Rapallo's gang by jumping through a window, he is wearing white socks, but when he runs away the socks have changed to black (*Killer's Kiss,* DVD, scene 16, 55:01–4, 20–30, 31–34; Phillips, *Stanley Kubrick,* 22).

28. Seesslen and Jung, *Stanley Kubrick,* 92. The duel in *Rashomon* ends in similar fashion to that in *Killer's Kiss,* with the bandit skewering the samurai lying on his back in the bushes. The weapons used in *Killer's Kiss* anticipate the short ax and long trident used in the gladiator duel in *Spartacus,* while Rapallo's dying scream transforms into the scream of a train whistle as in Hitchcock's *The Thirty-Nine Steps* (1935) (Phillips, *Stanley Kubrick,* 23).

29. Kagan, *Cinema of Stanley Kubrick,* 26.

30. *Killer's Kiss,* DVD, scene 20, 1:07.10–11.

31. *Killer's Kiss,* DVD, scene 11, 35.06–09.

32. *Killer's Kiss,* DVD, scene 11, 35.26–28; Department of Prints, Photographs, and Architectural Collections, New York Historical Society; Roger A. Fischer, *Them Damned Pictures: Explorations in American Political Cartoon Art* (New York: Archon, 1996), 76–100; Matthew Frye Jacobson, *Whiteness of a Different Color: European Immigrants and the Alchemy of Race* (Cambridge, Mass.: Harvard University Press, 1998), 48, 147; *What Do Those Old Films Mean?* vol. 2, *Tomorrow the World* (Channel 4, 1987); Herr, *Kubrick,* 45. The hats in the illustration are also similar to that worn by the caricatured Jewish peddler in Disney's *Three Little Pigs.*

33. *Killer's Kiss,* DVD, scenes 13, 47.40; 15, 49.11–52, 52.59–53.00; 18, 59.34–59.49, 1:02.12.

34. See the illustration from *Hitler's Madman* (1943), in Dick, *Star-Spangled Screen,* 194; Kagan, *Cinema of Stanley Kubrick,* 24, 25; Ciment, *Kubrick,* 7; Robert Polito, *Savage Art: A Biography of Jim Thompson* (New York: Knopf, 1995), 354; Patrick Villiers, personal communication, April 27, 2000; Charles Kenyon, Jr., *Lugers at Random* (Chicago: Handgun Press, 1969).

35. Frank M. Robinson and Lawrence Davidson, *Pulp Culture: The Art of Fiction Magazines* (Portland, Ore.: Collectors Press, 1998), 62; Auguste le Breton, *Du Rififi Chez Les Femmes* (n.p., [1953] 1967), 72, 188, 205, 228–29. See also Dassin's war films: *Nazi Agent* (1942), starring Conrad Veidt as both the good and the evil German twin; and *Reunion in France* (1942), about resistance to the Nazi occupation of France.

36. *Killer's Kiss,* DVD, scene 18, 59.46-47. Whether significant or not, the fragments of an address on the box read: "From E. H. Jacobs [a reference to Kubrick's father?], Motion Picture for T.V.——Walter Rus[??]—Tit[??]."

37. Nelson, *Kubrick,* 198.

38. LoBrutto, *Stanley Kubrick,* 16–17, 104, 148–49.

39. Tim Cole, "Scales of Memory, Layers of Memory: Recent Works on Memories of the Second World War and the Holocaust," *Journal of Contemporary History* 37:1 (2002): 133.

40. Claude Lanzmann, *Shoah: An Oral History of the Holocaust* (New York: Pantheon, 1985), 13; *Killer's Kiss,* DVD, scene 18, 1:02.12.

41. *Killer's Kiss,* DVD, scenes 5, 6, passim; scene 11, 34.46–35.25.

42. *Killer's Kiss,* DVD, scene 12, 38.30–43.

43. Baxter, *Stanley Kubrick,* 65; www.users.sisna.com/ruthsobotka/kubrickmarriage.html July 24, 2002.

44. Nelson, *Kubrick,* 28.

45. Baxter, *Stanley Kubrick,* 33, 60, 76; Christiane Kubrick, *Stanley Kubrick,* 58.
46. Phillips, *Stanley Kubrick,* 20.
47. *Killer's Kiss,* DVD, scenes 2, 4.12–19; 3, 4.40–49, 5:12–18. A clock reads 10 minutes to 7 in Gloria's apartment, the same time that appears on a clock in one scene in *The Shining*. In another scene (16, 54.27–28) Rapallo makes a remark about not being a "14-carat sucker." In Dassin's *The Naked City* a character lies about serving in the Seventy-seventh Division during the Second World War.
48. Nelson, *Kubrick,* 27.
49. Herr, *Kubrick,* 27; Nelson, *Kubrick,* 28; cf. Seesslen and Jung, *Stanley Kubrick,* 88; and LoBrutto, *Stanley Kubrick,* 104.
50. Kagan, *Cinema of Stanley Kubrick,* 31; LoBrutto, *Stanley Kubrick,* 109–28; Baxter, *Stanley Kubrick,* 70–84; Phillips, *Stanley Kubrick,* 26–38; Mario Falsetto, "Patterns of Filmic Narration in *The Killing* and *Lolita*," 100–108; Seesslen and Jung, *Stanley Kubrick,* 93–100; Nelson, *Kubrick,* 29–37; LoBrutto, "Written Word."
51. Baxter, *Stanley Kubrick,* 73; Thompson, "The Flaw in the System," in *Fireworks: The Lost Writings of Jim Thompson,* ed. Robert Polito and Michael McCauley (New York: Fine, 1988), 224–31; Polito, *Savage Art,* 344, 393–98.
52. Polito, *Savage Art,* 397–400.
53. LoBrutto, *Stanley Kubrick,* 120.
54. Philip Kemp, "John Huston (1906–1987)," in Nowell-Smith, ed., *Oxford History of World Cinema,* 448; Nelson, *Kubrick,* 29.
55. "29 and Running, the Director with Hollywood by the Horns Dissects the Movies," *Newsweek,* December 2, 1957, 97.
56. James Harvey, *Movie Love in the Fifties* (New York: Knopf, 2001), 226.
57. Harvey, *Movie Love in the Fifties,* 105.
58. *The Killing,* DVD, scenes 4, 9.16–45; 11, 24.44–54; 17, 41.04–43.49; Nelson, *Kubrick,* 31.
59. LoBrutto, *Stanley Kubrick,* 220; Baxter, *Stanley Kubrick,* 250; Seesslen and Jung, *Stanley Kubrick,* 121; *Dr. Strangelove,* DVD, scene 14, 45.41–47.43.
60. Lionel White, *Clean Break,* 150–53.
61. *The Killing,* DVD, scene 25, 57.17–58.24, 58.49–59.28, 1:00.20–1:01.15; Nelson, *Kubrick,* 32.
62. Nelson, *Kubrick,* 30; Hughes, *Complete Kubrick,* 40; Walker, *Stanley Kubrick,* 19.
63. Baxter, *Stanley Kubrick,* 100; Seesslen, *Stanley Kubrick,* 96.
64. Nelson, *Kubrick,* 32; Seesslen and Jung, *Stanley Kubrick,* 93, 98.
65. *The Killing,* DVD, scene 32, 1:23.46–51; scene 14; Nelson, *Kubrick,* 32.
66. *The Killing,* DVD, scene 32, 1:22.49–23.04.
67. James George Frazer, *The Golden Bough: A Study in Magic and Religion* (New York: Macmillan, 1951), 281–82, 483–84, 706, 732; Sikov, *Mr. Strangelove,* 197; Southern "Strangelove Outtake," 75.
68. Phillips, ed., *Interviews,* 14.
69. White, *Clean Break,* 89.
70. *The Killing,* DVD, scene 25, 1:00.13–15, 1:00.23–1:01.13, 1:01.28–1:02.12. Nikki's license plate number has one 7 in it.
71. *The Killing,* DVD, scenes 4, 7.01–2; 13, 29.21; 16, 37.16; 17, 40.56–41.00, 43.00; Falsetto, *Stanley Kubrick,* 11–12; Walker, *Stanley Kubrick,* 52.
72. *The Killing,* DVD, scene 30, 1:18.21–31, 1:21.04–9; Mainar, *Narrative and Stylistic Patterns,* 7, 15–17.

73. *The Killing*, DVD, scene 31, 1:23.17-33. The measurement of a doorway, "78×29," is written in a door (scenes 15 and 18), but it seems purely coincidental, unless one wants to make something of "the measure of a man."
74. Douglas, *Ragman's Son*, 273.
75. Louis Henry Cohn, "Zero Hour," *Saturday Review of Literature*, June 1, 1935, 5–6; Marshall A. Best, "The Facts in 'Paths of Glory,'" *Saturday Review of Literature*, June 8, 1935, 9.
76. Baxter, *Stanley Kubrick*, 105; Andrew Kelly, "The Brutality of Military Incompetence," 220; LoBrutto, *Stanley Kubrick*, 154–55; Harlan, *A Life in Pictures*, DVD, scene 8, 23. 46–54; Hughes, *Complete Kubrick*, 60.
77. "French Acquit 5 Shot for Mutiny in 1915," *New York Times*, July 2, 1934, 5; Phillips, ed., *Interviews*, 144; Baxter, *Stanley Kubrick*, 84.
78. Polito, *Savage Art*, 402–10; Baxter, *Stanley Kubrick*, 84; Douglas, *Ragman's Son*, 274–75; LoBrutto, *Stanley Kubrick*, 133, 136; Baxter, *Stanley Kubrick*, 94–95.
79. Kagan, *Cinema of Stanley Kubrick*, 63.
80. Walker, *Stanley Kubrick*, 69.
81. Phillips, ed., *Interviews*, 72.
82. Baxter, *Stanley Kubrick*, 104.
83. Kagan, *Cinema of Stanley Kubrick*, 64; Arthur Marwick, *The Sixties: Cultural Revolution in Britain, France, Italy, and the United States, c. 1958–c.1974* (Oxford: Oxford University Press, 1998), 159.
84. Seesslen and Jung, *Stanley Kubrick*, 44–47; Kirchmann, *Stanley Kubrick*, 26; Kinney, "Text and Pretext," 38–64.
85. Bier, "Cobb and Kubrick," 456. Bier (461–66) in fact misspells the name as "General Brouillard"; cf. Christiane Kubrick, *Stanley Kubrick*, 178.
86. Kagan, *Cinema of Stanley Kubrick*, 55.
87. Stanley Kubrick, "Now Kubrick Fights Back," 11.
88. *Paths of Glory*, DVD, scene 4, 11.22–38; Kagan, *Cinema of Stanley Kubrick*, 49; Kelly, "Brutality of Military Incompetence," 225.
89. Cobb, *Paths of Glory*, 33, 34, 46; Bier, "Cobb and Kubrick," 464.
90. Benjamin C. Truman, *The Field of Honor* (New York: Fords, Howard, & Hulbert, 1884), 56–69; Hughes, *Complete Kubrick*, 61; Vincent LoBrutto, personal communication, August 8, 2003.
91. Bier, "Cobb and Kubrick," 464; William Lee Nothstine, "George S. Patton and the Slapping Incidents, a Content Analytic Investigation of Media Image" (Master's thesis, Miami [Ohio] University, 1977), 6; *Paths of Glory*, DVD, scene 3, 7.40–8.29.
92. Polito, *Savage Art*, 406; Walker, *Stanley Kubrick*, 101; Baxter, *Stanley Kubrick*, 94–95; Nelson, *Kubrick*, 41; Herr, *Kubrick*, 48; Gabbard and Sharma, "Art Cinema," 95.
93. *Paths of Glory*, DVD, scene 14, 41.45–53.
94. *Paths of Glory*, DVD, scene 14, 43.10–19.
95. Cobb, *Paths of Glory*, 178; on Feról's (and Meyer's) negative attributes, see 176; see also Bier, "Cobb and Kubrick," 457.
96. Bier, "Cobb and Kubrick," 467.
97. *Paths of Glory*, DVD, scene 26, 1:04.06–39; Nelson, *Kubrick*, 52; cf. the publicity still in Ciment, *Kubrick*, 66.
98. *Paths of Glory*, DVD, scenes 26, 29, 30.
99. *Paths of Glory*, DVD, scenes 7, 24.07–25.25; 15, 45.01–25; 21, 55.46–56.29; cf. Cobb, *Paths of Glory*, 31, 195.

100. Phillips, ed., *Interviews*, 70; Kelly, "Brutality of Military Incompetence," 220; Kagan, *Cinema of Stanley Kubrick*, 65; cf. Ferro, *Cinema and History*, 119, 160–61.
101. Phillips, *Stanley Kubrick*, 78; Douglas, *Ragman's Son*, 316–18; Ciment, *Kubrick*, 80; Floyd Collins, "Implied Metaphor in the Films of Stanley Kubrick," 99; Henry Sheehan, "Roman Games," 24; LoBrutto, *Stanley Kubrick*, 166–93; Baxter, *Stanley Kubrick*, 123–41; Phillips, ed., *Interviews*, 81, 102, 145–46, 190; Walker, "Inexactly Expressed Sentiments," 289; Kagan, *Cinema of Stanley Kubrick*, 73; Howard Fast, *Spartacus* (New York: Simon and Schuster, 2000), 87.
102. Phillips, ed., *Interviews*, 179–80.
103. Davis, "Trumbo and Kubrick Argue History," 180–81.
104. Sheehan, "Roman Games," 23–24; Douglas, *Ragman's Son*, 317; Phillips, *Stanley Kubrick*, 71; Baxter, *Stanley Kubrick*, 124, 134; LoBrutto, *Stanley Kubrick*, 167; Dalton Trumbo, "Report on Spartacus," *Cineaste* 18:3 (1991): 30–33; Ina Rae Hark, "Animals or Romans: Looking at Masculinity in *Spartacus*," in *Screening the Male: Exploring Masculinities in Hollywood Cinema*, ed. Steven Cohan and Ina Rae Hark (London: Routledge, 1993), 170n4; Peter Hanson, *Dalton Trumbo, Hollywood Rebel: A Critical Survey and Filmography* (Jefferson, N.C.: McFarland, 2001), 135–36; Walker, "Inexactly Expressed Sentiments," 289; Ferro, *Cinema and History*, 151.
105. Arthur Koestler, *The Gladiators*, trans. Edith Simon (New York: Macmillan, 1947), 46–47. Koestler speculates that Spartacus derived communist ideals from "the Judaic sect of the Essenes—the only sizeable civilized community that practiced primitive Communism at that time" ("Postscript to the Danube Edition of 'The Gladiators'," in *The Gladiators* [London: Hutchinson, 1965], 317, 318–19; and *The Gladiators*, 90–91, 214–15).
106. Fast, *Spartacus*, 97, 98–99, 108, 114–15, 118, 121, 126, 127, 147, 151–52, 248, 263, 290; *Spartacus*, DVD, scene 9, 37.38; Natalie Zemon Davis, "Resistance and Survival: *Spartacus*," 21, 24–38; Ciment, *Kubrick*, 151.
107. *Spartacus*, DVD, scene 41, 2:49.57–59; Davis, "Trumbo and Kubrick Argue History," 185; Margot A. Henrikson, *Dr. Strangelove's America*, 242–43.
108. Phillips, *Stanley Kubrick*, 78; Davis, "Trumbo and Kubrick Argue History," 184, 188; Baxter, *Stanley Kubrick*, 137.
109. Davis, *Slaves on Screen*, 38–40.
110. Davis, "Trumbo and Kubrick Argue History," 186.
111. Baxter, *Stanley Kubrick*, 112–16, 142–74; LoBrutto, *Stanley Kubrick* 197–229; Kroll, "Kubrick's Brilliant Vision," 32; Phillips, *Stanley Kubrick*, 83–84; Sikov, *Mr. Strangelove*, 191; James Mason, *Before I Forget: Autobiography and Drawings* (London: Sphere Books, 1982), 426–38; Walker, *Peter Sellers*, 134–36; Kagan, *Cinema of Stanley Kubrick*, 81–109.
112. Vladimir Nabokov, *The Annotated Lolita*, 46, 60, 73.
113. *Lolita*, DVD , scene 2, 5.33–36; Paul Schrader, "'Lolita,'" 19.
114. *Lolita*, DVD, scene 25, 1:19.21–25; Schrader, "'Lolita,'" 18; Seesslen and Jung, *Stanley Kubrick*, 121–22, 137; Sikov, *Mr. Strangelove*, 160. Nabokov had written part of *Lolita* at the Enchanted Hunters Hotel in Lugano, Switzerland (Vladimir Nabokov, *Lolita: A Screenplay*, x).
115. Nabokov, *Lolita: A Screenplay*, xiii; Vladimir Nabokov, *Strong Opinions* (New York: McGraw-Hill, 1973), 21, 217; Jenkins, *Stanley Kubrick*, 34; Dan E. Burns, "Pistols and Cherry Pies."
116. Nabokov, *Annotated Lolita*, 7, 56, 326, 327; Nabokov, *Lolita: A Screenplay*, 167; Nabokov, *Strong Opinions*, 115–16.
117. *Lolita*, DVD, scenes 5, 16.53–17.00; 17, 53.56–54.04; 14, 23, 26, 38, 39.

118. *Lolita,* DVD, scenes 4–5, 7, 11, 13.
119. *Lolita,* DVD, scene 2, 11.43–12.03; Schrader, "'Lolita,'" 20. Whether Sellers knew it or not, there was an electric chair in Alabama named "Yellow Mama." Just before this sequence, Quilty plays a Chopin polonaise on the piano, a coincidence of Poland and incipient death that Kubrick would exploit musically and visually in *The Shining.*
120. Nabokov, *Annotated Lolita,* 87; *Lolita,* scenes 17–18, 54.55–55.30.
121. Nabokov, *Annotated Lolita,* 17, 20, 37, 42, 120, 125, 129, 250, 290, 373.
122. Nabokov, *Lolita: A Screenplay,* 13, 26, 69, 83, 97, 111, 112, 116, 198, 199.
123. Nabokov, *Annotated Lolita,* 178, 255, 264; Nabokov, *Lolita: A Screenplay,* 39; *Lolita,* DVD, scene 5, 17.12–18.
124. *Lolita,* DVD, scenes 4, 16.29; 24, 1:15.41–42. Humbert finds Zempf in his home at 7:10 P.M. as indicated by a clock that remains at that time throughout (scene 31, 1:44.53–54ff).
125. Nabokov, *Annotated Lolita,* 256; see also 76–77, 81, 299.
126. *Lolita,* DVD, scene 2, 7.37–47; Schrader, "'Lolita,'" 19; Nabokov, *Annotated Lolita,* 299.
127. *Lolita,* DVD, scene 13, 42.32–34; scene 31, 1:44.22; Nelson, *Kubrick,* 77–78; Phillips, *Stanley Kubrick,* 98–100.
128. Nabokov, *Strong Opinions,* 149; Nabokov, "Foreword" (1973), in Nabokov, *Lolita: A Screenplay,* xii.
129. Seesslen and Jung, *Stanley Kubrick,* 133; Nabokov, *Annotated Lolita,* 129.
130. Walker, *Stanley Kubrick,* 47; Seesslen and Jung, *Stanley Kubrick,* 136.
131. Nabokov, *Annotated Lolita,* 293, 295.
132. Bob Gaffney, quoted in LoBrutto, *Stanley Kubrick,* 211; *Lolita,* scene 2, 2.10–18.
133. Walker, *Stanley Kubrick,* 28.

# Chapter 6

1. Brownlow, *How It Happened Here,* 147.
2. *Stanley and Us* (Mauro Di Flaviano and Federico Greco, 1999).
3. Southern, "Strangelove Outtake," 69.
4. Phillips, *Stanley Kubrick,* 126; Marwick, *The Sixties,* 472; Maland, "*Dr. Strangelove.*"
5. *Inside the Making of Dr. Strangelove,* 3.45–4.00; Boyer, "Dr. Strangelove," 266; Phillips, ed., *Interviews,* 28.
6. Walker, *Stanley Kubrick,* 224. Kubrick hired German émigré Arthur Fellig, a New York crime photographer whose work he admired, as the stills photographer for *Dr. Strangelove* (Sikov, *Mr. Strangelove,* 194–95; Christiane Kubrick, *Stanley Kubrick,* 35, 94–95; Baxter, *Stanley Kubrick,* 184–85; *The Art of Stanley Kubrick from the Short Films to Strangelove, Dr. Strangelove,* DVD).
7. Peter Bryant, *Two Hours to Doom,* 191.
8. Stanley Kubrick, "How I Learned to Stop Worrying and Love the Cinema," 12; Baxter, *Stanley Kubrick,* 171–72, 175–80; LoBrutto, *Stanley Kubrick,* 228, 229, 231.
9. Walker, *Stanley Kubrick,* 30; Phillips, ed., *Interviews,* 148–51; Paul Williamson, "Hogarth and the Strangelove Effect," *Eighteenth-Century Life* 23 (February 1999): 83, 93; Ferro, *Cinema and History,* 151.
10. *Dr. Strangelove,* DVD, scene 7, 23.50–24.12; "*Dr. Strangelove:* A Continuity Transcript," 13; Kagan, *Cinema of Stanley Kubrick,* 111–44.

11. *Dr. Strangelove*, DVD, scene 9, 34.18-24; "Continuity Transcript," 19; Kubrick et al., *Dr. Strangelove*, 49; on Plan R, see also Bryant, *Two Hours to Doom*, 19, 26, 50-53; and Walker, *Stanley Kubrick*, 120.
12. "Continuity Transcript," 11.
13. Thomas Pynchon, *Gravity's Rainbow* (New York: Viking, 1973), 521; Sherrill E. Grace, "Fritz Lang and the 'Paracinematic Lives' of *Gravity's Rainbow*," *Modern Fiction Studies* 29:4 (1983): 655-70.
14. Henriksen, *Dr. Strangelove's America*, 320; Harriet and Irving Deer, "Kubrick and the Structures of Popular Culture," 240.
15. *Dr. Strangelove*, DVD, scene 4, 12.07, 12.14-16; Nelson, *Kubrick*, 89-92; Hughes, *Complete Kubrick*, 113; Walker, *Stanley Kubrick*, 127; Southern, "Strangelove Outtake," 75.
16. Nelson, *Kubrick*, 92; for example, Ripper, when ordering Mandrake to help him operate the machine gun, "feed me this belt, boy!" and Mandrake echoing "You with the old gun, and me with the belt and the ammo, feeding you, Jack! Feed me, you said, and I was feeding you, Jack" (*Dr. Strangelove*, DVD, scenes 16, 54.54-56; 17, 1:00.17-21; "Continuity Transcript," 28, 35).
17. Peter Baxter, "The One Woman," 36; F. Anthony Macklin, "Sex and Dr. Strangelove," 55; Walker, *Stanley Kubrick*, 121.
18. Mainar, *Narrative and Stylistic Patterns*, 54-57, 72, 84.
19. Baxter, "The One Woman," 41; Pollan, "Materiality and Sociality," 94; *Dr. Strangelove*, DVD, scene 3, 6.35-48. *Foreign Affairs* was the leading journal of the American foreign policy and defense establishment. For a naturalistic treatment of a woman's emotional suffering as a result of marriage into the nuclear warfare business, see Tony Richardson's film *Blue Sky* (1994).
20. *Dr. Strangelove*, DVD, scene 21, 1:10.13-18, 43-44, 1:10.51-13.02; Andrew Grossman, *Neither Dead nor Red: Civilian Defense and American Political Development During the Early Cold War* (New York: Routledge, 2001), 41-106. In the screenplay published in 1963 and (under only George's name) 1988, *The Leper Colony* drops its bombs on "Missile Complex 69" (Kubrick et al., *Dr. Strangelove*, 141).
21. Nicholas Christopher, *Somewhere in the Night: Film and the American City* (New York: Free Press, 1997), 49; the motion picture *Gilda* (1946) starred Hayworth. The *Leper Colony* is looking to ditch at "weathership tango delta," another possible erotic reference: the delta of Venus and tango, the sexually charged Argentine dance; and also perhaps the abbreviation "td" for "touchdown," to "score" in American football and to land in aviation; see "Continuity Transcript," 39, 43.
22. *Dr. Strangelove*, DVD, scene 16, 56.36-57.19; "Continuity Transcript," 33.
23. Victor Davis Hanson, "The Right Man," *Military History Quarterly* 8:3 (1996): 62; Michael S. Sherry, *The Rise of American Air Power: The Creation of Armageddon* (New Haven: Yale University Press, 1987), 1-21, 177-356; Ronald Takaki, *Hiroshima: Why America Dropped the Atomic Bomb* (Boston: Little, Brown, 1995), 109-20; Carol Cohn, "Sex and Death in the Rational World of Defense Intellectuals," *Journal of Women in Culture and Society* 12 (1987): 717.
24. Kubrick, "How I Learned to Stop Worrying," 12-13.
25. Nelson, *Kubrick*, 81, 84; Baxter, *Stanley Kubrick*, 186; Walker, *Peter Sellers*, 137; *Inside the Making of Dr. Strangelove*, 17.20-27; LoBrutto, *Stanley Kubrick*, 239; Sikov, *Mr. Strangelove*, 196; David Halberstam, *The Fifties* (New York: Random House, 1993), 234-35.

26. *Dr. Strangelove*, DVD, scene 9, 34.25-28; "Continuity Transcript," 19; cf. Bryant, *Two Hours to Doom*, 81.
27. *Dr. Strangelove*, DVD, scene 21, 1:09.34-49; "Continuity Transcript," 39-40; Walker, *Stanley Kubrick*, 145, 147.
28. Marwick, *The Sixties*, 31, 472, 535.
29. Gary K. Wolfe, "*Dr. Strangelove*, *Red Alert*, and Patterns of Paranoia in the 1950s," *Journal of Popular Film* 5:1 (1976): 60-61; Garry Wills, "The New Revolutionaries," *New York Review of Books*, August 10, 1995, 54.
30. Quoted in Nat Frankel and Larry Smith, *Patton's Best: An Informal History of the 4th Armored Division* (New York: Hawthorn Books, 1978), 41; *Dr. Strangelove*, DVD, scenes 3, 6.07-21; 7, 22.31-33; 14, 18.40-42; 17, 58.58-59.43; "Continuity Transcript," 13, 28, 34. Sellers himself had served in the RAF during the war (Sikov, *Mr. Strangelove*, 190; Phillips and Hill, eds., *Encyclopedia*, 317).
31. Howard, *Stanley Kubrick Companion*, 46-47; Sterling Hayden, *Wanderer* (New York: Norton, 1977), 92-93, facing 201, 298-333, 348-50, 377-91; Boyer, "Dr. Strangelove," 268; Sherry, *Rise of American Air Power*, 157-58, 178-82, 256-316. Scott originally disliked the fact that Kubrick forced him to play Turgidson over the top, but later came to regard the role as one of his best (Howard, *Stanley Kubrick Companion*, 70; Walker, "Inexactly Expressed Sentiments," 291; Baxter, *Stanley Kubrick*, 187; Phillips and Hill, eds., *Encyclopedia*, 314-15).
32. *Dr. Strangelove*, DVD, scenes 20, 1:08.14-18; 23, 1:18.30-40.
33. Baxter, *Stanley Kubrick*, 180; Hughes, *Complete Kubrick*, 128; Magid, "Quest for Perfection," 42; Seesslen and Jung, *Stanley Kubrick*, 149; *Inside the Making of Dr. Strangelove*, 12.31-13.58. Ironically, Taylor's B-17 was once forced to land in Iceland as a result of violating the air space of an American airbase.
34. Baxter, *Stanley Kubrick*, 178.
35. Kinney, "Text and Pretext," 82-83; James Earl Jones, quoted in *Inside the Making of Dr. Strangelove*, 30.06-13; Seesslen and Jung, *Stanley Kubrick*, 152. An interesting coincidence in terms of issues of ethnic identity and prejudice important to Kubrick was the fact that Kubrick got the idea of casting George C. Scott in *Dr. Strangelove* as a result of having seen him in the role of Shylock in a New York production of *The Merchant of Venice*, a coincidence compounded by his discovery of James Earl Jones, who was playing the Prince of Morocco in the same production (LoBrutto, *Stanley Kubrick*, 236; Baxter, *Stanley Kubrick*, 173; *Inside the Making of Dr. Strangelove*, 24.46-57, 29.51-30.05). The two bombs in *The Leper Colony* have "Hi-There" and "Dear John" written on them, a Second World War female greeting and rejection, respectively, addressed to military men; in George's *Dr. Strangelove*, instead of "Dear John" one of the messages is "Lolita" (6).
36. Shandler, *While America Watches*, 83, 104-5, 166-67, 211-12, 276n1; Novick, *Holocaust in American Life*, 133-34; Leon A. Jick, "The Holocaust: Its Uses and Abuses within the American Public," *Yad Vashem Studies* 14 (1981): 313; Carr, "Holocaust in the Text," 52; see also Leon Uris, *Armageddon: A Novel of Berlin* (Garden City, N.Y.: Doubleday, 1964).
37. Henriksen, *Dr. Strangelove's America*, 270.
38. Novick, *Holocaust in American Life*, 110, 112, 309n37.
39. Quoted in Ciment, *Kubrick*, 156; Walker, *Stanley Kubrick*, 62.
40. Quoted in James W. Harper, "Images of Armageddon: Nuclear War in Three Mass Audience Films," in *War and Peace: Perspectives in the Nuclear Age*, ed. Ulrich Goebel

and Otto Nelson (Lubbock: Texas Tech University Press, 1988), 28; Hughes, "The Alienated and the Demonic in the Films of Stanley Kubrick," 17.
41. Pierre Giuliani, *Stanley Kubrick*, 46; *Inside the Making of Dr. Strangelove*, 19.40–20.05.
42. *Dr. Strangelove*, DVD, scene 22, 1:14.13–17; "Continuity Transcript," 42; Nelson, *Kubrick*, 97; Walker, *Stanley Kubrick*, 116.
43. John Hofsess, "From *Take One* Magazine," in Agel, ed., *Making of Kubrick's 2001*, 235.
44. Quoted in Baxter, *Stanley Kubrick*, 178–79; Walker, *Peter Sellers*, 137–38.
45. Kubrick, "How I Learned to Stop Worrying," 12.
46. "Continuity Transcript," 30; *Inside the Making of Dr. Strangelove*, 2.32–46.
47. *Inside the Making of Dr. Strangelove*, 2.22–46, 5.31–33; Albert Wohlstetter, "The Delicate Balance of Terror," *Foreign Affairs* 37 (1959): 211–34.
48. Paul Boyer, "Dr. Strangelove," 267–68; Walker, *Peter Sellers*, 137; LoBrutto, *Stanley Kubrick*, 239; Maland, "*Dr. Strangelove*," 699.
49. Quoted in Halberstam, *The Fifties*, 614; see also Seesslen and Jung, *Stanley Kubrick*, 154.
50. *Dr. Strangelove*, DVD, scene 15, 53.30–31; cf. Baxter, *Stanley Kubrick*, 178; and Nelson, *Kubrick*, 91. In a scene cut from the film, Strangelove brandishes a Luger (Pierre Giuliani, *Stanley Kubrick*, 46; Baxter, *Stanley Kubrick*, 190; Southern, "Strangelove Outtake," 75).
51. Kubrick et al., *Dr. Strangelove*, 65; see also Henriksen, *Dr. Strangelove's America*, 428n42.
52. *Dr. Strangelove*, DVD, scene 27; Kinney, "Text and Pretext," 61; Walter, "Entretien avec Stanley Kubrick," 38.
53. Kubrick et al., *Dr. Strangelove*, 141 (emphasis in original); Henriksen, *Dr. Strangelove's America*, 428n43. There seems to be little or no use of symbolic numbers in the film, probably because the many numbers in it are related to specific military and strategic concepts and systems. There is a 7 above General Turgidson's head as he outlines his belief in a "monstrous commie plot" (*Dr. Strangelove*, DVD, scene 14, 46.35–44). There is also the CRM 114, but it comes from the novel; see Bryant, *Two Hours to Doom*, 29.
54. Nelson, *Kubrick*, 95, 98.
55. *Dr. Strangelove*, DVD, scenes 15, 51.56, 52.22; 27, 1:28.56, 1:29.28–46, 1:31.46, 1:31.50–53; Nelson, *Kubrick*, 93; *Inside the Making of Dr. Strangelove*, 36.47–37.18; Alec Nevala-Lee and J. Kastof, "Strangelove's Erection: A Parody of Pal?" www.netins.net/showcase/sahaja/pal.html, October 7, 1996, 2.
56. Baxter, *Stanley Kubrick*, 204; Arthur C. Clarke, *Childhood's End* (New York: Harcourt, Brace & World, 1953), 207, 209–10, 213, 216–17, 218.
57. Baxter, *Stanley Kubrick*, 205–13.
58. Marcel Chion, *Kubrick's Cinema Odyssey*, v; Phillips, ed., *Interviews*, 78; Baxter, *Stanley Kubrick*, 223–24; Christiane Kubrick, *Stanley Kubrick*, 113–30; Seesslen and Jung, *Stanley Kubrick*, 185; Kagan, *Cinema of Stanley Kubrick*, 145–66; Hobbs FAQ.
59. Baxter, *Stanley Kubrick*, 210, 212; Walker, *Stanley Kubrick*, 193; Seesslen and Jung, *Stanley Kubrick*, 157; Kael, "Trash, Art, and the Movies," 81–82; William Kloman, "In 2001, Will Love Be a Seven-Letter Word?". See also John Carpenter's satiric film homage, *Dark Star* (1974).
60. Quoted in Phillips, ed., *Interviews*, 73; see also 53; Walker, *Stanley Kubrick*, 193; Leonard F. Wheat, *Kubrick's 2001*, 87–137; Ciment, *Kubrick*, 105, 128, 130, 177, 265; LoBrutto, *Stanley Kubrick*, 308; Chion, *Kubrick's Cinema Odyssey*, 91–92.

61. Phillips, ed., *Interviews*, 50; Stephen E. Hefling, "Miners Digging from Opposite Sides: Mahler, Strauss, and the Problem of Program Music," in *Richard Strauss: New Perspectives on the Composer and His Work*, ed. Bryan Gilliam (Durham: Duke University Press, 1992), 47; Agel, ed., *Making of Kubrick's 2001*, 231–32; on the source for Nietzsche being Clarke and not Kubrick, see Kinney, "Text and Pretext," 142.
62. Stanley Kubrick and Arthur C. Clarke, "2001: A Space Odyssey Screenplay," 1; Seesslen and Jung, *Stanley Kubrick*, 160–62. It is not certain that this screenplay from the Internet is authentic; see also Arthur C. Clarke, *The Lost Worlds of 2001*, 29–40.
63. *2001: A Space Odyssey*, DVD, scene 3, 15.14–16.57, 19.41–56; Miller, "Cold Descent."
64. Phillips and Hill, eds., *Encyclopedia*, 31.
65. Chion, *Kubrick's Cinema Odyssey*, 93, 174–85; Phillips, *Stanley Kubrick*, 136; Joseph Gelmis, "'Space Odyssey' Fails Most Gloriously," 264–65.
66. Kinney, "Text and Pretext," 153.
67. Seesslen and Jung, *Stanley Kubrick*, 174; Chion, *Kubrick's Cinema Odyssey*, 146; Kinney, "Text and Pretext," 148, 157; Robert Burgoyne, "Narrative Overture and Closure in *2001: A Space Odyssey*," 176.
68. Baxter, *Stanley Kubrick*, 225–27; Ciment, *Kubrick*, 282; Chion, *Kubrick's Cinema Odyssey*, 93–95, 110n16; Walter, "Entretien avec Stanley Kubrick," 23; Jan Harlan, personal communication, December 9, 2002; Howard, *Stanley Kubrick Companion*, 110; Hughes, *Complete Kubrick*, 142–43; Hefling, "Miners Digging from Opposite Sides," 47–48; Michaela Williams, "*2001*: Where Did It Go Right?" 279–80.
69. Lloyd Schwartz, "By György," *Boston Phoenix*, March 26, 1993, 20.
70. Quoted in Schwartz, "By György," 20; Richard C. Cumbow, "Music of the Spheres: *2001: A Space Odyssey*," liner notes, *2001: A Space Odyssey*, CD (Turner Entertainment Company, 1996), 18.
71. Victor Yuzefovich, *Aram Khachaturian*, trans. Nicholas Kournikoff and Vladimir Bobrov (New York: Sphinx, 1985), 84; Grigory Shneerson, *Aram Khachaturian* (Moscow: Foreign Languages Publishing House, 1959), 55–67; Chion, *Kubrick's Cinema Odyssey*, 93; Mainar, *Narrative and Stylistic Patterns*, 152; *2001*, DVD, scenes 12–16, 54.41–58.06, 1:03.29–1:07.19.
72. Walter, "Entretien avec Stanley Kubrick," 23; Chion, *Kubrick's Cinema Odyssey*, 93; Nelson, *Kubrick*, 112; Baxter, *Stanley Kubrick*, 226; *2001*, DVD, scene 32, 2:23.07–12.
73. Michael H. Kater, *The Twisted Muse: Musicians and Their Music in the Third Reich* (New York: Oxford University Press, 1997), 57, 60, 258n101; Walter, "Entretien avec Stanley Kubrick," 23.
74. Novick, *Holocaust in American Life*, 109, 308n25; Kater, *Twisted Muse*, 61.
75. Michael H. Kater, *Composers of the Nazi Era: Eight Portraits* (New York: Oxford University Press, 2000), 213, 215, 220–21, 255–56.
76. Ernst Krause, *Richard Strauss: The Man and His Work* (London: Collet's, 1964), 241–43; Henry T. Finck, *Richard Strauss: The Man and His Works* (Boston: Little, Brown, 1917), 180–90.
77. Kater, *Composers of the Nazi Era*, 113.
78. Kater, *Composers of the Nazi Era*, 131.
79. Kater, *Composers of the Nazi Era*, 112–13, 125–31, 137.
80. Miller, "Cold Descent"; Phillips, ed., *Interviews*, 78; Chion, *Kubrick's Cinema Odyssey*, 94; *2001*, DVD, scenes 4–10; Nelson, *Kubrick*, 117.

81. Nelson, *Kubrick*, 118; John Charlot, "From Ape-Man to Space-Baby," 85; Carl Freedman, "Kubrick's 2001 and the Possibility of a Science-Fiction Cinema," 313–15; *2001*, DVD, scene 7.
82. *2001*, DVD, scenes 12, 56.09–57.19; 18, 1:19.07–20.11; Bizony, *2001*, 42, 53; Nelson, *Kubrick*, 122.
83. See also Kubrick and Clarke, "2001: Space Odyssey Screenplay," 62–63, 81; Seesslen and Jung, *Stanley Kubrick*, 166, 178; Nelson, *Kubrick*, 112; Walker, *Stanley Kubrick*, 187; Baxter, *Stanley Kubrick*, 215; Arthur C. Clarke, *2001: A Space Odyssey*, 94, 141–47; Clarke, *Lost Worlds of 2001*, 76–78. Clarke had heard a computer sing this song (Chion, *Kubrick's Cinema Odyssey*, 103), ostensibly in a "German-American accent" (Miles, *Paul McCartney*, 207).
84. Miller, "Cold Descent"; Baxter, *Stanley Kubrick*, 221; Mainar, *Narrative and Stylistic Patterns*, 72; *2001*, DVD, scenes 5; 6; 10, 46.53–49.06; 30; 12–19.
85. Miller, "Cold Descent"; *2001*, DVD, scene 5, 27.08–22.
86. Seesslen and Jung, *Stanley Kubrick*, 178; *2001*, DVD, scenes 5; 7; 8, 40–13–41.06; 19, 1: 23.50–53, 1:24.22–1:27.16.
87. *2001*, DVD, scenes 16–18, 22–27, 30. Unlike colors, numbers again do not appear to play a significant role in *2001*. Finck, *Richard Strauss*, 187; Kloman, "Will Love Be a Seven-Letter Word?" in which presumably the "seven-letter word" is "machine"; cf. Wheat, *Kubrick's 2001*, 83–85, 87–88, 110–11.
88. Judith Spector, "Science Fiction and the Sex War: A Womb of One's Own," *Literature and Psychology* 31:1 (1981): 21–32; Zoë Sofia, "Exterminating Fetuses: Abortion, Disarmament, and the Sexo-Semiotics of Extraterrestrialism," *Diacritics* 14:2 (Summer 1984): 47–59; Chion, *Kubrick's Cinema Odyssey*, 2, 6, 118; *2001*, DVD, scenes 4, 8, 12, 29.
89. Seesslen and Jung, *Stanley Kubrick*, 182; Nelson, *Kubrick*, 130; Agel, ed., *Making Kubrick's 2001*, 215; John Russell Taylor, "On Seeing 2001 a Second Time," 272; Wheat, *Kubrick's 2001*, 76, 86, 157–58.
90. David Boyd, "Mode and Meaning in *2001*," 207–8; Feldmann, "Kubrick and His Discontents," 193.
91. Cumbow, "Music of the Spheres," 12; Agel, ed., *Making of Kubrick's 2001*, 159; Wheat, *Kubrick's 2001*, 29; Norman N. Holland, "*2001*: A Psychosocial Explication," 23; Richard W. Noland, "Individuation in *2001: A Space Odyssey*," 308.
92. Wheat, *Kubrick's 2001*, 89; Holland, "Psychosocial Explication," 22. Athena, Athene, Pallas Athene, and Minerva (Roman) are all names for the same goddess.
93. Clarke, *2001* (1968), [222] (1999), [235].
94. Miller, "Cold Descent"; Nelson, *Kubrick*, 132; Wheat, *Kubrick's 2001*, 79–80. Kubrick had also originally planned to begin and end *Dr. Strangelove* with the observations of an alien history, *The Dead Worlds of Antiquity* (Kubrick et al., *Dr. Strangelove*, 1–3, 145; *Inside the Making of Dr. Strangelove*, 5.35–40).
95. Phillips, ed., *Interviews*, 74.
96. Nelson, *Kubrick*, 141; Feldmann, "Kubrick and His Discontents," 195, 196; Kagan, *Cinema of Stanley Kubrick*, 167–87.
97. Kroll, "Kubrick's Brilliant Vision," 29; Anthony Burgess, *A Clockwork Orange* (1963), 75, 79; *A Clockwork Orange*, DVD, scene 16, 47.52–55. An aerial shot shows one of Britain's Panoptican prisons proposed by Utilitarian jurist Jeremy Bentham as an effective way of observing prisoners' behavior. Phillips argues that the year may be 1985, the year *after* 1984 (Phillips, *Stanley Kubrick*, 157–58).

98. David Wheatley, personal communication, January 13, 2003; *A Clockwork Orange*, DVD, scenes 5, 7.48–8.06; 29; 30; LoBrutto, *Stanley Kubrick*, 353; Burgess, *A Clockwork Orange* (1963), 18.
99. Burgess, *A Clockwork Orange* (1963), 92; Baxter, *Stanley Kubrick*, 240–43, 257; Vincent LoBrutto, "The Old Ultra-Violence," 53; Phillips, ed., *Interviews*, 111.
100. Burgess, "A Clockwork Orange Resucked," viii.
101. Burgess, *A Clockwork Orange* (1963), 92; see also 127 for Alex's use of "a clockwork orange," a London Cockney expression; Anthony Burgess, "Clockwork Orange Resucked," x; Gehrke, "Deviant Subjects in Foucault and *A Clockwork Orange*"; see also Stanley Kubrick, *A Clockwork Orange*.
102. Burgess, "A Clockwork Orange Resucked," v, viii; Anthony Burgess, "Juice from a Clockwork Orange," 188–89; John W. Tilton, *Cosmic Satire in the Contemporary Novel* (Lewisburg, Pa.: Bucknell University Press, 1977), 24; *An Examination of Kubrick's A Clockwork Orange* (Kalb, Conn.: Creative Arts Television, 1972); McDougal, "Questioning Kubrick's *Clockwork*, 2; Janet Staiger, "The Cultural Productions of *A Clockwork Orange*." Burgess's novel also features two "nymphets" of ten with whom Alex has sex. As in *Lolita*, Kubrick makes the girls older: cf. Burgess, *A Clockwork Orange* (1963), 43; *A Clockwork Orange*, DVD, scenes 10–11.
103. Burgess, *A Clockwork Orange* (1963), 42; see also 34, 43, 47, 79, 89, 113, 115, 138–39, 167. Kubrick even shows a close-up of the Deutsche Grammophon label of the Beethoven's Ninth that Alex owns (*A Clockwork Orange*, DVD, scene 8, 18.43), with Ferenc Fricsay (1914–1963) conducting the Berlin Philharmonic recorded at the Jesus Christus Church in Berlin in April 1958. DGG recorded von Karajan conducting the Ninth in 1961, 1962, and 1963, but it might have been that the Fricsay recording was cheaper while also highly regarded (Jan Harlan, personal communication, January 13, 2003; cf. Gabbard and Sharma, "Art Cinema," 103).
104. Robert Hughes, "The Décor of Tomorrow's Hell," 186 (also in Stuart Y. McDougal, ed., *Stanley Kubrick's A Clockwork Orange*, 131–33).
105. Peter J. Rabinowitz, "'A Bird of Like Rarest Spun Heavenmetal': Music in *A Clockwork Orange*," 114, 118–127; *A Clockwork Orange*, DVD, scene 26.
106. *A Clockwork Orange*, DVD, scenes 4, 6, 14; Hughes, "Décor of Tomorrow's Hell," 186; Gabbard and Sharma, "Art Cinema," 102. An accelerated electronic rendition of Rossini's *William Tell* Overture (1829) accompanies Alex's sex with two young girls. This not only parodies the 1950s American television Western *The Lone Ranger*, which used this music for its theme of vigorous and valiant horseback riding ("Hi-o, Silver!"), but also contrasts the state of future society with the noble political aspirations in the play *Wilhelm Tell* (1804) by Schiller.
107. Marwick, *The Sixties*, 17, 694, 740; Phillips, ed., *Interviews*, 111; Nelson, *Kubrick*, 133; Vivian S. Sobchack, "Décor as Theme," 97; Kolker, "Ticking," 23–24, 31, 34–35; Gabbard and Sharma, "Art Cinema," 88–89.
108. Anthony Burgess, *Earthly Powers* (New York: Simon and Schuster, 1988), 343; Kolker, "Ticking," 30; Rabinowitz, "Music in *A Clockwork Orange*," 128–29n10.
109. *A Clockwork Orange*, DVD, scenes 18, 56.20–31; 22, 1:15.38–1:17.05; 31; Kinney, "Text and Pretext," 132–34; Burgess, *A Clockwork Orange* (1963), 113, 166–67. The scourging scene recalls Crixus in *Spartacus* wearing a light blue breastplate adorned with eagle wings (Floyd Collins, "Implied Metaphor in the films of Stanley Kubrick," 98–99).

110. *A Clockwork Orange,* DVD, scene 17, 54.42–45. I am grateful to Mark Crispin Miller for first drawing my attention to this tableau. On Nazi regalia, see scenes 2, 4, 7, and Ciment, *Kubrick,* 153.
111. Burgess, *A Clockwork Orange* (1963), 119.
112. *A Clockwork Orange,* DVD, scene 31, 1:56.29–35.
113. *A Clockwork Orange,* DVD, scenes 13, 36.59–37.04; 18, 56.52–55; Burgess, *A Clockwork Orange* (1963), 56–64, 79; on Big Jew, 84, 88, 90.
114. Judith Condon, "Miriam Karlin Talks to Women's Voice," *Women's Voice* 14 (February 1978): 11–12; see also later, 144 and 292n211.
115. John Clive, personal communication, September 27, 1999; *A Clockwork Orange,* DVD, scene 23, 1:22.54–23.06; Christiane Kubrick, *Stanley Kubrick,* 133.
116. Kroll, "Startling Vision of Stanley Kubrick," 29; George Orwell, *Nineteen Eighty-Four* (New York: Harcourt, Brace, 1949), 271.
117. Nelson, *Kubrick,* 159; Collins, "Implied Metaphor," 96; see Chapter 11 on *Nevsky.*
118. *A Clockwork Orange,* DVD, scenes 6, 9.46–10.00; 30, 1:43.29–52; Nelson, *Kubrick,* 147, 162. One wonders if Kubrick, by using an IBM typewriter, was having fun with those many who assumed that HAL in *2001* was intentionally chosen because the letters are those one ahead in the alphabet of IBM. Clarke and Kubrick always denied any intention of this on their part; see LoBrutto, *Stanley Kubrick,* 267–68.
119. *A Clockwork Orange,* DVD, scene 31, 1:59.47–2:00.12.
120. Burgess, "Clockwork Orange Resucked," vi; cf. *A Clockwork Orange,* DVD, scenes 20, 1:10.22–25; 28, 1:39.00, 1:39.51.
121. Michael Eric Stein, "The New Violence," *Films in Review* 46:1–2 (January–February 1995): 43.
122. Quoted in LoBrutto, *Stanley Kubrick,* 152.
123. Burgess, *A Clockwork Orange* (1963), 158; *A Clockwork Orange,* DVD, scenes 30–31; Nelson, *Kubrick,* 162; *A Clockwork Orange,* DVD, scene 30, 1:48.19–24; Phillips, *Stanley Kubrick,* 167.
124. *A Clockwork Orange,* DVD, scene 35; Kagan, *Cinema of Stanley Kubrick,* 181; Burgess, *A Clockwork Orange* (1963), 169–79; Nelson, *Kubrick,* 163; Margaret DeRosia, "An Erotics of Violence: Masculinity and (Homo)Sexuality in Stanley Kubrick's *A Clockwork Orange.*"
125. Walker, *Stanley Kubrick,* 234–35, 238; Baxter, *Stanley Kubrick,* 277–80; Christiane Kubrick, *Stanley Kubrick,* 146–51.
126. François Mauriac, foreword to Elie Wiesel, *Night* (Paris: Editions de Minuit, 1958), 7.
127. Alan Spiegel, "Kubrick's *Barry Lyndon,*" 205–6, 207; cf. Mark Crispin Miller, "*Barry Lyndon* Reconsidered," 828; Miller, "Kubrick's Anti-Reading," 226–42; Sarah Kozloff, *Invisible Storytellers: Voice-Over Narration in American Fiction Film* (Berkeley: University of California Press, 1988), 117–26; Walter Coppedge, "*Barry Lyndon:* Kubrick's Elegy for an Age," 173, 174–75; Kinney, "Text and Pretext," 174–77; Nelson, *Kubrick,* 169–70; Ciment, *Kubrick,* 170; cf. Stanley Kubrick, "Barry Lyndon"; and Jan Harlan, personal communication, September 16, 2003.
128. Nelson, *Kubrick,* 165–66, 170, 171, 176; Benjamin Ross, "Eternal Yearning," 42; Coppedge, "Kubrick's Elegy for an Age," 177–78; Friedman, "Kubrick and His Discontents," 197–98.
129. Miller, "*Barry Lyndon* Reconsidered," 831; Kagan, *Cinema of Stanley Kubrick,* 189–202.

130. *Barry Lyndon*, DVD, scene 3, 3.26–28; Burgess, *A Clockwork Orange* (1963), 1; chapter 7 also begins with these words: Burgess, *A Clockwork Orange* (1962), 140.
131. Frank Cossa, "Images of Perfection," 82; Nelson, *Kubrick*, 187n; *A Clockwork Orange*, DVD, scenes 35, 2:05.16–20, 2:06.46; 38, 2:18.39; 46, 2:59.25–42. And it is *December 1789*: Philippe Pilard, *Barry Lyndon, Stanley Kubrick: Étude Critique*, 43; Seesslen and Jung, *Stanley Kubrick*, 226.
132. Miller, "*Barry Lyndon* Reconsidered," 830–42; Miller, "Kubrick's Anti-Reading," 226–35.
133. Miller, "*Barry Lyndon* Reconsidered," 851.
134. Miller, "*Barry Lyndon* Reconsidered," 846.
135. Baxter, *Stanley Kubrick*, 285–90. Scenarist Ken Adam wanted to film in Germany as well, but Kubrick refused to travel there, although he did send a second-unit crew there near the end of production to shoot buildings and streets in Potsdam and East Berlin; see LoBrutto, *Stanley Kubrick*, 380; Baxter, *Stanley Kubrick*, 287.
136. William Makepeace Thackeray, *The Luck of Barry Lyndon*, 201, 213–36, 295, 377, 379; Miller, "*Barry Lyndon* Reconsidered," 344n; Siegbert Prawer, *Breeches and Metaphysics: Thackeray's German Discourse* (Oxford: Legenda, 1997), 499.
137. *Barry Lyndon*, DVD, scene 4, 6.51–7.11, see also 18, 59.05–09; Hummel et al., *Stanley Kubrick*, 269; Phillips, ed., *Interviews*, 163; Call Sheet, *The Luck of Barry Lyndon*, October 31, 1973.
138. Miller, "Kubrick's Anti-Reading," 228.
139. Elise F. Knapp and James Pegolotti, "Music in Kubrick's *Barry Lyndon*," 93.
140. *Barry Lyndon*, DVD, scenes 1, 0.07–0.57; 8, 21.12–25.57; 39, 2:20.47–25.24; 40, 2:27.14–33.46; 42, 2:40.00–51.04; 47, 3:01.35–04.55; Knapp and Pegolotti, "Music in Kubrick's *Barry Lyndon*," 96–97.
141. *Barry Lyndon*, DVD, scenes 31, 1:44.50–47.53; 32, 1:49.53–53.38; 38, 2:16.28–20.16.
142. *Barry Lyndon*, DVD, scenes 20–21, 1:10.30–11.12, 1:13.27–14.52; 24, 1:27.00–17.
143. *Barry Lyndon*, DVD, scenes 16, 51.16–52.28; 17, 58.07–59.28; 18, 1:01.11–54; 20, 1:04.34–1:08.39.
144. *Barry Lyndon*, DVD, scenes 24, 1:18.39–22.30; 25, 1:27.17–30.28.
145. Quoted in Ciment, *Kubrick*, 174; Knapp and Pegolotti, "Music in Kubrick's *Barry Lyndon*," 93–94; Michael Klein, "Narrative and Discourse in Kubrick's Modern Tragedy," 102–3; Miller, "*Barry Lyndon* Reconsidered," 839–40n; Hummel et al., *Stanley Kubrick*, 159–61; *Barry Lyndon*, DVD, scenes 26–27, 32.02–39.09; 28–29, 1:42.01–25, 1:42.44–43.05; 34, 1:56.43–2:00.06; 35, 2:04.01–6.12.
146. Bille Wickre, "Pictures, Plurality, and Puns"; Mainar, *Narrative and Stylistic Patterns*, 195; John Engell, "*Barry Lyndon*: A Picture of Irony," 83–84, 85, 87; Nelson, *Kubrick*, 167, 176, 184; Cossa, "Images of Perfection," 80; LoBrutto, *Stanley Kubrick*, 381–82.
147. *Barry Lyndon*, DVD, scene 26, 1:37.51–38.15; LoBrutto, *Stanley Kubrick*, 387–90; Ciment, *Kubrick*, 176; John Alcott, "Photographing Stanley Kubrick's *Barry Lyndon*," 223–25.
148. Engell, "A Picture of Irony," 83.
149. *Barry Lyndon*, DVD, scene 15, 48.22–38; William Thackeray, *Luck of Barry Lyndon*, 121.
150. *Barry Lyndon*, DVD, scene 15; Paul Fussell, *The Great War and Modern Memory* (New York: Oxford University Press, 1975), 299–309; Ciment, *Kubrick*, 171–72.
151. Blackbourn, *Long Nineteenth Century*, 61. The kiss between Grogan and Barry takes place in a muddy trench reminiscent of the First World War; there is a similar trench scene in the Prussian lines (*Barry Lyndon*, scenes 14, 46.31–47.39; 20, 1:06.28–35).

152. Prawer, *Breeches and Metaphysics*, 494, 496, 498, 501.
153. *Barry Lyndon*, DVD, scenes 17, 58.28–55;19; 20, 1:05.23–32; Thackeray, *Luck of Barry Lyndon*, 135; Gordon A. Craig, *The Politics of the Prussian Army, 1640–1945* (New York: Oxford University Press, 1955), 22; Peter H. Wilson, "Social Militarization in Eighteenth-Century Germany," *German History* 18:1 (2000): 10, 12, 20, 33. Coincidentally, actor Hardy Kruger, who plays Captain Potzdorf, was one of the many German children, including Christiane and Jan Harlan, who were evacuated from German cities during the Second World War; see Larass, *Zug der Kinder*, 16.
154. Seesslen and Jung, *Stanley Kubrick*, 211, 216; *Barry Lyndon*, DVD, scene 20, 1:05.06–21, 1:05.32–47; Miller, "*Barry Lyndon* Reconsidered," 833; Walker, *Stanley Kubrick*, 245, 253; Nelson, *Kubrick*, 181; Ciment, *Kubrick*, 23.
155. Nancy Mitford, *Frederick the Great* (New York: Harper & Row, 1970), 155; Walker, *Stanley Kubrick*, 261.
156. Miller, "*Barry Lyndon* Reconsidered," 838–39, 842n; *Barry Lyndon*, DVD, scene 17; Prawer, *Breeches and Metaphysics*, 195–209, 491–501.
157. *Barry Lyndon*, DVD, scene 17, 57.39–58.04; Thackeray, *Luck of Barry Lyndon*, 123–26; Miller, "*Barry Lyndon* Reconsidered," 839–41.
158. Baxter, *Stanley Kubrick*, 336–37, see also 326, 348–49; Nicolas Saada, "*The Shining*, une Histoire de Famille," 36; Phillips, ed., *Interviews*, 180, 181, 182, 184; Ciment, *Kubrick*, 241, 250, 308; LoBrutto, *Stanley Kubrick*, 459, 469, 485–86; Herr, *Kubrick*, 29–32, 40–46, 56–59; Jenkins, *The Art of Adaptation*, 107–47; Christiane Kubrick, *Stanley Kubrick*, 160–67; Bartov, *Murder in Our Midst*, 151, 233n7.
159. Gustav Hasford, *The Short-Timers*, 37; Baxter, *Stanley Kubrick*, 335; Herr, *Kubrick*, 91; Nelson, *Kubrick*, 232.
160. Walker, *Stanley Kubrick*, 315; Phillips, ed., *Interviews*, 182–83; Nelson, *Kubrick*, 229–30; Kagan, *Cinema of Stanley Kubrick*, 217–30; Stanley Kubrick et al., *Full Metal Jacket: The Screenplay*.
161. Michael Herr, *Dispatches* (New York: Knopf, 1977), 18, 20; Maggie Gordon, "Appropriation of Generic Convention: Film as Paradigm in Michael Herr's *Dispatches*," *Literature/Film Quarterly* 28 (2000): 16–27; Ciment, *Kubrick*, 250; Hasford, *Short-Timers*, iii, 42, 109; Phillips, ed., *Interviews*, 173, 183; Nelson, *Kubrick*, 233, 234; Greg Jenkins, *Art of Adaptation*, 108; Henrikson, *Dr. Strangelove's America*, 243–256.
162. Phillips, ed., *Interviews*, 181, 185; Gilliatt, "Heavy Metal," 22; Nelson, *Kubrick*, 235; *Full Metal Jacket*, DVD, scenes 21, 27, 29.
163. Nelson, *Kubrick*, 250–51, 257, 259; Phillips, ed., *Interviews*, 185; Kagan, *Cinema of Stanley Kubrick*, 228. But cf. James A. Stevenson, "Beyond Stephen Crane: *Full Metal Jacket*," 242, 243n3; Gerri Reaves, "The Fracturing of Identification," 235. On Jung, see *Full Metal Jacket*, DVD, scene 21, 1:05.05–11; Nelson, *Kubrick*, 236–37, 245, 248; Ciment, *Kubrick*, 234; Phillips, ed., *Interviews*, 184.
164. *Full Metal Jacket*, DVD, scenes 21, 1:02.50–3.39, 3.42–45; 37, 1:48.51–49.59; Hughes, *Complete Kubrick*, 227; LoBrutto, *Stanley Kubrick*, 480–81; Nelson, *Kubrick*, 257–58; Phillips, ed., *Interviews*, 182, 184–85, 186; Arthur H. Barlow, "The Films of Stanley Kubrick: A Study in Generative Aesthetics," 191–99. Mead's score is heavy on drums (scenes 5, 7, 21, 26) and thereby similar to the martial music in *The Killing* and *Paths of Glory*.
165. *Full Metal Jacket*, DVD, scene 12, 38.05–17; Hasford, *Short-Timers*, 17.
166. Paula Willoquet-Maricondi, "Full-Metal-Jacketing, or Masculinity in the Making"; Susan White, "Male Bonding, Hollywood Orientalism, and the Repression of the

Feminine in Kubrick's *Full Metal Jacket*," 122–23, 128; Richard Rambuss, "Machinehead," 109; Thomas Doherty, "Full Metal Genre: Kubrick's Vietnam Movie," 311–12; Michael Pursell, "*Full Metal Jacket:* The Unravelling of Patriarchy," 321–22; LoBrutto, *Stanley Kubrick*, 461–64.

167. *Full Metal Jacket*, DVD, scene 12, 34.51–35.51; White, "Male Bonding," 123, 125; Rambuss, "Machinehead," 101–4, 106; Nelson, *Kubrick*, 246–47; Willoquet-Maricondi, "Full-Metal-Jacketing." The name Pyle also recalls the protagonist in Graham Greene's *The Quiet American* (1955), Alden Pyle, who goes to Vietnam to save the Vietnamese from Communism, thereby forging, intentionally or not, links to other subjects and sources for active and ongoing audience investigation; see also *Full Metal Jacket*, DVD, scene 21, 1:05.28–32.

168. *Full Metal Jacket*, DVD, scenes 15–16, 32–37; Pursell, "Unravelling of Patriarchy." 324; Rambus, "Machinehead," 107, 109–10; Willoquet-Maricondi, "Full-Metal-Jacketing"; Nelson, *Kubrick*, 246–47.

169. *Full Metal Jacket*, DVD, scene 37, 1:50.47–52; Nelson, *Kubrick*, 258.

170. *Full Metal Jacket*, DVD, scenes 7; 20; 38, 1:52.17–24; Hasford, *Short-Timers*, 59, 65, 102; Stanley Kubrick and Michael Herr, "Full Metal Jacket," 112, 114–18; Baxter, *Stanley Kubrick*, 338; Hughes, *Complete Kubrick*, 236–38; Herr, *Dispatches*, 35; Willoquet-Maricondi, "Full-Metal-Jacketing"; Kagan, *Cinema of Stanley Kubrick*, 229; Jenkins, *Art of Adaptation*, 155.

171. *Full Metal Jacket*, DVD, scenes 1, 18, 23, 27, 39; Rich Schweitzer, "Born to Kill: S. Kubrick's *Full Metal Jacket* as Historical Respresentation of America's Experience in Vietnam," 68; Phillips, ed., *Interviews*, 192–93; Pursell, "Unravelling of Patriarchy," 321.

172. *Full Metal Jacket*, DVD, scenes 2, 1.36–52, 3.06–20; 6, 11, 12, 14, 22, 23, 31; Hasford, *Short-Timers*, 14, 15, 16, 26, 31, 52, 70–71.

173. *Full Metal Jacket*, DVD, scenes 13, 39.32–35; 37, 1:46.08; Kubrick and Herr, "Full Metal Jacket," 32; cf. Hasford, *Short-Timers*, 22; "Vietnam-Era MOS Codes: Marine Corps," www.noquarter.org/html/usmc_mos.html, January 23, 2003. The numbers in 3092, the Parris Island training platoon, coincidentally add up (like 68) to 14.

174. *Full Metal Jacket*, DVD, scene 26, 1:13.8–11, 1:13.23–29, 1:13.59–1:14.01; Nelson, *Kubrick*, 247.

175. Rambuss, "Machinehead," 100, 103; Mario Falsetto, *Stanley Kubrick*, 83; *Full Metal Jacket*, DVD, scene 9; Hasford, *Short-Timers*, 14–15; Kubrick and Herr, "Full Metal Jacket," 21–22; White, "Male Bonding," 124 Claude J. Smith, "Full Metal Jacket and the Beast Within," 227, 228; *Barry Lyndon*, DVD, scene 20, 1:04.34–5.05.

176. Hasford, *Short-Timers*, 3, 23, 50, 124.

177. *Full Metal Jacket*, DVD, scenes 29, 1:22.46–52; 36, especially 1:43.38–44.06, 44.39–56; 37; Walker, *Stanley Kubrick*, 334; Claude Humbert, *Ornamental Design* (New York: Viking, 1970), 17, 39, 40, 42; Nelson, *Kubrick*, 259; Ciment, *Kubrick*, 244; Steven Heller, *The Swastika: Symbol Beyond Redemption?* (New York: Allworth Press, 2000), 18–19, 22–23, 28–31, 148–157.

178. *Full Metal Jacket*, DVD, scene 25, 1:12.14–15; Carl B. Feldbaum and Ronald J. Bee, *Looking the Tiger in the Eye: Confronting the Nuclear Threat* (New York: Harper & Row, 1999), 6.

179. *Full Metal Jacket*, DVD, scene 30, 1:25.12–15; such racism does not prevent Animal Mother from risking his life for Eightball in combat (Schweitzer, "Born to Kill," 66).

180. *Full Metal Jacket,* DVD, scenes 1, 2.28; 20; Kubrick and Herr, "Full Metal Jacket," 4, 10, 28; Hasford, *Short-Timers,* 72, 85, 148; Smith, "Beast Within," 230; cf. Seesslen and Jung, *Stanley Kubrick,* 270.
181. *Full Metal Jacket,* DVD, scenes 1, 1.32–37; 35, 1:40.05–42.06; Walker, *Stanley Kubrick,* 340–41; Phillips, ed., *Interviews,* 182; Nelson, *Kubrick,* 257; LoBrutto, *Stanley Kubrick,* 488.
182. Nelson, *Kubrick,* 253; Pursell, "Unravelling of Patriarchy," 321; Ciment, *Kubrick,* 236; Stephen King, *The Shining,* 159.
183. Kubrick and Herr, "Full Metal Jacket," 62; *Full Metal Jacket,* DVD, scenes 20, 23, 31; White, "Male Bonding," 132–39; Pursell, "Unravelling of Patriarchy, " 320, 324; Willoquet-Maricondi, "Full-Metal Jacketing"; Phillips, ed., *Interviews,* 195–96; Rambuss, "Machinehead," 107; Gilliatt, "Heavy Metal," 22; LoBrutto, *Stanley Kubrick,* 469–71; Baxter, *Stanley Kubrick,* 341–42. Seesslen and Jung argue that the use of the gasworks at Beckton as a location represents a repudiation of 1980s neo-liberalism of the Thatcher government (*Stanley Kubrick,* 279).
184. *Full Metal Jacket,* DVD, scene 10, 31.04–32.24; Kubrick and Herr, "Full Metal Jacket," 24; Hasford, *Short-Timers,* 15.
185. *Full Metal Jacket,* DVD, scene 7, 22.21–26; Willoquet-Maricondi, "Full-Metal-Jacketing."
186. White, "Male Bonding," 128.
187. *Full Metal Jacket,* DVD, scenes 2, 2.03–5; 10, 31.41–43; 11, 32.55–56; Kubrick and Herr, "Full Metal Jacket," 24.
188. Ciment, *Kubrick,* 259, 264; Christiane Kubrick, *Stanley Kubrick,* 168–72; *The Last Movie,* part 3; coincidentally, Kubrick, like the Jewish Nathanson in the film, died in his sleep (Michel Chion, *Eyes Wide Shut,* 34, 58).
189. Quoted in Jack Kroll, "Kubrick's View," 67; Ciment, *Kubrick,* 259. Kubrick had had the flu a couple of weeks before his death and, according to Christiane, was "pale and tired" (quoted in Hughes, *Complete Kubrick,* 249). According to Warner Bros.'s Julian Senior (quoted in the *Guardian,* March 9, 1999), however, there seemed to be no trace of illness the day before he died in his sleep of a heart attack on March 7, 1999. His personal and premonitory commitment to *Eyes Wide Shut* would likely be the only possible reason why Kubrick would have for the first time appeared in one of his own films. Kubrick's family has firmly denied that he (and, according to some reports, Christiane) did a cameo in the Sonata Café, which bears the sign "All Exits Are Final" (*Eyes Wide Shut,* DVD, scene 13, 55.41–45); see Hobbs FAQ, 22. Nelson has argued that if this were the case it would be consistent with the extremely personal nature of *Eyes Wide Shut,* in particular that Kubrick, "like Bill Harford, had also benefited from the company of women" (*Kubrick,* 328n). Nelson also argues that such a cameo appearance would also make sense in terms of the film's setting in Manhattan, where Kubrick began his career as a photographer and then as a filmmaker—as well as the location of the Sonata Café in Greenwich Village, where Kubrick used to live. Anticipation that *Eyes Wide Shut* might be his last film might have contributed to a decision to appear onscreen. Another possibility is that in the planning, filming, or editing, the appearance, accidental or not, in the scene of someone who looked like Kubrick could have been a sly, reflexive joke on overly attentive audiences. In fact, there is a man who resembles Kubrick, but the hair is grayer and the woman with him is too young to be Christiane (*Eyes Wide Shut,* DVD, scene 13, 55.59–56.10, 57.00–12).

290 | The Wolf at the Door: Stanley Kubrick, History, and the Holocaust

190. *A Clockwork Orange*, DVD, scene 10, 26.23–26, 27.36–39; *Eyes Wide Shut*, DVD, scenes 1; 5; 6, 21.24–28; 23, 24, 28, 36.
191. Phillips, ed., *Interviews*, 67.
192. Arthur Schnitzler, *My Youth in Vienna*, trans. Cather Hutter (New York: Holt, Rinehart and Winston, 1970), 50; Arthur Schnitzler, *Dream Story*, 212–13; *Eyes Wide Shut*, DVD, scene 15, 1:05.12–1:08.39; Reinhard Urbach, *Arthur Schnitzler* (New York: Ungar, 1973), 14–15, 23, 25; George Sylvester Viereck, *Glimpses of the Great* (London: Duckworth, 1930), 333; Nata Minor, "Freud, Schnitzler et la Reine de la Nuit," *Etudes freudiennes* 5–6 (June 1971): 207–24; Loewenberg, "Freud, Schnitzler, and *Eyes Wide Shut*"; Ciment, *Kubrick*, 259, 264–65; Žižek, *Looking Awry*, 17, 85; Peter Gay, *Schnitzler's Century: The Making of Middle-Class Culture, 1815–1914* (New York: Norton, 2001); Chion, *Eyes Wide Shut*, 41, 88.
193. Nelson, *Kubrick*, 267; Phillips and Hill, eds., *Encyclopedia*, 104; Ciment, *Kubrick*, 259, 266; Loewenberg, "Freud, Schnitzler, and *Eyes Wide Shut*"; Chion, *Eyes Wide Shut*, 21; Arthur Schnitzler, "Traumnovelle," filmscript (n.d.), Deutsches Literaturarchiv, Marburg.
194. Stanley Kubrick and Frederic Raphael, "Eyes Wide Shut: A Screenplay," 17, 35, 36, 37, 44, 62, 82, 90, 91, 92, 100, 102, 105, 106, 116; Chion, *Eyes Wide Shut*, 20–21, 24, 69–74, 84.
195. *Eyes Wide Shut*, DVD, scenes 11, 47.53–48.00; 30, 1:55.30–52.
196. *Eyes Wide Shut*, DVD, scenes 5, 15, 17, 19, 21, 25, 26, 27, 30, 32; Stanley Kubrick and Frederic Raphael, *Eyes Wide Shut*, 26–32, 89–93, 98–110, 117–21, 123–25, 137–41, 143–45; Schnitzler, *Dream Story*, 213–16, 220–29, 251–52, 265–71, 279–80; Sigmund Freud, *The Interpretation of Dreams*, in *The Standard Edition of the Complete Psychological Works of Sigmund Freud*, ed. and trans. James Strachey (London: Methuen, 1955), 4:214, 242–48, 273–76; 5:395; Larry Gross, "Too Late the Hero," 20, 21; Van de Castle, *Our Dreaming Mind*, p. 123.
197. Kubrick and Raphael, *Eyes Wide Shut*, 93, 98; *Eyes Wide Shut*, DVD, scenes 15, 1:08.29–31; 17, 1:12.03–36, 1:12.45–1:18.07.
198. Loewenberg, "Freud, Schnitzler, and *Eyes Wide Shut*."
199. *Eyes Wide Shut* resembles other recent films of dangerous, mysterious, and fruitless search such as *Blow-Up* (1966), *Psycho* (1960), *Vertigo* (1958), *After Hours* (1985), *Blue Velvet* (1986), *Chinatown* (1974), and *Se7en* (1995); those exploring dreams like *Last Year at Marienbad* (1961), *Wild Strawberries* (1957), *Persona* (1965), and *Belle du Jour* (1967); as well several predecessors or referents including *Smiles of a Summer Night* (1957, which Kubrick admired [Haine, "Bonjour Monsieur Kubrick," 17]), *The Wizard of Oz* (1939, which he hated [Hobbs FAQ, 8]), and *Casanova* (1976); see Gross, "Too Late the Hero," 22, 23; Laurence Giavarini, "Puissance des Fantasmes," 42; Ciment, *Kubrick*, 261; and Seesslen and Jung, *Stanley Kubrick*, 284. Kubrick himself makes a classical reference, as in *2001*, by means of the Hotel Jason (scene 26) to the quest for the Golden Fleece by the Argonauts, perhaps a choice that also contains sexual innuendo in terms of the object of the search; see Terry Southern, *Blue Movie* (New York: New American Library, 1970), 148.
200. *Eyes Wide Shut*, DVD, scenes 2, 4, 7, 9, 10, 20; Kubrick and Raphael, *Eyes Wide Shut*, 17, 25, 50, 57, 69–70, 106–9; Schnitzler, *Dream Story*, 184, 186–92, 229; Freud, *Interpretation of Dreams*, 4:332–33; Nelson, *Kubrick*, 271.
201. Kubrick and Raphael, *Eyes Wide Shut*, 117–21, 145–46; Ciment, *Kubrick*, 266; Loewenberg, "Freud, Schnitzler, and *Eyes Wide Shut*"; Jonathan Rosenbaum, "In Dreams Begin Responsibilities"; Giavarini, "Puissance des Fantasmes," 41; Mark Pizzato,

"Beauty's Eye: Erotic Masques of the Death Drive in *Eyes Wide Shut*," in *Lacan and Contemporary Film*, ed. Todd MacGowan and Sheila Kunkle (New York: Other Press, 2004), 83–109; Nelson, *Kubrick*, 288, 295; Schnitzler, *Dream Story*, 275–79; *Eyes Wide Shut*, scenes 10, 15, 26, 27, 32.
202. Raphael, *Eyes Wide Open*, 26–27; see also 61; Ciment, *Kubrick*, 269.
203. Giavarini, "Puissance des Fantasmes," 42; Timothy Kreider, "Introducing Sociology"; Ciment, *Kubrick*, 266; *Eyes Wide Shut*, DVD, scenes 1, 1.06–9; 6; 11, 51.00–13; beautiful naked women (and, once, naked men) appear (voyeuristically?) in scenes 1, 5, 6, 7, 16, 17, 18, 19, 20, 22, 32; Kubrick and Raphael, *Eyes Wide Shut*, 34, 101.
204. Walker, *Stanley Kubrick*, 347; Ciment, *Kubrick*, 261, 266; Chion, *Kubrick's Cinema Odyssey*, 164–65; Loewenberg, "Freud, Schnitzler, and *Eyes Wide Shut*"; *Eyes Wide Shut*, DVD, scenes 2, 3, 4, 5, 12, 13, 25.
205. William Hays, ed., *Twentieth-Century Views of Music History* (New York: Scribner, 1972), 275; Nelson, *Kubrick*, 268–69, 277n, 288n; Ronald Taylor, *Franz Liszt: The Man and the Musician* (London: Grafton, 1986), 234; Franz Liszt, *Selected Letters*, ed. and trans. Adrian Williams (Oxford: Clarendon, 1988), 859; *Eyes Wide Shut*, DVD, scenes 12, 51.00–13; 13, 32, 38. The scenes in the Sonata Café recall James B. Harris's *Some Call It Loving* (1973); see Rosenbaum, "In Dreams Begin Responsibilities"; and LoBrutto, *Stanley Kubrick*, 229. Again an interesting coincidence is the advertisement for Fidelio Tonic on a billboard next to a 1940s Bronx movie theater; see Christiane Kubrick, *Stanley Kubrick*, 33.
206. Raphael, *Eyes Wide Open*, pp. 59, 70–76, 89–90; Jenny and Wolf, "Er war einfach schüchtern," 198. He had also considered making it a comedy starring Steve Martin, whose work in *The Jerk* (1979) he had enjoyed; that film contains a parody of the bone-tossing sequence in *2001* as well as a motorcycle girl in an SS cap.
207. Schnitzler, *Dream Story*, 202–7, 218, 254; Ciment, *Kubrick*, 153; Loewenberg, "Freud, Schnitzler, and *Eyes Wide Shut*."
208. Raphael, *Eyes Wide Open*, 119; Frederic Raphael, personal communications, May 23, 2000, March 14, 2002; Schnitzler, *Dream Story*, 184–85; Kubrick and Raphael, *Eyes Wide Shut*, 50–53; *Eyes Wide Shut*, DVD, scene 8; Nelson, *Kubrick*, 275. There is a Dr. Adler ("eagle" in German) in the novella but not in the film; see Schnitzler, *Dream Story*, 272–78; Frederic Raphael, *The Glittering Prizes* (Harmondsworth: Penguin, 1976), 14, 19.
209. *Eyes Wide Shut*, DVD, scene 8, 38.40–39.55; Hannah Arendt, "On Humanity in Dark Times: Thoughts about Lessing," in Arendt, *Men in Dark Times* (New York: Harcourt, Brace & World, 1968), 3–31; Schnitzler, *Dream Story*, 194–95; John Milfull, "The German and the Jewish Selves: Arthur Schnitzler's *Der Weg ins Freie*," in *The German-Jewish Dilemma: From the Enlightenment to The Shoah*, ed. Edward Timms and Andrea Haimmel (Lewiston: Edwin Mellen Press, 1999), 165–92; Urbach, *Arthur Schnitzler*, 25–28. The *fleur-de-lis* motif is also present in the Cat Lady's home in *A Clockwork Orange* (scene 14; Nelson, *Kubrick*, 161n). In *Eyes Wide Shut*, *fleur-de-lis* wallpaper is seen outside the Harfords' apartment when Bill returns shamed from the orgy and from a conversation with Ziegler that had told him nothing but reasserted the unassailable power of the elites Ziegler represents and thus again the defeat of humane idealism represented by Nathan and the Enlightenment (*Eyes Wide Shut*, DVD, scenes 23, 36). There is also Joseph Kreisch Knish Bakery ("Since 1910") next to The Lotto Store on the way to Domino's apartment. Is it accidental that the German verb *kreischen* means "shriek, scream, hiss, sizzle" (*Eyes Wide Shut*, DVD, scene 30, 1:55.30–52)?

210. Burgess, *A Clockwork Orange* (1963), 84, 88, 89, 90; George L. Mosse, *The Image of Man: The Creation of Modern Masculinity* (New York: Oxford University Press, 1996); George L. Mosse, *Nationalism and Sexuality: Respectability and Abnormal Sexuality in Modern Europe* (New York: Fertig, 1985); Schnitzler, *Dream Story,* 195, 205.
211. Tom Conley, *Film Hieroglyphs: Ruptures in Classical Cinema* (Minneapolis: University of Minnesota Press, 1911), 26; *Eyes Wide Shut,* DVD, scene 10, 45.57–46.08; Joël Dor, *Introduction to the Reading of Lacan* (New York: Other Press, 1998), 6. Does *Scarlett Street* contain the Nazi referent "SS" as well as reference to blood? On street sets, see Rosenbaum, "In Dreams Begin Responsibilities"; and "Diamond Jewelry" and "38," *Eyes Wide Shut,* DVD, scene 31 ("Stalker"), 2:02.03-10.
212. Quoted in Stephen Pizzello, "A Sword in the Bed," 31; *Eyes Wide Shut,* DVD, scene 10, 45.13–46.49; Kubrick and Raphael, *Eyes Wide Shut,* 60–61; Schnitzler, *Dream Story,* 194–95; Raphael, *Eyes Wide Open,* 59; Leonard Dinnerstein, *Antisemitism in America* (New York: Oxford University Press, 1994), 85, 87; William F. Buckley, *God and Man at Yale: The Superstitions of "Academic Freedom"* (South Bend: Gateway, 1951), 30, 112; William F. Buckley, *In Search of Anti-Semitism* (New York: Continuum, 1992), 8; cf. Rosenbaum, "In Dreams Begin Responsibilities."
213. Nelson, *Kubrick,* 295n; *Eyes Wide Shut,* DVD, scenes 5, 6, 7, 8, 9, 10, 16, 23, 36.
214. *Eyes Wide Shut,* DVD, scenes 1, 8, 33–35; Kubrick and Raphael, *Eyes Wide Shut,* 7–9, 29, 51; Pizzello, "Sword in the Bed," 31, 37–38; Rosenbaum, "In Dreams Begin Responsibilities." Numbers, by contrast, seem to play no special role in *Eyes Wide Shut.* The party and orgy sequences last seventeen minutes apiece (Nelson, *Kubrick,* 275, 288n; Schnitzler, *Dream Story,* 199, 253), daughter Helena is seven (cf. six in Schnitzler, *Dream Story,* 206), and there are references to 7:00 P.M. (Kubrick and Raphael, *Eyes Wide Shut,* 7, 75, 130–31; Schnitzler, *Dream Story,* 263, 281; Ciment, *Kubrick,* 144, 146). A painting in Bill's office has a seven (or the Hebrew letter *khaf*) at its center, but since the office was a location shoot and the picture was already in place, there is probably little or nothing to be made of this (*Eyes Wide Shut,* DVD, scenes 6, 20.52-21.01; 29, 1: 54.17-27; Jan Harlan, personal communication, January 30, 2003).
215. Kubrick and Raphael, *Eyes Wide Shut,* 10–12, 25–28, 29–32, 100, 146–59; *Eyes Wide Shut,* DVD, scenes 2, 5, 17, 33–35; Frederic Raphael, personal communications, May 23, 2000, March 14, 2002.
216. Amy Taubin, "Stanley Kubrick's Last Film," 31; Chion, *Eyes Wide Shut,* 21, 56.
217. David Denby, "Last Waltz," 84; Richard T. Jameson, "Sonata," 28; *Eyes Wide Shut,* DVD, scenes 5, 16; Kubrick and Raphael, *Eyes Wide Shut,* 95. Somerton was a small market town in southwest England used only in the summer when the land was dry.
218. Schnitzler, *Dream Story,* 256.
219. Herr, *Kubrick,* 84; Elizabeth Wilson, *Shostakovitch: A Life Remembered* (Princeton: Princeton University Press, 1994), 102, 292. Alice's tempter is played by German actor Sky Dumont, a Nazi officer in *The Boys from Brazil* (1978), *The Boat* (1981), *Inside the Third Reich* (1982), and *War and Remembrance* (1989).
220. György Ligeti, quoted in Harlan, *A Life in Pictures,* DVD, scene 25, 2:10.51-11.24; Lutz Lesle, "Ligeti im 'neuen werk,'" *Melos* 4 (1978): 118; *Eyes Wide Shut,* DVD, scenes 21, 22, 28, 31, 36; *ricercato:* "affected, farfetched, studied, sought after, (much) in demand."
221. Nelson, *Kubrick,* 296–97.
222. Joseph Lanza, *Fragile Geometry: The Films, Philosophy, and Misadventures of Nicolas Roeg* (New York: PAJ Publications, 1989), 55–58, 103–5, 119, 131–32, 148.

223. Gerald C. Wood, "Gender, Caretaking, and the Three Sabrinas," *Literature/Film Quarterly* 28 (2000): 73–77; Charles H. Helmtag, "Dream Odyssey: Schnitzler's *Traumnovelle* and Kubrick's *Eyes Wide Shut*," *Literature/Film Quarterly* 31:4 (2003): 282; Kubrick and Raphael, *Eyes Wide Shut*, 161; *Eyes Wide Shut*, DVD, scene 37; Ciment, *Kubrick*, 254; Chion, *Eyes Wide Shut*, 57–59; Chion, *Kubrick's Cinema Odyssey*, 164–73.

# Chapter 7

1. PCA Files, Margaret Herrick Library; Stang, "Film Fan to Filmmaker," 36, 38; Baxter, *Stanley Kubrick*, 74, 107–8; LoBrutto, *Stanley Kubrick*, 229; Ciment, *Kubrick*, 36, 154; Phillips, ed., *Interviews*, 101; Douglas, *Ragman's Son*, 324; James A. Ramage, *Gray Ghost: The Life of Col. John Singleton Mosby* (Lexington: University of Kentucky, 1999).
2. Felix Jackson, *So Help Me God* (New York: Viking, 1955), 50, 120–21, 194, 214–15, 235.
3. PCA Files.
4. Ciment, *Kubrick*, 105; Kolker, "Ticking," 23–24.
5. PCA Files.
6. Calder Willingham, *Natural Child* (New York: Dial Press, 1952), 88.
7. *Killer's Kiss*, DVD, scene 16, 54.28–38; Baxter, *Stanley Kubrick*, 117.
8. Quoted in Baxter, *Stanley Kubrick*, 121; LoBrutto, *Stanley Kubrick*, 158–65; Raphael, *Eyes Wide Open*, 156–57.
9. Charles Neider, "The Novel and the Film" (1984), in Neider, *The Authentic Death of Hendry Jones* (1956; Reno: University of Nevada Press, 1993), xiii; Stephen Tatum, "Commentary," in Neider, *Authentic Death*, 206–11; Michael Coyne, *The Crowded Prairie: American National Identity in the Hollywood Western* (London: Tauris, 1997), 55.
10. Neider, *Authentic Death*, 176; see also 19–22, 27, 57, 115, 121, 123; on yellow as a color of decay, see 71, 116, 123, 140, 141, 184, 199; Tatum, "Commentary," 208. The Punta del Diablo is based on central California's Point Lobos (Spanish for "wolves").
11. LoBrutto, *Stanley Kubrick*, 329–30; Herr, *Kubrick*, 90; Baxter, *Stanley Kubrick*, 179, 194–95, 248, 249, 274; Mel Gussow, "Terry Southern Literary Archives Go to New York Public Library," *New York Times*, April 3, 2003; Southern, *Blue Movie*, 5; coincidentally, Andy Warhol, *Blue Movie: A Film* (New York: Grove, 1970).
12. Baxter, *Stanley Kubrick*, 306–7; LoBrutto, *Stanley Kubrick*, 413.
13. Baxter, *Stanley Kubrick*, 275, 332, 360; LoBrutto, *Stanley Kubrick*, 497–99; Jenny and Wolf, "Er war einfach schüchtern," 198; Hairapetian, "Stanley hätte applaudiert!"; James, "At Home with the Kubricks," 18.
14. Walker, *Stanley Kubrick*, 363; Baxter, *Stanley Kubrick*, 275–76.
15. Quoted in Thissen, *Stanley Kubrick*, 262; see also Baxter, *Stanley Kubrick*, 276; Ciment, *Kubrick*, 253; and Walker, *Stanley Kubrick*, 107, 363.
16. Jan Harlan, personal communication, December 9, 2002; cf. Ciment, *Kubrick*, 253; and Baxter, *Stanley Kubrick*, 332, 360; Jeffrey Adams, "Narcissism and Creativity in the Postmodern Era: The Case of Patrick Süskind's *Das Parfum*," *Germanic Review* 75:4 (Fall 2000): 259–79.
17. PCA Files; Ciment, *Kubrick*, 154; Baxter, *Stanley Kubrick*, 86–89; LoBrutto, *Stanley Kubrick*, 131; Richard Laermer, "Filming a Sort of 'Peter Pan,' Only in Reverse," *New York Times*, December 18, 1988.

18. Ciment, *Kubrick*, 144, 146.
19. Stefan Zweig, *The World of Yesterday: An Autobiography by Stefan Zweig* (1943; Lincoln: University of Nebraska Press, 1964), 367–68; Kater, *Composers of the Nazi Era*, 172, 227, 241, 243, 246–47, 249.
20. Colin Young, "The Hollywood War of Independence" (1959) in Phillips, ed., *Interviews*, 6; Baxter, *Stanley Kubrick*, 87; LoBrutto, *Stanley Kubrick*, 155. There is no evidence one way or the other about whether Adams and Kubrick were influenced by August Strindberg's antiwar story, "The German Lieutenant" (1915), set during and after the Franco-Prussian War from 1870 to 1872. It may be that Kubrick was familiar with the story and decided to adopt its title for his screenplay, since it resembles *Paths of Glory* in that it concerns three French *francs-tireurs* to be shot since the Prussians did not recognize such irregular volunteer formations as soldiers under the rules of war. Strindberg also quotes Rousseau: "Man is good but men are bad' said our friend Jean Jacques and he was right" (*The German Lieutenant and Other Stories* [Chicago: McClurg, 1915], 60).
21. Richard Adams and Stanley Kubrick, "The German Lieutenant," 16. I am grateful to Glenn Perusek for his reading of the screenplay.
22. Adams and Kubrick, "The German Lieutenant," 31.
23. Adams and Kubrick, "The German Lieutenant," 120–21.
24. Adams and Kubrick, "The German Lieutenant," 161.
25. Jan Harlan, personal communication, January 21, 2003.
26. Adams and Kubrick, "The German Lieutenant," 161.
27. David Downing, *Jack Nicholson*, 169–170; Baxter, *Stanley Kubrick*, 240; LoBrutto, *Stanley Kubrick*, 329; Ciment, *Kubrick*, 196–97, 297; Thissen, *Stanley Kubrick*, 255–57; Perusek, "Kubrick's Armies"; Stanley Kubrick, "Napoleon: A Screenplay," 12, 14, 27–28, 63, 92, 96, and Stanley Kubrick, "Napoleon: Production Notes," November 22, 1968, 1–3, www.filmforce.net, August 1, 2000; Christiane Kubrick and Jan Harlan, *Stanley Kubrick's Napoleon: His Greatest Film Never Made* (forthcoming). Both Jan Harlan (personal communication, January 21, 2003) and Vincent LoBrutto (personal communication, September 26, 2000) affirm that this script is genuine.
28. LoBrutto, *Stanley Kubrick*, 322.
29. Phillips, ed., *Interviews*, 84; Herr, *Kubrick*, 23. Schnitzler, too, was fascinated by Napoleon (Viereck, *Glimpses of the Great*, 335).
30. Kubrick, "Napoleon," 65; Jan Harlan, personal communication, December 9, 2002.
31. Felix Markham, *Napoleon and the Awakening of Europe* (London: English Universities Press, 1954), 173; Felix Markham, *Napoleon* (New York: New American Library, 1963), xii.
32. Quoted in A. A. DeVitis, *Anthony Burgess* (New York: Twayne, 1972), 112.
33. Anthony Burgess, *Napoleon Symphony* (New York: Knopf, 1974), 48, 134–35; DeVitis, *Anthony Burgess*, 113, 115; Burgess, "Juice from a Clockwork Orange," 189; Burgess, *Earthly Powers*, 555–57; Jürgen Osterhammel, "In Search of a Nineteenth Century," *Bulletin of the German Historical Institute* 32 (Spring 2003): 15.
34. Kubrick, "Napoleon," 98, 106, 119.
35. Pieter Geyl, *Napoleon, For and Against*, trans. Olive Renier (New Haven: Yale University Press, 1949), 8.
36. Geyl, *Napoleon, For and Against*, 10.
37. Geyl, *Napoleon, For and Against*, 9, 10.

38. Louis Begley, *Wartime Lies*, 84, 192.
39. "Pressekonferenz zu 'Stanley Kubrick: A Life in Pictures,'" 4–5; www.rauschen.de/artikel/Festivals/festival4.htm, July 26, 2002; Jan Harlan, personal communication, February 5, 2003.
40. Janet Malcolm, "A Matter of Life and Death," *New York Review of Books*, June 13, 1991, 16, 17; Begley, *Wartime Lies*, 61, 66, 93–94, 148, 197. A passage about early Nazi victories in Russia may have caught Kubrick's eye: "My grandfather stopped making jokes about Napoleon and field marshal snow" (Begley, *Wartime Lies*, 49).
41. Begley, *Wartime Lies*, 58.
42. Begley, *Wartime Lies*, 7–8, 50.
43. Louis Begley, personal communication, November 4, 1996.
44. LoBrutto, *Stanley Kubrick*, 496–99; Baxter, *Stanley Kubrick*, 360–61.
45. Quoted in Raphael, *Eyes Wide Open*, 107; LoBrutto, *Stanley Kubrick*, 499; Cole, *Selling the Holocaust*, 73–94; Miriam Bratu Hansen, "*Schindler's List* Is Not *Shoah*: Second Commandment, Popular Modernism, and Public Memory," in *Visual Culture and the Holocaust*, ed. Barbie Zelizer (New Brunswick: Rutgers University Press, 2001), 127–51; Frank Manchel, "A Reel Witness: Steven Spielberg's Representation of the Holocaust in *Schindler's List*," *Journal of Modern History* 67 (1995): 83–100; Raphael, *Eyes Wide Open*, 45; Michael Wilmington, "Long Decades Journey into Light," *Film Comment* 36:2 (March–April 2000): 9–10; Annette Insdorf, *Double Lives, Double Chances* (New York: Hyperion, 1999), 107–14.
46. Raul Hilberg, personal communication, April 15, 1999.
47. Raul Hilberg, personal communication, September 3, 2003; Jan Harlan, personal communication, December 9, 2002; Christiane Kubrick, personal communication, November 20, 2002.
48. Leonard J. Leff, "Hollywood and the Holocaust: Remembering *The Pawnbroker*," *American Jewish History* 84 (1996): 361; Alan Mintz, *Popular Culture and the Shaping of Holocaust Memory in America* (Seattle: University of Washington Press, 2001), 107–24.
49. Tim Kreider, "A.I.: Artificial Intelligence," 33.
50. Carl Collodi, *Pinocchio: The Adventures of a Marionette*, trans. Walter S. Cramp (Boston: Ginn, 1904), 28.
51. Gregory Feeley, "The Masterpiece a Master Couldn't Get Right," 22; Ian Watson, "My Adventures with Stanley Kubrick," 159; James Hoberman, "The Dream Life of Androids," 17; Kreider, "A.I.," 36, 37.
52. John C. Tibbetts, "Robots Redux: *A.I. Artificial Intelligence (2001)*," *Literature/Film Quarterly* 29: 4 (2001): 260.
53. "A.I. Shot Similarities to Kubrick-Directed Films," www.freespace.virgin.net/d.Corcoran/aianalysis.htm, April 15, 2002; Kreider, "A.I.," 34, 36, 37, 39.
54. *A.I.*, DVD, Disc 2, "Music," scene 1, 1:32–2:35; *A.I.*, DVD, scene 19, 1:23.13–40.
55. *A.I.*, DVD, scenes 24, 1:42.19–22; 25, 1:45.06–51; Kreider, "A.I.," 36.
56. Kreider, "A.I.," 35; *A.I.*, DVD, scene 15; see also Todd Ford, The Mysteries of Jewish Symbolism, www.mysteries of ai.com/jewishsymbolism/index.htm, June 7, 2002, 3–5.
57. Quoted in Baxter, *Stanley Kubrick*, 356. There are two notable instances of the number 7: seven words to imprint David on his mother (*A.I.*, DVD, scene 6, 21.53) and seven questions for Dr. Know (scene 20); see also Collodi, *Pinocchio*, 129.

## Chapter 8

1. Jan Harlan, personal communications, December 9, 2002, October 6, 2003.
2. Herr, *Kubrick*, 10.
3. Quoted in Herr, *Kubrick*, 5, 6, 7–8, 10 (emphasis in original).
4. Raul Hilberg, personal communications, June 4, 1991, April 15, 1999; Raul Hilberg, *The Politics of Memory: The Journey of a Holocaust Historian* (Chicago: Dee, 1996), 22–23, 176–88; Hilberg, *Destruction of the European Jews*, 145, 154, 319.
5. Baxter, *Stanley Kubrick*, 298–99, 302; Phillips, ed., *Interviews*, 161–62, 171; Herr, *Kubrick*, 46–47; Marwick, *The Sixties*, 455–65.
6. Carr, "Holocaust in the Text," 52.
7. Metz, "Notorious Ranch," 75.
8. Shandler, *While America Watches*, 63, 64, 73, 77–78; Cole, "Scales of Memory, Layers of Memory," 133.
9. Novick, *Holocaust in American Life*, 103, 144; Friedman, "Exorcising the Past," 514; Jean Cayrol, "Night and Fog," in *Film: Book 2*, ed. Robert Hughes (New York: Grove Press, 1962), 237.
10. Novick, *Holocaust in American Life*, 133; Walter, "Entretien avec Stanley Kubrick," 30.
11. Novick, *Holocaust in American Life*, 134–41.
12. Cole, *Selling the Holocaust*, 99–100.
13. Novick, *Holocaust in American Life*, 188–89; Todd M. Endelman, *The Jews of Britain, 1656–2000* (Berkeley: University of California Press, 2002), 234, 237–39.
14. Jick, "Holocaust: Use and Abuse," 314.
15. Quoted in Baigell, *Jewish-American Artists and the Holocaust*, 43.
16. Phillips, ed., *Interviews*, 168; Anton Kaes, "Holocaust and the End of History," in Saul Friedlander, ed., *Probing the Limits of Representation: Nazism and the "Final Solution"* (Cambridge, Mass.: Harvard University Press, 1992), 208–9; Friedman, "Exorcising the Past," 514–19; Susan Sontag, "Syberberg's Hitler," in Sontag, *Under the Sign of Saturn* (New York: Farrar, Straus, and Giroux, 1980), 137–165; Bruno Bettelheim, "Surviving," *New Yorker*, August 2, 1976, 1–52; Insdorf, *Indelible Shadows*; Ciment, *Kubrick*, 289–90; Bartov, *Murder in Our Midst*, 128; LoBrutto, *Stanley Kubrick*, 198, 201, 338–39, 355; Baxter, *Stanley Kubrick*, 244–46.
17. Susan Sontag, "Fascinating Fascism," in Sontag, *Under the Sign of Saturn*, 91. An interesting coincidence is the appearance of Sontag's name in *The Shining* on the cover of the *New York Review of Books* (*The Shining*, DVD, scene 6, 14.39–45, 15.09–18) as author of an article titled "Illness as Metaphor." The periodical documents Jack's status as a private school teacher in New England, and its date, January 26, 1978, places the film in the present, as does the cover of another issue with a reference to then-president Jimmy Carter. *If* Kubrick had also been concerned with content, then he was probably more interested in the title of Sontag's piece than in Sontag herself as the author of "Fascinating Fascism," since Jack's "illness" is certainly metaphorical for larger disorder in the world. The reference to Carter is, however, also consistent with subsequent mention of presidents as among "all the best people" who have stayed at the Overlook Hotel.
18. Sontag, "Fascinating Fascism," 91, 94, 100–101; Saul Friedländer, *Reflections of Nazism: An Essay on Kitsch and Death*, trans. Thomas Weyr (New York: Harper & Row, 1984), 74–78.

19. Sebastian Haffner, *The Meaning of Hitler,* trans. Ewald Osers (New York: Macmillan, 1979), 143; Herbert S. Levine, "Beyond Watergate: The Culture of Fascism," *Nation,* August 17, 1974, 103–7.
20. John G. Cawelti, "*Chinatown* and Generic Transformation in Recent American Films," in Barry Keith Grant, ed., *Film Genre Reader* (Austin: University of Texas Press, 1986), 188.
21. John Brown, "The Impossible Object: Reflections on *The Shining,*" 119; Russell, "Stanley Kubrick," 73.
22. Robert Caserio, "The Name of the Horse: *Hard Times,* Semiotics, and the Supernatural," *Novel* 20 (1986): 19; Cawelti, "*Chinatown* and Generic Transformation," 190; cf. Frederic Jameson, "Historicism in *The Shining,*" 88; and Kathleen K. Rowe, "Class and Allegory in Jameson's Film Criticism," *Quarterly Review of Film and Video* 12:4 (1991): 1–18.
23. LoBrutto, *Stanley Kubrick,* 368–71; Christiane Kubrick, *Stanley Kubrick,* 140.
24. Kael, "Stanley Strangelove," 470, 475.
25. "Kubrick: News a Hitler on Public Morals," *Detroit News,* April 9, 1972, E3.
26. Fred Hechinger, quoted in Stanley Kubrick, "Now Kubrick Fights Back," 4:1, 11.
27. Kubrick, "Now Kubrick Fights Back," 11; Walker, *Stanley Kubrick,* 212.
28. Shandler, *While America Watches,* 155–78; Novick, *Holocaust in American Life,* 209–14; Insdorf, *Indelible Shadows,* 3–6; Don Kowat, "The Holocaust Breakthrough," *TV Guide,* April 28, 1979, 3–6; Manchel, "Reel Witness," 91; cf. the lesser effect in East Germany, whose citizens could watch the series on West German television; see Mary Fulbrook, *German National Identity after the Holocaust* (Cambridge: Polity Press, 1999), 160; Jeffrey Herf, *Divided Memory: The Nazi Past in the Two Germanies* (Cambridge, Mass.: Harvard University Press, 1997), 384–85; and even an East German Holocaust film, *Jakob the Liar* (1974).
29. Diane Johnson, *The Shadow Knows,* 273–74; Burgess, *A Clockwork Orange* (1963), 17.
30. Doneson, *Holocaust in American Film,* 4.
31. James B. Twitchell, *Dreadful Pleasures: An Anatomy of Modern Horror* (New York: Oxford University Press, 1985), 50.
32. Twitchell, *Dreadful Pleasures,* 65–104.
33. James Diedrick, "The Sublimation of Carnival in Ruskin's Theory of the Grotesque," *Victorian Newsletter* 74 (February 1988): 14.
34. Twitchell, *Dreadful Pleasures,* 28, 29; Charlene Bunnell, "The Gothic: A Literary Genre's Transition to Film," in Grant, ed., *Planks of Reason,* 81–84.
35. Geoffrey Cocks, "Bringing the Holocaust Home," 108, 115.
36. Skal, *Monster Show,* 39.
37. Skal, *Monster Show,* 65–66, 127, 185–86, 205–6.
38. Angus Calder, "Propaganda and the Arts," in *The Experience of World War II,* ed. John Campbell (New York: Oxford University Press, 1989), 208; Skal, *Monster Show,* 224–25; Twitchell, *Dreadful Pleasures,* 14–15; Ciment, *Kubrick,* 241.
39. Skal, *Monster Show,* 247–53; Jeremy Dyson, *Bright Darkness: The Lost Art of the Supernatural Horror Film* (London: Cassell, 1997), 189–94.
40. *Eyes Wide Shut,* DVD, scene 5; *The Shining,* DVD, scenes 8, 9, 21, 24, 33; *Dr. Strangelove,* DVD, scene 17; *A Clockwork Orange,* DVD, scene 30; Douglas Fowler, "*Alien, The Thing* and the Principle of Terror," *Studies in Popular Culture* 4 (1981): 16–19; Robin Wood, *Hollywood from Vietnam to Reagan* (New York: Columbia

298 | The Wolf at the Door: Stanley Kubrick, History, and the Holocaust

University Press, 1986), 83, 85, 87; Dick, *Star-Spangled Screen*, 207; Gross, "Too Late the Hero," 20.
41. Twitchell, *Dreadful Pleasures*, 104; Baxter, *Stanley Kubrick*, 302.
42. Wood, *Hollywood from Vietnam to Reagan*, 70-80.
43. Vivian Sobchack, "Child/Alien/Father," 7, 10-11; Skal, *Monster Show*, 292-94. Kubrick admired both *Rosemary's Baby* and *The Exorcist* (1973) (Ciment, *Kubrick*, 196).
44. Greg Keeler, "The Shining: Ted Kramer Has a Nightmare."
45. Prawer, *Caligari's Children*, 60; Sobchack, "Child/Alien/Father," 13-15.
46. Prawer, *Caligari's Children*, 61-62.

## Chapter 9

1. Mark Schwed, "The Shining: It Lives Again," 20, 21; Stephen King, "Before the Play"; Hughes, *Complete Kubrick*, 210-11.
2. Peter S. Perakos, "Stephen King on Carrie, The Shining, etc.," *Cinefantastique* (Winter 1978): 13; Jim Albertson and Peter S. Perakos, "The Shining," 74; Darrell Ewing and Dennis Myers, "King of the Road," *American Film* 11 (June 1986): 46-47; Clare Hanson, "Stephen King: Powers of Horror," in Brian Docherty, ed., *American Horror Fiction: From Brockden Brown to Stephen King* (New York: Macmillan, 1990), 145-49; James F. Smith. "Kubrick's or King's—Whose *Shining* Is It?" 181-82. For an interpretation of King's own "happy" ending to *The Shining*, see the introduction to Anthony Magistrale, ed., *The Shining Reader*, viii.
3. Quoted in Jack Kroll, "Stanley Kubrick's Horror Show," 99; Ciment, *Kubrick*, 181.
4. Kroll, "Stanley Kubrick's Horror Show," 99; Ciment, *Kubrick*, 181, 186.
5. Ciment, *Kubrick*, 293; Harmetz, "Kubrick Films 'The Shining'," 72; LoBrutto, *Stanley Kubrick*, 409-54; Baxter, *Stanley Kubrick*, 301-28. King wrote a script for Warner Bros., which apparently Kubrick never saw (Harlan Kennedy, "Kubrick Goes Gothic," 50).
6. Walker, *Stanley Kubrick*, 270-71; Stephen King, *On Writing: A Memoir of the Craft* (New York: Scribner, 2000), 138.
7. Seesslen and Jung, *Stanley Kubrick*, 235. Kubrick also believed that available special effects could not reproduce the movement of topiary animals (LoBrutto, *Stanley Kubrick*, 414).
8. King, *The Shining*, 432; Nelson, *Kubrick*, 205; James Hala, "Kubrick's *The Shining*," 209.
9. King, *The Shining*, 32, 55, 65, 132, 218, 426; Hanson, "Powers of Horror," 147; *The Shining*, DVD, scene 11; see also Chapter 11.
10. *The Shining*, DVD, scene 3, 10.19-31.
11. Salinger, *Catcher in the Rye*, 14; *The Shining*, DVD, scenes 2, 4.19-45; 6, 15.28-33; Hala, "Kubrick's *The Shining*," 21. Salinger's novel, like Kubrick's film, is the opposite of a *Bildungsroman*, a story of the education and improvement of a human being. Nelson argues that the Salinger and the Virginia Slims, along with Jack's reading of *Playgirl* (*The Shining*, DVD, scene 7, 19.56-20.28) represent the thin veneer of liberalism, education, and liberation over the traditional sexism of the Torrance relationship (*Kubrick*, 216). This is a valid interpretation that does not, however, exclude others. Jack's reading of *Playgirl* also represents Kubrick's habitual representation of sexual

ambiguity, in *The Shining* also possibly suggested in the characters of Stuart Ullman and Bill Watson. On the identical front and back covers of the paperback Wendy reads as another example of a mirror of the two sides of Jack's character, as is her being halfway through the book, see Rick Munday, The Shining FAQ, 17.

12. Ciment, *Kubrick,* 189, 294, 301; Johnson, "Writing *The Shining*"; Larry McCaffery, "Talking About *The Shining* with Diane Johnson," 78; Hala, "Kubrick's *The Shining,*" 205, 207; Emery, "U.S. Horror," 156–57; Jackie Eller, "Wendy Torrance: One of King's Women"; Perakos, "Stephen King," 15; LoBrutto, *Stanley Kubrick,* 451; Smith, "Kubrick's or King's," 182–83, 186–88, 190.

13. [Stanley Kubrick,] "The Shining," 66, 67; LoBrutto, *Stanley Kubrick,* 412; Diane Johnson, personal communication, July 15, 2002; Perakos, "Stephen King," 13; Greg Weller, "The Redrum of Time," 74.

14. Diane Johnson, quoted in Ciment, *Kubrick,* 294.

15. King, *The Shining,* 431, 437–38; *The Shining,* DVD, scene 39; Ciment, *Kubrick,* 301.

16. *The Shining,* DVD, scene 39; Mann, *The Magic Mountain,* 470, 486.

17. King, *The Shining,* 157.

18. Patricia Ferreira, "Jack's Nightmare at the Overlook: The American Dream Inverted"; Burton Hatlen, "Good and Evil in Stephen King's *The Shining,*" 87.

19. *The Shining,* no.145381, Warner Bros. Archives; [Kubrick,] "The Shining," 43, 44, 68; King, *The Shining,* vii, 345–59; Nelson, *Kubrick,* 200, 202; Bunnell, "The Gothic," 98–99; Jameson, "Kubrick's Shining," 250; cf. Metz, "Intertextuality and *The Shining,*" 50.

20. Baxter, *Stanley Kubrick,* 311, 320–21; John Hofsess, "'The Shining' Example of Kubrick," 25; Jenkins, *Art of Adaptation,* 69–105; Christiane Kubrick, *Stanley Kubrick,* 152–59; cf. Jameson, "Historicism in *The Shining,*" 95.

21. Quoted in Ciment, *Kubrick,* 81; Madigan, "'Orders from the House'," 193–94; Walter Metz, "Toward a Post-structural Influence in Film Genre Study: Intertextuality and *The Shining,*" 58; Walker, "Inexactly Expressed Sentiments," 299; Jenkins, *Art of Adaptation,* 100; King, *The Shining,* 383; Eller, "Wendy Torrance," 11.

22. Nelson, *Kubrick,* 198, 199–200, 216; Bunnell, "The Gothic," 81, 83–84, 87, 93–99; Jeanne Campbell Reesman, "Stephen King and the Tradition of American Naturalism in *The Shining*"; Brian Kent, "Canaries in a Gilded Cage"; Baxter, *Stanley Kubrick,* 302; Brown, "Impossible Object," 109, 114, 118.

23. Fridman, *Words and Witness,* 12.

24. Fridman, *Words and Witness,* 15, 20.

25. Falsetto, *Narrative and Stylistic Analysis,* 140.

26. Amelunxen, "Points de Vue Imaginaires et Réels," 198–99.

27. *The Shining,* DVD, scenes 2, 3; Richard Kohnstamm, personal communication, May 22, 1994; Ciment, *Kubrick,* 114, 186, 208, 294; Walker, *Stanley Kubrick,* 107, 290; Baxter, *Stanley Kubrick,* 309; LoBrutto, *Stanley Kubrick,* 415; Nelson, *Kubrick,* 206; Kroll, "Stanley Kubrick's Horror Show," 97; Jim Albertson, "Stanley Kubrick Films *The Shining* at EMI Elstree Studios in England," *Cinefantastique* (Winter 1978): 13; Dennis Sharp, *A Visual History of Twentieth-Century Architecture* (Greenwich, Conn.: New York Graphic Society, 1972), 79; *Great Lodges of the National Parks* (Mark Mitchell, 2002).

28. Sontag, "Fascinating Fascism," 94; Avisar, *Screening the Holocaust,* 162. Ken Adam used Art Deco for just this historical and thematic purpose in his design of *Salon Kitty.*

29. Michael James Emery, "U.S. Horror: Gothicism in the Work of William Faulkner, Thomas Pynchon, and Stanley Kubrick," 119.

30. James Agee, "The Blue Hotel," 393–488; Baxter, *Stanley Kubrick*, 52, 306; LoBrutto, *Stanley Kubrick*, 82, 88.
31. Ray Allen Billington, *Land of Savagery, Land of Promise: The European Image of the American Frontier* (New York: Norton, 1978), 272–78.
32. William Bysshe Stein, "Stephen Crane's *Homo Absurdus*," *Bucknell Review* 7 (1959): 174; Hugh N. MacLean, "The Two Worlds of 'The Blue Hotel,'" *Modern Fiction Studies* 5 (1959): 262–64; Ciment, *Kubrick*, 301; Piotr Wioryma, "A Sample Contrastive Analysis of 'The Blue Hotel' by Stephen Crane and 'The Nigger of the Narcissus' by Joseph Conrad," *Studia Anglica Posnansiensia* 30 (1996): 159–68.
33. Edwin H. Cady, *Stephen Crane* (New York: Twayne, 1962), 156; James R. Fultz, "Heartbreak at the Blue Hotel: James Agee's Scenario of Stephen Crane's Story," *Midwest Quarterly* 21 (1980): 423–34.
34. Agee, "The Blue Hotel," 428–29, 463–64.
35. Agee, "The Blue Hotel," 467.
36. Agee, "The Blue Hotel," 487; Stephen Crane, "The Blue Hotel," 131.
37. MacLean, "Stephen Crane's *Homo Absurdus*," 174.
38. Friedman, "'Canyons of Nightmare,'" 142–43.
39. Alfred Kazin, "On Stephen Crane and 'The Blue Hotel,'" in *The American Short Story*, ed. Calvin Skaggs (New York: Dell, 1977), 78.
40. Kazin, "On Stephen Crane," 78.
41. "Interview with Jan Kadar," in Skaggs, ed., *American Short Story*, 70–71, 73, 74; Richard Keenan, "The Sense of an Ending: Jan Kadar's Distortion of Stephen Crane's *The Blue Hotel*," *Literature/Film Quarterly* 16 (1988): 265–68; see also *Das blaue Hotel* (1973).
42. Ciment, *Kubrick*, 185; cf. Daniel Weiss, "'The Blue Hotel': A Psychoanalytic Study," in *Stephen Crane: A Collection of Critical Essays* (Englewood Cliffs, N.J.: Prentice-Hall, 1967), 154–64.
43. Crane, "The Blue Hotel," 93.
44. Joseph Petite, "Expressionism and Stephen Crane's 'The Blue Hotel,'" *Journal of Evolutionary Psychology* 10 (1989): 325–36, 327; Woryma, "Sample Contrastive Analysis," 161.
45. MacLean, "Two Worlds," 263, 265, 277; Cady, *Stephen Crane*, 156; Crane, "The Blue Hotel," 94, 102, 103, 105, 107, 120.
46. Crane, "The Blue Hotel," 94.
47. Stefan Zweig, *The Burning Secret*, 9, 152.
48. Agee, "The Blue Hotel," 393, 488; Crane, "The Blue Hotel," 94.
49. Agee, "The Blue Hotel," 463; see also 394–95, 464, 481–82.
50. Chester L. Wolford, "The Eagle and the Crow: High Tragedy and Epic in 'The Blue Hotel,'" *Prairie Schooner* 51 (1977): 273.
51. Crane, "The Blue Hotel," 117.
52. Alfred Kazin, *A Lifetime Burning in Every Moment* (New York: HarperCollins, 1996), 107.
53. Hilberg, *Destruction of the European Jews*, 296–300, 309–555.
54. Catherine Cocks, *Doing the Town: The Rise of Urban Tourism in the United States, 1850–1915* (Berkeley: University of California Press, 2001), 73, 81, 85, 86, 96–98; Peter Fritzsche, "Specters of History: On Nostalgia, Exile, and Modernity," *American Historical Review* 106 (2001): 1605, 1616; Stephen King, *Everything's Eventual: 14 Dark Tales* (New York: Scribner, 2002).

55. Charles Derry, *Dark Dreams: A Psychological History of the Modern Horror Film* (New York: Barnes, 1977), 24; Jean-Claude van Italie, "Motel: A Masque for Three Dolls," in van Italie, *America Hurrah* (New York: Coward-McCann, 1966), 135–43; Kurt Brown and Laure-Anne Bosselaar, eds., *Night Out: Poems About Hotels, Motels, Restaurants, and Bars* (Minneapolis: Milkweed, 1997).
56. Henry Bromell, "The Dimming of Stanley Kubrick," *Atlantic* 246:2 (1980): 82.
57. Siegfried Kracauer, "The Hotel Lobby," in Kracauer, *The Mass Ornament: Weimar Essays*, ed. and trans. Thomas Y. Levin (Cambridge, Mass.: Harvard University Press, 1995), 177, 179.
58. Zweig, *The Burning Secret*, 128; Christopher Alexander, "The City as a Mechanism for Sustaining Human Contact," in *People and Buildings*, ed. Robert Gutman (New York: Basic Books, 1972), 412–13; Charles Rosenberg, *The Care of Strangers: The Rise of America's Hospital System* (New York: Basic Books, 1987), 138–44; Terry Lawson, "Evil Takes Many Forms in Spanish 'Devil,'" *Detroit Free Press*, December 21, 2001, 9E.
59. McCaffery, "Talking About *The Shining*," 75, 77; see also Bizony, *2001*, 163.
60. Vicki Baum, *Es war alles ganz anders: Erinnerungen* (Berlin: Ullstein, 1962), 341.
61. Vicki Baum, *Hotel Berlin '43* (Garden City, N.Y.: Doubleday, Doran, 1944), 5; Gottfried Korff and Reinhard Rürup, *Berlin, Berlin: Ausstellung zur Geschichte der Stadt* (Berlin: Nicolai, 1987), 462; Hans-Georg von Studnitz, *While Berlin Burns: The Diary of Hans-Georg von Studnitz, 1943–1945* (Englewood Cliffs, N.J.: Prentice-Hall, 1963), 113, 139, 140, 144, 145, 159, 170, 197, 207, 214, 236–37, 241, 250.
62. Compare "like a stadium or a big hotel" in the English translation of the original screenplay (Cayrol, "Night and Fog," 235); there is a Grand Hotel in Kadar's *The Shop on Main Street; Hotel Imperial* (Mauritz Stiller, 1927), MoMA, July 1945, Exhibition 32, Box 2.
63. Irwin Chusid, "The 5,000 Fingers of Dr. T," *Film Comment* 39:3 (May–June 2003): 16; Bernard Welt, "Nightmare Fun: Dr. Seuss' The 5000 Fingers of Dr. T," www.hometown.aol.com/seivadj18/5000fingers.html, February 11, 2002; Judith and Neil Morgan, *Dr. Seuss and Mr. Geisel* (New York: Random House, 1995), 131–38; Ruth K. MacDonald, *Dr. Seuss* (Boston: Twayne, 1988), 100–117.
64. Quoted in Ciment, *Kubrick*, 301.
65. Mayersberg, "The Overlook Hotel," 256–57; Metz, "Intertextuality and *The Shining*," 44–45; Wood, "American Horror," 185; Brown, "Impossible Object," 114; P. L. Titterington, "Kubrick and 'The Shining,'" 120; Jameson, "Historicism in *The Shining*," 89; Jean-Pierre Oudart, "Les Inconnus dans la maison," 10; King, *The Shining*, 219–20; *The Shining*, DVD, scenes 17, 29, 37.
66. Derry, *Dark Dreams*, 24; cf. Titterington, "Kubrick and 'The Shining,'" 120.
67. Derry, *Dark Dreams*, 24; Juan Carlos Polo, *Stanley Kubrick* (Madrid: Ediciones JC, 1986), 149.
68. Johnson, "Writing *The Shining*."
69. McGilligan, *Fritz Lang*, 438; Heinz Höhne, *Canaris*, trans. J. Maxwell Brownjohn (Garden City, N.Y.: Doubleday, 1979), 190, 191; Walter Schellenberg, *The Labyrinth*, trans. Louis Hagen (New York: Harper, 1956), 17–19; Prawer, *Caligari's Children*, 18.
70. Jean Douchet, "L'etrange Obsession," *Cahiers du Cinema* 122 (August 1961): 52; Luc Mollet, *Fritz Lang* (Paris: Editions Seghers, 1963), 123.
71. Gunning, *Films of Fritz Lang*, 470.
72. *The Shining*, DVD, scene 19, 1:04.05–11.
73. Gunning, *Films of Fritz Lang*, 473.

74. Michel Estève, "*The Exterminating Angel:* No Exit from the Human Condition," in Joan Mellen, ed., *The World of Luis Buñuel: Essays in Criticism* (New York: Oxford University Press, 1978), 248.
75. Raymond Durgnat, *Luis Bunuel* (Berkeley: University of California Press, 1970), 125–29; Juan Buñuel, "A Letter on *The Exterminating Angel*," in Mellen, ed., *World of Luis Buñuel*, 256; Peter William Evans, *The Films of Luis Buñuel: Subjectivity and Desire* (Oxford: Clarendon Press, 1995), 81–82, 144.
76. Evans, *Films of Luis Buñuel*, 83–84; Carlos Fuentes, "The Discreet Charm of Luis Buñuel," in Mellen, ed.,*World of Luis Buñuel*, 65; Ciment, *Kubrick*, 162, 193, 202, 243.
77. Prawer, *Caligari's Children*, 74–75; Nelson, *Kubrick*, 198.
78. Jeff Smith, "Careening Through Kubrick's Space," 65 (emphasis in original). Cf. wind in *The Shining*, DVD, scenes 14, 16, 20, 22, 25, 35, 37; and King, *The Shining*, passim.
79. Geoffrey Cocks, "Modern Pain and Nazi Panic," in *Pain and Prosperity: Reconsidering Twentieth-Century German History*, ed. Paul Betts and Greg Eghigian (Palo Alto: Stanford University Press, 2003), 106; Prawer, *Caligari's Children*, 75; Sigmund Freud, "'The Uncanny,'" 244, 246, 252.
80. Gaetana Marrone, *The Gaze and the Labyrinth: The Cinema of Liliana Cavani* (Princeton: Princeton University Press, 2000), 107; Insdorf, *Indelible Shadows*, 138.
81. Pauline Kael, "Stuck in the Fun," in Kael, *Reeling* (Boston: Little, Brown, 1976), 342; Grace Lichtenstein, "In Liliana Cavani's Love Story, Love Means Always Having to Say Ouch," *New York Times*, October 13, 1974, 2:15; Alexander Walker, "Two for the Pipshow," *Evening Standard*, January 17, 1974, 19; cf. Teresa De Lauretis, "Cavani's *Night Porter:* A Woman's Film?" *Film Quarterly* 30 (Winter 1976): 35–38.
82. Primo Levi, *The Drowned and the Saved*, trans. Raymond Rosenthal (New York: Simon and Schuster, 1988), 36–69.
83. Marrone, *Gaze and Labyrinth*, 90.
84. De Lauretis, "Cavani's *Night Porter*," 36–37; the butcher who delivers food to Max and Lucia is named Jacob, perhaps also an oneiric conflation of persecutor and victim.
85. Christiane Kubrick has no memory of Kubrick seeing Cavani's film (Jan Harlan, personal communication, February 28, 2003).
86. Žižek, *Looking Awry*, 100; Marrone, *Gaze and Labyrinth*, 94–95, 104, 110; Marguerite Waller, "Signifying the Holocaust: Liliana Cavani's *Portiere di notte*," in Laura Pietrapaolo and Ada Testaferri, eds., *Feminisms in the Cinema* (Bloomington: Indiana University Press, 1995), 214–15.
87. Irving Howe, "Writing and the Holocaust," *New Republic*, October 27, 1986, 36.
88. Aharon Appelfeld, *Badenheim 1939*, trans. Dalya Bilu (Boston: Godine, 1980), 5, 55.
89. Appelfeld, *Badenheim 1939*, 51, 57.
90. Appelfeld, *Badenheim 1939*, 23, 29–30; Fridman, *Words and Witness*, 41–42.
91. Appelfeld, *Badenheim 1939*, 106.
92. Paul Woods, ed., *Joel and Ethan Coen: Blood Siblings*, ed.(London: Plexus, 2000), 96, 100, 114; Mark Horowitz, "Coen Brothers A-Z," *Film Comment* 27:5 (September-October 1991): 30; Joel Levine, *The Coen Brothers* (Toronto: ECW Press, 2000), 83, 86, 93; Michael Dunne, "*Barton Fink*, Intertextuality, and the (Almost) Unbearable Richness of Viewing," *Literature/Film Quarterly* 28 (2000): 306. See also the Coen reference to *Dr. Strangelove* (DVD, scene 19, 1:05.26–7.06) in *Raising Arizona* (1987), in the "P.O.E." and "O.P.E." written on the back of a bathroom door, which were Jack Ripper's (anal) doodlings of the variations for "Purity of Essence" and "Peace on Earth" as the recall code for the bombers (Rick Lyman, "Making the Wit Seem Unwitting,"

Ironically, Jack Nicholson, who plays the lead in *The Shining*, had his first role in Roger Corman's *Little Shop of Horrors* (1960), which was a satire on Jewish-Gentile relations (Friedman, "'Canyons of Nightmare'," 143–44).

93. Faulkner's *Sanctuary* (1931), which Kubrick was on record as disliking (Haine, "Bonjour Monsieur Kubrick," 14), is a Gothic horror tale in which "the terrible house" is both "the Old Frenchman place" and a brothel: "In fact, all the buildings portrayed in the novel blur into one immense enclosure that represses human feeling and imprisons the spirit" (Emery, "U.S. Horror," 58). See also Herr, *Kubrick*, 13.
94. Zweig, *The Burning Secret*, 128, 133.
95. Richard T. Jameson, "What's in the Box?" *Film Comment* 27:5 (September–October 1991): 26; Emmanuel Levy, *Cinema of Outsiders: The Rise of American Independent Film* (New York: New York University Press, 1999), 227.
96. Diane Johnson, personal communication, July 1, 2002; Frank Noack, personal communication, February 17, 2001, from an interview with Christiane Kubrick and Jan Harlan in Berlin, February 17, 2001. I am grateful to Peter Loewenberg for first pointing out the similarity between *The Shining* and *The Magic Mountain* at the Pacific Coast Branch Meeting of the American Historical Association, Honolulu, August 15, 1986.
97. *The Shining*, DVD, scene 12, 40.41–51; King, *The Shining*, 212–13; Mann, *The Magic Mountain*, 469–98. There is also a brief snow sequence in Johnson's *The Shadow Knows*, 226–32, which is set in Sacramento, California. The *Weather Almanac* (8th ed.), shows two inches of snow there in 1976, and Diane Johnson (personal communication, January 27, 2000) has said that it snowed in Davis, near Sacramento, when she was living there while writing *The Shadow Knows*.
98. Cynthia Ozick, "The Impossibility of Being Kafka," *New Yorker*, January 11, 1999, 80–87.
99. Günther Schwarberg, *Es war einmal ein Zauberberg: Thomas Mann in Davos—Eine Spurensuche* (Göttingen: Steidl, 2001), 26; Nigel Hamilton, *The Brothers Mann: The Lives of Heinrich and Thomas Mann, 1871–1950 and 1875–1955* (New Haven: Yale University Press, 1979), 200; *Letters of Heinrich and Thomas Mann, 1900–1949*, ed. Hans Wysling, trans. Don Reneau (Berkeley: University of California Press, 1998), 112–15.
100. Thomas Mann, "The Making of 'The Magic Mountain,'" 43–44.
101. Stephen Dowden, "Mann's Ethical Style," in *A Companion to Mann's The Magic Mountain*, ed. Dowden (Columbia, S.C.: Camden House, 1999), 35–36.
102. Avisar, *Screening the Holocaust*, 162.
103. Eugene Goodheart, "Thomas Mann's Comic Spirit," in Dowden, ed., *Mann's Magic Mountain*, 48.
104. Mann, *The Magic Mountain*, 441.
105. Schwarberg, *Es war einmal ein Zauberberg*, 153–59; Mann, *The Magic Mountain*, 385, 683–85.
106. Mann, *The Magic Mountain*, 3; see also 10, 11, 108, 125, 192, 203, 286, 305, 576; King, *The Shining*, 64.

# Chapter 10

1. Paul Banks, "Coherence and Diversity in the *Symphonie fantastique*," *19th-Century Music* 8:1 (Summer 1984): 37.

2. Fenichel, *Psychoanalytic Theory of Neurosis*, 78, 248. In *Making The Shining*, Kubrick is shown filming a decapitated woman's head, a shot that did not make it into the film.
3. D. Kern Holoman, *Berlioz* (Cambridge, Mass.: Harvard University Press, 1989), 99, 105; "Wendy Carlos Open Letter," www.wendycarlos.com/open.html, 7–8, September 3, 1999.
4. *The Shining*, DVD, scene 1, 0.15–3.01; outtakes from this sequence were used for the "happy ending" (!) of the original release of *Blade Runner* (1982) (Hughes, *Complete Kubrick*, 209); the Beatles used aerial outtakes from *Dr. Strangelove* for the television film *Magical Mystery Tour* (1967) (Miles, *Paul McCartney*, 364).
5. *The Shining*, DVD, scene 3, 6.17–19; King, *The Shining*, 25.
6. Eisenstein, "Color and Meaning," 137; cf. Baxter, *Stanley Kubrick*, 327; and Munday, Shining FAQ, 6–8.
7. Rupprecht Mattaei, ed., and Herb Aach, trans., *Goethe's Color Theory* (New York: Van Nostrand Reinhold, 1971), 170.
8. William Gass, *On Being Blue: A Philosophical Inquiry* (Boston: Godine, 1976), 11, 75–76; hear also *A Color Symphony* (1932) by Arthur Bliss.
9. Mann, *The Magic Mountain*, 4, 5, 8, 286, 301, 306; *The Shining*, DVD, scene 7, 17.59–18.11; see also Johnson, *The Shadow Knows*, 272.
10. Nelson, *Kubrick*, 200; *The Shining*, DVD, scenes 1, 2.45–58; 7, 19.31–40; 11, 34.12–19; King, *The Shining*, 11, 34, 35, 61, 115, 190; Mann, *The Magic Mountain*, 7; Kagan, *Cinema of Stanley Kubrick*, 203–16. A Volkswagen inhabits the same socioeconomic niche in Johnson, *The Shadow Knows*, 53.
11. Franz Kafka, *The Castle*, 225.
12. William Paul, *Laughing, Screaming: Hollywood Horror and Comedy* (New York: Columbia University Press, 1994), 339, 348; Hughes, "Alienated and Demonic," 21; Kafka, *The Castle*, 78.
13. Gabbard and Sharma, "Art Cinema," 94; Falsetto, *Narrative and Stylistic Analysis*, 132.
14. Janet Maslin, "Screen: Nicholson and Duvall in Kubrick's 'The Shining,'" 8; Denis Barbier, "Entretien avec Diane Johnson," 22; Lanza, *Fragile Geometry*, 154.
15. Johnson, *The Shadow Knows*, 31.
16. Quoted in Ciment, *Kubrick*, 192.
17. John Beebe, "*The Shining*," 58; Nelson, *Kubrick*, 30, 35, 57.
18. Christiane Kubrick, quoted in Bogdanovich, "Stanley Kubrick," 25–26, 40.
19. LoBrutto, *Stanley Kubrick*, 430, 434; Baxter, *Stanley Kubrick*, 324, 328; Munday, Shining FAQ, 58–59; Christiane Kubrick, *Stanley Kubrick*, 44, 54, 60, 69, 71, 72, 82, 98, 121, 128, 129, 150, 153, 156, 161, 165, 170; "Commentary by Vivian Kubrick," 26.59–27.18, *The Shining*, DVD; *The Shining*, DVD, scene 23, 1:22.45–57, 24.27–39.
20. Douglas Brode, *The Films of Jack Nicholson*, 209.
21. Johnson, "Writing *The Shining*."
22. Diane Johnson, "Pesky Themes Will Emerge When You're Not Looking," *New York Times*, September 11, 2000.
23. Vicente Molina Foix, "Entretien avec Stanley Kubrick," 8.
24. Hummel, *Stanley Kubrick*, 184.
25. *The Shining*, DVD, scene 10, 29.12–14; see also scene 10, 28.51–55. Dissolves are thus more thematically important in *The Shining* than crosscuts or shot/reverse shots (Metz, "Intertextuality and *The Shining*," 55).
26. Quoted in Ciment, *Kubrick*, 186–87.

27. Barbier, "Entretien avec Diane Johnson," 20, 21, 22; Harmetz, "Kubrick Films 'The Shining' in Secrecy at English Studio," 72; Saada, "Une Histoire de Famille," 35–36.
28. Freud, "The 'Uncanny,'" 220, 241.
29. *The Shining*, DVD, scene 8, 22.38–23.08; S. Schoenbaum, "Eek!" *New York Review of Books*, January 30, 1986, 24; Freud, "The 'Uncanny,'" 220–26, 245.
30. Freud, "The 'Uncanny,'" 235; Noel Carroll, "Nightmare and the Horror Film: The Symbolic Biology of Fantastic Beings," *Film Quarterly* 34:3 (1981): 21; Prawer, *Caligari's Children*, 118–20; Nelson, *Kubrick*, 198.
31. E. T. A. Hoffmann, "The Sandman," in *Selected Writings of E. T. A. Hoffmann*, ed. and trans. Leonard J. Kent and Elizabeth C. Knight (Chicago: University of Chicago Press, 1969), 1:137; *The Shining*, DVD, scene 3, 5.59–6.06.
32. Freud, "The 'Uncanny,'" 238.
33. *The Shining*, scenes 11, 35.39–36.51; 16, 53.22–45; 19, 1:02.52–54; 22, 1:17.07–10; 32, 2: 00.15–2:01.01; Freud, "The 'Uncanny,'" 234–35.
34. *A.I.*, DVD, scene 13, 51.57–59; Joe M. Abbott, "Family Survival: Domestic Ideology and Destructive Paternity in the Horror Fictions of Stephen King," (Ph.D. diss., University of Southern California, 1994), 160.
35. Ciment, *Kubrick*, 144, 189; *The Shining*, DVD, scenes 6, 16.28–17.19; 20, 1:07.59–8.56; cf. Kennedy, "Kubrick Goes Gothic," 51; Wilson, "Riding the Crest," 48, 63; Frank Manchel, "What About Jack?" 69; Baxter, *Stanley Kubrick*, 306, 312; Christopher Hoile, "The Uncanny and the Fairy Tale in Kubrick's *The Shining*," 8–9; Bruno Bettelheim, *The Uses of Enchantment*, 74.
36. *The Shining*, DVD, scenes 20, 21, 22; Nelson, *Kubrick*, 223.
37. Quoted in Ciment, *Kubrick*, 192.
38. Christiane Kubrick, *Stanley Kubrick*, 186; *The Shining*, DVD, scene 31, 1:55.25–28.
39. Rick Lyman, "A Perfectionist's Pupil with a Major in Creepy," B7.
40. Diedrick, "Sublimation of Carnival," 14.
41. *The Shining*, DVD, scenes 8, 11 (twice), 36, 37, 38, 39; see also 32, 1:59.00–2:00.49; Walker, *Stanley Kubrick*, 311; Titterington, "Kubrick and 'The Shining,'" 118.
42. Alain Cohen, "Stanley Kubrick's *The Shining*," 186, 187, 191–92; Nelson, *Kubrick*, 205–6.
43. Judie Newman, "Shirley Jackson and the Reproduction of Mothering: *The Haunting of Hill House*," in Docherty, ed., *American Horror Fiction*, 120–34; Dyson, *Bright Darkness*, 242.
44. *The Shining*, DVD, scenes 11, 17, 21; Richard Jameson, "Kubrick's Shining," 247; Foix, "Entretien avec Stanley Kubrick," 11; Ciment, *Kubrick*, 146.
45. Hala, "Kubrick's *The Shining*," 211; *The Shining*, DVD, scenes 4, 15, 22, 29, 37.
46. *The Shining*, DVD, scene 16, 55.49–55; Pipolo, "Modernist and Misanthrope," 16; Žižek, *Looking Awry*, 5–6, 83–85.
47. Freud, "The 'Uncanny,'" 245; Chodorow, *Reproduction of Mothering*, 183.
48. *The Shining*, DVD, scenes 5–6, 11, 12, 13, 14, 17, 18, 27; John Demos, *Entertaining Satan: Witchcraft and the Culture of Early New England* (New York: Oxford University Press, 1982), 200; Chodorow, *Reproduction of Mothering*, 181, 189, 196, 212, 214; cf. King, *The Shining*, 392, 393, 403–6: Durkin is not friend, owner, or African-American.
49. *The Shining*, DVD, scene 22, 1:19.48–20.13.
50. Jameson, "Kubrick's Shining," 247.
51. Dennis Bingham, "Masculinity and Hallucination," 143–44; Chodorow, *Reproduction of Mothering*, 194, 196; Klaus Theweleit, *Male Fantasies*, trans. Stephen Conway et al. (Minneapolis: University of Minnesota Press, 1987).

52. *The Shining*, DVD, scene 9, 28.09–14, 45–47. A similar construction appears behind Larry Durkin, with a dog cartoon on a television and an adjoining product display for "Perky Pooch Air Fresheners" (scene 27, 1:37.52–38.41).
53. *The Shining*, DVD, scenes 24, 31.
54. *The Shining*, DVD, scenes 4, 8, 9, 10, 13, 17, 21, 24, 31, 32, 1:14.40–46; 33; Freud, *Interpretation of Dreams*, 4:238–40; 5:355, 364–66, 369–72, 399–401; Fenichel, *Psychoanalytic Theory of Neurosis*, 62–66.
55. Fenichel, *Psychoanalytic Theory of Neurosis*, 273; Hughes, "Alienated and Demonic," 17; Caldwell and Umland, "'Come and Play with Us.'"
56. *The Shining*, DVD, scenes 29, 30; see note 99; Metz, "Intertextuality and *The Shining*," 45, 52–53.
57. *The Shining*, DVD, scene 11, 37.44–40.28; cf. Gilles Deleuze, *Cinema 2: The Time Image*, trans. Hugh Tomlinson and Robert Galeta (Minneapolis: University of Minnesota Press, 1989), 205–6; Cocks, "Bringing the Holocaust Home," 121–22. Disney cartoons, such as *Three Little Pigs*, are also filled with infantile and adolescent anal humor (Schickel, *Disney Version*, 174; Lears, "Mouse that Roared," 32).
58. *The Shining*, DVD, scene 28.
59. Madigan, "'Orders from the House,'" 200; Manchel, "What About Jack?" 77n11; Ronald Gray, *Franz Kafka* (Cambridge: Cambridge University Press, 1973), 84, 85, 90; Kafka, *The Castle*, 26. It is no coincidence that Kubrick reflexively has the Overlook closed for the winter as of October 31, Halloween (*The Shining*, DVD, scene 3, 5.59–6.02).
60. Kael, "Devolution," 147; Jean-Loup Bourget, "Le Territoire du Colorado," 19.
61. Seesslen and Jung, *Stanley Kubrick*, 232; Randy Rasmussen, *Stanley Kubrick: Seven Films Analyzed*, 233.
62. Paul, *Laughing, Screaming*, 337; Freud, "The 'Uncanny,'" 250.
63. Bettelheim, *Uses of Enchantment*, 42; Sigmund Freud, "The Occurrence in Dreams of Material from Fairy Tales" in *Standard Edition*, 12:279–87.
64. Bettelheim, *Uses of Enchantment*, 161; *The Shining*, DVD, scenes 9, 25.23–36, 25.47–49; 21, 1:12.12–21; King, *The Shining*, 73.
65. *The Shining*, DVD, scene 7, 18.32–19.13; Nelson, *Kubrick*, 217–18.
66. *The Shining*, DVD, scene 11, 34.52–57; Nelson, *Kubrick*, 214n2; Stephen Mamber, "Parody, Intertextuality, Signature: Kubrick, DePalma, and Scorsese," *Quarterly Review of Film and Video* 12 (1990): 31; Garrett Brown, "The Steadicam and *The Shining*."
67. Deer and Deer, "Structures of Popular Culture," 235; cf. the one instance of Expressionistic lighting, for uncanny effect, as Jack exits room 237 into a hall that was brightly lit when he went in (*The Shining*, DVD, scene 21, 1:15.55–16.09).
68. *The Shining*, DVD, scene 28, 1:43.44–44.07.
69. Bettelheim, *Uses of Enchantment*, 24.
70. *The Shining*, DVD, scenes 2, 4, 5, 9, 10, 16, 28, 31.
71. Donna J. Haraway, *Simians, Cyborgs, and Women: The Reinvention of Nature* (New York: Routledge, 1991), 199, 201. Since Warner Bros. owns the Roadrunner series, it is possible that Kubrick chose it in order not to incur clearances or expenses, which would not preclude the selection for reasons of meaning or exclude audience constructions.
72. King, *The Shining*, 75; *The Shining*, DVD, scenes 2, 8; *What's Up, Doc?* (1972) possibly further piqued his interest in King's book (King, *The Shining*, 75; Bogdanovich, "Stanley Kubrick," 20; LoBrutto, *Stanley Kubrick*, 385; Baxter, *Stanley Kubrick*, 280–81).

73. Fritz Moellenhoff, "Remarks on the Popularity of Mickey Mouse," *American Imago* 1: 3 (1940): 19–32; *The Shining,* DVD, scene 16; Kubrick reprises Mickey at the end of *Full Metal Jacket* through television's "Mickey Mouse Club Song"; *Mickey's Choo-Choo* (1929) and *Mickey's Grand Opera* (1936), MoMA, 1944, Exhibition 30, Box 2.
74. *The Shining,* DVD, scenes 2, 3, 8, 14, 18, 27, 28, 29, 30. There is also a flag of Colorado shown behind Danny in the game room (scene 8).
75. *The Shining,* DVD, scenes 2, 3.38–4.11; 11, 35.50–37.30; 14, 47.55–49.15; 26, 1:34.20–51.
76. *The Shining,* DVD, scene 10, 32.21–23.
77. Flo Leibowitz and Lynn Jeffress, "The Shining," 45; David A. Cook, "American Horror: *The Shining*"; Metz, "Intertextuality and *The Shining,*" 54, 55–56; Titterington, "Kubrick and 'The Shining,'" 118; *The Shining,* DVD, scene 8, 21.05–23.
78. *The Shining,* DVD, scenes 1, 8, 20.51–59; 9, 27.45–55; 14, 23, 27, 31, 1:55.48–57.43; 36, 2: 13.50–14.24; Bill Blakemore, "The Family of Man"; Leibowitz and Jeffress, "The Shining," 46; Jenkins, *Art of Adaptation,* 79.
79. Leibowtiz and Jeffress, "The Shining," 50; Rasmussen, *Seven Films Analyzed,* 246; King, *The Shining,* 196, 290.
80. *The Shining,* DVD, scenes 12, 40.39–41; 17, 18, 21, 35; Cocks, "Bringing the Holocaust Home," 108; Metz, "Intertextuality and *The Shining,*" 52, 57–58.
81. King, *The Shining,* 6, 7–9.
82. Bettelheim, *Uses of Enchantment,* 84; Gunnar Qvarnström, *Poetry and Numbers: On the Structural Use of Symbolic Numbers* (Lund: CWK Gleerup, 1966), 27.
83. Ciment, *Kubrick,* 34; Christiane Kubrick, quoted in Bogdanovich, "Stanley Kubrick," 25; Van de Castle, *Our Dreaming Mind,* 12.
84. *Full Metal Jacket,* DVD, scenes 21, 1:01.56–57; 23, 1:05.53–54; Kubrick and Herr, "Full Metal Jacket," 62.
85. Mann, *The Magic Mountain,* 706.
86. Norman Mailer, *The Naked and the Dead* (New York: Picador, 1998), 342.
87. Mann, "Making of 'The Magic Mountain,'" 42.
88. Mann, *The Magic Mountain,* 10, 29, 49, 56, 57, 58, 66, 68, 78, 91, 95, 106, 109, 149, 150, 166, 175, 189, 190, 191, 212, 223, 268, 269, 291, 295, 307, 322, 324, 328, 351, 359, 370, 411, 418, 426, 430, 472, 534, 538, 544, 556, 562, 633, 664, 702, 706; Christiane Pritzlaff, *Die Zahlensymbolik bei Thomas Mann* (Hamburg: Buske, 1972), 27–42; Dowden, "Mann's Ethical Style," 35–36; Kenneth Weisinger, "Distant Oil Rigs and Other Erections," in Dowden, ed., *Mann's Magic Mountain,* 177; Dowden, "Introduction," in Dowden, ed., *Mann's Magic Mountain,* xvii–xviii; Schwarberg, *Es war einmal ein Zauberberg,* 111; Ignace Feuerlicht, *Thomas Mann* (Boston: Twayne, 1968), 29–30.
89. *The Shining,* DVD, scenes 19, 23, 2, 3.53–56, 6.18–21; 10, 29.07–12; 37, 2:12.03–12; 12, 40.44–41.13, 44.43–55, 45.00–21, 45.24–30; 22, 1:20.34–40; 33, 2:02.51–53. The first time we see the stacks of 7-Up is during the tour (scene 10) just as Wendy compares the hotel in winter to a ghost ship (*The Ghost Ship,* R, February 1944).
90. Oudart, "Les Inconnus dans la Maison," 6.
91. *The Shining,* DVD, scene 4, 10.59–11.15. The clip was taken from a group provided by Warner Bros. that required no fees or clearances (Jan Harlan, personal communication, January 13, 2003); see also Donald K. Meisenheimer, "Machining the Man: From Neurasthenia to Psychasthenia in Sf and the Genre Western," *Science-Fiction Studies* 24 (1997): 448–50; and Richard Slotkin, *Gunfighter Nation: The Myth of the Frontier in Twentieth-Century America* (New York: Atheneum, 1992), 637–38.

92. *The Shining,* DVD, scenes 11, 37.29–44; 18, 59.13–21; *Full Metal Jacket,* DVD, scene 17, 48.12–49.00; *Eyes Wide Shut,* DVD, scenes 10, 46.10–14; 25, 1:38.49–27; Richard Kluger, *Ashes to Ashes: America's Hundred-Year Cigarette War* (New York: Knopf, 1996), 94.
93. Franz Kafka, *The Castle,* 179; *The Shining,* DVD, scenes 12, 43.03–17, 43.28–44.00, 44.06–13, 44.19–27, 45.36–59; 14, 46.58–47.09; 28, 1:41.13–46, 1:42.02–11; 29, 1:43.50–44.21, 1:44.42–55, 1:45.03–10
94. *The Shining,* DVD, scene 18, 59.13–29, 59.39–45, 1:00.47–1.50, 1:01.53–2.01, 2.05–11.
95. *The Shining,* DVD, scene 12, 43.55–44.00, 44.06–13, 44.19–29, 45.48–59. The chair is there again in scenes 14, 46.59–47.08; and 29, 1:41.46.
96. *The Shining,* DVD, scenes 8, 15, 23, 24, 31; King, *The Shining,* 154–68, 181–84; in "Family of Man," Blakemore argues that the British accents represent the British military that formed the basis for American imperialism in the New World.
97. *The Shining,* DVD, scene 19, 1:04.01–43; Saada, "Histoire de Famille," 36; Leibowitz and Jeffress, "The Shining," 46.
98. Elliott Currie, *Confronting Crime: The American Challenge* (New York: Pantheon, 1985).
99. *The Shining,* DVD, scenes 11, 36.19–23; 12, 44.20–25; 16, 55.01–06; 22, 1:19.54–55; 29, 1:46.59–47.41.
100. Kafka, *The Castle,* 118; Frederick R. Karl, *Franz Kafka: Representative Man* (New York: Ticknor & Fields, 1991), 709n.
101. *The Shining,* DVD, scenes 11, 12, 13, 14, 16, 17, 27, 31; Nelson, *Kubrick,* 211; Fridman, *Words and Witness,* 24.
102. *The Shining,* DVD, scenes 1, 7, 11.
103. *The Shining,* DVD, scenes 2, 3, 10, 14, 26; Kafka, *The Castle,* 21–22, 120–25.
104. *The Shining,* DVD, scenes 2, 3, 4, 7, 8, 9, 10, 17, 24, 25, 31; Kafka, *The Castle,* 15–16, 20, 33, 187, 196.
105. Kafka, *The Castle,* 66–67.
106. Karl, *Representative Man,* 707.
107. Kafka, *The Castle,* 137–38, 140. The most famous of Kubrick's very few attempts at slapstick comedy, a pratfall by General Turgidson in *Dr. Strangelove* (DVD, scene 15, 50.19–24), fails badly (Lyman, "Making the Wit Seem Unwitting").

## Chapter 11

1. Michael Klein and Gillian Parker, eds., *The English Novel and the Movies* (New York: Ungar, 1981), 4; Dennis Bingham, "The Displaced Auteur: A Reception History of *The Shining,*" 288.
2. David Stannard, *American Holocaust: Columbus and the Conquest of the New World* (New York: Oxford University Press, 1992); Windschuttle, *Killing of History,* 41–67.
3. Miklos Nyiszli, *Auschwitz: An Eyewitness Account of Mengele's Infamous Death Camp,* trans. Tibère Kremer and Richard Seaver (New York: Fell, 1960), 56–65, 134–37; see also the long shots of the Overlook from below that can be seen to resemble the gateway to the Auschwitz-Birkenau extermination camp (*The Shining,* DVD, scenes 7, 14, 17, 31, 33); in Adrian Lyne's film *Lolita* (1998), Humbert is once called Himmler as a Nabokovian expression of Humbert's own feelings of guilt.
4. Hilberg, *Destruction of the European Jews,* 607, 710.

5. Dinitia Smith, "Hollywood Loves Writers (If They Suffer)," *New York Times*, September 27, 1998, B26; LoBrutto, *Stanley Kubrick*, 445; *The Shining*, DVD, scene 11, 36.25–28.
6. Nelson, *Kubrick*, 209.
7. Combs, "Kubrick Talks!" 84; Brown, "Impossible Object," 109.
8. Freud, *Interpretation of Dreams*, 4:283.
9. Quoted in Perusek, "Kubrick's Armies"; Nelson, *Kubrick*, 207.
10. Hilberg, *Destruction of the European Jews*, v; see also Zygmunt Bauman, *Modernity and the Holocaust* (Ithaca: Cornell University Press, 1991); Bingham, *Acting Male*, 147; and *Eagle Squadron* (L, September 1942). One is also tempted to see the German word for eagle in the first and last syllables of the name "*Ad*olf Hit*ler*."
11. *The Shining*, DVD, scenes 11, 37.27–47; 30, 1:50.47–53; 9, 27.38–39.
12. *The French Yellow Book: Diplomatic Documents (1938–1939)* (New York: Reynal & Hitchcock, 1940), 19.
13. Ernest Jones, *The Life and Work of Sigmund Freud* (New York: Basic Books, 1957), 1: 335, 3:146, 148; Michael John Burlingham, *The Last Tiffany: A Biography of Dorothy Tiffany Burlingham* (New York: Atheneum, 1989), 195, 196; Bernhard Frank, *Die Rettung von Berchtesgaden und der Fall Göring* (Berchtesgaden: Plenk, 1984), 85, 95; Geoffrey Cocks, *Psychotherapy in the Third Reich: The Göring Institute*, 2nd ed. (New Brunswick: Transaction, 1997), 177–350.
14. Karl Ludvigsen, *Battle for the Beetle* (Cambridge, Mass.: Bentley, 2000), 30–31, 101; Manchel, "What About Jack?" 77n11; Seesslen and Jung, *Stanley Kubrick*, 230. In *The Pawnbroker*, a prominently parked Volkswagen, signs for Rheingold and Budweiser beer, and a pile of shoes in a window are similar nightmarish symbols of the Holocaust.
15. Hans-Jörg Wohlfromm and Gisela Wohlfromm, *Deckname Wolf: Hitlers letzter Sieg* (Berlin: edition q, 2001), 8–9, 246–309, 315.
16. George Steiner, *The Portage to San Cristobal of A. H.* (New York: Simon and Schuster, 1981), 51; Boria Sax, *Animals in the Third Reich: Pets, Scapegoats, and the Holocaust* (New York: Continuum, 2000), 72–80.
17. *The Shining*, DVD, scene 27, 1:38.59–39.02; LoBrutto, *Stanley Kubrick*, 40, 51; Nelson, *Kubrick*, 226. There is an accident in the novel, but no red Volkswagen involved (King, *The Shining*, 365). In the film, just as Hallorann approaches the accident scene, we view a lighted freeway sign with an arrow pointing in the opposite direction to Boulder (an apparently peaceful interlude in the Torrances' past). In the novel, Danny's toy "Violent Violet Volkswagen" is smashed (King, *The Shining*, 119, 309, 380). The television weather map of the storm resembles the map of a military operation, with three large red arrows showing its direction (*The Shining*, DVD, scene 21, 1:10.14–20).
18. LoBrutto, *Stanley Kubrick*, 444; Ciment, *Kubrick*, 187; Baxter, *Stanley Kubrick*, 311; Vivian Kubrick, *Making The Shining*, DVD, 34.10–16; Hilberg, *Destruction of the European Jews*, 566.
19. *The Shining*, DVD, scenes 4, 11. 43–12.07; 22, 1:19.42–47; 29, 1:45.28–45; 37, 2:14.40–56.
20. *The Shining*, DVD, scene 2, 4.12–54; Hilberg, *Destruction of the European Jews*, 298–99.
21. *The Collected Poems of Roy Campbell* (London: Bodley Head, 1949), 1:177; *The Shining*, DVD, scene 6, 14.34–36; Helen J. Dow, *The Art of Alex Colville* (Toronto: McGraw-Hill Ryerson, 1972), 156; Stephen Snyder, "Family Life and Leisure Culture in *The Shining*," 7.
22. Dow, *Art of Alex Colville*, 41, 90, 93, 179.

23. *The Shining*, DVD, scene 4, 11.00–02, 13–14.
24. *The Shining*, DVD, scenes 6, 16.16–17.38; 20, 1:07.58–08.53; Nelson, *Kubrick*, 211; King, *The Shining*, 48–50.
25. *The Shining*, DVD, scene 6, 14.56–15.06, 15.29–58, 16.09–11. The only book found with that title, by Jessica Stirling, is the third installment of the story of a marriage plagued by betrayal and poverty apparently published only in 1990; see also Celeste De Blasis, *The Night Child* (1975), in which a girl named Brandy accepts a job in Maine as teacher of a psychologically disturbed child in rambling Grey Mansion. In Lyne's *Lolita*, the tipping up of the smoking ash of a cigarette signals the death of Charlotte Haze.
26. King, *The Shining*, 73; *The Shining*, DVD, scenes 2; 10, 30.15–22, 31.00–10.
27. Rasmussen, *Seven Films Analyzed*, 248; *The Shining*, DVD, scenes 2, 4.19–48, 4.54–56, 4.59–5.01; 3, 5.04–6; 11, 34.13–19, 37.32–46; 7, 48.18–49.11.
28. *The Shining*, DVD, scene 10, 32.45–48.
29. *The Shining*, DVD, scene 9, 26.14–41.
30. *The Shining*, DVD, scene 11, 38.16–40.27; Pascal Bonitzer, "Partial Vision: Film and the Labyrinth," *Wide Angle* 4:4 (1981): 56; Caldwell and Umland, "Play Metaphor," 107, 111.
31. *The Shining*, DVD, scenes 8, 21.13–23; 14, 46.59–47.08; 16, 51.57–52.00, 53.25–27; 27, 1:36.41–53. As in the novel, Grady tells Jack that one of his girls stole a book of matches and tried to burn the Overlook down (King, *The Shining*, 354; *The Shining*, DVD, scene 24).
32. Hilberg, *Destruction of the European Jews*, 249, 265–66, 270–73, 646–62.
33. Hilberg, *Destruction of the European Jews*, 10–11, 29, 33–39; Peter Loewenberg, "The Unsuccessful Adolescence of Heinrich Himmler," in Loewenberg, *Decoding the Past: The Psychohistorical Approach* (New York: Knopf, 1983), 209–39.
34. *The Shining*, DVD, scene 19, 1:05.23–28; Rasmussen, *Seven Films Analyzed*, p. 263. Even Hallorann, an African-American victim of the white patriarchal order, is critiqued as a male via the portraits of nude black women in the bedroom of his Miami home (*The Shining*, DVD, scene 21, 1:10.10–54); see also the black man looking at a half-naked white woman on a calendar at Durkin's (*The Shining*, DVD, scene 27, 1:37.22–26).
35. *The Shining*, DVD, scenes 23–24, 1:25.22–26; Loewenberg, "Unsuccessful Adolescence," 231–36.
36. Rasmussen, *Seven Films Analyzed*, 270.
37. *The Shining*, DVD, scene 24, 1:27.21–1:31.26; Greg Smith, "'Real Horrorshow,'" 302.
38. *The Shining* DVD, scene 11, 36.30–37.32; this scene begins with what might be the howl of a coyote; see Jenkins, *Art of Adaptation*, 82; see also Mann, *The Magic Mountain*, 241, 271, 311, 384, 555.
39. *The Shining*, DVD, scenes 12, 43.03–42; 14, 46.59–47.09; 27, 1:36.31–53; King, *The Shining*, 124.
40. *The Shining*, DVD, scenes 2, 11, 12, 14, 18, 27, 28, 29, 30.
41. *The Shining*, DVD, scenes 9, 25.33–36, 25.54–26.13, 26.08–13, 26.52–27.00; 10, 28.55–57, 29.00–03; 14, 49.21–24, 49.26–32; 22, 1:20.38; 34, 2:05.32–37, 2:05.51–57; Levi, *Drowned and Saved*, 65. The British terms (e.g., "bins," "tidy") are probably details overlooked in the course of making a film about America in Britain, unlike the English accents of the Gradys, which are too apparent to have been overlooked and are consistent with the function, character, and historical symbolism of Delbert Grady. The high-voltage sign is followed by a shot that includes a crate that has a large black

"X" drawn over the words "Overlook Hotel" (*The Shining*, DVD, scene 18, 58.43–59.10).
42. Elie Wiesel, "Never Shall I Forget," in *Holocaust Poetry*, comp. Hilda Schiff (New York: St. Martin's Press, 1995). 42; Martin Filler, "Into the Void," *New Republic*, October 1, 2001, 28; Laurence A. Rickels, *Aberrations of Mourning: Writing on German Crypts* (Detroit: Wayne State University Press, 1988), 320.
43. Nelson, *Kubrick*, 230n; Walters, "Stanley Kubrick's *The Shining*," 34; Stephen King, "1408," in King, *Everything's Eventual*, 365–403.
44. *The Shining*, scene 20, 1:09.44–45.
45. Browning, *Ordinary Men*, xv; Hilberg, *Destruction of the European Jews*, 263–314; Hilberg, *The Destruction of the European Jews*, rev. and definitive ed. (New York: Holmes & Meier, 1985), 3:1220.
46. Arnost Lustig, "The Second Round," in Lustig, *Diamonds of the Night*, trans. Jeanne Nemcova (Washington, D.C.: Inscape, 1978), 33–61. cf. Metz, "Notorious Ranch," 77; and 42 as "funny": M.J. Simpson, *Hitchhiker* (Boston: Justin Charles, 2003), 112–13.
47. Vasily Grossman, *Life and Fate: A Novel*, trans. Robert Chandler (New York: Harper & Row, 1985), 195.
48. Mann, *The Magic Mountain*, 19; on "six or seven wolves" in the dream of the "Wolf-Man" and on the Grimm fairy tale "The Wolf and the Seven Little Goats," see also Freud, "Occurrence in Dreams," 12:284–85.
49. Mann, *The Magic Mountain*, 194, 269, 344, 346, 418, 484, 573, 706; Fenichel, *Psychoanalytic Theory of Neurosis*, 92–93, 103, 108.
50. Hilberg, *Destruction of the European Jews*, 555–74. One great numbing horror of the Holocaust was the number of victims, in seven figures, more than even the allusion to thousands of fingers and eyes in *The 5000 Fingers of Dr. T* and *The 1000 Eyes of Dr. Mabuse* ("1,000,000 Jews Slain by Nazis, Report Says," *New York Times*, June 30, 1942).
51. *The Shining*, DVD, scene 39, 2:20.11–21. In this photograph Jack is shown holding up four fingers of his right hand with the thumb against the palm, while on his left hand only two fingers, thumb and forefinger, are visible. The number 21 is also mirrored in the two-way radio call number for the hotel, "KDK 12" (*The Shining*, DVD, scenes 14, 26).
52. *The Shining*, DVD, scenes 2; 4, 10.32–49, 11.19–32; 5, 12.43–13.56, 14.19–22; Baxter, *Stanley Kubrick*, 322–23; LoBrutto, *Stanley Kubrick*, 446. It is possible that 42 is a reference to 1842, the year of publication of the Poe story mentioned in King's novel, but this would not exclude it as a reference to the Holocaust, especially given the other years of the twentieth century referenced in the film that are multiples of 7. Dopey alone has disappeared from Danny's bedroom door at the end of scene 5.
53. *The Shining*, DVD, scene 21, 1:11.06.
54. *The Shining*, DVD, scene 16, 51.18–52.38; Rasmussen, *Seven Films Analyzed*, 257; Bingham, "Displaced Auteur," 292; Barlow, "Generative Aesthetics," 242.
55. *The Shining*, DVD, scenes 12, 40.57–41.13; 21, 1:10.50–11.02.
56. *The Shining*, DVD, scene 17, 57.07–58.27; Nelson, *Kubrick*, 212; Hoile, "Uncanny and Fairy Tale," 9.
57. Ciment, *Kubrick*, 186; Timberline Lodge, personal communication, March 20, 2000; King, *The Shining*, 214–20. The digits in 237 also add up to 12, the mirror of 21: www.krusch.com/Kubrick/Q52.html, 6, March 5, 2004.
58. Quoted in Munday, Shining FAQ, 21.

59. Harlan, *A Life in Pictures*, DVD, scene 19, 1:34.33–34; see also Kenneth Plume, "Interview with Producer Jan Harlan," 3. It is an interesting coincidence, in line with the Haze address in *Lolita* at 342 Lawn Street, that in *Roxie Hart*, the 1942 satire that was one of Kubrick's favorite films, Roxie's street address number is 1442.
60. Freud, "The 'Uncanny,'" 237–38.
61. Freud, "The 'Uncanny,'" 237.
62. Diane Johnson, personal communications, March 30, 2003, April 7, 2003; *The Basic Writings of Sigmund Freud*, ed. and trans. A. A. Brill (New York: Modern Library, 1938). Of course Kubrick could have used a copy of the *Standard Edition*, just happened to have noticed the coincidence, or even checked the page number in the process of constructing his pattern of numerical symbols.
63. The number 42 is mirrored once in the television news report of the twenty-four-year-old woman killed on a hunting trip with her husband; 24 is a possible reference to the year *The Magic Mountain* was published, falls within the span of years (1907–1970) represented by the numbers in *The Shining*, and could also represent the juxtaposition of a year of death and the symbol of life that are the hours of a day.
64. Nelson, *Kubrick*, 217–18; King, *The Shining*, 386.
65. *The Shining*, DVD, scene 31, 1:55.52–1:57.43. "Yellow" could also have carried a connotation for Kubrick of the Second World War American stereotype of the "yellow peril" represented by the Japanese, another common subject and trope in the war films that screened in the Bronx from 1941 on. Michelangelo Antonioni's *Blow-Up* uses 39 as a reference to murder in the past. A smaller box of "Pimiento Pieces" that rests on top of the box of canned peaches that has one small number on it, 25786, the individual numbers of which, when added, equal 28, another multiple of seven that in the chronological scheme of numbers in *The Shining* would constitute a reference to 1928, the year Kubrick was born. This is probably, though not necessarily, a coincidence.
66. Tad Michel, personal communication, July 7, 1994; *The Shining*, DVD, scene 40, 2:22.55–2:23.00.
67. Nelson, *Kubrick*, 219; John Alcott, "Photographing Stanley Kubrick's *The Shining*," 267, 271; Ciment, *Kubrick*, p. 216; Avisar, *Screening the Holocaust*, 157; *The Shining*, DVD, scenes 17–20.
68. *The Shining*, DVD, scene 19, 1:03.13–19.
69. *The Shining*, DVD, scenes 8, 21.47–22.10; 9, 26.43–27.02, 28.09–54, 29.06–13; 11, 34.39–35.17; 12, 41.14–43.03; 17, 57.38–58.00; Rasmussen, *Seven Films Analyzed*, 244, 253, 258, 259. The red fire alarm bell in scene 8 behind the Grady girls is located between a poster for a ski spot named Monarch and a green exit light.
70. *The Shining*, DVD, scenes 2, 4, 8, 15, 21, 27, 30; Munday, Shining FAQ, 17.
71. Mattaei, ed., *Goethe's Color Theory*, 168.
72. Wiesel, "Never Shall I Forget," 42.
73. King, *The Shining*, 217–18; Paul Miers, "The Black Maria Rides Again," 1365–66; Prawer, *Caligari's Children*, 136.
74. George Steiner, *In Bluebeard's Castle: Some Notes Toward the Redefinition of Culture* (New Haven: Yale University Press, 1971).
75. *The Shining*, DVD, scenes 11, 12, 14, 18.
76. *The Shining*, DVD, scenes 4, 11:58; 8, 21.47–22.10; 12, 42.22; 15, 49.39–50.16.; Ciment, *Kubrick*, 182. See also Mann, *The Magic Mountain*, 301: "The dying girl was indeed a charming blond creature, with eyes of true forget-me-not blue."

77. *The Shining,* DVD, scene 8, 22.23–28; scene 7, 19.51–53; Donald Williams, "An Interview with Diane Johnson," 5; King, *The Shining,* 353–54.
78. LoBrutto, *Stanley Kubrick,* 444, photograph facing 278; Christiane Kubrick, *Stanley Kubrick,* 21- 26, 128–29, and especially 113; Walker, *Stanley Kubrick,* 287; Baxter, *Stanley Kubrick,* 40; Ciment, *Kubrick,* 241; Bourget, "Territoire du Colorado," 18.
79. LoBrutto, *Stanley Kubrick,* 445; *Look,* May 25, 1948, 67.
80. Hilberg, *Destruction of the European Jews,* 627–28; "Allies Are Urged to Execute Nazis," *New York Times,* July 2, 1942, 6. Bełżec apparently switched to Zyklon B, but Hilberg makes no mention of this in the book Kubrick read; see Reder, *Bełżec,* 127, and Hilberg, *Destruction of the European Jews* (1985), 3:878.
81. Hilberg, *Destruction of the European Jews,* 566.
82. Paul Weindling, *Epidemics and Genocide in Eastern Europe, 1890–1945* (Oxford: Oxford University Press, 2000), 46; Hilberg, *Destruction of the European Jews,* 565; Robert Ergang, *The Potsdam Führer: Frederick William I, Father of Prussian Militarism* (New York: Columbia University Press, 1941), 66, 167.
83. *A Clockwork Orange,* DVD, scene 5, 8.26–29.
84. On the "gaseous blue" filling a bathroom in *Eyes Wide Shut,* an image and atmosphere of multiple meanings, see Laleen Jayamane, "The Ornamentation of Nicole Kidman (Eyes Wide Shut) and Mita Vashisht (Kasba): A Sketch," *Senses of Cinema* 23 (November–December 2002),www.sensesofcinema.com, April 19, 2003; Phillips, ed., *Interviews,* 58.
85. Hughes, *Complete Kubrick,* 205; Kubrick might also have been influenced by the 1970s Italian horror film series called *giallo,* from the yellow covers of the publications on which they were based.
86. Titterington, "Kubrick and 'The Shining,'" 118.
87. Quoted in Ciment, *Kubrick,* 301.
88. *The Shining,* DVD, scenes 2, 4, 5, 12.
89. Nelson, *Kubrick,* 219.
90. Johnson, *The Shadow Knows,* 185; *The Shining,* DVD, scene 32, 1:58.45–2:01.19.
91. *"The Yellow Wall-Paper" and Selected Stories of Charlotte Perkins Gilman,* ed. Denise D. Knight (Newark: University of Delaware Press, 1994), 52; see also 39; Diane Johnson, personal communication, April 10, 2003.
92. Sergei Eisenstein, "Color and Meaning," 113, 114; Phillips, ed., *Interviews,* 7, 79, 103–4, 135, 154.
93. Walt Whitman, "The Wound Dresser," in *Leaves of Grass* (1892), quoted in Eisenstein, "Color and Meaning," 131.
94. Havelock Ellis, "The Psychology of Yellow," *Popular Science Monthly,* May 1906, quoted in Eisenstein, "Color and Meaning," 126.
95. Agee, "The Blue Hotel," 468–71; Salinger, *The Catcher in the Rye,* 83.
96. Mattaei, ed., *Goethe's Color Theory,* 169, quoted in Eisenstein, "Color and Meaning," 136.
97. Eisenstein, "Color and Meaning," 136.
98. Melissa Müller, *Anne Frank: The Biography,* trans. Rita and Robert Kimber (New York: Metropolitan, 1998), 137; Hilberg, *Destruction of the European Jews,* 374.
99. Walker, *Stanley Kubrick,* 233.
100. Eisenstein, "Color and Meaning," 151; see chapter 6 on *A Clockwork Orange.*
101. LoBrutto, *Stanley Kubrick,* 56, 173; Walter, "Entretien avec Stanley Kubrick," 36; MoMA Exhibitions 27, 32, 44, Box 2.

102. Eisenstein, "Color and Meaning," 152 (emphasis in original).
103. Hilberg, *Destruction of the European Jews*, 5; Léon Poliakov, *The History of Anti-Semitism*, trans. Richard Howard (New York: Vanguard, 1965), 65–67.
104. George Axelsson, "Nazis Again Fan Hatred of Jews," *New York Times*, November 2, 1941, 24.
105. Hilberg, *Destruction of the European Jews*, 117–22, 444–45.
106. Weindling, *Epidemics and Genocide*, 75.
107. Weindling, *Epidemics and Genocide*, 104, 273–75; Hilberg, *Destruction of the European Jews*, 114, 148, 217, 312–13, 567, 657–58.
108. Weindling, *Epidemics and Genocide*, 9.
109. Diane Johnson, personal communication, May 26, 2000; Johnson, "Stanley Kubrick," 28.
110. *The Shining*, DVD, scene 23, 1:24.53–56.
111. Nelson, *Kubrick*, 225; Francis Shor, "Father Knows Beast," 64.
112. Hoffmann, "The Sandman," 1:140, 141; Prawer, *Caligari's Children*, 131.
113. *The Shining*, scene 23, 1:24.37–1:25.26; Hilberg, *Destruction of the European Jews*, 444. It is unlikely that Kubrick intended it, but Hilberg notes that in Latvia Jews were marked with a yellow star on both front and back (*Destruction of the European Jews*, 231), and it is the case that such marks were placed on the right breast and left back shoulder, the shoulder of Grady marked by Jack's yellowed hand (Martin Lowenberg, personal communication, April 10, 2003).
114. Eisenstein, "Color and Meaning," 127 (emphasis in original); Ferro, *Cinema and History*, 140; Norman O. Brown, *Life Against Death: The Psychoanalytical Meaning of History* (Middletown, Conn.: Wesleyan University Press, 1970); Tim Fulmer and Road Munday, "*The Shining* and Transcendence," www.visualmemory.co.uk/amk/doc/0091.html, 3, February 3, 2002.
115. Titterington, "Kubrick and 'The Shining,'" 118; *The Shining*, DVD, scene 3, 9.20–32; King, *The Shining*, 9.
116. Mann, "Making of 'The Magic Mountain,'" 41.
117. David Blumberg, "From Muted Chords to Maddening Cacophony: Music in *The Magic Mountain*," in Dowden, ed. *Mann's Magic Mountain*, 90, 91.
118. Hobbs FAQ, 6.
119. Ciment, *Kubrick*, 153.
120. Paul Griffiths, "Music that Switches Its Gaze, from Future to the Past."
121. Michel Sineux, "La Symphonie Kubrick," 36; *The Shining*, DVD, scenes 1, 7, 8, 23, 24; among the Carlos/Elkind pieces omitted is a rendering (1978) of Jean Sibelius's "Valse Triste" (1904) from *Kuolema* (Death); see "Commentary by Vivian Kubrick," 33.07–34.50.
122. Bence Szabolcsi, *Bélá Bartók: His Life in Pictures*, ed. Ferenc Bónis (London: Boosey & Hawkes, 1964), 51, 52; Halsey Stevens, *The Life and Music of Bélá Bartók*, rev. ed. (London: Oxford University Press, 1964), 274; *Bélá Bartók Essays*, ed. Benjamin Suchoff (Lincoln: University of Nebraska Press, 1976), 518; Leon Botstein, "Out of Hungary: Bartók, Modernism, and the Cultural Politics of Twentieth-Century Music," in Peter Laki, ed., *Bartók and His World* (Princeton: Princeton University Press, 1995), 51.
123. *The Shining*, DVD, scenes 11, 38.12–40.28; 12 41.19–43.49; 16, 52.39–57.00.
124. *The Shining*, DVD, scene 40, 2:21.43–52; cf. the listing of Penderecki, Carlos and Elkind, and Ligeti, 2:21.53–2:22.02; Wolfgang Sedat, Deutsche Grammophon, per-

sonal communication, August 12, 1999; Jan Harlan, personal communication, January 13, 2003.
125. King, *The Shining*, 223; Nelson, *Kubrick*, 216; Gabbard and Sharma, "Art Cinema," 107n7; Edward Rothstein, "Karajan: The Nazi Recordings," *New Republic*, November 7, 1988, 27–33.
126. "250,000 in Poland Reported Killed," *New York Times*, July 27, 1942, 3.
127. Quoted in Julian Haylock, "Anaklasis, etc.," liner notes, *Matrix 5* (London: EMI Classics, 1994), 3; Wolfram Schwinger, *Krzysztof Penderecki: His Life and Work*, trans. William Mann (London: Schott, 1989), 214–17. The 1967 ceremony at Auschwitz was, however, in line with the Communist and Catholic dismissal of the unique exterminatory fate of the Jews at the hands of the Nazis, which, ironically perhaps, fit with Penderecki's emphasis on a universal message in his music (Cole, *Selling the Holocaust*, 99–100).
128. *The Shining*, scenes 28, 1:41.56–1:42.01; 29, 1:44.30–35, 1:44.57–1:45.02, 1:45.14–17, 1:45.52–55, 1:46.08–15, 1:46.19–20, 1:46.25–26, 1:46.31–33, 1:46.38–41, 1:46.46–47, 1:46.50–54, 1:47.09–10, 1:47.28–33.
129. King, *The Shining*, 281 (misspelled "Fiske"); Carl Yastrzemski and Gerald Eshkenazi, *Yaz: Baseball, the Wall, and Me* (New York: Doubleday, 1990), Chapter 2.
130. Mayersberg, "The Overlook Hotel," 258; Paul, *Laughing, Screaming*, 344.
131. *The Shining*, DVD, scenes 29, 32, 33, 34, 35, 36, 37, 38; *De Natura Sonoris No. 1:* scenes 15, 30, 39; *De Natura Sonoris No. 2:* scenes 18–19, 31, 32, 38; *Polymorphia:* scenes 28–29, 30, 35, 37, 38; *Kanon:* 32, 33, 34, 36, 37, 38; www.crash.simplenet.com/shining/charts.html, December 12, 1998; Schwinger, *Krzysztof Penderecki*, 219.
132. *The Shining*, DVD, scenes 3–5, 10.28–12.11; 17; 18, 1:00.03–5; 21.
133. Quoted in Ciment, *Kubrick*, 192.
134. Timothy K. Beal, "Our Monsters, Ourselves," *Chronicle of Higher Education*, November 9, 2001, B18; Žižek, *Looking Awry*, 87; Jacob also served seven years for Rachel (Genesis 28:22); see Bettelheim, *Uses of Enchantment*, 237.
135. Rubenstein, *After Auschwitz*, 42.
136. Rubenstein, *Cunning of History*, 22–35.
137. *The Shining*, DVD, scenes 18–19, 1:01.04–1:04.04.
138. *The Shining*, DVD, scene 18, 58.39–1:02.31.
139. Prawer, *Caligari's Children*, 136–37; Schwinger, *Krzysztof Penderecki*, 156.
140. John Fiske, *Understanding Popular Culture* (Boston: Unwin Hyman, 1989), 125; Shor, "Father Knows Beast," 60–61; Metz, "Intertextuality and *The Shining*," 57.
141. *The Shining*, DVD, scene 40, 2:22.53–2:23.35.
142. *The Shining*, DVD, scene 23, 1:22.13–1:23.06, 1:24.26–1:25.11; The Dance in Film, 1909–1936, MoMA, November 1945, Exhibition 32; see also Exhibition 41 (October 1953), Box 2.

# FILMOGRAPHY

*Fear and Desire*. dir. Stanley Kubrick. Joseph Burstyn, 1953.
*Killer's Kiss*. dir. Stanley Kubrick. United Artists, 1955. DVD, MGM, 1999.
*The Killing*. dir. Stanley Kubrick. United Artists, 1956. DVD, MGM, 1999.
*Paths of Glory*. dir. Stanley Kubrick. United Artists, 1957. DVD, MGM, 1999.
*Spartacus*. dir. Stanley Kubrick. Universal Pictures, 1960. DVD, Criterion, 2001
*Lolita*. dir. Stanley Kubrick. MGM, 1962. DVD, Warner Bros., 2001.
*Dr. Strangelove, or: How I learned to Stop Worrying and Love the Bomb*. dir. Stanley Kubrick. Columbia Pictures, 1964. DVD, Warner Bros., 2001.
*2001: A Space Odyssey*. dir. Stanley Kubrick. MGM, 1968. DVD, Warner Bros., 2001.
*A Clockwork Orange*. dir. Stanley Kubrick. Warner Bros., 1971. DVD, Warner Bros., 2001.
*Barry Lyndon*. dir. Stanley Kubrick. Warner Bros., 1975. DVD, Warner Bros., 2001.
*Making The Shining*. dir. Vivian Kubrick. Eagle Films, 1980. DVD, Warner Bros., 2001.
*The Shining*. dir. Stanley Kubrick. Warner Bros., 1980. DVD, Warner Bros., 2001.
*Full Metal Jacket*. dir. Stanley Kubrick. Warner Bros., 1987. DVD, Warner Bros., 2001.
*Eyes Wide Shut*. dir. Stanley Kubrick. Warner Bros., 1999. DVD, Warner Bros., 2001.
*Stanley Kubrick: A Life in Pictures*. dir. Jan Harlan. Warner Bros., 2000. DVD, Warner Bros., 2001.
*A.I.* dir. Steven Spielberg. prod. Stanley Kubrick. Warner Bros., 2001. DVD, Warner Bros., 2002.

# BIBLIOGRAPHY

Adams, Richard, and Stanley Kubrick. "The German Lieutenant: An Original Screenplay" (1956-1957). Box 22, Folder 2. Department of Defense Film Collection, Special Collections, Georgetown University, Washington, D.C.
Agee, James. "The Blue Hotel" (1949). In *Agee on Film, Volume Two: Five Film Scripts by James Agee*, 393-486. New York: Grosset & Dunlap, 1967.
Agel, Jerome, ed. *The Making of Kubrick's 2001*. New York: New American Library, 1970.
Albertson, Jim, and Peter S. Perakos. "The Shining." *Cinefantastique*, Fall 1978, 74.
Alcott, John. "Photographing Stanley Kubrick's *Barry Lyndon*." In Falsetto, ed., *Perspectives on Stanley Kubrick*, 214-25.
Amelunxen, Hubertus von. "Points du Vue Imaginaires et Réels." In Crone and Schaesberg, eds., *Stanley Kubrick: Still Moving Pictures*, 198-201.
Anger, Cédric. "Le Dernier Expressioniste." *Cahiers du Cinema* 534 (April 1999): 28-29.
Barbier, Dennis. "Entretien avec Diane Johnson." *Positif* 238 (January 1981): 20-25.
Barlow, Arthur H. "The Films of Stanley Kubrick: A Study in Generative Aesthetics." Ph.D. diss., Pennsylvania State University, 1996.
Baxter, John. *Stanley Kubrick: A Biography*. New York: Carroll & Graf, 1997.
Baxter, Peter. "The One Woman." *Wide Angle* 6:1 (1984): 34-41.
Beebe, John. "*The Shining*." *San Francisco Jung Institute Library Journal* 1:4 (Summer 1980): 57-61.
Begley, Louis. *Wartime Lies*. New York: Knopf, 1991.
Bettelheim, Bruno. *The Uses of Enchantment: The Meaning and Importance of Fairy Tales*. New York: Knopf, 1976.
Bier, Jesse. "Cobb and Kubrick: Author and *Auteur*." *Virginia Quarterly Review* 61 (1985): 453-71.

Bingham, Dennis. *Acting Male: Masculinities in the Films of James Stewart, Jack Nicholson, and Clint Eastwood*, 136–48. New Brunswick: Rutgers University Press, 1994.

———. "The Displaced Auteur: A Reception History of *The Shining*." In Falsetto, ed., *Perspectives on Stanley Kubrick*, 284–306.

Bizony, Piers. *2001: Filming the Future*. London: Aurum, 2000.

Blakemore, Bill. "The Family of Man." *San Francisco Chronicle*, July 29, 1987.

Bogdanovich, Peter. "What They Say About Stanley Kubrick." *New York Times Magazine*, July 4, 1999, 18–25, 40, 47–48.

Bourget, Jean-Loup. "Le Territoire du Colorado." *Positif* 234 (September 1980): 15–19.

Boyd, David. "Mode and Meaning in *2001*." *Journal of Popular Film and Television* 6:3 (1978): 202–15.

Brode, Douglas. *The Films of Jack Nicholson*. New York: Citadel, 1987.

Brown, Garrett. "The Steadicam and "The Shining." In Falsetto, ed., *Perspectives on Stanley Kubrick*, 273–83.

Brown, John. "The Impossible Object: Reflections on *The Shining*." In *Cinema and Fiction: New Modes of Adapting, 1950–1990*, edited by John Orr and Colin Nicholson, 104–21. Edinburgh: Edinburgh University Press, 1992.

Brustein, Robert. "Out of This World." In Falsetto, ed., *Perspectives on Stanley Kubrick*, 136–40.

Bryant, Peter. *Two Hours to Doom*. London: TV. Boardman, 1958.

Burgess, Anthony. *A Clockwork Orange*. 1962. New York: Norton, 1963.

———. "A Clockwork Orange Resucked." In Burgess, *A Clockwork Orange*. New York: Norton, 1987), v–xi.

———. "Juice from a Clockwork Orange." In Falsetto, ed., *Perspectives on Stanley Kubrick*, 187–90.

Burgoyne. Robert. "Narrative Overture and Closure in *2001: A Space Odyssey*." *Enclitic* 5 (Fall–Spring 1981–1982): 172–80.

Burns, Dan E. "Pistols and Cherry Pies: *Lolita* from Page to Screen." *Literature/Film Quarterly* 12 (1984): 245–50

Caldwell, Larry W., and Samuel J. Umland. "'Come and Play with Us': The Play Metaphor in Kubrick's Shining." *Literature/Film Quarterly* 14 (1986): 106–11.

Charlot, John. "From Ape-Man to Space-Baby: *2001*, an Interpretation." *East-West Film Journal* 1 (December 1986): 84–89.

Chion, Marcel. *Eyes Wide Shut*. Translated by Trista Selous. London: British Film Institute, 2002.

———. *Kubrick's Cinema Odyssey*. Translated by Claudia Gorbman. London: British Film Institute, 2001.

Ciment, Michel. *Kubrick: The Definitive Edition*. Translated by Gilbert Adair and Robert Bonnono. New York: Faber and Faber, 2001.

Clarke, Arthur C. *The Lost Worlds of 2001*. 1964. New York: New American Library, 1972.

———. *2001: A Space Odyssey*. New York: New American Library, 1968.

Cobb, Humphrey. *Paths of Glory*. London: Heinemann, 1935.

Cocks, Geoffrey. "Bringing the Holocaust Home: The Freudian Dynamics of Kubrick's *The Shining*." *Psychoanalytic Review* 78:1 (Spring 1991): 103–25.

———. "Death by Typewriter: Stanley Kubrick, the Holocaust, and *The Shining*." In Cocks, Diedrick, and Perusek, eds., *Depth of Field*.

———. "The Hinting: Holocaust Imagery in Kubrick's *The Shining*." *Psychohistory Review* 16:3 (Fall 1987): 115–36.

———. "Kubrick Confronted Holocaust—Indirectly." *Los Angeles Times*, March 12, 1999.
———. "Stanley Kubrick's Dream Machine: Psychoanalysis, Film, and History." *Annual of Psychoanalysis* 31 (2003): 35–45.
———, James Diedrick, and Glenn Perusek, eds. *Depth of Field: Stanley Kubrick, Film, and the Uses of History*. Madison: University of Wisconsin Press, 2005.
Cohen, Alain J.-J. "Stanley Kubrick's *The Shining*: Semiotics of the Labyrinth." In *Semiotics 2000: "Seebok's Century,"* edited by Scott Simpkins, 183–95. New York: Legas, 2001.
Collins, Floyd. "Implied Metaphor in the Films of Stanley Kubrick." *New Orleans Review* 16 (Fall 1989): 96–100.
Combs, Richard. "Kubrick Talks!" *Film Comment* 32 (September–October 1996): 81–84.
Cook, David A. "American Horror: *The Shining*." *Literature/Film Quarterly* 12 (1984): 2–4.
Coppedge, Walter. "*Barry Lyndon*: Kubrick's Elegy for an Age." *Literature/Film Quarterly* 29:3 (2001): 172–78.
Cossa, Frank. "Images of Perfection: Life Imitates Art in Kubrick's *Barry Lyndon*." *Eighteenth-Century Life* 19 (1995): 79–82.
Coyle, Wallace. *Stanley Kubrick: A Guide to References and Resources*. Boston: Hall, 1980.
Crane, Stephen. "The Blue Hotel." In Crane, *Maggie, together with George's Mother and The Blue Hotel*. New York: Knopf, 1931.
Crone, Rainer, and Petrus Graf Schaesberg. *Stanley Kubrick: Still Moving Pictures, Photographies, 1945–1950*. Regensburg: Schnell + Steiner, 1999.
Davis, Natalie Zemon. "Resistance and Survival: *Spartacus*." In Davis, *Slaves on Screen: Film and Historical Vision*, 17–40. Cambridge, Mass.: Harvard University Press, 2000.
———. "Trumbo and Kubrick Argue History." *Raritan* 22 (Summer 2002): 173–90.
Deer, Harriet, and Irving Deer. "Kubrick and the Structures of Popular Culture." *Journal of Popular Film* 3 (1974): 232–44.
Denby, David. "Death Warmed Over." *New Yorker*, June 9, 1980, 61.
———. "Last Waltz." *New Yorker*, July 26, 1999, 84–86.
DeRosia, Margaret "An Erotics of Violence: Masculinity and (Homo)Sexuality in *A Clockwork Orange*." In McDougal, ed., *Stanley Kubrick's A Clockwork Orange*, 61–84.
*Dr. Strangelove:* A Continuity Transcript. May 15, 1999. www.161.210.220.100/doc/0055.html, 2001.
Doherty, Thomas. "Full Metal Genre: Kubrick's Vietnam Combat Movie." In Falsetto, ed., *Perspectives on Stanley Kubrick*, 317–26.
Downing, David. *Jack Nicholson*. New York: Stein & Day, 1984.
Eisenstein, Sergei. "Color and Meaning," 113–53. In Eisenstein, *The Film Sense*. Edited and translated by Jay Leyda. New York: Harcourt, Brace, 1942.
Eller, Jackie. "Wendy Torrance, One of King's Women: A Typology of King's Female Characters." In Magistrale, ed., *The Shining Reader*, 11–22.
Emery, Michael James. "U.S. Horror: Gothicism in the Work of William Faulkner, Thomas Pynchon, and Stanley Kubrick." Ph.D. diss., State University of New York, Binghamtom, 1989.
Engell, John. "*Barry Lyndon*: A Picture of Irony." *Eighteenth-Century Life* 19 (1995): 83–88.
Falsetto, Mario. "Patterns of Filmic Narration in *The Killing* and *Lolita*." In Falsetto, ed., *Perspectives on Stanley Kubrick*, 100–123.
———. *Stanley Kubrick: A Narrative and Stylistic Analysis*. Westport, Conn.: Greenwood, 1994.
———, ed. *Perspectives on Stanley Kubrick*. New York: Hall, 1996.
Feeley, Gregory. "The Masterpiece a Master Couldn't Get Right." *New York Times*, July 18, 1999.

Feldmann, Hans. "Kubrick and His Discontents." In Falsetto, ed., *Perspectives on Stanley Kubrick*, 191-200.
Ferreira, Patricia. "Jack's Nightmare at the Overlook." In Magistrale, ed., *The Shining Reader*, 23-32.
Foix, Vincente Molina. "Entretien avec Stanley Kubrick." *Positif* 319 (January 1980): 5-11
Freedman, Carl. "Kubrick's *2001* and the Possibility of a Science-Fiction Cinema." *Science Fiction Studies* 25 (1998): 300-318
Freud, Sigmund. "The Uncanny" (1919). In *The Standard Edition of the Complete Psychological Works of Sigmund Freud*, edited and translated by James Strachey, 17: 218-252. London: Methuen, 1955.
Gabbard, Krin, and Shalija Sharma. "Stanley Kubrick and the Art Cinema." In McDougal, ed., *Stanley Kubrick's A Clockwork Orange*, 85-108.
Garsault, Alain. "Les Deux Visages du Fantastique." *Positif* 238 (January 1981): 17-19.
Gehrke, Pat J. "Deviant Subjects and *A Clockwork Orange*: Congruent Critiques of Criminological Constructions of Subjectivity." In Cocks, Diedrick, and Perusek, eds., *Depth of Field*.
———, and Gina Ercolini. "Subjected Wills: The Anti-Humanism of Kubrick's Later Films." In Cocks, Diedrick, and Perusek, eds., *Depth of Field*.
Gelmis, Joseph. "'Space Odyssey' Fails Most Gloriously." In Agel, ed., *Making of Kubrick's 2001*, 263-65.
George, Peter. *Dr. Strangelove Or, How I Learned to Stop Worrying and Love the Bomb*. (1963). New York: Oxford University Press, 1988.
Giavarini, Laurence. "Puissance des Fantasmes." *Cahiers du Cinema* 542 (January 2000): 41-43.
Gilliatt, Penelope. "Heavy Metal." *American Film* 12 (September 1987): 20-23.
Ginna, Robert Emma. "The Odyssey Begins." *Entertainment Weekly*, April 9, 1999, 16-22.
Giuliani, Pierre. *Stanley Kubrick*. Paris: Rivages, 1990.
Griffiths, Paul. "Music that Switches Its Gaze, from Future to Past." *New York Times*, July 21, 2002.
Gross, Larry. "Too Late the Hero." *Sight and Sound* 9:9 (September 1999): 20-23.
Haine, Raymond. "Bonjour Monsieur Kubrick." *Cahiers du Cinema* 73 (July 1957): 10-18.
Hairapetian, Marc. "Stanley hätte applaudiert." *Film-Dienst* 9 (2000).
———, and Claudia Tour-Sarkissian. "Ohne ihn ist die Welt viel kälter geworden." *Die Welt*, September 9, 1999.
Hala, James. "Kubrick's *The Shining*: The Specters and the Critics." In Magistrale, ed., *The Shining Reader*, 203-16.
Harmetz, Aljean. "Kubrick Films 'The Shining' in Secrecy in English Studio." *New York Times*, November 6, 1978.
Hasford, Gustav. *The Short-Timers*. New York: Harper & Row, 1979.
Hatlen, Burton. "Good and Evil in Stephen King's *The Shining*." In Magistrale, ed., *The Shining Reader*, 81-104.
Henrikson, Margot A. *Dr. Strangelove's America: Society and Culture in the Atomic Age*. Berkeley: University of California Press, 1997.
Herr, Michael. *Kubrick*. New York: Grove, 2000.
Hilberg, Raul. *The Destruction of the European Jews*. Chicago: Quadrangle, 1961.
Hoberman, James. "The Dream Life of Androids." *Sight and Sound* 11 (2001): 16-19.
Hofsess, John. "How I Learned to Stop Worrying and Love 'Barry Lyndon.'" *New York Times*, January 11, 1976.
———. "'The Shining' Example of Kubrick." *Los Angeles Times*, June 1, 1980.

Hoile, Christopher. "The Uncanny and the Fairy Tale in Kubrick's *The Shining*." *Literature/Film Quarterly* 12 (1984): 6–12.
Holland, Norman H. "*2001:* A Psychosocial Explication." *Hartford Studies in Literature* 1 (1969): 20–25.
Howard, James. *Stanley Kubrick Companion*. London: Batsford, 1999.
Hughes, David. *The Complete Kubrick*. London: Virgin, 2000.
Hughes, Philip. "The Alienated and Demonic in the Film of Stanley Kubrick: Cinemanalysis with a Freudian Technophobic Argument." *Journal of Evolutionary Psychology* 3:1–2 (April 1982): 12–27.
Hughes, Robert. "The Décor of Tomorrow's Hell." In Falsetto, ed., *Perspectives on Stanley Kubrick*, 185–86.
Hummel, Christoph, et al. *Stanley Kubrick*. Munich: Hanser, 1984.
James, Nick. "At Home with the Kubricks." *Sight and Sound* 9:9 (September 1999): 12–18.
Jameson, Frederic. "Historicism in *The Shining*." In Jameson, *Signatures of the Visible*, 82–98. New York: Routledge, 1990.
Jameson, Richard T. "Kubrick's Shining." In Falsetto, ed., *Perspectives on Stanley Kubrick*, 243–52.
———. "Sonata." *Film Comment* 35 (September 1999): 27–28.
Jenkins, Greg. *Stanley Kubrick and the Art of Adaptation*. Jefferson, N.C.: McFarland, 1997.
Jenny, Urs, and Martin Wolf. "Er war einfach schüchtern." *Der Spiegel*, August 30, 1999, 196, 198.
Johnson, Diane. *The Shadow Knows*. New York: Knopf, 1974.
———. "Stanley Kubrick (1928–1999)." *New York Review of Books,* April 22, 1999, 28.
———. "Writing *The Shining*." In Cocks, Diedrick, and Perusek, eds., *Depth of Field*.
Johnson, Jeffrey L. L. "The Eighteenth-Century Ape: *Barry Lyndon* and the Darwinian Pessimism of Stanley Kubrick." *Eighteenth-Century Life* 19 (May 1995): 89–91.
———. "Stanley Kubrick (1928–1999)." *New York Review of Books,* April 22, 1999, 28
Kael Pauline. "*A Clockwork Orange:* Stanley Strangelove." In McDougal, ed., *Stanley Kubrick's A Clockwork Orange*, 134–39.
———. "Devolution." *New Yorker,* June 9, 1980, 130f.
Kafka, Franz, *The Castle*. Translated by Willa and Edwin Muir. 1922. New York: Knopf, 1992.
Kagan, Norman. *The Cinema of Stanley Kubrick*. Expanded ed. New York: Continuum, 1997.
Katharina Kubrick Hobbs FAQ. www.alta.demon.co.uk/faq/kckh.html, 2000.
Keeler, Greg. "The Shining: Ted Kramer Has a Nightmare." *Journal of Popular Film and Television* 8:4 (Winter 1981): 2–8.
Kelly, Andrew. "The Brutality of Military Incompetence: 'Paths of Glory' (1975)." *Historical Journal of Film, Radio and Television* 13 (1993): 215–27.
Kennedy, Harlan. "Kubrick Goes Gothic." *American Film* 5 (June 1980): 49–52.
King, Stephen. "Before the Play." *TV Guide* April 26, 1997, 22–25, 49–57.
———. *The Shining*. New York: Doubleday, 1977.
Kinney, Judy Lee. "Text and Pretext: Stanley Kubrick's Adaptations." Ph.D. diss., University of California, Los Angeles, 1982.
Kirschmann, Kay. *Stanley Kubrick: Das Schweigen der Bilder*. Marburg: Hitzeroth, 1993.
Klein, Michael. "Narrative and Discourse in Kubrick's Modern Tragedy." In *The English Novel and the Movies*, edited by Michael Klein and Gillian Parker, 95–107. New York: Ungar, 1981.

Kloman, William. "In 2001, Will Love Be a Seven-Letter Word?" *New York Times*, April 14, 1968.
Knapp, Elise, and James Pegolotti. "Music in Kubrick's *Barry Lyndon:* 'A Catalyst to Manipulate.'" *Eighteenth-Century Life* 19 (May 1995): 92–97.
Kolker, Robert. *A Cinema of Loneliness*. 3rd ed. New York: Oxford University Press, 2000.
———. "*A Clockwork Orange* . . . Ticking." In McDougal, ed., *Stanley Kubrick's A Clockwork Orange*, 19–36.
Kreider, Tim. "Introducing Sociology." In Cocks, Diedrick, and Perusek, eds., *Depth of Field*.
———. "A.I.: Artificial Intelligence." *Film Quarterly* 56:2 (2003): 32–39.
Kroll, Jack. "Kubrick's Brilliant Vision." *Newsweek*, January 3, 1972, 28–33.
———. "Kubrick's View." *Newsweek*, March 22, 1999, 65–68.
———. "Stanley Kubrick's Horror Show." *Newsweek*, May 26, 1980, 96–99.
Kubrick, Christiane. *Paintings*. New York: Warner, 1990.
———. *Stanley Kubrick: A Life in Pictures*. Boston: Little, Brown, 2002.
Kubrick, Stanley. "Barry Lyndon." February 18, 1973. www.hundland.com/scripts/Barry Lyndon.txt, 2003.
———. A Clockwork Orange. 1971. www.geocities.com/Hollywood/Theater/9590/ACOSCRIPT.html, 2001.
———. *A Clockwork Orange*. 1972. Southwold: Screenpress, 2000.
———. "Director's Notes: Stanley Kubrick Movie Maker." In Falsetto, ed., *Perspectives on Stanley Kubrick*, 23–25.
———. "How I Learned to Stop Worrying and Love the Cinema." *Films and Filming* 9 (June 1963): 12–13.
———. "Napoleon: A Screenplay." September 29, 1969. www.filmforce.net, 2000.
———. "Now Kubrick Fights Back." *New York Times*, February 27, 1972.
[———.] "The Shining." n.d. The James Boyle Collection 135/S, Warner Bros. Archives, School of Cinema and Television, University of Southern California, Los Angeles.
———. "Words and Movies." *Sight and Sound* 30 (1960/1961): 14.
———, and Arthur C. Clarke. "2001: A Space Odyssey." October–December 1965. www.palantir.net/2001/script.html, 2001.
———, and Michael Herr. "Full Metal Jacket." February 4, 1985. www.alta.demon.co uk/amk/doc/0065.html, 2000.
———, Michael Herr, and Gustav Hasford, *Full Metal Jacket: The Screenplay*. New York: Knopf, 1987.
———, and Frederic Raphael. "Eyes Wide Shut: A Screenplay." August 4, 1996. www.godamongdirectors.com/scripts/eyeswideshu.htm, 1999.
———. *Eyes Wide Shut*. New York: Warner, 1999.
Leibowitz, Flo, and Jeffress, Lynn. "The Shining." *Film Quarterly* 34:3 (Spring 1981): 45–51.
Leyda, Jay, ed. and trans. *Film Form: Essays in Film Theory and The Film Sense*. Cleveland: World, 1967.
Lightman, Herb. "Photographing Stanley Kubrick's *The Shining*: An Interview with John Alcott." In Falsetto, ed., *Perspectives on Stanley Kubrick*, 260–72.
LoBrutto, Vincent. "The Old Ultra-Violence." *American Cinematographer* 52 (October 1999): 52–60.
———. *Stanley Kubrick: A Biography*. New York: Fine, 1997.
———. "The Written Word and the Very Visual Stanley Kubrick." In Cocks, Diedrick, and Perusek, eds., *Depth of Field*.

Loewenberg, Peter. "Freud, Schnitzler, and *Eyes Wide Shut.*" In Cocks, Diedrick, and Perusek, eds., *Depth of Field*.
Lyman, Rick, "Making the Wit Seem Unwitting." *New York Times,* March 29, 2002.
———. "A Perfectionist's Pupil with a Major in Creepy." *New York Times,* February 22, 2002.
Macklin, F. Anthony. "Sex and Dr. Strangelove." *Film Comment* 1 (Summer 1965): 55–57.
Madigan, Mark J. "'Orders from the House': Kubrick's *The Shining* and Kafka's 'The Metamorphosis.'" In Magistrale, ed., *The Shining Reader,* 193–201.
Magid, Ron. "Quest for Perfection." *American Cinematographer* 40 (October 1999): 40–51.
Magistrale, Anthony, ed. *The Shining Reader*. Mercer Island, Wash: Starmont, 1991.
Mainar, Luis M. Garcia. *Narrative and Stylistic Patterns in the Films of Stanley Kubrick*. Rochester, N.Y.: Camden House, 1999.
Maland, Charles. "*Dr. Strangelove* (1964): Nightmare Comedy and the Ideology of Liberal Consensus." *American Quarterly* 31 (1979): 697–717.
Manchel, Frank. "What About Jack? Another Perspective on Family Relationships in Stanley Kubrick's *The Shining*." *Literature/Film Quarterly* 23 (1995): 68–78.
Mann, Thomas. *The Magic Mountain*. Translated by H. T. Lowe-Porter. 1924. New York: Knopf, 1955.
———. "The Making of 'The Magic Mountain.'" *Atlantic Monthly,* January 1953, 41–45.
Maslin, Janet, "Flaws Don't Dim 'The Shining.'" *New York Times,* June 8, 1980.
———. "Screen: Nicholson and Shelley Duvall in Kubrick's 'The Shining.'" *New York Times,* May 23, 1980.
Mayersberg, Paul. "The Overlook Hotel." In Falsetto, ed., *Perspectives on Stanley Kubrick,* 253–59.
McCaffery, Larry. "Talking About *The Shining* with Diane Johnson." *Chicago Review* 33 (1981): 75–79.
McDougal, Stuart Y., ed. *Stanley Kubrick's A Clockwork Orange*. New York: Cambridge University Press, 2003.
———. "'What's It Going to be then, eh?': Questioning Kubrick's *Clockwork*." In McDougal, ed., *Stanley Kubrick's A Clockwork Orange,* 1–18.
McGregor, Craig. "Nice Boy from the Bronx?" *New York Times,* January 30, 1972.
Metz, Walter. "Toward a Post-structural Influence in Film-Genre Study: Intertextuality and *The Shining*." *Film Criticism* 22:1 (Fall 1997): 38–61.
———. "A Very Notorious Ranch, Indeed: Fritz Lang, Allegory, and the Holocaust." *Journal of Contemporary Thought* 13 (Summer 2001): 71–86.
Miers, Paul. "The Black Maria Rides Again: Being a Reflection on the Present State of American Film with Special Respect to Stanley Kubrick's *The Shining*." *Modern Language Notes* 95 (1980): 1360–66.
Miller, Mark Crispin. "*Barry Lyndon* Reconsidered." *Georgia Review* 30 (Winter 1976): 827–53.
———. "Kubrick's Anti-Reading of *The Luck of Barry Lyndon*." In Falsetto, ed., *Perspectives on Stanley Kubrick,* 226–42.
———. "*2001:* A Cold Descent." In Cocks, Diedrick, and Perusek, eds., *Depth of Field*.
Moraz, Patricia. "Il Faut Courir le risque de subtilité." *Le Monde,* October 23, 1980, 20.
Munday, Rod. The Shining FAQ. www.alta.demon.co.uk/faq/html/shining/shining.html, 2000.
Nabokov, Vladimir. *The Annotated Lolita*. Edited by Alfred Appel, Jr. 1955. New York: McGraw-Hill, 1970.
———. *Lolita: A Screenplay*. New York: McGraw-Hill, 1974.

Nelson, Thomas Allen. *Kubrick: Inside a Film Artist's Maze*. Bloomington: Indiana University Press, 2000.
Noack, Frank. *Veit Harlan: "Des Teufels Regisseur."* Munich: belleville, 2000.
Noland, Richard W. "Individuation in *2001: A Space Odyssey*." *Journal of Evolutionary Psychology* 15: 3–4 (August 1994): 302–9.
Novick, Peter. *The Holocaust in American Life*. Boston: Houghton Mifflin, 1999.
Ott, Susanna. "Reshaping Life." In Crone and Schaseberg, eds., *Stanley Kubrick: Still Moving Pictures*, 202–18.
Oudart, Jean-Pierre. "Les Inconnus dans la Maison." *Cahiers du Cinema* 317 (November 1980): 5–11.
Owen, Iris. "'It's Movies for Me'." *Modern Photography*, September 1953, 84–85, 98–99.
Perusek, Glenn. "Kubrick's Armies: Strategy, Hierarchy, and Motive in the War Films of Stanley Kubrick." In Cocks, Diedrick, and Perusek, eds., *Depth of Field*.
Phillips, Gene D. *Stanley Kubrick: A Film Odyssey*. New York: Popular Library, 1975.
———, ed. *Stanley Kubrick Interviews*. Jackson: University of Mississippi Press, 2001.
———, and Rodney Hill, eds. *The Encyclopedia of Stanley Kubrick*. New York: Facts on File, 2002.
Pilard, Philippe. *Barry Lyndon, Stanley Kubrick, Étude Critique*. Paris: Nathan, 1990.
Pipolo, Tony. "The Modernist and the Misanthrope: The Cinema of Stanley Kubrick." *Cineaste* 27 (Spring 2002): 4–15, 49.
Pizzello, Stephen. "A Sword in the Bed." *American Cinematographer* 52 (October 1999): 33–38.
Plume, Kenneth. "Interview with Producer Jan Harlan." June 28, 2001. www.filmforce.ign.com/articles/300920p1.html, 2002.
Pollan, Dana. "Materiality and Sociality in *Killer's Kiss*." In Falsetto, ed., *Perspectives on Stanley Kubrick*, 87–99.
Pudovkin, Vsevolod. *Film Technique*. Tranlated by Ivor Montagu. London: Newness, 1933.
Pursell, Michael. "*Full Metal Jacket:* The Unravelling of Patriarchy." In Falsetto, ed., *Perspectives on Stanley Kubrick*, 317–26.
Rabinowitz, Peter J. "'A Bird of Like Rarest Spun Heavenmetal': Music in *A Clockwork Orange*." In McDougal, ed., *Stanley Kubrick's A Clockwork Orange*, 109–30.
Rambuss, Richard. "Machinehead." *Camera Obscura* 14 (September 1999): 97–123.
Raphael, Frederic. *Eyes Wide Open: A Memoir of Stanley Kubrick*. New York: Ballantine, 1999.
———. "The Pumpkinification of Stanley Kubrick." In Cocks, Diedrick, and Perusek, eds., *Depth of Field*.
Rasmussen, Randy. *Stanley Kubrick: Seven Films Analyzed*. Jefferson, N.C.: McFarland, 2001.
Reaves, Gerri. "The Fracturing of Identification." *Literature/Film Quarterly* 16:4 (1988): 232–37.
Reesman, Jeanne Campbell. "Stephen King and the Tradition of American Naturalism in *The Shining*." In Magistrale, ed., *The Shining Reader*, 121–38.
Rosenbaum, Jonathan. "In Dreams Begin Responsibilities." In Cocks, Diedrick, and Perusek, eds., *Depth of Field*.
Ross, Benjamin. "Eternal Yearning." *Sight and Sound* 5 (October 1995): 42.
Rother, Rainer. "Das Kunstwerk als Konstruktionsaufgabe." *Merkur* 43 (May 1989): 384–96.
Saada, Nicolas. "Scènes de L'envie Conjugale." *Cahiers du Cinema* 538 (September 1999): 32–35.

———. "*The Shining*, une Histoire de Famille. Entretien avec Diane Johnson, Scenariste." *Cahiers du Cinema* 534 (April 1999): 34–37.
Schnitzler, Arthur. *Dream Story*. Translated by J. M. Q. Davies. 1926. New York: Warner, 1999.
Schrader, Paul. "'Lolita': Rapier Innuendos and Roman Ping-Pong." *American Film* 15:1 (October 1989): 18–20, 22.
Schwed. Mark. "The Shining: It Lives Again." *TV Guide*, April 26–May 2, 1997, 18–21.
Schweitzer, Rich. "Born to Kill: S. Kubrick's *Full Metal Jacket* as Historical Representation of America's Experience in Vietnam." *Film and History* 20:3 (1990): 62–70.
Seesslen, Georg, and Fernand Jung. *Stanley Kubrick und seine Filme*. Marburg: Schüren, 1999.
Shor, Francis. "Father Knows Beast: Patriarchal Rage and the Horror of Personality Film." *Journal of Criminal Justice and Popular Culture* 3:3 (June 15, 1995): 60–85.
Sineux, Michel. "La Symphonie Kubrick." *Positif* 239 (February 1981): 34–36
Smith, Claude J. "Full Metal Jacket and the Beast Within." *Literature/Film Quarterly* 16:4 (1988): 226–31.
Smith, Greg. "'Real Horrorshow': The Juxtaposition of Subtext, Satire, and Audience Implication in Stanley Kubrick's The Shining." *Literature/Film Quarterly* 25 (1997): 300–306.
Smith, James F. "Kubrick's or King's—Whose *Shining* Is It?" In Magistrale, ed., *The Shining Reader*, 181–91.
Smith, Jeff. "Careening Through Kubrick's Space." *Chicago Review* 33:1 (Summer 1981): 62–74.
Snyder, Stephen. "Family Life and Leisure Culture in *The Shining*." *Film Criticism* 7:1 (Fall 1982): 4–13.
Sobchack, Vivian. "Child/Alien/Father: Patriarchal Crisis and Generic Exchange." *Camera Obscura* 15 (1986): 7–35.
Southern, Terry. "Strangelove Outtake: Notes from the War Room." *Grand Street* 13:1 (Summer 1994): 65–80.
Spiegel, Alan. "Kubrick's *Barry Lyndon*." In Falsetto, ed., *Perspectives on Stanley Kubrick*, 201–13.
Staiger, Janet. "The Cultural Productions of *A Clockwork Orange*." In McDougal, ed., *Stanley Kubrick's A Clockwork Orange*, 37–60.
Stang, Joanne. "Film Fan to Film Maker." *New York Times Magazine*, October 12, 1958, 35–38.
*Stanley Kubrick Ladro di Sguardi: Fotografie di Fotografie, 1945–1949*. Rome: Bompiani, 1994.
Stevenson, James A. "Beyond Stephen Crane: *Full Metal Jacket*." *Literature/Film Quarterly* 16:4 (1988): 238–43.
Taubin, Amy. "Stanley Kubrick's Last Film." *Film Comment* 35 (September 1999): 25–26, 30–33.
Taylor, John Russell. "On Seeing *2001* a Second Time." In Agel, ed., *Making of Kubrick's 2001*, 272–74.
Thackeray, William Makepeace. *The Luck of Barry Lyndon*. Edited by Martin F. Anisman. 1844. New York: New York University Press, 1970.
Thissen, Rolf. *Stanley Kubrick: Der Regisseur als Architekt*. Munich: Heyne, 1999.
Titterington, P. L. "Kubrick and 'The Shining.'" *Sight and Sound* 50 (Spring 1981): 117–21.
Vitali, Leon. "Kubrick Questions Finally Answered." www.dvdtalk.com/leonvitaliinterview.html, 2002.

Walker, Alexander. "Inexactly Expressed Sentiments About the Most Private Person I Know." In Walker, *"It's Only a Movie, Ingrid,"* 285–302.
———. *"It's Only a Movie, Ingrid": Encounters On and Off Screen*. London: Headline, 1988.
———. *Stanley Kubrick, Director*. New York: Norton, 1999. `
Walter, Renaud. "Entretien avec Stanley Kubrick." *Positif* 101 (January 1969): 19–39.
Walters, C. T. "Stanley Kubrick's *The Shining*: A Study in the Terror of Abstractionism." *Forum* 26:3 (Summer 1985): 21–38.
Watson, Ian. "My Adventures with Stanley Kubrick." *Playboy*, August 1999.
Weller, Greg. "The Redrum of Time: A Meditation on Francisco Goya's 'Saturn Devouring His Children.'" In Magistrale, ed., *The Shining Reader*, 61–78.
Wheat, Leonard F. *Kubrick's 2001: A Triple Allegory*. Lanham, Md.: Scarecrow, 2000.
White, Lionel. *Clean Break*. New York: Dutton, 1955.
White, Susan. "Male Bonding, Hollywood Orientalism, and the Repression of the Feminine in Kubrick's *Full Metal Jacket*." *Arizona Quarterly* 44 (Autumn 1988): 120–44.
Wickre, Bille. "Pictures, Plurality, and Puns: A Visual Approach to *Barry Lyndon*." In Cocks, Diedrick, and Perusek, eds., *Depth of Field*.
Williams, Donald. "An Interview with Diane Johnson, Screenwriter for Stanley Kubrick's Film *The Shining*." 1992. www.cgjungpage.org/films/shining.html, 2003.
Williams, Michaela. "2001: Where Did It Go Right?" In Agel, ed., *Making of Kubrick's 2001*, 274–81.
Willoquet-Maricondi, Paula. "Full-Metal-Jacketing, or Masculinity in the Making." In Cocks, Diedrick, and Perusek, eds., *Depth of Field*.
Wilson, William. "Riding the Crest of the Horror Craze." *New York Times*, May 11, 1980.
Zweig, Stefan. *The Burning Secret*. London: Allen & Unwin, 1914.

# INDEX

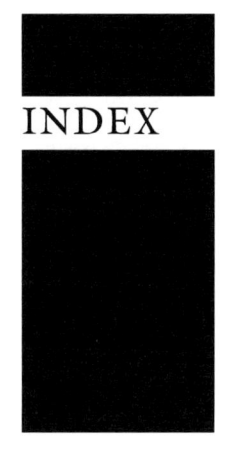

*A.I. Artificial Intelligence,* 60, 158–160, 208
Adam, Ken, 56, 60, 61, 286n35
Adams, Richard, 151–152
Adorno, Theodor, 15–16, 244
Agee, James, 64, 67, 79, 179, 182, 198
Aldiss, Brian, 158–159, 160
Aldrich, Robert, 88
*Alexander Nevsky,* 127, 243
Anti-Nazi League, 41, 126
anti-Semitism, 24, 27, 29, 35, 37–38, 41–46, 54–55
anti-Semitic groups, 35–36
Anya Productions, 102
*Apocalypse Now,* 114, 133, 165
Arbus, Diane, 237
Arnold, Matthew, 64, 94
"Aryan Papers", 14, 15, 69, 156–158
*The Asphalt Jungle,* 88, 90
Auschwitz, 10, 15, 21–22, 29, 45, 114, 127, 137, 198, 219, 231, 308n3, 315n27
Avery, Tex, 37

Bacon, Francis, 169

*Bad Timing: A Sensual Obsession,* 147
*Badenheim 1939,* 190–191, 241
Baigell, Matthew, 46
Ballard, Lucien, 88
*Barry Lyndon,* 2, 11, 43, 56, 92, 121, 133, 140, 146, 151
*Barry Lyndon,* 199, 212, 240
army in, 60, 132
Bryan, 131
Captain Grogan, 89, 132
Captain Quin, 131
Chevalier, 131
ending, 94
filming, 131
Holocaust references in, 167, 240
homosexuality in, 89, 132
humor in, 132
Lady Harriet Lyndon, 131
music in, 131, 132
Lischen, 132–133
narration, 13, 131, 133
Nora Brady, 130, 131
number 7, 131

*Barry Lyndon (continued)*
  opening scene, 130
  Redmond Barry/Barry Lyndon, 26, 60, 89, 131–132, 147
  use of color in, 131
Barthes, Roland, 3
Bartók, Béla, 146, 206, 236, 248–250
*Barton Fink,* 190–193
Bauer, Fritz, 69
Baum, Vicki, 183, 187
Baxter, John, 30, 94
Bazin, André, 13
*The Beast with Five Fingers,* 188–189
Beethoven, Ludwig van, 63, 74, 125, 126, 128, 146
Bergman, Ingmar, 182, 213
Berlin Philharmonic, 118, 119
Berlioz, Hector, 196–197
Bethmann, Sabine, 99
Bettelheim, Bruno, 164, 174, 201, 210–211
"Blue Danube Waltz," 117, 118
"The Blue Hotel," 179–182, 198
*Blume in Love,* 143
Bogdanovich, Peter, 32
Boulanger, General Georges, 96
Brando, Marlon, 148–149, 152
Brecht, Bertolt, 8, 13, 57
Bresson, Robert, 50
Bryant, William Cullen, 24
Bryant, Peter. SEE Peter George
Bryna Productions, 99, 102
Buñuel, Luis, 187–188, 244
Burgess, Anthony, 29, 75, 123, 125, 126, 130
Burnett, Murray, 53
*The Burning Secret,* 31, 53, 146, 150–151, 181–182, 192
Burstyn, Joseph, 25, 78

*The Cabinet of Dr. Caligari,* 51, 97, 169, 171
Capra, Frank, 43, 47
Cartier, Walter, 66
Cartier-Bresson, Henri, 50
*Casablanca,* 45, 50, 53
*The Castle,* 2, 64, 198–199, 207, 216–217
*The Castle of Otranto, a Gothic Story,* 168
*Cat People,* 17, 37
*Catch-22,* 94
*The Catcher in the Rye,* 174, 236, 273n12

Céline, Louis-Ferdinand, 81
Chaplin, Charlie, 44–45, 50, 60, 246
*Chinatown,* 165–166, 290n199
Chodorow, Nancy, 4–5, 142
Christian, Susanne. SEE Kubrick, Christiane
Ciment, Michel, 23, 27, 49–50, 54, 76, 223
Clarke, Arthur C., 116, 118, 122–23, 283n83
*Clean Break,* 29, 87, 91–92
Clive, John, 127
*A Clockwork Orange,* 29, 60, 123, 129
*A Clockwork Orange,* 2, 8–10, 31, 75, 125–126, 130, 133, 139, 140. 170–172, 199, 240
  Alex DeLarge, 8, 26, 28, 30, 31, 54, 89, 123–126, 127, 147
  Deltoid, 89
  ending, 128
  Dr. Brodsky, 28
  Dr. Rubinstein, 28
  German version, 70
  Frank Alexander, 29, 125, 128
  Georgie, 126
  "HOME," 128
  homosexuality in, 89
  Korova Milkbar, 125–126, 159
  language of, 124, 125
  Ludovico Technique, 124, 125, 127
  Miss Weathers, the "Cat Lady," 8, 126
  music in, 74, 76, 123–125, 132
  Nazi imagery in, 125–129, 167
  use of color in, 128
Cobb, Humphrey, 29, 93–94, 97
Cold War, 34, 70, 107, 113, 115, 149, 169
Colville, Alex, 224–225
Conrad, Joseph, 10, 15, 64–66, 76, 78, 96–97, 114, 139, 177, 179
Coppola, Francis Ford, 114, 133, 165
Coughlin, Father Charles, 35
Crane, Stephen, 179–180, 182
Cruise, Tom, 1
Curtis, Tony, 26, 35–36

*The Damned,* 165, 189
Dassin, Jules, 32, 84, 149
Davis, Natalie Zemon, 70, 98
*Day of the Fight,* 25, 43, 66
de Maupassant, Guy, 63
de Rochement, Richard, 78

*Der Reigen,* 62
*The Destruction of the European Jews,* 2, 161, 221, 226, 227, 231, 238, 243, 244, 253
Dieterle, William, 53
"Disorder and Early Sorrow," 39–40
*Dispatches,* 133, 136
*Dr. Strangelove, or: How I Learned to Stop Worrying and Love the Bomb,* 2, 28, 43, 59, 77–79, 88, 107–118, 138
  "Bland Corporation," 115
  Ambassador Alexander de Sadesky, 108
  Dmitri Kissoff, 108
  Dr. Strangelove, 60, 108, 114–116, 147
  "Doomsday Machine," 108, 115, 116
  "Doomsday shroud," 108
  ending, 59, 81, 116
  General Buck Turgidson, 108, 114
  General Jack D. Ripper, 98, 107, 108, 147
  Holocaust subtext in, 116
  Lieutenant Goldberg, 29
  Miss Scott, 110
  music, 110, 113, 116
  President Merkin Muffley, 108, 115
  sexism in, 110, 116
  Strategic Air Command, 108
  War Room, 60
  "Wing Attack Plan R", 108
doubles, 66, 82, 120, 128, 140, 146, 153, 201, 202–203, 205, 213, 216, 219, 233, 237–239
Douglas, Kirk, 93, 99
*Dream Story,* 29, 139–146
  Albertine, 140, 142
  Fridolin, 140, 141–145
Dreyer, Carl-Theodor, 50
Dreyfus Affair, 29, 97

Eagle Films, 6, 212
eagles, symbolism of, 6, 10, 13, 95, 120, 125, 139, 212, 216–217, 222, 273–274n27, 309n10
*The Earrings of Madame De . . . ,* 63
Eichmann, Adolf, 106, 113–114, 163
Eisenhower, Dwight, 111, 149, 223
Eisenstein, Sergei, 13, 127, 197, 242–243
"Elegy Written in a Country Churchyard," 93, 94
Enlightenment, 11, 15–16, 24, 63–64, 144
*The Eternal Jew,* 69

*Everybody Comes to Rick's,* 53
Expressionistic lighting, 53–54
*The Exterminating Angel,* 187–188, 244
*Eyes Wide Shut,* 1, 2, 6–7, 15, 28, 29–31, 139–147, 151, 199
  Alice Harford, 141, 142, 143
  anti-Semitism in, 90, 144–145
  Bill Harford, 28, 90, 141–147
  blue Mercedes-Benz in, 1, 6, 145
  changes from source material, 29
  color, 1, 6, 145
  Domino, 142
  gay hotel desk clerk, 90
  homosexual references in, 29, 89–90, 141, 144–145
  Holocaust reference in, 146
  Italian references, 143
  Lou Nathanson, 28, 143–144, 289n188
  Mandy, 142, 146
  Marion Nathanson, 28
  Milich, 141
  music, 142–143, 146–147
  orgy, 142, 143, 146
  paintings in, 140
  Sally, 142
  setting, 139, 142
  "Somerton" mansion, 95, 146, 151
  Victor Ziegler, 28, 142, 145–146
  Yellow Cabs, 145

Fast, Howard, 100
*Fear and Desire,* 2, 25, 43, 64, 78–81
  details in, 79–80
  filming of, 78–79
  Fletcher, 79
  Lieutenant Corby, 79
  location, 78
  Mac, 79
  narration, 78
  Proteus, 79
  Sidney, 28–29, 78
*Fidelio,* 143, 146, 190
Filbert, Alfred, 71
film noir, 14, 80–81, 84, 88
*Film Technique,* 13
*Five Graves to Cairo,* 53–56, 189
Flynn, Errol, 42
*The 5000 Fingers of Dr. T,* 184–185, 187, 188

Foucault, Michel, 4
*42nd Street,* 86
Frank, Anne, 68, 73, 163, 164
French Revolution, 128–129, 130, 196–197
Freud, Sigmund, 4, 9, 22, 63–65, 74, 102, 110, 130, 186, 188, 198–199, 201–202, 206, 212, 220–221, 222, 227, 231, 233–234, 245
Fried, Gerald, 25, 27
*Full Metal Jacket,* 2, 15, 25, 27, 32, 43, 79, 133–139, 196–197, 202, 226
  Animal Mother, 138
  "Chaplain Charlie," 139
  Eightball, 138
  Gunnery Sergeant Hartman, 89, 138, 139, 147
  homosexuality in, 89
  Holocaust references in, 138
  Joker, 138
  music in, 136
  number 7, 139
  racism in, 138
  swastikas in, 138
  use of color, 139

George, Peter, 107
German Expressionism, 14, 50–51, 53, 54, 58–62, 80, 87–88, 107, 133, 177, 187
"The German Lieutenant," 84, 151–154, 294n20
Gilman, Charlotte Perkins, 34, 241
*The Gladiators,* 99, 100
Goebbels, Joseph, 53, 57, 70, 137, 187, 249
Göring, Hermann, 137, 222
Goethe, Johann Wolfgang von, 197, 215, 236
*Grand Illusion,* 50, 60
*Gravity's Rainbow,* 109, 166
Gray, Thomas, 93, 94
*The Great Dictator,* 44–45
Griffith, D. W., 27, 50
Grimm's fairy tales, 33–34, 57, 118, 120
Grosz, Georg, 52, 168
*Gulliver's Travels,* 109

Hadas, Moses, 64, 243
Halliwell, J. Q., 33
Handel, Georg Friedrich, 131
*Hangmen Also Die,* 45, 57

Harlan, Dominic, 69
Harlan, Fritz, 71–73
Harlan, Ingeborg, 72–74
Harlan, Jan, 67, 68, 69, 158, 161, 233
Harlan, Manuel, 68–69
Harlan, Maria, 68
Harlan, Susanne Christiane. SEE Kubrick, Christiane
Harlan, Thomas, 70–71, 246
Harlan, Veit, 70–71, 246
Harrier Films, 6
Harris, James B., 2, 87, 93, 101, 291n205
Harris-Kubrick Pictures, 2, 87, 101–102, 148–149, 152
Hasford, Gustav, 133, 134, 136, 137
*The Haunting,* 17, 182
Hawk Films, 6, 107, 130, 212
Hayden, Sterling, 90
*Heart of Darkness,* 10, 65, 65–66, 96, 114, 138, 177
Hegel, Georg Wilhelm Friedrich, 5
*Heimat,* 69
Heine, Heinrich, 151
Heller, Joseph, 94
Herr, Michael, 14–15, 35, 74, 87, 133, 136, 146
Heydrich, Reinhard, 57, 230
Hilberg, Raul, 2, 161, 218, 221, 226, 227, 231, 238, 243, 244, 253
Himmler, Heinrich, 126, 230, 308n3
Hippler, Fritz, 69
Hiroshima, 114
Hitchcock, Alfred, 6, 169, 186, 188
Hitler, Adolf, 20, 23, 30, 101, 112, 116, 150, 154–156, 164–165, 166, 187, 193, 198, 222, 227, 230
Hobbs, Katharina Kubrick, 68, 140, 142
Hobby Films, 6
"Holocaust," 113–114
*Holocaust,* 166–167
Holocaust Martyrs and Heroes Remembrance Authority, 20
horror, 167–171
House Un-American Affairs Committee, 99
*Humanism: The Greek Idea and Its Survival,* 64
Huston, John, 88–89
Huxley, Aldous, 69

"I Stole 16 Million Dollars"/"The Theft," 148
Industrial Revolution, 11, 94
*Inferno*, 91
International Society for the Suppression of Savage Customs, 66

*J'Accuse*, 169
Jackson, Felix, 148–149
Jackson, Sam. SEE Dalton Trumbo
*Jew Süss*, 69–70, 246
Jewish Telegraphic Agency, 46
John Birch Society, 108
Johnson, Diane, 12, 32, 174–175, 186–199, 234, 240
Jones, Chuck, 210–211
*Judgment at Nuremburg*, 114, 163
Jung, Carl, 63, 134, 202, 252

Kadar, Jan, 180, 182, 198
Kael, Pauline, 166, 189
Kafka, Franz, 2, 14, 64–65, 120, 139, 177, 182, 188, 199, 207–208, 210, 215–218, 244, 246
Kagan, Norman, 94
Kahn, Herman, 114–115
Karlin, Miriam, 126–127
Karski, Jan, 46
Katzmann, Friedrich, 22
Kazin, Alfred, 164, 180
Khachaturian, Aram, 118
*The Killer Inside Me*, 88
*Killer's Kiss*, 2, 25, 32, 82–87, 138, 139, 203, 226
  Aunt Grace, 81
  Davy Gordon, 26, 81–87
  changes from source material, 32
  ending, 83, 87
  filming of, 80
  Gloria Price, 81–82, 83, 86–87
  Iris Price, 81, 82
  music in, 81–82, 84
  number 7, 87
  number 42, 87
  Pleasureland, 81, 82, 84
  Uncle George, 81
  Vincent Rapallo, 32, 81–82, 83, 84
*The Killing*, 2, 25, 43, 80, 84, 86, 87–89, 145, 149

*The Killing (continued)*
  dog, 92–93
  ending, 91
  Fay, 91, 92
  filming of, 87
  George Peatty, 90
  Johnny Clay, 90–91, 92–93, 178
  lighting in, 53–54
  Marvin Unger, 90, 92
  Maurice Oboukhoff, 90
  Mike O'Reilly, 90
  Mr. Grimes, 91
  Nikki Arane, 90, 92
  narrator, 92
  number 7, 91–93
  racism in, 90
  Randy Kennan, 90
King, Stephen, 1–2, 177–178, 180, 182, 188, 198, 212, 215, 223
*Kiss Me Deadly*, 88
Kissinger, Henry, 114
Klein, Georges Antoine, 65–66
Koestler, Arthur, 99, 277n105
*Kolberg*, 69
Köllner, Kurt, 22
Körber, Maria, 70
Korean War, 34, 48, 148
Kramer, Stanley, 114
*Kramer vs. Kramer*, 170
Kreider, Tim, 158
"Kubrick Under the Lens," 30
Kubrick, Anya, 237
Kubrick, Barbara, 18, 31, 231
Kubrick, Christiane, 10, 15, 23, 26, 28, 40, 47, 67–75, 97, 102, 146, 237
Kubrick, Gertrude, 18
Kubrick, Jacob (Jack), 11, 18, 23–24, 26–27, 199, 253, 255
Kubrick, Stanley
  and anti-Semitism, 23, 29–31, 35, 37–38, 41, 116, 138, 144–145
  attention to detail, 1, 9, 12–14, 16
  censored, 101–102
  childhood, 10, 14–15, 18–19, 23–27, 29, 39–41, 53, 55
  classic period, 88
  color used in films, 121, 131, 145, 212, 238–246

Kubrick, Stanley *(continued)*
  and crime, 88–89
  death, 74, 289n188, 289n189
  death of parents, 32
  documentaries, 66–68, 107
  during World War II, 39–48
  early influences, 40–44
  education, 23–25, 40, 64–66, 94
  and evil, 70, 74–75
  family history, 18–19, 32, 45, 46, 101
  and Germans, 56, 65–71, 74–76, 132–133
  Holocaust subtext in films, 2–3, 14–17, 23, 48, 56–57, 59, 66, 69, 84, 87, 114, 126, 127, 133, 138
  homosexual theme in films, 26–27, 132, 144–145
  humor in films, 59, 109, 126, 131, 132
  hypermasculinity in films, 4, 11–12, 28, 43, 60, 109–112, 132, 144
  Jewish heritage, 20–32, 56–57, 107–108, 126, 127
  language/narrative, 11–12, 16
  lighting in films, 53–54
  at *Look* magazine, 44, 47, 50, 52, 64, 66, 238
  music in films, 63, 74, 76, 81–82, 84, 98, 110, 117–118, 118–121, 131–132, 136, 146–147, 159, 196, 251–256
  number 7, 87, 91–92, 98, 103, 131, 136–137, 231–233
  number 42, 86–87, 90, 233, 234
  obsession with eyes, 30–31
  Oedipal references in films, 6, 10, 16, 26, 28, 31, 81–82, 110, 130–131, 202, 231
  as photojournalist, 24, 27, 30, 32, 40, 44, 47, 50, 52, 66, 67, 80, 107
  racism in films, 39, 97, 116, 138, 149
  and religion, 12, 23–24
  and technology, 60–61
  sexism in films, 2, 8, 91, 133, 139–140, 151
  violence in films, 8, 11–16, 28, 30–31, 81, 84, 88, 91, 98, 111, 131, 148, 151, 197
Kubrick, Toba, 78
Kubrick, Vivian, 32, 135, 212
Kurosawa, Akira, 50, 78, 90
Kwariani, Kola, 90

*La Ronde*, 62, 63
Lacan, Jacques, 5–6, 142, 204
Laemmle, Carl, 29, 41
Lang, Fritz, 30, 45, 52, 53, 57–58, 59, 60, 62, 80, 109, 121, 144, 162, 187, 226
  influence on Kubrick, 57–59
Lanzmann, Claude, 16, 223
*The Last Laugh*, 51
*The Last Parallel: A Marine's War Journal*, 148
*Le Plaisir*, 63, 81
Lessing, Gotthold, 144
Lewton, Val, 17, 37
Ligeti, György, 118, 143, 146, 247, 249
LoBrutto, Vincent, 238
Loewenberg, Peter, 303n96
*Lolita*, 87, 104
  Dr. Zempf, 28
  "McFate," 103, 233
  number 42, 103–104
*Lolita*, 2, 75, 84, 88, 101–104, 106, 144, 151, 233
  Charlotte, 102, 103
  Clare Quilty, 90, 102, 103, 104
  Dr. Zempf, 28, 102, 104, 114
  Enchanted Hunters Hotel, 102, 103, 187
  filming of, 101–102, 104
  George Swine, 90, 91
  Holocaust reference in, 103, 104, 231
  homosexuality in, 90
  Humbert Humbert, 58, 102, 103, 104, 178, 233
  Lolita, 58, 103, 104
  number 42, 103–104
  opening shot, 104
*Look* magazine, 23, 32, 44, 47, 50, 52, 64, 66, 238
Lorre, Peter, 53, 186, 187–188
Lubitsch, Ernst, 45, 50, 53
Lumet, Sidney, 158
Lynn, Vera, 110, 236

MGM, 41, 102
*The Magic Mountain*, 2, 193–195, 199, 231, 240, 241, 246–247
Mahler, Gustav, 63, 118
Mailer, Norman, 213
Maimon, Solomon, 64

Index | 335

*Making The Shining,* 32, 49, 200
*The Man in the Glass Booth,* 145, 165
Mann, Anthony, 99
Mann, Thomas, 2, 39–41, 193–195, 199, 231, 239–241, 246–247
Mason, James, 101, 268n41
Mayer, Louis B., 29, 41
Mazursky, Paul, 29, 78
McDowell, Malcolm, 30
*The Memoirs of Barry Lyndon, Esq.,* 29, 129, 131–132
Mendelssohn, Felix, 118, 120
Mengele, Dr. Josef, 219–220
"Metamorphosis," 207–208, 244
*Metropolis,* 57–60, 121
   Hel, 121
   influence on Kubrick, 58–59
   robot Maria, 60, 121
   Rotwang, 58, 60, 121
Metz, Toba, 24–25, 40
"A Midsummer Night's Dream," 118, 120
Miller, Mark Crispin, 132, 285n110
*Ministry of Fear,* 58, 226
Minotaur Production, 80, 203
*Mr. Skeffington,* 44, 220
*Modern Times,* 60
modernism, 6–8
*A Modest Proposal . . . ,* 108
Morgue, Olivier, 121
Moritz, Fritz, 68
Mosby, John Singleton, 148
*Mother Night,* 114
Mozart, Wolfgang Amadeus, 63, 131, 190
Mulvey, Laura, 5
Mumford, Lewis, 114
Murnau, Friedrich Wilhelm, 50, 51, 60
Museum of Modern Art (MoMA), 50, 52, 54, 55, 58

Nabokov, Vladimir, 87, 101, 102, 103, 104, 233
   number 42, 103–104, 233, 234
*The Naked City,* 32, 84
   changes from source material, 32
   Daniel Muldoon, 32
   Davy Gordon, 32
"Napoleon," 11, 154–156
*Nathan der Weise,* 144
*Natural Child,* 149

*Niagara,* 213
Nazi Final Solution, 10, 15, 22, 57, 61, 86, 113–114, 186, 188, 218–219, 226, 227, 251
Nelson, Thomas Allen, 115, 241
New Objectivity (*Neue Sachlichkeit*), 51–53, 58, 88
*New York Times* coverage of Holocaust, 46–47
Nicholson, Jack, 165, 200, 203, 255, 303n92
Nietzsche, Friedrich, 7, 65, 117, 168
Night of Broken Glass, 46
*The Night Porter,* 165, 189–190
*Nineteen Eighty-four,* 69, 123, 127, 138
"Ninth Symphony," 125, 126
Noack, Frank, 272n135
North, Alex, 118
*Notes from Underground,* 65
*Nuit et Brouillard* (*Night and Fog*), 95, 163, 230, 301n62
number 7, 87, 98, 103, 131, 213–214, 231-32, 275n47, 292n214
number 42, 86–87, 90, 103–104, 230–235
*Nursery Rhymes and Nursery Tales,* 33

Olivier, Laurence, 99
*The 1000 Eyes of Dr. Mabuse,* 57, 60, 186–187
*One-Eyed Jacks,* 149
Ophuls, Max, 52, 53, 62–63, 81
Oppenheimer, J. Robert, 138
Oppenheimer, Süss, 69
Orenstein, Catherine, 34
Orff, Carl, 118–120
Orwell, George, 69, 123, 127
Oswald, Lee Harvey, 139

Pabst, Georg, 51, 52
Paisiello, Giovanni, 131
Paramount Pictures, 41
"The Passion Flower Hotel," 148
*Paths of Glory,* 2, 25, 26, 29, 43, 50, 62, 79, 84, 88, 93–99, 130, 132, 149, 151
   beginning, 95
   Captain Rousseau, 95, 96
   changes from source material, 29
   "Château d'Aigle" (Eagle Castle), 94
   Colonel Dax, 26, 95, 96, 97, 98
   Corporal Paris, 97

*Paths of Glory (continued)*
 ending, 93, 97
 Férol, 97
 filming of, 67–68, 94–95
 General Broulard, 95, 98
 General Mireau, 94–96, 98
 German army, 96
 Lieutenant Roget, 96–97
 Major Saint-Auban, 96
 number 7, 98
 Private Arnaud, 97
 Private Lejeune, 97
 racism in, 97
 Schleissheim, 94, 146
 Sergeant-Major Boulanger, 96
Patton, George, 96, 112
*The Pawnbroker,* 158, 309n14
Peckmann, Heinrich, 22
"The Penal Colony," 246
Penderecki, Krzysztof, 1, 199, 248–249, 251–252
Peregrine Productions, 6, 130, 212
*Perfume: The Story of a Murderer,* 150
Perrault, Charles, 34
Perveler, Martin, 25, 80
*Pinocchio,* 158–159
*Platoon,* 133
Polanski, Roman, 165, 171, 214
Polish National Council in London, 46
Pollack, Sydney, 147
postmodernism, 7, 8, 15–16
Production Code Administration (PCA), 41–42, 44, 148–149, 151
*Psycho,* 169, 175, 182, 186
Pudovkin, Vsevolod, 13

RKO-Pathé, 66
RAND Corporation, 115
*Rancho Notorious,* 162
Raphael, Frederic, 7, 15, 16, 29, 30, 56, 144
*Rashomon,* 78, 82, 90, 179, 274n28
Rathenau, Walter, 55–56
Ray, Man, 86
Reich Music Chamber, 119
Reitz, Edgar, 69
Renoir, Jean, 50
Resnais, Alain, 95, 163, 230
Richter, Hans, 86

"Ride of the Valkyries," 114
Riefenstahl, Leni, 38, 42 , 125
*Rififi,* 84
Robinson, Edward G., 42
Rommel, Erwin, 53, 54, 56, 189, 268n41
Roosevelt, Franklin, 46, 47
*Rosemary's Baby,* 171
*Der Rosenkavalier,* 159, 190
Rossellini, Roberto, 50
Rousseau, Jean-Jacques, 96, 166, 294n20
*Roxie Hart,* 59
Russ, Martin, 148
"Ruth, Roses, and Revolvers," 86

Sackler, Howard, 25, 78, 80
Sahl, Mort , 115
*Salon Kitty,* 165, 299n28
Sarris, Andrew, 63
*Scarlet Street,* 58, 144, 162
Schickel, Richard, 34
Schiller, Friedrich, 125
Schindler, Oskar, 72
*Schindler's List,* 150, 157, 160, 191, 221
Schinoski, Walter J., 138
Schnitzler, Arthur, 29, 62, 63, 139–146
Schubert, Franz, 131
Schwartz, Bernard. SEE Tony Curtis
Schwarzkopf, Elisabeth, 119
Seesslen, Georg, 121
Sellers, Peter, 60, 101, 102, 127
Seven Arts UK, 101
Seven Years War, 131, 150, 240
Seyss-Inquart, Artur, 71
*The Shadow Knows,* 150, 167, 199, 241
Shakespeare, William, 64, 78, 93, 120
Shaw, Irwin, 152
*The Shining,* 131–133, 187–188, 215, 233
*The Shining,* 1–4, 6, 8, 11, 12, 14, 16–17, 28, 32, 60, 87, 103, 121, 131–133, 144–240
 Bill Watson, 89
 Dick Halloran, 38–39, 204, 205, 212, 225, 226, 227, 310n34
 Danny Torrance, 11, 26, 27, 39, 170–240
 fairy tales and, 33
 ghosts, 170–240
 Grady, 76, 205, 213, 215, 226, 227, 235
 Holocaust subtext, 31, 103, 104, 110, 139, 167, 170, 220–240

*The Shining (continued)*
  Jack Torrance, 11, 31, 33, 34, 38–39, 49, 85, 104, 146, 151, 158, 170–240
  Larry Durkin, 204, 305n48
  music in, 1, 119, 144, 176, 220–230
  number 7, 203, 213–214, 216, 229, 231–232, 311n48, 311n50, 311n52, 311n57, 312n65
  number 42, 86, 103, 104
  Overlook Hotel, 11, 38–39, 49, 57, 74, 89, 95, 104, 146, 151, 170–240
  typewriter in, 49, 55, 170, 174, 215, 221–222, 228
  Wendy Torrance, 39, 170, 174–175, 180–220
*The Shop on Main Street*, 180, 301n62
*The Short-Timers*, 133, 136
Shostakovich, Dmitri, 142, 146
"Silly Symphonies" series, 33
Simmons, Jean, 99
Silvera, Frank, 79
Silverman, Donald, 25
Singer, Alexander, 25, 87, 243
Siodmak Robert, 53, 61, 80
Skelton, John, 34
Smith, Gerald L. K., 35
Smith, Larry, 145
*So Help Me God*, 148–149
Sobchack, Vivian, 170
Sobotka, Ruth, 25, 82, 86
*Some Call It Loving*, 291n205
Sontag, Susan, 165, 166, 178, 296n17
Southern, Terry, 107, 149–150
*Spartacus*, 2, 26, 43, 88, 99, 149
  difficulties with script, 99–100
  Draba, 99–100
  marriage scene, 101, 116
  Spartacus, 99–100
Speer, Albert, 60, 150, 177
Spielberg, Steven, 60, 157–159
Stadtmueller, Fred, 66
Stainforth, Gordon, 233
Stalin, Joseph, 30, 99
Stanislavsky, Konstantin, 77
Steiner, George, 222, 236
Stone, Oliver, 133
"The Story of the Three Little Pigs," 33
Strauss, Johann, 63, 97, 117, 119
Strauss, Richard, 117, 118, 119, 151, 159, 184

Strode, Woody, 99
Stroheim, Erich von, 50, 53, 54–56, 60, 62, 97, 160, 189
Stroheim, Erich Oswald. SEE Stroheim, Erich von
Summering, 146, 151
"Supertoys Last All Summer Long," 158
swastikas, 125, 137–138, 190, 226
Swift, Jonathan, 108–109, 166

Taylor, Gilbert, 113
Teller, Edward, 115
*The Tempest*, 78
*The Tenant*, 171, 190, 214
*The Testament of Dr. Mabuse*, 57, 187–188
Thackeray, William, 29, 131–133
Thompson, Jim, 88, 93, 148
"Thus Spake Zarathustra," 7, 118, 119
Tolstoy, Leo, 65
Traister, Aaron, 23, 40
Trilling, Lionel, 64–65, 94
Trumbo, Dalton, 56, 99, 101, 116, 123, 149
"Try a Little Tenderness," 109, 110
*Twelve O'Clock High*, 113
*Two Hours to Doom*, 107, 108, 113
  Brigadier General Quinten, 107
*2001: A Space Odyssey*, 2, 7, 10–11, 30, 32, 74–75, 110, 116, 171, 205
  apes, 120
  Andrezj Smyslov, 120
  Dave Bowman, 120, 121, 122, 123
  Discovery, 118–119, 120, 122
  ending, 122
  Frank Poole, 120, 121
  HAL "Heuristically Programmed Algorithmic Computer," 60, 119–122
  Halvorsen, 121
  Heywood Floyd, 120, 121
  Holocaust reference in, 121
  music in, 76, 118–120
  relevance of names, 120
  Star-Child, 27–28, 30, 121, 122, 123
  Star Gate, 81
  use of color, 120–121

United Artists, 80, 87, 93, 101
Universal Pictures, 37, 41, 99
Ustinov, Peter, 63, 99

Van Doren, Mark, 64–65
Veidt, Conrad, 53, 274n35
*Verdict for Tomorrow*, 113–114
Vietnam War, 27, 114, 136, 138
*Village Voice*, 63
Visconti, Luchino, 189
Vivaldi, Antonio, 131
von Braun, Wernher, 61, 115
von Harbou, Thea, 57, 58
von Karajan, Herbert, 118, 119, 249–250
"von Karajan effect," 119
von Sternberg, Josef, 50
Vonnegut, Kurt, 114

Wagner, Richard, 114, 125, 165, 246–247
Walker, Alexander, 11, 22, 51, 57, 104
Wallant, Edward, 158
Walpole, Horace, 168
Walt Disney, 33–34, 36–38, 158, 211, 232
Walter, Bruno, 119
Waldteufel, Emile, 179
Warner Bros., 2, 29, 41, 173
  campaign against Nazis, 41–45
Weber, Max, 10, 94, 109, 221

"We'll Meet Again," 110, 116
Wellman, William, 59
White, Lionel, 29, 87, 92, 148
*The White Hotel*, 189
Whitman, Charles, 139
"Who's Afraid of the Big Bad Wolf?" 33–34, 36, 37
*Wild Strawberries*, 213, 290n199
Wilder, Samuel "Billy," 53, 54, 80, 147, 186
Willingham, Calder, 93, 149, 151
Wilson, Herbert Emerson, 148
Wise, Robert, 17
Wohlstetter, Albert, 115
"The Wolf at the Door," 34
wolves, symbolism of, 34–38, 41, 211, 222–223
*The Wolf Man*, 37
Woolf, Virginia, 63
*Wound Passage*, 71
Writers Guild, 88

Zucker, Adolph, 29, 41
Zweig, Stefan, 31, 53, 150–151, 181
Zygielbojm, Szmul, 46

**Contemporary Film, Television, and Video**

Joanne Hershfield
*General Editor*

*Contemporary Film, Television, and Video Studies* is a series that seeks to publish serious, scholarly materials about contemporary American and international film, television, and video practices. Topics of interest include studies of national media practices, the globalization of media production and consumption, and studies of important and influential media practitioners. We invite submissions of single author manuscripts and edited collections of essays from a wide range of theoretical and methodological perspective.

For further information about the series and submitting manuscripts, please contact:

> Peter Lang Publishing, Inc.
> Acquisitions Department
> 29 Broadway, 18th floor
> New York, NY 10006

To order other books in this series, please contact our Customer Service Department at:

> (800) 770-LANG (within the U.S.)
> (212) 647-7706 (outside the U.S.)
> (212) 647-7707 FAX

Or browse online by series at:

> www.peterlang.com